Reading and All That Jazz

Tuning Up Your Reading, Thinking, and Study Skills

SIXTH EDITION

Peter Mather
Retired from Glendale Community College
Glendale, Arizona

Rita McCarthy
Glendale Community College
Glendale, Arizona

READING AND ALL THAT JAZZ, SIXTH EDITION

Published by McGraw-Hill Education, 2 Penn Plaza, New York, NY 10121.

Some ancillaries, including electronic and print components, may not be available to customers outside the United States.

This book is printed on acid-free paper.

1 2 3 4 5 6 7 8 9 0 RMN/RMN 1 0 9 8 7 6 5

ISBN: 978-0-07-351358-4 (student edition)
MHID: 0-07-351358-X (student edition)

ISBN: 978-0-07-776847-8 (instructor's edition)
MHID: 0-07-776847-7 (instructor's edition)

Senior Vice President, Products & Markets: *Kurt L. Strand*
Vice President, General Manager, Products & Markets: *Michael Ryan*
Vice President, Content Design & Delivery: *Kimberly Meriwether David*
Managing Director: *David S. Patterson*
Executive Brand Manager: *Kelly Villella*
Director of Development: *Lisa Pinto*
Editorial Coordinator: *Dana Wan*
Executive Marketing Manager: *Jaclyn Elkins*
Marketing Manager: *Nancy Baudean*
Senior Market Development Manager: *Suzie Flores*
Director, Content Design & Delivery: *Terri Schiesl*
Full-Service Manager: *Faye Herrig*
Content Project Managers: *Jane Mohr and Judi David*
Buyer: *Sandy Ludovissy*
Designer: *Studio Montage*
Cover Image: *Gilbert Mayers/Getty Images*
Compositor: *MPS Limited*
Typeface: *10/13 Palatino Lt Std*
Printer: *R. R. Donnelly*

All credits appearing on page or at the end of the book are considered to be an extension of the copyright page.

Library of Congress Cataloging-in-Publication Data

Mather, Peter.
Reading and all that jazz : tuning-up your reading, thinking, and study skills / Peter Mather, Retired from Glendale Community College, Glendale, Arizona, Rita McCarthy, Glendale Community College, Glendale, Arizona. --Sixth edition.
pages cm
ISBN 978-0-07-351358-4 (alk. paper)
1. Reading (Higher education)--United States. 2. English language--Rhetoric. 3. Critical thinking--Study and teaching (Higher)--United States. 4. Study skills--United States. I. McCarthy, Rita. II. Title.
LB2395.3.M28 2016
428.4071'1--dc23

2014035250

The Internet addresses listed in the text were accurate at the time of publication. The inclusion of a website does not indicate an endorsement by the authors or McGraw-Hill Education, and McGraw-Hill Education does not guarantee the accuracy of the information presented at these sites.

www.mhhe.com

Peter dedicates this book to his late parents,
Carl and Dorothy; and his brother and sister-in-law,
John and Peggy.

Rita dedicates this book to her sons, Ryan and Steve;
her daughters-in-law, Bonnie and Raquel; her grandchildren,
Zachary, Kate, Dylan, and Sofia; and especially her husband, Greg.

About the Authors

Dr. Peter Mather—Dr. Mather earned his B.A. in government from the University of Redlands; his first M.A. in African studies from the University of California, Los Angeles; his second M.A. in reading from California State University, Los Angeles; and his Ed.D. in curriculum and instruction from the University of Southern California. Before recently retiring, he taught reading at the secondary, adult education, and community college levels for close to 30 years. While at Glendale Community College, he taught both developmental and critical and evaluative reading. He also taught American government and was the college director of the America Reads/Counts program. In addition to being the coauthor of *Reading and All That Jazz,* now in its sixth edition, and *Racing Ahead with Reading,* he has published articles in the *Journal of Reading.*

MS. Rita Romero McCarthy—Ms. McCarthy earned her B.A. in sociology and history from the University of California, Berkeley, and her M.A. in education from Arizona State University. She has taught at the elementary, secondary, and college levels. For the past 27 years, she has taught English as a second language, developmental reading, and critical and evaluative reading at Glendale Community College. She is the coauthor of *Reading and All That Jazz* and *Racing Ahead with Reading*. Ms. McCarthy has also published articles in professional journals and other media; most of these have been concerned with the use of bibliotherapy. She has also published reading lists for beginning and remedial readers.

Brief Contents

Contents

The Learning Support System of *Reading and All That Jazz*, Sixth Edition

Reading and All That Jazz: The Text

- **Text chapters:** 14 foundational chapters and a dedicated unit on vocabulary available in national edition
- **Custom option:** McGraw-Hill CREATE™ allows you to tailor a custom text with selected chapters of your choice as well as readings of your own choice from among hundreds of selections in the CREATE database

Connect Reading and *Reading and All That Jazz*

- **Learn Smart Achieve:** Adaptive assessment, learning, and practice assignments in reading skills that align with chapter topics
- **Power of Process:** Guided reading assignments support holistic application of multiple reading strategies and metacognition about the reading process
- **The E-Book Reader:** Selection of 90-plus readings across a range of themes
- **Writing Assignments with Outcomes-Based Assessment:** Tools to facilitate rubric assessment, data collection and reports, and feedback around performance outcomes
- **Tegrity:** Lecture capture service that allows students to replay instructor recordings
- **Connect Insight™:** Analytics tool that provides a series of visual data displays—each framed by an intuitive question—to provide instructors at-a-glance information regarding how their classes are doing.

Teaching Resources and Digital Support

- **Annotated Instructor's Edition:** Includes on-page teaching tips
- **Teaching Resources:** Includes an Instructor's Manual with Test Bank and PowerPoint presentations for classroom use

Preface

"Reading furnishes the mind only with materials of knowledge; it is thinking that makes what we read ours."—John Locke

Why *Reading and All That Jazz?*

The theme of jazz is interwoven in the title and concept of this book in order to emphasize a positive, exciting, and engaging approach to reading and learning. Just as jazz relies on improvisation, instructors should feel free to improvise in their use of this book so that it becomes an effective learning tool for classes of varying skill levels and with different interests. And, just as jazz musicians bring their individual backgrounds to bear on the music they play, instructors should encourage students to draw from their individual backgrounds when they read and interpret the selections in the book. Jazz, an American art form, grew from many diverse influences—African, Spanish, European. Similarly, this text attempts to reflect the cultural diversity and varying interests of its student audience.

In this edition the music theme has been broadened to include other kinds of music and musicians. This expanded music focus reflects even more accurately the varying interests of students. This greater range of topics and perspectives will further enable students to clarify their own values and experience events through the eyes of others.

The Instructional Framework of *Reading and All That Jazz*

Reading and All That Jazz allows students to take control of their study plan while providing engaging and diverse reading selections, multiple assessment opportunities, in-context essential vocabulary content, and an integrated print and digital program designed to prepare students for reading in college and beyond.

Hallmarks of this esteemed title include the following:

Engaging and diverse reading selections. Reading selections were chosen for their excellence, their contemporary relevance and interest, and their overall diversity.

- There are 44 readings in the text, 90-plus readings in Connect Reading, and hundreds of additional readings available in McGraw-Hill's custom database, CREATE.

Multiple assessments. Multiple assessments in the book and online help students test their knowledge so they can understand what their next steps will be in advancing their reading skills.

- Assessments are placed after each reading and at the end of chapters.
- Each chapter contains a series of exercises arranged sequentially, progressing from easy to difficult.
- Review tests are included throughout the book.
- LearnSmart Achieve offers students a continually adaptive learning experience, on ten core reading topics.

- The Power of Process guides students through performance-based assessment activities that require them to apply active reading strategies and demonstrate critical thinking and analysis of a reading selection in their own writing.

In-context and essential vocabulary. Chapter 1 focuses on vocabulary development techniques and provides context practice. Part 5, dedicated to vocabulary development, consists of eight units, each introducing a set of Latin or Greek word parts or homonyms. Students learn college-level words associated with these word parts and then practice using the key words through context exercises and crossword puzzles.

- Each reading includes vocabulary-in-context exercises, and each chapter summary includes vocabulary review. Chapters and dedicated vocabulary units (Part 5) include crossword puzzles for additional practice.
- Connect Reading teaches multiple vocabulary strategies and includes many learning objectives and questions designed to build vocabulary.

Essential study techniques. *Reading and All That Jazz* shows students how to take control of their study plan through integral study techniques, helping them study more effectively and manage their schedules throughout the term.

- Through multiple activities within the book, students are given an opportunity to learn the key skills necessary for success in school and in life.
- Thirteen highlighted study techniques are presented in the book. Examples include skimming, scanning, underlining and annotating, taking lecture notes, and outlining.

Methodical, step-by-step instruction to facilitate student learning. Students get the most out of the pedagogy and activities through a variety of strategically designed paths.

- Each chapter contains a series of exercises arranged to progress from the relatively easy to the quite difficult.
- Pre-reading material that accompanies reading selections is organized in a consistent format. A section titled "Tuning In to Reading" contains questions designed to actively engage the student with the subject of the upcoming selection. A "Bio-sketch" provides information about each author's background. "Notes on Vocabulary" offers a discussion of unusual words that appear in the selection.
- Readings are formatted as they would appear in their original source. Selections from magazines or newspapers are formatted to look like magazine or newspaper articles; textbook selections are formatted to look like textbooks. This gives the text a more varied appearance and eases students' transition to readings they will encounter in other classes as well as outside school.
- "Comprehension Checkup" sections follow a standardized format. Objective questions, written in the style of those found on many standardized tests, come first, followed by "Vocabulary in Context" questions designed to test knowledge of vocabulary used in the selection. A series of open-ended questions for critical thinking follow, titled "In Your Own Words." Next, a section titled "Written Assignment" calls for more in-depth writing

from the students, and finally "Internet Activity" asks students to do Internet research on topics or issues raised by the selection.

- Power of process supports holistic application of multiple reading strategies and metacognition about the reading process with guided reading assignments.

What's New in the Sixth Edition of *Reading and All That Jazz*

This book is organized along two dimensions. First, the successive parts of the book focus on skills and strategies that an effective learner and reader must master. Second, the book begins with a narrow perspective—focusing on the student as learner—and then becomes increasingly broad, focusing in turn on interpersonal, social, national, and global issues.

Part 1, Getting a Handle on College, is designed to capture students' attention and interest by helping them discover more about themselves as learners.

- New: Coverage of reading rate (in Introduction)
- New: Coverage of skimming and scanning as study techniques (in Introduction)
- New: Timed reading: "Speaking of Success: Sonia Sotomayor," excerpt from *P.O.W.E.R. Learning and Your Life,* by Robert S. Feldman (in Introduction)
- New: Chapter 1 devoted to vocabulary development, including vocabulary in context, word structure, dictionary use, and making picture vocabulary note cards
- New: Excerpt from *Understanding Business,* "Learning the Skills You Need to Succeed Today and Tomorrow," by William G. Nickels (chapter 2)

Part 2, Discovering Meaning Through Structure, is directed at developing the basic skills needed to make reading easier and more productive.

- New: Deeply revised chapter 3 on topics, main ideas, and details with a new section on formulating implied ideas and paraphrasing
- New: Excerpt from *Concepts of Biology* by Sylvia S. Mader, "Fire Ants Have a Good Defense" (chapter 3)
- New: Excerpt from *Parenting Without Borders* by Christine Gross-Loh, "Global Food Rules" (chapter 3)
- New: *"Ban Cell Phones, Unless Under Squid Attack"* by Dave Barry (chapter 3)
- New: Chapter 4 on organizing textbook information and understanding visual aids, focused on the topic of memory
- New: Excerpt from *Essentials of Understanding Psychology* by Robert S. Feldman, "The Foundations of Memory" (chapter 4)
- New: Excerpt from *Power Learning Strategies for Success in College and Life* by Robert S. Feldman, "The Secret of Memory" (chapter 4)
- New: Chapter 5 that consolidates coverage of author's purpose with modes of writing
- New: Excerpt from *Personal Finance* by Jack Kapoor, "Consumer Credit" (chapter 5)

- New: Introduction to Chapter 6 on transition words and patterns of organization
- New: Discussion of patterns of organization in reading selections (Chapter 6)
- New: Introduction to transition words and patterns of organization (chapter 7)
- New: "My World Now" by Anna Mae Halgrim Seaver (chapter 7)
- New: Excerpt from *Computing NOW* by Glen J. Coulthard, "Identity Theft and How to Avoid It" (chapter 7)
- New: Review Test in Chapter 7 on transition words and patterns
- New: Excerpt from *Interpersonal Communication* by Kory Floyd, "Getting In, Getting Out" (chapter 7)

Part 3, Interpreting What We Read, emphasizes reading as an interpretive process.

- New: Introduction to inference (chapter 8)
- New: Discussion of drawing inferences from a mystery, from fables, and from textbook material (chapter 8)
- New: "Abraham Lincoln Denies a Loan," by Abraham Lincoln (chapter 8)
- New: Introduction to figures of speech (chapter 9)
- New: Introduction to inferring tone (chapter 10)
- New: "The Old Grandfather and His Little Grandson," by Leo Tolstoy (chapter 10)
- New: "Whale of a Rescue" by Anita Bartholomew" (chapter 10)

Part 4, Reading Critically, concentrates on developing critical reading and thinking skills.

- New: Excerpt from *Experience History: Interpreting America's Past* by James West Davidson et al., "Jackie Robinson Integrates Baseball" (chapter 11)
- New: Excerpt from *Marriages and Families* by David H. Olson, "Factors Affecting Happiness" (chapter 11)
- New: "The Dinner Party" by Mona Gardner (chapter 12)
- New: Chapter 13 with a streamlined discussion of propaganda techniques, logical fallacies, and argument
- New: Creating Venn diagrams as a study technique (chapter 13)

Part 5, Vocabulary Units, provides an in-depth exploration of vocabulary.

- New: Eight units on homonyms and categories of word parts with exercises and crossword puzzles

Features of the Learning Support System of *Reading and All That Jazz*

Together, *Reading and All That Jazz,* Connect Reading, the Annotated Instructor's Edition, McGraw-Hill's CREATE, and the Online Learning Center address specific needs of developmental reading courses.

Connect Reading

Connect Reading is a comprehensive and engaging digital program built from the ground up to address the specific needs of reading courses and various redesign models of instruction. Its innovative content and revolutionary learning technology complements *Reading and All That Jazz* with the following:

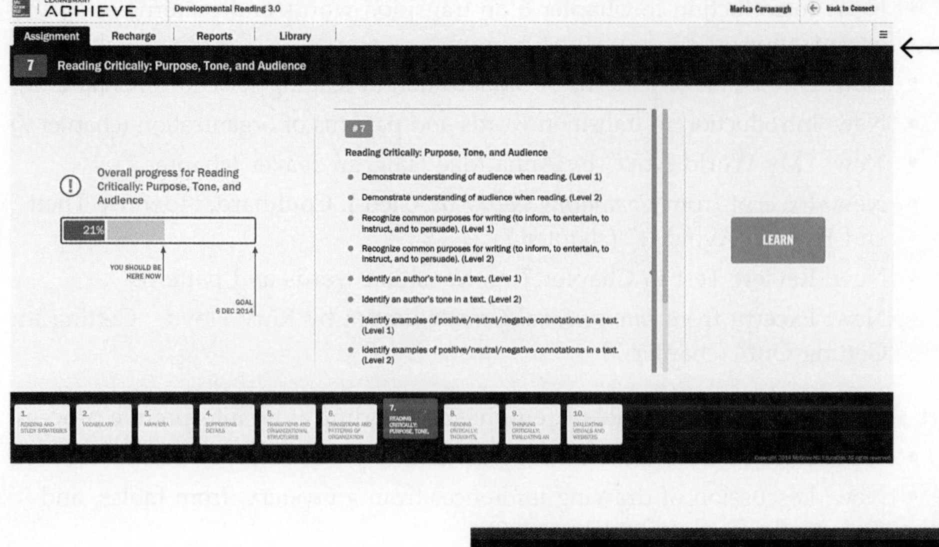

• *LearnSmart Achieve* offers an adaptive learning experience designed to ensure mastery of reading skills. By targeting particular strengths and weaknesses, *LearnSmart Achieve* facilitates high-impact learning at an accelerated pace.

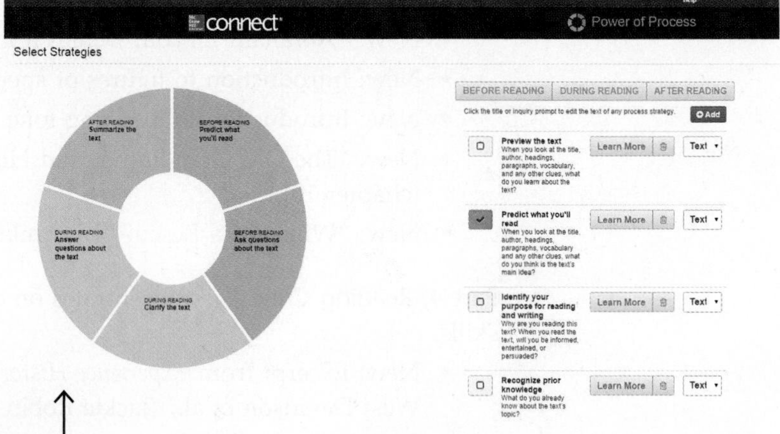

• *Power of Process* guides students through performance-based assessment activities using the pedagogy of strategies instruction, in which students use strategies to read and respond to the text, and then instructors can assess students' depth of engagement with the text.

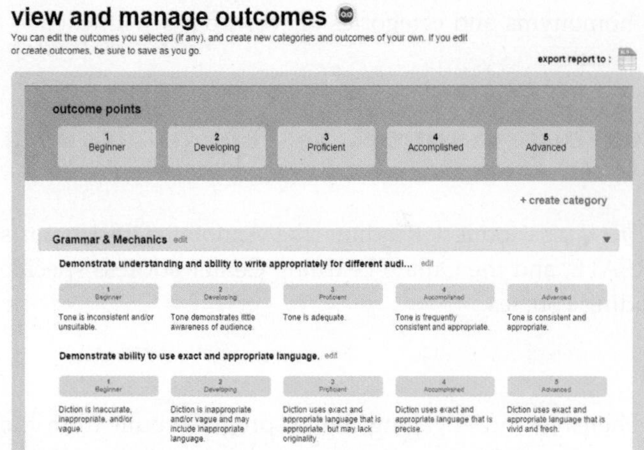

• *Writing Assignments* **with Outcomes Based Assessment** allow instructors and departments to assess written assignments with custom rubrics built around learning outcomes and to generate detailed reports that support formative assessment and improve efficacy at the student, section, and program levels.

- **A thematic, leveled e-book reader and question bank** provide approximately 140 compelling readings and assessment options that instructors can incorporate into their syllabuses. Four pre-built assessments, aligned with the same topics and learning objectives in *LearnSmart Achieve,* may be used as static pre- and posttests for lower- and upper-level courses.
- **McGraw-Hill Campus** is a Learning Management System (LMS) integration service that offers instructors and students universal single sign-on, automatic registration, and gradebook synchronization of McGraw-Hill Connect products.
- **Connect Insight**™ is an analytics tool within Connect that provides a series of visual data displays—each framed by an intuitive question—to provide instructors at-a-glance information regarding how their classes are doing.

Annotated Instructor's Edition

The *Annotated Instructor's* Edition includes on-page teaching tips as well as answers to questions in the text.

McGraw-Hill's CREATE

Through the McGraw-Hill CREATE platform, instructors can easily arrange chapters to align with their syllabus, eliminate chapters they do not wish to assign, and arrange any of the *Reading and All that Jazz* content into a print or e-book text. Instructors can also add their own material, such as a course syllabus, a course rubric, course standards, and any specific instruction for students.

Teaching Resources

The author draws on her own extensive experience in the classroom—as well as the experiences of many other seasoned reading faculty—to offer pedagogical ideas that are effective and easy to use. The Instructor's side of the Online Learning Center, written by the author, contains the following:

- An Instructor's Manual, divided into four sections: (1) Get-acquainted activities; (2) additional chapter exercises, answer keys, and teaching tips, organized by chapter; (3) a test bank, with chapter quizzes, unit tests, a posttest, and final exam; and (4) answer keys.
- Numerous PowerPoints for each chapter.

Acknowledgments

No textbook can be created without the assistance of many people. I relied on the thoughtful reactions and suggestions of colleagues across the country who reviewed the project at various stages.

Elizabeth Brock, City College of San Francisco
Elizabeth Earle, Valencia College–Osceola
James Fusaro, Moreno Valley College
Kathleen Gregory, Morehead State University
Jennifer Levinson, City College of San Francisco
Virginia Mix, Portland Community College

Sonya Syrop, Moreno Valley College

Jacqueline Shehorn, West Horns College–Lemoore

Brenda Tuberville, Rogers State University

Robert Vettese, Southern Maine Community College

I owe a special thanks to the honest and valuable criticism from my colleagues in the Maricopa Community College District. In particular, I would like to thank Cindy Ortega, Mary Jane Onnen, Gwen Worthington, Viva Henley, Gina Desai, Gaylia Nelson, Pam Hall, and Karen Irwin. Others who helped in this edition and in previous editions are Cindy Gilbert, Marilyn Brophy, Nancy Edwards, Arlene Lurie, Carol Jones, Lynda Svendsen, and Jim Reynolds.

My sincere gratitude goes to those at McGraw-Hill involved in the production of the sixth edition of *Reading and All That Jazz*. These include Lisa Pinto, Executive Director of Development; Kelly Villella, Executive Brand Manager, Developmental English; Dana Wan, Coordinator, Developmental English; Jane Mohr, Full Service Content Project Manager; LouAnn Wilson, photo researcher; Wesley Hall, literary permissions; and Ruma Khurana, Senior Project Manager. I am especially grateful to my developmental editor, Susan Messer, for all her hard work and sound advice to make *Jazz* 6e as good as it can possibly be.

I also wish to thank my students, who in addition to reading the selections and completing the exercises, made many helpful suggestions.

Rita McCarthy

Getting a Handle on College

P
1

CHAPTERS IN PART 1

I Your First Week in Class

CHAPTER PREVIEW

In this chapter, you will

- Learn how to keep track of assignments.
- Learn about reading rate.
- Learn how to skim written material.
- Examine your motivation for attending college.
- Learn how to scan material quickly to locate specific information.

"There are no secrets to success. It is the result of preparation, hard work, and learning from failure."

—Colin Powell

Some of you just recently graduated from high school. Others have been out in the "real world" and now realize the importance of a college education. Each of you decides what is important in your life, and you have decided that going to college is important. Besides investing your time, you are investing money, and so you want to get as much benefit as you can out of college. In high school, perhaps many of you did well in your classes without trying very hard. This won't happen in college, because college is more demanding. Whether you succeed in college is up to you. It is your responsibility to attend class, study, and turn in your work on time. No one else can do it for you.

Reading and studying will be an important part of your college career. You can't expect to do well in college without having good reading and studying skills. In this book, we will provide you with techniques for improving these skills. Using these techniques will make the time you spend in college more enjoyable and productive.

Assignment Sheets

Success in college requires an organized and disciplined approach. So, one of the first things you need to think about is how to organize yourself as a serious student. Perhaps the easiest way to improve your college performance is to take charge of your assignments. Many of your assignments will be listed in the class syllabi, while other assignments will be announced in class. In some classes, late assignments will receive less credit, and in others, they will not be accepted at all—no excuses!

The best way to keep a record of your classroom assignments is by using assignment sheets. Developing the habit of carefully recording your assignments is crucial not only in this class but in your other classes as well. On the next page are samples of three types of assignment sheets. The first sample shows a weekly format, the second a monthly format, and the third a "continuous log" format. You can find a copy of each type of assignment sheet in the Appendices. Whichever format you prefer, be sure to make additional copies of it for future use.

Your First Assignment

Now you can write down your first assignment for this class. This assignment will be due the next class session. On page 5 you will find a crossword puzzle that will introduce you to the material covered in this book. Read the clues, use the table of contents and index to find the answers in the book, and record the answers in the puzzle. Bring your completed puzzle the next time class meets.

A Discussion of Reading Rate

Good readers learn to read flexibly—that is, they adjust their speed according to the difficulty of the material and their specific purpose in reading it. For example, if you are already familiar with the topic of a reading and none of the ideas are new to you, you might read the material rapidly. If, however, the subject is especially important to you and also unfamiliar, you probably need to read it slowly and carefully, and maybe even more than once.

The average adult reading rate on material of moderate difficulty is 250 words per minute with 70 percent comprehension. College-level readers typically read at a rate of 300 words per minute. Many of you want to become faster readers without sacrificing your ability to comprehend the material. The following are some suggestions you might try to speed up your reading.

- Time yourself reading relatively easy material such as your local newspaper, *USA Today*, or *People* magazine. The selections are usually short, interesting, and topical. Set a timer and keep track of the number of pages you read.
- Many of the best authors today write in the young adult category, including J. K. Rowling (*Harry Potter*), Stephenie Meyer (*Twilight*), and Suzanne Collins (*The Hunger Games*). These novels would all be appropriate to practice on as would many of the shorter novels by John Steinbeck. You might also want to practice on short nonfiction selections. The important thing is to read for at least 20 minutes each day with no distractions.

Weekly Assignment Sheet

ASSIGNMENTS
MONDAY
TUESDAY
WEDNESDAY
THURSDAY
FRIDAY
OTHER ASSIGNMENTS, TESTS, ETC.

Monthly Assignment Sheet

MONTH ________________

SUNDAY	MONDAY	TUESDAY	WEDNESDAY	THURSDAY	FRIDAY	SATURDAY

Continuous Log Assignment Sheet

ASSIGNMENT SHEET

Subject(s) ________________________________

Date	Assignments	Due	Finished

Introduction Crossword Puzzle

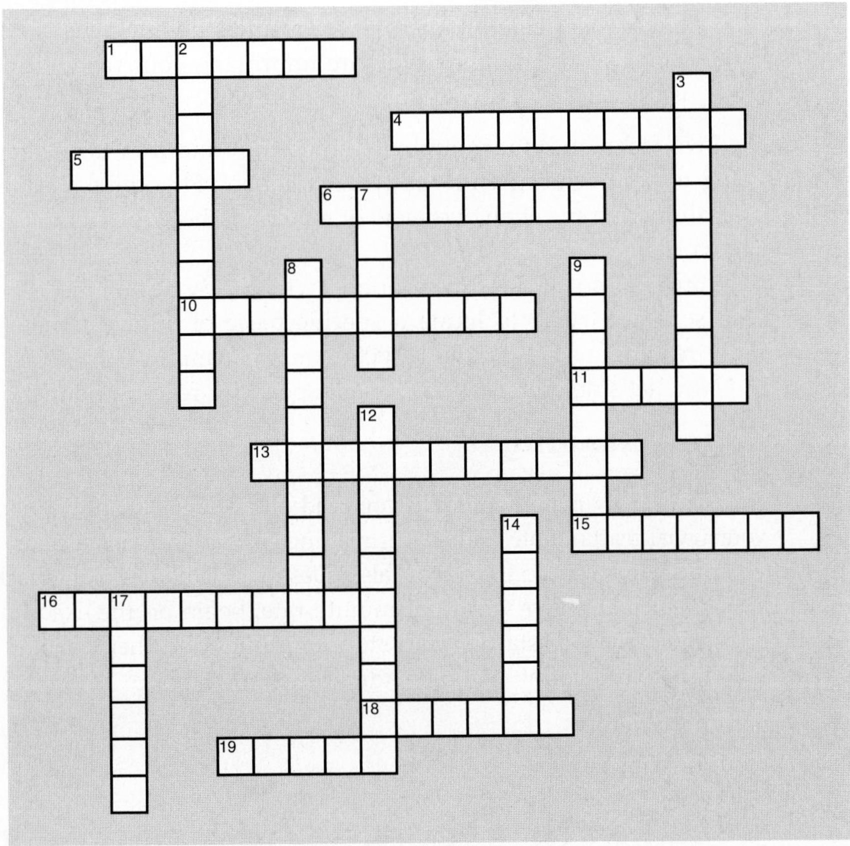

ACROSS CLUES

1. ______ are one type of figure of speech. They use words such as *like* and *as*.
4. "Notes on ______" will introduce you to difficult words in the reading selections.
5. A word part meaning "four." (Vocabulary Unit 2 in Part 5)
6. One type of pattern of organization in Chapter 6 is the comparison-______ pattern.
10. Chapter 8 contains information about ______(s).
11. In the Introduction, you will be introduced to ______ Skills Technique 1: Skimming.
13. One type of learning style discussed in Chapter 1.
15. In Chapter 2, there is an excerpt by William G. ______.
16. Both authors of this textbook attended colleges in ______.
18. The author of "A Hanging" is George ______.
19. A Robert Frost poem in Chapter 9 is titled "The Road Not ______."

DOWN CLUES

2. The publisher of this book is ______. (Don't use a hyphen.)
3. Chapter 13 discusses ______ techniques.
7. Chapter 6 introduces you to the spatial ______ pattern of organization.
8. The first type of context clue discussed in "Vocabulary: Words in Context" in Chapter 1.
9. The "Q" in SQ3R stands for ______.
12. In Chapter 5, "Students Who Push Burgers" is listed as reading ______.
14. Chapter 4 covers ______ aids.
17. Chapter 2 has a reading by ______ Ponte.

- Go to the Appendix of this textbook. We have provided you with seven timed readings on music-related topics. All the readings have approximately the same number of words and the same level of difficulty, so you can easily determine if you are improving your reading rate. All you need is a timer and a pen or pencil.

Two techniques for rapid reading are introduced in this chapter. First, you are going to be practicing with Study Technique 1: Skimming. Readers who skim are typically trying to get an overview of material. They read at a rate of approximately 800 words per minute.

You are also going to be working with Study Technique 2: Scanning. Readers who scan are trying to locate a specific piece of information. Again, scanning is rapid reading, usually around 1,000 words per minute.

Now let's determine your present speed for reading nonfiction.

Timed Reading

Directions: How many words do you read on average? Read the following selection at your usual reading rate. Time your reading so that you can calculate your rate. When you finish, answer the 10 true or false questions without looking back at the selection.

To calculate your word-per-minute rate, begin on the exact minute (zero seconds). Record your starting and stopping times and then consult the instructions on Page 7, to determine your reading rate.

Starting time: ___________________

Stopping time: ___________________

SPEAKING OF SUCCESS: SONIA SOTOMAYOR

U.S. Supreme Court Justice Sonia Sotomayor's educational journey was not an easy one, but hard work, determination, and a supportive family helped her to become the first Latina and the third woman to serve in the Supreme Court's 220-year history.

Sotomayor's parents moved from Puerto Rico to New York City in the 1950s, and she grew up in a working-class Bronx neighborhood where both of her parents worked. At the age of 9, her father's death was an emotional blow, but she immersed herself in books—particularly the Nancy Drew series, which started her thinking about crime solving. That, and doing her homework in front of the TV while watching lawyer Perry Mason, ignited her goal of pursuing law. 2

She went on to graduate from Cardinal Spellman High School in New York City and was able to earn a scholarship to college. Although her undergraduate years were challenging, she was ultimately successful, graduating with honors. After graduation, she went on to law school. 3

"Although I grew up in very modest and challenging circumstances, I consider my life to be immeasurably rich," Sotomayor said. 4

"My mother taught us that the key to success in America is a good education," Sotomayor said at her Senate confirmation hearing. "And she set the example, studying alongside my brother and me at our kitchen table so that she could become a registered nurse." 5

Close to her family, the Supreme Court Justice notes that her mother, who worked six days a week as a nurse to support her and her brother, is her greatest inspiration. And while her achievements have been attained through hard work, she points to an appreciation for the opportunities she has had. 6

"It is our nation's faith in a more perfect union that allows a Puerto Rican 7
girl from the Bronx to stand here now," she said during her swearing-in ceremony. "I am struck again by the wonder of my own life and the life we in America are so privileged to lead."

(Robert S. Feldman, *P.O.W.E.R. Learning and Your Life: Essentials of Student Success*, 2/e, McGraw-Hill, 2014, p. 73)

Calculating Your Reading Rate

To calculate your reading speed (words per minute), you need to know the number of words in the selection. We have provided the number of words for our timed reading selections. There are 336 words in the "Sonia Sotomayor" selection.

1. Take the number of words in the selection and divide it by the number of minutes it took you to read the material. For example, if you read the selection in two minutes, you divide 336 by 2. Your reading rate is 168 words per minute.
2. If your time does not come out evenly, convert everything into seconds, and then back into minutes. Let's assume you read the selection in 1 minute and 30 seconds. Take the number of minutes (1) and multiply by 60. This gives you 60 seconds. Now add the seconds (30) for a total of 90 seconds (60 + 30). Divide the number of words (336) by the number of seconds (90). So 336/90 = 3.73 words per second. Now multiply by 60 to get to the words per minute. So 3.73 × 60 = 228 words per minute.

True or False Questions

_____ 1. Sonia Sotomayor's father served as her inspiration.
_____ 2. Sonia Sotomayor is of Puerto Rican descent.
_____ 3. Sonia Sotomayor's mother wanted to become a registered nurse.
_____ 4. The Harry Potter books were Sotomayor's particular favorites.
_____ 5. Sonia Sotomayor grew up in a working-class neighborhood in New York.

STUDY TECHNIQUE 1: SKIMMING

Skimming (sometimes called previewing or surveying) is a means of familiarizing yourself with the content and organization of reading material before you begin to read it carefully.

The following assignment provides an example of how to skim. On pages 7–9, read only the material that is underlined, which includes the pre-reading sections (Tuning In to Reading, Bio-Sketch, and Notes on Vocabulary), the title of the selection, the headings and subheadings, the first sentence of each paragraph, and the print in bold and italics. Then answer the true-or-false questions in the Comprehension Checkup at the end of the reading.

READING

"Effort produces success."

TUNING IN TO READING Did you know that approximately half of those who begin taking classes at a community college will drop out by the end of the first year? Notice how many cars there are in the parking lot now. As the days and weeks pass, you will see more empty parking spaces as students drop out for one reason or another. You are the one who decides whether you are going to be a survivor. *Decide to be a survivor!*

READING *(continued)*

BIO-SKETCH The author of the following selection, Robert S. Feldman, remembers being overwhelmed when he first started college. He wondered whether he was capable of meeting the challenges of college, and he realized he had no idea what it took to be successful. Feldman, the author of numerous books, went on to receive a doctorate in psychology and today teaches at the University of Massachusetts.

NOTES ON VOCABULARY

swollen head an exaggerated sense of self-importance. Someone who has a *swollen head* thinks he is more intelligent or more important than he actually is.

MOTIVATION

Robert S. Feldman

Finding the Motivation to Work

"If only I could get more motivated, I'd do so much better with my ________" (insert *schoolwork, diet, exercising,* or the like—you fill in the blank).

All of us have said something like this at one time or another. We use the concept of **motivation**—or its lack—to explain why we just don't work hard at a task. But when we do that, we're fooling ourselves. We all have some motivation, that inner power and psychological energy that directs and fuels our behavior. Without any motivation, we'd never get out of bed in the morning. 2

We've all seen evidence about how strong our motivation can be. Perhaps you love to work out at the gym. Or maybe your love of music helped you learn to play the guitar, making practicing for hours a pleasure rather than a chore. Or perhaps you're a single mother, juggling work, school, and family, and you get up early every morning to make breakfast for your kids before they go off to school. 3

All of us are motivated. The key to success in and out of the classroom is to tap into, harness, and direct that motivation. 4

If we assume that we already have all the motivation we need, learning becomes a matter of turning the skills we already possess into a habit. It becomes a matter of redirecting our psychological energies toward the work we wish to accomplish. 5

But there's a key concept that underlies the control of motivation—viewing success as a consequence of effort. 6

Effort produces success. Suppose, for example, you've gotten a good grade on your mid-term. The instructor smiles at you as she hands back your test. How do you feel? 7

You will undoubtedly be pleased, of course. But at the same time you might think to yourself, "Better not get a swollen head about it. It was just luck. If she'd asked other questions I would have been in trouble." Or perhaps you explain your success by thinking, "Pretty easy test." 8

If you often think this way, you're cheating yourself. Using this kind of reasoning when you succeed, instead of patting yourself on the back and thinking with satisfaction, "All my hard work really paid off," is sure to undermine your future success. 9

A great deal of psychological research has shown that thinking you have no 10
control over what happens to you sends a powerful and damaging message to your self-esteem—that you are powerless to change things. Just think of how different it feels to say to yourself, "Wow, I worked at it and did it," as compared with "I lucked out" or "It was so easy that anybody could have done well."

In the same way, we can delude ourselves when we try to explain our failures. 11
People who see themselves as the victims of circumstance may tell themselves, "I'm just not smart enough" when they don't do well on an academic task. Or they might say, "Those other students don't have to work five hours a day."

The way in which we view the causes of success and failure is, in fact, 12
directly related to our success. Students who generally see effort and hard work as the reason behind their performance usually do better in college. It's not hard to see why: When they are working on an assignment, they feel that the greater the effort they put forth, the greater their chances of success. So they work harder. They believe that they have control over their success, and if they fail, they believe they can do better in the future.

Here are some tips for keeping your motivation alive: 13

- **Take responsibility for your failures—and successes.** When you do poorly on a test, don't blame the teacher, the textbook, or a job that kept you from studying. Analyze the situation and see how you could have changed what you did to be more successful in the future. At the same time, when you're successful, think of the things you did to bring about that success.
- **Think positively.** Assume that the strengths that you have will allow you to succeed, and that, if you have difficulty, you can figure out what to do, or get the help you need to eventually succeed.
- **Accept that you can't control everything.** Seek to understand which things can be changed and which cannot. You might be able to get an extension on a paper due date, but you are probably not going to be excused from a college-wide requirement.

(Robert S. Feldman, *P.O.W.E.R. Learning and Your Life: Essentials of Student Success,* 2/e, McGraw-Hill, 2014)

COMPREHENSION CHECKUP

True or False

Directions: Without referring back to the reading, answer the following questions. Write **T** or **F** in the space provided.

______ 1. To stay motivated, it is important to remain positive.

______ 2. You are harming your self-esteem when you think you have no control over your future.

______ 3. The amount of effort you put into something has very little to do with your eventual success.

______ 4. Professor Feldman never had any doubts about whether or not he would be successful in college.

______ 5. To stay motivated, you must learn to accept responsibility for your failures as well as your successes.

Was your previewing successful? How many of the true-or-false questions did you get right? You likely discovered that you were able to acquire a great deal of information about the topic of motivation and the organization of the reading excerpt in a short amount of time. Now go back and read "Motivation" carefully. Drawing on your broader understanding of the reading, answer the questions below with an appropriate phrase or sentence.

Short Answer

1. Of the three tips presented by Robert Feldman, which one do you find the most helpful? Why?

____

____

____

2. What are your motivators—the things that will get you going when things become difficult? Try to list at least three things below.

____

____

____

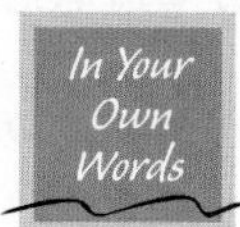

In Your Own Words

Explain the following quotations.

1. "Many of life's failures are people who did not realize how close they were to success when they gave up."—Thomas Alva Edison, inventor
2. "Opportunity is missed by most people because it is dressed in overalls and looks like work."—Thomas Alva Edison, inventor

Written Assignment

The motivational quiz below is designed for assessing how difficult you many find it to stay in college. This quiz is just for you and is not to be turned in. Place a check mark beside each statement that applies to you.

Motivational Quiz

______ 1. I have not yet really decided what my career objective is. Or it is difficult for me to visualize what I will be doing in five years.

______ 2. High school was easy for me, and I never really had to study to get good grades. Or I never really studied in high school and got average or above-average grades.

______ 3. My main reason for being here is athletics.

______ 4. I have small children at home I must take care of.

______ 5. I need to stay in school so that I can remain on my parents' health insurance.

______ 6. My parents want me to go to college, and I want to please them.

______ 7. I am working 30 to 40 hours a week and taking 12 to 15 units. (Consider unpaid activities such as athletics as part of those 30 to 40 hours.)

______ 8. I am living with two or more roommates and plan to do most of my studying at home or in my dorm room.

______ 9. I need to work part-time to pay for my car, clothes, stereo, etc.

______ 10. This is the first time I have been away from home on my own.

______ 11. I plan to get married soon. Or I am going through a divorce.

Now take a look at the number of statements you checked. The more you checked, the greater your chances of not making it. If you checked a lot, this does not mean that you will drop out. But it does mean that you need to do some thinking about your priorities and goals. Your chances of not making it are greater if you are here for the wrong reasons or if you have too many other commitments.

Now write a short paragraph giving your assessment of whether you will be able to complete college.

The following reading features CBS correspondent Byron Pitts. Pitts accepted the many adversities in his life as challenges. He is an example of a person who refused to be defeated.

READING

"I'm sorry, Mr. and Mrs. Pitts. Byron is functionally illiterate."

TUNING IN TO READING CBS *60 Minutes* correspondent Byron Pitts did not learn to read until he was 12 years old, and he had a debilitating stutter until he was 20. He was bullied throughout elementary and junior high school and placed in remedial classes. As a result of those circumstances, he had problems with anger and suffered from low self-esteem. And yet today, after a great deal of hard work, he has a career that many aspire to and very few achieve.

BIO-SKETCH In his memoir, *Step Out on Nothing,* Pitts describes how, with faith and the help of family, friends, and mentors, he overcame illiteracy to become an award-winning correspondent. As a correspondent for CBS News, Pitts has interviewed five presidents of the United States, reported from 33 countries, and covered three wars. He won an Emmy Award for his coverage of the 9/11 attacks. Pitts graduated from Ohio Wesleyan University with a B.A. in journalism.

NOTES ON VOCABULARY

finagled obtained or achieved by indirect, usually devious, methods

warehoused placed or stored. The author is referring to the practice of placing people where they receive only minimal care and opportunities.

sheepish meek. Sheep are noted for their tendency to follow others in the flock and for their fearfulness.

Keep Your Head Up

BYRON PITTS

THE ST. KATHARINE'S STAFF MEMBER AND I, along with my parents, were all sitting in our living room. He asked to speak to my parents privately, but Mother assured him that whatever he had to say was fine to say in front of me. He had brought the results of some tests my parents had not yet seen. His words will always ring in my ears.

"I'm sorry, Mr. and Mrs. Pitts. Byron is functionally illiterate." 2

My father frowned, my mother raised her hand to her mouth, and I looked 3
puzzled. What does "functionally illiterate" mean? My parents were finding out

that in all the years in school I hadn't learned to read. I'd faked and finagled. It wasn't that I couldn't do the math: I could not read the directions. All these years and no one had noticed. Sweet, polite, quiet Byron could not read. I could recognize some words, identify names of certain locations, remember the words I'd memorized at the kitchen table, the name of my school on the side of the building, and the names of my siblings attached to magnets on the refrigerator. I could function, but I could not read. My mother would say years later that it was one of the few nights she cried herself to sleep. Usually knowing is better than not knowing, but initial shock has a pain all its own. She'd been asked on more than a few occasions, why didn't you know sooner that Byron couldn't read? The short answer: when did she have time? Two jobs, three kids, night school, and a cheating husband usually made for a very full day.

The anger and tension that often curled through our house like smoke up a chimney was suddenly replaced by sadness. Everyone felt it. Everyone dealt with it in different ways. My brother treated me like his best friend. My mother, whom I used to follow around the house, was now following me. This went on for weeks. As we searched for some resource, some long-term solution, my mother set out the short-term course. 4

"Okay, honey, if we've spent two hours on homework, we'll try four hours. We will pray when we start. We'll pray when we get tired. And we'll pray when we're done." 5

Just the idea of working longer hours seemed to make her happy. As sad as I was at the time, I remember the joy I felt in anticipating the journey. I had no control over how poorly I read at the time, but I did have control over how hard I worked. That's what you do if you're Clarice Pitts's child. You work hard. 6

"Smart people can think their troubles to the ground, honey," she'd say. "We have to wrestle ours." 7

Soon my father seemed disengaged from the process. He worked more overtime, or at least that's what he told my mother, and stayed away from the house for longer hours. I don't recall a single conversation we ever had after my diagnosis. Maybe he really was embarrassed. Relatives had long teased me, "You're a Momma's boy." From that moment and every day since, I've been proud to be a Momma's boy. 8

These were the darkest days of my life. It wasn't simply the shame of not knowing how to read: it was not knowing where to start. Unsure where the bottom was, it felt as if I was falling. My mother was holding my hand, but we were both just falling. How easy it would have been for her to give up. Give up on me, give up on her abilities or responsibilities as a parent. That was a vulnerable time for both of us. A working-class family, we lacked the resources to do much more than pray and look to others for help. There wasn't much help around, but the power of prayer was immeasurable. It created comfort where none existed. It revealed a path when earthly avenues seemed closed. And it provided strength that could be explained in no other way. 9

As the family prayed and looked for answers, a decision was made in school. I was removed from a regular classroom and placed in all remedial 10 classes. I was about to spend fifth grade as one of "the basement boys." Smart kids were taught aboveground; children like me were sent to the basement.

When I had taken classes aboveground, there were those giant glass windows to look through to the street below. The kids in the basement looked up at a window and saw only the feet of people passing by. Deep in my heart, I knew I didn't belong there, or at the very least I had to escape. But I didn't know how. The classroom size was smaller, and these were kids with whom I had rarely spent time. Many often seemed angry, some were violent, and none seemed hopeful. In my regular class, my friends talked and dreamed of becoming teachers, doctors, lawyers, or sports stars. In my new class, the answer was always "I `ont know." I don't know. It's the slogan for those without dreams or a path to follow. 11

For all the gloom of being a basement boy, this time also proved to be one of life's great teachable moments. I truly believe that it is possible to find good in every moment, especially the difficult ones. Until this point, my academic life was mostly one failure after another. Each day the new challenge had been to find a way to hide. Once I was assigned to the basement, the days of hiding were finally just about over. I can still remember the glance from classmates in the morning. The bright kids, or at the very least, the normal kids walked upstairs, and my kind headed to the basement. I could feel the looks of disdain at the back of my head. Worse still, I could sometimes hear the whispers of pity or contempt. "There go the dummies . . . " 12

I once overheard two adults in the basement chatting in the hallway. "Today the basement, tomorrow prison." It was clear the basement wasn't a place you went to learn. It's where you were warehoused until fate or the legal system had a place for you. 13

Many of those in the basement doubted their future, and so did many of those who were paid to be there to help us. Hopelessness breeds more hopelessness. It was the same for many of us in the basement. We tried covering up our academic deficiencies with attitude and bravado. At about five feet four and ninety pounds, thank God I was never able to pull off the tough guy act. My grandmother always said, "The good Lord gives us what we need." I guess He knew I needed to remain skinny and sheepish until He got me through middle school. 14

There was a whole new look, language, and protocol in the basement. And there was a different approach to learning. We rarely had homework; assignments were completed in the classroom as a group. Even blackboard assignments were done as a group. Upstairs, I always dreaded going to the blackboard alone, now we would go up two or three at a time. 15

Unlike many of my classmates, I still had an optimistic spirit. I still believed that, with hard work, success was possible. Upstairs my optimism was met with skepticism and the clear sense I was naïve or even stupid, but oddly, in the basement, at least some of my new friends welcomed me. Though shy and frequently bullied, I was mostly cheerful and could keep people entertained with humor or encouragement. Classmates often chose to work with me because I could make them laugh or lift their spirits. A favorite line from childhood on a ball field was always "We got this." In other words, we can win. 16

Upstairs I was always alone and afraid at the blackboard, but here I could be the encourager.

"If John went to the store with three dollars and bought cereal for a dollar forty and gum for fifty cents, how much money would he have left?" the teacher would ask. We were to write out her question and answer it on the blackboard. 17

"We got this," I'd say through a ragged smile. 18

One boy would write; the other two would repeat the teacher's sentence and help with spelling. I treated those exercises like a sporting event. We were a team. The question was the opponent. It was easier to rally the group around a sports challenge than an academic problem. We often got the answer wrong, but I took joy in the effort. Upstairs, success was almost always measured by achievement (getting the right answer; passing the test), but here, at least in my heart, success could be measured by effort. No one can always know the right answer, but you can always give your best effort. 19

Those days in the basement were an early lesson on how to redefine success. Take life in small bites, until you can take on more. Find your own pace and stick to it. In a regular classroom, I was a kid on a tricycle trying to keep pace with cars on a highway. In the basement, some of us had tricycles and some had even less. Admittedly, I had one major advantage over most of my classmates. I had Clarice Pitts. Life has taught me there is a fast-moving river that separates success from failure. It's called giving up. Too many people drown in that river. As a boy in the basement, I was often caught in its undertow, but my mother was always nearby, screaming, encouraging, threatening, praying, and on occasion she'd dive in and pull me out. 20

Regardless of the obstacles in your way, one of the great wedges to get you past an obstacle is hard work. There's almost a renewable fuel you get from working hard. The harder you push, the further you realize you can go. As I see it, success is just your work made public. Through the years I've come to enjoy the hard work on the way to success more than the actual achievement. It's the joy of being in the midst of it. It's like a great glass of ice water. Water's good for the body almost any day, but after you've worked hard in the sun, is there anything better than a cold glass of ice water? 21

Hard work never lies. It may not always reward you in the ways and in the time you'd like, but it's always honest. When you've worked hard, you know where you stand. You know what you've given. I've always believed that someone else could outthink me or outmaneuver me, but I only feared the person who could outwork me. Fortunately, I haven't come across that person too often. It's actually a pretty small fraternity: hard workers. Look at almost any successful person in any field, and you'll find at least this one trait: an ability and willingness to work hard. It's the great equalizer. It's the one gift we can give to ourselves, too often overlooked as we "trade up" for a sexier approach. It's not a shortcut; rather, it's the straightest line to success. It's also a great building block for acquiring other important life skills. 22

Every door that's ever opened for me in life started by my knocking hard and sometimes even kicking, putting my shoulder against it, and if not patiently, 23 then prayerfully, waiting for it to open or fall off its hinges. Even as a kid who couldn't read, I knew I was fortunate. I had the gift. I knew how to work hard because my mother taught me.

And so it began. The first steps to overcoming my childhood shame of 24
illiteracy. Pure, raw, uncomplicated hard work. Except for a few school administrators and teachers, no one outside my immediate family ever knew I couldn't read. Most days I was deathly afraid of failure, but I refused to let the outside world see it. The mask was coming off . . . but ever so slowly.

Years later after that horrible diagnosis, I can still remember my mother's 25
words: "Keep your head up, son. . . . We'll pray about it. Work our way through it." She rubbed the top of my head, pulled at my chin, and then took my hand. I've never walked with my head down since that day.

(Byron Pitts, "Keep Your Head Up," 2009)

COMPREHENSION CHECKUP

Multiple Choice

Directions: For each item, write the letter corresponding to the best answer.

_____ 1. The author's primary reason for writing this selection is
- a. to encourage those who are unable to read well to seek professional help.
- b. to share a personal story in order to motivate others to tackle their own personal difficulties.
- c. to focus attention on the staggering rate of illiteracy in the United States.
- d. to thank his mother, family members, and friends for their unwavering support.

_____ 2. The key point of the selection is that
- a. Byron Pitts pulled himself up by his own bootstraps to achieve great things.
- b. Byron Pitts owes a huge debt of gratitude to his mother.
- c. through hard work and the assistance of others, Byron Pitts overcame illiteracy.
- d. mentors provide a valuable service.

_____ 3. Based on the information in the selection, the author would agree with which of the following statements?
- a. Believing in yourself is an important key to success.
- b. Slow learners can't become successful.
- c. His difficulties with reading should have been recognized by his mother much earlier.
- d. Reading is unimportant in many endeavors in life.

_____ 4. All the following statements demonstrate that Byron Pitts is an optimistic person *except* for which one?
- a. He frequently used the phrase "we got this" to indicate to his fellow classmates that they can solve problems.
- b. He thinks good can be found in even difficult moments.
- c. He believes that success is possible with enough hard work.
- d. He measures success by achievement rather than by effort.

_____ 5. Byron Pitts did all the following *except*
a. hide his illiteracy from his closest family members.
b. confront his father over his lack of support and encouragement.
c. refuse to attend remedial classes.
d. both b and c.

True or False

Directions: Indicate whether each statement is true or false by writing **T** or **F** in the space provided.

_____ 6. After Byron Pitts's diagnosis, the family reacted with anger.

_____ 7. The encouragement of Byron Pitts's father helped Byron to overcome illiteracy.

_____ 8. Byron Pitts's mother endorsed the value of working hard to achieve a goal.

_____ 9. Byron Pitts is proud to be a so-called Momma's boy.

_____ 10. The students in the basement had twice as much homework as those upstairs.

_____ 11. Byron Pitts's mother never gave up on him.

_____ 12. Byron Pitts fears only the person who can outwork him.

Vocabulary in Context

Directions: Without consulting a dictionary, write a definition in the blank for each of the following phrases.

1. always ring in my ears (paragraph 1) ______________________________
2. disengaged from the process (paragraph 8) ______________________________
3. darkest days of my life (paragraph 9) ______________________________
4. pull off the tough guy act (paragraph 14) ______________________________
5. lift their spirits (paragraph 16) ______________________________
6. a ragged smile (paragraph 18) ______________________________
7. redefine success (paragraph 20) ______________________________
8. great equalizer (paragraph 22) ______________________________

____

Understanding the Words in the Selection

Directions: In the blanks below, write the word from the list that best completes the sentence. Use each word only once.

assured	initial	protocol
bravado	obstacle	skepticism
disdain	outmaneuvered	vulnerable
immeasurable		

1. Irving's __________ desire to be a pilot faded when he discovered he didn't like to fly.
2. Because Andrea didn't know how to swim, she felt very __________ whenever she was around a swimming pool.

3. Maria has done so much for me; her kindness is __________.
4. Teresa has complete __________ for those who are mean to children.
5. The young bullfighter was very nervous, but he faced the bull with swaggering __________.
6. Jon __________ his mother that he intended to visit his sister in the hospital in the next couple of days.
7. There is a specific __________ for storing and displaying the American flag.
8. When someone says that astrologists can predict the future, I feel only __________.
9. A lack of a good education can be a large __________ to success.
10. Eduardo __________ me and scored the winning goal.

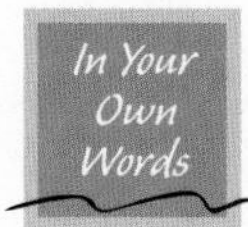

In Your Own Words

Explain the meaning of each of the following quotes.

1. "Smart people can think their troubles to the ground, honey," she'd say. "We have to wrestle ours."
2. "Today the basement, tomorrow prison."
3. "Take life in small bites, until you can take on more."
4. "Success is just your work made public."
5. "Hard work never lies."

Written Assignment

1. What advice would you give someone who is having difficulty learning how to read? What are some concrete steps an individual can take to solve reading problems? Write a short letter giving your advice.
2. Byron Pitts had an "optimistic spirit." According to Alan McGinnis, author of *The Power of Optimism,* pessimists may be overwhelmed by their problems, whereas optimists are challenged by them. "Optimists think of themselves as problem-solvers, as trouble-shooters," he says. This does not mean they see everything through rose-colored glasses. Rather, they have several traits that help them have a positive attitude while still remaining realistic and tough-minded.

Optimists . . .

1. Look for partial solutions.
2. Believe they have control over their future.
3. Interrupt their negative trains of thought.
4. Heighten their powers of appreciation.
5. Are cheerful even when they can't be happy.
6. Like to swap good news.
7. Accept what cannot be changed.

Write a few paragraphs describing how these traits helped Byron Pitts overcome his challenges.

Internet Activity

Visit the Literacy Volunteers of America Web site at

http://www.literacyvolunteers.org/conference

Write a paragraph describing what you learned about the organization.

STUDY TECHNIQUE 2: SCANNING

Scanning is a technique for reviewing reading material quickly to find answers to specific questions. When you scan, you run your eyes rapidly over the material to find the information that you need. Most of us use scanning techniques when we search the telephone book for a number or the TV guide for the time and channel of a show we want to watch.

Now scan "Warren Buffett Offers Advice to Students," pages 18–19, to find answers to the following questions.

1. Scan the first paragraph. What kind of advice does Warren Buffett offer students? ______________
2. Scan paragraph 2. Whom does Buffett advise students to invest in? ______________
3. Scan paragraph 3. According to Buffett, what sort of people should students surround themselves with? ______________
4. Scan paragraph 6. What course was valuable to Buffett? ______________
5. Scan paragraph 7. What kind of person does Buffett advise students to strive to become? ______________
6. Scan paragraph 8. What does Buffett encourage students to use? ______________

READING

Buffett encourages students to "use all their horsepower."

TUNING IN TO READING Do you ever wonder what advice a very successful person would offer to a student such as yourself? In the following reading, Warren Buffett, who has been very successful not only financially but also as a person, offers his advice.

BIO-SKETCH Warren Buffett started his business career delivering newspapers and working at his grandfather's grocery store. Today, the chairman of Berkshire Hathaway is known not only for his investments but also for his philanthropy, primarily with the Gates Foundation.

NOTES ON VOCABULARY

oracle a person or thing regarded as an infallible authority or guide. In the ancient world, people seeking advice would go to oracles, who were believed to speak for particular gods or goddesses.

Warren Buffett Offers Advice to Students

WARREN BUFFETT, THE BILLIONAIRE CEO of Berkshire Hathaway, is considered to be a financial visionary. In fact, Buffett, one of the wealthiest people in the world, is often referred to as the "Oracle of Omaha." Although he has always said that his vast fortune would go to charity, it wasn't until 2006 that he actually began giving it away. More than

$13 billion has already been donated to various foundations. Always interested in philanthropy, Buffett sees it as his duty to give back to society. "All along, I've felt the money was just claim checks that should go back." He also sees it as his duty to nurture the next generation. Buffett says that trees don't grow to the sky; instead, new saplings form. As a result of his philosophy, Buffett has made a habit of offering "life-changing" advice to students. In this way, he is helping new saplings take root.

In difficult economic times when many college graduates are unable to find jobs that match their skills, Buffett says "investing in yourself is the best thing you can do—anything that improves your talents. No matter what happens in the economy, if you have true talent yourself, and you have maximized your talent, you have a terrific asset." 2

Speaking with students at Rice University's Graduate School of Business, he gave the following advice: "Unconditional love is more valuable than any amount of wealth. Students need to surround themselves with people who love them, and to give love in return." When asked what he thought about the correlation between wealth and happiness, he explained that "success is getting what you want, and happiness is wanting what you get." 3

When speaking at Columbia University, Buffett said: "Find what turns you on, what you're passionate about. Do what you would do if the money meant nothing to you. You'll have more fun and be more successful. I'm doing what I would most like to be doing in the world, and I have been since I was 20." 4

Speaking with Emory University students, he offered the following advice: "I enjoy what I do. I tap dance to work every day. I work with people I love, doing what I love. I spend my time thinking about the future, not the past. The future is exciting. To focus on what you don't have is a terrible mistake." 5

At Notre Dame, Buffett told students that taking a public speaking course had been extremely helpful to him. As a young man, Buffett was so terrified of giving speeches that he became physically sick. He actually arranged his life so that he would never have to get up and speak in front of others. Realizing that being proficient in public speaking was important to success, he forced himself to take a public speaking course. Today, of course, Buffett gives speeches with ease. In fact, he credits the ability to feel comfortable in front of an audience as responsible for a large part of his success. 6

On a more general note, Buffett advised one MBA student to "be a nice person. It's so simple that it's almost too obvious to notice. Look around at the people you like. Isn't it a logical assumption that if you like certain traits in other people, then other people would like you if you developed those same traits?" 7

Buffett encourages students to "use all their horsepower." "How big is your engine and how efficiently do you put it to work?" Buffett says that "many people have 400 horsepower engines, but 100 horsepower of output." According to Buffett, "the person who gets full output from a 200-horse-power engine is a lot better off." 8

COMPREHENSION CHECKUP

Directions: Answer the questions below. If you're not sure about the answers, go back and find the information you need.

1. What does Buffett mean when he says that "success is getting what you want, and happiness is wanting what you get?"
2. What does Buffett mean when he says, "I tap dance to work every day?"
3. What does Buffet mean when he says, "Many people have 400 horsepower engines, but 100 horsepower of output?"

Internet Activity

Do a search to find out more about Warren Buffett. Then use the information you collect to write a short biography of him.

Chapter Summary and Review

In this chapter, you were given an introduction to college. You learned how to keep track of your assignments, analyzed your motivation for attending college, learned some ways to increase reading speed, and practiced the study techniques of skimming and scanning.

Short Answer

Directions: Answer the questions briefly, in a few sentences or paragraphs.

1. Which type of assignment sheet works best for you? Explain what you like about it. If you want to use another method of keeping track of your assignments, describe the method you are going to use.
2. What are some ways for improving your reading rate?

Vocabulary in Context

Directions: Choose one of the following words to complete the sentences below. Use each word only once.

assignment sheets flexible scan skimming motivation

3. ___________ (surveying) is a study technique that helps you become familiar with reading material before you begin to read it carefully.
4. If you want to find a specific piece of information, such as a date or a person's name, you can ___________ the material.
5. The best way to keep track of assignments is to use ___________.
6. ________ reading means adjusting your reading rate according to the difficulty of the material and your purpose for reading it.
7. __________ is the inner power and psychological energy that directs our behavior.

CHAPTER 1

Improving Your Vocabulary

CHAPTER PREVIEW

In this chapter, you will

- Learn why it's important to develop a college-level vocabulary.
- Learn techniques for developing a larger vocabulary.
- Learn how to use context clues and word structure to determine the meaning of a word.
- Master the fundamentals of dictionary usage.
- Learn how to make vocabulary cards.

Introduction to College-Level Vocabulary

Why is it important for you as a college student to have a large vocabulary? Knowing more words will improve your ability to communicate effectively in both speaking and writing. When you are speaking to others, if you have many words to choose from, you can pick the exact words you need to express your thoughts. Knowing many words enables you to make fine distinctions between them so that people know precisely what you mean. Further, if you have a large vocabulary, you can more easily understand what others are saying.

Your reading comprehension also depends on your knowing the meaning of words. A large vocabulary enables you to read and understand a wider range of material.

Your ability to think critically and communicate well will also influence your success in your chosen field. A large vocabulary is a common characteristic of successful people. In fact, a person's vocabulary level is one of the best predictors of occupational success. But having a large vocabulary is also essential to being a good citizen. The more you improve your vocabulary in such areas as geography, politics, and ecology, among others, the better you will be able to understand what's happening in the world. Keep in mind that building a large vocabulary is a lifelong pursuit. Following are some general tips that will assist you in developing a larger vocabulary.

- Be aware of words. Make a daily practice of noting words that are unfamiliar to you or catch your interest. You will pick up these words from many sources, such as friends, teachers, magazines, and mass media.
- Read challenging material, both fiction and nonfiction. When you have questions about words you read and hear, write them down. Use note cards, or enter the words in your smartphone. Find out what the words mean. Ask somebody or go to a dictionary. When you look up a word in the dictionary, be sure to note the pronunciation, so that you can say your word correctly.
- Use your new words in conversation as soon as you can. But use them appropriately, at the right place and time. As Mark Twain often said, "Don't use a five-dollar word when a fifty-cent word will do."
- Be patient. Research has shown that we have to notice a word and use it about five to seven times before we really master it.

The next section in this textbook will introduce you to four techniques for building a larger vocabulary.

1. **Context Clues.** Guess the meaning of the word from how it is used.
2. **Word Structure**. Decipher the meaning of the word by looking at its parts—roots, prefixes, and suffixes.
3. **Dictionary**. Don't overlook your most reliable and accurate resource—the dictionary. Look up the words to discover meaning and pronunciation.
4. **Word Cards**. Put your new words on a note card. The act of writing the word will help you remember it. Keep the note cards in a file box so that you can review your words from time to time. Keep track of your progress.

Context Clues

When you encounter an unfamiliar word, your job is made easier if you can use the context to help you determine its meaning. The context of a word is what surrounds it and includes the sentence it appears in, other nearby sentences, and even the whole article in which it appears. Try placing your finger over the unfamiliar word and see if you can supply a word you know that gives the sentence meaning, or at least enough meaning for your purposes.

For example, see if you can figure out the meaning of the italicized word below from the context of the sentence:

> Imagine Sue's *chagrin* when she realized that all of the other women at the office party were wearing long dresses and she was wearing shorts.

You can probably guess from context clues that *chagrin* in this sentence means "embarrassment."

Keep in mind that the exact meaning of a word may not be as important when you are reading a light novel or cartoon for enjoyment as it is when you are reading one of your college textbooks.

There are several kinds of context clues. Familiarizing yourself with all of them will go a long way to helping you study your college textbooks without having to interrupt your reading to look up a specific word. When having a precise definition is not necessary, the use of context clues can be sufficient and save time.

Here are some common techniques for using context to determine the meaning of new words.

Definition: Sometimes a writer simply provides us with a definition of a word somewhere within the sentence, especially if the word is one that we are unlikely to be familiar with:

> A *thesaurus,* or dictionary that lists synonyms, antonyms, and other related words, can help you express your ideas more clearly and effectively.

You can see that the author defines a *thesaurus* as a special type of dictionary.

Synonym: A synonym, which is another word with a similar meaning, may be used elsewhere in the sentence.

> Four types of objects *revolve* around the sun; however, the planets are the largest objects that circle our fiery star.

"The first book of the nation is the dictionary of its language."

—Contanitin, Count de Volney

If you did not know the meaning of *revolve,* you could determine its meaning from the word *circle.* To circle and to revolve mean approximately the same thing.

The cartoon below uses the word *tranquility*. Notice the synonyms "peace and quiet" help you understand that the word *tranquility* means "peaceful and restful."

HAGAR © 2009 by King Features Syndicate, Inc. World rights reserved

Antonym: Sometimes you can determine the meaning of a word by finding an antonym, a word with an opposite meaning, somewhere in the sentence.

Gustavo was a very skillful soccer player, but Pedro was *inept.*

You can see that the writer is making a contrast, and that skillful is the opposite of *inept.*

The cartoon below illustrates the use of an antonym. Notice that the phrase *filters out* helps you understand that the antonym *amplifies* must mean "increases."

"It's a special hearing aid. It filters out criticism and amplifies compliments."

Examples: Sometimes examples illustrate the meaning of a word.

In a *brazen* act of defiance, Marco lit his cigarette while standing in front of a "No Smoking" sign and then refused to put it out when asked to do so.

This example suggests to you that a *brazen* act is one that is bold and shameless.

Look at the cartoon below. Notice that an example of *flexible* is provided. Someone who is *flexible* is "capable of stretching." The cartoon character Gumby, made of green clay, is a good example of something very *flexible.*

"We're looking for someone who can stretch with the demands of this job. Are you flexible?"

Explanation: Sometimes a writer simply gives an explanation of what a word means.

> In your communications class, you will probably have to give an *impromptu* speech. For this type of speech, you will be given a topic and only a few minutes to prepare your talk.

The writer is telling you that an *impromptu* speech is one that is given with very little preparation.

Experience: This way of discovering the meaning of a word draws on your personal experience.

> Have your efforts to complete a paper for a class ever been *thwarted* because your computer broke down?

Perhaps you have experienced this or a similar situation, and you remember that your efforts were "hindered" or "frustrated" at least for the time being.

Knowledge of Subject: In this technique, you have just enough familiarity with the subject the writer is discussing to enable you to figure out the meaning of the unknown word.

> Although many Americans often diet, many have difficulty maintaining a *svelte* shape for more than a few months.

You know that people often diet to make themselves "slim" or "slender."

Combination: Can you use a number of these techniques at the same time to detect the meaning of a word? You bet!

> The man at the party was a real *extrovert.* He acted like a clown and had everyone laughing the whole evening.

Here you probably used explanation, experience, and familiarity with the subject to determine that an *extrovert* is a very outgoing person.

Now work with a partner on the following exercises. Remember, no peeking at your dictionary.

Context Clue Practice 1

Directions: On the first line, write your own definition for the italicized word. Then on the second line, note the technique you used to arrive at the definition. The first item is done for you. ______

1. Everyone in the family was *elated* to discover that Howard had the winning million-dollar lottery ticket in his pocket.

   Definition: jubilant; overjoyed

   Technique(s) used: knowledge of subject, explanation, maybe experience

2. Believing the 12-year-old offender to be *contrite,* the judge decided to give him another chance before putting him in juvenile detention.

   Definition: ______

   Technique(s) used: ______

3. Should football games be canceled because of *inclement* weather?

   Definition: ______

   Technique(s) used: ______

4. Should sexually *explicit* scenes be deleted from movies when they are shown on television?

   Definition: ____________________

   Technique(s) used: ____________________

5. Carol was extremely relieved to discover that her tumor was *benign* rather than malignant and so she would require no further treatment.

   Definition: ____________________

   Technique(s) used: ____________________

6. Her house was so *immaculate* that you could literally eat off the floor.

   Definition: ____________________

   Technique(s) used: ____________________

7. Many boys in high school *aspire* to be professional athletes, but very few are actually good enough to make it to the professional ranks.

   Definition: ____________________

   Technique(s) used: ____________________

8. The FBI conducted *covert,* or secret, operations to find out information about the drug-smuggling ring.

   Definition: ____________________

   Technique(s) used: ____________________

9. Many students are not *affluent* enough to attend college without working part-time or receiving some type of financial assistance.

   Definition: ____________________

   Technique(s) used: ____________________

Context Clue Practice 2

Directions: Use the context clues in the second sentence to define the italicized word in the first. Circle the clue word (or words) in the second sentence that provided the clue(s).

1. "Yes, this computer is *obsolete,*" said Matt. "But out of date or not, it's too expensive to replace."
2. "I can't accept any *remuneration* for taking care of your dog while you were in the hospital," said Carrie. "Nonsense dear," said Mrs. Watson, "you should get paid for doing a good deed."
3. It would be *presumptuous* to accuse him of the crime. Taking him in for questioning without solid evidence would simply be too bold.
4. Mountain climbing is full of *hazards.* However, the adventure is worth all of the risks.
5. He considered it an *indignity* for his parents to ignore his college graduation. He couldn't envision a worse insult.
6. Martha complained that she was getting tired of *goading* her son to do his homework. At his age, he should be able to finish it without her urging.
7. Some people *feign* injuries after their car is rear-ended. They don't stop pretending until they have received a cash settlement.

8. Todd, the pilot of our small airplane, seemed very *apprehensive* about taking off during the storm. His anxious behavior was upsetting the passengers.
9. I was certain he was *despondent* because he hadn't smiled all week. Perhaps he had good reason to be so depressed.
10. The teacher was *cognizant* of the difficulties involved in learning a new language. Her awareness was based on the fact that she too had once emigrated from her homeland.
11. In the United States, many families celebrate Thanksgiving with a *sumptuous* meal. However, after the lavish feast, many Americans begin dieting in earnest.

Context Clue Practice 3

Directions: Use the context clues in each sentence to help determine the missing word. Briefly describe the clue or clues that helped you.

1. If you believe that you control your own destiny, you have an internal locus of control; however, if you believe that your fate is determined by chance or outside forces, you have an __________ locus of control.

   Clue: ______________________________

2. Successful students are naturally __________ because they have a hopeful attitude and believe that effort, good study habits, and self-discipline will make their grades go up. "They can because they think they can."

   Clue: ______________________________

3. Students exhibit what is called self-serving bias. When they get an exam grade back, if they did well they tend to accept personal credit. They consider the exam to be a valid indication of their abilities. However, if they did very poorly, they are much more likely to __________ the teacher or the exam.

   Clue: ______________________________

4. Interestingly enough, teachers do the same thing. They are likely to take credit for whatever success is associated with their students and blame the student for any __________. "Teachers, it seems, are likely to think, 'With my help, Maria graduated with honors. Despite all my help, Melinda flunked out.'"

   Clue: ______________________________

5. College students need to be especially careful about those with whom they associate. Researchers have verified that students learn more from their friends and other students than they do from their __________ or from books. Out-of-class relationships are clearly the major influence in a student's life.

   Clue: ______________________________

(David G. Myers, *Social Psychology*, 8/e, 2005)

Context Clue Practice 4

1. Consumers are easy prey for land swindlers. Instead of a *lucrative* investment, they end up with a purchase of worthless or overvalued land.

(Freda Adler et al., *Criminal Justice*, 5/e, McGraw-Hill, 2009, p. 64)

Definition: ______________________________

Technique used: ______________________________

2. *Fair use* allows the copying of a work for a noncommercial use, as long as that copying does not interfere with sales by the copyright holder.

(George Rodman, *Mass Media in a Changing World*, 4/e, McGraw-Hill, 2012, p. 410)

Definition: ______________________________

Technique used: ______________________________

3. The term *disaster* refers to a sudden or disruptive event or set of events that overtaxes a community's resources, so that outside aid is necessary.

(Richard T. Schaefer, *Sociology*, 12/e, McGraw-Hill, 2010, p. 478)

Definition: ______________________________

Technique used: ______________________________

4. When trying to detect a lie, the polygraph operator begins by asking *irrelevant* questions such as, "Did you eat lunch today?" However, even starting with unimportant questions is not enough to put some people at ease.

(Freda Adler et al., *Criminal Justice*, 5/e, McGraw-Hill, 2009, p. 389)

Definition: ______________________________

Technique used: ______________________________

5. Human activities have altered almost all ecosystems and reduced *biodiversity*, or the number of different species present in a given area.

(Sylvia Mader and Michael Windelspecht, *Human Biology*, 13/e, McGraw-Hill, 2014, p. 9)

Definition: ______________________________

Technique used: ______________________________

6. *Hoaxes* have long been used to sell newspapers. In fact, these personal deceptions were so commonplace that when the telegraph was invented in 1848, many readers thought it was just another media prank.

(George Rodman, *Mass Media in a Changing World*, 4/e, McGraw-Hill, 2012, p. 510)

Definition: ______________________________

Technique used: ______________________________

7. Until recently, *monetary sanctions* were not used much in the American legal system, but today the use of fines is increasing.

(Freda Adler et al., *Criminal Justice*, 5/e, McGraw-Hill, 2009, p. 405)

Definition: ______________________________

Technique used: ______________________________

8. The colon is subject to the development of *polyps*, small growths arising from the lining.

(Sylvia Mader and Michael Windelspecht, *Human Biology*, 13/e, McGraw-Hill, 2014, p. 123)

Definition: ______________________________

Technique used: ______________________________

9. Victims of white-collar crime range from the *savvy* investor to the unsuspecting consumer.

(Freda Adler et al., *Criminal Justice*, 5/e, McGraw-Hill, 2009, p. 60)

Definition: ______________________________

Technique used: ______________________________

10. If you claim that an innocent person is guilty of criminal or unethical behavior, that would be *defamation.* If you engage in any type of false communication that injures the reputation of an individual, you are *defaming* them.

(George Rodman, *Mass Media in a Changing World,* 4/e, McGraw-Hill, 2012, p. 406)

Definition: ______________________________

Technique used: ______________________________

11. "Punch $200 into the machine or I'll blow you away." With these words Curtis K. Taylor would approach customers at automated teller machines throughout California. Taylor was *prolific,* perhaps the most *prolific* of all teller-machine bandits in the United States. When apprehended in 1988, he pleaded guilty to 37 robbery and attempted robbery charges.

(Freda Adler et al., *Criminal Justice,* 5/e, McGraw-Hill, 2009, p. 295)

Definition: ______________________________

Technique used: ______________________________

12. Not all telemarketing is *genuine.* The New York State Attorney General estimates that approximately 10 percent of the over 140,000 New York businesses using telemarketing to sell their products are frauds.

(Freda Adler et al., *Criminal Justice,* 5/e, McGraw-Hill, 2009, p. 64)

Definition: ______________________________

Technique used: ______________________________

Word Structure: Roots, Prefixes, and Suffixes

The second method of determining what a word means is to examine its parts. Many words in English are based on Latin and Greek words. The Greeks and Romans devised a system of word parts that is still in use today. If you know the meaning of enough of these word parts, you can discover a word's meaning without referring to the dictionary.

The three types of word parts are roots, prefixes, and suffixes.

The **root** is the basic part of the word and usually comes in the middle. Many English words are composed of at least one root. Learning common roots will help you remember words and allow you to learn whole families of words at one time.

Here's an illustration of how it works.

The word *dictatorial* means acting like a dictator—someone who rules with absolute authority. It comes from the Latin root *dict,* which means "to say, speak, or tell."

Now let's look at other words from the same family. Take the word *dictate.* When you *dictate* something, somebody else has to write it down. The word also means to "speak" orders.

A *benediction* is a form of speech in which a person speaks well of somebody or something, and *diction* has to do with speaking or pronouncing words.

As you can see, you can learn many words from just one root and remember them more easily, too.

The root gives the basic clue to the meaning of a word. A **prefix** comes at the beginning of the word and a **suffix** at the end. Let's examine another word from the same family—*predicted.* Look at the following sentence:

> Tom *predicted* the winner of this year's Kentucky Derby.

The sentence means that Tom said ahead of time who the winner was going to be. Let's examine the word parts for *predicted. Pre* means "before"; *dict* means "to say, speak, or tell"; and *ed* is the suffix indicating past tense. Now, see how the prefix (along with the context) helps you get the meaning of the italicized words in the next example:

> The witness *contradicted* the story told by the defendant.

Contra is a prefix meaning "against." The literal meaning of *contradict* is "say against someone or something."

Suffixes consist of a syllable or syllables placed at the end of a word to form particular parts of speech. Suffixes can change words into adjectives, adverbs, nouns, or verbs. For example, by adding different suffixes to the root *agree,* the part of speech and the meaning of the word are changed, as you can see in these examples:

agreeable He was *agreeable* to a change in plans. (adjective)

agreeably He worked *agreeably* with his coworkers on the project. (adverb)

agreement The two countries were trying to forge a trade *agreement.* (noun)

Exercise 1: Prefixes, Roots, and Suffixes

Directions: In the following list, combine each root with a prefix or suffix to make a common word. You may use prefixes and suffixes more than once. Write a definition for each of the words you create.

Prefixes	Roots	Suffixes
un	break	ful
re	read	ed
non	law	ive
in	pay	able
over	sight	ment
pre	take	less
mis	grace	ness
de	part	en
dis	know	er
im	remark	s/ion
	measure	t/ion
	prove	

1. ____________________ Definition: ____________________

2. ____________________ Definition: ____________________

3. ____________________ Definition: ____________________

4. ____________________ Definition: ____________________

5. ______________________ Definition: ______________________
6. ______________________ Definition: ______________________
7. ______________________ Definition: ______________________
8. ______________________ Definition: ______________________
9. ______________________ Definition: ______________________
10. ______________________ Definition: ______________________
11. ______________________ Definition: ______________________
12. ______________________ Definition: ______________________

The vocabulary units in Part 5 will give you additional practice in using more than 75 word parts.

Dictionary Usage

It is essential that you have access to a good college dictionary, whether it is printed or online. A dictionary is an invaluable resource provided you have one that suits your purposes and you know the basics of how to use it. Dictionaries define words, show how they are spelled, show how they are pronounced, identify their parts of speech, and give their etymologies, or histories of words. Some dictionaries include examples showing the correct usage of words in phrases or sentences.

Advantages and Disadvantages of Online Dictionaries

Many students use online dictionaries, which often have an audio feature that lets you hear a word's correct pronunciation. Just type the word you want and press "search." Following are some good online dictionaries.

www.merriam-webster.com
www.onelook.com
www.yourdictionary.com
www.encarta.com

These dictionaries have advantages over print books, but they also have disadvantages.

Advantages

1. Entries are not cluttered with multiple definitions.
2. The font is large enough to be easily readable.
3. Information is provided quickly.
4. Content is frequently updated, so the definitions stay current.
5. Users can more easily find words when they do not know the correct spelling.

Disadvantages

1. Entries may list only the most common definitions.

2. Entries may not offer variant forms of words—for example, how one word can be used as either a noun or an adjective.
3. Etymologies are not always provided.
4. Archaic or obsolete meanings are not always provided. This is a disadvantage if you are reading older material.

The exercises in the next section are designed to give you practice mastering the fundamentals of dictionaries, both print and online.

Dictionary Organization

The discussion and examples below will often refer to the sample dictionary page found on page 33. We have taken an excerpt from the *Random House Webster's College Dictionary,* 2nd ed., 2000, enlarged the print, and adapted the pages for your use.

1. Entry words
Dictionaries are organized like telephone books, in alphabetical order. Each entry word is usually in **boldface** type. Often dictionaries will also give common two- or three-word phrases as entry words.

What boldface entry comes after "sawbones"? ____________________

2. Guide words
As in a telephone book, there are guide words at the top of each page that indicate the first and last entries on that page.

What are the guide words for this page? ____________________

3. Entry word division versus pronunciation—syllabication division
For each entry, the word division and the pronunciation and syllabication division are usually the same.

How many syllables are there in the word "saxophone"? ____________________

You should realize that some dictionaries divide their entry words as you would for printers and typesetting, so the entry word and pronunciation divisions may not be exactly the same. Take a look at the word "curious." Notice that the entry word is divided differently than its pronunciation.

> **cu•ri•ous** (kyŏŏr′ē əs), *adj.* **1.** eager to learn or know. **2.** taking an undue interest in others' affairs; prying. **3.** arousing attention or interest through being unusual or hard to explain; odd; strange; novel. **4.** *Archaic.* **a.** made or done skillfully or painstakingly. **b.** careful; fastidious. **c.** marked by intricacy or subtlety. [1275–1325; ME < L *cūriōsus* careful, inquisitive, prob. back formation from *incūriōsus* careless, der. of *incūria* carelessness]—**cu′ri•ous•ly,** *adv.* —**cu′ri•ous•ness,** *n.*
>
> (*Random House Webster's College Dictionary,* 2/e, 2000)

4. Pronunciation
Notice how most dictionary entries are followed by their pronunciations but the words are written quite differently. Dictionaries will use letters and symbols that represent sounds. Usually you will find a complete key to these sounds in the front part of the dictionary. On pages 34–35 is the Random House pronunciation key.

savvy to sayyid

sav•vy (sav′ē), *n., adj.,* **-vi•er, -vi•est,** *.v.,* **-vied, -vy•ing.** —*n.* **1.** Also, **sav′vi•ness.** practical understanding; shrewdness or intelligence; common sense: *political savvy.* —*adj.* **2.** shrewdly informed; experienced and well-informed; canny. —*v.t., v.i.* **3.** to know; understand. [1775–85; prob. orig. < *sábi* "know" in E creoles (< Pg *sabe,* pres. 3rd sing. of *saber* to know < L *sapere* to be wise; see SAPIENT)] **—sav′vi•ly,** *adv.*

saw[1] (sô), *n., v.,* **sawed, sawed** or **sawn, saw•ing.** —*n.* **1.** a tool or device for cutting, typically a thin blade of metal with a series of sharp teeth. **2.** any similar tool or device, as a rotating disk, in which a sharp continuous edge replaces the teeth. —*v.t.* **3.** to cut or divide with a saw. **4.** to form by cutting with a saw. **5.** to make cutting motions as if using a saw: *to saw the air with one's hands.* **6.** to work (something) from side to side like a saw. —*v.i.* **7.** to use a saw. **8.** to cut with or as if with a saw. —***Idiom.*** **9. saw wood,** to snore loudly while sleeping. [bef. 1000; ME *sawe,* OE *saga,* c. MLG, MD *sage* (D *zaag*), OHG *saga,* ON *sǫg;*] —**saw′er,** *n.*

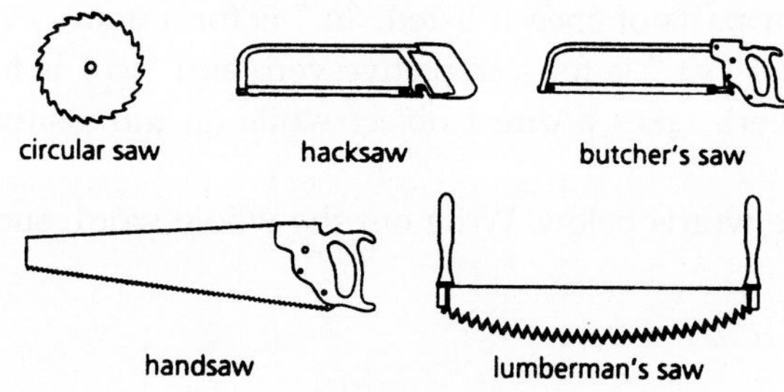

saws (def. 1)

saw[2] (sô), *v.* pt. of SEE[1].

saw[3] (sô), *n.* a maxim; proverb; saying; *an old saw.* [bef. 950; ME; OE *sagu;* c. OFris *sege,* OHG, G *sage,* ON *saga* (cf. SAGA); akin to SAY]

Sa•watch (sə′wäch′), *n.* a mountain range in central Colorado: part of the Rocky Mountains. Highest peak, Mt. Elbert, 14,431 ft. (4400 m).

saw•bones (sô′bōnz′), *n., pl.* **-bones, -bones•es.** (*used with a sing. v.*) *Slang.* a surgeon or physician. [1830–40]

saw•buck (sô′buk′), *n.* **1.** a sawhorse. **2.** *Slang.* a ten-dollar bill. [1860–65, *Amer.;* cf. D *zaagbok;* (def. 2) so called from the resemblance of the Roman numeral X to the crossbars of a sawhorse]

saw•dust (sô′dust′), *n.* fine particles of wood produced in sawing.

sawed′-off′, *adj.* **1.** cut off at the end, as a shotgun. **2.** *Slang.* smallish; of less than average size or stature. [1865–70, *Amer.*]

saw•fish (sô′fish′), *n., pl.* (*esp. collectively*) **-fish,** (*esp. for kinds or species*) **-fish•es.** any large, sharklike ray of the genus *Pristis,* living along tropical coasts and lowland rivers, with a bladelike snout edged with strong teeth. [1655–65]

saw•fly (sô′flī′), *n., pl.* **-flies.** any of numerous insects of the family Tenthredinidae, the female of which has a sawlike ovipositor for inserting the eggs in the tissues of a host plant. [1765–75]

saw•horse (sô′hôrs′), *n.* a movable frame or trestle for supporting wood while it is being sawed. [1770–80]

saw•mill (sô′mil′), *n.* a place or building in which timber is sawed into planks, boards, etc., by machinery. [1545–55]

sawn (sôn), *v.* a pp. of SAW[1].

saw-off (sô′ôf′, -of′), *n. Canadian.* **1.** an arrangement between political rivals by which each agrees not to run for the same office as another. **2.** any arrangement that involves concessions. [1905–10]

saw′palmet′to, *n.* a shrublike palmetto, *Serenoa repens,* native to the southern U.S., having green or blue leafstalks set with spiny teeth.

saw•tooth (sô′tooth′), *n., pl.* **-teeth** (-tēth′), *adj.* —*n.* **1.** one of the cutting teeth of a saw. —*adj.* **2.** having a zigzag profile, like that of the cutting edge of a saw; serrate. [1595–1605]

saw′-toothed′, *adj.* having sawlike teeth; serrate. [1580–90]

saw′-whet′owl′, *n.* a small North American owl, *Aegolius acadicus,* with a persistently repeated, mechanical sounding note. [1825–35, *Amer.;* from its cry being likened to a saw being whetted]

saw•yer (sô′yr, soi′ər), *n.* **1.** a person who saws wood, esp. as an occupation. **2.** any of several long-horned beetles, esp. one of the genus *Monochamus,* the larvae of which bore in the wood of coniferous trees. [1300–50; ME *sawier* = *sawe* saw[1] + *-ier* -IER[1]]

sax (saks), *n.* a saxophone. [by shortening]

Sax., **1.** Saxon. **2.** Saxony.

sax•a•tile (sak′sə til), *adj.* living or growing on or among rocks; saxicoline. [1645–55; < L *saxātilis* frequenting rocks, der. of *sax(um)* rock]

Saxe (SAKS), *n.* French name of SAXONY.

Saxe-Co•burg-Go•tha (saks′kō′bûrg gō′thə), *n.* **1.** a member of the present British royal family, from the establishment of the house in 1901 until 1917 when the family name was changed to Windsor. **2. Albert Francis Charles Augustus Emanuel, Prince of,** ALBERT, Prince.

sax•horn (saks′hôrn′), *n.* any of a family of brass instruments close to the cornets and tubas. [1835–45; after A. *Sax* (1814–94), a Belgian who invented such instruments]

sax•ic•o•line (sak sik′ə lin, -līn′) also **sax•ic•o•lous** (-ləs), *adj.* living or growing among rocks. [1895–1900; < NL *saxicol(a)* (L *saxi-,* comb. form of *saxum* rock + *-cola* dweller; see -COLOUS) + -INE[1]]

sax•i•frage (sak′sə frij), *n.* any of numerous plants of the genus *Saxifraga,* certain species of which grow wild in the clefts of rocks, other species of which are cultivated for their flowers. [1400–50; late ME < L *saxifraga* (*herba*) stone-breaking (herb) = *saxi-,* comb. form of *saxum* stone + *-fraga,* fem. of *-fragus* breaking; see FRAGILE]

sax•i•tox•in (sak′si tok′sin), *n.* a neurotoxin produced by the dinoflagellate *Gonyaulax catenella,* the causative agent of red tide. [1960–65; < NL *Saxi(domus),* a clam genus infected by the dinoflagellates (L *sax(um)* stone + *-i-* -i- + *domus* house) + TOXIN]

Sax•o Gram•mat•i•cus (sak′sō grəmat′i kəs), *n.* c1150–1206?, Danish historian and poet.

Sax•on (sak′sən), *n.* **1.** a member of a Germanic people or confederation of peoples, occupying parts of the North Sea littoral and adjacent hinterlands in the 3rd–4th centuries A.D.: later notorious as sea raiders, groups of whom invaded and settled in S Britain in the 5th–6th centuries. **2.** a native or inhabitant of Saxony. **3.** a native of England, or person of English descent, esp. as opposed to an inhabitant of the British Isles of Celtic descent. —*adj.* **4.** of or pertaining to the early Saxons. **5.** of or pertaining to Saxony or its inhabitants. [1250–1300; ME, prob. < LL *Saxō, Saxonēs* (pl.) < Gmc; r. OE *Seaxan* (pl.)]

sax•o•ny (sak′sə nē), *n.* **1.** a fine, three-ply woolen yarn. **2.** a soft-finish, compact fabric for coats. [1825–35; from SAXONY]

Sax•o•ny (sak′sə nē), *n.* **1.** a state in E central Germany, 4,900,000; 6561 sq. mi. (16,990 sq. km). *Cap.:* Dresden. **2.** a former state of the Weimar Republic in E central Germany. 5788 sq. mi. (14,990 sq. km). *Cap.:* Dresden. **3.** a medieval division of N Germany with varying boundaries: extended at its height from the Rhine to E of the Elbe. German, **Sachsen;** French, **Saxe.** —**Sax•o′ni•an** (-sō′nēən), *n., adj.*

Sax′ony-An′halt, *n.* a state in central Germany. 3,000,000; 9515 sq. mi. (24,644 sq. km). *Cap.:* Magdeburg. German, **Sachsen-Anhalt.**

sax•o•phone (sak′sə fōn′), *n.* a musical wind instrument consisting of a conical, usu. brass tube with keys or valves and a mouthpiece with one reed. [1850–55; *Sax* (see SAXHORN) + -o- + -PHONE]—**sax′o•phon′ic** (-fon′ik), *adj.* —**sax′o•phon′ist,** *n.*

saxophone

say (sā), *v.,* **said, say•ing,** *adv., n., interj.* —*v.t.* **1.** to utter or pronounce; speak: to *say a word.* **2.** to express in words; state; declare: *Say what you think.* **3.** to state as an opinion or judgment: *I say we should wait here.* **4.** to recite or repeat. **5.** to report or allege; maintain. **6.** to express (a message, viewpoint, etc.), as through a literary or other artistic medium. **7.** to indicate or show: *What does your watch say?* —*v.i.* **8.** to speak; declare; express an opinion, idea, etc. —*adv.* **9.** approximately; about: *It's, say, 14 feet long.* **10.** for example. —*n.* **11.** what a person says or has to say. **12.** the right or opportunity to state an opinion or exercise influence: *to have one's say in a decision.* **13.** a turn to say something. —*interj.* **14.** (used to express surprise, get attention, etc.) —***Idiom.*** **15. go without saying,** to be completely self-evident. [bef. 900; ME *seyen, seggen,* OE *secgan;* c. D *zeggen,* G *sagen,* ON *segja;* akin to SAW[3]] —**say′er,** *n.*

say•a•ble (sā′ə bəl), *adj.* **1.** of the sort that can be said or spoken. **2.** capable of being said or stated clearly, effectively, etc. [1855–60]

Sa•yan′Moun′tains (sä yän′), *n.pl.* a mountain range in the S Russian Federation in central Asia. Highest peak, 11,447 ft. (3490 m).

Say•ers (sā′ərz, sârz), *n.* **Dorothy L(eigh),** 1893–1957, English detective-story writer, dramatist, essayist, and translator.

say•est (sā′ist) also **sayst** (sāst), *v. Archaic.* 2nd pers. sing. of SAY.

say•ing (sā′ing), *n.* something said, esp. a proverb or maxim.

sa•yo•na•ra (sī′ə när′ə), *interj., n.* farewell. [1870–75; < Japn]

says (sez), *v.* 3rd pers. sing. pres. indic. of SAY.

say′-so′, *n., pl.* **say-sos. 1.** one's personal statement or assertion. **2.** right of final authority. **3.** an authoritative statement. [1630–40]

say•yid or **say•ed** or **say•id** (sä′yid, sā′id), *n.* **1.** a supposed descendant of Muhammad through his grandson Hussein. **2.** an Islamic title of respect, esp. for royal personages. [1780–90; < Ar: lord]

From *The Random House Webster's College Dictionary* (1995).

Sometimes variant pronunciations will also be given for dictionary entry words. For example, the word "sawyer" has two pronunciations (see page 33).

What words show how "oi" is pronounced? ____________________

Write out the pronunciations for the following words:

sayable ____________________

sawyer (both pronunciations) ____________________

sawtooth ____________________

5. Parts of speech

Each word will also have its part or parts of speech listed: "n." is for a noun, "v." is for a verb, and so forth. Note that "v.t." is for a transitive verb and "v.i." is for an intransitive verb. A transitive verb takes a direct object while an intransitive does not.

Find the parts of speech for the words below. Write out the whole word, such as "adjective" for "adj."

Saxe ____________

sayable ____________

sayyid ____________

6. Etymology

We have been studying word etymologies, or word histories, in the vocabulary units throughout this book. We will not list all the abbreviations used for different languages, but "L" is the abbreviation for Latin and "Gk" stands for Greek.

Find out the Latin meaning for

savvy ____________________

saxicoline ____________________

Many words in English come from other languages. From what language does the word "sayonara" come? ____________________

ENGLISH SOUNDS

a	**a**ct, b**a**t, m**a**rry	**l**	**l**ow, me**ll**ow, bott**le** (bot'l)	**th**	**th**at, ei**th**er, smoo**th**
ā	**a**ge, p**ai**d, s**ay**	**m**	**m**y, su**mm**er, hi**m**	**u**	**u**p, s**u**n
âr	**air**, M**ar**y, d**are**	**n**	**n**ow, si**nn**er, butto**n** (but'n)	**ûr**	**ur**ge, b**ur**n, c**ur**
ä	**ah**, b**a**lm, st**a**r	**ng**	si**ng**, Washi**ng**ton	**v**	**v**oice, ri**v**er, li**v**e
b	**b**ack, ca**b**in, ca**b**	**o**	**o**x, b**o**mb, w**a**sp	**w**	**w**itch, a**w**ay
ch	**ch**ild, pit**ch**er, bea**ch**	**ō**	**o**ver, b**oa**t, n**o**	**y**	**y**es, oni**o**n
d	**d**o, ma**dd**er, be**d**	**ô**	**o**rder, b**a**ll, r**aw**	**z**	**z**oo, la**z**y, tho**se**
e	**e**dge, s**e**t, m**e**rry	**oi**	**oi**l, j**oi**nt, j**oy**	**zh**	trea**s**ure, mira**g**e
ē	**e**qual, b**ee**, prett**y**	**o͝o**	**oo**mph, b**oo**k, t**ou**r	**ə**	used in unaccented syllables to indicate the sound of the reduced vowel in **a**lone, syst**e**m, eas**i**ly, gall**o**p, circ**u**s
ēr	**ear**ring, ch**eer**ful, app**ear**	**o͞o**	**oo**ze, f**oo**l, t**oo**	**ᵊ**	used between **i** and **r**
f	**f**it, di**ff**er, pu**ff**	**ou**	**ou**t, l**ou**d, c**ow**		
g	**g**ive, tri**gg**er, be**g**	**p**	**p**ot, su**pp**er, sto**p**		
h	**h**it, be**h**ave	**r**	**r**ead, hu**rr**y, nea**r**		
hw	**wh**ich, no**wh**ere				

i if, big, mirror	**s** see, passing, miss	and between **ou** and **r**		
ī ice, bite, deny	**sh** shoe, fashion, push	to show triphthongal		
j just, tragic, fudge	**t** ten, matter, bit	quality, as in **fire** (iᵊr),		
k keep, token, make	**th** thin, ether, path	**hour** (ouᵊr)		

NON-ENGLISH SOUNDS

A	as in French **ami** (A mē′)	R	[a symbol for any non-English **r** sound, including a trill or flap in Italian and Spanish and a sound in French and German similar to KH but pronounced with voice]		
KH	as in Scottish **loch** (lôKH)			Y	as in French **tu** (tY)
N	as in French **bon** (bôN) [used to indicate that the preceding vowel is nasalized]			ᵊ	as in French **bastogne** (ba stôn′yᵊ)
Œ	as in French **feu** (FŒ)				

From *The Random House Webster's College Dictionary* (1995).

7. Words in phrases

Some dictionaries, such as the *Random House Webster's College Dictionary,* give some words in sample phrases. Take a look at the definitions for "say" and see how this word is used in sample phrases.

What are some of the phrases used for this word? ____________________

____

____

8. Geographical and biographical information

Most dictionaries place this information in with the regular entries. Other dictionaries, such as the Merriam-Webster dictionaries, give this information at the end of the dictionary.

Where is Saxony and what is its capital city? ____________________

____

Exercise 2: Dictionary Usage

Directions: Use the dictionary page provided to answer the following questions.

1. How many syllables does each of the following entry words have?

   sawyer ____________________

   saxicoline ____________________

   sayable ____________________

2. Write the part(s) of speech for each of the following entry words:

   saw ____________________

   Saxon ____________________

3. Write the plural forms for the following words:

   sawbones ____________________

   sawfly ____________________

   sayso ____________________

   sawtooth ____________________

4. Find an entry word that is an example of each of the following:

   a place ______________________

   a person ______________________

   ____

   an animal ______________________

5. Name two entries that have pictures as aids to understand their meanings.

   ____

   ____

6. How many meanings are given for each of the following entry words?

   saw[1] ______________________

   sawyer ______________________

   Saxon ______________________

7. What suffixes are used to change "savvy" to different parts of speech?

   ____

8. What is the origin of the word "saxatile"? ______________________

   ____

9. Pronounce the following words. Then write each word using correct spelling.

   sak si tok sin ______________________

   sā ing ______________________

   sez ______________________

   saks ______________________

Directions: Indicate whether the following statements are true or false by writing **T** or **F** in the space provided.

______ 10. **Sawbones** is slang for a surgeon or physician.

______ 11. To **saw wood** means to sing loudly.

______ 12. A **savvy** person is dull-witted.

______ 13. The British royal family no longer uses the name **Saxe-Coburg-Gotha.**

Exercise 3: Abbreviations

Directions: Most dictionaries use many abbreviations. Using any available dictionary, write what the following abbreviations and symbols mean.

1. ME ______________________
2. pl. ______________________
5. v.i. ______________________
6. adj. ______________________
7. adv. ______________________
8. prep. ______________________
9. conj. ______________________

3. n. ______________________
4. v.t. ______________________
18. Ger. ______________________
19. It. ______________________
20. L ______________________
21. Gk. ______________________
22. sing. ______________________

10. pron. ______
11. fem. ______
12. masc. ______
13. OE ______
14. < ______
15. E. ______
16. etym. ______
17. Fr. ______
23. obs. ______
24. orig. ______
25. poss. ______
26. pres. ______
27. Russ ______
28. Sp. ______
29. Syn. ______
30. Heb. ______

Word Cards

One of the best ways to build a larger vocabulary is to make word cards. All you need are packs of plain or ruled index cards and a file box. Write the word you want to learn on the front of the card and draw a picture that you associate with the word. Even a simple stick-figure illustration will help you remember the meaning of the word.

On the back of the card, write a definition of the word and the part of speech. Then write a meaningful sentence using your new word. Personalize your sentence by making it something you might say or by referring to something in your life.

Keep your word cards together in a file box or with rubber band. This makes it easy to pick them up for review purposes. Review your cards periodically. When you have mastered a card, throw it away or put it in another stack. Add new cards as you encounter more unfamiliar words.

See the examples below.

Vocabulary Word Card 1

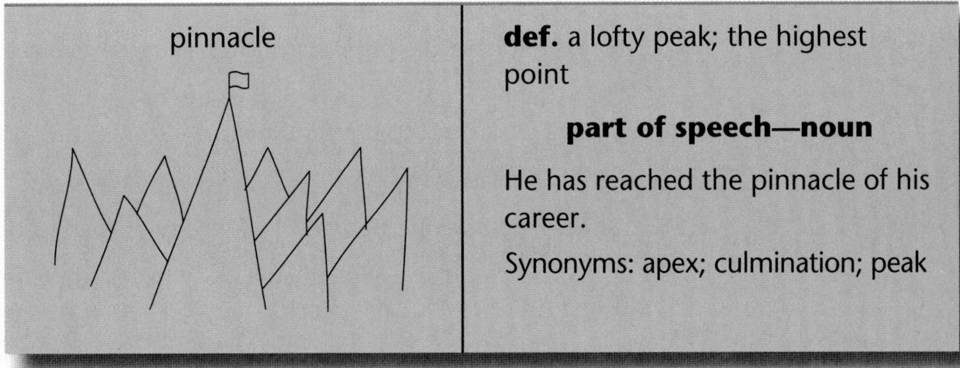

pinnacle
def. a lofty peak; the highest point
part of speech—noun
He has reached the pinnacle of his career.
Synonyms: apex; culmination; peak

Vocabulary Word Card 2

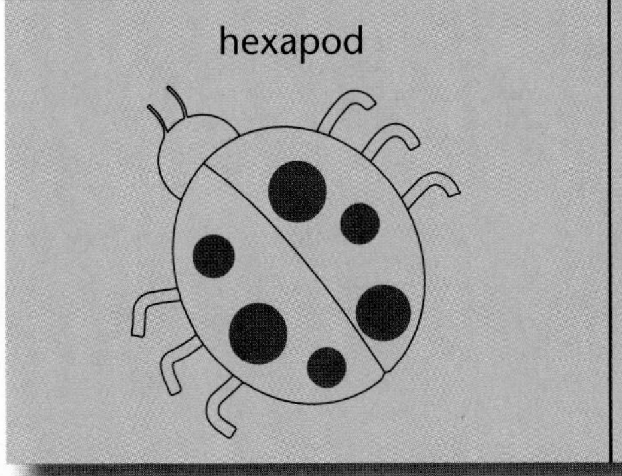

def. an insect having six feet

part of speech—noun

A ladybug is a hexapod.

Vocabulary Summary and Review

In Chapter 1, you learned techniques to develop a larger vocabulary. You became familiar with context clues, word structure, and the fundamentals of using a dictionary.

Short Answer

Directions: Answer the questions briefly, in a sentence or two.

1. What are four techniques for discovering the meaning of words from context clues?

   ____

2. Why is it important for a student to develop a college-level vocabulary?

   ____

   ____

   ____

Vocabulary in Context

Directions: Choose one of the following words to complete the sentences below. Use each word only once.

alphabetical	antonyms	context clues	etymology
guide words	prefixes	root synonyms	suffixes

3. The __________ of a word tells you its history.
4. __________ are a syllable or syllables placed at the beginning of a word to change its meaning.
5. Words that have the opposite meaning to each other are called __________.
6. When having a precise definition of a word is not necessary, the use of __________ can be sufficient and save time.
7. Dictionaries list words in __________ order.
8. __________ are the first and last entries at the top of each dictionary page.
9. __________ consist of a syllable or syllables placed at the end of a word to form a different part of speech.
10. A __________ is the main part of a word to which prefixes and suffixes are attached.
11. Words that are similar in meaning to each other are called __________.

CHAPTER

2

Becoming an Effective Learner

Finding Out about Yourself

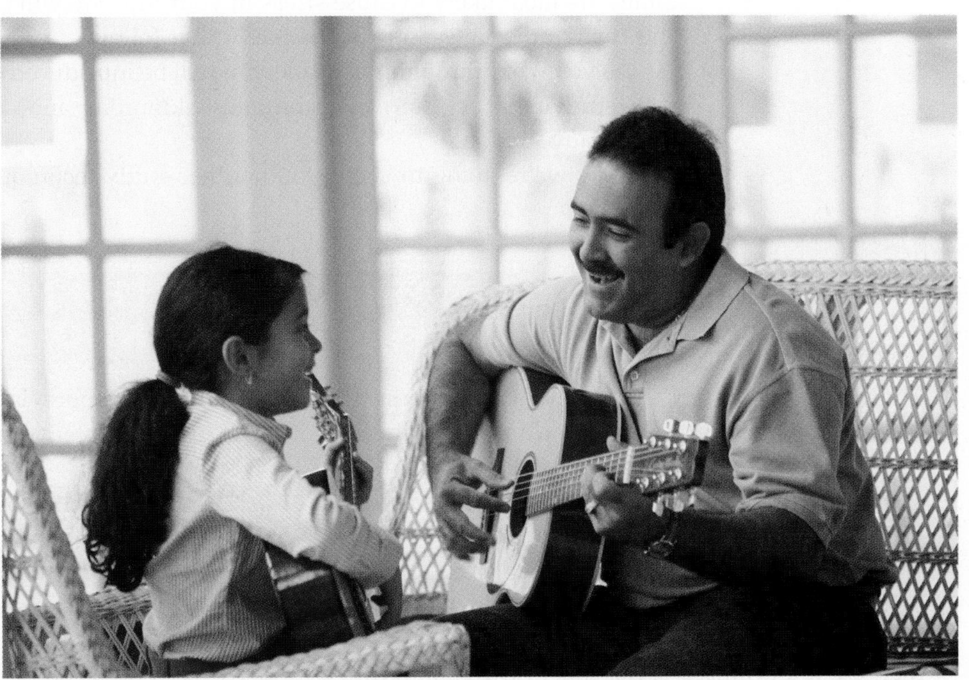

CHAPTER PREVIEW

In this chapter, you will

- Practice marking written material.
- Discover your preferred learning style.
- Assess your stress level and learn ways of dealing with stress.
- Develop a study schedule compatible with your learning style.
- Practice using SQ3R techniques.
- Learn tips for taking effective lecture notes.

How You Learn

"In Jazz the essential quality is the right to be an individual."
—Ornette Coleman

In this chapter, you are going to discover a little more about yourself so that you may become a better learner. Are you the kind of person who works best at night or during the day? Are you a visual learner or an auditory one? What kinds of things are most likely to cause stress in your life? We will be trying to answer these and many other questions in the pages that follow.

As you work through this book, you will be introduced to techniques to improve your studying. The first two techniques, skimming and scanning, were discussed in the Introduction.

Now we're going to show you another study technique.

STUDY TECHNIQUE 3: MARKING WRITTEN MATERIAL—UNDERLINING, HIGHLIGHTING, AND ANNOTATING

The common ways of marking written material are underlining, highlighting, and making notes in the margins (called annotating). Marking is something you may want to begin doing the first time you read a selection.

When marking, keep in mind that less is often better. If you underline, highlight, or annotate too much, you're defeating your purpose, because then the important material that you've marked no longer stands out.

One reason for marking is that it gets you involved right away in the material you are reading by requiring you to think about what is important. Strive to underline or highlight key ideas or concepts, or ones that you have questions about or may want to refer to later. Do you strongly agree or disagree with something you've read? Say so in the margin. Do you have a specific question about something? Put your question in the margin. In this way, you're beginning to develop your thoughts and feelings about the material.

The following is a list of techniques for marking written material. These are only suggestions. You can adapt them to suit your own purposes or create your own abbreviations and symbols to make a personal system of marking.

- Underline or highlight important terms and concepts.
- Write **MI** in the margin next to main ideas.
- Circle definitions and meanings or write **Def.** (definition) in the margin.
- Write key words and definitions in the margin or write **KV** (key vocabulary) beside important words.
- Use **EX** to indicate an example.
- Signal in the margin where important information can be found with **IMP** or a symbol such as an asterisk (*).
- Signal summaries with **SUM** or write your own short summaries in the margin.
- Use a question mark (?) in the margin to indicate a point that needs further explanation.
- Indicate where the answers to particular questions in the text can be found by writing **ANS** (answer).

"A human being's name is a principal component in his person, perhaps a piece of his soul."
—Sigmund Freud

Look at the following reading, titled "Naming Defines and Differentiates Us," and note the markings we have supplied for the "Naming and Identity" section. Try your hand at marking the rest of the material ("Naming Practices") as if you are preparing for a test. There is no single correct way to mark, but try to identify the key ideas or concepts and avoid overmarking. Compare your work with that of a fellow student. In your opinion, which one would be more helpful for you in preparing for a test?

READING

"To an extent, then, your name tells your story."

TUNING IN TO READING In the next couple of weeks, most of your instructors will be trying hard to learn the names of their students. They do this not only for convenience but also out of politeness—they know your name is important to your sense of identity. Think about how annoyed you become when your name is forgotten or mispronounced by someone who should know better. Many of you were given your name by a close relative who chose it because it had some personal significance. Perhaps it was the relative's name, or the name of a movie star or an athlete the relative admired. Some people are even named after special places or the day of the week on which they were born. How did you get your special name?

BIO-SKETCH Kory Floyd is a professor of communication at Arizona State University. His primary research focuses on the communication of affection in families.

NOTES ON VOCABULARY

demographics the statistical data of a group of people arranged according to such factors as age, income, and education

surname the family name, or last name

NAMING DEFINES AND DIFFERENTIATES US

Kory Floyd

What's something that belongs to you yet is constantly used by others?
The answer to this riddle is: *your name*. A name is simply a linguistic Def
device that identifies something or someone. Your name does more, however,
than just differentiate you from others—it's also an important component of
your sense of self. Naming is one way we represent ourselves to others and
one way we gain information about other people. Let's examine how names
relate to identity and look at some common ways that names come about.

Naming and Identity

First impressions are often critical to the perception we form of someone. 2
Although impressions are influenced by factors such as a person's appearance or
behaviors, they can also be shaped by his or her name. A person's first name,
for instance, frequently suggests information about the person's demographic
characteristics. One such characteristic is the person's sex. In Western societies,
for instance, we usually assign names such as Jacob, Michael, and Caleb only to EX
males and names such as Emma, Savannah, and Nicole to females. EX

Names can also provide clues about a person's ethnicity. For example, you 3
might infer that LaKeisha is African American, Huong is Asian, and Santiago is EX
Latino. Some names even suggest a person's age group, so you might assume
that Emma, Madison, and Hannah are younger than Edna, Mildred, and Bertha. EX

In addition to demographic information, names can suggest information about 4
our disposition and sense of self. For instance, we might perceive an adult man
who goes by the name William differently than one who goes by Billy, even though EX
those are two forms of the same name. Indeed, research shows that we do make

assumptions about people—whether accurately or not—on the basis of their names. Perhaps as a result, people sometimes adopt completely different names to project a different identity. Internet screen names, for instance, allow people to create their own identities for the purpose of interacting online. To enhance their distinctiveness, some celebrities have adopted the practice of being known by a single name, such EX
as Bono, Cher, Madonna, Sting, and Oprah. EX

In one study, for instance, people made more positive evaluations of men 5
named David, Jon, Joshua, and Gregory than they did of men named Oswald, Myron, Reginald, and Edmund, even though they were given no information about the men other than their names. Other studies have shown that people whose first names strongly suggest a nonwhite ethnicity sometimes experience discrimination based only on their names.

Naming Practices

In the United States, the Social Security Administration keeps track of the most 6
popular first names given to newborns throughout the country. Some names have remained fashionable for quite some time. Beginning in 1880, for example, Mary and John were the most popular female and male first names nearly every year until 1926, when Robert took over the top spot for boys. Mary dominated the list for girls until 1947, when it was replaced with Linda. As times change, though, so do naming preferences. By 1985, Jessica and Michael were the most popular first names. Sophia and Aiden topped the list in 2010.

Practices of naming also vary according to culture and religion. In predomi- 7
nantly Catholic communities around the world, for instance, males are often given a feminine middle name, such as Marie or Maria. Among the Sikh of India, boys are given the surname *Singh* and girls the surname *Kaur,* although adults of both sexes often take these as middle names instead. This practice of giving common surnames to all boys and girls is meant to symbolize the abolition of class inequalities. In many parts of the world, it is also traditional for women to adopt their husband's last name when they marry, or at least to add his name to hers. So, when marrying George Rogers, Jean Levitt might become Jean Rogers, or Jean Levitt Rogers, or Jean Levitt-Rogers. Alternatively, she might choose to remain Jean Levitt. What factors might influence that decision?

To an extent, then, your name tells your story. Like your clothes or your hairstyle, 8
it is a part of how you present yourself to others and how others relate to you.

(Kory Floyd, *Interpersonal Communication,* 2/e, 2012)

COMPREHENSION CHECKUP

"Names" Group Exercise

Almost all English and Continental surnames (last names) fall into four basic categories: place names, patronyms, occupational names, personal descriptions. Place names derive from names of actual places or descriptions of places close to where an ancestor lived. Patronyms are derived from the name of a father or some other ancestor. Patronyms are often created by adding a suffix or prefix indicating descent, as in Johnson (son of John) or McDonald (son of Donald). Occupational names derive from the occupations of the ancestor. Thus, if someone was called Baker, that person probably made bread. If a person's last name was Smith, that person was probably a blacksmith. Personal description names derive from physical characteristics of ancestors such as height. For example, John Long probably had a tall ancestor. Following are several other examples.

Place Names	Patronyms	Occupational Names	Personal Descriptions
Winston Churchill (church on a hill)	Ronald McDonald	Anne Archer Karen Carpenter	Henry Wadsworth Longfellow Martin Short

Directions: Go through this list of well-known individuals, and place each surname under the appropriate heading in the chart below.

Betty White
Bill Gates
Chris Rock
Christina Applegate
Clint Eastwood
Conan O'Brian
David Letterman
Faith Hill
Carrie Underwood
George W. Bush
Harry Truman
Holly Hunter
John McCain
John Goodman
Justin Timberlake
Lance Armstrong
Amy Smart
Martin Luther King Jr.
Michael Jackson
Pamela Anderson
Paul Newman
Taylor Swift
Tiger Woods
Will Smith
Harrison Ford

NAME CATEGORY CHART

Place Names	Patronyms	Occupational Names	Personal Description
____________	____________	____________	____________
____________	____________	____________	____________
____________	____________	____________	____________
____________	____________	____________	____________
____________			____________
____________			____________
____________			____________
____________			
____________			
____________			

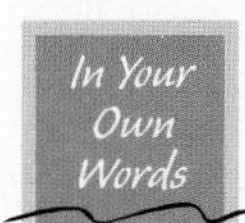

In Your Own Words

1. What are some reasons that last names might change?
2. How do people go about choosing an Internet screen name?
3. Why have some celebrities adopted the practice of being known by a single name, such as Bono, Cher, Madonna, Sting, and Oprah?

Written Assignment

Directions: Choose one of the following activities to complete.

1. Do you ever wish that you had a different name? Choose a new name for yourself, and explain in a paragraph the reasons behind your choice. For instance, you might choose the name Dawn because that is your favorite part of the day.
2. What are your feelings about nicknames? Do you like or dislike them? Did you have any nicknames while you were growing up? Did they affect you in any way? If you could choose your own nickname, what would it be, and why? Write a paragraph on this issue.

3. In your culture, how do you address people to show respect? How do you address people who are older than you? People in positions of authority? When do you address people by their first name only? Their last name? Using personal examples as illustrations, write a paragraph in which you discuss these issues.
4. Use the Internet to explore the meaning of your name and then write a paragraph describing your findings. Go to a search engine and type in "names and meanings." There are a variety of Web sites devoted to the meanings of names. One of the more complete Web sites related to names is www.behindthename.com. See if you can locate your name and its meaning. Did the people who named you take the meaning of your name into account when they gave it to you? If not, what were their reasons for giving you your name?

Internet Activity

1. Do you want to find out how popular your first name is? Visit www.babynamewizard.com/voyager and click on "NameVoyager." Has your name become more or less fashionable over time? What year was your name the most popular? Write a short paragraph discussing your results.
2. Find out more about the naming practices of other cultures. For instance, how do people in Spanish-speaking countries construct "last names"? How are Arabic names constructed? Write a paragraph discussing what you learned.

What Is Your Learning Style?

Auditory, Visual, or Kinesthetic

Each of us is an individual with particular strengths and weaknesses. If you want to do better in school, you must learn how to use your strengths and minimize your weaknesses. Research is beginning to demonstrate that most of us have a learning style that will work best for us.

Your learning style is partially dependent on whether you are a visual, auditory, or kinesthetic learner. The following test will help you determine your learning style. Keep in mind that there are no right or wrong answers.

ADULT LEARNING STYLES INVENTORY

Directions: Read each question and place a check mark on the appropriate line. If the question doesn't directly apply to you, think of a similar situation that might apply to you.

	Often	Sometimes	Seldom
1. I need to see a map or written directions to drive to someone's house.	_______	_______	_______
2. I remember material from a lecture without studying, or I have to tape the lecture and play the tape.	_______	_______	_______
3. I feel comfortable touching others, shaking hands, etc.	_______	_______	_______

	Often	Sometimes	Seldom
4. I would rather learn a new recipe from a TV show than from a recipe book.	______	______	______
5. When I watch sports on TV, I pay more attention to the play than to the explanation of the play by the announcers.	______	______	______
6. I enjoy sewing, cooking, gardening, or working with tools.	______	______	______
7. I remember a news event best by reading about it in a newspaper or magazine.	______	______	______
8. I am good at making and interpreting graphs and charts.	______	______	______
9. In order to learn material, I write notes over and over again.	______	______	______
10. Without writing them down, I remember oral directions for assignments well.	______	______	______
11. I smoke, chew gum, or play with coins or keys in my pockets.	______	______	______
12. In order to learn material, I read notes out loud to myself.	______	______	______
13. When taking a trip, I would rather drive than be responsible for giving directions or reading a map.	______	______	______
14. When I encounter a new word while I am reading, I usually sound it out.	______	______	______
15. When I am trying to learn something, I form pictures in my mind.	______	______	______
16. When I am studying for a test, I can visualize my notes on the page.	______	______	______
17. When I study, I tend to tap my pencil or my pen.	______	______	______
18. When oral introductions are made at a party, I am likely to remember the names of people I have not met before.	______	______	______

See page 46 to score your test. For each question, give yourself 5 points if you answered "often," 3 points if you answered "sometimes," and 1 point if you answered "seldom." For example, if you answered "often" to question 1, you would place a 5 on the line next to that question. When you have finished, add up the points for each column.

Visual		Auditory		Kinesthetic	
1.	______	2.	______	3.	______
5.	______	4.	______	6.	______
7.	______	10.	______	9.	______
8.	______	12.	______	11.	______
15.	______	14.	______	13.	______
16.	______	18.	______	17.	______
Totals	______		______		______

Now look at the differences between the totals for each learning style. A small difference—say, less than 4 points—doesn't mean much, but larger differences do. The larger the difference, the more dominant your learning style. For example, if your total for visual learning far exceeds the other two totals, this would be a good indication that you are basically a visual learner.

You just finished marking "Naming Defines and Differentiates Us." You are now going to annotate (place notes in the margins of the text) the information on visual, auditory, and kinesthetic learners. Look at the sample margin notes for visual learners and then fill in the blanks for the other two types of learners.

EYE SMART

Visual Learner
Definition: learns best by seeing
Application: highlights key points, and recopies notes

What does it mean to be a visual learner? A **visual learner** is one who learns best by seeing. Visual learners like to use textbooks, course outlines, maps, diagrams, charts, and pictures. Their goal is to be able to visualize the subject they are trying to learn. Visual learners prefer teachers who use a whiteboard, an overhead projector, or PowerPoint slides over ones who primarily talk. Visual learners often have a superior ability to visualize pages of print. They learn material well by highlighting key points and by copying and recopying their notes. Most people are visual learners.

EAR SMART

Auditory Learner
Definition: ______________
____
Application: ______________
____
____
____

What does it mean to be an auditory learner? An **auditory learner** is one who learns best through hearing. Auditory learners have a superior ability to hear and remember sounds in their mind. Auditory learners like to listen, and they prefer teachers who lecture and encourage discussion. They learn material well by talking to themselves and repeating words and phrases out loud. If you are an auditory learner, you might learn best by reading your textbook out loud or by studying with a friend and talking through the key points. Auditory learners might do very well in class group activities. Many people are auditory learners.

ACTION SMART

Kinesthetic Learner
Definition: ______________
____
Application: ______________
____
____
____

What does it mean to be a kinesthetic learner? **Kinesthetic learners,** who are the smallest group, learn best by doing and performing. They are hands-on, or tactile, learners. They have a superior ability to remember their actions. Kinesthetic learners like to be in movement while learning. Their special talent is in associating ideas and concepts with motion. When learning material, they may prefer to gesture or walk around. These students need to take frequent short study breaks. It is a good idea for kinesthetic learners to take notes and underline key points as they read. Kinesthetic learners might benefit from taking part in classroom skits and role-playing activities.

Keep in mind, though, that even if one of your scores was way above the other two, all that the test results show is a *tendency* on your part. For example, if you have a high score for auditory learning, this just means that you tend to be an auditory learner, but you are still likely to have a significant ability to learn in visual and kinesthetic ways. Most of us learn best by using some combination of all three learning styles. Suppose, for example, you want to learn how to ski. You might attend a lecture where someone discusses how to ski (auditory). Or you might watch a video in which someone demonstrates skiing techniques (visual). Or you might strap on a pair of skis and go down the beginner slope (kinesthetic). But the person who involves all three learning styles by doing all three things might learn to ski faster. The trick is to find the combination that works best for you.

Day versus Night People

ARE YOU MORE OF A MORNING LARK OR A NIGHT OWL?

You probably already have some idea whether you are more alert in the morning, afternoon, or evening. The following test is intended to determine whether you are a morning person or a night person. Answer the questions and then add up your points to determine your score.

	Points Possible	Points Earned
1. I feel best if I get up around		
5–6:30 A.M.	5	
6:30–7:30 A.M.	4	
7:30–9:30 A.M.	3	
9:30–11 A.M.	2	
11–noon	1	______
2. If I had to describe how easy it is for me to get up in the morning, I would say		
it is not easy at all!	1	
it is not very easy.	2	
it is fairly easy.	3	
it is very easy.	4	______
3. The way I feel for the first half-hour after I wake up is		
very tired.	1	
fairly tired.	2	
fairly refreshed.	3	
very refreshed.	4	______
4. If I could choose the best time to take a difficult test, it would be		
8–10 A.M.	4	
10 A.M.–1 P.M.	3	
1–5 P.M.	2	
7–9 P.M.	1	______
5. If my job would require that I work from 4 to 6 A.M. one day, I would choose to		
not go to bed until after I worked.	1	
take a nap before and sleep after.	2	
sleep before work and nap after.	3	
get all the sleep I need before work.	4	______
6. If someone asked me to jog with them at 7 A.M. one morning, I would perform		
well.	4	
reasonably well.	3	
not very well.	2	
not well at all.	1	______

(*continued*)

	Points Possible	Points Earned
7. If I have to wake up at a specific time each morning, I		
don't depend on my alarm at all.	4	
depend on my alarm slightly.	3	
depend on my alarm quite a lot.	2	
depend on my alarm desperately.	1	______
8. I am usually tired and wanting to go to bed by		
8–9 P.M.	5	
9–10:30 P.M.	4	
10:30 P.M.–12:30 A.M.	3	
12:30–2 A.M.	2	
2–3 A.M.	1	______
Total Number of Points Earned		______

An average score would be 17. The higher the score, the more of a morning or day person you are; the lower the score, the more of an evening person you are.

(Gary Funk and Jan Bradley, *Thrills, Spills, and Study Skills,* 1992)

In another section, we will show you how to use this information in making a study schedule. If at all possible, you should plan the activities that require the most concentration when you are the most alert. For example, if math is a difficult subject for you and you are a morning person, plan to take that class in the morning and do your homework while you are still fresh.

READING

"By understanding our body clocks, we can improve our health and continue to foster our survival."

TUNING IN TO READING Before we see how your circadian cycle might affect how you set up your class and study schedule, read the following article from *Reader's Digest*. The article describes our circadian, or daily, cycles, and how these cycles affect us.

BIO-SKETCH Lowell Ponte currently hosts a national talk radio show on the Genesis Communication Network and writes for FrontPageMag.com. He was formerly the roving science and technology editor for *Reader's Digest*. He has written essays for the *New York Times*, the *Los Angeles Times*, and the *Wall Street Journal* and has been a correspondent in 32 countries.

NOTES ON VOCABULARY

circadian rhythm A person's circadian rhythm, popularly known as one's "body clock," is a biological rhythm that governs our routine of working, eating, and sleeping through a 24-hour period. *Circadian* is derived from the Latin words *circa,* meaning "about," and *dies,* meaning "day."

dexterity skill in using the body or hands; cleverness. The word *dexterity* is derived from the Latin word *dexter,* meaning "right." The origin suggests a bias in favor of right-handed people. In the 15th century, you were not considered "skillful" unless you were right-handed.

endurance ability to bear pain, hardship, or adversity. *Endurance* is derived from the French word endurer, meaning "harden" or "make hard." The meaning has changed little over time. Today we talk about *enduring* pain and about *endurance* training for long-distance runners.

THE TWO MOST DANGEROUS HOURS OF YOUR DAY BY LOWELL PONTE

You awaken after a good night's sleep and start to climb out of bed. Take care! You are beginning the most dangerous time of your day.

2 For the next two hours or so, you are two to three times more likely to suffer a heart attack or a stroke than you are in the late evening, the safest cardiovascular time of your day. According to a study headed by Merrill Mitler of Scripps Clinic and Research Foundation in La Jolla, California, 6 A.M. to 10 A.M. is the average peak time for many other major causes of death: ischemic heart disease, cancer, bronchitis, emphysema and asthma.

3 Until recently doctors were taught that the human body lives in homeostasis, changing little during the day. The science of chronobiology—the study of how time affects life—is sparking a medical revolution by revealing how much our bodies change through circadian (daily) rhythms.

4 "These natural biological rhythms are as vital as our heartbeat," says Lawrence E. Scheving of the University of Arkansas for Medical Sciences in Little Rock. "By learning their secrets, we are discovering new ways to prevent and cure illness. There isn't a function in your body that doesn't have its own rhythm. The absence of rhythm is death."

5 While you sleep, your blood pressure falls, your temperature drops more than a degree from its daily afternoon high, and some blood pools in your body's extremities. Come morning, the body has to "jump start" itself from its sleeping to waking stages with a surge of excitation chemicals called catecholamines. Heart rate increases and blood vessels constrict, raising blood pressure and reducing blood flow to the heart muscle; this might cause ischemia, or angina, as well as sudden death from myocardial infarction. If hardened plaques of cholesterol coat arteries, fragments may break loose, causing the clots that lead to heart attacks.

Also, your blood swims with cell granules called platelets that are most likely to stick together during these morning hours. When a leap from bed and a surge of catecholamines combine to "get your blood moving," your blood is near its daily peak in thickness and tendency to clot. Packing kids off to school and rushing to get ready for work add emotional tension to the physical stress. 6

This circadian cardiovascular risk comes not from your bedside clock but from your interior biological clock. "Whatever hour you get up," says Dr. James Muller, chief of cardiology for New England Deaconess Hospital in Boston, "your peak risk of myocardial infarction will come within two to three hours after awakening." 7

The master timekeepers in our bodies help synchronize us with such outside cycles as day and night. Like orchestra conductors, they coordinate hundreds of functions inside us. Our body dances through the day to complex inner rhythms of rising and falling tides of hormones, immune cells, electrolytes and amino acids. 8

The long-held belief that some of us are "larks," or morning people, and others are "owls," or evening people, has now been confirmed. Measurements of circadian rhythms in morning people show heart rates peaking between 1 and 2 P.M., while evening people peak between 5 and 6:30 P.M. Larks produce more of the stimulating hormone adrenaline during the morning hours, followed by decreasing levels of performance through the day. Owls start the day more slowly, produce more nearly level amounts of adrenaline, and improve performance through the day and into early evening. 9

Most people enjoy a peak in short-term memory and mental quickness in 10 the late-morning hours until shortly after noon. Then a measurable dip in energy and efficiency begins around 1 P.M. In some Mediterranean cultures, shops close during the afternoon for a period of siesta.

11 In the afternoon, exercise endurance, reaction time and manual dexterity are at their highest. Some research indicates that from then until early evening, athletes put in their best performances. From 6:30 P.M. until 8:30 P.M. is the sharpest time of day for long-term memory, an optimal time to study.

12 Our daily rhythms can bring a dark side to the early evening, however. These hours include a second daily peak in heart attacks, although smaller than the morning's. Around 7 P.M., alcohol takes longer to be cleared by your liver, and hence can be more intoxicating and performance-impairing than at other times of day—except 11 P.M., which brings a second peak of high ethanol susceptibility.

13 Students often cram during late-night and early-morning hours. Research, however, shows this is the time of the circadian cycle when long-term memory, comprehension and learning are at their worst.

14 Sensitivity to pain has generally increased throughout the day; it reaches its peak late at night. But by early morning the body may have almost doubled its nighttime levels of beta endorphins, which help relieve pain. Researchers theorize that this is what increases the body's pain tolerance during the hours after awakening.

15 For most of us, sleep is a time of life's renewal. Within the first 90 minutes or so of sleep, we reach our daily peak of growth hormone, which may help regenerate our bodies. And among pregnant women, the hours between midnight and 4 A.M. most commonly mark the start of labor. "Early morning labor and birth may be part of our genetic inheritance and may have had some survival value for the species," speculates chronobiologist Michael Smolensky of the University of Texas Health Science Center in Houston.

By understanding our body clocks, we can improve our health and continue to foster our survival. Without grasping, for instance, that our natural temperature rises one to two degrees from morning until evening, we could misjudge thermometer readings. A temperature of 99 degrees might signal perfect health at 5 P.M. but augur illness at 7 A.M. 16

The effects of drugs are also subject to our rhythms. For instance, many doctors are learning to give powerful cancer drugs with the patient's biological clocks in mind. A given chemotherapy drug may be highly toxic to the kidneys at one time of day, for example, and far less harmful at another. "For every one of more than 20 anticancer drugs, there is an optimal time of day," says Dr. William Hrushesky of the Stratton Veterans Administration Medical Center in Albany, New York. 17

Some prescription drugs can reduce morning heart-attack risk, as can aspirin. One major study found that taking an aspirin *every other day* reduced overall incidence of heart attack in men by almost 45 percent and morning risk by more than 59 percent. You should, of course, consult your doctor about the use of aspirin. 18

Aside from using medicine, there are ways to make your mornings less stressful and, perhaps, less risky. Set the alarm clock a bit earlier to give yourself time to stretch arms and legs slowly while still lying down, the way your dog or cat does. This gets the pooled blood in your extremities moving. Move slowly. Don't subject yourself to the thermal shock of a very hot or cold shower, which could boost blood pressure. Then eat breakfast. Dr. Renata Cifkova at Memorial University of Newfoundland at St. John's says, "Skipping breakfast apparently increases platelet activity and might contribute to heart attacks and stroke during morning hours." 19

20 To avoid the "Monday morning blues," don't change your schedule on weekends. Your body's clock naturally runs on a cycle of about 25 hours. During the week, your body uses mechanical clocks, mealtimes, work schedules and other cues to reset itself to 24 hours each day. On weekends it is tempting to let the clock "free run" forward by staying up late Friday and Saturday, then sleeping late Saturday and Sunday. This action will leave you "jet-lagged," an unnecessary stress.

21 By turning the cycles of your biological clock in your favor, you may reduce your daily danger and increase your days of life.

(Lowell Ponte, "The Two Most Dangerous Hours of Your Day," *Reader's Digest*, 1992)

COMPREHENSION CHECKUP

Multiple Choice

Directions: For each item, write the letter corresponding to the best answer.

_____ 1. Your circadian rhythm is
a. a daily cycle.
b. a 1-hour cycle.
c. a 1-month cycle.
d. none of the above.

_____ 2. Which of the following statements is true based on paragraph 9?
a. Owls are awake at night.
b. Larks are more lively during the morning.
c. Some people are morning people and some are evening people.
d. All of the above.

_____ 3. When do you think you would be least likely to suffer a heart attack or stroke?
a. just after you wake up
b. early evening
c. late evening
d. 2 hours after you wake up

_____ 4. Which of the following statements is true based on the information in the article?
a. Orchestra conductors can help coordinate the functions of our body.
b. Babies are most likely to be born in the early morning hours.
c. It's best to sleep in on Saturday and Sunday mornings to readjust to the 25-hour cycle.
d. None of the above.

_____ 5. The human body
a. changes little during the day.
b. lives in homeostasis.
c. changes a lot through daily rhythms.
d. has no rhythm.

True or False

Directions: Indicate whether each statement is true or false by writing **T** or **F** in the space provided.

_____ 6. Cramming for exams late at night is unlikely to benefit most students.

_____ 7. Most people show a decline in energy around 1 P.M.

______ 8. For most people, alcohol is more intoxicating in the morning.

______ 9. If you need to have surgery, you should plan on having it in the early evening when you are least sensitive to pain.

______ 10. Your body temperature increases as you go through the day.

______ 11. If someone *speculates* about something, he or she is sure to know the answer.

______ 12. If you're *sensitive* to pain, be sure to tell the dentist to avoid the use of all anesthetics.

Vocabulary in Context

Directions: In a previous section you were introduced to finding the meaning of new words by using context clues. In the following exercise, try to discover the meaning of each of the italicized words by using a technique called **scanning,** which was introduced in the Introduction. In this exercise, we have indicated the specific paragraph in which the vocabulary word is located. Quickly scan the paragraph for the context clues that will give you the answer.

1. In paragraph 2, the word *cardiovascular* refers to what specific organ of the body? ______
2. In paragraph 3, what is a synonym, or word that has a similar meaning, for *circadian?* ______
3. After scanning paragraph 3, what do you think *chronobiology* means? ______
4. According to the context of paragraph 3, what does *homeostasis* mean? ______
5. In paragraph 6, what is the synonym for *platelets?* ______
6. In paragraph 9, if something is *stimulating* to you, does it depress or energize you? ______
7. In paragraph 10, is a *peak* a high point or a low point? ______
8. In paragraph 10, what is a *siesta?* ______
9. In paragraph 11, define *optimal.* ______
10. In paragraph 15, what do you think the prefix *re-* means? As another example, one might need to *renew* a library book. ______
11. In paragraph 16, if we *misjudge,* are we judging badly or well? ______
12. In paragraph 16, what is the synonym for *augur?* ______
13. Use the context of paragraph 17 to define the word *toxic.* ______
14. According to the context of paragraph 17, if you are *anti* something, are you for it or against it? ______
15. After scanning paragraph 19, name some parts of your body that would be considered *extremities.* ______

In Your Own Words

The *Zits* cartoon that follows illustrates what happens when teenagers are sleepy at the start of the school day.

Zits

As the cartoon suggests, teenagers appear to have a different circadian cycle. New research suggests that they are "wired" to stay up later at night and to sleep longer in the morning. Many prominent educators are saying that the traditional high school day is out of sync with teenagers' body clocks. These educators feel that the school day should not begin before 9 or 10 A.M. What is your opinion on this issue?

Internet Activity

Did you know that many college students have sleep patterns that are detrimental to their academic performance? Use a search engine of your choosing to find out more about the topic of "sleep and college students." Write a paragraph discussing your findings.

Left-Brain and Right-Brain Orientation: Which One Are You?

Over the past 20 years, psychologists have been studying how the two hemispheres of the brain operate. Research shows that the two sides of the brain think in quite different ways. In general, the left half is more analytical, logical, and likely to break down thoughts into parts. The right half is more likely to focus on the whole picture, to think in analogies, and to interpret things imaginatively. We use both halves of the brain together, but one side may be dominant. Being right-brain oriented or left-brain oriented has little to do with whether you are right-handed or left-handed.

Frank and Ernest

Take the following test to see which half of your brain is dominant.

WHICH SIDE OF YOUR BRAIN IS DOMINANT?

Directions: Check the statements that apply to you.

_____ 1. When reading or watching TV, I prefer a true story to one that is fictional.

_____ 2. I like to read or write poetry.

_____ 3. I prefer to take tests that have no right or wrong answers rather than tests having objective and definite answers.

_____ 4. I find myself solving a problem more by looking at the individual parts than by looking at the big picture.

_____ 5. I usually do several tasks at once rather than one task at a time.

_____ 6. I would prefer a job with a set salary over one such as sales where my income might vary considerably.

_____ 7. I usually follow new directions step by step rather than improvising or taking steps out of order.

_____ 8. When planning a vacation, I usually like to just go, without doing much planning in advance.

_____ 9. The papers in my notebook are usually neat and orderly and not simply thrown in every which way.

_____ 10. When listening to someone else's problems, I usually become emotional instead of trying to come up with logical solutions.

To Score Your Test

To score your test, circle the number for each statement that you checked.

Right-brain hemisphere	2	3	5	8	10
Left-brain hemisphere	1	4	6	7	9

Now compare the results. Which hemisphere has the most circled numbers? The bigger the difference between the two scores, the greater your right-brain dominance or left-brain dominance. If you circled about the same number for both hemispheres, neither one of your hemispheres is dominant.

What does all this mean? One hemispheric orientation is not better than the other, but the thinking processes are different. People who are more left-brain oriented tend to be more organized, be more analytical, and use more logic. So, it is not surprising that engineers, accountants, scientists, and auto mechanics are more likely to have a dominant left hemisphere.

Those with a dominant right hemisphere, on the other hand, tend to focus on the whole more than individual parts, be imaginative, jump to conclusions, and be emotional. Poets, artists, musicians, and inventors are more likely to have a dominant right hemisphere.

"Intuition becomes increasingly valuable in the new information society precisely because there is so much data."
—John Naisbitt

We will apply this information later on when we discuss study techniques. Students with a dominant left hemisphere will probably do better organizing material by outlining, while those with a dominant right hemisphere might find mapping easier. Those who are left-brain oriented will probably find study schedules easier to stick to than those who are right-brain oriented.

Left-brain-oriented students will probably find it easier to do well in classes that require analysis and linear thinking than will students who are right-brain oriented. Examples of such classes are algebra, science, accounting, logic, computers, and engineering. Those who are more right-brain oriented might do better in classes such as art, social science, music, English, history, and geometry.

Multiple Intelligences: What Are Your Strengths?

Merriam-Webster's Collegiate Dictionary defines intelligence as "the ability to learn or understand" and "the ability to cope with a new situation."* We have discovered in the previous sections that we are all unique individuals who learn in different ways. Some psychologists believe that intelligence can also be expressed in a variety of ways. Many of you may remember taking the Stanford-Binet IQ test. After completing the test, you were assigned a score and then evaluated based on that score. If your mental age, as measured by the test, and your age in years were the same, you had an IQ of 100. This meant that you were considered "average." The higher the score above 100, the more intelligent you were considered to be, while a score of 80 meant that you were below average.

Critics argue that one problem with this test is that it is based on the principle that our intelligence is one-dimensional. Howard Gardner, a Harvard professor, has proposed the idea that there are eight types of intelligence. His theory is based on biological research showing different parts of the brain to be the sites of different abilities. He says that "the concept of 'smart' and 'stupid' doesn't make sense. . . . You can be smart in one thing and stupid in something else." As you read a description of each type of intelligence, try to determine your own strengths and weaknesses.

"The art of writing is the art of discovering what you believe."

—David Hare

Practice your marking skills by highlighting (or underlining) the definition for each of the following types of intelligences. Follow the example given below for verbal/linguistic intelligence.

*By permission. From *Merriam-Webster's Collegiate® Dictionary, 11th Edition* © 2011 by Merriam-Webster, Incorporated (www.merriam-webster.com).

WORD SMART—VERBAL/LINGUISTIC INTELLIGENCE

This intelligence relates to language skills. It includes the ability to express yourself verbally, to appreciate complex meanings, and to detect subtle differences in the meanings of words. It is considered to be a key intelligence for success in college.

People with this type of intelligence are likely to be good writers and good spellers. For recreation, they often like to do crossword puzzles or play word games, such as Scrabble. They have good memories for names and dates. They are often good at telling stories or giving speeches. To learn best: Talk, read, or write about it.

LOGIC SMART—LOGICAL/MATHEMATICAL INTELLIGENCE

This intelligence involves the ability to reason, solve abstract problems, and understand complex relationships. Intelligence in this area is also a good predictor of academic success.

People with this type of intelligence are logical, orderly thinkers. It is easy for them to comprehend factual material. In school, they often ask a lot of questions. They like working with equations in subjects such as math and chemistry. They are often proficient with the computer. For recreation, they like board games such as Clue, Battleship, and chess, or computer games. To learn best: Think critically about it.

PICTURE SMART—VISUAL/SPATIAL INTELLIGENCE

This is the ability to think in three dimensions and to re-create experiences visually. Painters, sculptors, and architects are all able to manipulate a form in space.

People who have this type of intelligence like to visualize each step in their mind when they are given a set of directions. They are the "finders." Many can readily retrieve missing objects in the home by tapping a visual memory of where the objects were last seen. To process complex information, they like to draw pictures, graphs, or charts. They learn more in class when information is given by means of videos, movies, or PowerPoint slides. For recreation, they often like to do puzzles or mazes. To learn best: Draw, sketch, or visualize it.

MUSIC SMART—MUSICAL/RHYTHMIC INTELLIGENCE

This is the ability to hear pitch, tone, and rhythm.

People with this type of intelligence may sing or hum throughout the day. They enjoy dancing and can keep time with the music. They often need to listen to music when they study. It is very easy for them to remember the words and melodies of songs. To learn best: Sing, rap, or play music.

BODY SMART—BODILY/KINESTHETIC INTELLIGENCE

This intelligence places the emphasis on control of the body and the skillful handling of objects. The mind clearly coordinates the movements of the body. Athletes, pianists, and dancers might excel in this area.

People with this type of intelligence are often Mr. or Ms. Fix-it. They enjoy repairing things, they use many gestures when they speak, and they are good at competitive sports. For recreation, they prefer physical activities such as bicycling, rollerblading, skateboarding, and swimming. To learn best: Do hands-on activities.

"You're wise, but you lack tree smarts."

PEOPLE SMART—INTERPERSONAL INTELLIGENCE

This is the ability to interact well with people. People who excel in this area are especially skillful in detecting the moods and intentions of others. Politicians might display this type of intelligence.

People with this type of intelligence are often found in leadership positions. They tend to be empathic individuals who communicate well with others. They often make good mediators and are called upon to help settle other people's problems and conflicts. To learn best: Join a group, get a study partner, or discuss the subject matter with friends.

SELF SMART—INTRAPERSONAL INTELLIGENCE

This is the ability to understand one's own feelings and to use the insight gained to guide actions.

People with this type of intelligence set reasonable goals for themselves and take steps to accomplish those goals. They often study by themselves, and they need time to be alone with their thoughts. To learn best: Relate the material to your personal experiences.

ENVIRONMENT SMART—NATURALISTIC INTELLIGENCE

This is the ability to appreciate and respect the environment and nature.

People with this type of intelligence probably enjoy being outdoors and participating in hiking, camping, and gardening. They tend to notice and value diversity among plants and animals. They like studying such subjects as astronomy, zoology, and geology. Farmers or oceanographers might display this type of intelligence. To learn best: Go on field trips or walks.

Is there a relationship between these intelligences and the learning styles we have been studying? Probably, but our knowledge of how the brain functions is still in the early stages. One problem, of course, is that although we are all human beings, we are all distinctly different, making it difficult for scientists to generalize.

Another problem concerns the controversy over how much of our intelligence is fixed at birth and how much is determined by our environment. More than likely, our intelligence is a combination of these two factors, but the nature-versus-nurture debate is far from resolved. In the meantime, many educators and psychologists are not only attempting to define intelligence more broadly but also devising new methods to teach thinking skills once thought to be fixed for life.

Exercise 1: Working with Multiple Intelligences

Directions: Match the examples to the specific intelligence.

______	1. Playwright William Shakespeare	a. Intrapersonal
______	2. Microsoft founder Bill Gates	b. Visual/Spatial
______	3. Quarterback Drew Brees	c. Interpersonal
______	4. Architect Maya Lin	d. Verbal
______	5. Singer Beyoncé Knowles	e. Logical/Mathematical
______	6. Talk show host David Letterman	f. Naturalistic
______	7. Conservationist Dr. Akoi Kauadio	g. Bodily/Kinesthetic
______	8. His Holiness the Dalai Lama	h. Musical/Rhythmic

Internet Activity

In this chapter, you have been trying to improve your understanding of yourself by taking various assessment tests. Go to one of the following Web sites and take one of the tests. Try to take a test that is different from one that you have already taken. What can you conclude about yourself after taking the test?

www.intelligencetest.com

www.iqtest.com

www.queendom.com

Stress Inventory: How Much Stress Is There in Your Life?

Although there is no exact correlation between how well students do in college and the stress in their lives, students need to pay attention to personal stress. To be successful in college, you must be able to give full attention to your studies. This means that you must come to terms with all facets of your life, including whatever is causing you stress. If the stress in your life is controlling you, you need to do something about it. You may be able to solve the problem yourself, or you might want to consider seeking professional help. Most college campuses have a counseling center to help students deal with too much stress and other emotional problems. When we have physical problems, most of us are willing to consult a doctor. On the other hand, many of us have difficulty seeking help for other personal problems. But if you need help and help is available, why not take advantage of it?

The following test is meant to be confidential and is for your use only.

ADD IT UP: STUDENT STRESS SCALE

If you have experienced any of the events listed here in the last 12 months, check that item.

Event	Check	Points
1. Death of a close family member	_______	100
2. Death of a close friend	_______	73
3. Divorce of parents	_______	65
4. Jail term	_______	63
5. Major personal injury or illness	_______	63
6. Marriage	_______	58
7. Firing from a job	_______	50
8. Failure in an important course	_______	47
9. Change in health of a family member	_______	45
10. Pregnancy	_______	45
11. Sex problems	_______	44
12. Serious argument with close friend	_______	40
13. Change of financial status	_______	39
14. Change of major	_______	39
15. Trouble with parents	_______	39
16. New girlfriend or boyfriend	_______	37
17. Increase in workload at school	_______	37
18. Outstanding personal achievement	_______	36
19. First quarter/semester in college	_______	36
20. Change in living conditions	_______	31
21. Serious argument with an instructor	_______	30
22. Lower grades than expected	_______	29
23. Change in sleeping habits	_______	29
24. Change in social activities	_______	29
25. Change in eating habits	_______	28
26. Chronic car trouble	_______	26
27. Change in the number of family get-togethers	_______	26
28. Too many missed classes	_______	25
29. Change of college	_______	24
30. Dropping of more than one class	_______	23
31. Minor traffic violations	_______	20
TOTAL	_______	

Scoring

Now total your points. A score of 300 or more is considered high and puts you at risk for developing a serious health-related stress problem. A score between 150 and

300 is considered moderately high, giving you about a 50-50 chance of developing a stress-related health problem. Even a score below 150 puts you at some risk for stress-related illness. If you do have an accumulation of stressful life events, you can improve your chances of staying well by practicing stress-management and relaxation techniques.

(Adapted from Thomas H. Holmes and Richard H. Rahe, "Social Readjustment Rating Scale," 1967)

Exercise 2: Context Clue Practice Using Textbook Material (Why Students Get the Blues)

Directions: Use the context clues to determine the meaning of the italicized word, and write a definition for that word in the space provided.

1. During the school year, up to 78 percent of all college students suffer some symptoms of depression. At any given time, from 16 to 30 percent of the student population is depressed. Why should so many students be "blue"? Various factors contribute to depressive feelings. Here are some of the most *prevalent:*

   prevalent: ______________________________

2. Stresses from the increased difficulty of college work and pressures to make a career choice often leave students feeling that they are missing out on fun or that all their hard work is *for naught.*

   for naught: ______________________________

3. *Isolation* and loneliness are common when a student leaves his or her support group behind. In the past, family, a circle of high school friends, and often a boyfriend or girlfriend could be counted on for support or encouragement.

   isolation: ______________________________

4. Problems with studying and grades frequently trigger depression. Many students enter college with high *aspirations* and little experience with failure. At the same time, many lack *rudimentary* skills necessary for academic success.

   aspirations: ______________________________

   rudimentary: ______________________________

5. Another common cause of college depression is the breakup of an *intimate* relationship with a boyfriend or girlfriend.

   intimate: ______________________________

6. Students who find it difficult to live up to their idealized images of themselves are especially *prone* to depression.

   prone: ______________________________

7. Stressful events frequently *trigger* depression. An added danger is that depressed students are more likely to abuse alcohol, which is a depressant.

   trigger: ______________________________

(Dennis Coon, *Introduction to Psychology,* 8/e, 1998)

Internet Activity

Do a search on the Internet about how stress affects college students. Write a paragraph about what you learned.

READING

"I just want to be the best I can be—to live up to my fullest potential."

TUNING IN TO READING Inventor Thomas Alva Edison once said, "Success is 10 percent inspiration and 90 percent perspiration." In the excerpt that follows, Kurt Warner typifies the kind of work ethic that not only leads to success on the football field, but to success in school and life. Even for someone as successful in his chosen career as Warner, life has not been easy. Yet, he clearly believes in trying his best and not giving up even when the odds are stacked against him. In his case, persistence, hard work, and holding on to a dream have paid off. Perhaps this excerpt will inspire you to take advantage of your own opportunities in college and help you to set your own standards for excellence.

BIO-SKETCH Kurt Warner, who was born in Iowa on June 22, 1971, graduated from the University of Northern Iowa, where he was a backup quarterback until his senior year. Because he was not drafted by the National Football League (NFL), Warner worked as a stock boy in a local grocery store until the Iowa Barnstormers of the Arena Football League signed him to a contract in 1995. Then, in 1998, the NFL's St. Louis Rams signed him. In 1999, he was both the NFL MVP and the Super Bowl MVP. Warner became an Arizona Cardinal in 2005 and retired after multiple injuries in 2010. Shortly thereafter he began a career in broadcasting, working as an analyst for FOX and the NFL network. Warner competed on *Dancing with the Stars,* coming in fifth. He has been married to his wife Brenda since 1997. Together they are raising seven children. Kurt and Brenda are the co-authors of *First Things First,* from which this excerpt is taken.

NOTES ON VOCABULARY

underdog a person, team, or side that is losing or is expected to lose

benched kept from playing in a game

stats an abbreviated form of the word statistics

MVP most valuable player

Strive to Be the Best You Can Be

BY KURT AND BRENDA WARNER

THE CARDINALS WERE THE WORST TEAM in NFL history. In their sixty-year existence, they'd never been to a Super Bowl and had played in only a handful of playoff games.

When we entered the 2008 season playoffs, no one expected much. We 2
were 9–7. People called us the worst team ever to go to the playoffs. We were the underdogs in *every* game.

And yet we got to the Super Bowl. 3

We even had a chance to win it in the end. 4

When I was in St. Louis, the Rams were considered one of the worst teams 5
of the nineties, and yet in one year, we went from worst to first, winning the 1999 Super Bowl. In my years as a player, I've been a part of some real come-from-behind stories.

There have also been times in my career when I've had personal comebacks. There were times when I was benched through no fault of my own, and times when injuries prevented me from playing. Times when I did everything I could but still got booed coming off the field. Let me just say, it's never good when you're booed in your profession. Those were the low moments in my career. Moments when I would ask God, *What are you doing? Why am I here?* 6

I had some of those same questions when I was benched two years after coming to Arizona. I worried that my entire future as a player would be limited to holding a clipboard, just waiting to see if the starter got injured. I considered retirement in those days, but I also hoped that by working hard I could change the situation. Before I got into the NFL, I was naïve. I believed the best players would always play because coaches wanted to win games. But once I got into the league, I learned it's also about other things—money, draft picks, politics, and marketing. But despite the low times—no matter how much the fans or coaches turned against me—I've always tried my best, and I will continue to do my best. 7

That's what I want my kids to see. 8

Yes, I'm proud of my accomplishments. My quarterback rating is in the top five all-time, better than some of my heroes, like Joe Montana and Roger Staubach. I'm one of the most accurate passers in NFL history, which makes me happy because I believe that's my greatest strength. Throughout my career, there have been other accomplishments that have stood out, such as fastest to throw for ten thousand yards, second fastest to a hundred touchdowns, and second all-time to throw forty touchdown passes in a season—with my name in the record books alongside Dan Marino's. My stats are up there with some of the best ever to have played the game. 9

But beyond the statistics, I'm even more proud that I took two different teams to the Super Bowl. Regardless of the odds against me, or the accolades I've received, I've always done my best to be a leader on the field and to inspire other players to greatness. So, on the one hand, if my career ended today, I would be satisfied. But the truth is, I'm not done and there's more I want to accomplish. I want to become an even better quarterback. I want to throw more touchdown passes, break more records, and win more Super Bowls. I want to play the perfect game. 10

I'm not saying I want to accomplish these things so people will look at me and say, "Oh, he's the best quarterback that ever played," or whatever. I'm not really worried about what other people think or say. I just want to be the best I can be—to live up to my fullest potential. And I hope that in doing so, I inspire the people who watch me to be the best at what they're supposed to be. 11

After the Super Bowl, it would have been so easy to pick one of those two pivotal plays—the interception to James Harrison or the touchdown to Larry Fitzgerald—and have that define me. But those aren't the moments that play over and over in my head. The moments I relive are the conversations I've had with people who stopped to tell me that I inspired them. 12

For example, I remember one of my first years in Phoenix. Larry Fitzgerald and his girlfriend were having dinner with Brenda and me. Sometime during 13 the main course, Larry and I got into a heated discussion about something related to football, and I said to him, "You've got to get better."

I'll never forget his response: "Kurt, I'm good enough." 14

Brenda was there, and she will tell you that I couldn't believe he'd said 15
that. It blew me away that "good enough" would be okay.

"Don't you want to be the best?" I asked. 16

That conversation stuck with me. When I disagree with someone on a topic, 17
I'm the kind of person who always asks a lot of questions—like, "Why do you believe what you believe?" I want to understand their thinking and how they arrived at the conclusion they did. That's what I did when Brenda and I were dating and she kept talking about religion.

That's probably also why I still remember that conversation with Larry. I had 18
no idea why Larry would think it was okay for him just to be "good enough."

Over the next few years, Larry and I became pretty good friends. We 19
worked closely together, both on and off the field, and I got to watch him grow from a good player into a great player.

After the Super Bowl, Larry and I were traveling together on a plane, and 20
we had another conversation I'll never forget. He locked eyes with me and said, "Kurt, you made me better. You made me want to be better."

That's it. 21

That's what I live for. 22

I want my life to encourage others. Whether as the leader of a football 23
team, as a husband to my wife, or as a father to my kids, I always strive to do my best in hopes that by doing so, the people around me will strive to do their best. I want a spirit of excellence to surround everything I do. When my kids see me loving them, when they watch how I treat my wife, or when they see me preparing for football, I want them to know that I'm doing my best. I also hope that pushes them to do better in what they're doing. I want to be great. And I hope to inspire others to want the same.

(Kurt and Brenda Warner, *First Things First*, 2009, pp. 65–69)

COMPREHENSION CHECKUP

Multiple Choice

Directions: Write the letter of the correct answer in the blank provided.

______ 1. According to the selection, all of the following are important to Warner *except*

a. being the best that he can be.
b. setting a good example for his children.
c. paying attention to what his fans think.
d. inspiring others to be the best that they can be.

______ 2. In the selection, Kurt Warner discusses

a. encouraging others.
b. considering retirement.
c. getting angry at hecklers.
d. Both a and b.

______ 3. Which of the following is *not* discussed in the selection?
a. Warner's success as a passer
b. Warner's success as a motivator
c. Warner's success as a coach
d. Warner's success as a team leader

______ 4. Which of the following words best describe Kurt Warner now?
a. lazy
b. naïve
c. motivated
d. cautious

______ 5. The word *strive* in "I always *strive* to do my best . . ." means
a. fight against.
b. overexert.
c. make every effort.
d. bother.

True or False

Directions: Indicate whether each statement is true or false by writing **T** or **F** in the blank provided.

______ 6. A person who is *naïve* is not likely to be sophisticated.

______ 7. Kurt Warner has won two Super Bowls.

______ 8. This selection is primarily about Warner's personal philosophy of life.

______ 9. Warner has taken two different teams to the Super Bowl.

______ 10. Warner takes his profession seriously.

______ 11. Being benched was one of the high points in Warner's career.

______ 12. Warner is motivated to perform well because of public opinion.

Scanning

Directions: Scan the reading to find the word (or words) that correctly completes each statement.

1. Two of Kurt Warner's football heroes are ______________________.
2. Warner won the __________ Super Bowl.
3. Warner remembers a conversation with ____________ about improving football skills.
4. As quarterback of the Cardinals in the 2009 Super Bowl, Warner threw an interception to ____________.
5. Before the 2008 playoffs, the Cardinals had a win-loss record of __________.
6. Prior to the Cardinals, Warner played for the St. Louis __________.

Vocabulary in Context

Directions: Try to determine the meaning of the italicized words and then write the definition on the line provided. The paragraph in which the words appear in the reading selection is indicated in parentheses.

1. personal *comebacks* (6) ______
2. two *pivotal* plays (12) ______
3. have that *define me* (12) ______
4. a *heated* discussion (13) ______
5. It *blew me away* (15) ______
6. conversation *stuck with me* (17) ______

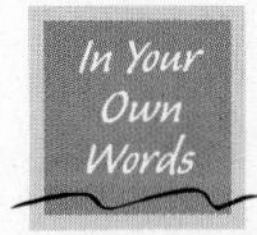

In Your Own Words

1. What general statement is Warner making in this selection?
2. How does Warner describe the Cardinals before their Super Bowl performance?
3. Kurt Warner received a number of accolades throughout his lengthy career. Do you think that earning awards and recognition can also cause stress? In what ways?
4. What are some stresses that commonly affect professional athletes or their families?

Written Assignment

1. What qualities do you think Warner values in people? Write a few paragraphs giving your opinion.
2. The Warner family was featured in an article by Karen Crouse of the *New York Times*. When asked by Crouse to come up with a few rules for being a Warner daughter or son, the children quickly came up with the following:

Eight Rules for Being a Warner Daughter or Son

1. Everyone has to agree on which stranger's meal to pay for when dining at a restaurant.
2. At dinner, share the favorite part of your day.
3. Hold hands and pray before every meal.
4. After ordering at a restaurant, be able to tell Mom the server's eye color.
5. Throw away your trash at the movie theater and stack plates for the server at restaurants.
6. Spend one hour at an art museum when on the road.
7. Hold hands with a sibling for ten minutes if you can't get along.
8. If you can't get along holding hands, sit cheek to cheek. (If you can't get along cheek to cheek, then it's lips to lips!)

(Kurt and Brenda Warner, *First Things First*, pp. 48–49)

What is your reaction to the Warner rules? What are the rules for your particular family? Write a short paragraph describing a few of these rules and giving the reason for each one.

Internet Activity

Karen Crouse's article, "The Rules of the Family," (September, 25, 2008) can be found at

http://www.nytimes.com/2008/09/26/sports/football/26rules.html?ref=football.

Write a paragraph reporting new information you learn about the Warners.

Study Schedules

"Dost thou love life? Then do not squander time; for that's the stuff life is made of."
—Benjamin Franklin

"It takes time to save time."
—Joe Taylor

How do you create a study schedule that makes you more efficient?

When to Study

Now let's begin to put some more of this information you have learned about yourself to practical use. Would you like to be prepared for a test two nights before the test is given? Would you like to have that paper written a day early? If so, follow along. The purpose of this section is to show you how to organize yourself so that you can take charge of your life and do better in school.

You will find a practice weekly study schedule form on page 66. Another copy is located in the Appendices.

COMPLETING A WEEKLY STUDY PLAN

Step 1: Fill in your class schedule. For example, if your math class is MWF from 9 to 10, write "math" in the three blocks for those days and times. You have no control over these items; you have to go to class.

Step 2: Now fill in your work schedule. We hope it is fairly regular, because if it is not, keeping a regular study schedule from week to week is going to be more difficult. Write "work" in the appropriate blocks. If your schedule changes from week to week, try to approximate it. If some weeks you work more than others, go to your busier weeks.

Step 3: Fill in time for school activities such as sports events, clubs, and student council.

Step 4: Fill in time for other regularly scheduled activities such as church, meetings, laundry, and grocery shopping. If it's something you do almost every week, put it in. If you do something only every once in a while, leave it out.

Step 5: Fill in time commitments to your family, spouse, and friends. These people also need your attention. Include such things as putting children to bed or doing social activities with friends. Keep in mind that it often does not work out very well to mix family or social activities with academic obligations. Try not to study and cook dinner simultaneously. If you can arrange things so that you can have time to concentrate solely on your school assignments, that would be better. And your friends and family may be happier too, now that they get your full attention at other moments.

Step 6: Fill in other times when you are not likely to be studying, maybe Friday and Saturday evenings, the time of your favorite TV show, or times when you exercise. Exercise is important to your health and sense of well-being, which will benefit you in many ways, including academically.

Step 7: At the bottom of the schedule sheet, list the classes you are taking. For each of the classes, estimate how much time you will need to spend working on it each week to obtain an A or a B. This number will, of course, vary from class to class, since some classes will be more difficult than others or will simply require more time to do the assignments. Generally, in college courses, you need to devote two hours outside the class to course work for each hour spent in the class. You will want to include time for reviewing notes, writing your

WEEKLY STUDY SCHEDULE

	Monday	Tuesday	Wednesday	Thursday	Friday	Saturday	Sunday
6:00–7:00							
7:00–8:00							
8:00–9:00							
9:00–10:00							
10:00–11:00							
11:00–12:00							
12:00–1:00							
1:00–2:00							
2:00–3:00							
3:00–4:00							
4:00–5:00							
5:00–6:00							
6:00–7:00							
7:00–8:00							
8:00–9:00							
9:00–10:00							
10:00–11:00							
11:00–12:00							
12:00–1:00							

papers, and studying for tests. If you're unsure how much time to put down, say 4 or 6 hours, go with the larger number.

Step 8: Now determine which of your classes is the most difficult and so will demand more of your time. Recall the test you took on your circadian cycle. If math is going to be your most difficult subject, try to give it your best study hours—when you have the most patience and the clearest mind. Maybe this will be early in the morning, or at noon, or in the early evening. Also keep in mind your most effective style of learning—visual, auditory, or kinesthetic. For example, if you are mostly a visual learner but have a class that emphasizes lectures, allow sufficient time for going over your lecture notes and reviewing the textbook. That way you bring your strengths into play.

Step 9: Keep in mind the limits of your attention span in setting up blocks of time to study particular courses. Some will be more interesting to you than others. Some will require more concentrated effort than others. For example, if biology is going to be difficult for you, you don't want to assign yourself a block of time for studying it that will exceed your attention span. Otherwise, you will be wasting your time. So instead of fewer, longer sessions, it may make sense for you to schedule more numerous, shorter sessions. Experiment in your academic scheduling so that your study time will be most productive.

Step 10: You now have a guide for your daily and weekly routine. You have to go to class on a regular basis, so why not study on a regular basis? What should you be doing during your scheduled study time? You can read the chapter to be covered in class, review your notes from previous days' classes, begin to study for an upcoming test, or work on a paper that is coming due. Each time you sit down to study, ask yourself how you can best use that time to master the course material or meet the course requirements. The ideal place for studying is somewhere comfortable and free of unwanted distractions. Try to come as close to this as you can.

STUDY TECHNIQUE 4: SQ3R A CLASSIC WAY TO STUDY

SQ3R (**S**urvey, **Q**uestion, **R**ead, **R**ecite, **R**eview) is a system for reading and studying textbook material that was developed by Dr. Francis P. Robinson more than 50 years ago. Most "new" study techniques are variations of this old classic.

Step 1: Survey

You survey a reading selection by looking it over before actually beginning to closely read it. When you complete your survey, you should have a general understanding of what the selection is about. Surveying is very similar to skimming. Following are some suggestions for surveying:

1. Read the title or subtitle and any information given about the author.
2. Read the first paragraph or the introduction.
3. Scan the headings or subheadings.
4. Notice any boldfaced or italicized words.
5. Read the first sentence of each paragraph.
6. Notice the charts, diagrams, pictures, or other graphical material.
7. Read the last paragraph, the conclusion, or the summary.
8. Read any questions at the end of the selection.
9. Think about what *you* already know about the topic.

Step 2: Question

After completing your survey, you should have some questions in mind about the material. If you can't think of any questions, try turning a subheading into a question. For a section with the title "SQ3R," you might ask, "What is SQ3R?" or, "Why is it a classic technique of studying?" If the material you are reading doesn't have subheadings, try turning the first sentence of every paragraph into a question. It is much easier to keep yourself actively involved in the material if you are reading to answer specific *how, why,* or *what* questions. Your attention is less likely to wander if you actually write down the questions, and their answers, on a separate sheet of paper, or even in the textbook. You might want to try conducting an imaginary conversation with the author—talk to the author, ask her or him for answers, and keep a continuous conversation going.

Step 3: Read

Now carefully read the entire selection from beginning to end. Look for main ideas and the answers to your questions. You may also want to mark key points by underlining, highlighting, or jotting notes in the margins. Remember, most textbook material will need to be read more than once. The first reading will give you only a limited understanding of the material. If the material is particularly long, divide it into sections, read a section at a time, and perhaps take a short break between sections.

Step 4: Recite

To do this step, you must put the information you have learned into your own words, and then say it either to yourself or out loud. While it might seem odd at first, talking out loud can be a very effective technique for remembering material because it involves hearing and speaking at the same time. You might pretend someone has asked you a question about the material and then respond (out loud or to yourself) by giving the answer. Or you might pretend that you are the teacher giving a lecture on the material. Be sure you can recite the answers to *who, what, where, when, why,* and *how* questions. When you organize the material mentally and put it into your own words, you are demonstrating your understanding of the material.

Step 5: Review

In this last step, look over your questions, notes, and highlighted material. Practice giving the answers to the questions you originally posed. By now you should be able to define special terms and give relevant examples. You might want to do your review with a classmate by explaining the material to that person or by taking turns quizzing each other on the material. Review frequently so the material will stay with you.

In the following exercise, you have a chance to practice your SQ3R techniques with the excerpt from *Understanding Business* (pages 69–72). Follow all the steps carefully. You may also wish to highlight or underline the key ideas. Use the margins for any notes you wish to make.

Exercise 3: SQ3R Practice

STEP 1: SURVEY

1. Write a few sentences about what you already know about succeeding in your college classes.

____

____

2. What is the title of the selection?

____

3. What is the overall message of the first paragraph?

____

4. How many jobs are people likely to have in a lifetime?

____

5. What is the second heading? ____

6. In the second numbered item, what does the author urge you to focus on?

____

7. The fifth numbered item is concerned with

____

STEP 2: QUESTION

After surveying the selection, you should have at least two questions about it. Write your questions below.

8. _______________

9. _______________

STEP 3: READ

Now read the entire selection and answer the questions you posed previously. Then do the **Comprehension Checkup** located on p. 72.

STEP 4: RECITE

Can you recite the answer to the following question?

10. What are some benefits of a college education? _______________

____

STEP 5: REVIEW

Now you should be able to answer your own questions from step 2. Write the answers below.

11. _______________

12. _______________

13. Why is being on time important? _______________

____

14. Why is how you dress important? _______________

READING

An old saying goes, "You never get a second chance to make a good first impression."

TUNING IN TO READING William G. Nickels, author of the popular college textbook *Understanding Business,* says that in the working world a good presentation is everything. Nickels says that in dress "consistency is essential." Today, many businesses have adopted a policy of "business casual." Unfortunately, this term means different things to different people. Experts, though, agree that it doesn't mean "sloppy or sleazy." The selection below gives some guidelines on making a good impression.

BIO-SKETCH William Nickels is emeritus professor of business at the University of Maryland. He has taught business classes for over 30 years.

NOTES ON VOCABULARY

clinches decides; settles

succinct concise, compact. Succinct is derived from the Latin word *succinctus,* meaning "to tuck up short."

LEARNING THE SKILLS YOU NEED TO SUCCEED TODAY AND TOMORROW

William Nickels

Succeeding in This Course

Since you've signed up for this course, we're guessing you already know the value of a college education. The holders of bachelor's degrees make an average of $46,000 per year compared to $30,000 for high school graduates. That's 53 percent more for college graduates than those with just a high school diploma. Compounded over the course of a 30-year career, the average college grad will make nearly a half million dollars more than the high school grad! Thus, what you invest in a college education is likely to pay you back many times. That doesn't mean there aren't good careers available to non-college graduates. It just means those with an education are more likely to have higher earnings over their lifetime.

The value of a college education is more than just a larger paycheck. Other 2
benefits include increasing your ability to think critically and communicate your ideas to others, improving your ability to use technology, and preparing yourself to live in a diverse world. Knowing you've met your goals and earned a college degree also gives you the self-confidence to work toward future goals.

Experts say today's college graduates will likely hold seven or eight different 3
jobs (often in several different careers) in their lifetime. Many returning students are changing their careers and their plans for life. In fact, over 30 percent of the people enrolled in college today are 25 or older. In addition, over 60 percent of all part-time college students are 25 or older.

You may want to change careers someday. It can be the path to long-term 4
happiness and success. This means you'll have to be flexible and adjust your strengths and talents to new opportunities. Learning has become a lifelong job. You'll constantly update your skills to achieve and remain competitive.

If you're typical of many college students, you may not have any idea what 5
career you'd like to pursue. That isn't necessarily a big disadvantage to today's fast-changing job market. After all, many of the best jobs of the future don't even exist today. There are no perfect or certain ways to prepare for the most interesting and challenging jobs of tomorrow. Rather, you should continue your college education, develop strong computer and Internet skills, improve your verbal and written communication skills, and remain flexible when you explore the job market.

Learning to Behave Like a Professional

There's a reason good manners never go out of style. As the world becomes 6
increasingly competitive, the gold goes to teams and individuals with that extra bit of polish. The person who makes a good impression will be the one who gets the job, wins the promotion, or clinches the deal. Good manners and professionalism are not difficult to acquire; they're second nature to those who achieve and maintain a competitive edge.

Not even a great résumé or a designer suit can substitute for poor behav- 7
ior, including verbal behavior, in an interview. Say "Please" and "Thank you" when you ask for something. Open doors for others, stand when an older

person enters the room, and use a polite tone of voice. Of course, it's also critical to be honest, reliable, dependable, and ethical at all times.

Some rules are not formally written anywhere; instead, every successful 8
businessperson learns them through experience. If you follow these rules in college, you'll have the skills for success when you start your career. Here are the basics:

1. **Making a good first impression.** An old saying goes, "You never get a second chance to make a good first impression." You have just a few seconds to make an impression. Therefore, how you dress and how you look are important.
2. **Focusing on good grooming.** Be aware of your appearance and its impact. Wear appropriate, clean clothing and a few simple accessories. Be consistent too; you can't project a good image by dressing well a few times a week and then showing up like you're getting ready to mow the lawn.
3. **Being on time.** When you don't come to class or work on time, you're sending this message to your teacher or boss: "My time is more important than your time. I have more important things to do than be here." In addition to showing a lack of respect to your teacher or boss, lateness rudely disrupts the work of your colleagues. To develop good work habits and get good grades, arrive in class on time and avoid leaving (or packing up to leave) early.
4. **Practicing considerate behavior.** Listen when others are talking—for example, don't read the newspaper or eat in class. Don't interrupt others when they are speaking; wait your turn. Eliminate profanity from your vocabulary. Use appropriate body language by sitting up attentively and not slouching. Sitting up has the added bonus of helping you stay awake! Professors and managers alike get a favorable impression from those who look and act alert.
5. **Practicing good e-mail etiquette**. The basic rules of courtesy in face-to-face communication also apply to e-mail exchanges. Introduce yourself at the beginning of your first e-mail message. Next, let your recipients know how you got their names and e-mail addresses. Then proceed with your clear but succinct message, and always be sure to type full words (*ur* is not the same thing as *your*. Finally, close the e-mail with a signature. Do not send an attachment unless your correspondent has indicated he or she will accept it. Ask first!
6. **Practicing good cell phone manners.** Turn off the phone during class or in a business meeting unless you are expecting a critical call. If you are expecting such a call, let your professor know before class. Turn off your ringer and put the phone on vibrate. Sit by the aisle and near the door. If you do receive a critical call, leave the room before answering it.
7. **Practicing safe posting on social media.** Be careful what you post on your Facebook page or any other social media. While it may be fun to share your latest adventures with your friends, your boss, or future boss, may not appreciate your latest party pictures. Be aware that those pictures may not go away even if you delete them from your page. If anyone else downloaded them, they are still out there waiting for a recruiter to

discover. Make sure to update your privacy settings frequently. It's a good idea to separate your list of work friends and limit what that group can view. Also be aware that some work colleagues aren't interested in becoming your Facebook friend. To avoid awkwardness, wait for work associates to reach out to you first. Make sure you know your employer's policy on using social media on company time. Be mindful that social media accounts time-stamp your comments.

8. **Being prepared**. A businessperson would never show up for a meeting without having read the appropriate materials and being prepared to discuss the topics on the agenda. For students, acting like a professional means reading assigned material before class, asking and responding to questions in class, and discussing the material with fellow students.

(William G. Nickels, James M. McHugh, and Susan M. McHugh, *Understanding Business*, 10/e, McGraw-Hill, 2013, pp. 3, 5–7)

COMPREHENSION CHECKUP

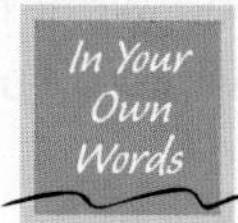

In Your Own Words

1. The author believes that people evaluate each other within a few minutes of meeting for the first time. And we tend to make an immediate judgment about the other person based on what we see. In your experience, how much do you think first impressions matter? Explain.
2. Do you think casual Fridays at the office are a good idea? Does informal clothing lead to informal behavior at work? How would you define "business casual"?
3. Do you think what employees wear to work can affect the success of their business? For instance, if an employee dresses sloppily, do you think a customer might assume that the business is poorly run?
4. Patricia T. O'Conner, author of *Woe Is I*, suggests that while it's one thing to be creative with grammar, spelling, and punctuation with friends, it's quite another to use "goofy English" when writing instant messages or e-mails to teachers and people in the business community. She suggests that the audience you're writing to should influence how you write the message. What do you think?
5. Everyone to whom you send e-mail will see your e-mail address. In a personal e-mail account, you often choose your own address, which says something about you similar to a vanity plate on a car. How important do you think it is to avoid having an e-mail address that is too cute or too personal? Do you think people should get into the habit of using different e-mail addresses for different purposes?

Written Assignment

1. It is said that what you wear on the outside is a reflection of who you are on the inside. What do you think your clothing says about who you are? Do you think your school clothing indicates that you are a capable person? Does the clothing you wear to job interviews say "Hire me. I'm the best person for the job"? Write a paragraph giving your answers to these questions.

2. The following are the most common netiquette (proper Internet etiquette) rules. Write a short essay giving your overall impression of their usefulness.
   - Use business language and write professionally in all work-related messages.
   - Remember that your message may be printed or forwarded to other people.
   - Proofread and correct errors in your message before sending it.
   - Do not use all capital letters because this connotes shouting.
   - Keep in mind that your reader does not have the benefit of hearing your tone of voice and seeing your facial clues.
   - The time, date, and reply address are added automatically to your e-mail message; therefore, you do not need to type this information.
   - Always include an appropriate subject line in your e-mail message.
   - Respond promptly to e-mail.

Internet Activity

Additional pointers on dressing appropriately can be found by conducting the following Internet searches: "tips on dressing for interviews," and "tips on appropriate business dress." Consult one of the sites and list some of the tips you find there

You can find much more information about proper Internet etiquette online—for example, at NetManners.com

STUDY TECHNIQUE 5: TIPS ON TAKING EFFECTIVE LECTURE NOTES

1. Don't attempt to write down everything your professor says.
2. There is no one best way to take notes. Find a method that works for you.
3. The format you choose should be the one that works best for your learning style.
4. If you are left-brain oriented, you might want to make a formal outline. If you are right-brain oriented, you might find mapping more helpful.
5. It helps to preview the material that is going to be covered in class so that you have some idea what the main points in the lecture are going to be.
6. Be sure to put the date at the top of your notes.
7. A loose-leaf binder works well because you can organize and reorganize your notes and add or take out material.
8. Use only one side of the paper and be sure to number each page. You can use the backs to write summaries, pose questions, and add information.
9. As you are taking notes, leave blank spaces between key concepts and ideas.
10. Develop your own system of abbreviating and stick to it.
11. Put question marks by information that you aren't sure about or have a question about.
12. Review your notes as soon as possible after class.
13. Compare your notes with those of fellow classmates who get good grades. What do their notes have that yours do not?

Chapter Summary and Review

In Chapter 2, you learned about various learning styles and how to develop a study schedule that suits your learning style. You also learned about the theory of multiple intelligences. Furthermore, you learned about SQ3R and how to apply it to a reading selection. Finally, you learned some tips on how to take effective lecture notes.

Short Answer

Directions: Answer the questions briefly, in a sentence or two.

1. What are your personal learning styles? How can you use them to do better in college?
2. What are four tips for taking effective lecture notes?
3. Are you more of a day or night person? How will this knowledge help you prepare for your classes?
4. Which multiple intelligences are your strengths? Your weaknesses?

Vocabulary in Context

Directions: Choose one of the following words to complete the sentences below. Use each word only once.

date	circadian	death	kinesthetic
left-brain	married	paragraphs	survey

5. Accountants and computer engineers are probably __________ oriented.
6. If you are a(n) __________ learner, you may want to take notes, highlight your textbook, or get up and walk around the room.
7. You can easily throw off your __________ cycle when you get on a plane and fly to a different time zone.
8. Two of the biggest stressors for people are a(n) __________ in the family and getting __________.
9. A good way to __________ a chapter in one of your textbooks is to read the first and last __________ and look at the headings and subheadings.
10. Always put the __________ at the top of your notes.

Discovering Meaning through Structure

PART 2

CHAPTERS IN PART 2

CHAPTER

3

Topics, Main Ideas, and Details

CHAPTER PREVIEW

In this chapter, you will

- Learn how to distinguish between general ideas and specific details.
- Learn how to identify the topic of a paragraph.
- Learn how to locate the stated main idea of a paragraph.
- Learn how to diagram a paragraph by identifying its main idea sentence and key details.
- Become familiar with paraphrasing.
- Learn how to formulate implied main ideas.

Description of Topics, Main Ideas, and Details

What do these people have in common? Below is a list of the names of the people pictured. Come up with a word or a few words to describe all of them. Write your heading for this list on the line.

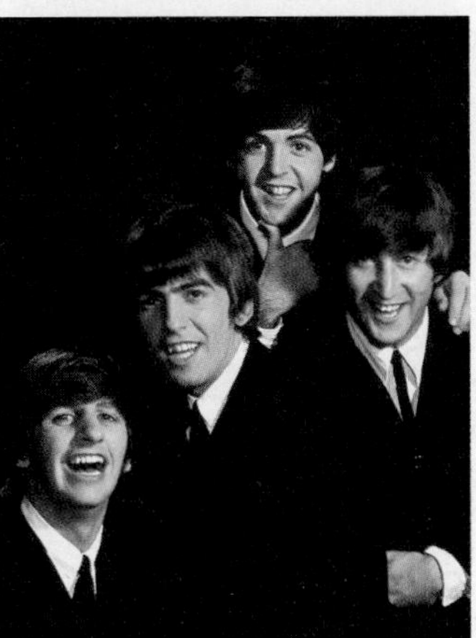

____

Kelly Clarkson
Beyoncé Knowles
The Beatles
Carrie Underwood

Write your own definition for each boldfaced term. Use your own words.
topic or subject: ________________ ________________

There are a number of possibilities, such as "entertainers," "famous singers," or even "performers." This heading tells the **subject** or the **topic**.

Most paragraphs are about a particular **topic** or **subject**. The topic is what the paragraph is about. It is the subject of the paragraph. The topic is not a complete sentence you can find in the paragraph. It can usually be summed up in a word or brief phrase similar to a title. It is often the noun that is mentioned most frequently in the paragraph or selection. You can identify the topic by asking the question: "What is this all about?" or "Who is this about?" The answer is the topic.

Exercise 1

Directions: For each group of items, cross out the one item that doesn't belong. Then write a word that tells the topic of all of the remaining items.

1. ________________	2. ________________	3. ________________
hot fudge sundae	apostrophe	Capricorn
strawberry shortcake	period	Pisces
pumpkin pie	colon	Aries
chocolate chip cookies	sentence	Moon
egg rolls	comma	Taurus

Once you have identified the topic, ask this question: What is the most important point the author wants me to know about the topic? The answer is the **main idea**. Paragraphs are supposed to be organized around a main idea, with all sentences supporting the main idea or key point. **Details** are supporting sentences that reinforce the main idea. While the main idea is a general statement, supporting details are specific bits of information that answer these question words: who, what, where, when, why, and how. Supporting details provide facts, reasons, and examples that support, explain, or elaborate on the main idea.

main idea: ________________

____

details: ________________

____

As an illustration of the difference between main ideas and details, study the *Baby Blues* cartoon.

Baby Blues

In this cartoon, Darryl provides Wanda with the main idea of the phone conversation, but he is unable to provide her with any of the supporting details.

In the following paragraph, the general topic is sensitivity to nonverbal communication. The main idea is given in the first sentence. The sentences following the main idea are all supporting details, serving as examples to illustrate the main idea. Notice how all the details directly back up and support the main idea, which is underlined.

> <u>Cultural diversity in the workplace has created a need for greater sensitivity among managers and employees regarding people's use of nonverbal communication.</u> For example, white Americans define eye contact in the course of a conversation as showing respect. But many Latinos do not, and many Americans of Asian ancestry find eye contact with an employer to be exceedingly disrespectful behavior. Potential conflicts may arise when white supervisors consider Hispanic or Asian employees furtive or rude for casting their eyes about the room.
>
> (Michael Hughes and Carolyn J. Kroehler, *Sociology*, 9e, McGraw-Hill, 2009)

major supporting details:

____

____

minor supporting details:

____

____

Those supporting details that directly reinforce the main idea are called **major supporting details,** and those sentences that serve only to reinforce the major supporting details are called **minor supporting details.** To gain an understanding of how main ideas and major and minor supporting details work in a paragraph, read the following paragraph on posture as body language. Then study the outline and the diagram that follows.

> Posture often indicates feelings of tension or relaxation. We take relaxed posture in nonthreatening situations and tighten up in threatening situations. Based on this observation, we can tell a good deal about how others feel by simply watching how tense or loose they seem to be. For example, watching tenseness is a way of detecting status differences. The lower-status person is generally the more rigid, tense-appearing one, whereas the higher status person is more relaxed. This is the kind of situation that often happens when an employee sits ramrod straight while the boss leans back in her chair. The same principle applies to social situations, where it's often possible to tell who's uncomfortable by looking at pictures. Often you'll see someone laughing and talking as if he were perfectly at home, but his posture almost shouts nervousness.
>
> (Albert Mehrabian, *Silent Messages,* Communication Research, 1981)

In the outline, **MI** refers to the main idea, **MSD** to major supporting details, and **msd** to minor supporting details.

I. Posture often indicates feelings of tension or relaxation (MI)
  A. Person displays relaxed posture when not threatened. (MSD)
  B. Person displays tense posture when feeling threatened. (MSD)
  C. Tension or relaxation in posture may indicate status. (MSD)
    1. Tense-appearing person has low-status. (msd)
    2. Relaxed-appearing person has high status. (msd)
  D. Posture indicates who's comfortable in a social setting. (MSD)

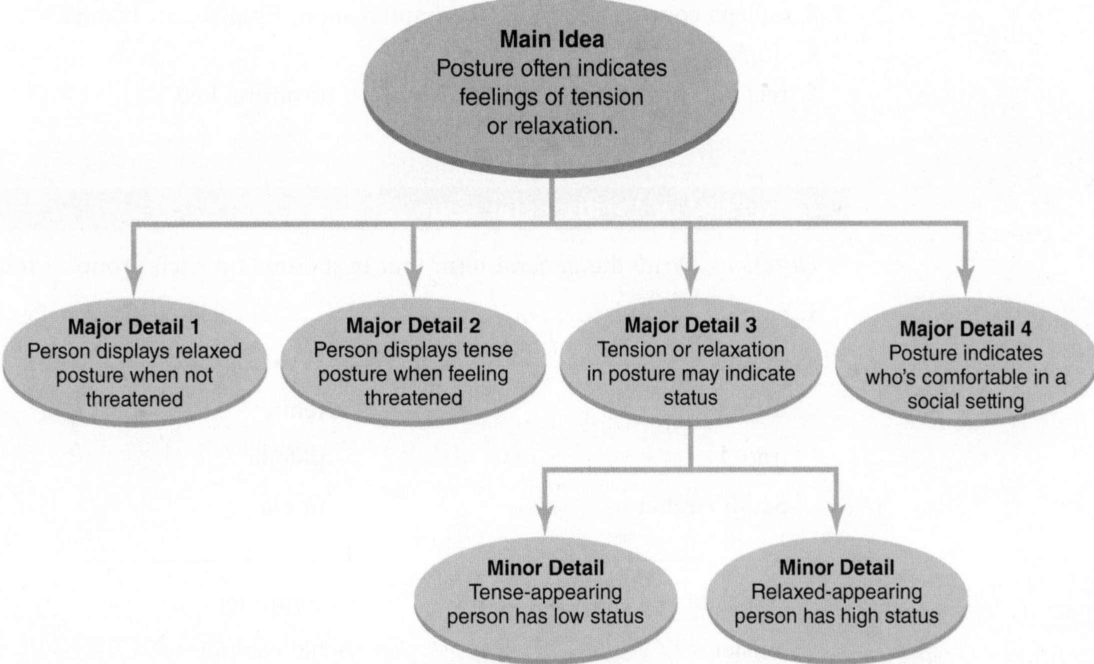

The main idea in both of these sample paragraphs is **directly stated**, meaning that you can locate it somewhere in the passage or selection. Main ideas can also be **implied**, meaning that you, the reader, are responsible for coming up with a general statement that unites the author's key supporting details. This general statement should be no more than one sentence long. In the pages that follow, we will be working with both types of main ideas: directly stated and implied.

In summary, a paragraph is about a specific **topic** or **subject**. Most paragraphs have a **main idea,** either **directly stated** or **implied.** All of the sentences in a paragraph must directly relate to the topic and main idea. **Supporting details** explain the main idea by providing facts, reasons, or examples.

If you had difficulty with this material, don't be discouraged. This chapter will provide you with the skills you need to readily identify main ideas and supporting details as you read. You will also have an opportunity to practice writing effective implied main ideas.

Distinguishing Between General and Specific

In order to recognize a topic, a main idea, and supporting details, you must be able to determine the difference between something that is general and something that is specific.

Exercise 2: Underlining the Most General Term

Directions: Underline the most general term in each group of words.

1. Los Angeles Dodgers, New York Yankees, professional baseball teams, Arizona Diamondbacks, New York Mets
2. Abraham Lincoln, U.S. presidents, Harry Truman, Barack Obama, George Washington
3. college courses, sociology, communication, English, art history
4. dogs, cats, goldfish, pets, hamsters
5. recliner, dining room table, television, furniture, bed

Exercise 3: Writing the General Term

Directions: Write the general term that best sums up each group of items.

1. ____________________

Egypt

Iran

Iraq

Saudi Arabia

2. ____________________

associate

master's

bachelor's

doctoral

3. ____________________

vertebrae

femur

patella

fibula

4. ____________________

computer

file cabinet

printer

fax machine

Exercise 4: Going from the Most General to the Most Specific

Directions: Number the following lists from the most general (1) to the most specific (4).

A.

_____ entertainment

_____ television shows

_____ *Big Bang Theory*

_____ comedies

B.

_____ star

_____ constellation

_____ North Star

_____ galaxy

C.

_____ community college

_____ public speaking

_____ communication classes

_____ Department of Communication

D.

_____ Spanish male names

_____ male names

_____ Guillermo

_____ names

Exercise 5: Choosing the Best Topic

Directions: Choose the best topic for each list of words. Place the correct letter in the space provided.

_____ 1. May
July
December
October
August

a. summer months
b. winter months
c. calendar
d. months with 31 days

_____ 2. Labor Day
Presidents' Day
Thanksgiving Day
Memorial Day
New Year's Day

a. patriotic holidays
b. summer holidays
c. holidays
d. winter holidays

_____ 3. violin
harp
guitar
trumpet
drum

a. string instruments
b. marching band instruments
c. brass instruments
d. musical instruments

_____ 4. Sacramento
Juneau
Little Rock
Springfield
Boise

a. U.S. state capitals
b. western cities
c. cities
d. small cities

Exercise 6: Identifying Topics in Textbook Paragraphs

Now apply what you have learned about general and specific to help you identify the topic of a paragraph. A good topic is comprehensive because it covers all of the ideas mentioned in the paragraph. Sometimes it helps to think of the topic as a title for the paragraph.

Directions: For each paragraph, determine the best topic and put a **T** on the line. Put a **G** on the line of the topic that is too general or broad and an **S** on the line of the topic that is too specific.

1. There is no doubt that advertisers have zeroed in on the child audience. The last few years have seen the growth of kid-specific media: Nikelodeon, Web sites, kid-oriented magazines, movie tie-ins, and even hamburger wrappers. Part of the reason behind this increase is the fact that kids have become important factors in family buying decisions. First, they have more money to spend. The under-14 set gets allowances, earns money, and receives gifts to the tune of about $20 billion per year. In addition, kids probably influence another $200 billion worth of shopping decisions. Second, the increase in single-parent families and dual-career families means that kids are now making some of the purchasing decisions that were once left to Mom and Dad. It is not surprising, then, to find that companies are intensifying their efforts to reach this market segment.

   (Joseph R. Dominick, *The Dynamics of Mass Communication,* 11/e, 2011)

   Example:

   __G__ a. Audiences (This is too broad—it covers all types of audiences, not just child audiences.)

   __S__ b. The increase in single parent families and dual-career families (This provides one specific detail from the paragraph.)

   __T__ c. Advertisers target child audiences (This covers all the ideas in the paragraph.)

2. Which sex is healthier: women or men? We know that women have a higher life expectancy than men and lower death rates throughout life. Women's greater longevity has been attributed to genetic protection given by the second X chromosome (which men do not have). However, factors such as men's greater propensity for risk taking and their preference for meat and potatoes rather than fruits and vegetables, also may play a part. Despite their longer life, women are more likely than men to report being in fair or poor health, go to doctors or seek outpatient or emergency room care more often, are more likely to seek treatment for minor illnesses, and report more unexplained symptoms. Men are *less* likely to seek professional help for health problems, but they have longer hospital stays, and their health problems are more likely to be chronic and life-threatening. Women's greater tendency to seek medical care does not necessarily mean that they are in worse health than men, nor that they are imagining ailments or are preoccupied with illness. They may simply be more health conscious. Men may feel that illness is not "masculine," and seeking help means a loss of control. Research suggests that a man is least likely to seek help when he perceives a health problem as a threat to his self-esteem or if he believes his male peers would look down on him. It may well be that the better care women take of themselves helps them live longer than men.

   (Diane E. Papalia, and Ruth Duskin Feldman, *Experience Human Development,* 12/e, 2012)

______ a. Men and women

______ b. Which sex is healthier?

______ c. Men and longer hospital stays

3. Engineers and inventors often appropriate their best ideas directly from the natural world. Perhaps the best example of this is the development of Velcro fasteners. Today, Velcro has hundreds of uses in diapers, running shoes, and space suits, even in sealing the chambers of artificial hearts. But it all started in 1948, when George de Mestral, a Swiss hiker, observed the manner in which cockleburs clung to clothing and thought that a fastener could be designed using the pattern. Cockleburs have up to several hundred curved prickles that function in seed dispersal. These tiny prickles tenaciously hook onto clothing or the fur of animals and are thus transported to new areas. De Mestral envisioned a fastener with thousands of tiny hooks, mimicking the cocklebur prickles on one side, and on the other side thousands of tiny eyes for the hooks to lock onto. It took 10 years to perfect the original concept of the "locking tape" that has become Velcro, and is so common in modern life.

(Estelle Levetin and Karen McMahon, *Plants and Society,* 6/e, 2012)

______ a. Velcro use in diapers and shoes

______ b. Inventions

______ c. The development of Velcro

4. Women absorb and metabolize alcohol differently than men do. A woman cannot metabolize much alcohol in the cells that line her stomach. Women also have less body water in which to dilute the alcohol than do men. So, when a man and a woman of similar size drink equal amounts of alcohol, a larger proportion of the alcohol reaches and remains in the woman's bloodstream. Overall, women develop alcohol-related ailments such as cirrhosis of the liver more rapidly than men do with the same alcohol consumption habits.

(Gordon Wardlaw, *Contemporary Nutrition,* 6/e, 2007)

______ a. Alcohol

______ b. The development of cirrhosis of the liver in women

______ c. Gender differences in alcohol effects

5. Ethnocentrism is the belief that our own group or culture—whatever it may be—is superior to all other groups or cultures. If you were born and raised in the United States, you may find it strange that most people in India regard the cow as a sacred animal and forgo using it as a source of food. On the other hand, if you were born and raised in India, you might well be shocked at the use of cows in the United States for food, clothing, and other consumer goods. If you are a Christian, you most likely think of Sunday as the "normal" day of worship. But if you are Jewish, you probably regard Saturday as the "correct" Sabbath. And if you are Muslim, you doubtless see both Saturday and Sunday as unusual times for worship. For you, Friday is the "right" day.

(Stephen E. Lucas, *The Art of Public Speaking,* 10/e, 2009)

______ a. The meaning of ethnocentrism

______ b. Cows as a sacred animal in Indian culture

______ c. Feeling superior to others

Exercise 7: Identifying Topics and Main Ideas

Directions: The main idea sentences are missing from the following paragraphs on nonverbal communication. Locate the letter of the main idea sentence for each paragraph in the Main Ideas box on page 86 and write it on the line provided.

1. Chinese tradition associates red with good fortune, but Korean Buddhists use red to announce death. In the United States, red is associated with a stop sign or a warning light but also symbolizes love, as in Valentine's Day. Black is the color of joy in Japan, but it is the color of death in the United States. White is the color of funerals and mourning in eastern countries, but in the United States it is the color of brides. Green is perceived to be a very lucky color in western countries like Britain, Ireland, and the United States. During the uncertain, tension-filled times following 9/11, green became a favored color. Green is perceived as being safe and serene, and it makes people feel better. Even the Department of Homeland Security put green at the bottom of the terrorist alert code, meaning we're safe. In Japan, green is associated with youth and energy.

   (Kitty O. Locker and Donna S. Kienzler, *Business and Administrative Communication,* 8/e, 2008)

   Main idea: ______

2. The intense aroma of spicy curry or barbecue may strike you differently if you are European American than if you are Arab American. At first you may find these new odors unpleasant. But as you get to know the culture and the people, you become accustomed to the new smells and may even find them inviting. People in the United States are especially concerned with body smells, spending a great deal of money to prevent bad breath and natural body odors. In the United States, we equate such smells with the lack of personal hygiene. Most other cultures, however, find body smell natural and are bewildered by our attempt to disguise such odors with deodorant, mouthwash, and toothpaste.

   (Bethami A. Dobkin and Roger C. Pace, *Communication in a Changing World,* 2006)

   Main idea: ______

3. Our clothes, jewelry, cars, houses, and other objects or possessions all say something about us and are sometimes important expressions of our personalities, values, and interests. A large house, expensive car, and designer clothes all convey the nonverbal message of privilege and wealth. Military uniforms convey very precise ranks and status. Similarly, high school letter jackets convey specific ranks or awards, with a series of bars, letters, or patches. At commencement, students graduating with honors sometimes wear robes or chords, and those with PhDs wear special hoods. Objects or possessions can also communicate inclusion in or identification with a group. Students often wear caps or sports jerseys from their favorite team or school. License plates can communicate a person's home state while bumper stickers reveal a person's favorite music group, political party, religious preference, or social cause.

   (Bethami A. Dobkin and Roger C. Pace, *Communication in a Changing World,* 2006)

   Main idea: ______

4. The handshake is the most common greeting in the United States, but in Japan people bow with hands at their waists. The depth of the bow is a sign of social status, gender, or age. The Thai, Laotians, and Khmer make a slight bow at the waist while placing their hands, palms together, under the chin. The Finnish, New Zealander, Bedouin, Polynesian, and Inuit touch noses. The

tip of the nose is brought into contact with the tip of another person's nose or with another part of his or her head. Hawaiians raise their arms and wiggle the hand gently. The thumb and little finger are extended with the other fingers curled. North Africans place their index fingers side by side.

(Bethami A. Dobkin and Roger C. Pace, *Communication in a Changing World,* 2006)

Main idea: ______

5. Some Muslim women wear a veil to express their strongly held convictions about gender differences and the importance of distinguishing men from women. Others wear a veil, which can cover just the head or the entire body, as a sign of disapproval of an immodest Western culture or to protect themselves from the unwanted sexual advances of men. However, the primary reason for wearing a veil is that it is believed to be commanded in the Koran and is thus a symbol of devotion to Islam.

   (Mary Kay DeGenova, *Intimate Relationships, Marriages, & Families,* 8/e, 2011)

   Main idea: ______

6. Some years ago, during the Olympic games in Mexico, some African-American athletes raised clenched fists to protest racial discrimination and symbolize Black power. It is all too common for professional athletes to make obscene gestures at officials, members of the opposing team, or fans. Even more to the point, one college basketball player, Toni Smith, elected to symbolize her displeasure with U.S. foreign policy by turning her back on the U.S. flag and looking down at the floor during the playing of the national anthem before games. Others in Smith's presence signaled their support for U.S. policy and expressed their patriotism by choosing to use different non-verbal cues. Some carried flags onto the court to counter Smith's actions. Others wore American flag lapel pins. Still others indicated their support for or opposition to Smith's behavior with their cheers or boos.

   (Terry Kwal Gamble and Michael Gamble, *Communication Works,* 9/e, 2006)

   Main idea: ______

7. Typically, we respond more positively to those we perceive to be well dressed than we do to those whose attire we find questionable or unacceptable. The National Basketball Association (NBA) has long had a dress code for coaches, requiring them to wear a jacket and tie during games. Now the commissioner of the NBA, David Stern, is requiring players and all other personnel to wear a jacket and tie when traveling to or from a game, home and away. The thinking is that these clothes will improve the players' image. Among the items players are prohibited from wearing are T-shirts, chains or pendants, sunglasses when indoors, headphones, and jerseys and baseball caps.

   (Terry Kwal Gamble and Michael Gamble, *Communication Works,* 9/e, 2006)

   Main idea: ______

8. In an effort to enhance the relationships between the external environment and the inner self, the Chinese, and now others, use feng shui (pronounced "fung SHWAY"), the ancient Chinese art of placement, to add harmony and balance to living spaces. Feng shui introduces the five elements in nature into design: earth, fire, water, wood, and metal. For example, it uses green plants to bring the outdoors inside, and red candles and fabrics to increase energy.

The goal is to arrange space, furniture, walls, colors, and objects to promote blessings and to harness the life force (chi).

(Terry Kwal Gamble and Michael Gamble, *Communication Works*, 9/e, 2006)

Main idea: ______

9. The numerous signs indicating city, country, state, and national borders are examples of our strong need to communicate the boundaries of our territory. In our personal lives, we communicate boundaries by building fences around homes or putting names on office doors. National and state parks always post signs indicating their boundaries. Landscaping not only beautifies one's yard but also communicates, "This is my land." Gangs "tag" territory with graffiti or other recognizable symbols. Even universities construct elaborate entrances to identify the boundaries of campus and to restrict access from unwanted visitors. Territorial markers also extend to personal space. For example, you might place your coat or books on the chair or seat next to you at the library or on a bus. Finally, territorial markers personalize and distinguish space. For instance, many office workers mark their computer monitors with pictures, stickers, or drawings. Similarly, many university students mark their apartment or dorm room with pictures, posters, or other personal items.

(Bethami A. Dobkin and Roger C. Pace, *Communication in a Changing World*, 2006)

Main idea: ______

10. The voice can be used to produce a wide range of nonverbal behaviors such as sounds that are not words, laughter, pauses, silence, breathing patterns, and voice qualities. Laughter is an almost universal sign of happiness and good feelings. Pauses during a conversation can convey a variety of meanings, including confusion, concentration, thoughtful reflection, anger, nervousness, or suspense. The way you breathe often reflects your emotional state. Breathing quickly and loudly might signal arousal, physical exertion, or anxiety, whereas breathing slowly might communicate that one is relaxed or tired.

(Bethami A. Dobkin and Roger C. Pace, *Communication in a Changing World*, 2006)

Main idea: ______

Main Ideas

A. Objects and possessions can be forms of nonverbal communication.

B. Culture affects the treatment of space.

C. Reasons for wearing a veil (hijab) when out in public vary among Muslim women.

D. The voice itself can be used to communicate nonverbally.

E. How people dress affects how others respond to them.

F. Sometimes people deliberately use nonverbal cues to send specific messages.

G. Humans mark and defend their territory by communicating with objects or signs.

H. Culture plays a big role in determining what smells people consider pleasant and what smells they find repugnant.

I. Countries around the world have different gestures for friendly greetings.

J. Colors can have varying meanings in different cultures.

Exercise 8: Identifying Topics and Main Ideas

Directions: Now locate the topic of each paragraph and the main idea sentence. The main idea can be identified by asking, "What key point does the author want me to know about the topic?"

1. Physical motions and gestures provide signals. The "preening behavior" that accompanies courtship is a good illustration. Women frequently stroke their hair, check their makeup, rearrange their clothes, or push the hair away from the face. Men may adjust their hair, tug at their tie, straighten their clothes, or pull up their socks. These are signals that say, "I'm interested in you. Notice me. I'm an attractive person."

   Topic: ____________________

   Main idea: ____________________

2. Students who sit in the front rows of a classroom tend to be the most interested, those in the rear are more prone to mischievous activities, and students on the aisles are primarily concerned with quick departures. As you can see, the way we employ social and personal space also contains messages.

   Topic: ____________________

   Main idea: ____________________

3. Through physical contact such as touch, we convey our feelings to one another. However, touch can also constitute an invasion of privacy, and it can become a symbol of power when people want to make power differences visible. For example, a high-status person might take the liberty of patting a low-status person on the back or shoulder, something that is deemed inappropriate for the subordinate.

   Topic: ____________________

   Main idea: ____________________

   ____

   (James W. Vander Zanden, *Sociology*, 4/e, 1996)

4. Gestures that mean approval in the United States may have different meanings in other countries. The "thumbs up" sign, which means "good work" or "go ahead" in the United States and most of western Europe, is a vulgar insult in Greece. The circle formed with the thumb and first finger that means OK in the United States is obscene in southern Italy and can mean you're worth nothing in France and Belgium. And in Japan the circle gesture is associated with money.

   (Kitty O. Locker and Donna S. Kienzler, *Business and Administrative Communication*, 8/e, 2008)

   Topic: ____________________

   Main idea: ____________________

   ____

5. Even the gestures for such basic messages as "yes" and "no," "hello" and "good-bye" are culturally based. In the United States people nod their heads up and down to signal "yes" and shake them back and forth to signal "no." In Thailand the same actions have exactly the opposite meaning! To take

another example, the North American "good-bye" wave is interpreted in many parts of Europe and South America as the motion for "no," while the Italian and Greek gestures for "good-bye" is the same as the U.S. signal for "come here."

(Stephen E. Lucas, *The Art of Public Speaking,* 10/e, 2009)

Topic: ______________________________

Main idea: ______________________________

____

Exercise 9: Writing Supporting Detail Sentences

Directions: In the exercise below, a main idea sentence is given to you. Come up with two sentences that directly support the main idea. Your sentences should provide specific details by giving reasons or examples.

Example: Many people do not use antibiotics properly.

a. They stop taking the antibiotic when they start feeling better.

b. They pass them around to their friends like candy.

1. Children today don't treat their parents with much respect.

   a. They ______________________________

   b. They ______________________________

2. Young boys are more interested in active, aggressive play than little girls.

   a. Boys play ______________________________

   b. Girls play ______________________________

3. In the last 10 years, a new kind of father has emerged.

   a. Fathers now ______________________________

   b. Fathers now ______________________________

4. For a student in the United States, school is just like a job.

   a. Students have to ______________________________

   b. Students have to ______________________________

5. Holding a part-time job can benefit students.

   a. They learn ______________________________

   b. They learn ______________________________

6. People are more isolated from their neighbors today than they were 50 years ago.

   a. They no longer ______________________________

   b. They no longer ______________________________

7. The traditional family (husband as breadwinner, wife as homemaker) has all but disappeared.

   a. Today ______________________________

   b. Today ______________________________

Exercise 10: Working with Book Titles

BOOK TITLES

The (Honest) Truth About Dishonesty by Dan Ariely
Animal Wise by Virginia Morell
Cooked by Michael Pollan
Salt Sugar Fat by Michael Moss
The Myths of Happiness by Sonja Lyubomirsky
The Sibling Effect by Jeffrey Kluger
Parenting Without Borders by Christine Gross-Loh

Directions: Read each of the tables of contents below to determine the topic of the book it came from. Then, choose the title from the list above that best matches the topic and the chapter titles. Write the title on the line provided.

1. Contents

a. Topic: ______________________________

b. Title of Book: ______________________________

2. Contents

a. Topic: ______________________________

b. Title of Book: ______________________________

3. Contents

a. Topic: ______________________________

b. Title of Book: ______________________________

4. Contents

a. Topic: ______________________________

b. Title of Book: ______________________________

5. Contents

a. Topic: ____________________

b. Title of Book: ____________________

6. Contents

a. Topic: ____________________

b. Title of Book: ____________________

7. Contents

a. Topic: ______________________________

b. Title of Book: ______________________________

Varying Positions for Main Ideas

In previous exercises, we saw that the main idea in a paragraph is frequently located at either the beginning or the end of the paragraph. However, the main idea also may appear in other locations within a paragraph, such as in the middle, or at both the beginning and the end. Wherever the main idea is located, it must be supported by details. Most authors provide examples, illustrations, major points, reasons, or facts and statistics to develop their main idea. While a main idea can be either directly stated somewhere in the paragraph or implied, supporting details are always directly stated. The ability to recognize supporting details is of crucial importance in the reading process. Locating supporting details will tell you whether you have correctly identified the main idea.

Paragraph Diagrams

For those of you who are visual learners, graphic organizers may be helpful. The following diagrams, a type of graphic organizer, show the development of a paragraph by indicating the position of the main idea and supporting details. The topic of each of the following paragraphs is the healing power of laughter.

Directions: After reading the explanation for each type of paragraph, write several key supporting details on the line provided.

1. Humor can be used inappropriately and can actually cause distress. Anyone who has seen the hurt and puzzled expression on another's face in response to an ironic remark, or remembers how she or he may have felt as an object of a joke, has witnessed humor's power to cause distress. Because humor's effects are not always predictable, experts recommend that humor be used carefully when helping someone else cope with stress so as not to make the situation worse.

(Jerrold S. Greenberg, *Comprehensive Stress Management*, 13/e, 2013)

Main Idea Sentence

Details

In paragraph 1, the main idea is stated in the first sentence. The supporting details are examples illustrating the main idea. A diagram of this type of paragraph would be a triangle with the point aiming downward. The main idea is represented by the horizontal line at the top.

Supporting detail: ______________________________

Supporting detail: ______________________________

Details

Main Idea Sentence

(Summary)

2. A deep laugh temporarily raises pulse rate and blood pressure and tenses the muscles. After a good laugh, however, pulse rate and blood pressure go down and muscles become more relaxed. Laughter works in two ways. Being able to laugh at a situation reminds you that life is seldom perfect or predictable. Laughing helps keep events in perspective. Laughing also works to reinforce a positive attitude. Laughing or even smiling can improve mood. As you can see, laughter is a powerful stress-reducing agent.

(David J. Anspaugh et al., *Wellness, 7/e,* 2009)

In paragraph 2, the author gives examples at the beginning and uses the main point to draw a conclusion. A diagram for this type of paragraph places the main idea at the bottom of the triangle.

It takes 17 muscles to smile, 43 muscles to frown.

Supporting detail: ______________________________

Supporting detail: ______________________________

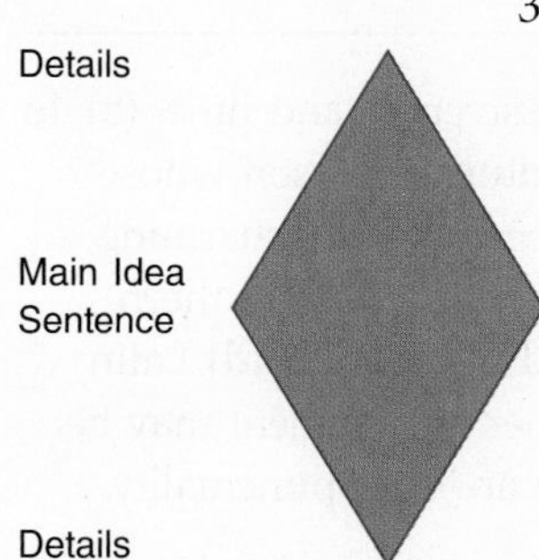

3. Research suggests that while both sexes laugh a lot, females laugh more. In male-female conversations, females laughed 126 percent more than their male counterparts, meaning that women tend to do the most laughing while males tend to do the most laugh-getting. There are strong gender differences in laughter. Across cultures, from early childhood on, men seem to be the main instigators of humor. Think back to your high school class clown—most likely he was a male. The gender pattern of everyday laughter also suggests why there are more male than female comedians.

(Robert Provine, "The Science of Laughter," *Psychology Today*, 2000)

In paragraph 3, the author begins with examples, states the main idea, and then concludes with additional examples. Because the main idea is in the middle, the diagram resembles a diamond.

Supporting detail: ______________________________

Supporting detail: ______________________________

Main Idea Sentence

Details

Main Idea Sentence

(Restatement)

4. Pain reduction is one of laughter's promising benefits. Rosemary Cogan, a professor of psychology at Texas Tech University, found that subjects who laughed at comedy videos or underwent a relaxation procedure tolerated more discomfort than other subjects. James Rotton, a professor at Florida International University, reported that orthopedic patients who watched comedy videos requested fewer aspirin and tranquilizers than the group that viewed dramas. It appears that humor may help alleviate intense pain.

(Robert Provine, "The Science of Laughter," *Psychology Today,* 2000)

In paragraph 4, the author begins with the main idea, provides a detailed explanation of it, and concludes with a restatement of the main idea. A diagram of this type of paragraph would have an hourglass shape.

Supporting detail: ______________________________

Supporting detail: ______________________________

Exercise 11: Locating the Main Idea

Directions: The main idea sentence appears at different locations in the following paragraphs. Write the letter of the main idea sentence on the line. Then draw a diagram of the paragraph and list the supporting details.

1. (a) American males may feel uncomfortable when Middle Eastern heads of state greet the U.S. president with a kiss on the cheek. (b) A German student, accustomed to speaking rarely to "Herr Professor," considers it strange that at American colleges most faculty office doors are open and students stop by freely. (c) An Iranian student on her first visit to an American McDonald's restaurant fumbles around in her paper bag looking for the eating utensils until she sees the other customers eating their French fries with, of all things, their hands. (d) In many areas of the globe, your best manners and my best manners may be exceedingly offensive to people of different nationalities and may cause us to make a serious breach of etiquette. (e) Foreigners visiting Japan often struggle to master the rules of the social game—when to take their shoes off, how to pour the tea, when to give and open gifts, how to act toward someone higher or lower in the social hierarchy.

   Main idea sentence: ________________ Diagram: ________________

   Supporting details: ____

   ____

2. (a) Cultures also vary in their norms for personal expressiveness and time. (b) To someone from a relatively formal northern European culture, a person whose roots are in an expressive Mediterranean culture may seem "warm, charming, inefficient, and time-wasting." (c) To the Mediterranean person, the northern European may seem "efficient, cold, and over concerned with time." (d) Latin American business executives who arrive late for a dinner engagement may be mystified by how obsessed their American counterparts are with punctuality.

   Main idea sentence: ________________ Diagram: ________________

   Supporting details: ____

3. (a) Adults maintain more distance from each other than children. (b) Men keep more distance from one another than do women. (c) Cultures near the equator prefer less space and more touching and hugging. (d) Thus the British and Scandinavians prefer more distance than the French and Arabs; North Americans prefer more space than Latin Americans. (e) As you can see, individuals and groups differ in their need for personal space.

   (David G. Myers, *Social Psychology*, 9/e, 2008)

   Main idea sentence: ________________ Diagram: ________________

   Supporting detail: ____

4. (a) Once in Mexico I raised my hand to a certain height to indicate how tall a child was. (b) My hosts began to laugh. (c) It turned out that Mexicans have a more complicated system of hand gestures to indicate height: one for people, a second for animals, and a third for plants. (d) What had amused them was that I had ignorantly used the plant gesture to indicate the child's height.

   Main idea sentence: ________________ Diagram: ________________

   Supporting detail: ____

5. (a) When Big Boy opened a restaurant in Bangkok, it quickly became popular with European and American tourists, but the local Thais refused to eat there. (b) Instead they placed gifts of rice and incense at the feet of the Big Boy statue (a chubby boy holding a hamburger) because it reminded them of Buddha. (c) In Japan, customers were forced to tiptoe around a logo painted on the

floor at the entrance to an Athlete's Foot store because in Japan, it is considered taboo to step on a crest. (d) And in Russia, consumers found the American-style energetic happiness of McDonald's employees insincere and offensive when the company opened its first stores there. (e) As these examples illustrate, many businesspeople engaged in international trade underestimate the importance of social and cultural differences.

(O. C. Ferrell, Geoffrey Hirt, and Linda Ferrell, *Business*, 9/e, 2014)

Main idea sentence: ________________ Diagram: ________________

Supporting details: ________________________________

6. (a) Coor's slogan "Turn it loose" was translated into Spanish where it was read as "Suffer from diarrhea." (b) Colgate introduced Cue toothpaste in France, only to discover that Cue is a French pornographic magazine. (c) Translated into Chinese, Pepsi's "Come alive with the Pepsi generation" became "Pepsi brings back your ancestors from the grave." (d) Clairol introduced the Mist Stick curling iron in Germany where "mist" is German slang for manure. (e) These examples underscore that firms that want to market a product globally and reach consumers of varying cultures need to become thoroughly acquainted with the language, customs, prejudices, and tastes of the intended market.

   Main idea sentence: ________________ Diagram: ________________

   Supporting details: ________________________________

7. (a) Even numbers have different meanings in different countries. (b) Marketers should avoid using the number four when addressing Chinese, Korean, and Japanese consumers. (c) Although advertising that says "four times the savings" would probably appeal to American consumers, it would not appeal to an Asian audience because four is the number for death in Asian numerology.

   Main idea sentence: ________________ Diagram: ________________

   Supporting details: ________________________________

8. (a) Westerners consider direct eye contact important, but many cultures see it as a personal affront, conveying a lack of respect. (b) In Japan, for example, when shaking hands, bowing, and especially when talking, it is important to glance only occasionally into the other person's face. (c) One's gaze should instead focus on fingertips, desk tops, and carpets. (d) In the words of one American electronics representative, "Always keep your shoes shined in Tokyo. (e) You can bet a lot of Japanese you meet will have their eyes on them."

   (David H. Olson and John DeFrain, *Marriages and Families*, 6/e, 2008)

   Main idea sentence: ________________ Diagram: ________________

   Supporting details: ________________________________

Internet Activity

To discover more about nonverbal communication, visit the following Web site sponsored by the University of California at Santa Cruz:

http://nonverbal.ucsc.edu/

You can test your skill at "reading" samples of nonverbal communication in the areas of gestures and personal space. Write a short paragraph explaining what you learned.

Exercise 12: Locating Topics, Main Ideas, and Details

Directions: In the following passages from Kitty Locker's *Business and Administrative Communication,* locate the topic of each paragraph and the main idea sentence, and write them on the designated lines. One supporting detail has been omitted from each paragraph. Look at the supporting details list at the end of the exercise, match each one to its correct paragraph, and then enter the paragraph number on the line.

1. In the United States smiling varies from region to region. Thirty years ago, Ray Birdwhistell found that "middle-class individuals" from Ohio, Indiana, and Illinois smiled more than did people from Massachusetts, New Hampshire, and Maine, who in turn smiled more than did western New Yorkers. People from cities in southern and border states—Atlanta, Louisville, Memphis, and Nashville—smiled most of all. Students from other countries who come to U.S. universities may be disconcerted by the American tendency to smile at strangers—until they realize that the smiles don't "mean" anything.

   Topic: ______________________________

   Main idea: ______________________________

2. Repeated studies have shown that older people are healthier both mentally and physically if they are touched. It is well-documented that babies need to be touched to grow and thrive. Touch, while necessary for optimum health, can communicate many messages. A person who dislikes touch may seem unfriendly to someone who's used to touching. A toucher may seem overly familiar to someone who dislikes touch. Studies in the United States have shown that touch is interpreted as power: more powerful people touch less powerful people.

   Topic: ______________________________

   Main idea: ______________________________

   ____

3. People who don't know each other well may feel more comfortable with each other if a piece of furniture separates them. For example, a group may work better sitting around a table than just sitting in a circle. Lecterns and desks can be used as barricades to protect oneself from other people. One professor normally walked among his students as he lectured. But if anyone asked a question he was uncomfortable with, he retreated behind the lectern before answering it. Spatial arrangements mean different things within a culture and between cultures. In the United States, the size, placement, and privacy of one's office connotes status. Large corner offices have the highest status. An individual office with a door that closes connotes more status than a desk in a common area. Japanese firms, however, see private offices as "inappropriate and inefficient," reports Robert Christopher. Only the very highest executives and directors have private offices in the traditional Japanese company, and even they will also have desks in the common area.

   Topic: ______________________________

   Main idea: ______________________________

   ____

4. People in many cultures want to establish a personal relationship before they decide whether to do business with each other. For example, to do business in Mexico, you need to develop a personal relationship. Tell me about you as a person. That's very important. Then I tell you about me, and we do this

sometimes not just one time, but several times. Then I will trust you and I will value your qualities. Then I will like to work with you.

Topic: ______________________________

Main idea: ______________________________

____

5. Many North Americans measure time in five-minute blocks. Someone who's five minutes late to an appointment or a job interview feels compelled to apologize. If the executive or interviewer is running half an hour late, the caller expects to be told about the likely delay upon arriving. Some people won't be able to wait that long and will need to reschedule their appointments. But in other cultures, 15 minutes or half an hour may be the smallest block of time. To someone who mentally measures time in 15-minute blocks, being 45 minutes late is no worse than being 15 minutes late to someone who is conscious of smaller units. Different cultures also have different lead times. In some countries, you need to schedule important meetings at least two weeks in advance. In other countries, not only are people not booked up so far in advance, but a date two weeks into the future may be forgotten. Various cultures mentally measure time differently.

Topic: ______________________________

Main idea: ______________________________

6. Symbols (clothing, colors, and age) carry nonverbal meanings that vary from culture to culture. In North America, certain styles and colors of clothing are considered more "professional" and more "credible." In Japan, clothing denotes not only status but also occupational group. Students wear uniforms. Workers wear different clothes when they are on strike than they do when they are working. In the United States, youth is valued. Some men as well as some women color their hair and even have face-lifts to look as youthful as possible. In Japan, younger people defer to older people. Americans attempting to negotiate in Japan are usually taken more seriously if at least one member of the team is noticeably gray-haired.

Topic: ______________________________

Main idea: ______________________________

____

7. Height connotes status in many parts of the world. Executive offices are usually on the top floors; the underlings work below. Even being tall can help a person succeed. Studies have shown that employers are more willing to hire men over 6 feet tall than shorter men with the same credentials. In one study, every extra inch of height brought in an extra $1,300 a year.

Topic: ______________________________

Main idea: ______________________________

8. Differences in eye contact can lead to miscommunication in the multicultural workplace. For example, North American whites see eye contact as a sign of honesty. But in many cultures, dropped eyes are a sign of appropriate deference to a superior. Puerto Rican children are taught not to meet the eyes of adults, and in Korea, prolonged eye contact is considered rude. The lower-ranking person is expected to look down first. Arab men in laboratory experiments looked at each other more than did two American men or two Englishmen. Eye contact is so important that Arabs dislike talking to someone wearing dark glasses or

while walking side by side. It is considered impolite not to face someone directly. In Muslim countries, women and men are not supposed to make eye contact.

(Kitty O. Locker and Donna S. Kienzler, *Business and Administrative Communication,* 8/e, 2008)

Topic: ______________________________

Main idea: ______________________________

____

Supporting Details

(*See directions on pqge 96.*)

_____ In Arab countries, appointments are scheduled only three or four days in advance.

_____ In North America, a person sitting at the head of a table is generally assumed to be the group's leader.

_____ North Americans who believe that "time is money" are often frustrated in negotiations with people who place more emphasis on personal relationships.

_____ Company badges indicate rank within the organization.

_____ Superiors may feel that subordinates are being disrespectful when they look down, but the subordinate is being fully respectful—according to the norms of his or her culture.

_____ When the toucher had higher status than the recipient, both men and women liked being touched.

_____ Some scholars speculate that northerners may distrust the sincerity of southerners who smile a lot (like former President Jimmy Carter).

_____ Studies of real-world executives and graduates have shown that taller men make more money.

REVIEW TEST 1: Topics, Main Ideas, and Details

Directions: Each of the following groups contains a series of related statements: One of the statements gives a topic, another gives a main idea, and the rest give supporting details. Identify the role of each statement in the space provided using the following abbreviations: **T** for Topic, **MI** for Main Idea, and **SD** for Supporting Detail.

Group 1

_____ a. A four-leaf clover means good luck.

_____ b. Red roses convey passionate love.

_____ c. The symbolic meaning of plants.

_____ d. Even today, several plants have symbolic meanings.

_____ e. An olive branch indicates peace.

Group 2

_____ a. Red indicates passion.

_____ b. White indicates sympathy.

_____ c. The meaning of floral colors.

_____ d. Floral colors also can communicate feelings.

_____ e. The color orange signifies friendship.

Group 3

_____ a. In the 1870s, an ardent suitor might have sent his beloved a bouquet of flowers that expressed a complete message.

_____ b. The symbolism of flowers reached its peak during the Victorian era, when almost every flower and plant had a special meaning.

_____ c. A bouquet of forget-me-nots conveyed the sentiment "remember me."

_____ d. A bouquet of jonquils, white roses, and ferns indicated that a suitor desired a return of affection, was worthy of his intended's love, and was fascinated by her.

_____ e. The "language" of flowers.

Group 4

_____ a. In 1875, in Switzerland, Daniel Peter and Henri Nestle created milk chocolate by adding condensed milk to chocolate liquor.

_____ b. In the 1890s, the first candy bar was created by adding nuts, fruits, caramels, and other ingredients to the chocolate liquor.

_____ c. For the love of chocolate.

_____ d. There have been many changes in chocolate candy since it was created in 1847.

_____ e. Milton Hershey modified the Peter process by adding whole milk.

Group 5

_____ a. Food of the gods.

_____ b. According to Aztec mythology, the god Quetzalcoatl gave cacao beans to the Aztec people.

_____ c. The beans were later offered as gifts to the gods.

_____ d. The cacao tree, the source of chocolate, has long been cultivated by native peoples of Central and South America for religious purposes.

_____ e. The beans also were used to make a beverage consumed by priests on ceremonial occasions.

Group 6

_____ a. Originally chocolate candy bars were promoted as health foods.

_____ b. A high energy treat.

_____ c. In World War I, candy bars were given to the soldiers as a source of quick energy.

_____ d. In the 1920s, many candy bars claimed to aid the digestion and had names like Vegetable Sandwich.

(Estelle Levetin and Karen McMahon, *Plants and Society*, 6/e, 2012)

REVIEW TEST 2: Topics, Main Ideas, and Details

Directions: The following group contains a series of related statements: One of the statements gives a topic, another gives a main idea, and four give supporting details. Identify the role of each statement in the space provided using the following abbreviations: **T** for Topic, **MI** for Main Idea, and **SD** for Supporting Detail.

Group 1

______ a. Between 9 and 12 months of age, for example, Maika pointed to things to show that she wanted an object, nodded her head to mean *yes,* and shook her head to mean *no.*

______ b. Babies develop a rich repertoire of nonverbal gestures before saying their first words.

______ c. At 13 months, she was using representational gestures such as holding up her arms to show that she wanted to be picked up, or holding an empty cup to her mouth to show that she wanted a drink.

______ d. Symbolic gestures of babies.

(Diane E. Papalia and Ruth Duskin Feldman, *Experience Human Development,* 12/e, 2012)

Group 2

______ a. Demonstration of affection.

______ b. For example, middle-class Brazilians teach their male and female children to kiss every adult relative they ever see.

______ c. While females continue kissing throughout their lives, Brazilian men greet each other with a hearty handshake and a traditional male hug.

______ d. Brazilians do not fear demonstrations of physical contact and affection.

(Conrad Phillip Kottak, *Anthropology,* 12/e, 2008)

Group 3

______ a. In a suit brought by New Jersey importer, John Nix, tomatoes were legally declared vegetables in 1893 by the U.S. Supreme Court.

______ b. The Spanish conquistadors introduced the tomato to Europe, where it was first known as the "Apple of Peru."

______ c. What is a fruit?

______ d. Later it was known as *pomo doro,* golden apple in Italy, and *pomme d'amour,* love apple (it was believed by many to be an aphrodisiac) in France.

______ e. Tomatoes, one of the most common, popular, and versatile "vegetables," is technically a fruit.

______ f. Justice Horace Gray said that although tomatoes are considered to be the fruits of the vine, they are usually served at dinner, and not, like fruits, generally as dessert.

(Estelle Levetin and Karen McMahon, *Plants and Society,* 6/e, 2012)

REVIEW TEST 3: Topics, Main Ideas, and Details

Directions: The main idea sentence appears at different locations in the following paragraphs. Write the letter of the main idea sentence on the line. Then draw a diagram of the paragraph and list the supporting details by letter.

1. (a) Americans eat oysters but not snails. (b) The French eat snails but not locusts. (c) The Zulus eat locusts but not fish. (d) The Jews eat fish but not pork. (e) The Hindus eat pork but not beef. (f) The Russians eat beef but not snakes. (g) The Chinese eat snakes but not people. (h) The Jalé of New Guinea find people delicious. (i) The diversity of our customs and expressive behavior suggests that much of our behavior is socially programmed, not hardwired.

   (David G. Myers, *Social Psychology*, 9/e, 2008)

   Main idea sentence: ________________ Diagram: ________________

   Supporting details: ____

2. (a) Most North Americans value "fairness." (b) "You're not playing fair" is a sharp criticism calling for changed behavior. (c) In some countries, however, people expect certain groups to receive preferential treatment. (d) Most North Americans accept competition and believe that it produces better performance. (e) The Japanese, however, believe that competition leads to disharmony. (f) U.S. business people believe that success is based on individual achievement and is open to anyone who excels. (g) However, in England and in France, success is more obviously linked to social class. (h) Many people in the United States value individualism, but other countries may value the group. (i) In traditional classrooms, U.S. students are expected to complete assignments alone; if they get much help from anyone else, they're "cheating." (j) In Japan, in contrast, groups routinely work together to solve problems. (k) It appears that values and beliefs, often unconscious, affect our response to people and situations.

   (Kitty O. Locker and Donna S. Kienzler, *Business and Administrative Communication*, 8/e, 2008)

   Main idea sentence: ________________ Diagram: ________________

   Supporting details: ____

3. (a) The world's nations and cultures have strikingly different notions about displays of affection and personal space. (b) Cocktail parties in international meeting places such as the United Nations can resemble an elaborate insect mating ritual as diplomats from different countries advance, withdraw, and sidestep. (c) When Americans talk, walk, and dance, they maintain a certain distance from others. (d) Italians or Brazilians, who need less personal space, may interpret such "standoffishness" as a sign of coldness. (e) In conversational pairs, the Italian or Brazilian typically moves in, while the American "instinctively" retreats from a "close talker." (f) How people show affection and respect personal space varies greatly from culture to culture.

   (Conrad Phillip Kottak, *Anthropology*, 14/e, 2011)

   Main idea sentence: ________________ Diagram: ________________

   Supporting details: ____

Writing a Paraphrase

When you **paraphrase** something, you express the author's meaning *using your own words.* Often you will substitute synonyms for some words, but key words such as names are usually left the same. A paraphrase typically keeps the same sequence of ideas as the original. Don't be surprised if your paraphrase is longer than the original. The ability to paraphrase is important when you are trying to formulate a main idea.

Paraphrasing is also a useful study technique. When you can put the author's thoughts into your own words, you have truly understood the material. When you write a paraphrase for your classes, you want to put only the information that is key to your subject in your own words.

Examples of Paraphrases

Quotation: The man who most vividly realizes a difficulty is the man most likely to overcome it.

Sample Paraphrase: The person who can clearly recognize a problem is the one likely to solve it.

Textbook Paragraph: Honeybees use a combination of communication methods, but especially tactile ones, to impart information about the environment. When a foraging bee returns to the hive, it performs a waggle dance that indicates the distance and the direction of a food source. Inside the hive, it is dark, and other bees have to follow and touch the dancer in order to get the message.

(Sylvia Mader, *Concepts of Biology*, 2009, p. 735)

Sample Paraphrase: Honeybees rely heavily on touch to communicate environmental information. A bee returning to the hive does a certain kind of dance, called a waggle dance, to indicate to other bees how far away food is and where it is. Because the hive is dark, the other bees need to touch the dancer to get the message.

Exercise 1: Paraphrasing Modern Proverbs

Directions: Paraphrase the following proverbs. When you are finished, check to make sure the meaning of both statements is the same.

1. You can't unring a bell.

 ____

2. It takes a village to raise a child.

 ____

3. Old age isn't for sissies.

 ____

4. Labels are for cans, not people.

 ____

5. Free advice is worth exactly what you pay for it.

 ____

6. Don't let the same bee sting you twice. ______________________________

 ____

7. Follow your own bliss.

____

8. Keep your friends close and your enemies closer.

____

9. You don't get defeated unless you quit.

____

10. It isn't whether you win or lose that counts, it's how you play the game.

____

Exercise 2: Paraphrasing Rhymes

Directions: Working with a partner, paraphrase each of these nursery rhymes using your *own* words. Leave the key names, such as Humpty Dumpty, the same.

Example: There was an old woman who lived in a shoe,
She had so many children she didn't know what to do;
She gave them some broth without any bread;
She whipped them all soundly and put them to bed.

An elderly woman, who was residing in a shoe, felt so overwhelmed by her large family that she fed all the children clear soup, spanked them, and sent them to bed.

1. Jack Sprat could eat no fat,
His wife could eat no lean,
And so betwixt them both, you see,
They licked the platter clean.

____

____

2. Humpty Dumpty sat on a wall,
Humpty Dumpty had a great fall.
All the king's horses, and all the king's men,
Couldn't put Humpty together again.

____

____

3. Tom, Tom, the piper's son,
Stole a pig and away did run!
The pig was eat, and Tom was beat,
And Tom went howling down the street.

____

____

4. Three wise men of Gotham
Went to sea in a bowl;
If the bowl had been stronger
My song had been longer.

____

____

5. Little Polly Finders
Sat among the cinders,
Warming her pretty little toes;
Her mother came and caught her,
And whipped her little daughter
For spoiling her nice new clothes.

____

____

6. Jack and Jill
Went up the hill,
To fetch a pail of water;
Jack fell down,
And broke his crown,
And Jill came tumbling after.

____

____

Exercise 3: Paraphrasing a Poem

Directions: Read the poem by Tran Thi Nga carefully, noting the key words and main ideas. Try to explain the meaning of the poem in your own words, and then write a paraphrase of it.

Grandmother's Fable

Once upon a time there lived a farming family.
The mother died, leaving three sons
to live with their father.
When the father became ill
and thought he was going to die, he called his children to his bedside
and handed each of them
a large bunch of chopsticks tied together.

He said, "Whoever can break this,
I will reward."
Not one was able to.

The father then handed each of them
only one set.
This they broke easily.

The father said, "If you remain united,
no one can harm you,
but if you separate, then you will be hurt.
This is the advice I leave with you.
The heritage I have for you
is in the rice fields."

After the father's death,
the three brothers stayed together
even after they married.
They did not find any golden treasures
buried in the rice fields.

They plowed and planted
and the ground gave successful harvests.
They realized working together
and working hard were life's riches.

Nga emigrated to the United States in 1975.

(Tran Thi Nga, "Grandmother's Fable")

Exercise 4: Paraphrasing a Fable

Directions: First, read the fable by Aesop below. Then answer the following questions. Finally, rewrite the fable in your own words.

A lion used to prowl about a field in which four oxen lived. Many a time he tried to attack them. But, whenever he came near, they turned their tails to one another, so that whichever way he approached them, he was met by the horns of one of them. At last, however, they fell to quarreling among themselves, and each went off to the pasture alone in a separate corner of the field. Then the lion attacked them one by one and soon put an end to all four.

1. How would you express the moral of this fable? ______
2. How is this fable similar to the previous fable? ______
3. In what ways are the advice of Tran Thi Nga and that of Aesop the same?

READING

"The message could be 'food is available' or 'be alert for possible danger.'"

TUNING IN TO READING The fire ant is considered the most aggressive of all varieties of ants. It is also one of the most dangerous because it can sting many times in succession. Most people who live in locations where these ants are found are especially cautious, because the bite of the ant lives up to its name. It burns like fire.

BIO-SKETCH Dr. Sylvia S. Mader is the author of several highly respected college biology textbooks. She is noted for her entertaining writing style and her ability to motivate students who are hesitant to take science courses.

NOTES ON VOCABULARY

mandible lower jaw

READING (continued)

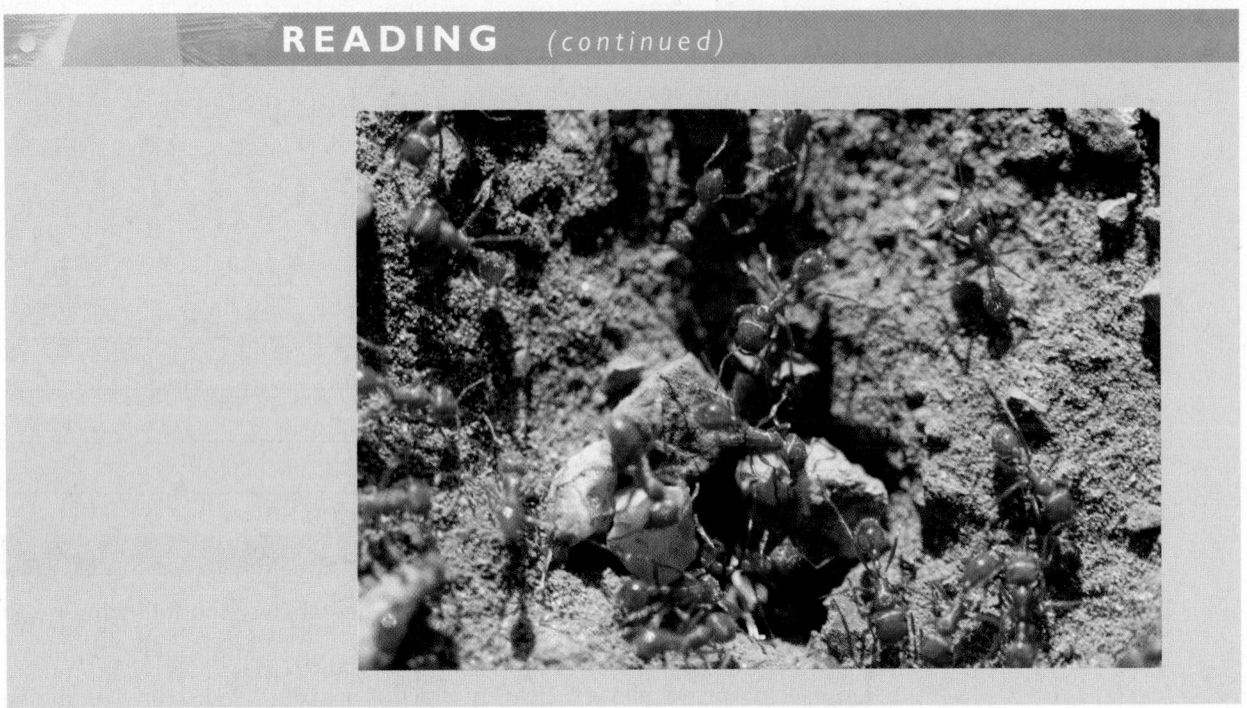

FIRE ANTS HAVE A GOOD DEFENSE

Sylvia S. Mader

Fire ants have a red to reddish-brown color, but even so, they most likely take the name from the ability to STING. Their stinger protrudes from the rear, but in a split second, they can grab the skin of a person with their mandibles and position the stinger between their legs to sting from the front. The stinger injects a toxin into the tiny wound, and the result is a burning sensation. The next day, the person will end up with a white pustule at the site of the sting.

The success of this defense mechanism is clear because most animals try 2
to stay away from bees, wasps, and ants—and any other animal that can sting.

Living usually in an open, grassy area, fire ants sting in order to defend 3
their home, which is a mound of soil that they have removed from subterranean tunnels. They use the tunnels to travel far afield safely when searching for food, which they bring back to their nest mates. The queen and many worker ants live in chambers within the mound or slightly below it.

The queen ant is much larger than the other members of the colony, and 4
she has only one purpose: to produce many thousands of small, white eggs. First, the eggs develop into cream-colored, grublike larvae, which are lavishly tended by worker ants to keep them clean and well fed. When the larvae become encased by a hard covering, they are pupae. Inside a pupa, an amazing transformation takes place, and eventually, an adult breaks out. Most of these adults are worker ants, but in the spring a few are winged "sexuals," which are male and female ants with the ability to reproduce. The sexuals remain inside the colony with nothing to do until the weather is cooperative enough for them to fly skyward to mate. A few of the fertilized females manage to survive the perils of an outside existence long enough to start another colony.

All the ants in a colony have the same mother, namely the queen ant who produces the eggs. The workers are sterile, closely related sister ants. Because of their genetic relationship, we can view the members of a colony as a superorganism. The queen serves as the reproductive system, while the workers serve as the digestive, urinary, and, indeed, all the systems that keep the superorganism functioning. 5

What fosters cooperation between the members of the superorganism? The answer is pheromones, chemicals excreted externally that influence the behavior and even development of other species members. Fire ants, like other ants, produce several different pheromones that send messages when released into the air. The message could be "food is available" or "be alert for possible danger." The queen even releases pheromones that cause workers to attend her. 6

(Sylvia S. Mader, *Concepts of Biology*, McGraw-Hill, 2009, pp. 2–3)

COMPREHENSION CHECKUP

Paraphrase

Directions: Here are some sentences from the selection. Paraphrase them by rewriting each one in your own words in the space provided.

1. The queen ant is much larger than the other members of the colony, and she has only one purpose: to produce many thousands of small, white eggs.

____

____

____

2. The queen serves as the reproductive system, while the workers serve as the digestive, urinary, and, indeed, all the systems that keep the superorganism functioning.

____

____

____

Directions: Read paragraphs 1 and 2 again. Then paraphrase them by putting the information into your own words.

____

____

____

____

____

____

____

____

Multiple Choice

Directions: Write the letter of the correct answer on the blank provided.

_____ 1. The worker ants are
  a. able to fly.
  b. able to reproduce.
  c. larger than the queen.
  d. females.

_____ 2. All of the following apply to the queen ant **except**
  a. She lives inside a mound of soil.
  b. She is a winged sexual.
  c. She is much larger than the other ants.
  d. She carefully tends her baby ants to make sure they are clean and well fed.

_____ 3. The queen ant
  a. is the mother of all of the ants in her colony.
  b. is the digestive system of her colony.
  c. is willing to tend to her workers' needs if other ants aren't available.
  d. is willing to share her colony with another queen if necessary.

_____ 4. The eggs develop first as
  a. pupae.
  b. larvae.
  c. fertilized females.
  d. workers.

_____ 5. Pheromones have all of the following characteristics **except**
  a. They are chemicals released into the air.
  b. They help foster communication between members of the ant colony.
  c. They are released only by the workers.
  d. They influence ant behavior.

True or False

Directions: Indicate whether the statement is true or false by writing **T** or **F** on the blank provided.

_____ 6. Fire ants received their name because of their reddish color.

_____ 7. If something *protrudes,* it likely sticks out.

_____ 8. A fire ant can't sting from the front.

_____ 9. A *toxin* is a poisonous substance.

_____ 10. As a defense mechanism, the sting of a fire ant has proven to be inadequate.

_____ 11. A *subterranean* tunnel is located above ground.

_____ 12. Fire ants are located in rocky, mountainous regions.

_____ 13. Tunnels allow the ants to safely forage for food.

_____ 14. The much larger queen is solely responsible for producing eggs.

_____ 15. If something is *perilous,* it is likely to be dangerous.

Vocabulary in Context

Directions: Choose one of the following words to complete each of the sentences below. Use each word only once. Be sure to pay close attention to the clues provided.

afield	encased	inject	sterile
chambers	excrete	lavishly	tended
defense	fosters	species	transformation

1. She ____________________ the development of many children at her daycare center.
2. Washing your hands thoroughly is the best ____________________ against disease.
3. He recently learned how to ____________________ insulin using a pen syringe.
4. When Peter Parker is bitten by a spider, he begins the ____________________ into Spider Man.
5. The warrior roamed far ____________________ looking for new lands to conquer.
6. The billionaire's home was ____________________ decorated.
7. It was a ____________________ environment; nothing would grow there.
8. The king's ____________________ were furnished with all of the finest materials.
9. There are many threatened ____________________, such as great apes, whales, and tigers.
10. The nurses selflessly ____________________ their patients throughout the flu outbreak.
11. When we ____________________ sweat, does it help the body to cool down?
12. After walking for hours barefoot in the storm, his feet were ____________________ in mud.

In Your Own Words

1. What is your opinion about applying pesticides to reduce fire ant infestations?
2. Can you think of another approach that might be more environmentally friendly? What about introducing a natural predator of fire ants?

Written Assignment

Did you know that there's a variety of ant that's even worse than the fire ant? It's called the "crazy ant." It can wipe out a colony of fire ants and take over an area. Unlike the fire ant, it doesn't stay outside of buildings. Instead, it enters homes by invading crawl spaces, walls, and electrical outlets. Although its bite is less severe, the devastation it causes is much worse. Should anything be done to control crazy ants? Presently they are most common in coastal regions of southern states. Should measures be taken to guard against their spreading to other areas of the country?

Internet Activity

Fire ants have a peculiar locomotive style. They can quickly run through tunnels (and evacuate them quickly, if necessary) without smacking into each other. They even use their antennae as additional limbs. Researchers believe that new discoveries about fire ants could aid engineers in developing search-and-rescue robots. To find out more about this topic, search for "fire ants as models for rescue robots." Write a paragraph about your findings.

Introduction to Implied Main Ideas

Not all main ideas are directly stated, as you can see in the cartoon above. Instead, some main ideas are **implied**, which means that you must figure out the most important point the author is making from the details provided. You may recall that the first step in identifying a directly stated main idea is to identify the topic. You do this by asking, "What is this about?" or "Who is this about?" The first step in determining an implied main idea is exactly the same. In the cartoon, the topic is "a delivery mistake." Following are the key details in the cartoon that will help you determine the main idea.

- First, notice the man near the zoo entrance returning the box marked "computer monitor." He mentions that he ordered a "monitor lizard."

© Mark Parisi, permission granted for use. www.offthemark.com

- Then notice the people fleeing the computer store across the street.
- Finally, notice the "UH, OH" expressed by the driver.

Together these details suggest an implied main idea that is stated something like this: The driver (dispatcher) has delivered a monitor lizard to the computer store and a computer monitor to the zoo.

To be able to write an implied main idea, you need to understand the difference between something that is implied, meaning that it is hinted at or suggested in the text, and something that is directly stated. Look at the following two statements. Which statement is implying something? Which one is directly stating it?

Statement 1. Don, I've had a really hard day. I didn't do well on my first test in biology, and the kids left the house a mess. I just don't feel like cooking tonight. I'm much too tired.

Statement 2. Don, I need to go out to dinner tonight.

The first sentence is implying what the second sentence is directly stating. Now let's take a look at some strategies to try to identify the implied main idea.

Asking Questions to Determine Supporting Details

Read the paragraph below on the topic of personality differences between boys and girls.

In general, young boys tend to be more aggressive than girls. They play more loudly; they roughhouse more, and are more apt to try to dominate other children and challenge their parents. Boys argue and fight more often and are more apt to use force or threats of force to get their way, while girls try to solve conflicts by persuasion rather than confrontation. Girls are more likely to cooperate with their parents and they tend to set up rules to avoid clashes. Girls are more likely to be empathic, that is, to identify with other people's feelings.

(Diane E. Papalia, *Experience Human Development,* 12/e, 2012)

Ask yourself who, what, where, when, why, and how questions about the topic of the paragraph. This will give you the following answers.

Who: boys and girls

What: display different personality characteristics

Where: in social settings

When: during interactions with others

Why: boys are more aggressive; girls are more cooperative and empathic

How: boys dominate, fight, threaten; girls persuade, cooperate, set up rules

By combining these key details, the main idea looks something like this:

Implied Main Idea: Young boys are more likely to display an aggressive personality, and young girls are more likely to display an empathic, cooperative personality.

Combining Sentences

Sometimes the implied main idea can be constructed by combining two or more sentences in a paragraph. Read the following paragraph on the topic of male and female friendships.

In North American culture, most male friendships are activity-based. Men tend to do things together—a pattern that provides companionship without closeness. In general, men live their friendships "side by side." On the other hand, the friendships of women are more often based on shared feelings and confidences. If two female friends spent an afternoon together and did not reveal problems, private thoughts and feelings to one another, they would assume that something was wrong. For women, friendship is a matter of talking about shared concerns and intimate matters. Women tend to live their friendships "face to face."

(Dennis Coon, *Introduction to Psychology,* 8/e, 1998)

The main idea for this paragraph can be found in the two underlined sentences. The rest of the sentences have details that support these two sentences. Combining the third and last sentences results in a main idea that reads like this:

Implied Main Idea: In general, men live their friendships "side by side" while women live their friendships "face to face."

Summing Up Important Ideas into One Sentence

This strategy involves summing up the important information from the paragraph into one main idea sentence. Read the paragraph below on the topic of tag questions.

Women are more likely than men to use tag questions. A tag question is a short phrase that turns a statement into a question. For example, "That was a hard test, wasn't it?" instead of simply saying, "That was a hard test." One interpretation of this is that women's tendency to use tag questions reflects uncertainty. A tag question is seen as weakening the statement being made. Another interpretation, however, is that the tag question encourages the other person to express an opinion. This view says that rather than reflecting uncertainty, a woman's use of tag questions might reflect greater sensitivity and warmth.

(Curtis O. Byer, *Dimensions of Human Sexuality*, 6/e, 2002)

Implied Main Idea: The fact that women use tag questions more often than men reflects either uncertainty or warmth and sensitivity.

Making Sure You Have Correctly Identified the Implied Main Idea

Some key points to remember:

1. **Make sure you have correctly identified the topic.** What is the main thing the author is talking about in the paragraph?
2. **Look at the details in the paragraph.** What one idea do they all relate to?
3. **Make sure the implied main idea you write covers all the supporting details in the paragraph but does not go beyond them.**
4. **Remember that when you write an implied main idea—as you would with a directly stated main idea—you always write it in one complete sentence.**

Exercise 1: Determining the Topic and Implied Main Ideas

Directions: Read each paragraph below and identify the topic. Write the topic on the given line. Then find the implied main idea in the choices listed below. Put the correct letter on the line provided.

A. Avoid issuing ultimatums in fights.

B. Using credit has both advantages and disadvantages.

C. How people greet each other can vary greatly from culture to culture.

D. Alcohol exacts a great toll on American families.

E. As education increases, income also increases.

F. Involved fathers are good for their children.

G. When fighting, resist giving the silent treatment.

H. The average income of men differs from that of women, with men making more than women.

1. According to a U.S. Census Bureau report, the average American male working full time earned $47,100, whereas the average American woman working full time earned only $36,300, a difference of about $11,000. Economists and other social observers cite a number of reasons for these income differences. Women often drop out of the labor force to have children and then stay at home to care for them for a few years. Meanwhile, men gain seniority in the labor force and get more job-related experience. Although it is illegal to pay women less for doing the same job, women have little legal recourse when they are paid lower wages for jobs that may require essentially the same skills.

   Topic: ______________________ Implied Main Idea: __________

2. Individuals completing 9 years of schooling or less averaged $23,000 in yearly income. Those with 9 to 12 years of schooling averaged $28,000. High school graduates averaged $38,000. College graduates averaged $77,000. Individuals with professional degrees beyond college make even a larger increase in salary, some almost double those of a college graduate. When you look at the total income individuals achieve in a lifetime of working full-time, individuals with a high school education earn about $1.2 million in a lifetime, while those with a college degree earn almost twice that amount, $2.1 million. Those with a master's degree earn about $2.5 million, with a doctorate about $3.4 million, and with a professional degree, the total annual income is about $4.4 million over a lifetime.

   Topic: ______________________ Implied Main Idea: ____________

3. Buying on credit is very popular for a number of reasons. It is convenient, and it also allows people to enjoy something while paying for it, to take advantage of sales, and to have something in case of an emergency. The disadvantages of credit include the generally high interest charges and the potential for overuse. Credit should be used with caution. Unfortunately, it is a very seductive luxury.

   Topic: ______________________ Implied Main Idea: ____________

4. Don't get into the game of saying things like, "If you do that again I will *never ever* … " or "You had better do this *or else!*" This is one of the most heavily confrontational ways people have for arguing with each other and such a strategy does not cool things down; it tends to heat things up. When someone gives an ultimatum they are trying to put themselves in an adult position, looking down on the other person, who is supposed to feel like a child. However, the response usually is anger and defiance, and the battle escalates.

   Topic: ______________________ Implied Main Idea: ____________

5. When couples get into the game of "What's wrong?"—"Nothing …" the likelihood of successfully resolving the conflict goes down dramatically. The silent treatment does not end a conflict. To end a conflict, the partners have to sit down and listen to each other and talk with each other in a respectful and kind manner.

   Topic: ______________________ Implied Main Idea: ____________

6. In most Latin countries, from Venezuela to Italy, the *abrazo* (hug) is as common as a handshake. Men hug men; women hug women; men hug women. In Slavic countries, this greeting is better described as a bear hug. In France, the double cheek-to-cheek greeting is common among both men and women. A traditional bow from the waist is the standard greeting for the Japanese, who are averse to casual touching. Many Americans, however, feel uncomfortable with bowing, but to the Japanese it means, "I respect your experience and wisdom."

   Topic: ______________________ Implied Main Idea: ____________

7. Fathers can have a very positive impact on their children's development—whether or not the father lives with the children or is a noncustodial partner. The more fathers are involved in the routine activities of their children, the more likely the children will have fewer behavior problems, be more sociable, and do better in school. Across different ethnic groups, fathers tend to assume the important role of economic provider, protector, and caregiver. When fathers provide economically for their children, they also stay more involved with their children, even if they live apart. In addition, fathers who pay child support tend to have children who behave better and do better in school.

   Topic: ______________________ Implied Main Idea: ____________

8. More than one-half of American adults have a close family member who has or has had alcoholism or was a problem drinker. That is to say, about half of all adults in this country grew up with an alcoholic or problem drinker or had a blood relative who was an alcoholic or problem drinker. Alcohol is the most widely used psychoactive drug in the United States. It contributes to the death of 100,000 people every year, making it the third leading cause of preventable death in this country after tobacco and diet/activity patterns. It is estimated that more than 7 million children live with a parent with alcohol problems. Alcohol is commonly associated with marital disruption, domestic violence, and many other family problems. Alcohol abuse and family violence are statistically related. A national sample of more than 2,000 couples found, in general, that the more often a spouse was drunk, the greater likelihood there was of physical violence in the marital relationship. Even if there is no violence in the family of an alcoholic, there is likely to be a high degree of marital dissatisfaction and a large number of disagreements. Tension and verbal conflict are likely to be frequent. Researchers have estimated that half the divorces and half the juvenile arrests for delinquency in the United States occur in families with at least one alcohol-abusing member. Finally, spouses and children of alcohol abusers are at risk for developing serious physical and emotional problems.

(David Olson, John DeFrain, and Linda Skogrand, *Marriages and Families,* 8/e, McGraw-Hill, 2014)

Topic: ______________ Implied Main Idea: ______________

Exercise 2: Practice with Implied Main Idea Strategies

Directions: Read each of the passages below and then write your answers on the lines provided. Use the indicated strategies.

Baby Blues

BABY BLUES © 2002 Baby Blues Partnership. Dist. by King Features Syndicate.

STRATEGY 1: ASKING QUESTIONS

1. Boys' play illustrates why men tend to be on the lookout for signs they are being put down or told what to do. The chief commodity that is bartered in the boy's hierarchical world is status, and the way to achieve and maintain status is to give orders and get others to follow them. A boy in a low-status position finds himself being pushed around. So boys monitor their relations for subtle shifts in status by keeping track of who's giving orders and who's taking them.

(Deborah Tannen, *You Just Don't Understand,* 1990)

Who: ____________________

What: ____________________

Where: ____________________

When: ____________________

Why: ____________________

How: ____________________

Implied Main Idea: ____________________

____

2. A popular urban legend tells the following story of an instructor and his students. Whenever the instructor walked to the left side of the room, they seemed to lose interest in what he said. They yawned, wrote notes, whispered, and paid little or no attention. When he moved to the right, they sat up straight. They listened carefully, took notes, and asked questions. After a while, the instructor began to lecture only from the right side of the classroom.

(Rhonda Atkinson and Debbie Longman, *Choosing Success in Community College and Beyond,* 2012, p. 40)

Who: ____________________

What: ____________________

Where: ____________________

When: ____________________

Why: ____________________

How: ____________________

Implied Main Idea: ____________________

____

3. In many cultures, both past and present, people have pierced and tattooed their bodies. These markings often commemorated a rite of passage such as puberty, marriage, or a successful hunt. Just a short time ago, a pierced nose, tongue, eyebrow, lip, navel, or other body part was virtually unheard of in mainstream society; however, that has changed. Today, tattooing and body piercing have become a popular trend, especially among adolescent and young adults. The American Academy of Dermatology reports that 36 percent of 18- to 29-year-olds have a tattoo. Yet, despite their popularity, tattoos and body piercings continue to create unintended impressions. In fact, cities and school districts across the country are forcing their employees to cover up tattoos if they want to keep their jobs. In addition, many young job-seekers find themselves having to conceal tattoos and remove body piercings for job interviews.

(Isa N. Engleberg et al., *Think Communication,* 2011)

Who: ____________________

What: ____________________

Where: ____________________

When: ____________________

Why: ____________________

How: ____________________

Implied Main Idea: ____

____

____

STRATEGY 2: COMBINING SENTENCES

1. Conversational differences between men and women begin early in childhood. Deborah Tannen summarizes a variety of studies showing that boys use talk to assert control over one another, while girls' conversations are aimed at maintaining harmony. Transcripts of conversations between preschoolers aged 2 to 5 showed that girls are far more cooperative than boys. They preceded their proposals for action by saying "let's," as in "Let's go find some," or "Let's turn back." By contrast, boys gave orders like "Lie down," or "Gimme your arm."

   (Ronald B. Adler, Russell F. Proctor II, and Neil Towne, *Looking Out, Looking In,* 11/e, 2005)

   Implied Main Idea: ____

   ____

2. Women tend to speak and hear a language of intimacy. In contrast, men tend to speak and hear a language of status and independence. As a result, the stage is set for misunderstandings and misinterpretations. Not seeing style differences for what they are, people draw faulty conclusions about each other, such as "You don't listen," "You are putting me down," or "You don't care about me."

   (Curtis O. Byer et al., *Dimensions of Human Sexuality,* 6/e, 2002)

   Implied Main Idea: ____

   ____

3. One nonverbal communication difference between the sexes is in the area of smiling. For example, women tend to smile more than men. We can only speculate on why this is, but smiling appears to be a part of the stereotypical female role. People tend to expect women to smile. A woman's smile does not necessarily reflect happiness or friendliness and can even be associated with fear or other negative feelings. Another nonverbal communication difference is that women tend to prefer to stand or sit closer to other people while men tend to prefer a greater distance.

   (Curtis O. Byer et al., *Dimensions of Human Sexuality,* 6/e, 2002)

   Implied Main Idea: ____

   ____

STRATEGY 3: SUMMING UP IMPORTANT IDEAS INTO ONE SENTENCE

1. It had been a long day at the office, and the going-home traffic was bumper to bumper. By the time Jason Whitehawk pulled his late-model car into the driveway at home, he was exhausted. As he trudged into the house, he routinely asked his wife, "How did things go with you at work today?"

   "Oh, pretty well," she replied, "except for the attack by space aliens in the morning and the outbreak of bubonic plague in the afternoon."

   Jason nodded his head as he made his way to the sofa. "That's nice," he said. "At least someone had a good day. Mine was awful."

   (Stephen E. Lucas, *The Art of Public Speaking,* 7/e, 2001)

Implied Main Idea: ____

____

2. Authoritarian parents are rigid and punitive and value unquestioning obedience from their children. They have strict standards and discourage expressions of disagreements. Permissive parents give their children lax or inconsistent direction and, although warm, require little of them. Authoritative parents are firm, setting limits for their children. As the children get older, these parents try to reason with and explain things to them. They also set clear goals and encourage their children's independence.

(Robert S. Feldman, *Essentials of Understanding Psychology,* 10/e, 2013)

Implied Main Idea: ____

____

3. Facebook has over 350,000,000 registered users. If Facebook were its own country, it would be the third most populous country in the world, after China and India. Although Facebook began in the United States, 70 percent of users today are from other countries. Facebook is available in 70 different languages. More than 3.5 billion pieces of content are shared on Facebook every week.

(Kory Floyd, *Interpersonal Communication,* 2/e, McGraw-Hill, 2012, p. 39)

Implied Main Idea: ____

Exercise 3: Identifying the Topic and Supporting Details, and Formulating the Implied Main Idea

Directions: Read the following passages and then write the requested information on the lines provided.

1. How can you tell if you're at risk for Internet addiction? Watch for the following signs:
   - You lose track of the time you spend online. You're frequently on the Internet for longer than you realize. You find yourself running late for school, work, or appointments because of time spent online.
   - You have trouble completing tasks at work or home. You get so busy online that household chores, such as laundry and grocery shopping, don't get done. You sometimes stay late at work to surf the Web.
   - You feel isolated from your friends and family. You start to feel that no one in your face-to-face life understands you the way your online friends do. You skip social engagements to spend time on the Internet.
   - You lie about your Internet use. You find ways to hide your online activities. You lie to friends, relatives, and colleagues about how much time you spend on the Internet or what you do online.

   (Kory Floyd, *Interpersonal Communication,* 2/e, McGraw-Hill, 2012, p. 84)

   Topic: ____

   Major Supporting Detail: 1. ____

   Minor Supporting Detail:

   a. ____

   b. ____

   Major Supporting Detail: 2. ____

Minor Supporting Detail:

a. ______

b. ______

Major Supporting Detail: 3. ______

Minor Supporting Detail:

a. ______

b. ______

Major Supporting Detail: 4. ______

Minor Supporting Detail:

a. ______

b. ______

Implied Main Idea: ______

______

2. Cell Phone Etiquette

Cell phones have invaded our classrooms and our bedrooms, our restaurants and our theaters, our offices and our streets. CellPhones.org has put together a helpful list of cell phone etiquette tips.

- Lower your voice when taking calls in public. Tilt your chin downward so that your voice doesn't carry as far. It's impolite to force others to hear your private conversations.
- Avoid taking calls and texting when you're already engaged in face-to-face conversation. If you do take a call, ask permission of the people with you. Put your phone's ringer on silent mode in enclosed public places. This list includes elevators, waiting rooms, libraries, restaurants, places of worship, classrooms, and theaters. Don't light up your phone's screen in a dark theater.
- Avoid cell phone conversations when you are engaging in other tasks such as driving or shopping. At any given time about 3 percent of people driving are simultaneously talking on their cell phones.
- Keep a distance of at least ten feet from the nearest person when talking on a cell phone.
- Choose your ring tone wisely (no loud or distracting tones).

Topic: ______

Major Supporting Detail: 1. ______

Minor Supporting Detail:

a. ______

b. ______

Major Supporting Detail: 2. ______

Minor Supporting Detail:

a. ______

Major Supporting Detail: 3. ______________________

____

Minor Supporting Detail:

a. ______________________

b. ______________________

Major Supporting Detail: 4. ______________________

Minor Supporting Detail:

a. ______________________

Major Supporting Detail: 5. ______________________

____

Major Supporting Detail: 6. ______________________

Implied Main Idea: ______________________

____

Exercise 4: Writing General or Main Idea Sentences

Directions: Two specific detail sentences are given to you. Working in a group, try to write a main idea sentence that will cover both of the details.

Example: Dying today has become more lonely and impersonal.

a. Today people are more likely to die in a hospital hooked up to a machine.

b. At the time of death, people are often surrounded by strangers, such as hospital personnel, instead of loved ones.

1. ______________________

a. Research shows that a 15-minute nap can improve concentration.

b. Truck drivers who pull over to the side of the road whenever they feel sleepy are less likely to have an accident on long-haul trips.

2. ______________________

a. Air bags have been responsible for the deaths of 31 young children.

b. Air bags deploy with a 200-pound force, sometimes injuring children and small adults in minor fender-bender accidents.

3. ______________________

a. A local minister was caught telling a lie to a member of his church.

b. Kids as young as two years of age routinely lie to avoid punishment.

4. ______________________

a. Americans exercise very little and watch too much TV.

b. Americans eat far too many foods classified by nutritionists as "junk."

5. ______________________

a. Pet owners enjoy better health and have fewer visits to the doctor.

b. Pet owners recover more quickly from surgery.

6. ______________________________

a. After a divorce, boys are more likely to be low achievers in school.

b. After a divorce, many boys suffer from a poor self-image.

7. ______________________________

a. Toothpaste contains unappetizing ingredients like chalk, detergent, seaweed, and formaldehyde.

b. Toothpaste can actually create cavities.

8. ______________________________

a. College athletes spend enormous amounts of time and energy on their sport.

b. Although individual athletic departments generate large sums from team sports, the individual student-athlete receives no compensation.

Exercise 5: Aunt Caroline—Determining the Implied Main Idea

Directions: Aunt Caroline is a fictional advice columnist who tries to help people solve personal problems. Read each paragraph below and then write the main idea. Because the main idea is not stated directly in just one sentence, you must identify the key details and unite them to form the main idea. The first one is done for you as an example.

Dear Aunt Caroline,

Do you think my boyfriend really loves me? He gives me a present every Saturday. However, he always asks me to return the one he gave me the week before.

Main idea: My boyfriend gives me gifts but asks me to return the old ones.

1. Last Saturday, my boyfriend was really furious with me for using up half a bottle of perfume in a week. I told him that I had spilled some on my floor. He took the perfume from me anyway.

   Main idea: ______________________________

2. Yesterday, on my way to work, I eavesdropped on the conversation of the woman sitting behind me on the subway. She told her friend that her boyfriend had given her a half-empty bottle of perfume last Sunday. She told her friend that her boyfriend gives her a new gift every Sunday.

   Main idea: ______________________________

3. I became very curious. So, before I could stop myself, I turned around and asked her if he makes her return the gifts to him the next week. She indignantly replied, "Of course not!"

   Main idea: ______________________________

4. Then I asked her if he had given her a half-eaten box of candy the week before, and she replied, "How on earth did you know?" I didn't tell her, but I'm positive my boyfriend is giving my used gifts to her.

   Main idea: ______________________________

5. What do you think, Aunt Caroline? Who does a man usually love more, the woman he gives a fresh gift to, but takes it away from, or the woman he lets keep the used gift? And how can I get my boyfriend to love only me?

   Half-loved Helen

   Main idea: ______________________________

   ____

(*Finding the Main Idea,* 1982)

Written Assignment

What advice would you give "Half-loved Helen"? Write a short paragraph providing Helen with an answer to her dilemma.

Exercise 6: Urban Legends—Determining the Implied Main Idea

Most of you are familiar with urban legends, those bizarre stories that are just too good to be true. Maybe you've heard the one about the man who unsuspectingly eats a fried rat at a local fast-food restaurant. Or the one about the mice in Coca-Cola bottles. Or how about the one about the babysitter who receives a threatening phone call that turns out to be coming from inside the house where she's sitting. All of these stories have one thing in common: They happened to a friend of a friend's next-door neighbor's brother-in-law. Although these tales are widely believed, easily spread by word of mouth, and ever present on talk radio and the Internet, most require you to suspend all logic and just go along. And most of us are willing to suspend disbelief because the world is, after all, a scary place. The tales, many with a strong cautionary note, exploit our fears that danger lurks everywhere—even in our own homes. And like folktales, urban legends often impart real lessons by serving as warnings.

Directions: After reading each urban legend, write the lesson or moral. Then write the implied main idea.

1. OLD VERSUS YOUNG

An older woman drives her Mercedes into a crowded parking lot. After searching in vain for a parking space she spies another car getting ready to leave, so she pulls up nearby and waits. But just as the other car pulls out a shiny blue sports car zips into the space. The young driver smiles as he gets out and shouts, "You've got to be young and fast!" The woman thinks about this a moment, then rams the sports car. She backs up and rams it again and again. The young man comes running in horror. "What are you doing?" he shouts. The woman smiles and says, "You've got to be old and rich." Then she drives away.

Jan Harold Brunvand, The Mexican Pet: More "New" Urban Legends and Some Old Favorites, 1986.

Example:

Moral: ______________________________

Implied main idea: ______________________________

____

2. THE KILLER IN THE BACK SEAT

Phoenix (UPI)—As the woman walked to her car in a parking lot, she noticed a man following her. She jumped in her car and tore off, only to notice to her dismay that the man was following her in his car. The woman drove through downtown Phoenix trying to elude him, passing stores, houses, and bars. When that failed, she drove across town to the home of her brother-in-law, a policeman. Horn honking, she pulled up and her brother-in-law came running out. She explained that a man was following her and "There he is, right there!" The policeman ran up to the man's car and demanded to know what he was doing. "Take it easy. All I wanted to do was tell her about the guy in her back seat," the man said. And, indeed, there was a man huddled in the woman's back seat.

Jan Harold Brunvand, The Mexican Pet: More "New" Urban Legends and Some Old Favorites, 1986.

Moral: ______________________________

Implied main idea: ______________________________

____

3. THE BUMP IN THE RUG

A carpet layer could not find his pack of cigarettes. He had just finished laying a customer's carpet when he reached for his pack of Winstons. They were gone. He then noticed a small mound under the carpet in the middle of the room. He concluded that his pack must have slipped out of his pocket. Rather than rip up his day's work, the carpet layer hammered the lump flat and walked out to his van. To his amazement, there on the dash, were his cigarettes. Confused, he reentered the house only to have the lady of the house ask if he had seen her precious pet parakeet that minutes ago crawled out of its cage.

Moral: ______________________________

Implied main idea: ______________________________

____

4. MESSAGE TO STUDENTS

Students beware!!!! My neighbor's son's best friend went to a fraternity party and was offered a cup of red punch. He thought it had alcohol in it so he drank it slowly. After a couple of sips he began to feel woozy, and he passed out. When he woke up, he found he was sitting in a hotel room bathtub full of ice. A cellular phone was next to the tub. On the mirror there was a message scrawled in lipstick, "Do not move. Call 911 immediately or you will die." He called 911 and was instructed by the operator to reach behind him and see if there was a tube coming out of his lower back. He found the tube and answered yes. The 911 operator told him to lie still and that paramedics were on the way. When the paramedics arrived, they examined him and said that both of his kidneys had been removed, probably to be sold for medical use.

(Joseph R. Dominick, *The Dynamics of Mass Communication,* 6/e, 1999)

Moral: ______________________________

Implied main idea: ______________________________

____

____

READING

"It's not just what kids eat, but how much."

TUNING IN TO READING Before Michelle Obama became First Lady, she struggled as a working mother to provide her daughters with healthy, nutritious meals. She said her daughters only liked three things: pasta, pasta with cheese, and pizza. According to the First Lady, the earlier parents introduce healthy foods to children, the easier it will be to do so. Then the children will grow up accustomed to having healthy eating habits. While in the White House, the First Lady started a Let's Move! anti-obesity campaign. The goal is not only for children to eat healthy food at home and at school, but also for children to become physically fit.

BIO-SKETCH Christine Gross-Loh, a writer and expert on parenting, has a Ph.D. from Harvard University. She currently writes for mothering.com.

NOTES ON VOCABULARY

empty calories calories from food that supplies energy but has few nutrients

Excerpt from Parenting Without Borders

CHRISTINE GROSS-LOH

Global Food Rules

As a culture, we don't do a great job supporting healthy eating or parents who want to feed their kids well. Evidence suggests that in the last few decades American children's diets, notoriously poor, have actually been getting worse. Nearly 40 percent of the calories American kids consume are empty calories—sugar and fat—and half of those are from junk food and fast food. People in our nation eat more packaged food than people from any other country—lots of it frozen pizza and snack foods. Processed foods are full of unhealthy ingredients such as high-fructose corn syrup, which pumps our bodies full of more glucose than we can process, and petroleum-based artificial food dyes, which require warning labels in European countries. This kind of diet may even negatively affect our brains: A study of nearly four thousand children in the UK (where kids are susceptible to similar food temptations as our own) found that eating a fat, sugar, or processed-food diet at age three was directly linked to lower IQ at age eight.

2 Food manufacturers spend enormous amounts of money to market their products to even the youngest eaters. "Dora!" a two-year-old cries when she sees her favorite explorer (and sidekick Boots) on a Yoplait Kids yogurt package. The labels are brightly colored and appealing, and the foods are advertised directly to children on television and the Internet. Supermarkets often put these kid-friendly foods at a child's eye level so a child will be more likely to take them off the shelves and put them in the grocery cart when a parent's back is turned. There are even popular Cheerios board books for toddlers that teach

them to recognize the cereal brand while learning how to count or helping monkeys juggle by putting the cereal in the right spaces.

It's not just what kids eat, but how much. In the past 30 years, portion sizes have grown astronomically: a cookie today is 700 percent bigger than it was in the 1970s. Our kids get used to eating more—one study shows young children eat more when they're given larger portions. American children today eat almost two hundred more calories daily than they did in 1977, and most of this increase comes from unhealthy foods. Though the processed and unhealthy foods in the school cafeterias or school vending machines have gotten a lot of blame for American children's poor diet, a recent study showed that children's dietary habits are more likely to be formed outside school, in their homes and neighborhoods. Their diets get even worse as they get older and have more opportunities to eat on their own. 3

The price our children pay for their poor eating habits is dear. Today about one out of three kids is overweight or obese, which puts them at risk for a range of serious health issues. Our children are the first in centuries who might live shorter lives than their parents as a direct result of childhood obesity. Even children who aren't necessarily overeating or who don't look obese are suffering ill effects from unhealthy eating. 4

(Christine Gross-Loh, *Parenting Without Borders*, Penguin, 2013, pp. 57–58)

COMPREHENSION CHECKUP

Completion

1. What is the topic of the first paragraph?

____

2. What does the author have to say about the topic in the first paragraph?

____

____

____

3. Write the main idea of paragraph 2 below.

____

____

4. List three supporting details that back up the main idea of paragraph 2.

Supporting Detail 1: _______________

Supporting Detail 2: _______________

Supporting Detail 3: _______________

5. In paragraph 3, the author discusses the poor dietary habits of American children. According to the author, who or what is to blame?

a. _______________

b. _______________

c. _______________

6. Where is the main idea of paragraph 4 located? ______________________

7. List three supporting details that back up the main idea of paragraph 4.

   Supporting Detail 1: ______________________

   Supporting Detail 2: ______________________

   Supporting Detail 3: ______________________

8. According to the author, what are the problems associated with childhood obesity?

   ____

   ____

9. Define the word *dear* as used in paragraph 4. ______________________

10. Give a synonym for *dear* as used in paragraph 4. ______________________

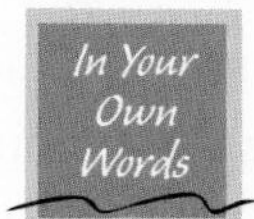

In Your Own Words

1. Do you think it's possible to be overweight but still healthy?
2. Could the negative focus on weight become a form of bullying?

Written Assignment

Answer the following questions in a short essay.

Are there drawbacks to calling society's attention to the problem of overweight children? Is this something that could harm the self-esteem of a heavier child? Are some ways better than others for discussing this issue and encouraging overweight children to eat a healthier diet and get more exercise?

Internet Activity

Consult one of the following Web sites and summarize the information.

1. Five ways grocery stores try to trick you

   www.rodale.com/supermarkets-and-healthy-food

2. Generation XL: portion sizes

   www.parenting.com/article/fat-kids

3. Various school lunches around the world

   http://whatsforschoollunch.blogspot.com/

READING

"The good news is, some politicians want to ban cell-phone use."

TUNING IN TO READING Lifehacker.com recently invited readers to share the most annoying things people do on cell phones. Among the top irritants are talking on the phone while driving, checking Facebook at the dinner table, and taking pictures of *everything*. However, the number one gripe is the one discussed in the selection below: treating the world as your own personal phone booth.

READING (continued)

BIO-SKETCH Dave Barry, a Pulitzer Prize–winning columnist, is the author of numerous best-selling books, including *Lunatics*, published in 2012. He began his career as a newspaper reporter and later developed a column for the *Miami Herald* that depicted the humor in everyday life. The *New York Times* called Barry "the funniest man in America."

NOTES ON VOCABULARY

Federal Communications Commission a U.S. government agency overseen by Congress that regulates interstate and international communications

BAN CELL PHONES, UNLESS UNDER SQUID ATTACK BY DAVE BARRY

It was a beautiful day at the beach—blue sky, gentle breeze, calm sea. I knew these things because a man sitting five feet from me was shouting them into his cellular telephone, like a play-by-play announcer.

2 "IT'S A BEAUTIFUL DAY," he shouted. "THE SKY IS BLUE, AND THERE'S A BREEZE, AND THE WATER IS CALM, AND . . ."

3 Behind me, a woman, her cell phone pressed to her ear, was pacing back and forth.

4 "She DIDN'T," she was saying. "No. She DIDN'T. She DID? Really? Are you SERIOUS? She did NOT. She DID? No she DIDN'T. She DID? NO she . . ."

5 And so on. This woman had two children, who were frolicking in the surf. I found myself watching them, because the woman surely was not. A giant squid could have surfaced and snatched the children, and this woman would not have noticed. Or, if she had noticed, she'd have said, "Listen, I have to go, because a giant squid just . . . No! She didn't! She DID? No! She . . ."

6 And next to me, the play-by-play man would have said: ". . . AND A GIANT SQUID JUST ATE TWO CHILDREN, AND I'M GETTING A LITTLE SUNBURNED, AND . . ."

7 It used to be that the major annoyance at the beach was the jerk who brought a boom box and cranked it up so loud that the bass notes caused seagulls to explode. But at least you knew where these jerks were; you never know which beachgoers have cell phones. You'll settle next to what appears to be a sleeping sunbather, or even (you hope) a corpse, and you'll sprawl happily on your towel, and you'll get all the way to the second sentence of your 467-page book before you doze off to the hypnotic surge of the surf, and . . .

BREEP! BREEP! The corpse sits up, 8
gropes urgently for its cell phone, and shouts, "Hello! Oh hi! I'm at the beach! Yes! The beach! Yes! It's nice! Very peaceful! Very relaxing! What? She did? No she didn't! She DID? No she . . ."

Loud cell-phoners never seem to get 9
urgent calls. Just once, I'd like to hear one of them say: "Hello? Yes, this is Dr. Johnson. Oh, hello, Dr. Smith. You've opened the abdominal cavity? Good! Now the appendix should be right under the ... What? No, that's the liver. Don't take THAT out, ha ha! Oh, you did? Whoops! OK, now listen very, very carefully . . ."

The good news is, some politicians 10
want to ban cell-phone use. The bad news is, they want to ban it in cars, which is the one place where innocent bystanders don't have to listen to it. Granted, drivers using cell phones may cause accidents ("I gotta go, because I just ran over a man, and he's bleeding from the ... What? She DID? NO she didn't. She DID? No she . . ."). But I

frankly don't believe that drivers yakking on cell phones are nearly as dangerous as drivers with babies in the back seat.

11 I'm one of those drivers, and we're definitely a menace, especially when our baby has dropped her Elmo doll and is screaming to get it back, and we're steering with one hand while groping under the back seat with the other. ("Groping for Elmo" would be a good name for a rock band.)

12 So we should, as a long-overdue safety measure, ban babies. But that is not my point. My point is that there is good news on the cell-phone front, which is that several companies—including Image Sensing Systems and Netline—are selling devices that jam cell-phone signals. Yes! These devices broadcast a signal that causes every cell phone in the immediate vicinity to play the 1974 hit song "Kung Fu Fighting."

13 No, that would be too wonderful. But, really, these devices, which start at around $900, cause all nearby cellular phones to register NO SERVICE.

14 Unfortunately, there's a catch. Because of some outfit calling itself the "Federal Communications Commission," the cell-phone jamming devices are illegal in the United States. I say this stinks. I say we should all contact our congresspersons and tell them that if they want to make it up to us consumers for foisting those lousy low-flow toilets on us, they should . . . pass a law legalizing these devices, at least for beach use.

15 I realize some of you disagree with me. I realize you have solid reasons—perhaps life-and-death reasons—why you MUST have your cellular phone working at all times, everywhere. If you're one of those people, please believe me when I say this: I can't hear you.

(Dave Barry, "Ban Cell Phones, Unless Under Squid Attack," *Miami Herald,* August 19, 2001)

COMPREHENSION CHECKUP

Completion

1. What is the topic of the selection?

____

2. What is the main idea of the selection?

____

3. List three details supporting the author's main idea.
   a. ____
   b. ____
   c. ____

Multiple Choice

______ 1. Dave Barry's descriptions of what happened at the beach illustrates all of the following points except
   a. Some cell phone users are inconsiderate of people nearby.
   b. Talking on a cell phone can lead to inattentiveness.
   c. Cell phone users don't want others to overhear their private business.
   d. Many cell phone conversations lack urgency or importance.

______ 2. What concerns does Barry express about people talking on cell phones at vacation locations?
   a. They sometimes loudly relate a play-by-play description of what is happening.

b. They may create an annoying distraction.
c. They may ruin the peacefulness of the day for others.
d. All of the above

______ 3. According to Barry, how were things at the beach different in the past, before cell phones?
a. Beaches weren't as crowded.
b. Lifeguards were present to rescue drowning children.
c. Beachgoers could get away from noisy distractions.
d. Children stayed close to their parents.

______ 4. In the selection, Barry expresses a positive reaction to:
a. Elmo dolls
b. cell-phone jamming devices
c. low-flow toilets
d. both b and c

______ 5. Which of the following do you think is more likely a true statement?
a. Barry once saw a giant squid grab a child at the beach.
b. Barry believes that low-flow toilets are a good idea.
c. Barry thinks that cell-phone jamming devices should be allowed.
d. Barry is offended by loud, silly cell phone conversations at the beach.

Vocabulary in Context

Directions: The sentences below are taken from the selection. Try to determine the meaning of the italicized word from its context and then write your definition on the line.

1. I knew these things because a man sitting five feet from me was shouting them into his cellular telephone, like a *play-by-play* announcer. (paragraph 1)

____

2. The corpse sits up, *gropes* urgently for its cell phone . . . (paragraph 8)

____

3. Loud cell-phoners never seem to get *urgent* calls. (paragraph 9)

____

4. I'm one of those drivers, and we're definitely a *menace* . . . (paragraph 11)

____

5. So we should, as a *long-overdue* safety measure . . . (paragraph 12)

____

6. every cell phone in the immediate *vicinity* . . . (paragraph 12)

____

7. make it up to us consumers for *foisting* those lousy low-flow toilets on us . . . (paragraph 14)

____

8. I realize you have solid reasons . . . (paragraph 15)

____

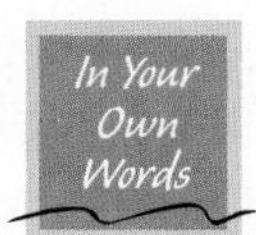

In Your Own Words

1. Discuss three ways that Barry uses humorous exaggeration to make his serious point about cell phone usage.
2. How do you think the problem that Barry describes could best be addressed?

Written Assignment

Lifehacker.com took a survey of people's cell phone annoyances. It then proposed a practical solution for each of the top pet peeves. What do you think of these solutions? Do you think they will work? Can you think of additional steps that could be taken? Write a couple of paragraphs answering these questions. Be sure to have a main idea sentence in each of your paragraphs.

Problem: The world is your phone booth (51 percent)

This issue only gets worse when that annoying someone goes on to talk loudly in public spaces, hold business conversations in the bathroom, or talk about a breakup on the bus.

Solution: Just because you don't care if your conversation remains private doesn't mean everyone wants to hear it. The basic rule of thumb here is pretty simple: if you're going to talk on the phone in a public spot, step away from other people. Always.

Problem: The multitasking driver (34 percent)

"Drivers who use hand-held devices are 4 times more likely to get into crashes serious enough to injure themselves." U.S. government

Solution: Remove the temptation. If your willpower for blocking out a cell phone ring is weak, silence your phone before you get in the car. Or get a Bluetooth headset for hands-free use or integrate your phone into your car.

Problem: The smartphone addict (10 percent)

You feel the urge to grab your phone to check social networks, texts, phone calls, or even play a game while you're in public with friends.

Solution 1: If you wouldn't work on a crossword puzzle in a situation, then it's probably not a good time to dawdle away on your smartphone. Essentially, if someone is in front of you and wants your attention, it's probably not the best time to tap away on your phone.

Solution 2: Wean yourself away. Make your own rules of use (no phone usage at social events, no answering calls on a date, etc.).

Problem: Cell phone photographer (1 percent)

Most people aren't annoyed if you snap a picture or two on your cell phone. That changes when you ignore what's going on around you to edit, annotate, crop, filter, and post that picture to a social network.

Solution: Take the picture now; edit and upload later.

Internet Activity

Check out one of the following Web sites and write a paragraph about the tip that seems most helpful to you. Be sure to have a main idea sentence.

1. www.realsimple.com/work-life/etiquette/manners/tech-etiquette
2. etiquettesurvival.com
3. netmanners.com

Chapter Summary and Review

In Chapter 3, you learned about the structure of paragraphs and how to identify topics, main ideas, and details. You also learned how to paraphrase directly stated main ideas and short paragraphs and how to formulate implied main ideas. Based on the material in Chapter 3, answer the following questions.

Short Answer

Directions: In a few words or a sentence, define each of the following terms.

1. Topic ______________________________
2. Main idea ______________________________
3. Major supporting details ______________________________
4. Minor supporting details ______________________________

Paragraph Diagramming

Directions: Insert the shape from pages 92–93 that best depicts the paragraph development described.

5. The author begins with examples, states the main idea, and then concludes with additional examples. ___________
6. The main idea is expressed in both the first and last sentences. ___________
7. The main idea is expressed in the last sentence. ___________

Vocabulary in Context

Directions: Choose one of the following words to complete the sentences below. Use each word only once.

implied last paraphrasing specific

8. When you put a sentence or paragraph into your own words, you are ___________.
9. Sometimes paragraphs have a main idea that is not explicitly stated in any one sentence. Such a main idea is ___________.
10. Main ideas are supported by ___________ details.
11. The main idea is usually found in the first or ___________ sentence.

CHAPTER

4 Organizing Textbook Information

CHAPTER PREVIEW

In this chapter, you will

- Improve your underlining, highlighting, and annotating skills.
- Improve your outlining and mapping skills.
- Improve your summarizing skills.
- Improve your strategies for memorizing material.
- Improve your skills for interpreting visual aids.

Working with Study Skills and Visual Aids

In this chapter you will have an opportunity to practice study skills such as annotating, outlining, mapping, and summarizing. These are very useful study techniques. Each one requires you to digest information and then transform it into a more abbreviated format that you can use to study and learn the material.

Included in this chapter is a section on memory from a psychology textbook by Robert S. Feldman. You will be practicing study skills techniques on this material, and at the same time you will be learning some valuable tips and strategies to aid in the process of memorization.

Concluding the chapter, you will be working with visual aids. A visual aid helps you to better understand the written material accompanying it. Too often readers skip over the visual aids. However, these graphics are provided to assist you with comprehending and retaining what you are reading.

STUDY TECHNIQUE 6: FURTHER PRACTICE WITH UNDERLINING, HIGHLIGHTING, AND ANNOTATING

Underlining with a pen or pencil or highlighting with a marker is the first step in transforming text into something more meaningful. You can use underlining and highlighting to identify the major points an author makes. However, you should underline or highlight only the most important points or key words. Underlining or highlighting a whole paragraph requires no thought on your part and makes it difficult to find the most important information later when you are studying. Look at the underlining that has been done to the reading about the foundations of memory on pages 132–134. Notice how it will assist you in learning and retaining the information.

Annotating is the second step in the process of transforming a textbook section into your own study and learning tool. Annotating requires you to think about the text and write notes in the margins as you read. Annotations identify the main points and indicate important examples. Annotations can also consist of your comments on the material and any questions you have about it. Now look at the reading on pages 132–134 and note the annotations in the margins.

You get the most out of this strategy if you skim the material first and then carefully read and annotate it. For a list of possible annotating techniques and symbols, see Study Technique 3 in Chapter 2.

Exercise 1: Underlining, Highlighting, and Annotating

Directions: The following excerpt titled "The Foundations of Memory" has been underlined and annotated for you. Use this as a model to annotate paragraphs 1–14 of the reading titled "The Secret of Memory" on pages 137–138.

The Foundations of Memory

There are three different memory storage systems or stages through which information must travel if it is to be remembered: sensory, short-term, and long-term. The first stage, **sensory memory**, refers to the initial, momentary storage of information, lasting only an instant. A momentary flash of lightning, the sound of a twig snapping, and the sting of a pinprick all represent stimulation

MI
DEF
Stage I

of exceedingly brief duration. Such stimuli are initially—and briefly—stored in
sensory memory, the first repository of the information the world presents to
us. Sensory memory in general is able to store information for only a very short
time. If information does not pass to short-term memory it is lost for good.
Sensory memory employs a "file or forget it" approach to its job. It operates
as a kind of snapshot that stores information for a brief moment in time. But
it is as if each snapshot, immediately after being taken, is destroyed and
replaced with a new one. Unless the information in the snapshot is transferred
to some other type of memory, it is lost.

Because the information that is stored briefly in sensory memory consists 2
of representations of raw sensory stimuli, it is not meaningful to us. For us to
make sense of it, the information must be transferred to the next stage of
memory: short term memory. **Short-term memory** is the memory store in Stage 2
which information first has meaning, although the maximum length of reten- EX
tion is relatively short. The specific amount of information that can be held in
short-term memory has been identified as seven items or "chunks" of information. For instance, we can hold a seven-digit phone number (like 226-4610) in
our short-term memory. Just how brief is short-term memory? If you've ever
looked up a telephone number in a phone directory, repeated the number to
yourself, put away the directory, and then forgotten the number after you've
tapped the first three numbers into your phone, you know that information
does not remain in short-term memory very long. Most psychologists believe
that information in short-term memory is lost after 15 to 25 seconds—unless
it is transferred to long-term memory. Stage 3

The transfer of material from short-term to long-term memory proceeds 3
largely on the basis of **rehearsal**, the repetition of information that has entered
short-term memory. Rehearsal accomplishes two things. First, as long as the DEF
information is repeated, it is maintained in short-term memory. More important,
however, rehearsal allows us to transfer the information into long-term memory.

Whether the transfer is made from short-term to long-term memory seems 4
to depend largely on the kind of rehearsal that is carried out. If the information
is simply repeated over and over again—as we might do with a telephone
number while we rush from the phone book to the phone—it is kept current
in short-term memory, but it will not necessarily be placed in long-term memory. Instead, as soon as we stop punching in the phone numbers, the number
is likely to be replaced by other information and will be completely forgotten.

In contrast, if the information in short-term memory is rehearsed, using a 5
process called **elaborative rehearsal**, it is much more likely to be transferred DEF
into long-term memory. *Elaborative rehearsal* occurs when the information is
considered and organized in some fashion. The organization might include
expanding the information to make it fit into a logical framework, linking it to
another memory, turning it into an image, or transforming it in some other
way. For example, a list of vegetables to be purchased at a store could be
woven together in memory as items being used to prepare an elaborate salad,
could be linked to the items bought on an earlier shopping trip, or could be
thought of in terms of the image of a farm with rows of each item. EX

Material that makes its way from short-term memory to long-term memory 6
enters a storehouse of almost unlimited capacity. Like a new file we save on a

hard drive, the information in long-term memory is filed and coded so that we can retrieve it when we need it.

(Adapted from Robert S. Feldman, *Essentials of Understanding Psychology*, 10/e, New York: McGraw-Hill, 2013, pp. 206–209)

STUDY TECHNIQUE 7: OUTLINING

Outlining is a formal method of indicating how material is organized. There are specific rules for outlining. Main headings are represented by Roman numerals (I, II, III, IV, V, etc.). The next level of headings is represented by capital letters (A, B, C, etc.), the next level by Arabic numbers (1, 2, 3, 4, etc.), and the next level by lowercase letters (a, b, c, etc.). In a topical outline, each division contains information that is more specific than the division that precedes it.

In an outline, you must have more than one subtopic—that is, there must always be two or more. For example, if you list a subtopic A, there must also be a B. If you list a subtopic 1, there must be a 2.

Here is a sample outline of the material you just read about the three types of memory. A good outline can serve as review material for a test

Main Idea: There are three different memory storage systems.

I. Sensory memory
   A. Momentary
      1. Flash of lightning
      2. Sound of twig snapping
      3. Sting of pinprick
   B. First repository
   C. File or forget it
II. Short-term memory
   A. Meaningful information
      1. Short—lost after 15–25 seconds unless transferred
      2. Seven items—like a 7-digit phone number
      3. Held if just repeated over and over
   B. Can proceed to long-term
III. Long-term memory
   A. Requires elaborative rehearsal
      1. Information considered
      2. Information organized
         a. Expanding information
         b. Linking to another memory
         c. Turning it into an image
   B. Unlimited capacity
   C. Can be retrieved when needed

Exercise 2: Outlining

Directions: Now it's your turn. Make an outline of paragraphs 1–14 of "The Secret of Memory" on pages 137–138. (These are the same paragraphs you just underlined—or highlighted—and annotated.)

STUDY TECHNIQUE 8: MAPPING

Mapping is like outlining but less formal and more visual. Although there are no formal rules for mapping, you will see that you include topics, main ideas, details, and so on, just as you have in an outline. Here is a sample map of the "Foundations of Memory" passage. Notice that with this map, you can actually see how each step in the memory process flows into the next, something it is more difficult to see in an outline than in a map.

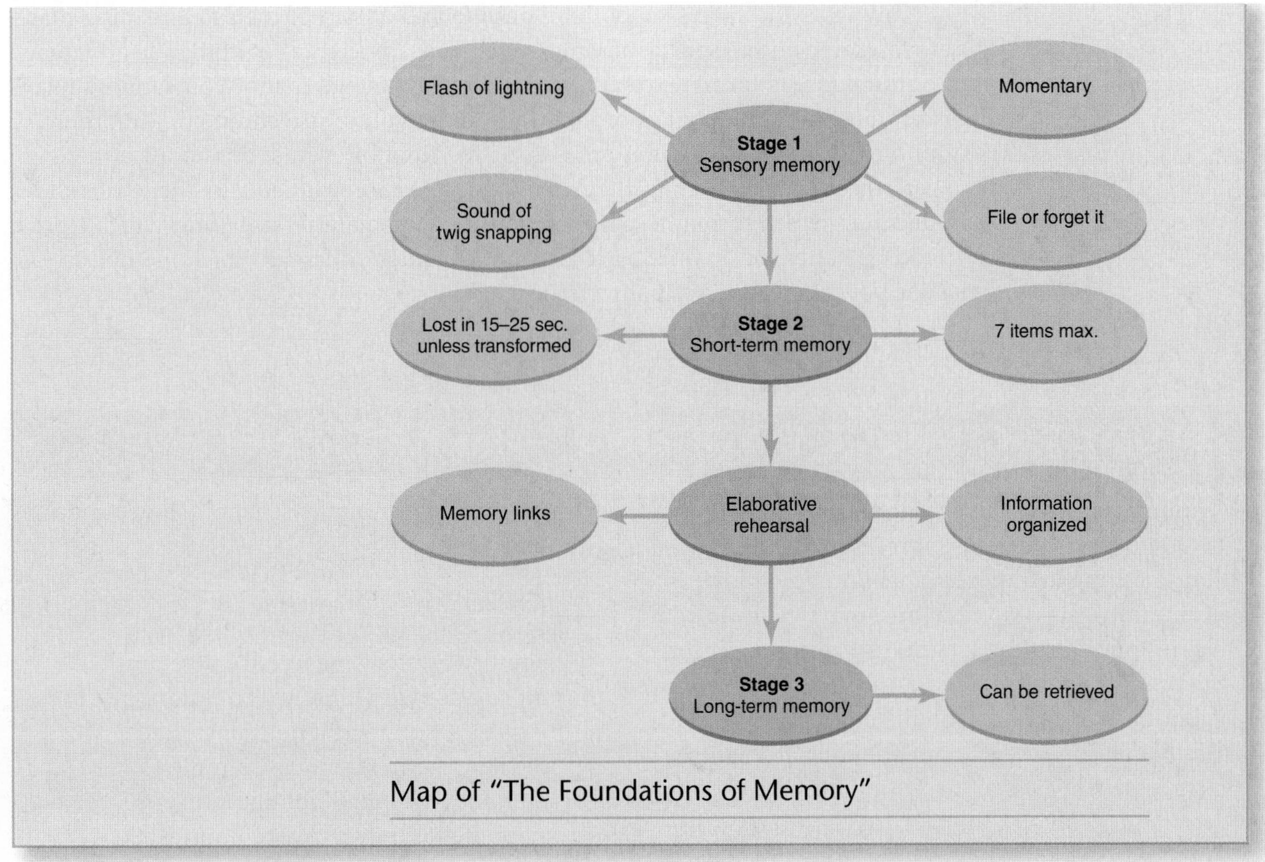

Map of "The Foundations of Memory"

Exercise 3: Mapping

Directions: Using paragraphs 1–14 of "The Secret of Memory," make a map of the main points in the reading.

Now that you have seen both an outline and a map of the same reading material, you can begin to see the advantages and disadvantages of both. The advantage of outlining is its formal structure, but its disadvantage is that you cannot always place points in chronological order. Maps allow you to use chronological order, for example, to see the steps in a process, or the flow of events, but because there are fewer rules for constructing them, they may be more difficult to create or follow. In deciding which format to use, first consider the material itself and which format would be better for organizing it. Second, consider yourself: Which method is easier for you to create as a tool for studying?

STUDY TECHNIQUE 9: WRITING SUMMARIES, METHOD I

Summarizing involves condensing what you read to only the most important information and writing it down using your own words. Generally speaking, a summary should be about one-third the length of the original information. It should include only what is written about an article and should not include any of your own opinions about the ideas the author expressed. You can use summaries to study from, just as you would study from an outline or a map.

Here are some guidelines for writing a summary.

- Identify the main ideas and supporting details in the reading and underline them, list them on a piece of paper, or make an outline of them as described above. This will serve as a guide as you write your summary.
- Start with a sentence that states the topic of the article and the main point the author is making about it.
- Be sure to include the name of the author and the title of the reading.
- List each of the main ideas and details in the order they appear in the reading.
- If the author expresses an opinion in the topic of the reading, include it in your summary.
- Use your own words, not the author's.
- Do not include your opinions about the material you are summarizing.

Here is a sample summary of the "The Foundations of Memory."

> There are three types of memory—sensory, short-term, and long-term memory. Sensory memory only retains information very briefly. That information is lost for good if not transferred into short-term memory. Examples might be a flash of lightning, a twig snapping, or the sting of a pinprick. Sensory memory is our first repository of information.
>
> Short-term memory is the second stage in the memory process. In short-term memory we begin to add meaning to the information, but the length of retention is still quite short, and the amount of information we can retain is quite small. The maximum amount of information we can retain in short-term memory is seven items or "chunks," as in a telephone number.
>
> Long-term memory is the third and permanent stage of holding memory. In order for memory to transfer from short-term to long-term memory, it must go through an elaborative rehearsal process. This process involves transforming information or linking it with other information or memories, or expanding it into a logical framework. Long-term memory has an almost unlimited capacity. In long-term memory, information is filed and coded so that we can retrieve it later.

Exercise 4: Summarizing

Directions: Write your own summary of paragraphs 1-14 of "The Secret of Memory" on a separate sheet of paper. After underlining, annotating, outlining, and mapping these paragraphs you should find it fairly easy to summarize the reading.

____

____

____

READING

"If you approach each new memorization task as something entirely new and unrelated to your previous knowledge, you'll have enormous difficulty recalling it."

TUNING IN TO READING What is the name of the third president of the United States? What states joined the Union in 1959? What is the difference between engraving and etching? What are the parts of a cell? Every day, we encounter information we would like to remember. This is especially true for students, who need to master the material in their classes. Most of us would like to have better memory skills. The selection below discusses how memory works and gives strategies for memorizing information more quickly and effectively.

BIO-SKETCH Robert Feldman, a professor of psychology at the University of Massachusetts, is a well-known author of textbooks on psychology and study skills.

NOTES ON VOCABULARY

visualizing to form a picture of something in the mind

abstract theoretical; separate from concrete reality

litmus a substance that turns red in an acid and blue in a base

Excerpt from

POWER LEARNING STRATEGIES FOR SUCCESS IN COLLEGE AND LIFE

by Robert S. Feldman

The Secret of Memory

Don't think of memorization as pumping gasoline (new information) into an almost-empty gas tank (your brain). You're not filling something that is empty. On the contrary, you are filling a container that already has a lot of things in it, that is infinitely expandable, and that never empties out.

If you approach each new memorization task as something entirely new and unrelated to your previous knowledge, you'll have enormous difficulty recalling it. On the other hand, if you connect it to what you already know, you'll be able to recall it far better. The way to get your brain to do this 2 organizational work for you is by thinking about the associations the new material has with the old.

Personalize Information

Suppose, for example, you need to remember information about the consequences of global warming, such as the fact that the level of the oceans is predicted to rise. You might think about the rising level of the ocean as it relates to your personal memories of visits to the beach. You might think what a visit to the beach would be like with dramatically higher water levels, visualizing a shrunken shoreline with no room for sunbathing. Then whenever you think about global warming in the future, your mind is likely to associate this fairly abstract concept with its concrete consequences for beaches. The association you made makes the information personal, long-lasting, and useful. 3

As critical thinking expert Diane Halpern points out, having an organized memory is like having a neat bedroom: Its value is that you know you'll be able to find something when you need it. To prove the point, try this exercise she devised. 4

Read the following 15 words at the rate of approximately one per second: 5

girl	finger	man	eagle
heart	flute	hawk	child
robin	blue	green	piano
purple	organ	lung	

Now, cover the list, and write down as many of the words as you can on a separate sheet of paper. How many words are there on your list? ________________ 6

7 After you've done this, read the following list:

green	girl	organ	eagle
blue	child	heart	hawk
purple	piano	lung	robin
man	flute	finger	

Now cover this second list and write down as many of the words as you can on the other side of the separate sheet of paper. 8

How many words did you remember this time? Did you notice that the words on both lists are identical? Did you remember more the second time? (Most people do.) Why do you think most people remember more when the words are organized as they are in the second list? 9

Organize Information by Place

Where you learn something makes a difference in how well you can recall it. 10
Memory researchers have found that people actually remember things better in the place where they first studied and learned them. Consequently, one of the best ways to jog your memory is to try to re-create the situation in which you first learned what you're trying to remember. If you memorized the colors that litmus paper turns when it is placed in acids and bases while you were in

your campus science library, it might be helpful during a test to recall the correct colors by imagining yourself in the science library thinking about the colors.

Another effective place-related strategy is to introduce new data into your 11
mind in the place that you know you're going to need to recall it at some future moment. For instance, suppose you know that you're going to be tested on certain material in the room in which your class is held. Try to do at least some of your studying in that same room.

One of the good things about the work of memorization is that you have 12
your choice of literally dozens of techniques. Depending on the kind of material you need to recall and how much you already know about the subject, you can turn to any number of methods.

As we sort through the various options, keep in mind that no one strategy 13
works by itself. (And some strategies don't seem to work: Forget about supplements like *ginkgo biloba*—there's no clear scientific evidence that they are effective.) Instead, try the following proven strategies and find those that work best for you. Feel free to devise your own strategies or add those that have worked for you in the past.

Rehearsal

Think it again: rehearsal. Say it aloud: rehearsal. Think of it in terms of the three 14
syllables that make up the word: re—hear—sal. OK, one more time—say the word "rehearsal."

If you're scratching your head over the last paragraph, it's to illustrate 15
the point of rehearsal: to transfer material that you encounter into memory. If you don't rehearse information in some way, it will end up like most of the information to which we're exposed: on the garbage heap of lost memory.

To test if you've succeeded in transferring the word "rehearsal" into your 16
memory, put down this book and go off for a few minutes. Do something entirely unrelated to reading this book. Have a snack, catch up on the latest sports scores on ESPN, or read the front page of the newspaper.

Are you back? If the word "rehearsal" popped into your head when you 17
picked up this book again, you've passed your first memory test. You can be assured that the word "rehearsal" has been transferred into your memory.

Rehearsal is the key strategy in remembering information. If you don't rehearse 18
material, it will never make it into memory. Repeating the information, summarizing it, associating it with other memories, and above all thinking about it when you first come across it will ensure that rehearsal will be effective in pushing the material into memory.

Mnemonics

This odd word (pronounced in an equally odd fashion, with the "m" silent—"neh MON ix") describes formal techniques used to make material more readily remembered. Mnemonics are the tricks-of-the-trade that professional memory experts use, and you too can use them to nail down the sort of information you will often need to recall for tests.

Among the most common mnemonics are the following:

Acronyms. You're already well acquainted with *acronyms,* words or phrases formed by the first letters of a series of terms. For instance, though you may not have known it, the word "laser" is actually an acronym for "light amplification by stimulated emissions of radiation," and "radar" is an acronym for "radio detection and ranging."

Acronyms can be a big help in remembering things. If you took music lessons, you may know that FACE spells out the names of the notes that appear in the spaces on the treble clef music staff ("F," "A," "C," and "E," starting at the bottom of the staff.) Roy G. Biv is a favorite of physics students who must remember the colors of the spectrum (red, orange, yellow, green, blue, indigo, and violet). 19

The benefit of acronyms is that they help us to recall a complete list of steps or items. The drawback, though, is that the acronym itself has to be remembered, and sometimes we may not recall it when we need it. For instance, Roy G. Biv is not exactly the sort of name that readily comes to mind. And even if we do remember Roy G. Biv, we might get stuck trying to recall what a particular letter stands for. (For example, we'd probably prefer not to spend a lot of time during a test trying to remember if the "B" stands for brown, or beige, or blue.) 20

Acrostics. After learning to use the acronym "FACE" to remember the notes on the spaces of the music staff, many beginning musicians learn that the names on the lines of the staff form the acrostic, "Every Good Boy Deserves Fudge." Acrostics are sentences in which the first letters spell out something that needs to be recalled. The benefits—as well as the drawbacks—of acrostics are similar to those of acronyms. As an example of the usefulness of acronyms try the following exercise: 21

1. Figure out an acronym to remind you of the names of the five Great Lakes, using the first letters of their names (which are Erie, Huron, Michigan, Ontario, Superior).
2. Devise an acrostic for the eight planets in order of their average distance from the sun. Their names, in order, are Mercury, Venus, Earth, Mars, Jupiter, Saturn, Uranus, Neptune.

How successful were you in devising effective acronyms and acrostics? Is the act of creating them an important component of helping to remember what they represent, or would having them created by someone else be as helpful in recalling them? For your information, a common acronym for the Great Lakes is HOMES (**H**uron, **O**ntario, **M**ichigan, **E**rie, **S**uperior), and a popular acrostic for the order of the planets is **M**y **V**ery **E**ducated **M**other **J**ust **S**erved **U**s **N**oodles. 22

Rhymes and Jingles. "Thirty days hath September, April, June, and November . . ." If you know the rest of the rhyme, you're familiar with one of the most commonly used mnemonic jingles in the English language. You may have also heard of the English spelling rule, "I before E, except after C." (The spelling rule will serve you well only when you want to make the sound of EE as in "Receive," and "Deceive.") 23

Although all these varieties of mnemonics are helpful in their own ways, 24
they also have a number of shortcomings. First, none of them focuses on the meaning of the items being remembered. Trying to retain information based on its surface characteristics—such as first letters—is an imperfect route to memorization.

Second, sometimes it takes as much effort to create a mnemonic device as 25
it would to memorize the material in the first place. And because the mnemonic itself has no meaning, it can be forgotten.

Despite these drawbacks, mnemonics can be useful. They are particularly 26
helpful when the material being memorized includes a list of items or a series of steps.

The Method of Loci: Special Help for Recalling Sequences and Lists

The ancient Greeks had a way with words. Their orators could deliver speeches that went on for hours, without notes. How did they remember what they wanted to say?

They used a procedure called the method of loci. *Loci* (pronounced "low 27
sigh") is the Latin word for "places," and it helps describe a procedure in which items in a sequence you wish to remember—such as the sections of a speech or a series of events—are thought of as "located" in a different place in a building.

Consider, for example, a speech that has three major sections: an introduc- 28
tion, a main body, and a conclusion. Each of the three sections has various points that you need to recall also.

To use the method of loci, you'd first visualize the living room, kitchen, 29
and bedroom of a house with which you were familiar. Next, you'd mentally "place" the introduction of the speech into the living room of the house. You would mentally place each of the *parts* of the introduction on a different piece of furniture, following the way the furniture was laid out in the room (for example, you might proceed clockwise from the door). The easy chair might contain the first point of the introduction, the sofa the next point, and an end table the last point. Then you'd move into the kitchen and do the same thing with the body of the paper, laying out your arguments on different pieces of kitchen furniture or appliances. Finally, you'd end up in the bedroom, where you'd "place" the conclusion.

Involve Multiple Senses

The more senses you can involve when you're trying to learn new material, 30
the better you'll be able to remember.

When you learn something, use your body. Don't sit passively at your 31
desk. Instead, move around. Stand up; sit down. Touch the page. Trace figures with your fingers. Talk to yourself. Think out loud. It may seem strange, but doing this increases the number of ways in which the information is stored. By involving every part of your body, you've increased the number of potential ways to trigger a relevant memory later, when you need to recall it. And when one memory is triggered, other related memories may come tumbling back.

Draw and diagram the material. In a concept map, each key idea is placed in a different part of the map, and related ideas are placed near it—above, below, or beside it. A "finished" concept map looks something like a map of the solar system, with the largest and most central idea in the center (the "sun" position), and related ideas surrounding it at various distances. It has also been compared to a large tree, with numerous branches and sub-branches radiating out from a central trunk. When we create a concept map, one of the things we're doing is expanding the modalities in which information can be stored in our minds. 32

Other types of drawing can be useful in aiding later recall. Creating drawings, sketches, and even cartoons can help us remember better. Your creations don't have to be great art, or detailed, involved illustrations. Even rough sketches are effective, because creating them gets both the visual and tactile senses involved. For practice see Exercise 5: "Harry and Bill." 33

Visualize. Visualization is a technique by which images are formed to ensure that material is recalled. Visualization is effective because it serves several purposes: it helps make abstract ideas concrete; it engages multiple senses; it permits us to link different bits of information together; it provides us with a context for storing information. 34

What kind of visualization works best? There's a simple rule: Weird is good. The more extreme, outlandish, and eccentric image you create, the more notable it will be and so the easier it will be to remember. And if you can remember the image, you'll probably remember the information that's attached to it. 35

(Robert S. Feldman, *P.O.W.E.R. Learning Strategies for Success in College and Life*, 6/e, New York: McGraw-Hill, 2014, pp. 207–216)

Exercise 5: Practice in Remembering What You Read: Involving Multiple Senses

I. Below are two people's names with a list of 10 descriptive details for each. Give yourself a second or two to look at each detail. Then cover the list with a sheet of paper and see how many details you can recall.

First person: Harry	Second Person: Bill
1. bald	1. glasses
2. red-faced	2. short hair
3. thin	3. necktie
4. laughing	4. sad
5. short-sleeved shirt	5. suit
6. shorts	6. wristwatch
7. small eyes	7. cuffs on pants
8. large ears	8. pipe in hand
9. sandals	9. dress shoes
10. heart tattoo	10. belt

First person's name	Second person's name
1.	1.
2.	2.
3.	3.
4.	4.
5.	5.
6.	6.
7.	7.
8.	8.
9.	9.
10.	10.

(Most people are able to recall fewer than eight of the details.)

II. Go back to the original lists and work through the following activities.

1. Think of two people you have known or whose pictures you have seen who remind you of Harry and Bill. Associate Harry's and Bill's special features with their features.
2. Mentally visualize Harry and Bill and then draw pictures of each of them. Label the 10 details in each picture.
3. Look away from the pictures you have drawn and see if you can recall the 10 features of Harry and Bill without looking. If you can't recall the information, look back at the pictures and try again. Now cover up everything and reproduce the details in the original lists.

First person's name	Second person's name
1.	1.
2.	2.
3.	3.
4.	4.
5.	5.
6.	6.
7.	7.
8.	8.
9.	9.
10.	10.

How did you do? Try tomorrow and a week from now to visualize Harry and Bill.

(Based on information in *Improving Reading* by Nancy V. Wood, New York: Holt, Rinehart and Winston, 1984, pp. 214–215)

Exercise 6: Visualize the Possibilities

You may have noticed how important visualization is to memory. In fact, many of the techniques discussed in the excerpt rely on some measure of visualization, especially your visualization of extreme or absurd images.

Test the truth of this statement by drawing a concept map—itself a visual form of organizing material—of the concept of visualization. Start with the word "Visualization" in the center of the map and link as many other memory and mnemonic techniques to it as you can. For example, you might start by adding the concept of "drawing an image"—and then adding "weird image" to that. You may be surprised at the richness of your map.

Visualization

How well does the concept map reflect what you know about visualization? Is it a useful tool for you? Do you think that the act of creating a concept map itself is helpful in memorizing the material? Would using someone else's concept map be less helpful than creating your own?

Compare your concept map with those of your classmates. What are the major similarities and differences? How do you account for them? Are some of your fellow students' concept maps more likely to help recall information than others? A sample concept map is located in the Appendix.

COMPREHENSION CHECKUP

Multiple Choice

______ 1. The author thinks that a brain
a. is usually empty.
b. already contains a lot of information.
c. always has the capacity to learn even more.
d. both b and c.

______ 2. Mnemonics are
a. acronyms.
b. acrostics.
c. rhymes and jingles.
d. all of the above

______ 3. ATV (all-terrain vehicle), NPR (National Public Radio), and NASCAR (National Association for Stock Car Auto Racing) are all examples of an
a. acrostic.
b. rhyme.

c. acronym.
d. jingle.

______ 4. You are having trouble remembering the signs of the zodiac: Aries, Taurus, Gemini, Cancer, Leo, Virgo, Libra, Scorpio, Sagittarius, Capricorn Aquarius, Pisces. In order to remember, you create the following: "As The Great Cook Likes Very Little Salt, She Compensates Adding Pepper." You have just created a(n)
a. homonym.
b. antonym.
c. acrostic.
d. acronym.

______ 5. The author would agree with all of the following **except**
a. People remember things better in the place where they first learned them.
b. It might be wise to study in the room where a future test will be held.
c. Rehearsing information you want to remember is the least valuable method.
d. Associating new material with other memories is a good way to recall it.

______ 6. The author states that "having an organized memory is like having a neat bedroom." He means that
a. a neat bedroom leads to a peaceful mind.
b. it doesn't matter whether your bedroom is clean because nobody is going to see it.
c. you can easily locate information when you need it.
d. you'll fall asleep faster in a neat bedroom.

______ 7. The point of rehearsal is to
a. transfer information into memory.
b. practice for a performance or play.
c. build physical stamina.
d. improve your listening skills.

______ 8. What would be the best dictionary definition for the word "bases" in paragraph 10?
a. the support on which things rest
b. parts of bodies or surfaces
c. the four corners of a baseball diamond
d. chemical compounds that react with acids to form salts

______ 9. Visualization is effective because
a. it helps make abstract concepts concrete.
b. the images formed help us in recalling material.
c. both a and b.
d. it involves moving around and using your body.

______ 10. The word "place" as used in paragraph 29 means
a. a particular portion of space.
b. any part of a body or surface.
c. to put or set in a particular location.
d. to finish among the first three competitors of a race.

True or False

______ 11. According to the author, it is easier to visualize odd images than ordinary ones.

______ 12. Drawing and diagramming material is similar to creating a concept map.

______ 13. The author compares memorization with filling an empty container.

______ 14. People remember things best when they lie on their beds.

______ 15. Research has demonstrated that *ginkgo biloba* improves memory.

Vocabulary in Context

Directions: Write a definition for each of the following words consistent with how the word is used in the paragraph. You may refer to a dictionary if necessary.

1. consequences (paragraph 3) ______
2. researchers (paragraph 10) ______
3. strategy (paragraph 11) ______
4. material (paragraph 12) ______
5. options (paragraph 13) ______
6. staff (paragraph 19) ______
7. spectrum (paragraph 19) ______

In Your Own Words

1. Describe briefly how you can take advantage of one or more of these memory strategies to learn material for one of your classes.
2. Talk to a classmate and find out what memorization strategies he or she likes.
3. Create a rhyme or jingle to help you remember something you need to know for one of your classes.

Written Assignment

1. What advice would you give to someone who keeps forgetting key information for tests? Write a paragraph describing your advice.
2. What do you think it would be like if we remembered everything? Would that be a benefit or a liability?

Internet Activity

Robert S. Feldman, the author of this selection, suggests three Web sites that can help you with memorizing. Go to one of them and write a paragraph about what you learned.

1. Concept mapping: The first Web site is written by the University of Victoria's Learning Skills Program.

   www.coun.uvic.ca/learning/critical-thinking/concept-mapping.html

2. Mnemonics: This Web site is also from the University of Victoria's Learning Skills Program.

   www.coun.uvic.ca/learning/memory/mnemonics.html

3. Mind Tools: This is a bookstore specializing in works on memory. Find one technique that works for you.

   www.mindtools.com/memory.html

Visual Aids: How to Use and Interpret Tables, Diagrams, Charts, and Graphs

Visual aids are useful tools that help us organize, understand, and remember written material. Visual aids can be as simple as a street map or as complex as a statistical table. Because textbook authors frequently use visual aids to explain complicated information, it is very important to look closely at all graphic illustrations and understand what they represent. Those of you who are strong in visual-spatial intelligence may find this section easier than those of you who have strengths in other areas. In this section, you will learn how to read and interpret the graphs and tables found online and in various books, magazines, and newspapers.

Here are some steps to follow when looking at a visual aid.

1. **Read the title and subtitle.** These will tell you what the table, chart, graph, or map is about.
2. **Read the key or legend.** These will explain how to interpret the visual aid.
3. **Determine the purpose of the visual aid.** Why did the author include it? Is it there to provide objective information? Or to support the author's bias?
4. **Determine the source of the information provided.** A table, chart, graph, or map published by a government agency may be more objective than one published by a special-interest group.
5. **Look at how the graph or chart is set up.** If there are horizontal or vertical scales, determine what they measure. If there is no scale, read the caption or look closely at the item to determine the scale. What is the unit of measurement? Thousands? Millions?
6. **Look for highs, lows, trends, and relationships.** What conclusions can you reach?

Diagrams

A **diagram** is a drawing or picture that is meant to illustrate how something works or how concepts relate to one another. Writers use diagrams when they realize that a visual aid would help explain a concept or process. Diagrams are especially useful in science textbooks. A biology textbook might have a diagram of the muscles of the arm, an astronomy textbook a diagram of the solar system, and a chemistry textbook a diagram showing how atoms group together to form molecules.

Exercise 1: Diagrams

The following diagram titled "Visualizing Memory" explains the three basic steps of memory: the initial recording of information, the storage of that information, and ultimately the retrieval of the stored information.

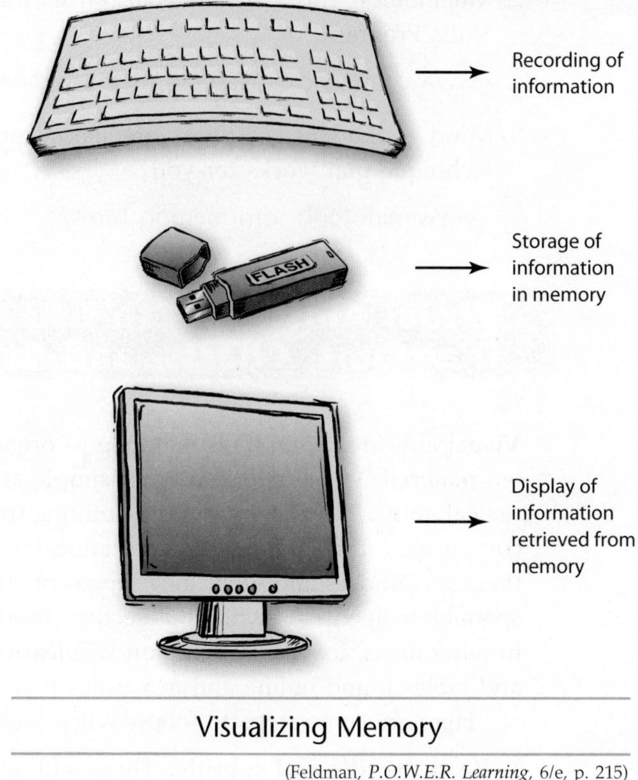

Visualizing Memory

(Feldman, *P.O.W.E.R. Learning*, 6/e, p. 215)

Directions: Study the diagram and then answer the following questions.

1. What does the keyboard represent? ______________________

____

2. What does the flash drive represent? ______________________

____

3. What does the monitor represent? ______________________

____

Flowcharts

The purpose of a **flowchart** is to visually explain cause-and-effect relationships, a sequence of events, or the steps in a complex process. The action moves, or flows, in the direction of arrows or numbers, or sometimes just from left to right or up to down. A biology textbook might have a flowchart showing the steps in photosynthesis. A criminal justice or American government textbook might have a flowchart to illustrate how criminal cases proceed through the state and federal courts. A health textbook might contain a flowchart depicting how food is digested and processed.

Exercise 2: Flowcharts

The following flowchart illustrates the three-system memory theory.

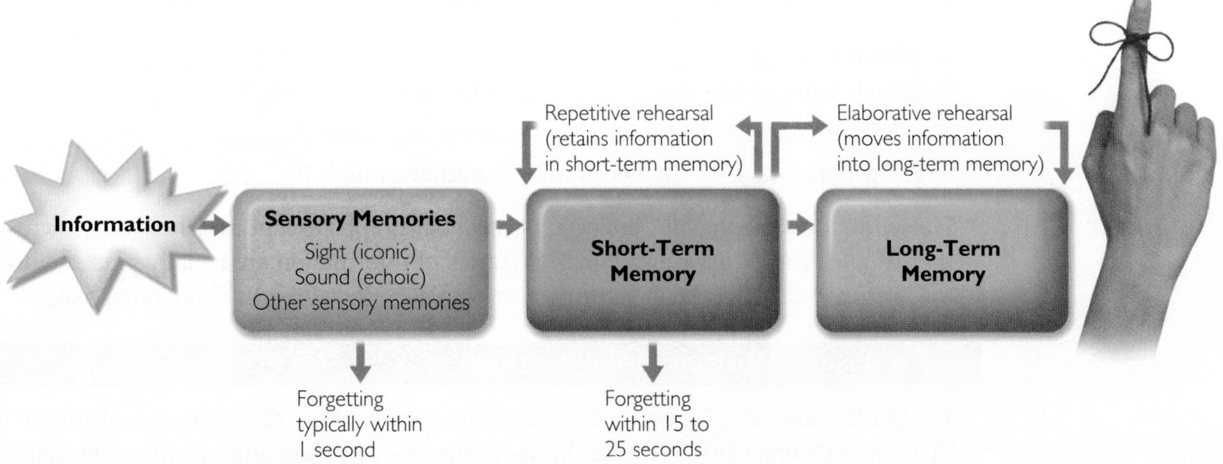

(Feldman, *Essentials of Understanding Psychology*, 10/e, p. 206)

Directions: Fill in the blank with the correct term.

1. ________ memory might last only an instant.
2. ________ memory holds information for 15 to 25 seconds.
3. ________ memory stores information on a relatively permanent basis.
4. ______________ determines whether something moves from short-term memory to long-term memory.

Bar Graphs

Bar graphs are one of the most common types of visual aids. They provide information by means of vertical (up and down) or horizontal (left to right) bars or columns. Bar graphs are an easy way to visualize statistical information.

In **vertical bar graphs,** units of measure usually appear along the left-hand or vertical axis, and items to be compared and contrasted appear along the bottom or horizontal axis.

Exercise 3: Vertical Bar Graphs

The vertical bar graph below illustrates the tendency many of us have to remember events more favorably than they really were. When college students were asked to recall their high school grades, the worse the grade was, the less often students remembered it accurately. Errors tended to be biased in a positive direction. Students recalled their Bs as having been As, their Cs as Bs, and their Ds as Cs.

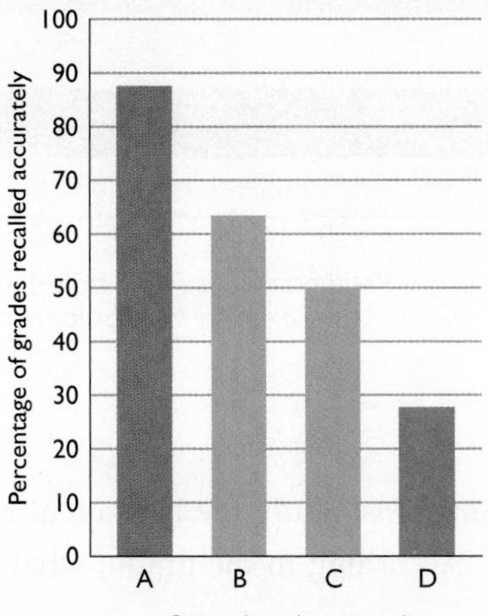

(Feldman, *Essentials of Understanding Psychology*, 10/e, p. 225 data from Bahrick et al., 1996)

Directions: Study the bar graph and then answer the following questions.

1. Which letter grade was correctly recalled most accurately? ______
2. Which letter grade was correctly recalled least accurately? ______
3. What percentage of Ds were remembered accurately? ______
4. What percentage of Cs were remembered accurately? ______

Horizontal bar graphs are similar to vertical bar graphs except that the bars go across the page instead of up and down. Categories of information are usually placed along the vertical axis and measurements of these categories along the horizontal axis.

Exercise 4: Horizontal Bar Graphs

Flashbulb memories" are vivid, "snapshot" recollections of an important moment in a person's life. Certain flashbulb memories are common among college students, such as the time they gave a speech and the night of high school graduation. The horizontal bar graph below identifies and measures some common flashbulb memories of college students.

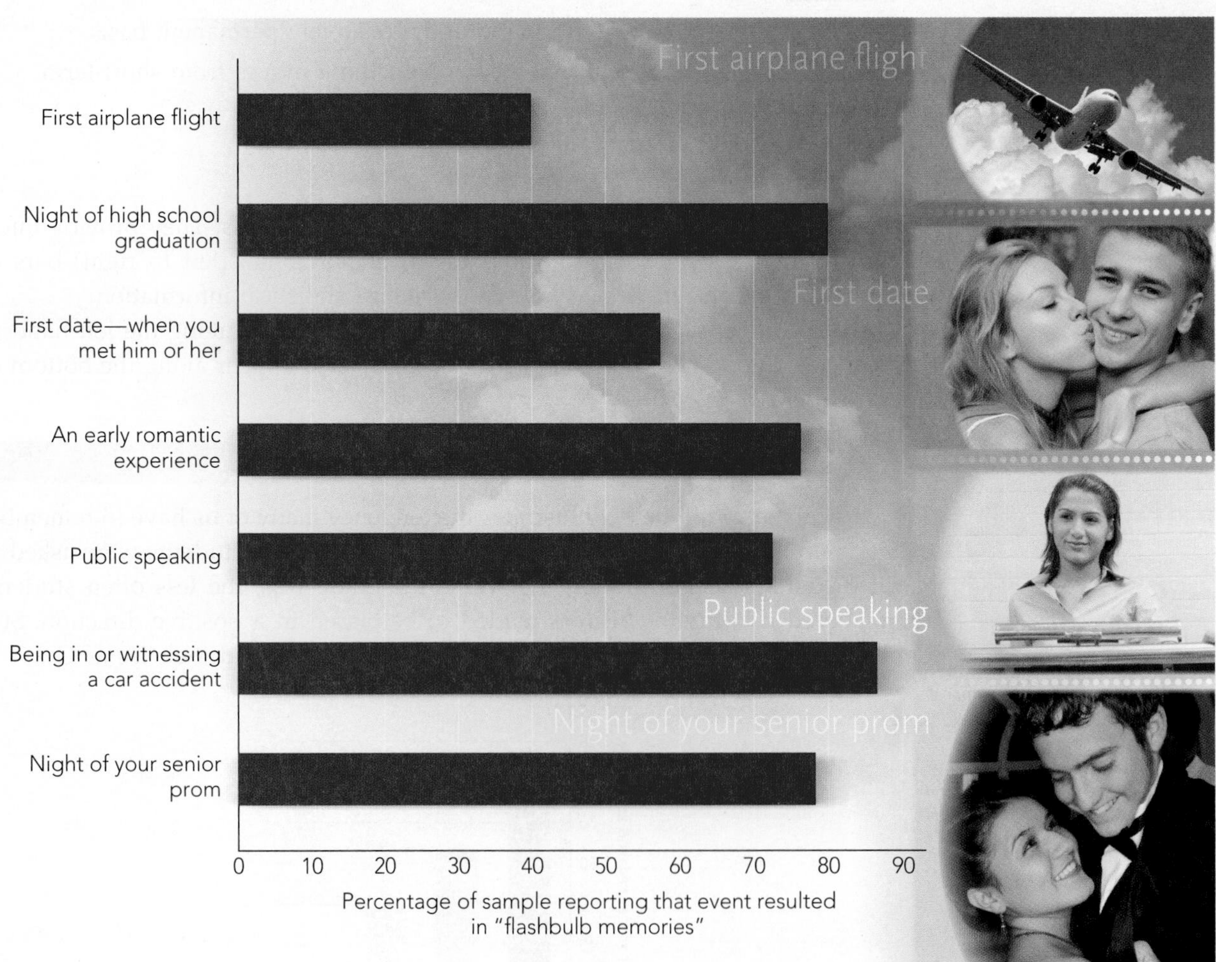

(Feldman, *Psychology and Your Life*, 2/e, p. 217; data from Rubin, 1985)

Directions: Study the horizontal bar graph and answer the questions that follow.

1. According to the graph, what is the most common flashbulb memory?

____

2. What percentage of college students had a flashbulb memory of their first airplane flight? ____________

3. What percentage of college students had a flashbulb memory of their high school graduation? ____________

4. What are some of your flashbulb memories? ____________

Line Graphs

A **line graph** is a way to depict the changing relationship between two variables or factors. A typical line graph has two scales—a horizontal one (left to right) and a vertical one (bottom to top). Line graphs are commonly used to show changes over time.

Exercise 5: Line Graphs

Below is a line graph that shows how memory fades with the passage of time. Participants in the experiment were given a list of words to learn. Some participants saw the word list only once, while others saw the list three times. In addition, some participants were quizzed on the list immediately, while others were asked to recall the words one, two, three, or four days later.

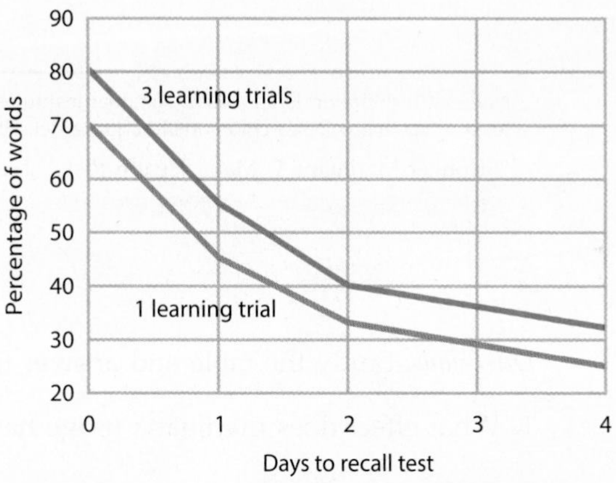

(Gregory J. Feist, *Psychology*, 2/e, p. 296; data from Slameka & McElree, 1983)

Directions: Study the line graph and then answer the questions that follow.

1. What percentage of words did those with one learning trial recall within one day? ____________

2. What percentage of words did those with three learning trials recall within one day? ____________

3. What percentage of words did those with one learning trial recall after three days? ____________

4. What percentage of words did those with three learning trials recall after three days? ____________

Tables

Another kind of visual aid is a **table.** Tables display information in rows (across) and columns (up and down).

Exercise 6: Tables

The table below titled "Effects of Marijuana" shows both the short-term and long-term effects of marijuana usage.

Effects of Marijuana

Short-Term Effects	Long-Term Effects
• Increased heart rate and blood pressure	• Lung damage
• Feeling of elation	• Increased risk of bronchitis
• Drowsiness and sedation	• Emphysema
• Increased appetite	• Lung cancer
• Red eyes	• Heart attack[†]
• Food cravings	• Loss of motivation and short-term memory
• Slow reaction time	• Increased panic or anxiety
• Feelings of depression, excitement, paranoia, panic, and euphoria	• May become tolerant to marijuana
• Problems with attention span, memory, learning, problem-solving, and coordination	• Damage to lungs, immune system, and reproductive organs
• Sleeplessness[*]	• Can remain in the body for up to a month
	• Can cause birth defects
	• Five times more damaging to the lungs than tobacco products[*]

[*]National Institute on Drug Abuse. National Institutes of Health, *NIDA Research Report—Marijuana Abuse*, www.nida.nih.gov/ResearchReports/Marijuana/default.html, February 15, 2005.

[†]"Stronger Marijuana Is Major Health Risk," *The Independent*, February 1, 2001.

(Dale B. Hahn, *Focus on Health*, 9/e, p. 181)

Directions: Study the table and answer the questions that follow.

1. What effect does marijuana usage have on short-term memory?

____

2. What effect does marijuana usage have on motivation?

____

Pie Charts

Pie charts show percentages or proportions of a whole as pie-shaped sections of a circle. The whole of the circle represents 100 percent, and each pie-shaped piece represents a percentage of the whole.

Exercise 7: Pie Charts

The following pie chart, prepared by the Centers for Disease Control and Prevention (CDC), identifies the causes of traumatic brain injury (TBI) and the percentage of the total each cause represents. TBI, which may result in death or disability, is a serious public health issue.

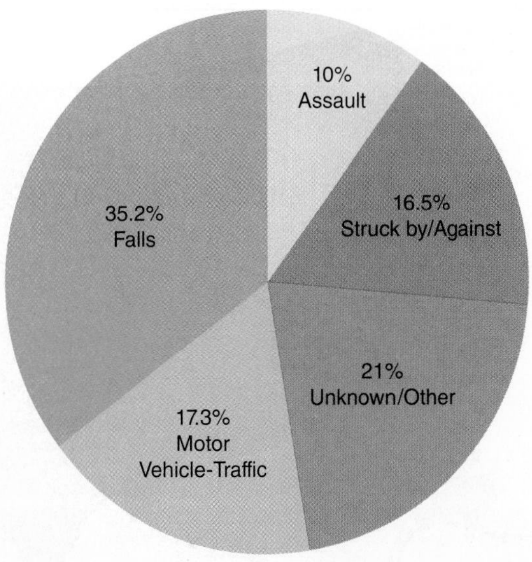

Estimated Average Percentage of Annual TBI by External Cause in the United States, 2002–2006

(CDC.gov)

Directions: Study the pie chart and then answer the questions that follow.

1. What percentage of traumatic brain injury is caused by falls? ______________
2. What percentage of traumatic brain injury is caused by motor vehicle or traffic accidents? ______________
3. What ideas does the chart give you for reducing your chances of suffering a TBI? ______________

____

Maps

Maps can be used for a variety of purposes. As you are aware, they are commonly used to show geographical locations such as countries, oceans, and mountain ranges. They are also useful for showing comparisons between such things as population density, rates of rainfall, and rates of disease.

Exercise 8: Maps

The map on the following page is from the Centers for Disease Control and Prevention (CDC). It depicts the U.S. mortality rate for Alzheimer's disease on a state-by-state basis from 2000 to 2010.

Alzheimer's disease is the sixth leading cause of death in the United States. The risk of dying from Alzheimer's disease is 26 percent higher among the non-Hispanic white population than among the non-Hispanic black population. The Hispanic population has a 30 percent lower risk than the non-Hispanic white population.

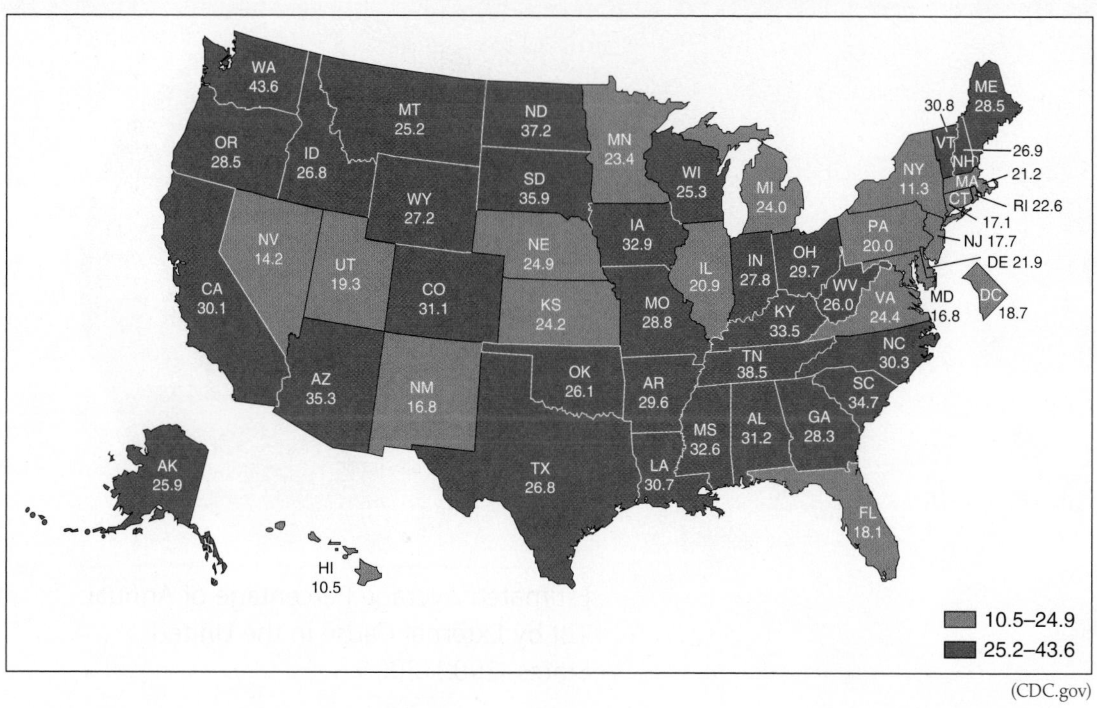

(CDC.gov)

Directions: Study the information on the map and then answer the questions that follow.

1. Which state had the lowest death rate for Alzheimer's disease?

____

2. Which state had the highest death rate for Alzheimer's disease?

____

3. What is Nevada's death rate for Alzheimer's disease? ____________________

Photos

Photos are a common kind of visual aid. They may illustrate, highlight, or explain a point made in the text. Another function of photos may be to make the material more visually appealing.

Exercise 9: Photos

How could anyone lose something as large as a car? Yet, it happens all the time. If you often park your car in different locations, you may have experienced the frustration of not knowing where it is when you go to get it. Your memory of where you parked it yesterday, or the day before, may interfere with your memory of where you parked it today. The photo is meant to illustrate the psychological concept of memory interference. Study the photo and then answer the question that follows.

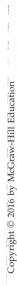

1. Can you think of another circumstance when you were unable to remember something because of memory interference?

____

Cartoons

Cartoons may be used as visual aids. These drawings, which usually have a humorous, amusing, or eye-catching slant, are sometimes used by writers to illustrate a main point.

Some cartoons, called strip cartoons, move from left to right through a series of panels. These are what often appear in the comics section of newspapers. On the editorial page, you may find political cartoons.

Exercise 10: Cartoons

Directions: Study the following cartoon and then answer the question that follows.

Dan Reynolds/www.CartoonStock.com

1. According to the cartoonist, what is the reason elephants never forget?

____

Chapter Summary and Review

In Chapter 4, you practiced a variety of study skill techniques with textbook material on the topic of memory. In addition, you learned how to interpret visual aids. Based on the material in Chapter 4, answer the following.

Vocabulary in Context

Directions: Choose one of the following words to complete the sentences below. Use each word only once.

annotating horizontal mapping outline percentages summary vertical

1. Each division in a(n) __________ must contain information that is more specific than the division before it.
2. A less formal and more visual way of outlining information is called __________
3. A(n) __________ bar goes from top to bottom.
4. A(n) __________ bar goes from side to side.
5. Writing notes in the margins and highlighting important information is called __________.
6. Pie charts are illustrations that show __________ or proportions as pie-shaped sections of a circle.
7. A(n) __________ of a reading condenses the original material.

CHAPTER

5 Determining an Author's Purpose

CHAPTER PREVIEW

In this chapter, you will

- Learn how to determine whether the author's purpose is to entertain, inform, or persuade.
- Learn the difference between a general and a specific purpose.
- Become familiar with the narrative, expository, persuasive, and descriptive modes of writing.
- Learn how to summarize short articles.

Author's Purpose: To Entertain, Inform, or Persuade?

Most writers create a story, essay, article, or poem with at least one **general purpose** in mind. Because most writers do not directly state their general purpose, readers must use indirect clues to determine it. We can identify the general purpose by asking "Why did the author write this?" or "What did the author want to accomplish?" Usually, this purpose will fall into one of three broad categories: to entertain, to inform, or to persuade.

To Entertain

Highlight or underline several words that define each boldfaced term.

An author whose purpose is to **entertain** will tell a story or describe someone or something in an interesting way. A piece of writing meant to entertain will often make an appeal to readers' imagination or sense of humor. If the writing is humorous, the author might say things in an exaggerated fashion or use understatement. Witty, unusual, dramatic, or exciting stories usually have entertainment as their purpose. A romance, suspense, or mystery novel is usually meant to entertain. Writing meant to entertain may be either fiction or nonfiction. The following is an example of a paragraph whose purpose is to entertain:

1. I assume you are on the Internet. If you are not, then pardon my French, but *vous êtes un big loser.* Today EVERYBODY is on the Internet, including the primitive Mud People of the Amazon rain forest. In the old days, when the Mud People needed food, they had to manually throw spears at wild boars, whereas today they simply get on the Internet, go to www.spearaboar.com and click their mouse a few times (the Mud People use actual mice). Within three business days, a large box (containing a live boar) is delivered to them by a UPS driver, whom they eat.

(Dave Barry, *Dave Barry Is Not Taking This Sitting Down,* 2000).

To Inform

An author whose purpose is to **inform** will explain something to readers or provide them with knowledge they did not possess before. Ordinarily, the material will be presented in an objective, unemotional fashion. Authors who write textbooks presenting factual material usually have this purpose in mind. Encyclopedias, research studies, and articles in newspapers are usually meant to inform. The following is an example of a paragraph whose purpose is to inform:

2. In the United States, the most "wired" nation in the world, only 65 percent of Americans have Internet access at home. In many developing countries almost no one has Internet access. According to a recent report by the United Nations, 88 percent of all Internet users live in industrialized countries. One of the major barriers to Internet use in developing countries is the cost. In 1999 it cost $10.50 an hour to use the Internet in the African nation of Chad, where the average annual income was $187. The Web is also largely limited to people who read English, since 80 percent of the world's web sites are in English. Another barrier in many countries is that there is no way to log on. Consider that in the industrialized nations there are about 50 phone lines for every 100 people, while developing nations average 1.4 phone lines per 100 people. According to the United Nations, half the world's population has yet to make a phone call, much less log on to the Internet.

(Ralph E. Hanson, *Mass Communication,* 1/e, 2005)

To Persuade

Finally, the author's purpose may be to **persuade.** Persuasion goes beyond merely entertaining or providing information. This kind of writing tries to change readers' opinions by appealing to their emotions or intellect. If the author is making an emotional argument, vivid descriptive passages may be used to manipulate readers' feelings. If the author is making an appeal to intelligence, a rational or logical argument may be used. Political literature is a common example of writing meant to persuade. While articles in newspapers are usually meant to inform, newspaper editorials ordinarily have persuasion as their purpose. The following is an example of a paragraph whose purpose is to persuade:

POP-UPS AND SPAM: THE EVIL TWINS OF INTERNET ADVERTISING

3. Suppose you are doing online research when all of a sudden an ad appears: Order DVDs by mail! You close that one but another pops up: Find low fares! Get rid of that and there is another: Lower your mortgage rates! Click to close it and there is another. And another. Pretty soon you are doing the cyber equivalent of swatting flies as you try to get rid of those intrusive pop-up and pop-under ads. Pop-up ads are bad enough, but they pale in comparison to spam. The Internet is literally stuffed full of junk e-mail for low-cost prescription drugs, debt consolidation plans, schemes that will make you a millionaire in only six months, and various treatments to enlarge certain body parts. What, if anything, can you do about it? The ultimate solution might be a legal one. It's time for Congress to pass legislation to create a national Do-Not-Spam list that resembles the Do-Not-Call list that limited telemarketers.

(Joseph R. Dominick, *The Dynamics of Mass Communication*, 8/e, 2005).

General and Specific Purposes

To determine whether the author's general purpose is to entertain, inform, or persuade, look for clues in the title, in headings and subheadings, and in the introduction or conclusion. Also, pay attention to the source of the article.

Authors also take into account their **audience**—those they are writing for—when they choose their general purpose. Writers of fiction usually want to entertain readers by creating interesting characters and stories. If an author writes an article for a wellness magazine, the general purpose probably will be to provide information promoting good health. If an author writes a letter to solicit campaign contributions for a political candidate, the general purpose will be to persuade, because the author is trying to persuade people to give money.

In addition to a general purpose, authors usually have a **specific purpose,** which gives more information about the article than the general purpose does. Take the previous "wellness" example. The general purpose is to "inform." The specific purpose might be "to inform people about foods that protect against cancer."

Multiple Purposes

Sometimes an author may have more than one purpose in mind. For instance, an author might want to both entertain and persuade. Or the author might write an entertaining article that also provides information about something important. When an author has more than one purpose in mind, usually one of the author's purposes will be primary. To determine the author's primary purpose, first identify the main idea and the key details that support the idea. Then note the source of the article or passage. Often the publication that the article or passage appears in will help you identify the author's primary purpose. Finally, note the author's choice of words. Is the vocabulary neutral and unbiased? Is it meant to influence your judgment in some way? These steps should help you identify the author's primary purpose.

Read the paragraph below and identify the writer's topic, main idea, and general and specific purposes.

4. One of the reasons that occupational stress has been receiving so much attention lately is that businesses are genuinely beginning to care about employee welfare. You don't buy that? Well, how about this? Work stress is costing businesses billions of dollars. Sounds more plausible, doesn't it? It is estimated by the International Labor Organization that stress on the job costs businesses over $300 billion per year. These costs include salaries for sick days, costs of hospitalization and outpatient care, and costs related to decreased productivity. Other stress-related factors are catching the eyes of business leaders. For example, health benefit costs to employers have increased dramatically. Employees trained over a long period of time, at great cost, may break down when stressed on the job. They may make poor decisions, miss days of work, begin abusing alcohol and other drugs, or die and have to be replaced by other workers who need training. All of this is costly. These effects of occupational stress have caused companies to give high priority to stress management programs.

(Jerrold S. Greenberg, *Comprehensive Stress Management,* 13/e, 2011)

Topic: occupational stress

Main idea: businesses giving high priority to stress management programs because of the high costs of employee occupational stress

General purpose: to inform

Specific purpose: informing readers about why businesses are paying attention to employee stress

The following exercises will give you some practice in determining an author's general purpose.

Exercise 1: Determining the General Purpose

Directions: Label each sentence according to its general purpose: to inform (**I**), to entertain (**E**), or to persuade (**P**).

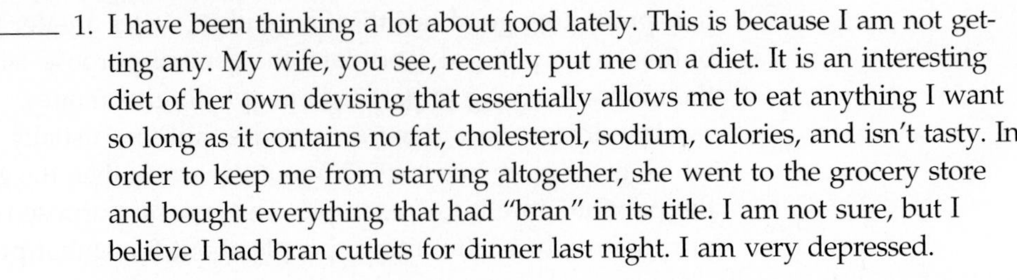

______ 1. I have been thinking a lot about food lately. This is because I am not getting any. My wife, you see, recently put me on a diet. It is an interesting diet of her own devising that essentially allows me to eat anything I want so long as it contains no fat, cholesterol, sodium, calories, and isn't tasty. In order to keep me from starving altogether, she went to the grocery store and bought everything that had "bran" in its title. I am not sure, but I believe I had bran cutlets for dinner last night. I am very depressed.

(Bill Bryson, *I'm a Stranger Here Myself,* 1999)

______ 2. Most sharks are harmless—at least to humans. Actually we threaten the survival of sharks more than they threaten us. They reproduce slowly, and their numbers are already being depleted by overfishing in many areas. This attitude toward sharks may be shortsighted, because they play an important role in marine communities. Some people catch shark only for the shark's fins or jaws. Others practice shark hunting for sport, leaving the meat to waste. A magnificent predator, the shark may soon be exterminated by humans, the fiercest predator of them all.

(Peter Castro and Michael E. Huber, "Sharks," *Marine Biology*, 8/e, 2010)

______ 3. The idea of a family consisting of a wage-earning husband and a wife who stays at home has largely given way to the dual-income household. Among married people between the ages of 25 and 34, 96 percent of the men and 69 percent of the women are in the labor force. Why has there been such a rise in the number of dual-income couples? A major factor is economic need. In 2003, the median income for households with both partners employed was 99 percent more than in households in which only one person was working outside the home. Of course, because of such work-related costs as child care, not all of a family's second wage is genuine additional income.

(Richard T. Schaefer, *Sociology*, 12/e, 2010)

Exercise 2: Determining an Author's Purpose

Directions: Label each paragraph according to its general purpose: to inform (**I**), to entertain (**E**), or to persuade (**P**).

______ 1. Since earliest times the fragrances of certain plants, owing to their essential oils, have been valued as a source of perfumes. It is difficult to pinpoint when people first began using plant fragrances to scent their bodies, but by 5,000 years ago the Egyptians were skilled perfumers, producing fragrant oils that were used by both men and women to anoint their hair and bodies. Fragrances were also used as incense to fumigate homes and temples in the belief that these aromas could ward off evil and disease. In fact, our very word *perfume* comes from the Latin *per* meaning through and *fumus* meaning smoke, possibly referring to an early use of perfumes as incense.

(Estelle Levetin and Karen McMahon, "Alluring Scents," *Plants and Society*, 6e, 2012)

______ 2. The images are vivid and appalling. Emaciated children with haunting eyes and distended stomachs, and too weak to cry, stare at us from news photos and television screens. Throughout the world, the problems of poverty and undernutrition are widespread and growing. The majority of undernourished people live in Asia. However, the largest increases in numbers of chronically hungry people occur in eastern Africa, particularly in Ethiopia, Sudan, Rwanda, Burundi, Sierra Leone, Kenya, Somalia, Eritrea, and Tanzania. Their eyes haunt us. If undernutrition is to be eradicated, the world's nations must examine the problem and assume responsibility. Life is not necessarily fair, but the aim of civilization should be to make it more so. The world has both enough food and the technical expertise to end hunger. What is lacking is the political will and cooperation to do so. It is time for leaders of rich and poor nations alike to come to an agreement on the best possible means to serve all of the world's citizens.

(Gordon Wardlaw, *Contemporary Nutrition*, 6/e, 2007)

______ 3. Are you lost in Cyberspace? You went away for three days and returned to find 1,892 messages in your mailbox. You just came out of the computer room and your dog is barking at you as if you were a stranger. You just missed your daughter's soccer game, your son's piano recital, or

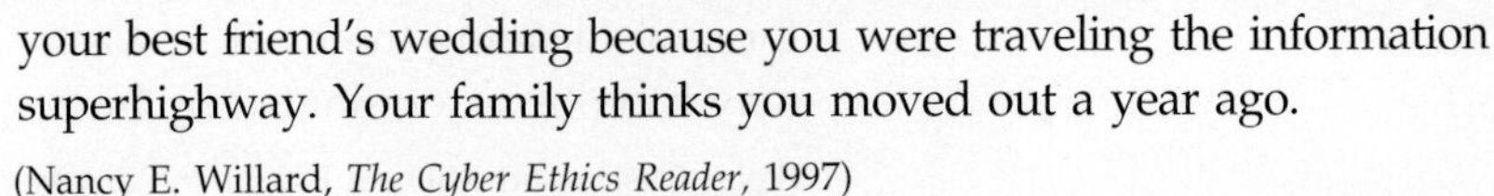

your best friend's wedding because you were traveling the information superhighway. Your family thinks you moved out a year ago.

(Nancy E. Willard, *The Cyber Ethics Reader,* 1997)

______ 4. U.S. society strongly supports marriage, and about nine out of ten people at some point "tie the knot." But many of today's marriages unravel. . . . Ours is the highest divorce rate in the world. At greatest risk of divorce are young couples—especially those who marry after a brief courtship, have little money, and have yet to mature emotionally. The chance of divorce also rises if a couple marries after an unexpected pregnancy or if one or both partners have substance abuse problems. People whose parents divorced also have a higher divorce rate themselves. Finally, people who are not religious are more likely to divorce than those who have strong religious beliefs.

(John J. Macionis, *Society,* 8/e, 2006)

______ 5. How would you describe the behavior of Bruce Damon, who held up the Mutual Federal Savings Bank near Brockton, Massachusetts? Using a gun, Damon demanded $40 million. When the teller explained that the bank kept only $40,000 on the premises, he said, "Okay, $40,000." Now get this: He demanded not cash, but a check! You can imagine the ending. He was arrested a short time later when he tried to deposit the check into his account in another bank. Way to go, Bruce! Not very smart!

(Hamilton Gregory, *Public Speaking for College and Career,* 7/e, 2005)

______ 6. Something must be done about high school dropouts. A student who drops out of high school not only hurts himself or herself, but the decision to leave high school before graduation also has harmful consequences for society. Dropping out of high school does not guarantee poverty, but dropouts do have to scramble harder to start a career—if they ever have one. Society suffers when many young people do not finish school. Dropouts are more likely to end up on welfare, to be unemployed, and to become involved with drugs, crime, and delinquency. In addition, the loss of taxable income burdens the public treasury. Fortunately, with a strong commitment by government, educators, and parents, it is possible to prevent dropping out. We can help millions of young people to have a brighter future. Doing nothing is a national tragedy.

(Diane E. Papalia, et al., *Human Development,* 10/e, 2007)

Exercise 3: Determining the Primary Purpose and Main Ideas

Directions: Read each of the following paragraphs to determine if the author's primary purpose is to entertain, persuade, or inform. Indicate the clues that enabled you to make your decision. In the space provided, write the directly stated or implied main idea.

1. Most crimes are committed in large urban areas rather than in small cities, suburbs, or rural areas. National Crime Victimization Survey data tell us the safest place to be is at home, however we are more likely to be victimized when we are in familiar territory. In 2009, only one-quarter of violent crimes took place near or at the victim's home, and three-quarters of violent crimes occurred within five miles of home. Common locations for violent crimes are streets other than those near the victim's home (15 percent), at school (14 percent), or at a commercial establishment (8 percent).

   (Freda Adler et al., *Criminology,* 8/e, 2013)

Purpose: ______________________ Clues: ______________________

Main idea: ____

2. You know how when you buy your pants, there's a piece of paper in one of the pockets that says "inspected by #47." Who ARE these people anyway? Has anyone out there met one of these inspectors? What do they inspect? I mean seriously, if someone bends over and their pants rip, should we say, "Oh no! Who inspected that? Number 63? Whew. That was close. Mine were done by number 34." If there was a problem, what are you supposed to do? Call up the manufacturer and say, "Hello. I hate to be the one to break it to you, but you know number 63? She just isn't going to cut it anymore."

   (Tom Mather, *The Cheeseburger Philosophy*, 1996)

   Purpose: ______________________ Clues: ______________________

   ____

   Main idea: ____

3. Child labor laws prohibit a 13-year-old from punching a cash register for 40 hours a week, but that same child can labor for 40 hours or more inside a gym or an ice skating rink without drawing the slightest glance from the government. The U.S. government requires the licensing of plumbers. It demands that even the tiniest coffee shop adhere to a fastidious health code. It scrutinizes the advertising claims on packages of low-fat snack food. But it never asks a coach, who holds the lives of his young pupils in his hands, to pass a minimum safety and skills test. Coaches in this country need no license to coach children, even in a high-injury sport like elite gymnastics.

   (Joan Ryan, *Little Girls in Pretty Boxes*, 1995)

   Purpose: ______________________ Clues: ______________________

   ____

   Main idea: ____

4. Alcohol abuse by college students usually takes the form of a drinking pattern called *binge drinking.* Binge drinking is defined as the consumption of five drinks in a row. One large study of more than 17,000 students on 89 campuses found that 49.7 percent of students engaged in binge drinking. The strongest predictors for binging were living in a fraternity or sorority, adopting a party-centered lifestyle, and engaging in other risky behavior. The study also suggested that many college students began binge drinking in high school.

   (Wayne A. Payne, et al., *Understanding Your Health*, 11/e, 2011)

   Purpose: ______________________ Clues: ______________________

   Main idea: ____

5. Tina was found dead last week—her neck broken by the jaws of a steel trap. I didn't know Tina. But John and Rachel Williamson knew her, and so did their children, Tyrone and Vanessa. Tina had been a beloved member of their family for 10 years. She was a Samoyed—a handsome, intelligent dog, pure white with soft, dark eyes. When she died she was only 200 yards from her back door. Tina had gone out to play that morning as usual, but this time she found something *un*usual—an odd-shaped box with delicious-smelling food inside. She put her head inside the box to get at the food. When she did, the trap closed and Tina was killed. Unless we crack down on illegal trapping within town property, this tragedy will be repeated. The next time it might be *your* family dog. Or your pet cat. Or your child.

Purpose: ______________________ Clues: ______________________

____

Main idea: ______________________

____

6. To keep an adequate supply of pennies in circulation, the U.S. Mint creates approximately 12 billion new pennies each year. The cost of manufacturing these new pennies is 0.66 of a cent apiece, which adds up to approximately $80 million a year. According to Treasury officials, when you add on storage and handling expenses, it costs the U.S. government more than a penny to transact a penny's worth of business.

Purpose: ______________________ Clues: ______________________

____

Main idea: ______________________

7. As we wait for the plane to climb to the jump altitude of 12,000 feet, my mind races with a frenzied jumble of thoughts: "Okay, this is the moment you've been waiting for. It's going to be great. Am I really going to jump out of an airplane from 12,000 feet? What if something goes wrong? Can I still back out? Come on now, don't worry. It'll be fine." My palms are sweating and my heart is pounding so hard I think it may burst. "Get ready," yells the instructor. As I jump into the blue, I wonder, "What am I doing here?" The blast of air resistance blows me backward like a leaf at the mercy of the autumn wind. In about ten seconds my body levels out and accelerates to a speed of 120 miles an hour. The air supports my body like an invisible flying carpet. Any fears or doubts I had are gone in the exhilaration of free flight. Every nerve in my body is alive with sensation; yet I am overcome by a peaceful feeling and the sense that I am one with the sky.

(Stephen E. Lucas, *The Art of Public Speaking*, 9/e, 2007)

Purpose: ______________________ Clues: ______________________

Main idea: ______________________

An Introduction to Modes of Writing (Rhetorical Modes)

In longer reading selections, the main idea is often referred to as the **thesis.** The thesis, just like the main idea in paragraphs, expresses the most important point the writer is trying to make. You may also hear the thesis referred to as the *controlling idea* because it is meant to hold the essay or story together.

In the process of creating written work, most writers select a mode of writing (sometimes called a *rhetorical mode*) that helps them achieve their purpose. In the following sections, we will explore the four most common rhetorical modes—narrative, expository, persuasive, and descriptive—and present examples of each. As you will see, the four rhetorical modes and the three purposes you just learned about work closely together.

- **Narrative Mode** Material written in a **narrative mode** tells a story, either true or fictional. In narrative writing, the events of a story are usually ordered by time.
- **Expository Mode** An author who is trying to explain something will likely use an **expository mode.** Expository writing explains ideas and how things

work. It is likely to be logical and factual. Much of the material that you read in your textbooks follows an expository mode.

- **Persuasive Mode** Material written in a **persuasive mode** is meant to convince you of something. Persuasive writing tends to be about controversial topics. It presents an argument and offers evidence. It is writing that is considered to be biased.
- **Descriptive Mode** With material written in a **descriptive mode,** the emphasis is on providing details that describe a person, place, object, concept, or experience. The writing may employ the use of figurative language and include material that appeals to one or more of the five senses. Descriptive writing most commonly deals with visual perceptions, but not always.

Narrative Mode with Purpose to Entertain

The following excerpt from *Farmworker's Daughter—Growing up Mexican in America* by Rose Castillo Guilbault is written in a narrative mode with entertainment as its purpose.

READING

"During that first summer, I learned to respect the conveyor belt ladies."

TUNING IN TO READING The excerpt below is taken from Rose Castillo Guilbault's memoir, *Farmworker's Daughter—Growing Up Mexican in America.* In it, Guilbault describes summer vacations during her teenage years working with migrant workers. What kind of jobs have you had? Did any of them profoundly affect you?

BIO-SKETCH When Rose Castillo Guilbault was 5, she and her mother left Mexico for California's Salinas Valley. Rose, with a great deal of hard work and help from mentors, gradually perfected her English and began writing for her school newspaper. After graduating from college, she became a writer for the *San Francisco Chronicle.* She entered broadcasting and has worked with both CBS and ABC, winning an Emmy for outstanding children's programming. She was appointed to serve on the California Community College Board of Governors.

NOTES ON VOCABULARY

cross to bear a heavy burden to carry in life or a serious problem to put up with. The phrase alludes to the cross Jesus carried to his crucifixion.

Excerpt from Farmworker's Daughter—Growing Up Mexican in America

ROSE CASTILLO GUILBAULT

The Conveyor Belt Ladies

The conveyor belt ladies were migrant women, mostly from Texas. I worked with them during the summers of my teenage years. I call them conveyor belt ladies because I got to know them while sorting tomatoes on a conveyor belt.

The women and their families arrived in May for the carrot season, spent the summer in the tomato sheds, and stayed through October for the bean harvest. After that, they emptied from town, some returning to their homes in Texas while others continued on the migrant trail, picking cotton in the San Joaquin Valley or grapefruits and oranges in the Imperial Valley. 2

Most of these women had started in the fields. The vegetable packing sheds were a step up, easier than the backbreaking jobs in the fields. The work in the sheds was often more tedious than strenuous, paid better, and provided fairly steady hours and clean bathrooms. Best of all, you didn't get rained on. 3

I had started sorting tomatoes with my mother in high school. I would have preferred working in a dress shop or babysitting like my friends, but I had a dream that would cost a lot of money—college—and the fact was that sorting tomatoes was the highest-paying work in town. The job consisted of picking out the flawed tomatoes on the conveyor belt before they rolled into the shipping boxes at the end of the line. These boxes were immediately loaded onto delivery trucks, so it was important not to let bad tomatoes through. 4

The work could be slow or intense, depending on the quality of the tomatoes and how many there were. Work increased when the company deliveries got backlogged or after rain delayed picking. During those times, it was not unusual to work from 7:00 A.M. until midnight. I never heard anyone complain about overtime, though. Overtime meant desperately needed extra money. 5

It would have been difficult not to like the women. They were an entertaining group, easing the long, monotonous hours with bawdy humor and spicy gossip. They poked fun at all the male workers and did hysterical impersonations of the supervisor. Although he didn't speak Spanish (other than "*¡Mujeres, trabajo, trabajo!* Women, work, work!"), he sensed he was being laughed at. He would stamp his foot and forbid us from talking until break time. But it would have been much easier to tie the women's tongues in knots than to keep them quiet. Eventually the ladies had their way and their fun, and the men learned to ignore them. 6

Pretty Rosa described her romances and her pending wedding to a handsome fieldworker. Berta told me that Rosa's marriage would cause her nothing but headaches because the man was younger and too handsome. Maria, large and placid, described the births of each of her nine children, warning me about the horrors of labor and delivery. 7

At other moments they could turn melancholic, telling of babies who died because their mothers couldn't afford medical care, the alcoholic husbands who were their "cross to bear," the racism they experienced in Texas, where they were referred to as "dirty Mexicans" or "Mexican dogs" and not allowed in certain restaurants. 8

I was appalled and deeply moved by these confidences, and the injustices they endured enraged me. I could do little but sympathize. My mother, no stranger to suffering, said I was too impressionable when I emotionally relayed to her the women's stories. 9

"If they were in Mexico, life would be even harder. At least there are opportunities here; you can work," she'd say. 10

11 During that first summer, I learned to respect the conveyor belt ladies.

12 The last summer I worked in the packing shed turned out to be the last I lived at home. I had just finished junior college and was transferring to a university. At this point I was "overeducated" for seasonal work, but if you counted the overtime, it was still the best-paying job. So I went back one last time.

13 The ladies treated me with warmth and respect. I was a college student and they thought I deserved special treatment.

14 Aguedita, the crew chief, moved me to softer and better-paying jobs within the plant. I moved from the conveyor belt to shoving boxes down a chute and finally to weighing boxes of tomatoes on a scale—the highest-paying position for a woman.

15 When the union representative showed up to collect dues, the women hid me in the bathroom. They had determined it was unfair for me to have to pay dues since I worked only during the summer. We played a cat-and-mouse game with him all summer. "You ladies aren't hiding students, are you?" he'd ask suspiciously.

16 "Why does *la unión* charge our poor students anyway?" The ladies would distract him with questions and complaints until he tired of answering them and had to leave for his next location.

17 Maria, with the nine children, tried to feed me all summer, bringing extra tortillas, which were delicious. I accepted them with some guilt, wondering if I was taking food away from her children. Others brought rental contracts or other documents for me to explain and translate.

18 The last day of work was splendidly beautiful, golden and warm. The conveyor belt's loud humming was turned off, silenced for the season. The women sighed as they removed their aprons. Some of them walked off, calling, "*¡Hasta la próxima!* Until next time."

19 But most of the conveyor belt ladies came over to me, shook my hand, and gave me a blessing or a big hug.

20 "Don't come back. Make us proud, *hija*."

(Rose Castillo Guilbault, *Farmworker's Daughter*, 2005)

COMPREHENSION CHECKUP

Short Answer

Directions: Answer each question briefly.

1. In this selection, the author's purpose is to entertain. Give some reasons to support this conclusion.
   a. ______________________________
   b. ______________________________
   c. ______________________________

2. The selection is an example of narrative writing.
   a. Who is narrating the significant events of the story? ______________________________
   ____
   b. Is the story true or fictional? ______________________________

Multiple Choice

Directions: For each item, write the letter corresponding to the best answer.

______ 1. Guilbault met the conveyor belt ladies while
a. canning tomatoes.
b. picking carrots.
c. sorting tomatoes.
d. harvesting lettuce.

______ 2. Working in the packing sheds provided all the following **except**
a. clean restroom facilities.
b. more money than a field job.
c. health insurance benefits.
d. shelter from the elements.

______ 3. Guilbault liked the conveyor belt ladies for all the following reasons **except** which?
a. They were entertaining.
b. They treated her with warmth and respect.
c. They gave her preferential treatment.
d. They listened to her gripes and complaints and offered advice.

______ 4. To entertain themselves at work, the conveyor belt ladies did all the following **except**
a. impersonate the supervisor.
b. gossip about their romances.
c. make fun of their male coworkers.
d. play tricks on one another.

______ 5. The conveyor belt ladies described all the following hardships **except**
a. lack of adequate food and shelter.
b. experiences with racial discrimination.
c. problems with husbands who drank too much.
d. babies dying because of lack of medical care.

______ 6. Guilbault experienced all the following with the conveyor belt ladies **except** for which?
a. They hid her from the union representative.
b. They needed her help in filing complaints over discrimination.
c. They brought her food.
d. They asked her help in deciphering documents.

______ 7. The main idea of the selection is that
a. migrant workers lead extremely difficult lives.
b. while working with the conveyor belt ladies, Guilbault came to respect and admire them.
c. the conveyor belt ladies were grateful for the jobs they held.
d. supervisors can be very hard to get along with.

______ 8. The author's purpose in writing the selection is to
a. Tell about the experiences she had working in vegetable packing sheds.
b. persuade the reader to lobby for reforms in the agricultural industry.
c. inform the reader of the hardships she endured as a child.
d. compare and contrast the lives of field-workers in Mexico with those in the United States.

______ 9. From reading the selection, you can conclude all of the following **except**
a. The workers Guilbault describes had less formal education than she did.
b. The conveyor belt ladies largely accepted their lot in life.
c. Guilbault's mother had less sympathy for the conveyor belt ladies than did Guilbault.
d. Guilbault's mother wished to return to Mexico.

______ 10. From reading the selection, you can conclude all of the following **except**
a. The author would have preferred a more traditional teenage job.
b. The conveyor belt women were easily intimidated by authority.
c. The author disliked working with her mother in the packing sheds.
d. Both b and c.

______ 11. How does the mother sound when she says the words in paragraph 10?
a. matter-of-fact.
b. unsympathetic.
c. sarcastic.
d. both a and b.

______ 12. The last words the conveyor belt ladies speak to Rose are meant to sound
a. encouraging.
b. disgusted.
c. befuddled.
d. ambivalent.

True or False

Directions: Indicate whether each statement is true or false by writing **T** or **F** in the space provided.

______ 13. The conveyor belt ladies were primarily local women trying to earn extra money.

______ 14. Guilbault worked year-round at a vegetable packing shed.

______ 15. A *backbreaking* job is one that demands great effort.

______ 16. Working in the packing sheds was more boring than exhausting.

______ 17. Guilbault could make more money by babysitting than by working in the packing sheds.

______ 18. An antonym of *flawed* is "perfect."

______ 19. The conveyor belt ladies disliked having to work overtime.

______ 20. A synonym for *monotonous* is "boring."

______ 21. A cat-and-mouse game is one in which someone is trying to elude discovery by someone else.

Vocabulary Matching

Directions: Match each word in column A with its definition in column B.

	Column A	Column B
______	1. appalled	a. postponed
______	2. bawdy	b. boring
______	3. delayed	c. communicated

______ 4. impressionable	d. requiring great effort or energy
______ 5. melancholic	e. calm; unruffled
______ 6. pending	f. dismayed
______ 7. placid	g. coarse; vulgar
______ 8. relayed	h. characterized by sadness
______ 9. strenuous	i. capable of being easily influenced
______ 10. tedious	j. about to happen; imminent

In Your Own Words

1. The conveyor belt ladies found a way to make their jobs seem less oppressive. What are some acceptable ways that office and retail workers can make their jobs less oppressive (without getting fired)?
2. At the end of the selection, the conveyor belt ladies told the author, "Don't come back. Make us proud, *hija* [daughter]." What do you think they meant? Why were the ladies so protective of the author?
3. The supervisor in Guilbault's story didn't speak Spanish and sensed that the ladies were making fun of him. Have you ever had a similar experience at work (either as a supervisor or as a worker)? Sometimes customers, employees, and employers complain that when some employees speak another language, they feel excluded and annoyed because they don't know what is being said and worry it might be something negative or personal about them. Do you think this is a problem? Do you think that requiring that only English be spoken in the workplace would be a good solution?

Written Assignment

1. A migrant worker moves from one geographic area to another in search of employment. Migrant workers often harvest crops, and as a result often move around the country following the seasons. What kinds of problems do you think migrant workers face? What kinds of problems do you think their children experience? Write a couple of paragraphs discussing this issue.
2. In a recent series of speeches, Guilbault shared lessons she learned. Her first lesson is to "find your passion." Guilbault says there is always something you can do with your own talent or gift. "It's important to find out what that gift or passion is and to find jobs to sustain it." The next lesson is to "face your fears and believe in yourself." The third lesson is to pay back. Guilbault says, "It's important to remember where you came from and pay back to your community." The fourth lesson is to be true to yourself. "You need to create your own definition of success. Determine what gives you joy, satisfaction, and balance in your life." The final lesson is to celebrate your successes, no matter how small they may be. Guilbault says that success is individualistic. It's what you want it to be. "Your dreams will direct the journey."

   In a few paragraphs, respond to Guilbault's lessons. Do you agree or disagree with them? Try to come up with a few of your own lessons.

Internet Activity

Cesar Chavez founded an organization that advocated for the rights of farmworkers. Use any search engine to find out more about Chavez's life and his organization. Write a few paragraphs summarizing your findings.

Expository Mode with Purpose to Inform

Read the following excerpt from *Personal Finance* by Jack Kapoor. Kapoor's purpose is to present information about consumer credit. The selection is written in the expository mode.

READING

"By her senior year, Wendy had amassed $9,000 in credit card debt and couldn't make the monthly payments of nearly $200."

TUNING IN TO READING This reading discusses the advantages and disadvantages of using credit cards. In addition to the regular questions following the article you will find questions related to a graph that pertains to the reading.

BIO-SKETCH Jack Kapoor, the lead author of this reading, has taught business and economics at the College of DuPage, Glen Ellyn, Illinois, since 1969. In addition to writing the textbook from which this reading is taken, he is the author of *Business: A Practical Approach; Business; Business and Personal Finance;* and *Focus on Personal Finance.*

NOTES ON VOCABULARY

credit receiving cash, goods, or services and paying for them in the future

vulnerable susceptible to temptation

Excerpt from

PERSONAL FINANCE

by Jack Kapoor

Consumer Credit

Uses and Misuses of Credit

Using credit to purchase goods and services may allow consumers to be more efficient or more productive or to lead more satisfying lives. There are many valid reasons for using credit. A medical emergency may leave a person strapped for funds. A homemaker returning to the workforce may need a car. It may be possible to buy an item now for less money than it will cost later. Borrowing for a college education is another valid reason. But it probably is not reasonable to borrow for everyday living expenses or finance a Corvette on credit when a Ford Focus is all your budget allows.

"Shopaholics" and young adults are most vulnerable to misusing credit. College students are a prime target for credit card issuers, and issuers make it very easy for students to get credit cards. Wendy Leright, a 25-year-old teacher in Detroit, knows this all too well. As a college freshman, she applied for and got seven credit cards, all bearing at least an 18.9 percent interest rate and a $20 annual fee. Although unemployed, she used the cards freely, buying expensive clothes for herself, extravagant Christmas presents for friends and family, and even a one-week vacation in the Bahamas. "It got to a point where I didn't even look at the price tag," she said. By her senior year, Wendy had amassed $9,000 in 2 credit card debt and couldn't make the monthly payments of nearly $200. She eventually turned to her parents to bail her out. "Until my mother sat me down and showed me how much interest I had to pay, I hadn't even given it a thought. I was shocked," Wendy said. "I would have had to pay it off for years."

Using credit cards increases the amount of money a person can spend to purchase goods and services now. But the trade-off is that it decreases the amount of money that will be available to spend in the future. However, many people expect their incomes to increase and therefore expect to be able to make payments on past credit purchases and still make new purchases. 3

Here are some questions you should consider before you decide how and when to make a major purchase, for example, a car: 4

- Do I have the cash I need for the down payment?
- Do I want to use my savings for this purchase?
- Does the purchase fit my budget?
- Could I use the credit I need for this purchase in some better way?
- Could I postpone the purchase?
- What are the opportunity costs of postponing the purchase (alternative transportation costs, a possible increase in the price of the car)?
- What are the dollar costs and the psychological costs of using credit (interest, other finance charges, being in debt and responsible for making a monthly payment)?

If you decide to use credit, make sure the benefits of making your purchase now (increased efficiency or productivity, a more satisfying life, etc.) outweigh the costs (financial and psychological) of using credit. Thus, credit, when effectively used, can help you have more and enjoy more. When misused, credit can result in default, bankruptcy, and loss of creditworthiness. 5

Advantages of Credit

Consumer credit enables people to enjoy goods and services now—a car, a home, an education, help in emergencies—and pay for them through payment plans based on future income. 6

Credit cards permit the purchase of goods even when funds are low. Customers with previously approved credit may receive other extras, such as advance notice of sales and the right to order by phone or to buy on approval. In addition, many shoppers believe it is easier to return merchandise they have purchased on account. Credit cards also provide shopping convenience and the efficiency of paying for several purchases with one monthly payment. 7

Credit is more than a substitute for cash. Many of the services it provides are taken for granted. Every time you turn on the water tap, flick the light switch, or telephone a friend, you are using credit. 8

It is safer to use credit, since charge accounts and credit cards let you shop and travel without carrying a large amount of cash. You need a credit card to make a hotel reservation, rent a car, and shop by phone. You may also use credit cards for identification when cashing checks, and the use of credit provides you with a record of expenses. 9

Finally, credit indicates stability. The fact that lenders consider you a good risk usually means you are a responsible individual. However, if you do not repay your debts in a timely manner, you will find that credit has many disadvantages. 10

Disadvantages of Credit

Perhaps the greatest disadvantage of using credit is the temptation to overspend. It seems easy to buy today and pay tomorrow. But continual overspending can lead to serious trouble. Failure to repay a loan may result in loss of income, valuable property, and your good reputation. It can even lead to court action and bankruptcy. Misuse of credit can create serious long-term financial problems, damage to family relationships, and a slowing of progress toward financial goals. Therefore, you should approach credit with caution and avoid using it more extensively than your budget permits. 11

Although credit allows more immediate satisfaction of needs and desires, it does not increase total purchasing power. Credit purchases must be paid for out of future income; therefore, credit ties up the use of future income. Furthermore, if your income does not increase to cover rising costs, your ability to repay credit commitments will diminish. Before buying goods and services on credit, consider whether they will have lasting value, whether they will increase your personal satisfaction during present and future income periods, and whether your current income will continue or increase. 12

Finally, credit costs money. It is a service for which you must pay. Paying for purchases over a period of time is more costly than paying for them with cash. Purchasing with credit rather than cash involves one very obvious tradeoff: the fact that it will cost more due to monthly finance charges and the compounding effect of interest on interest. 13

Summary: Advantages and Disadvantages of Credit

The use of credit provides immediate access to goods and services, flexibility in money management, safety and convenience, a cushion in emergencies, a means of increasing resources, and a good credit rating if you pay your debts back in a timely manner. But remember, the use of credit is a two-sided coin. An intelligent decision as to its use demands careful evaluation of your current debt, your future income, the added cost, and the consequences of overspending. 14

(Jack Kapoor et al., *Personal Finance,* 10/e, McGraw-Hill, 2012, pp. 172–174)

COMPREHENSION CHECKUP

Short Answer

Directions: Answer each question briefly.

1. In this selection, the author's purpose is to inform. Give some reasons to support this conclusion.

   a. ____________________

   b. ____________________

   c. ____________________

2. The selection is an example of expository writing.

   a. What is being explained to you? ____________________

   ____

   b. What are some examples of factual details? ____________________

   ____

Multiple Choice

Directions: Write the letter for the correct answer to each question on the lines provided.

______ 1. The author's purpose in writing this selection is
a. to persuade the reader not to use credit cards.
b. to present information on the advantages and disadvantages of credit cards.
c. to encourage the use of credit cards in most circumstances.
d. to give several examples of when credit cards have been misused.

______ 2. The example of Wendy is used to illustrate all of the following **except**
a. the ease with which students can obtain credit cards.
b. the wisdom of purchasing only what can be reasonably afforded.
c. the danger of leaving a balance on a credit card each month.
d. the problem with paying only the monthly minimum on each account.

______ 3. The author would agree with which of the following statements?
a. We should use our credit cards whenever possible.
b. We should have several credit cards so our total credit limit can be higher.
c. We should never use credit cards.
d. We should use credit cards when appropriate such as for traveling, shopping by phone, and making hotel reservations.

______ 4. The word "interest" in paragraph 2 means
a. state of curiosity or concern about something.
b. a right claim or legal share.
c. involvement with or participation in something.
d. a charge for a loan.

______ 5. All of the following are credit situations **except**
a. paying rent at the beginning of the month.
b. paying your electric bill.
c. charging a restaurant meal on a credit card.
d. buying a car over time.

True or False

Directions: Indicate whether each statement is true or false by writing **T** or **F** in the space provided.

______ 6. When used properly, credit cards can be used to indicate financial stability.

______ 7. College students find it difficult to obtain credit cards because of their lack of credit.

______ 8. The author would probably agree that using a credit card for needed purchases over the Internet would be appropriate.

______ 9. It's usually best to pay off your credit card bills when they come to you each month.

______ 10. This reading discusses the differences between debit cards and credit cards.

Vocabulary in Context

Directions: In the paragraphs indicated in parentheses, find the words that correctly match the definitions given, and write them in the spaces provided.

1. well grounded; just (1) ____________
2. lavish or imprudent expenditure (2) ____________
3. something that saves work (7) ____________
4. reliability; dependability (10) ____________
5. a general estimation in which a person is held (11) ____________

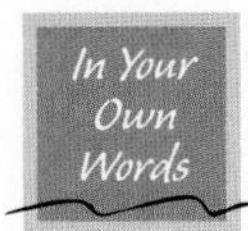

In Your Own Words

1. Do you think credit card companies want people to pay off their credit cards? Do you think credit card companies should advise people about the use and misuse of credit cards?
2. A new type of credit agency that has been popping up almost everywhere is the payday loan office. These companies typically give short-term loans at very high interest rates. Do you think these companies serve a purpose? Should their interest rates be regulated?

Written Assignment

Write a paragraph about a credit or loan situation that hurt you or someone you know financially.

Internet Activity

Go to www.creditcards.com. Click on one of the types of credit cards that is listed in the left-hand side of the screen. Write a few sentences about what you found out about these credit cards.

Credit Card Holders and Credit Cards Held

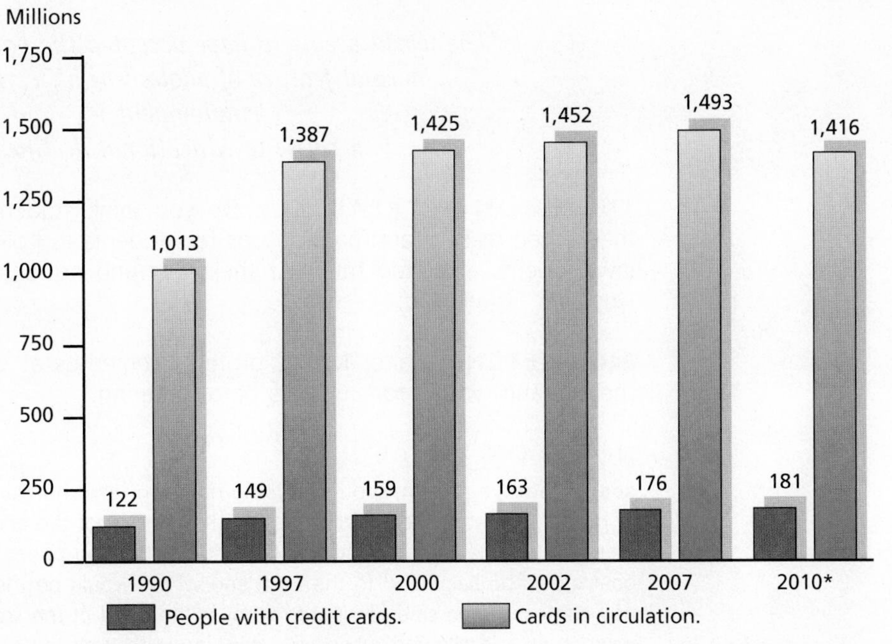

*Estimated.

(Jack R. Kapoor et al., Personal Finance, 10/e, McGraw-Hill, 2012, p. 177. Data from Statistical Abstract of the United States 2010)

Visual Aid

Directions: Look at the bar graph and then answer the questions that follow it.

1. Who publishes the annual *Statistical Abstract of the United States?*

   ____

2. The left-hand axis of the graph indicates that the numbers are in

   ____

3. How many people had credit cards in 1990? ____________________
   In 2007? ____________________
4. How many credit cards were in circulation in 1990? ____________________
   ____________ In 2007? ____________________
5. Did the number of credit cards increase or decrease per person between 1990 and 2007? ____________________ (Divide the total number of credit cards for those two years by the number of people with credit cards.)
6. Does this graph indicate how much money was actually being loaned per person or per card? ____________________

Persuasive Mode with Purpose to Persuade

The following article, "Students Who Push Burgers," was first published in *The Christian Science Monitor.* The author, Walter S. Minot, worries that too many students are working too many hours a week while also trying to be full-time students. He would like to see college students give a higher priority to their studies and work fewer hours. Although this article was written in 1988, the information presented is still relevant today. In fact, the actual percentage of working students has increased slightly. The selection, which presents an argument, is written in the persuasive mode, and its purpose is to persuade.

READING

"The world seems to have accepted the part-time job as a normal feature of adolescence. . . . But such employment is a cause of educational decline."

TUNING IN TO READING Do you think students should have jobs? Are there good reasons and bad reasons for students to hold down jobs? Do your fellow students work too much at their jobs and not put enough effort into their studies?

BIO-SKETCH Walter Minot, professor emeritus at Gannon University, taught rhetoric and writing for 36 years before retiring.

NOTES ON VOCABULARY

scapegoat a person, group, or thing made to take the blame for the crime or mistake of others. Under the law of Moses, the high priest of the ancient Jews would bring two goats to the altar on the Day of Atonement. The high priest then cast lots to see which goat would be sacrificed to the Lord and which would be the *scapegoat.* After the priest had confessed the sins of his people over the head of the *scapegoat,* it was taken to the wilderness and allowed to escape, carrying with it all the sins of the people. The other goat was then given in sacrifice. (Definition of *scapegoat* from William Morris and Mary Morris, *Morris Dictionary of Word and Phrase Origins*. Copyright © 1987 by William Morris and Mary Morris. Reprinted by permission of HarperCollins Publishers.)

tripe slang for nonsense, or anything offensive; part of the stomach of cattle, goats, and deer when used for food.

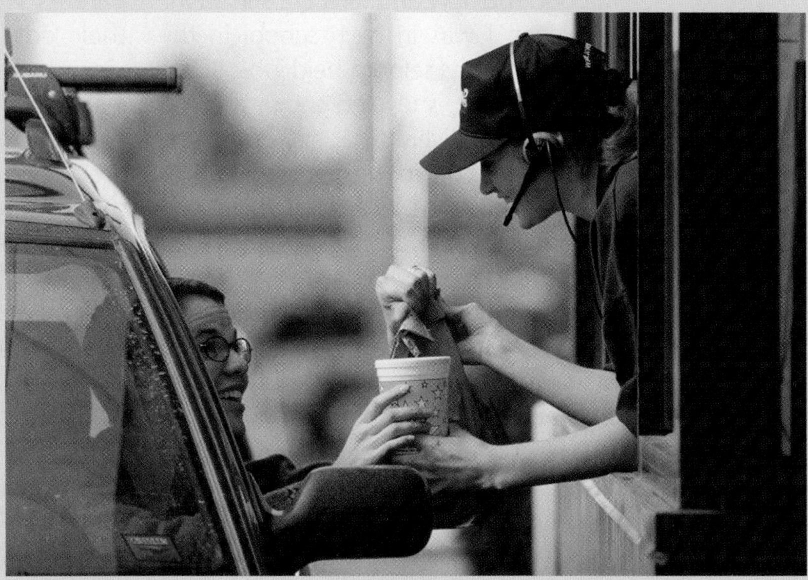

Minot argues that students today often work to support a luxurious lifestyle. Do you agree?

STUDENTS WHO PUSH BURGERS **BY WALTER MINOT**

A college freshman squirms anxiously on a chair in my office, his eyes avoiding mine, those of his English professor, as he explains that he hasn't finished his paper, which was due two days ago. "I just haven't had the time," he says.

2 "Are you carrying a heavy course load?"

3 "Fifteen hours," he says—a normal load.

4 "Are you working a lot?"

5 "No, sir, not much. About 30 hours a week."

6 "That's a lot. Do you have to work that much?"

7 "Yeah, I have to pay for my car."

8 "Do you really need a car?"

9 "Yeah, I need it to get to work."

10 This student isn't unusual. Indeed, he probably typifies today's college and high school students. Yet in all the lengthy analyses of what's wrong with American education, I have not heard employment by students being blamed.

I have heard drugs blamed and 11
television—that universal scapegoat. I have heard elaborate theories about the decline of the family, of religion, and of authority, as well as other sociological theories. But nobody blames student employment. The world seems to have accepted the part-time job as a normal feature of adolescence. A parochial school in my town even had a day to honor students who held regular jobs, and parents often endorse this employment by claiming that it teaches kids the value of the dollar.

12 But such employment is a major cause of educational decline. To argue my case, I will rely on memories of my own high school days and contrast them with what I see today. Though I do have some statistical evidence, my argument depends on what anyone over 40 can test through memory and direct observation.

13 When I was in high school in the 1950s, students seldom held jobs. Some of us baby-sat, shoveled snow, mowed lawns, and delivered papers, and some of us got jobs in department stores around Christmas. But most of us had no regular source of income other than the generosity of our parents.

14 The only kids who worked regularly were poor. They worked to help their families. If I remember correctly, only about five people in my class of 170 held jobs. That was in a working-class town in New England. As for the rest of us, our parents believed that going to school and helping around the house were our work.

15 In contrast, in 1986 my daughter was one of the few students among juniors and seniors who didn't work. According to Bureau of Labor statistics, more than 40 percent of high school students were working in 1980, but sociologists Ellen Greenberger and Laurence Steinberg in "When Teenagers Work" came up with estimates of more than 70 percent working in 1986, though I suspect that the figure may be even higher now.

16 My daughter, however, did not work; her parents wouldn't let her. Interestingly, some of the students in her class implied that she had an unfair advantage over them in the classroom. They were probably right, for while she was home studying, they were pushing burgers, waiting on tables, or selling dresses 20 hours a week. Working students have little time for homework.

17 I attended a public high school, while she attended a Roman Catholic preparatory school whose students are mainly middle class. By the standards of my day, her classmates did not "have to" work. Yet many of them were working 20 to 30 hours a week. Why?

They worked so that they could spend $60 to $100 a week on designer jeans, rock concerts, stereo and video systems, and, of course, cars. They were living lives of luxury, buying items on which their parents refused to throw hard-earned money away. Though the parents would not buy such tripe for their kids, the parents somehow convinced themselves that the kids were learning the value of money. Yet, according to Ms. Greenberger and Mr. Steinberg, only about a quarter of these students saved money for college or other long-term goals. 18

How students spend their money is their business, not mine. But as a teacher, I have witnessed the effects of their employment. I know that students who work all evening aren't ready for studying when they get home from work. Moreover, because they work so hard and have ready cash, they feel that they deserve to have fun—instead of spending all their free time studying. 19

Thus, by the time they get to college, most students look upon studies as a spare-time activity. A survey at Pennsylvania State University showed that most freshmen believed they could maintain a B average by studying about 20 hours a week. (I can remember when college guidebooks advised two to three hours of studying for every hour in class—30 to 45 hours a week.) 20

Clearly individual students will pay the price for lack of adequate time studying, but the problem goes beyond the individual. It extends to schools and colleges that are finding it difficult to demand quantity or quality of work from students. 21

Perhaps the reason American education has declined so markedly is because America has raised a generation of part-time students. And perhaps our economy will continue to decline as full-time students from Japan and Europe continue to outperform our part-time students. 22

(Walter S. Minot, "Students Who Push Burgers," 1988)

Short Answer

Directions: Answer each question briefly.

1. What is Minot's basic argument? Are you persuaded by it?

____

____

2. What is it about Minot's background that makes him an authority on this topic?

____

Multiple Choice

Directions: For each item, write the letter corresponding to the best answer.

_____ 1. The college freshman who spoke to Professor Minot
   a. has to work so much so that he can pay for his food and rent.
   b. takes a lighter course load than other college students.
   c. has completed his English paper on time.
   d. is fairly typical of today's college students, according to the author.

_____ 2. The main idea expressed in this article is that
   a. drugs and television are directly responsible for the decline in American education.
   b. the decline in religious values has led to a corresponding decline in American education.
   c. student employment in the United States is a major cause of educational decline.
   d. parochial schools, unlike public schools, are still able to provide a quality education.

_____ 3. Which of the following statements is true according to the author?
   a. Students in the 1950s rarely worked.
   b. The majority of students save their wages from part-time jobs for long-term goals.
   c. A parochial school honored students who had regular employment.
   d. Both a and c.

_____ 4. From Minot's article, we can conclude that many parents
   a. no longer believe that going to school and helping out at home should be a student's only work.
   b. are reluctant to spend their money on frivolous items such as designer jeans.
   c. are convinced that students learn the value of money by working at a part-time job.
   d. All of the above.

_____ 5. The author's primary purpose is to
   a. describe the educational system of the 1950s.
   b. argue that student employment contributes to educational decline.
   c. describe one student's academic dilemma.
   d. applaud the attitude of today's parents toward part-time student employment.

True or False

Directions: Indicate whether each statement is true or false by writing **T** or **F** in the space provided.

_____ 6. A Penn State survey indicates that college freshmen believe they can maintain an A average with only 20 hours of studying per week.

_____ 7. Minot believes that there is a correlation between student employment and a college's ability to maintain high academic standards.

_____ 8. Although Minot is opposed to student employment, he did allow his daughter to work while she was in high school.

_____ 9. According to the statistics given in the article, teenage employment has continued to rise over the years.

_____ 10. Minot has personally observed how student employment harms academic achievement.

Vocabulary in Context

Directions: Indicate whether the word in italics is used correctly or incorrectly by writing **C** or **I** in the space provided.

_____ 1. It's an act of *generosity* to refuse to help others.

_____ 2. After the well-known athlete *endorsed* the product, sales immediately rose.

_____ 3. The student became bored by the lecture and began to *squirm* about in his seat.

_____ 4. A person who strives for perfection is likely to be satisfied with an *adequate* performance.

_____ 5. Alejandro was walking down the sidewalk when he *witnessed* a car accident on the nearby street.

_____ 6. Tenssy made *elaborate* plans for her formal wedding ceremony, which was to have over 500 guests.

_____ 7. A person in the stage of *adolescence* is very close to retirement age.

_____ 8. Shawn *typifies* college student-athletes who work long hours at both their studies and their sports.

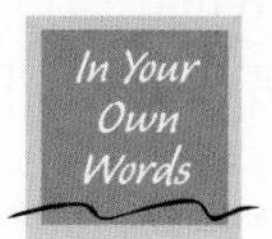

In Your Own Words

1. Do you think parents today still support the notion that a student's only "job" should be going to school and getting good grades? Why or why not?
2. In grade school, most students are in class until three or four in the afternoon. Most high school students are dismissed much earlier than this. Do you think high schools should require students to spend more time at school?
3. What do parents hope a student will learn from work experience? What do you think students learn from work experience? Would it be better for students with free time to do volunteer work or internships instead of working for a salary?
4. It is well known that students in the United States spend less time in school than do students in any other modern industrial country. What are the global implications of being a nation of part-time students?
5. Many high school and college teachers comment that they no longer require the same amount of work from their students. For example, where once two

research papers were required for English 101, now only one is required. What are some possible effects of these reduced standards?

6. Many teachers report that the number of students trying to do their homework in class has increased over the years. The main idea from paragraph 16 supports the observation of these teachers. Write the main idea below.

____

Written Assignment

Write an essay on your views about the factors in a student's life that make it difficult for the student to succeed.

STUDY TECHNIQUE 10: WRITING SUMMARIES METHOD 2

In your reading and English classes, you will be called upon to write summaries. **Summarizing** simply means restating the main ideas of a reading in your own words. Because many supporting details are omitted, a summary is much shorter than the original on which it is based. When you write summaries, you need to present the main ideas in order of importance in an objective fashion. Keep in mind that you are reporting the author's viewpoints and not your own. When writing a summary, you never write something like "I feel" or "I think" or "it seems to me." Instead, you always write only the author's opinions. In a summary, it is always the *author* who feels, thinks, or believes.

You just read an article by Walter S. Minot titled "Students Who Push Burgers." This is a relatively easy article to summarize because the author presents his main ideas in a logical sequence. Try to locate the directly stated main ideas. Because not all of the main ideas are stated directly, you will have to come up with several implied main ideas.

In order to identify the key supporting details, try to answer as many of the question words (*who, what, where, when, why,* and *how*) about the topic as possible.

Summarizing an Article

Directions:

1. Provide answers to *who, what, where, when, why,* and *how.* (Not all of these question words will apply to every article.)

   Who: ______________________________

   What: ______________________________

   Where: ______________________________

   When: ______________________________

   Why: ______________________________

   How: ______________________________

2. List four to five main ideas from the article, paraphrasing each main idea. The overall main idea of the article is: Student employment is a major cause of the decline in American education.

   1st main idea: ______________________________

   ____

   2nd main idea: ______________________________

   ____

   3rd main idea: ______________________________

   ____

   4th main idea: ______________________________

   ____

   5th main idea: ______________________________

   ____

3. Write at least a half-page summary of the article. Be sure to include the information from numbers 1 and 2 in your summary. Your completed summary should contain no trivia (useless information) and should not be redundant (give information more than once). Remember to present the information in an organized way. After writing your summary, compare your version to the student sample in the Appendices.

Descriptive Mode with Purpose to Inform

The following selection is written in the descriptive mode. Notice how the key details describe both the black widow spiders and the author's experience with them. Because of the emphasis on sensory images, readers can visualize the scene being depicted.

READING

"I hunt Black Widow. I have never been bitten."

TUNING IN TO READING What do you know about spiders? Did you know that they have been on Earth for millions of years and are important to our survival because of the large numbers of insects they consume? While all spiders are poisonous, most species don't cause serious harm to humans. The black widow, though generally shy and retiring, has a very toxic bite. To learn more about the habits of the black widow, read the following selection.

BIO-SKETCH Gordon Grice is the author of *The Red Hourglass* and *The Deadly Kingdom.* He has written for *The New Yorker, Harper's,* and other magazines. His work has been anthologized in *The Best American Essays* and *The Art of the Essay.* His published work includes memoirs, essays, short stories, and poems.

NOTES ON VOCABULARY

gargoyle A sculpture or decoration depicting grotesque human shapes, beasts, or evil spirits that was placed on many buildings in the Middle Ages, especially churches and cathedrals. Some gargoyles acted as spouts that drained rainwater from the roof of the building. The Gothic gargoyle was usually a grotesque bird or animal sitting on the back of a cornice and projecting forward for several feet in order to throw the water far from the building. This form of sculpture declined with the introduction of lead drainpipes in the 16th century. The term originates from the French *gargouille,* meaning "the throat or waterspout."

arthropod animals with jointed legs and segmented bodies, such as insects, centipedes, scorpions, crustaceans, and spiders

The Black Widow

By GORDON GRICE

I hunt Black Widow. When I find one, I capture it. I have found them in discarded wheels and tires and under railroad ties. I have found them in house foundations and cellars, in automotive shops and toolsheds, in water meters and rock gardens, against fences and in cinderblock walls. I have found them in a hospital and in the den of a rattlesnake, and once at the bottom of a chair I was sitting in.

2 Sometimes I raise a generation or two in captivity. The egg sacs produce a hundred or more pinpoint cannibals, each leaving a trail of gleaming light in the air, the group of them eventually producing a glimmering tangle in which most of them die, eaten by stronger sibs. Finally I separate the three or four survivors and feed them bigger game.

3 Once I let several egg sacs hatch out in a container about eighteen inches on a side, a tight wooden box with a sliding glass top. As I tried to move the box one day, the lid slid off and I fell, hands first, into the mass of young widows. Most were still translucent newborns, their bodies a swirl of brown and cream. A few of the females had eaten enough to molt; they had the beginnings of their blackness. Their tangle of broken web

clung to my forearms. They felt like trickling water in my arm hairs.

4 The black widow has the ugliest web of any spider. It is a messy-looking tangle in the corners and bends of things and under logs and debris. Often the web is littered with leaves. Beneath it lie the husks of insect prey, their antennae still as gargoyle horns, cut loose and dropped; on them and the surrounding ground are splashes of the spider's white urine, which looks like bird guano and smells of ammonia even at a distance of several feet. This fetid material draws scavengers—ants, sow bugs, crickets, roaches, and so on—which become tangled in vertical strands of silk reaching from the ground up into the web. The widow comes down and, with a bicycling of the hind pair of legs, throws gummy silk onto this new prey.

5 When the prey is seriously tangled but still struggling, the widow cautiously descends and bites the creature, usually on a leg joint. This is a killing bite; it pumps neurotoxin into the victim. The widow will deliver a series of bites as the creature dies, injecting substances that liquefy the organs. Finally it will settle down to suck the liquefied innards out of the prey, changing position two or three times to get it all.

6 Before the eating begins, and sometimes before the victim dies from the slow venom, the widow usually moves it higher into the web. It attaches some line to the prey with a leg-bicycling toss, moves up the vertical web strand, and here secures the line. It has thus dragged the prey's body up off the ground. The whole operation is like that of a person moving a load with block and tackle.

7 You can't watch the widow in this activity very long without realizing that the web is not a mess at all but an efficient machine. It allows complicated use of leverage and also, because of its complexity of connections, lets the spider feel a disturbance anywhere in the web—usually with enough accuracy to tell the difference at a distance between a raindrop or leaf and viable prey. The web is also constructed in a certain relationship to movements of air so that flying insects are drawn into it. An insect that is clumsy and flies in random hops, such as a June beetle, is especially vulnerable to this trap.

The architectural complexities of the widow web do not particularly impress the widows. They move around in these webs almost blind, yet they never misstep or get lost. Furthermore, widows never snare themselves, even though every strand of the web is a potential trap. A widow will spend a few minutes every day coating the clawed tips of its legs with the oil that lets it walk the sticky strands. It secretes the oil from its mouth, coating its legs like a cat cleaning its paws. 8

Widows reportedly eat mice, toads, tarantulas—anything that wanders into that remarkable web. I have seen them eat scarab beetles heavy as pecans; cockroaches more than an inch long; and hundreds of other arthropods of various sizes. Widows begin life by eating their siblings. An adult female will fight any other female; the winner often eats the loser. The widow gets her name by eating her lover, though this does not always happen. 9

The widow's venom is a soundly pragmatic reason for fear. The venom contains a neurotoxin that can produce sweats, vomiting, swelling, convulsions, and dozens of other symptoms. The variation in symptoms from one person to the next is remarkable. The constant is pain. A useful question for a doctor trying to diagnose an uncertain case: "Is this the worst pain you've ever felt?" A "yes" suggests a diagnosis of black widow bite. Occasionally people die from widow bites. The very young and the very old are especially vulnerable. Some people seem to die not from the venom but from the infection that may follow; because of its habitat, the widow carries dangerous microbes. 10

I have never been bitten. 11

(Gordon Grice, "The Black Widow," in Geoffrey C. Ward, ed., *The Best American Essays*, 1996, pp. 209–214)

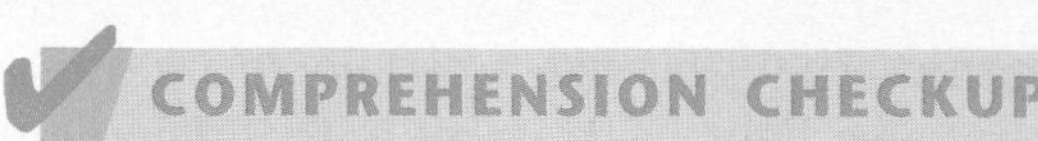

COMPREHENSION CHECKUP

Short Answer

Directions: Answer each question briefly.

1. What is the author's purpose? ________________________________

____

2. Give two reasons to support your choice.

a. ________________________________

b. ________________________________

3. Name four vivid details the author uses to describe the black widow.

a. ________________________________

b. ________________________________

c. ________________________________

d. ________________________________

Multiple Choice

Directions: For each item, write the letter corresponding to the best answer.

_____ 1. The author's purpose in writing this selection was to
a. describe how black widows are a threat to human beings.
b. explain how black widows are well suited to survive in their particular environments.
c. persuade the reader to exercise extreme caution in handling black widows.
d. entertain the reader with scary stories about the black widow.

_____ 2. The author suggests all of the following **except**
a. The black widow preys on insects.
b. The female black widow may eat the male.
c. The black widow has a venomous bite that is always fatal to humans.
d. The web of a black widow looks messy.

_____ 3. By describing baby black widow spiders as pinpoint cannibals the author is implying that they
a. are exceedingly small.
b. feed on each other.
c. are warriors.
d. both a and b.

_____ 4. From this excerpt you could conclude that the widow's web is all of the following **except**
a. capable of ensnaring the black widow in a trap.
b. ugly.
c. messy but efficient.
d. architecturally complex.

_____ 5. The black widow does all of the following to its prey **except**
a. throw gummy silk on it.
b. kill it by biting it.
c. lower it to the ground.
d. suck out its liquefied innards.

Vocabulary in Context

Directions: In the paragraphs indicated in parentheses, find a word that correctly matches the definition given and write it in the space provided.

1. cast-off (1) ____________________
2. extremely small (2) ____________________
3. allowing light to pass through (3) ____________________
4. shed part or all of a coat or outer covering (3) ____________________
5. the outer layers or shells (4) ____________________
6. upright (4) ____________________
7. foul-smelling (4) ____________________
8. sufficiently developed; living (7) ____________________
9. having no specific pattern or purpose (7) ____________________
10. practical (10) ____________________
11. capable of being wounded or hurt (10) ____________________
12. an environment providing the food and shelter required for an animal to survive (10) ____________________

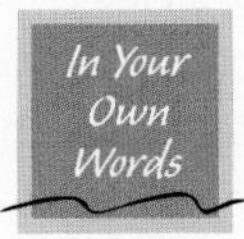

In Your Own Words

1. How many cultural references or literary allusions can you think of in regard to the spider? There are good spiders like Charlotte from *Charlotte's Web,* and there is the comic book hero Spider-Man. But there are also giant, nasty spiders, such as Shelob from *The Lord of the Rings* and Aragog from *Harry Potter.* Taken collectively, what do these references tell us about spiders?
2. What are your feelings about spiders? Do you think learning about spiders can help you appreciate them better and reduce the fear factor? Did this descriptive essay change your mind about spiders?

Written Assignment

Arachnophobia is an abnormal and persistent fear of spiders. It is among the most common of all phobias. People with arachnophobia feel uneasy in any area they believe could harbor spiders or that has signs of their webs. Their fear of spiders can produce panic attacks. Do you have any specific phobias? How do you think phobias are created? Could there be any advantages to having a specific phobia? Write a few paragraphs giving your opinion.

Internet Activity

1. Check out the following Web site to read an interview with Gordon Grice. Among other things, he discusses what led to his interest in spiders and how he came to marry his wife. You might want to read a fascinating excerpt from his book *The Red Hourglass,* describing the effects of a black widow bite. Write a paragraph discussing what you found most interesting about his interview.

www.randomhouse.com/boldtype/0598/grice/interview.html

2. Locate information about the black widow by typing "information about black widow spiders" into a search engine, or use one of the following Web sites:

   www.animals.nationalgeographic.com/animals/bugs/black-widow-spider.html

   www.desertusa.com/july97/du_bwindow.html

   Try to find information that was not covered in the reading selection. Briefly summarize your findings.

3. Do a search of Anansi tales and summarize your favorite. What is the moral or message of the tale that you selected?

REVIEW TEST 4: Topics, Main Ideas, Details, and Purpose

Multiple Choice

Directions: Read each passage. Then for each item, write the letter corresponding to the best answer.

A. If our business enterprises are to be as flexible and innovative at all levels as they need to be, our youngsters must be prepared to work with and through other people. While there will always be a need for a certain number of solo practitioners, the more usual requirement will be that combinations of individual skills are greater than their sums. Most of the important work will be done by groups, rather than by individual experts. . . . Young people must be taught how to work constructively together. Instead of emphasizing individual achievement and competition, the emphasis in the classroom should be on group performance. Students need to learn how to seek and accept criticism from their peers, to solicit help, and to give credit to others, where appropriate. They must also learn to negotiate—to articulate their own needs, to discern what others need and see things from others' perspectives, and to discover mutually beneficial outcomes.

(Robert Reich, "Dick and Jane Meet the New Economy," 1989)

______ 1. The main idea expressed in this passage is that
   a. most of the work in the future will be done by individuals working alone.
   b. there are advantages and disadvantages to working collectively.
   c. many students are capable of learning to work together productively.
   d. young people need to be taught how to work together productively so that our business enterprises can successfully meet new challenges.

______ 2. The author's primary purpose is to
   a. convince us of the necessity of emphasizing group activities in our educational systems.
   b. explain the dynamics of a business enterprise.
   c. entertain us with an interesting anecdote concerning the world of business.
   d. inform us of problems students are likely to face in the near future.

_____ 3. The examples of seeking and accepting criticism, soliciting help, and giving appropriate credit were used to illustrate
a. skills students need to develop in order to work individually.
b. skills students need to develop in order to work cooperatively.
c. requirements of a top-notch school system.
d. the complexity of a business organization.

_____ 4. The best title for the paragraph would be
a. "Group Dynamics in Action."
b. "Cooperative Learning."
c. "The Solo Practitioner."
d. "Group Learning and Business."

B. In the same way that doctors, janitors, lawyers, and industrial workers develop unique ways of looking at and responding to their work environment, so too do police officers. Police officers are often viewed as suspicious and authoritative. Police work is potentially dangerous, so officers need to be constantly aware of what is happening around them. They are frequently warned about what happens to officers who are too trusting. They learn about the many officers who have died in the line of duty because they did not exercise proper caution. On the street, they need to stay alert for signals that crimes may be in progress: an unfamiliar noise, someone "checking into" an alleyway, a secret exchange of goods. The working environment also demands that officers gain immediate control of potentially dangerous situations. They are routinely called on to demonstrate authority. Uniforms, badges, nightsticks, and guns signify authority—but officers soon learn that this authority is often challenged by a hostile public.

(Freda Adler, Gerhard O. W. Mueller, and William S. Laufer, *Criminal Justice*, 5/e, 2009)

_____ 5. The best title for this paragraph would be
a. "Jobs."
b. "The Outlook of Police Officers."
c. "The World of Work."
d. "Becoming a Police Officer."

_____ 6. All of the following were given as reasons for the effect of police work on an officer's outlook *except* for which?
a. a belief that courts are too lenient on criminals
b. a realization of what happens to officers when they are too trusting
c. the need to constantly monitor a situation
d. the need to assert authority

Written Assignment

Directions: Choose one of the following:

1. What kind of work gives you the most satisfaction? What kind of work do you find least rewarding? Write a paragraph discussing your answers.
2. Write a paragraph describing your job history. Explain why you liked or disliked your previous jobs. What did each of your previous jobs teach you about what you want to do as a future career?

3. Write a paragraph describing the difference between a "good" boss and a "bad" boss.
4. What kind of work do you want to do? Interview some people already active in the career of your choice. How do these people feel about their work? Write a paragraph discussing your findings.

Chapter Summary and Review

In this chapter, you learned how to determine whether the author's purpose is to entertain, inform, or persuade. You also learned how to summarize. Based on the material in Chapter 5, answer the following questions.

Short Answer

Directions: Answer the questions briefly.

1. What do you do when you summarize?
2. What question words should you keep in mind when writing a summary?

Vocabulary in Context

Directions: Choose one of the following words to complete the sentences below. Use each word only once.

audience	details	entertain	time-order
persuasive	purpose	textbooks	visual

3. An author needs to take into account the intended ______________, the people who will be reading the work.
4. An author who is telling a story or making an appeal to your imagination is probably trying to ______________ you.
5. What you read in your ______________ is probably informative writing.
6. Political advertisements that you receive in the mail before elections are good examples of ______________ writing.
7. A good summary of an article will include the main ideas and significant supporting ______________.
8. To determine an author's ______________, you should ask yourself why the author wrote the article.
9. An article written in the descriptive mode usually draws on ______________ perceptions.
10. Stories written in the narrative mode usually follow a(n) ______________ sequence.

CHAPTER

6 Transition Words and Patterns of Organization

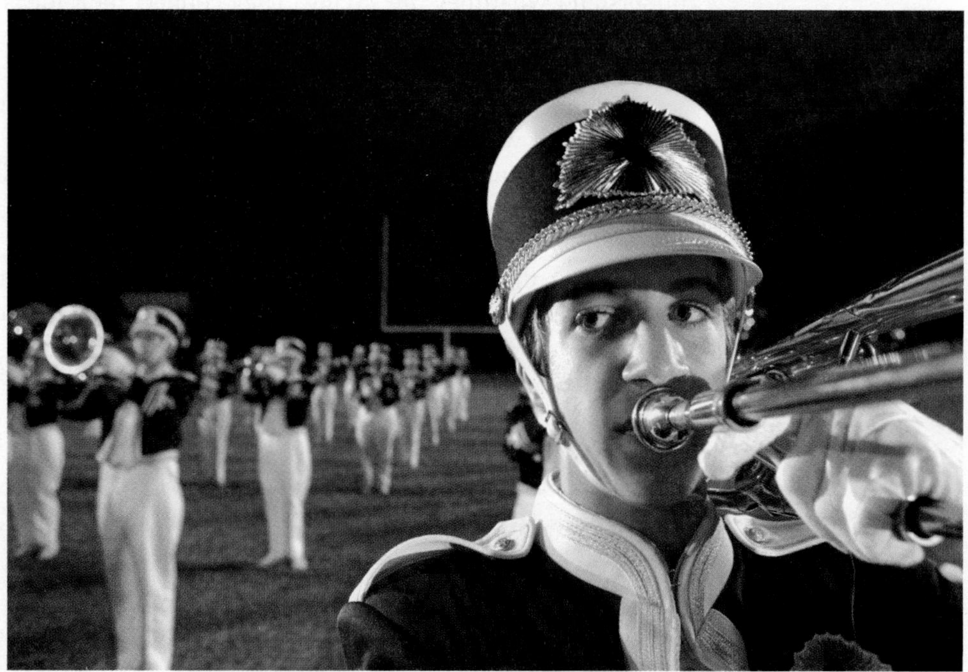

CHAPTER PREVIEW

In this chapter, you will

- Learn about transition words and phrases.
- Learn about patterns of paragraph organization.
- Learn about relationships within and between sentences.

Introduction to Transition Words and Patterns of Organization

Writers ordinarily try to write so that their thoughts flow smoothly and logically. They try to connect one idea with another in such a way that readers can easily understand what they are saying. They connect their ideas by means of **transition words.** In Latin, the prefix *trans* means "across." Transition words enable the author to carry you from one place in your reading "across" to another.

In your reading it is important to pay close attention to these transition words. These special words help show the relationships between ideas within sentences and ideas within paragraphs. Good drivers learn to closely watch the road ahead, using signposts or markers to make their trips easier and safer. Good readers learn to use the author's transition words, which signal what is ahead.

Look at the sentences below. The addition of a transition word signaling a contrast makes a big difference in our ability to understand Tom's situation.

1. Tom was very eager to leave for college. The thought of leaving familiar surroundings filled him with dread.
2. Tom was very eager to leave for college. **However,** the thought of leaving familiar surroundings filled him with dread.

The first example doesn't really make a lot of sense. If Tom is so eager to leave, why is he filled with dread? The addition of the transition word makes the situation clear in the second example. Although Tom wants to leave for college, he is understandably reluctant to give up his safe and comfortable surroundings.

Now look at these two sentences:

1. Karla did poorly in her English classes. She decided to switch her major to communication.
2. **Because** Karla did poorly in her English classes, she decided to switch her major to communication.

The first example makes us guess at the relationship between the two sentences. The addition of the transition word clarifies this relationship.

Following are two more examples. Study the two sentences. Which one is easier to read and understand?

1. Bill did everything he could think of to get a good grade in chemistry. He always attended class, did all of his homework assignments, and studied long hours. He hired a tutor.
2. Bill did everything he could think of to get a good grade in chemistry. He always attended class, did all of his homework assignments, and studied long hours. **In addition,** he hired a tutor.

The transition words *in addition* make the author's meaning easier to understand.

Now look at the next example.

1. Mary did not like to go to the dentist to have her teeth cleaned. She went anyway because she knew that it would be better for her in the long run.
2. **Although** Mary did not like to go to the dentist to have her teeth cleaned, she went anyway because she knew that it would be better for her in the long run.

The transition word *although* helps clarify the relationship between the two thoughts.

Transition Words

Words that can be used to show **classification or division (categories):**

break down	combine	lump
categorize	divide	split
class and subclass	group	type
classify	kind	

Words that can be used to show **cause-and-effect** relationships:

as a consequence	due to	resulting
as a result	for	since
because	for this reason	so
begin	hence	then
bring about	lead to	therefore
consequently	reaction	thus

Words that can be used to show **comparison:**

all	both	like
and	in comparison	likewise
as	just as	similarly

Words that can be used to show **contrast:**

although	in contrast	on the other hand
but	in opposition	rather than
despite	instead	though
even so	nevertheless	unlike
however	on the contrary	yet

Words that can be used to show **steps in a process:**

after	finally	process
afterward	first, second, third	step
at this point	next	then
at this stage	now	

Words that can be used to show **examples:**

for example	specifically	to illustrate
for instance	such as	
in particular	to demonstrate	

Words that can be used to **define:**

derives from	is described by	refers to
is called	means	term or concept
is defined as	originates from	

continued

Transition Words—*continued*

Words that can be used to show **chronological order:**

after	first, second, third	next
at last	finally	seasons
before	following	soon
currently	in a year, month, day	then
during	in the meantime	until

Words and symbols that can be used to show **listing (enumeration):**

follow, following	bullets(•)	functions
first, second, third	asterisks(*)	characteristics
colon (:)	numbers (1, 2, 3)	in addition
also	letters (a, b, c)	next, finally

Words that can be used to show **spatial order:**

above	front	on top
below	left	right
beyond	near	underneath
center	next to	

Words that can be used to show **addition**:

again	further	as well as
also	furthermore	besides
and	in addition	too
another	moreover	

The following transition words are often used in presenting an argument.

Words that can be used to show **summary and conclusion:**

finally	in short	therefore
hence	in summary	thus
in brief	overall	to conclude
in conclusion	so	to sum up

Words that can be used to show **reversal:**

granted that	nevertheless	unlike
instead	still	yet

Words that can be used to show **emphasis:**

as indicated	it's important	to repeat
as noted	once again	truly
certainly	to emphasize	unquestionably
here again	to remember	without a doubt

Words that can be used to show **concession:**

although	even though
despite	in spite of

Note: While lists of transition words are helpful, the groupings of the words given in this section are not perfect, and many of these words may be placed in more than one category. The only way to truly determine the function of a transition word is by studying the context of the sentence and the paragraph.

Exercise 1: Transitions

Directions: In the following sentences, provide an appropriate transition word. If you need help, use the transition words chart. Be sure your completed sentence makes sense.

1. (contrast) __________ he was failing all of his classes, he still had a positive attitude about school.
2. (cause) __________ she worked so many hours at her job, she had no time left for a social life.
3. We can (classification or division) __________ parents into two categories: those who are willing to use physical punishment on their children and those who are not.
4. Aggression is (definition) __________ any physical or verbal behavior that is directly intended to hurt someone.
5. (example) __________ a slap, a punch, and even a direct insult are all considered forms of aggression.
6. Suppose your boss insults you; (steps in a process) __________ you go home and yell at your wife, __________ she yells at your son, __________ he kicks his baby sister, __________ she pulls the dog's tail, and __________ the dog bites the mail carrier.
7. In the winter months of (months of the year in chronological order) __________, __________, and __________, assaults are at an all-time low. In the hotter seasons of __________, __________, and __________, violent crimes are more likely to occur.

Patterns of Organization

Writers organize their supporting sentences and ideas in ways called **patterns of organization.** The most common kinds of patterns of organization are (1) classification and division, (2) cause and effect, (3) comparison-contrast, (4) steps in a process, (5) examples, (6) definition, (7) chronological order, (8) listing, (9) spatial order, and (10) addition. A writer's chosen pattern of organization will affect the sort of transition words he or she uses. In the sections that follow, we will discuss patterns of organization and the relationships between patterns of organization and transition words.

Classification and Division

Classification is the process of organizing information into categories. We create a category by noting and defining group characteristics. The categories we create make it easier to analyze, discuss, and draw conclusions.

Have you ever scanned the classified ads section of the newspaper? If you have, you are already familiar with classification and division. Ads are not arranged randomly in the newspaper; otherwise, you would never be able to quickly locate the information you need. Instead, ads are grouped into categories, with each category further subdivided as much as needed.

Whenever you do the laundry, you are also probably putting things into categories. Many washers have categories such as: easy care, delicates, casuals, and cottons. Going to the grocery store is made a lot easier because the items are arranged by categories. Fresh fruits and vegetables are together in one location, canned goods in another, and household cleaning supplies in still another.

The following are the main categories of music according to iTunes.

Classical
Rock
Pop
Hip Hop or Rap
Jazz
Alternative

And then there are subgenres such as metal or rock ballads, and love songs.

(iTunes)

The details in many paragraphs are also organized using classification. Look at the three short paragraphs describing unhealthy expressions of anger. The author uses two specific categories to make it easier for us to understand the information being presented.

"Self-control is the quality that distinguishes the fittest to survive."
—George Bernard Shaw

According to psychologist Roger J. Daldrup, the unhealthy expression of anger can be **divided into two main types:** misdirection and suppression.

Misdirected anger, Daldrup says, "is the classic kicking the cat because you're angry at your spouse maneuver. Though people who misdirect their anger seem to be expressing it, they are just burying the real problem and creating more problems along the way."

Daldrup says, "complete suppression of anger doesn't work either because it creates a keyboard effect." If a person represses one emotion, "he begins repressing them all. This is similar to pressing down the soft pedal on the piano. That pedal will soften all the notes on the piano, just as dulling one emotion will dull them all."

(Roger J. Daldrup and Dodie Gust, *Freedom from Anger*, Pocket, 1988)

Now look at the following graphic organizer to gain a better understanding of this pattern.

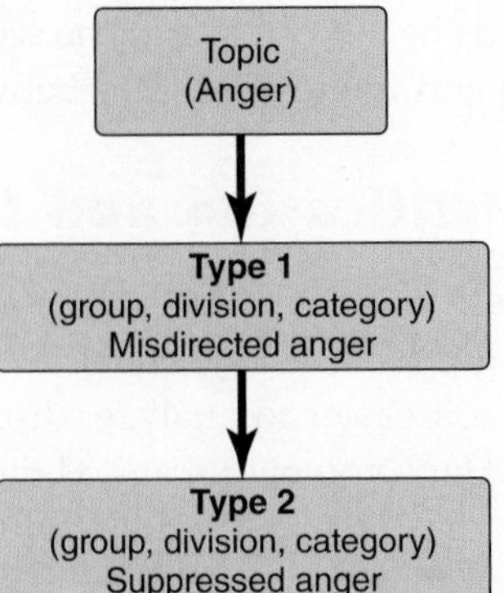

In recent years, many Americans have become fascinated with investigating their ancestral background. They use the information they gather to assemble family trees or genealogy charts showing the names, birth dates, marriages, and deaths of ancestors. In addition to being fun, studying the details of a family's medical past can provide early warning of health problems that might lie ahead

Three-Generation Genealogical Chart

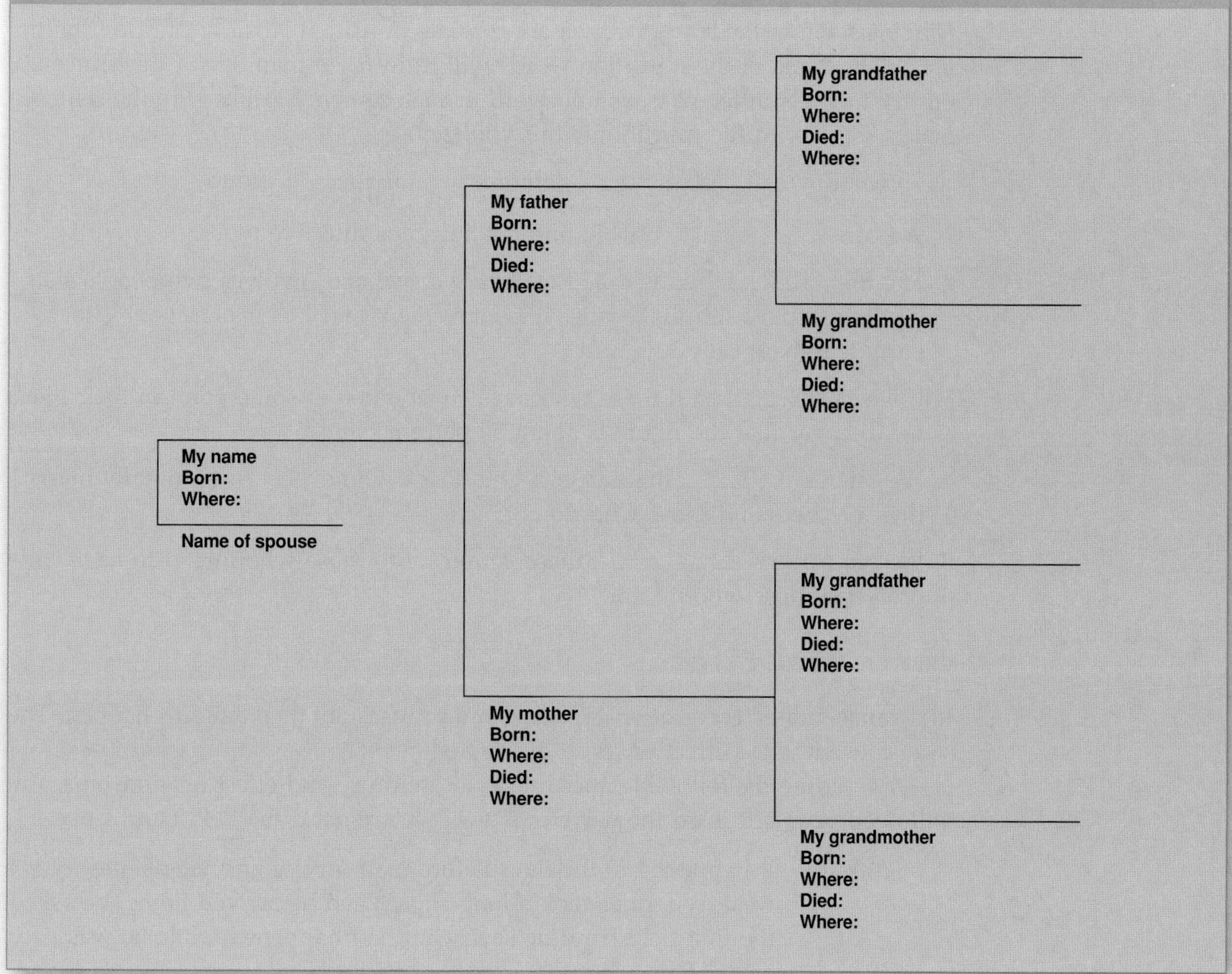

My name
Born:
Where:

Name of spouse

My father
Born:
Where:
Died:
Where:

My grandfather
Born:
Where:
Died:
Where:

My grandmother
Born:
Where:
Died:
Where:

My mother
Born:
Where:
Died:
Where:

My grandfather
Born:
Where:
Died:
Where:

My grandmother
Born:
Where:
Died:
Where:

for current family members. Many ailments are known to have genetic links, including cancer, diabetes, and alcoholism.

To practice classification, try making a genealogy chart or family tree. Talk with family members to try to gather information about your ancestors. Then record the information on a genealogical chart like the one above.

Written Assignment

In the process of doing your research, you may discover some interesting stories about your family. Some of these stories are likely true, but others may be part family myth. Write three of these stories in paragraph format, and share them with the class.

Internet Activity

Genealogy Web sites are available on the Internet. The following Web sites are especially helpful in looking up family tree information:

www.cyndislist.com
www.familysearch.org
www.ancestry.com
www.ellisislandrecords.org

Exercise 2: Classification and Division

Directions: Fill in the blank with an appropriate transition word or phrase from the list below. Some of the transition words will fit in more than one of the sentences, but try to use a different transition word in each sentence. Make sure the sentence makes sense with the transition word you choose.

break down   classify   combine   divide   group

1. We can ___________ cohabitating relationships into five types.
2. The first ___________ is called *temporary casual* and involves two people sharing living space simply because it is convenient and less expensive. Neither party is romantically involved.
3. If we ___________ all those who have cohabitated at some point in their lives, we discover that the figure is about 50 percent.
4. We can ___________ this category into those who expect to eventually marry their partners and those who do not.
5. We can further ___________ those couples into those who intend to have children and those who do not.

Cause and Effect

In a **cause-and-effect** relationship, one thing causes another thing to happen. The second event is the effect or result of the first event.

Try reading the following anecdote to locate cause-and-effect relationships. You will need people to read the narrator's, the farmer's, and the field hand's parts.

Narrator: It happened in the days before mail service and telephones. A wealthy farmer took a long trip. When he arrived home, he asked the first field hand he saw what had happened while he was away. This is how their conversation went:

Field hand: Well, the dog died.

Farmer: The dog died! How?

Field hand: The horses ran over him when they became frightened and ran out of the barn.

Farmer: What scared the horses? Why did they run?

Field hand: They were running from the flames when the barn caught on fire.

Farmer: My God! How did the barn catch on fire?

Field hand: Well, sir, flames jumped from the house and caught the barn on fire.

Farmer: From the house! Did the house burn down, too?

Field hand: Yep. The house is gone, too.

Farmer: How on earth did the house burn down?

Field hand: You see, one of the candles around your wife's casket fell over and caught the house on fire.

(*Contemporary's Building Basic Skills in Reading, Book I,* 1988)

Now complete the cause-and-effect sentences.

1. Because the candles on the wife's casket fell over, the ___________
2. Because flames jumped from the house, the ___________
3. Because the horses were scared, they ___________

You will encounter many cause-and-effect relationships in the textbooks you read for your various classes. The following paragraphs from a health textbook illustrate a cause-and-effect relationship; transition words are set in bold. Read the paragraphs and then study the graphic that follows.

"Angers are the sinners of the soul."
—Robert Fuller

Anger can have many **causes**, but its **effects** depend on your ability to manage it.

CAUSES

You cut yourself shaving. You burned the toast. You can't find the keys. Now the car won't start and you'll be late for work. No one did these things to you. They just happened. If you ask others, you'll find that such "disasters" are quite common and that they make almost everyone angry. We feel anger when we sense we've lost control, or when we feel vulnerable or afraid. We all have these feelings sometimes, and some of us are more easily irritated and annoyed than others.

EFFECTS

Anger signals your body to prepare for a fight. This **reaction** is commonly called "fight or flight." When you get angry, adrenaline and other hormones are released into the bloodstream. Then your blood pressure goes up, your heart beats faster, and you breathe faster. Anger can increase your chances of having another health problem, such as depression, heart attack, or stroke.

(http://www.cigna.com/healthwellness/hw/medical-topics/anger-hostility-and-violent-behavior-anger)

Paragraphs organized to show cause and effect are often structured in the following way.

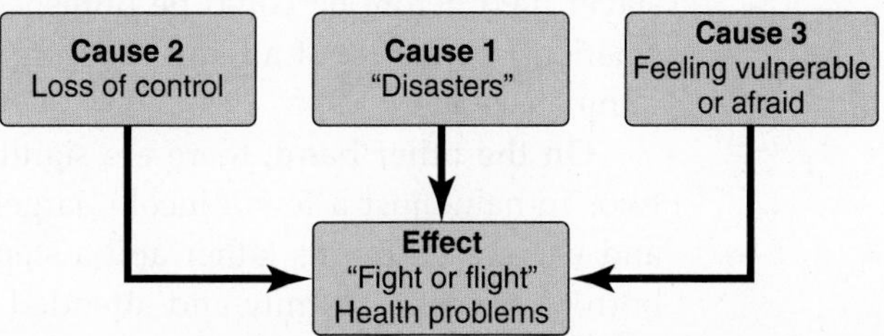

Exercise 3: Cause and Effect

Directions: Fill in the blank with an appropriate transition word or phrase from the list below. Some of the transition words will fit in more than one of the sentences, but try to use a different transition word in each sentence. Make sure the sentence makes sense with the transition you choose.

as a result because bring about reaction therefore

1. ___________ working moms with children under the age of five want a familiar face to care for their children, many are turning to grandparents and other relatives for help with child care.
2. Teens who begin drinking before they are old enough to drive have a higher chance of becoming alcoholics at some time in their lives. ___________, many organizations want to begin early-intervention programs with those teens who begin drinking early.
3. Last year, U.S. residents spent $207 billion on meals prepared by restaurants, with 51 percent of that total for takeout and delivery; ___________, online food order companies are beginning to see the potential for big business.

4. In ___________ to criticism by the Food and Drug Administration, R. J. Reynolds Tobacco Co. discontinued the use of Joe Camel, the cartoon character, in its ads.

5. In order to ___________ positive changes in race relations, more and more open forums discussing problems are being held around the country.

Comparison-Contrast

A **comparison** shows the similarities between two or more things, while a **contrast** shows the differences. Sometimes a writer compares (tells the similarities) and contrasts (tells the differences) at the same time. The following information from the Internet on Presidents Lincoln and Kennedy illustrates comparison-contrast, with transition words in bold.

> There are many curious parallels in the deaths of Presidents Abraham Lincoln and John Fitzgerald Kennedy. President Lincoln was elected in 1860. **And** exactly 100 years later, in 1960, Kennedy was elected president. **Both** were assassinated on a Friday in the presence of their wives. **Both** presidents were deeply involved in civil rights for blacks. **Both** President Lincoln and President Kennedy were succeeded by vice presidents named Johnson who were southern Democrats and former senators. **Both** men were killed by a bullet that entered the head from behind. Lincoln was killed in Ford's Theater. Kennedy met his death while riding in a Lincoln convertible made by the Ford Motor Company. **Both** assassins died before they could be brought to trial. In turn, each assassin's slayer died before he could be punished. Many believe that **both** assassinations were part of a giant conspiracy extending far beyond the one gunman.
>
> **On the other hand,** there are significant dissimilarities between the two. To name just a few: Lincoln, largely self-educated, was born poor and was raised by his father and a stepmother. **In contrast,** Kennedy was born to a wealthy family and attended elite private schools. Lincoln was president when the country was at war with itself during the Civil War. **In contrast,** Kennedy served during the Cold War when the country was unified against an enemy outside the United States.

To learn more about Ford's Theater and the Lincoln assassination, go to www.nps.gov/foth. To learn more about Kennedy, go to www.jfklibrary.org and take a virtual tour of the John Fitzgerald Kennedy Library and Museum in Boston.

In the two paragraphs that follow, the author explores how different cultures deal with strong emotions. Again, transition words are set in bold. After reading the paragraphs, study the comparison-contrast graphic organizer that follows.

> **Although** humans share four primary emotions—happiness, fear, anger, and sadness—we don't all express them in the same way. To express fear, Oriya women of Bhubansewar, India, extend their tongues out and downward, raise their eyebrows, and widen and cross their eyes. **In contrast**, Europeans and Americans tend to open their eyes wide, raise their eyebrows, and open their mouths wide. There are also significant cultural **differences** in how acceptable it is to express feelings. Some cultures (such as Asian cultures) are more emotionally restrictive. However, others (such as Italians) are more emotionally intense.

Expressing anger is rare for Tahitians and Utku Eskimos; **in contrast**, Americans and Western Europeans tend to frequently express this emotion. **Even though** cultures share the same emotions, not all situations evoke the same emotional response in all cultures. People from Bali laugh in response to grief and fall asleep in reaction to unfamiliar or frightening situations. Americans tend to see smiling at a stranger as a way to convey friendliness, **but** Japanese tend to interpret smiling at a stranger as being fake and shallow.

(Dale B. Hahn et al., *Focus on Health*, 9/e, McGraw-Hill, 2009, p. 31)

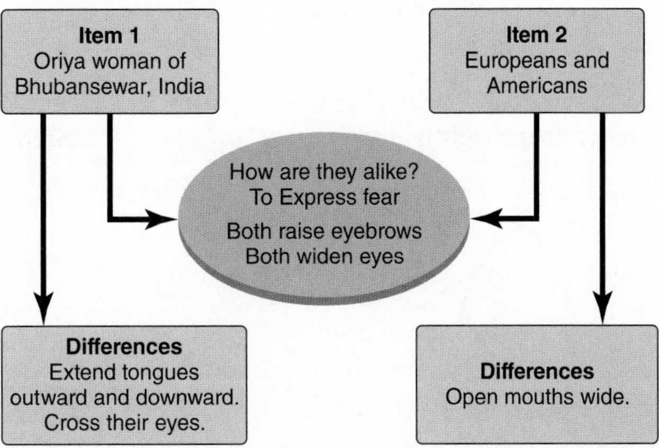

Exercise 4: Comparison-Contrast

Directions: Fill in the blank with an appropriate transition word or phrase from the list below. Some of the transition words will fit in more than one of the sentences, but try to use a different transition word in each sentence. Make sure the sentence makes sense with the transition you choose.

although both however just as on the other hand

1. In order to live a healthy lifestyle, people are increasingly being told to ____________ eat right and exercise.
2. Joan's advisor gave her some good reasons for going to graduate school, but, ________________, he also gave her some good reasons for directly starting her career.
3. There are two ways to go to get to the mall, and one way is ____________ good as the other.
4. ____________ linemen on a professional football team need to be large, they also need to be fast.
5. Judging by all the dark clouds in the sky, it looked like it was going to rain. ____________, around noontime the sun came out.

Written Assignment

For practice, write a short paragraph comparing and contrasting two ordinary household objects such as a pencil and a pen, or a fork and a spoon. Or you might want to try comparing and contrasting an iPod with CDs and records. Include some of the "compare and contrast" words found in the transition words chart.

Steps in a Process

In the **steps-in-a-process** pattern, something is explained or described in a step-by-step manner. The sequences are clearly identified by specific transition words. A lot of scientific writing uses this particular pattern. In addition, anytime we try to show how to make or do something, we are probably using this pattern of organization. Just for fun, try following these directions explaining how to draw cartoon characters. (You will need a separate piece of paper for your sketches.)

> It's easy to draw a cartoon. Just take it step by step. First, start by drawing a shape in pencil, and then lightly sketch in the features. Remember to exaggerate!

Step 1. Draw a basic shape lightly and loosely in pencil.

Step 2. Lightly sketch in the features.

Step 3. Go back over the drawing darkening some of your lines.

Step 4. Erase pencil lines and add details to make your drawing personal.

In the paragraph that follows, the author gives a step-by-step account of how to deal with anger in other people. Read the paragraph and then study the graphic organizer.

Anger can be infectious, and it disrupts cooperation and communication. If someone you're with becomes very angry, respond by reacting not with anger but with calm. **First,** try to validate the other person by acknowledging that he or she has some reason to be angry. This does not mean apologizing if you don't think you're to blame or accepting verbal abuse, which is always inappropriate. **At this point,** try to focus on solving the problem by allowing the person to explain why he or she is so angry and what can be done to alleviate the situation. **Finally,** if the person cannot be calmed, it may be best to disengage, at least temporarily. **Then** after a time-out, you may have better luck trying to solve the problem rationally.

(Paul M. Insel et al., *Connect Core Concepts in Health,* 13/e, McGraw-Hill, 2014, p. 52)

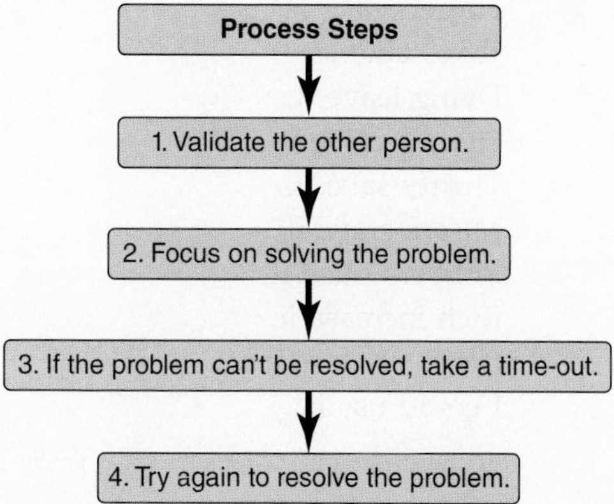

Exercise 5: Steps in a Process

Directions: Fill in the blank with an appropriate transition word or phrase from the list below. Some of the transition words will fit in more than one of the sentences, but try to use a different transition word in each sentence. Make sure the sentence makes sense with the transition you choose.

at this point   final   first   process   second   stages

1. The ___________ of sleeping is complicated, with people progressing through four distinct, 90-minute stages during a night's rest.
2. Each of these sleep ___________ is associated with a unique pattern of brain waves.
3. In the ___________ stage, as people begin to go to sleep, images sometimes appear, as if they were viewing still photos.
4. It is ___________, in stage 1, that rapid eye movement, or REM, sleep occurs. REM sleep is usually accompanied by dreams, which, whether people remember them or not, are experienced by *everyone* during some part of the night.
5. As sleep becomes deeper, people enter the ___________ stage, which is characterized by a slower, more regular wave pattern.
6. By the time sleepers arrive at the ___________ stage, they are least responsive to outside stimulation. Stage 4 sleep is most likely to occur during the early part of the night.

(Robert S. Feldman, *Essentials of Understanding Psychology,* 10/e, 2013)

Examples

A paragraph of **examples** usually gives a general statement of the main idea and then presents one or more concrete examples to provide support for this idea. Many writers place the most important or convincing example either first, as an attention-getter, or last, as a dramatic climax. While the terms *example* and *illustration* often are used interchangeably, an illustration is usually longer, and there may be only one in the paragraph.

In this poem, Richard Armour gives a series of short examples about the different ways people relate to money.

MONEY

Workers earn it,
Spendthrifts burn it,
Bankers lend it,
Women spend it,
Forgers fake it,
Taxes take it,
Dying leave it,
Heirs receive it,
Thrifty save it,
Misers crave it,
Robbers seize it,
Rich increase it,
Gamblers lose it . . .
I could use it.

(Richard Armour, "Money," *Yours for the Asking, a Book of Light Verse*, 1942)

The following paragraphs are on aggression, which is defined as "hostile assault intended to inflict harm." After studying the graphic organizer for paragraph 1, create your own graphic organizers for paragraphs 2 and 3. The main ideas in both paragraphs on aggression are underlined.

1. We need look no further than the daily paper or the nightly news to be bombarded with **examples** of aggression, both on a societal level (war, invasion, assassination) and on an individual level (crime, child abuse, and the many petty cruelties that humans are capable of inflicting on one another).

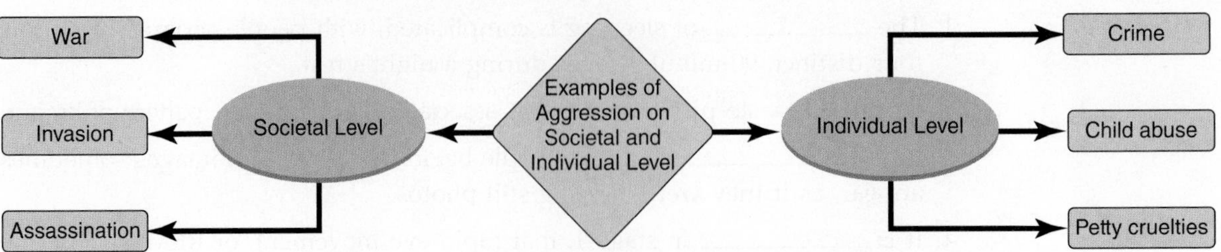

2. <u>Sometimes aggressive behavior is a reaction to frustration</u>. **For example,** suppose you've been working on a paper that is due for a class early the next morning, and your computer printer runs out of ink just before you can print out the paper. You rush to the store to buy more ink, only to find the sales clerk locking the door for the day. Even though the clerk can see you gesturing and begging him to open the door, he refuses, shrugging his shoulders and pointing to a sign that indicates when the store will open the next day. At that moment, the feelings you experience toward the sales clerk probably place you on the verge of real aggression, and you are

undoubtedly seething inside. Frustration produces anger, leading to a *readiness* to act aggressively.

(Robert S. Feldman, *Understanding Psychology*, 11/e, 2013)

3. It appears that temporary climate changes can affect human behavior. **For example,** William Griffitt found that compared with students who answered questionnaires in a room with normal temperature, those who did so in an uncomfortably hot room (over 90°F) reported feeling more tired and aggressive and expressed more hostility to strangers. In the real world, drivers without air conditioning in heat-stricken Phoenix, Arizona, are much more likely to honk at a stalled car. And, **in another instance,** during the 1986–1988 major league baseball seasons, the number of batters hit by a pitch was two-thirds greater for games played above 90°F than for games played below 80°F. Pitchers weren't wilder on hot days—they had no more walks and wild pitches. They just clobbered more batters! Across the Northern Hemisphere, not only do hotter days have more violent crimes, so do hotter seasons of the year, hotter summers, hotter years, hotter cities, and hotter regions. If a 4-degree Fahrenheit global warming occurs, scientists project that the United States alone would actually see at least 50,000 more serious assaults.

(David G. Myers, *Social Psychology*, 9/e, 2008)

Exercise 6: Examples

Directions: Fill in the blank with an appropriate transition word or phrase from the list below. Some of the transition words will fit in more than one of the sentences, but try to use a different transition word in each sentence. Make sure the sentence makes sense with the transition you choose.

for example   for instance   in particular   specifically   such as

1. Today's college classrooms include many different kinds of students, ____________ Donna, who entered college after working for eight years following high school.
2. One avenue of self-discovery in college is the exploration of new career choices. ____________, James was originally interested in a career in teaching, but has since decided to pursue a career in business.
3. ____________, James has decided to become a marketing major.
4. In the 1970s, high school girls were less likely to go to college. Today, girls ____________ are more likely than boys to go to college.
5. However, even today many women avoid taking academic risks. ____________, they stay away from taking mathematics and science classes.

Definition

A paragraph of **definition** will define, clarify, or explain a key term. Definitions can be developed by providing dictionary meanings or personal meanings. They can also be developed by means of examples or by comparing and contrasting the key word with other words.

In *The Adventures of Tom Sawyer,* Mark Twain **defines** work as "whatever a body is obliged to do while play consists of whatever a body is not obliged to do."

In the following paragraphs, an attempt is made to clarify the meaning of anger by describing its distinguishing characteristics and key components. Study the two paragraphs and the graphic organizer that follows.

Anger is a normal emotion with a wide range of intensity, from mild irritation and frustration to rage. It is a reaction to a perceived threat to ourselves, our loved ones, our property, our self-image, or some part of our identity. Anger is a warning bell that tells us that something is wrong.

Anger has three components: (1) Physical reactions, usually starting with a rush of adrenaline and responses such as increased heart rate, blood pressure, and tightening muscles. (2) The cognitive experience of anger, or how we perceive and think about what is making us angry. We might think that something that happened to us is wrong, unfair, and undeserved. (3) Behavior, or the way we express our anger. There is a wide range of behavior that signals anger. We may look and sound angry, turn red, raise our voices, clam up, slam doors, storm away, or otherwise signal to others that we are angry. We may also state that we are angry and why, ask for a time-out, request an apology, or ask for something to change.

(pbs.org/thisemotionallife/topic/anger)

Topic: Anger

Definition: Anger, an emotional reaction to a perceived threat, may range in severity from irritation to rage.

Characteristics/components: physical reactions, cognitive experience, behavior

Examples of Physical Reactions: Increased heart rate, blood pressure, and tightening muscles.

Examples of Cognitive Experience: Something that happened to us is wrong, unfair, undeserved.

Examples of Expression of Anger: Look and sound angry; ask for time-out, apologies, or changes

Exercise 7: Definition

Directions: Fill in the blank with an appropriate transition word or phrase from the list below. Some of the transition words will fit in more than one of the sentences, but try to use a different transition word in each sentence. Make sure the sentence makes sense with the transition you choose.

described as　　is called　　is defined as　　means　　term

1. Middle adulthood ____________ the years between 40 and 65.
2. A middle-aged person is sometimes ____________ someone with grown children and/or elderly parents.
3. Many people age 40 and older need reading glasses for presbyopia, a lessened ability to focus on near objects—a condition associated with aging. (The prefix *presby* ____________ "with age.")
4. The pressures created by a society that believes in looking young, acting young, and being young—added to the real physical losses that people may suffer as they get older—may contribute to what ____________ the midlife crisis.
5. The ____________ *empty nest* refers to the period when the last child leaves home.

(Diane E. Papalia and Ruth Duskin Feldman, *Experience Human Development*, 12/e, 2012)

Chronological Order

The word *chronological* comes from the Greek root *chron,* which means "time." The **chronological** pattern of organization involves arranging events in time in the order that they actually happened. For this reason, historical essays and articles that are date oriented are usually organized by this method. Paragraphs written with this pattern are usually very easy to recognize.

This short poem illustrates the key elements of the chronological pattern because the events are ordered by time.

Solomon Grundy

Solomon Grundy
Born on a **Monday,**
Christened on **Tuesday,**
Married on **Wednesday,**
Took ill on **Thursday,**
Worse on **Friday,**
Died on **Saturday,**
Buried on **Sunday,**
This is the end
Of Solomon Grundy.
—Anonymous

The following paragraphs from *Anger: The Misunderstood Emotion* are in the chronological order pattern. Study the paragraphs and the graphic organizer that follows.

Popular opinion has it that time heals all wounds, that human beings are naturally resilient. But some people do not heal from the wounds of divorce. In **1971,** Judith Wallerstein, then working with Joan Kelly, began a study of 131 children and adolescents from sixty families, and their divorcing parents, in Marin County, California. The researchers reinterviewed all family members **eighteen months later,** again **five years after** divorce, and again **ten and fifteen years after** divorce. The parents were upper-middle-class, mostly white, and had been married anywhere from four to twenty-three years. The children were all developmentally normal, doing well in school, and in good psychological health—**until** the divorce hit them.

Wallerstein found that even **after ten years,** half of the women and one-third of the men in her study were still intensely angry at their former spouses, and that the consequences of this anger and conflict for their children were often disastrous.

(Carol Tavris, *Anger: The Misunderstood Emotion,* 1989)

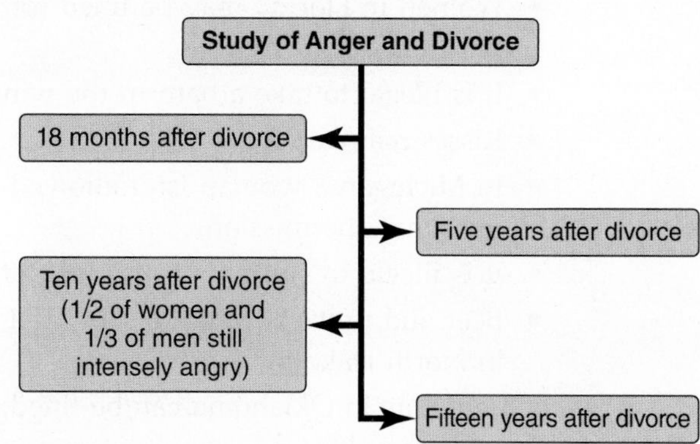

Exercise 8: Chronological Order

Directions: Fill in the blank with an appropriate transition word or phrase from the list below. Some of the transition words will fit in more than one of the sentences, but try to use a different transition word in each sentence. Make sure the sentence makes sense with the transition you choose.

following frequently 1853 1890 then until

1. In ___________, Vincent van Gogh was born to a Dutch Protestant minister in the town of Groot-Zundert, in Holland.
2. His early life was spent as a lay preacher to the miners of the region and so not ___________ the age of 27 did he begin to take a serious interest in art.
3. ___________ he went to live with his brother Theo, an art dealer in France, where he met the painter Paul Gauguin.
4. The two artists ___________ quarreled, and after one very intense argument, van Gogh cut off a portion of his ear.
5. ___________ that bizarre incident, van Gogh committed himself to an asylum where much of the work we now admire, including *Starry Night,* was created.
6. Unfortunately, his despair deepened, and so in July of ___________ he shot himself to death.

(Mark Getlein, *Living with Art,* 10/e, 2013)

Listing

When an author simply lists information without regard to order, the pattern of organization is referred to as simple **listing** or enumeration. Sometimes authors use numbers (1, 2, 3), letters (a, b, c), bullets (•), or asterisks (*) to show the individual items in the list. Or they will say *first, second, third,* and so on. Sometimes they use words such as *in addition, next,* or *finally.* Often a colon will be used at the start of a list. A variation of the word *follow* may indicate that a list is about to begin.

Below is a list of laws that were actually enforced at one time in the United States. Many are still "on the books." What do you think the original purpose of these laws might have been?

- It is illegal to buy a bag of peanuts after sunset and before sunrise the next day in Alabama.
- In California, it is illegal to trip horses for entertainment, to possess bear gall bladders, or to peel an orange in your hotel room.
- It is illegal to throw shoes at weddings in Colorado.
- In Connecticut, it is illegal to walk across the street on your hands.
- Women in Florida may be fined for falling asleep under a hair dryer, as can the salon owner.
- It is illegal to take a bath in the wintertime in Indiana.
- Kisses may last for as much as, but no more than, 5 minutes in Iowa.
- In Michigan a woman isn't allowed to cut her own hair without her husband's permission.
- It is illegal to slurp soup in New Jersey.
- Beer and pretzels can't be served at the same time in any bar or restaurant in North Dakota.
- Violators in Oklahoma can be fined, arrested, or jailed for making ugly faces at a dog.

- The state law of Pennsylvania prohibits singing in the bathtub.
- In Tennessee, it is illegal to shoot any game other than whales from a moving automobile.
- In Texas, it is illegal to take more than three sips of beer at a time while standing.
- It is an offense in Washington State to pretend your parents are rich.

(Robert H. Bohm and Keith N. Haley, *Introduction to Criminal Justice*, 6/e, 2010)

Spatial Order

The spatial order pattern is used to describe the location or placement of something. Many of the spatial order transition words are prepositions. The following anecdote illustrates spatial order, with transition words in bold.

> A poor man lived **inside** a crowded house, and he was very angry. **Within** his house, he had to contend with his wife, his six children, his mother-in-law, and a boarder. When he lay down to rest at night, there was no room to the **left** of him and no room to the **right.** He complained to a friend who lived **close** by, and the friend gave him one sentence of advice: "Bring your goat **into** the house." A week later the man returned and complained to his friend about the stench and dirt **within** his house from the goat. His friend listened and said: "Bring your chickens **into** the house." A week later, the poor man was a nervous wreck with chickens living **above** him in the rafters of his cottage and the goat making his bed **next to** him, keeping him awake all night. **Outside,** he again ran into his friend who listened closely to his complaints and then said: "Put out the goat." The man returned to his friend a few days later and announced that things were better, but he still felt too crowded. The friend said: "Put the chickens **outside**." When the man returned a week later, he said to his friend: "You are a genius! Now I have room all **around** me. My house is as big as a mansion!"

In the paragraph that follows, a description is given of the famous painting the *Third of May* by Goya. Again, transition words are set in bold.

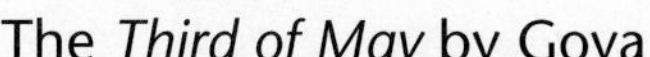

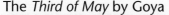

The *Third of May* by Goya

Goya, The *Third of May,* 1808

The *Third of May* by Spanish painter Francisco Goya is a powerful anti-war statement. The painting shows French troops shooting unarmed Spanish civilians. Goya lit the night-time scene with a lamp on the ground **near** the soldiers' feet, casting a harsh light. In the **rear**, the church is dark. In the **left foreground**, a bloody body falls **toward** the viewer. **Behind** is a line of other victims. The victims are the **center** of interest, with a white-shirted man throwing his arms wide in a defiant gesture. With their backs to the viewer, the faceless figures of the firing squad stand locked together directly **opposite** the victims.

Exercise 9: Spatial Order

Directions: Fill in the blank with an appropriate transition word or phrase from the list below. Some of the transition words will fit in more than one of the sentences, but try to use a different transition word in each sentence. Make sure the sentence makes sense with the transition you choose.

across beneath next to north-south under west

1. On December 26, 2004, an earthquake measuring 9.0 occurred ____________ of the Indonesian island of Sumatra.
2. The focus was about 6 miles ____________ the ocean floor.
3. The ocean floor was suddenly uplifted, triggering a tsunami that created a path of destruction ____________ the 2,800-mile-wide Indian Ocean.
4. If you are ever in an earthquake, stay indoors and seek protection ____________ a heavy desk or table. Be sure to protect your head.
5. You can also stand under door frames or ____________ inner walls, as these are the least likely to collapse.
6. The San Andreas fault runs ____________ for 807 miles through California.

Addition

The addition pattern is often used to discuss a topic in greater depth or to expand or elaborate on it.

In this poem, William Cole uses the addition pattern.

Lies, All Lies

There is no ham in hamburger,
And "allspice" is a cheat;
Applesauce is not a sauce,
And sweetbreads aren't sweet.
There is no horse in horseradish—
Why are we so misled?
There's no cheese in headcheese,
And sweetbreads aren't bread!

(William Cole, *A Boy Named Mary Jane, and Other Silly Verse,* Avon Books, 1979)

The following paragraph on jealousy illustrates the addition pattern. The addition transition words are in bold.

How common is jealousy? Very common. Many college students play jealousy games. They flirt openly **and** even manufacture tales to make their partners pay more attention to them. Feelings of jealousy can lead to perceiving anyone as a rival. When women are jealous, they turn to food. **In addition** they turn to friends for consolation. A small group of women **also** turn to vigorous exercise to relieve the stress of jealous feelings. Not only might exercise better reduce stress; **additionally** it will do so without adding pounds, which can lead to self-deprecation **as well as** depression. Women tend to **further** express sexual jealousy through behaviors such as improving their own physical appearance, demanding increased commitment from the partner, **as well as** trying to make the partner jealous himself. Jealousy in women may derive from low self-esteem, feelings of inadequacy **and** a lack of self-confidence.

(David Knox, *Choices in Relationships*, 9/e, 2008)

Exercise 10: Addition

Directions: Fill in the blank with an appropriate transition word or phrase from the list below. Some of the transition words will fit in more than one of the sentences, but try to use a different transition word in each sentence. Make sure the sentence makes sense with the transition you choose.

and also another furthermore in addition too

Want to have a happier life? Here are some practical suggestions based on recent research studies.

1. Develop strategies for coping with stress __________ hardship. Just thinking "this __________ shall pass" seems to help.
2. Count your blessings. __________, savor life's joys.
3. Practice acts of kindness __________.
4. __________ good suggestion is to learn to forgive those who have wronged you in the past.
5. __________, it's important to take care of your body by getting enough sleep and exercise.

Internet Activity

There is a great deal of material on the Internet on the topic of anger. Locate two Web sites that discuss anger, and determine the purpose of each site. The following sites might be a good place to start your search:

www.apa.org (then type in "anger")

www.angermgmt.com

The last three letters of any Internet address indicate the type of the site: "org" stands for organization, "net" for networking, and "com" for commercial. Other site types are "edu" for education, "gov" for government, and "mil" for military. This information may help you determine the sort of information found on each site.

Exercise 11: Practice with Transition Words: King Tutankhamen—The Celebrity Mummy

Directions: Write the correct word(s) in the blank provided.

1. The burial vault of King Tutankhamen was opened in 1923. The coffin was made of 242 pounds of pure gold and was sculpted into a jeweled effigy of

the king himself. When the mummy inside was unwrapped, it ____________ was covered with jewels.

a. despite
b. truly
c. also
d. besides

2. ____________, the mummy was in a state of extreme decay, possibly from use of excessive amounts of embalming oil. ____________, the flesh stuck to the inside of the coffin, meaning the mummy had to be cut up in order to remove it.

a. In spite of; Above
b. However; In fact
c. Again; Likely
d. As well as; Due to

3. The lengthy embalming process, which took over 70 days to complete, included thoroughly washing the body, removing the internal organs, covering the body with sodium, drying it, coating it with resin, and wrapping it in linen. ____________, the pharaoh was ready to be displayed to the public.

a. First
b. Finally
c. In short
d. All

4. The media was ecstatic ____________ this was the first time that a pharaoh's tomb had been discovered reasonably intact in the Valley of the Kings. They marveled at the precious objects the tomb contained, including gold sandals, rings, necklaces, bracelets, and amulets. And, in case the king wanted to travel, he was given two full-size gold chariots.

a. because
b. unlike
c. to emphasize
d. overall

5. ____________ robbers had tunneled into King Tutankhamen's tomb shortly after he was interred, they had taken very little. About all they accomplished was to desecrate the holy site.

a. Again
b. Although
c. Underneath
d. Hence

6. ____________, priests were called to purify the site. They quickly resealed the tomb, and then they left behind curses to intimidate those who would attempt to enter the sacred shrine again.

a. In spite of
b. As noted
c. So
d. Yet

7. Inside the tomb over a hundred *ushabti,* three-foot-high statues of servants, were lined up ______________ the king's body, ready to wait on him in death as they had waited on him in life.

a. as indicated

b. next to

c. further

d. right

8. King Tutankhamen ascended the throne at age 9, died at age 19, and never actually participated in a battle. ______________, his tomb is crowded with images of him as a great warrior.

a. Yet

b. Finally

c. Here again

d. Thus

9. Tutankhamen became pharaoh after his childhood marriage to the daughter of the pharaoh Akhenaten. ______________ his father-in-law Akhenaten, King Tutankhamen is not considered to be a great pharaoh.

a. Overall

b. Unlike

c. Furthermore

d. Without a doubt

10. ______________, he was a totally innocuous one.

a As well as

b. Once again

c. Hence

d. Instead

11. He has achieved fame solely ______________ his tomb was discovered intact. Debris from other nearby tombs had covered the entrance hiding the tomb from view. ______________ Carter removed the waste material on November 4, 1922, he discovered one stone step leading downwards. He uncovered 15 more steps and then a blocked doorway. As Carter slowly worked his way into the tomb, he described it this way: "My eyes grew accustomed to the light, details of the room within emerged slowly, and gold—everywhere the glint of gold."

a. again; Furthermore

b. because; After

c. nevertheless; Despite

d. still; Once again

Exercise 12: Predicting the Pattern

Directions: The following are headings in actual textbook chapters. Carefully study the given topic and the transition words used by the author in the heading. What type of pattern of organization would you expect the author to use in the chapter? Place the letter of your choice on the line.

a. classification or division (categories)

b. cause and effect

c. comparison and contrast
d. steps in a process
e. examples
f. definition
g. chronological order
h. listing
i. spatial order

______ 1. The Birth Process

______ 2. History of Prisons in America

______ 3. The Prison Experience: Men vs. Women

______ 4. Space Planning Considerations in Interior Design

______ 5. Examples of Major Life Changes and Daily Hassles

______ 6. How Living Things Are Classified

______ 7. The Causes of the Civil War

______ 8. What Are the Major Categories of Rock-Forming Minerals?

______ 9. The Following Are Some Tips on Handling a Stalker

______ 10. The Definition of Sport

______ 11. Comparing Cultural Variation within Societies

______ 12. Types of Crime

______ 13. Physiological Effects of Caffeine

______ 14. The History of Plants and Medicine

Exercise 13: Identifying Patterns of Organization and Transition Words

Directions: Identify the dominant pattern of organization for each paragraph. You may look at the transition words chart if necessary.

1. Quick French Onion Soup (serves 4–6)
In medium fry pan, first saute onion in butter until golden and tender, about 15 minutes. Next, stir in flour. Then add remaining ingredients. Simmer uncovered at least 20 minutes, stirring occasionally. Serve piping hot. For a final touch, if desired, top with melba toast and shredded Gruyere cheese.

____

Transition Words: ______________________________

2. In ancient Rome, whenever a man wished to be elected to a public office, he canvassed for votes wearing a white robe or toga. The purpose of this was to enable the populace to easily recognize him. The Latin word for white is *candidus,* so the potential official came to be known as a *candidatus,* which means "a person clothed in white." From this derivation comes our English word *candidate.*

____

Transition Words: ______________________________

3. If you were a child growing up in the 1950s and you used the f-word, there would probably have been at least a discussion, and more than

likely, a bar of soap would have been put to good use. In contrast, today this word is uttered routinely just about everywhere. Kids hear the word riding the bus to school, in class, in the lyrics of many songs, and on regular network TV. In the 1950s, profanity was a shocking rarity. But, in the 2000s, profanity has become part of our language. Some psychologists even say using curse words is healthy because it allows us to express our deepest emotions. Young people of today are so used to hearing the f-word that many linguists predict it will end up meaning as little as the standard curse word of the 1950s, "hell."

____

Transition Words: ____________________________

4. One hundred years ago, no one "exercised" because their daily life was strenuous enough. As a direct result of the many labor-saving devices we have today, the typical American's weight is rising. Most Americans don't participate in athletics, and many hire others to do their routine home-maintenance chores. Thus, they get almost no vigorous exercise. The most exercise many get is changing the channel on the remote control. The sad consequence of becoming a sedentary, TV-watching nation is that one in three adults is currently overweight.

____

Transition Words: ____________________________

5. The Ripley's Museum in Orlando, Florida, is apparently the place to go for those seeking to start a family. In late 1994, two ebony fertility statues were placed in the office lobby. Three employees immediately became pregnant after rubbing the belly of the statue. In another instance, three wives of office personnel all became pregnant despite the fact one was using birth-control pills. In another example, eight women who visited the office became pregnant, including a woman who accidentally bumped into the statue while delivering a package. One Texas woman with five daughters recently came to make the pilgrimage in the hope of having a son. She's convinced the "reproductive magic" will work for her.

____

Transition Words: ____________________________

6. In a study of workaholics, those people who work too much, Marilyn Machlowitz found that workaholics exhibited the following characteristics:

   1. Tend to be intense and energetic,
   2. Sleep less than most people,
   3. Have difficulty taking vacations,
   4. Spend most of their waking time working,
   5. Frequently eat while they work,
   6. Prefer work to play,
   7. Work hard at making the most of their time,
   8. Tend to blur the distinction between work and play,
   9. Can and do work anywhere and everywhere.

   (Jerrold S. Greenberg, *Comprehensive Stress Management*, 13/e, 2013)

____

Transition Words: ____________________________

7. Consider the gender differences market researchers observe when studying the food preferences of men and women. Women eat more fruit. On the other hand, men are more likely to eat meat. As one food writer put it, "Boy food doesn't grow. It is hunted or killed." Men are more likely to eat Frosted Flakes or Corn Pops, but women prefer multigrain cereals. Men are big root beer drinkers, but women account for the bulk of sales of bottled water.

(Michael R. Solomon, *Consumer Behavior*, 6/e, 2004)

____

Transition Words: ______________________________

Exercise 14: Identifying Patterns of Organization and Transition Words

Directions: Choose the correct pattern of organization by noting the transition words.

1. As the "global village" expands and Americans are exposed to an ever-greater variety of cultures and traditions, we find ourselves increasingly joining in the rituals of many ethnic groups and nations. Perhaps the most obvious example is St. Patrick's Day. On every 17th of March, a sea of green engulfs the streets, offices, retail establishments, and bars of all fifty states—and many "wearers o' the green" have not a trace of Irish in their background. Cinco de Mayo ("the fifth of May") is an example of a Mexican-American holiday just now coming into its own. The celebration commemorates Mexico's defeat of the French in the battle of Puebla in 1862. Cinco de Mayo is drawing ever-larger crowds of non-Hispanics who enjoy sharing traditional foods like tamales, roasted corn, and other ethnic specialties, and who love to sway to the beat of mariachi, ranchera, and banda music. Street vendors can't keep up with the demand for spicy Mexican food—and the taps flow freely with Dos Equis, Corona, and other popular Mexican beers.

(Wayne A. Payne and Dale B. Hahn, *Understanding Your Health*, 6/e, 2000)

____

Transition Words: ______________________________

2. If you want to break the caffeine habit, the following steps may help you to achieve your goal. First, gradually switch from regular to decaffeinated coffee by mixing them before brewing, or substitute decaffeinated instant coffee for some of the caffeinated instant you drink. Then, increase the decaffeinated proportion each day while using more low-fat milk in your coffee to reduce the amount of caffeinated beverage you consume. Next, switch little by little to smaller cups from larger mugs and glasses. If your favorite mug is a comfort to you, don't discard it, but fill it with a caffeine-free beverage. Change your daily routine by taking a walk instead of your usual coffee break. At this stage, if you find your coffee paraphernalia to be a temptation, get rid of those mugs, pots, filters, and grinders. If you get enough sleep, exercise regularly, and follow a healthy diet, you'll be less reliant on the artificial "pep" that caffeine provides.

(Wayne A. Payne and Dale B. Hahn, *Understanding Your Health*, 6/e, 2000)

____

Transition Words: ______________________________

3. Many of us experience anger and frustration at one time or another, but for some people these feelings represent a pervasive, characteristic set of personality traits defined as the Type A behavior pattern. Type A individuals are described by experts as being competitive, aggressive, and hostile, both verbally and nonverbally—especially when interrupted while trying to complete a task. They exhibit a driven quality regarding their work and show a constant sense of urgency about time.

   (Robert S. Feldman, *Understanding Psychology*, 8/e, 2008)

   ____

   Transition Words: ______________________________

4. On a more general level, the Internet has brought us both positive and negative consequences. On the one hand, it entertains us, informs us, links us with friends and family, provides us with the world's greatest reference library, and stimulates commerce. On the other hand, it opens up whole new areas of concern: identity theft, fraud, deceptive advertising, pornography, and invasion of privacy.

   (Joseph R. Dominick, *The Dynamics of Mass Communication*, 8/e, 2005)

   ____

   Transition Words: ______________________________

5. Because you are always the "author" of your dreams, it is not surprising that you often play a leading role. Thus, you have an active role in nearly three-fourths of your dreams, and you are absent from your own dreams only 10 percent of the time. About half of the other characters in your dreams are friends, acquaintances, or family members. The other half are people you do not know or cannot recognize—or are animals.

   (Benjamin B. Lahey, *Psychology*, 8/e, 2004)

   ____

   Transition Words: ______________________________

6. How many times have you asked yourself questions such as "Am I as smart as Jill?" "Is Bob better-looking than I am?" or "Is my taste as good as Carmen's?" We gain self-knowledge by comparing ourselves with others. We are more likely to compare ourselves with others who are similar to us. We develop more accurate self-perceptions by comparing ourselves with people in communities similar to where we live, with people who have similar family backgrounds, and with people of the same sex or sexual orientation.

   (John W. Santrock, *Psychology*, 7/e, 2003)

   ____

   Transition Words: ______________________________

7. If you're a traditional age student, ask some older students what they ate when they were growing up. You're likely to hear about American favorites that include meatloaf, mashed potatoes and gravy, chicken pot pie, hearty beef stew, and homemade fudge layer cake. Back then big meals served "family style," featuring red meat and lots of side dishes—plus a rich dessert—were considered healthy, as well as essential for growing, active children. Today, in contrast, our food focus is firmly on ethnic dishes, with their novel flavors and textures, their exotic spices, their alluringly foreign names. Unlike the meals of the past, ethnic cuisines feature generous

servings of vegetables, with just a bit of fish, meat, or poultry, plus spices for flavor. Dishes are often cooked with heart-healthy olive oil instead of cholesterol-heavy butter, shortening, or lard. Protein is more likely to come from legumes than from meat, and dessert may be a small wedge of cheese instead of seven-layer fudge cake or rocky road ice cream.

(Wayne A. Payne and Dale B. Hahn, *Understanding Your Health*, 6/e, 2000)

____

Transition Words: ______________________________

8. One of America's fastest-growing crimes, identity theft, is causing havoc for innocent people across the country. In a recent example, Theresa May, an English professor in Georgia, was victimized by a California woman of the same name who obtained her Social Security number and then applied for loans, defaulted on the payments, and filed for bankruptcy—all in the professor's name. In yet another example, in Ohio, a successful businesswoman's Social Security number was stolen by a thief who escaped to another state, where she used the Ohio woman's identity to obtain a driver's license and several credit cards, on which she ran up a slew of charges.

   (Stephen E. Lucas, *The Art of Public Speaking*, 8/e, 2004)

   ____

   Transition Words: ______________________________

Exercise 15: More Patterns of Organization and Transition Words

Directions: Identify the transition words and write them on the line. Now identify the pattern of organization and write it on the line.

1. At birth, most infants can turn their heads from side to side while lying on their backs. While lying chest down, many can lift their heads enough to turn them. Within the first two to three months, they lift their heads higher and higher, sometimes to the point where they lose their balance and roll over on their backs. After three months, the average infant begins to roll over deliberately—first from front to back and then from back to front. The average baby can sit without support by 6 months of age and can assume a sitting position without help about two and a half months later. Between 6 and 20 months, most babies begin to get around under their own power by means of creeping or crawling. By holding onto a helping hand or a piece of furniture, the average baby can stand at a little past 7 months of age. A little more than four months later, most babies let go and stand alone. The average baby can stand well about two weeks or so before the first birthday. Soon after they can stand alone well, most infants take their first unaided steps. Within a few weeks, soon after the first birthday, the average child is walking well.

   (Diane E. Papalia, and Ruth Duskin Feldman, *Experience Human Development*, 12/e, 2012)

   ____

   Transition Words: ______________________________

   ____

2. Our daily lives are enriched by other countries and by the diversity of American society. Consider this example of a typical American citizen. Each morn-

ing she wakes up in a bed (an invention from the Near East). She puts on clothes made in Taiwan, Mexico, and Jamaica, shoes from Spain and a wristwatch from Switzerland, jewelry from Kenya and perfume from France. She eats breakfast at a table made in Sweden, using plates from Korea and a tablecloth from India. Her breakfast includes a banana from Honduras and coffee from Colombia. While driving to work in a car made in Japan, she listens to music performed by a band from Cuba. For lunch at a restaurant, she can choose from a wide variety of ethnic cuisines—Thai, Italian, Chinese, Mexican, Korean, Vietnamese, Egyptian, and so on. Throughout the day, she is likely to use or benefit from products invented by immigrants to the United States and their descendants. Her health, for example, is protected by an oral polio vaccine, developed by Albert B. Sabin, a Polish immigrant.

(Hamilton Gregory, *Public Speaking for College and Career*, 7/e, 2005)

____

Transition Words: ____________________________________

3. Medical researchers have found that the average human needs about eight hours of sleep each night in order to function well on the job, on the highway, in school, and in the home. But the majority of Americans try to get by on less than eight hours; in fact, 80 percent get six hours of sleep or less each night. Perhaps the most insidious consequence of skimping on sleep is the irritability that increasingly pervades society. Weariness corrodes civility and erases humor, traits that ease the myriad daily frustrations, from standing in supermarket lines to refereeing the kids' squabbles. Because people go without sufficient sleep, tempers flare faster and hotter at the slightest offense.

   (Hamilton Gregory, *Public Speaking for College and Career*, 7/e, 2005)

   ____

   Transition Words: ____________________________________

4. One way we simplify our environment is to categorize—to organize the world by clustering objects into groups. A biologist classifies plants and animals. A human classifies people. Ethnicity and sex are, in our current world, powerful ways of categorizing people. Imagine Gina, a 45-year-old, New Orleans real estate agent. Your categories might be "female," "middle-aged," "businessperson," and "southerner."

   (David G. Myers, *Social Psychology*, 9/e, 2008)

   ____

   Transition Words: ____________________________________

5. Indian and U.S. cultures have produced different approaches to love and marriage. In India, about 95 percent of marriages are still arranged by the parents. In the U.S., individual mate selection matches the core values of individuality and independence, while arranged marriages match the Indian value of children's deference to parental authority. For Indians, love is a peaceful emotion, based on long-term commitment and devotion to family. Indians think of love as something that can be "created" between two people. For Indians, marriage produces love—however for Americans love produces marriage. Americans see love as having a mysterious element, a passion that suddenly seizes an individual. In contrast, Indians see love as a peaceful feeling that develops when a man and a woman are united in intimacy and share common interests and goals in life.

(James M. Henslin, *Essentials of Sociology*, 7/e, 2007)

____

Transition Words: ______________________________

Relationships Within and Between Sentences

Using transition words as clues, a good reader is able to recognize how one part of a sentence relates to another part of the same sentence. In addition, transition words help a reader recognize how the information in one sentence relates to the information in another sentence. Exercises 16 and 17 will give you practice in both of these skills.

Exercise 16: Identifying Transition Words and Sentence Relationships

Directions: Read the following paragraphs on the history of underwear and then identify the transition words in each paragraph.

A BRIEF HISTORY OF UNDERWEAR

(1) There is an old saying, "Don't air your dirty linen in public," which means don't spread private, unpleasant details about yourself for everyone to hear. Well, underwear in sixteenth-century England was the original "dirty linen." Shirts and shifts were gray with dirt and smelled of sweat. Underwear was alive with fleas, ticks, and mites because people rarely took baths. Nevertheless, underwear had an important job to do: It protected people's better outer clothes, which were hard to wash, from the dirt and smells of their bodies. It was easier to wash underwear—at least a few times a year.

1. In paragraph 1, what transition word is used to indicate a definition?

____

2. In paragraph 1, what transition word is used to indicate cause and effect?

____

3. In paragraph 1, what transition word is used to indicate reversal?

____

(2) Elizabeth I (1533–1603), queen of England, loved fine clothes. During her years as queen, women wore the "farthingale," which refers to a petticoat stiffened with hoops of wood or whalebone that held a dress from the body like a dome. Though hooped petticoats changed in size and shape, they continued to be worn in eighteenth-century Europe and America. In the middle of the century, they grew flat in front and back, but they were sometimes as wide as six feet across at the sides. (Imagine holding a yardstick out on either side of you!) Called "panniers," which derives from the French word for "basket," they made a woman look as if she had a basket on each hip. Doorways were difficult, carriages were a problem, and unquestionably sitting in an armchair was impossible.

4. In paragraph 2, which transition words are used to indicate definition?

____

5. In paragraph 2, which transition word indicates emphasis?

____

6. In paragraph 2, which transition words indicate spatial order?

____

(3) Toward the end of the century, young girls began wearing pantalettes underneath their dresses. Each leg was separate from the other and joined at the waist with drawstrings. Pantalettes would first slowly shrink to become "drawers" in the next century, then "bloomers," and finally women's underpants today.

7. In paragraph 3, which transition words are used to indicate steps in a process?

____

8. In paragraph 3, which transition word is used to indicate spatial order?

____

(4) Fashions are often not designed for the natural shape of the human body. In nineteenth-century England and France, women learned to live with bodies tightly bound in corsets to have the small, slender waists required by society. However, tightly laced corsets could change a woman's body permanently by altering the position of her internal organs. Since her lungs were compressed, she could take only short, shallow breaths.

______ 9. In paragraph 4, the relationship of the second sentence to the third sentence is one of
   a. chronological order.
   b. addition.
   c. contrast.
   d. example.

10. In paragraph 4, what transition word is used to indicate cause and effect?

____

(5) A few women decided they could do very well without corsets. In 1851 in Seneca Falls, New York, a magazine editor, Amelia Bloomer, published a new idea from her friend Elizabeth Smith Miller. The idea was to wear a comfortable tunic over pajama-style pants. Amelia and her friends, who supported women's rights, were free to go on a hike, jump over a fence, even work in the garden! But people were horrified by the sight of women wearing pants. They teased and laughed at the women; children threw snowballs and apple cores at them. However, years later "bloomers" reappeared as part of women's bathing suits and bicycle outfits.

11. In paragraph 5, what transition words are used to indicate contrast?

____

(6) Other ideas were also changing the way people dressed in the nineteenth century. In 1864, when Louis Pasteur discovered microbes, or germs, and proved that they cause disease, people became very health-conscious. Many theories for staying healthy circulated, some more scientific than others. In the 1870s Dr. Gustav Jaeger of Germany believed everyone should wear his Sanitary Woolen System for good health. He claimed his knit underwear would hold in the body's warmth, but let the "noxious exhalations of the body" (bad smells) out. Dr. Jaeger convinced so many people to wear his thick, scratchy "woolies" in winter and summer that he made a fortune selling underwear.

12. In paragraph 6, what words are used to indicate chronological order?

____

(7) Woolen "combinations" in England were called "union suits" in the United States. The bottom half of a union suit got the name "long johns" from John L. Sullivan, an American bare-knuckles boxing champion of the 1880s and 1890s. Besides being a prizewinning boxer, he was also known for fighting in his long underwear.

13. In paragraph 7, what transition words were used to indicate definition?

____

14. In paragraph 7, what transition words were used to indicate addition?

____

(8) As the nineteenth century ended and the twentieth century began, the end of the corset was coming. Women discovered bike riding in 1895 and the joy of getting around on their own. And by 1900 more than four million women in America were working outside the home.

15. In paragraph 8, what transition words indicate chronological order?

____

______ 16. In paragraph 8, the relationship of the second sentence to the third sentence is one of
a. definition.
b. addition.
c. spatial order.
d. comparison.

(9) As hemlines rose in the 1920s and 1930s, silk stockings were very popular. But by the late 1930s, getting silk was a problem. Japan controlled the Chinese silk market, and in the years leading to World War II, relations between the United States and Japan became more strained. Finally, in 1939, the DuPont Company came up with the answer. At the New York World's Fair that year, they introduced a man-made silk called "nylon," the world's first synthetic fiber.

17. In paragraph 9, what transition word indicates contrast?

____

18. In paragraph 9, what transition word was used to indicate a conclusion?

____

(10) In the 1950s and 1960s, underwear became lighter and more comfortable. By the 1960s parents could also buy disposable diapers. Disposable diapers are popular today not only for babies but for adults—such as astronauts—as well.

19. In paragraph 10, what words indicate chronological order?

____

20. In paragraph 10, what transition words indicate example?

____

(11) Because it just isn't possible to get to a toilet, astronauts wear long underwear and adult diapers under their space suits. Astronaut R. Mike Mullane once had to wait four hours for his space shuttle to take off. He said he remembers "lying in a very wet diaper, knowing why babies cry when they have wet diapers. It's gross!"

21. In paragraph 11, what word indicates cause and effect?

____

(12) What will happen to underwear in the future? Researchers are working hard to invent new fabrics that will absorb perspiration and take it away from the body. This process is called "moisture management." In addition T-shirt fabric containing tiny ceramic particles is being tested to see if it will block harmful rays from the sun. Supposedly a person wearing such a shirt will feel five degrees cooler than if he or she were wearing a normal shirt.

(Ruth Freeman Swain, *Underwear*, 2008)

22. In paragraph 12, what words indicate definition?

____

______ 23. In paragraph 12, which words indicate addition?
 a. contrast
 b. cause and effect
 c. in addition
 d. definition and example

Exercise 17: Patterns of Organization and Sentence Relationships

Directions: Read the paragraphs below and then answer the questions.

(1) You don't have to look very hard to see some high-profile examples of deception. (2) Marion Jones forfeited her Olympic medals after admitting she lied about taking performance-enhancing drugs. (3) Martha Stewart was sentenced to prison for lying to investigators. (4) Further, contestants on reality shows such as *Survivor*, *The Apprentice*, and *Big Brother* often lie to gain an advantage over their competitors. (5) Is deception that common in everyday life, or do these high-profile examples simply make us think it is?

______ 1. For this paragraph, the author uses an overall pattern of organization that
 a. analyzes the causes of lying.
 b. describes the types of lies people tell.
 c. gives examples of people lying.
 d. compares lies told by men with lies told by women.

______ 2. The relationship between sentence 3 and sentence 4 is one of
 a. contrast.
 b. addition.
 c. summary.
 d. spatial order.

(1) In a 2004 survey of 3,000 adults, 71 percent of participants reported they had lied to friends or relatives to spare their feelings; 63 percent had faked an illness to get out of work; 32 percent had lied to their spouse about a purchase; and 28 percent had lied to their spouse about their relationship with someone else.

______ 3. This paragraph is organized by
 a. identifying the effects of lying.
 b. listing certain lies and their frequency.
 c. analyzing the consequences of lying.
 d. listing suggestions for avoiding lying.

(1) After conducting 3.8 million background checks in April 2005, Automatic Data Processing found that 52 percent of job applicants had lied on their resumes. (2) However, a different survey by the Gillette Corporation found that, for men, the number was 86 percent.

______ 4. The relationship between the first sentence and the second sentence is one of

a. time order.
b. example.
c. summary.
d. contrast.

(1) Researchers at Cornell University wanted to know the frequency of lying behavior, so they asked college students to keep a diary on every social interaction they had for a week involving a lie. (2) As a result of the study, researchers determined that students lied on average in approximately 265 of their interactions, with lying behavior the most common in telephone conversations.

______ 5. The relationship between the first sentence and the second sentence is one of

a. cause and effect.
b. spatial order.
c. addition.
d. summary.

(1) Some people may be surprised at how high these figures are. (2) Conversely, others may be surprised at how low they are. (3) In either event, there's no question that we encounter deception regularly in our day-to-day interactions with people.

______ 6. The relationship between the first sentence and the second sentence is one of

a. comparison.
b. contrast.
c. definition.
d. spatial order.

(Kory Floyd, *Interpersonal Communication*, 2/e, 2011)

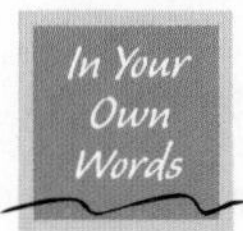

In Your Own Words

1. Do you think lying is more common today than it used to be? If so, why do you think this is so?
2. Do you believe that lying is sometimes justified? When?

READING

"Road rage now results in more highway deaths than drunk driving."

TUNING IN TO READING Widespread publicity campaigns emphasizing slogans such as "Steer clear of aggressive driving" and "Instead of trying to make good time, try to make time good" have failed to prevent aggressive driving. What kinds of things do you think will help law enforcement rid the streets and highways of the menace of aggressive driving? Do you think it would help if people were encouraged to have and use "I'm Sorry" placards? Or is it simply time for law enforcement to "get tough" on those who willfully endanger the lives of others?

BIO-SKETCH Freda Adler and Gerhard O. W. Mueller are both distinguished professors of criminal justice at Rutgers University. William S. Laufer is associate professor of legal studies at the Wharton School of the University of Pennsylvania. All three authors have written books and articles on criminal justice. Drs. Adler and Mueller have also been advisors in criminal justice to the United Nations.

NOTES ON VOCABULARY

boil over erupt in anger. The phrase alludes to the fact that when something is vigorously boiling, it is apt to spill over unless it is watched carefully or the heat is reduced.

anonymous with no name either known or acknowledged. *Anonymous* is derived from the Greek words *an* meaning "without" and *onoma* meaning "name." In ancient Greece, *anonymous* was used whenever an author was unknown.

aggressive driving the operation of a motor vehicle in an unsafe and hostile manner, without regard for others.

Note: For additional practice with transitions, read the following selection and then answer the questions that follow. You may need to refer to the transition words chart on pages 188–189.

ROAD RAGE

Freda Adler, Gerhard O. W. Mueller, and William S. Laufer

It has been known for years as aggressive driving. It is a factor in 28,000 highway deaths per year. It is a disorder that is said to affect over half of all drivers. Symptoms include speeding, tailgating, weaving in and out of busy traffic, passing on the right, making unsafe or improper lane changes, running stop signs and red lights, flashing lights or high beams at other drivers, using obscene gestures, swearing and yelling insults, honking or screaming at other drivers, throwing items at other vehicles, and shooting other drivers or passengers. "The symptoms are incredibly commonplace and sometimes boil over

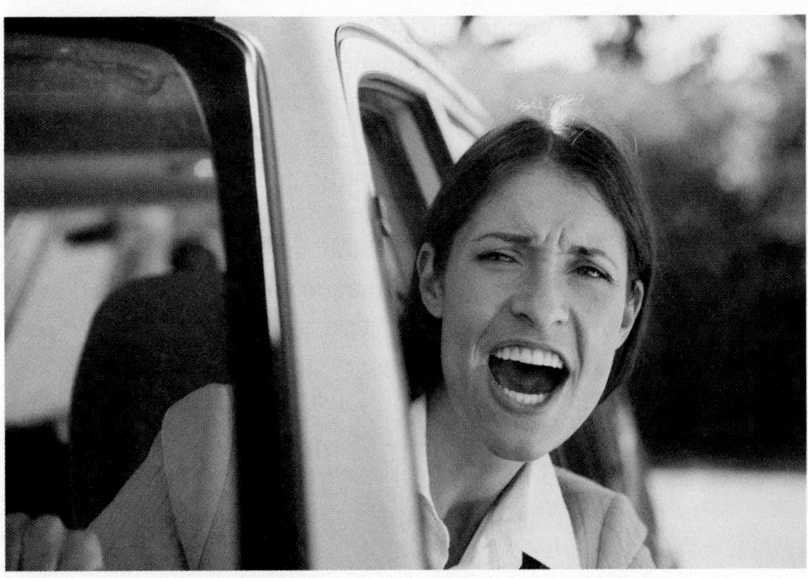

into actual assault and life-threatening situations," explains John Hagerty of the New Jersey State Police.

Road rage now results in more highway deaths than drunk driving. A national study by the AAA Foundation for Traffic Safety found that the majority of aggressive drivers were men aged eighteen to twenty-six, but that dangerous driving behavior is present in women also, and across age levels and economic classes. The same study concluded that from 1990 to 1996, "violent aggressive driving" increased by 7 percent per year. The reasons for this growth depend on whom you ask. 2

Psychiatrists look to deep-seated personal causes such as stress disorders, which result in impaired judgment. Sociologists see a connection between problems in society and aggressive driving. Others say that the car shields drivers, in effect making them anonymous. This anonymity allows those who become frustrated while driving to ignore society's rules for proper behavior and to behave recklessly. Some claim that drivers see the car as an extension of themselves, and they react angrily when cut off, passed on the highway, or forced to slow down. 3

As a consequence of young men "dueling" with their cars, two eerily similar accidents happened. The first occurred on the George Washington Memorial Parkway in the nation's capital region. As the two cars raced each other along the parkway, one car crossed the median and hit an oncoming car. Three people were killed. Two of them were drivers not involved in the duel. The second happened as two cars on the New Jersey Turnpike chased each other at speeds of up to 100 miles per hour. The cars wove in and out of lanes of traffic, until the occupant of one of the vehicles allegedly threw an object at the other car. This caused the car to slam into a tree and resulted in the death of two men. 4

Ricardo Martinez is head of the National Highway Traffic Safety Administration. He blames aggressive driving on a combination of an increase in a "me first" philosophy and reduced levels of traffic enforcement arising from budget cuts, as well as increased congestion and traffic in urban areas. Since 1987, traffic has increased by 35 percent, but new road construction has only increased 1 percent. Pam Fischer, spokeswoman for the New Jersey Automobile Club, also sees congestion on the roadways as a contributing factor. "Any time there is an accident or construction that slows down traffic, people tend to get more aggravated, and normal and rational people do some dumb things because they are running late or just don't want to sit there." 5

What can be done to prevent this carnage on our highways? In New Jersey, state troopers and municipal police first use plainclothes officers in unmarked cars to cruise dangerous highways during rush hours and spot aggressive drivers. Then, they relay the information to police in marked cars who stop the deviant motorists and give them tickets. In the District of Columbia, Maryland, and Virginia, police have a program called Smooth Operator. In two one-week periods, they issued 28,958 summonses and warnings, including nearly 12,000 for speeding, 3,300 for failing to obey traffic signals, 2,000 for failing to wear a seat belt, and 1,800 for failing to obey a traffic sign. 6

Another approach calls for making roads bigger. The reasoning is that wider roads reduce traffic congestion and the resulting frustration. But, as noted by 7

Congressman Earl Blumenauer, a Democrat from Oregon, building more roads is "the equivalent of giving a wife beater more room to swing." Instead, he advocates building bicycle lanes and planting trees. These are "features that soften the streets and let drivers know they have to share the road."

It's important to remember that America has faced a deadly threat on its 8 roadways before—drunk driving. Emphasis was placed on changing the laws and making it socially unacceptable to drink and drive. The experts say aggressive driving should be treated the same way. "We have to enforce the law, take bad drivers off the road, and make them pay for their mistakes," urged Colonel Peter J. O'Hagan, director of the New Jersey Division of Highway Safety. The time has come to address aggressive driving through better education, better enforcement, and a get-tough policy. Dr. Martinez warns that "aggressive drivers must get the message that their behavior will not be tolerated, and that they will be prosecuted."

(Freda Adler, Gerhard O. W. Mueller, and William S. Laufer, "Road Rage," *Criminal Justice*, 6/e, 2011)

COMPREHENSION CHECKUP

Short Answer

Directions: Answer the following questions briefly, using no more than a sentence or two.

1. What is the main idea of the selection? ______________________________

____

2. What is the author's overall purpose? ______________________________
3. What is the cause-and-effect relationship in the last two sentences of paragraph 4?

   Cause: ______________________________

   Effect: ______________________________
4. What is the cause-and-effect relationship in the last sentence of paragraph 5?

   Cause: ______________________________

   ____

   Effect: ______________________________
5. Paragraph 7 contains this analogy: Building more roads is "the equivalent of giving a wife beater more room to swing." In your own words, explain what this analogy means. ______________________________

____

6. Here are some sentences from the selection. Paraphrase them by writing each one in your own words in the space provided.

   a. "This anonymity allows those who become frustrated while driving to ignore society's rules for proper behavior and to behave recklessly."

   ____

   ____

   b. "He blames aggressive driving on a combination of an increase in a 'me first' philosophy and reduced levels of traffic enforcement arising from budget cuts, as well as increased congestion and traffic in urban areas."

   ____

   ____

Multiple Choice

Directions: For each item, write the letter corresponding to the best answer. You may refer to the transition words chart on pages 191–192.

_____ 1. A key idea expressed in this selection is that
a. the stress of modern society is solely responsible for road rage.
b. to get the message across to the public that aggressive driving is unsafe, law enforcement needs to deal with the problem in a manner similar to the way it deals with drunk driving.
c. making roads bigger is the answer to the problem of road rage.
d. road rage will be alleviated when there are fewer 16-year-olds and senior citizens on the highways.

_____ 2. The organizational pattern in paragraph 1 could be described as
a. listing pattern.
b. spatial order.
c. chronological order.
d. compare and contrast.

_____ 3. The transition word *but* in paragraph 2 indicates
a. conclusion.
b. contrast.
c. emphasis.
d. spatial order.

_____ 4. The transition word *also* in paragraph 2 indicates
a. reversal.
b. concession.
c. addition.
d. both a and c.

_____ 5. The transition words *such as* in paragraph 3 indicate
a. addition.
b. summary.
c. reversal.
d. example.

_____ 6. In paragraph 3, all of the following are given as possible reasons for the growth in aggressive driving *except*
a. intoxication.
b. anonymity.
c. problems in society.
d. stress disorders.

_____ 7. Read the first sentence of paragraph 4. What do the transition words *as a consequence* signal?
a. summary and conclusion
b. spatial order
c. cause and effect
d. comparison-contrast

_____ 8. Paragraph 6 uses the transition words *first* and *then*. What pattern of organization do these words signal?
a. chronological order
b. examples
c. cause and effect
d. comparison-contrast

______ 9. The relationship of the second sentence below to the first is one of
a. addition.
b. emphasis.
c. contrast.
d. summary.

But as noted by Congressman Earl Blumenauer, a Democrat from Oregon, building more roads is "the equivalent of giving a wife beater more room to swing." Instead, he advocates building bicycle lanes and planting trees. (paragraph 7)

True or False

Directions: Indicate whether each statement is true or false by writing **T** or **F** in the space provided.

______ 10. Road rage affects men and women in equal numbers.
______ 11. Drunk driving is the leading cause of highway deaths.
______ 12. Road construction has failed to keep pace with the increase in traffic.
______ 13. Experts give various reasons to account for aggressive driving.
______ 14. "Dueling" with cars can result in the loss of innocent lives.

Vocabulary in Context

Directions: Use context clues from the article to determine the meaning of the italicized words, and write a definition in the space provided. Then consult your dictionary to see how accurate your definition is.

1. Stress disorders, which result in *impaired* judgment (paragraph 3)
   Definition: ______________________________
2. The car *shields* drivers, in effect making them anonymous (paragraph 3)
   Definition: ______________________________
3. See the car as an *extension* of themselves (paragraph 3)
   Definition: ______________________________
4. Two *eerily* similar accidents happened (paragraph 4)
   Definition: ______________________________
5. Drivers not involved in the *duel* (paragraph 4)
   Definition: ______________________________
6. Increased *congestion* and traffic in urban areas (paragraph 5)
   Definition: ______________________________
7. What can be done to prevent this *carnage* (paragraph 6)
   Definition: ______________________________
8. Stop the *deviant* motorists and give them tickets (paragraph 6)
   Definition: ______________________________
9. Their behavior will not be *tolerated* (paragraph 8)
   Definition: ______________________________

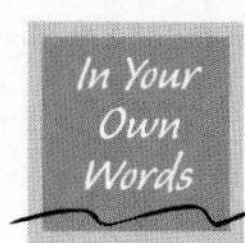

In Your Own Words

1. Have you ever engaged or been tempted to engage in aggressive driving? Have you ever been affected by someone else's aggressive driving? What do you think led to the behavior? How could it have been prevented?
2. Picture the area around your campus. Are there any problems with aggressive driving in this vicinity? What concrete steps could the college and local police take to address these problems?
3. What is a suitable punishment for someone who speeds? How about someone who screams obscenities at other drivers? Do you think it is possible to reduce or eliminate such misconduct through law enforcement?

Written Assignment

The following are three basic guiding principles from the AAA Foundation for Traffic Safety for avoiding the rage of other motorists. What's your opinion of these suggestions? Are they likely to help deter aggressive driving?

1. **Don't offend.** When surveys ask drivers what angers them most, the results are remarkably consistent. A few specific behaviors seem unusually likely to enrage other drivers:
   a. Cutting off
   b. Driving slowly in the left lane
   c. Tailgating
2. **Watch gestures.** Almost nothing makes another driver angrier than an obscene gesture. Keep your hands on the wheel. Avoid making any gestures that might anger another driver, even "harmless" expressions of irritation like shaking your head.
3. **Don't engage.** One angry driver can't start a fight unless another driver is willing to join in. You can protect yourself against aggressive drivers by refusing to become angry at them.

Internet Activity

Consult the following Web site for tips on not becoming the victim of aggressive driving:

www.danesheriff.com/roadrage.htm

Do you think these tips are likely to be effective? Can you think of other tips that might be effective?

Are You an Aggressive Driver?

The National Highway Traffic Safety Administration describes an aggressive driver as someone who "commits a combination of moving traffic offenses so as to endanger other persons or property." The NHTSA recommends avoiding the challenges and confrontations of such risk drivers. Do you ever exhibit any of the behaviors of an aggressive driver? To find out, answer yes or no to the following questions:

	Yes	No
1. Overtake other vehicles only on the left?	____	____
2. Avoid blocking passing lanes?	____	____
3. Yield to faster traffic by moving to the right?	____	____
4. Keep to the right as much as possible on narrow streets and at intersections?	____	____

(*continued*)

Are You an Aggressive Driver? (*continued*)

	Yes	No
5. Maintain appropriate distance when following other motorists, bicyclists, and motorcyclists?	____	____
6. Leave an appropriate distance between your vehicle and the one you have passed when cutting in after passing?	____	____
7. Yield to pedestrians?	____	____
8. Come to a complete stop at stop signs and before making a right turn on red?	____	____
9. Stop for red traffic lights?	____	____
10. Approach intersections and pedestrians slowly to show your intention and ability to stop?	____	____
11. Follow right-of-way rules at four-way stops?	____	____
12. Drive below posted speed limits when conditions warrant?	____	____
13. Drive at slower speeds in construction zones?	____	____
14. Maintain speeds appropriate for conditions?	____	____
15. Use vehicle turn signals for all turns and lane changes?	____	____
16. Make eye contact and signal intentions when necessary?	____	____
17. Acknowledge intentions of others?	____	____
18. Use your horn sparingly around pedestrians, at night, and near hospitals?	____	____
19. Avoid unnecessary use of high-beam headlights?	____	____
20. Yield and move to the right for emergency vehicles?	____	____
21. Refrain from flashing headlights to signal a desire to pass?	____	____
22. Drive trucks at posted speeds and in the correct lanes, changing lanes at proper speeds?	____	____
23. Make slow U-turns?	____	____
24. Maintain proper speeds around roadway crashes?	____	____
25. Avoid returning inappropriate gestures?	____	____
26. Avoid challenging other drivers?	____	____
27. Try to get out of the way of aggressive drivers?	____	____
28. Refrain from using high-occupancy-vehicle or carpool lanes to pass vehicles?	____	____
29. Focus on driving and avoid distracting activities such as smoking, using a cell phone, reading, or shaving?	____	____
30. Avoid driving when drowsy?	____	____
31. Avoid blocking the right-hand turn lane?	____	____
32. Avoid taking more than one parking space?	____	____
33. Avoid parking in a disabled space if you are not disabled?	____	____
34. Avoid letting your door hit the car parked next to you?	____	____
35. Avoid stopping in the road to talk with a pedestrian or other driver?	____	____
36. Avoid playing loud music that can be heard in neighboring cars?	____	____

(Michael L. Teague, Sara L. C. Mackenzie, and David M. Rosenthal, *Your Health Today*, 2/e, 2009)

REVIEW TEST 5: Main Idea, Details, Purpose, Transitions, and Patterns of Organization

Directions: Each of the following paragraphs related to aggressive behavior was adapted from commonly used psychology textbooks. Read each passage. Then choose the best answer for each item.

A. Psychologists define *aggression* as physical or verbal behavior intended to hurt someone. Throughout the world, hunting, fighting, and warring are primarily men's activities. In surveys, men admit to more aggression than women do. In laboratory experiments, men exhibit more physical aggression by administering what they believe are hurtful shocks. In Canada, the male-to-female arrest rate is 7 to 1 for murder and 6 to 1 for assault. In the United States, it is 9 to 1 for murder and 4 to 1 for assault. Across the world murder rates vary. Yet in all regions, men are roughly 20 times more likely to murder men than women are to murder women. However, in less violent forms of aggression—say, slapping a family member or verbally attacking someone—women are no less aggressive than men.

(David G. Myers, *Social Psychology,* 7/e, 2002)

______ 1. In the first sentence of this paragraph, the author uses a(n)
a. cause-and-effect relationship.
b. definition.
c. example.
d. contrast.

______ 2. The body of the paragraph is organized to
a. make a contrast.
b. show steps in a process.
c. show events in chronological order.
d. give a definition.

______ 3. The last sentence of the paragraph is written to
a. define what was described above it.
b. show a cause-and-effect relationship.
c. show steps in a process.
d. show a contrast with the body of the paragraph.

B. It is a warm evening. Tired and thirsty after two hours of studying, you borrow some change from a friend and head for the nearest soft-drink machine. As the machine devours the change, you can almost taste the cold, refreshing cola. But when you push the button, nothing happens. You push it again. Then you flip the coin return button. Still nothing. Again, you hit the buttons. You slam them. And finally you shake and whack the machine. You stomp back to your studies empty-handed and shortchanged. Should your roommate beware? Are you now more likely to say or do something hurtful?

(David G. Myers, *Social Psychology,* 9/e, 2008)

______ 4. The author has written this paragraph using which method?
a. definition
b. comparison
c. classification
d. chronological order

______ 5. The example of the student and the vending machine was used to illustrate
a. the difficulties of a student's life.
b. the relationship between frustration and aggression.
c. the problems with vending machines.
d. the wide variety of things that can go wrong in a day.

C. One of the first psychological theories of aggression, the popular frustration–aggression theory, says that a person who has suffered frustration is more likely to do or say something harmful. "Frustration always leads to some form of aggression," said John Dollard and his colleagues. *Frustration* is anything (such as the malfunctioning vending machine) that blocks our attaining a goal. Frustration grows when our motivation to achieve a goal is very strong, when we expected satisfaction, and when the blocking is complete.

(David G. Myers, *Social Psychology*, 9/e, 2008)

______ 6. The main purpose of this paragraph is to
   a. entertain.
   b. inform or explain.
   c. persuade.
   d. criticize.

______ 7. Which of the following best describes the organizational pattern of this paragraph?
   a. definition and explanation
   b. examples and classification
   c. comparison and contrast
   d. classification and division

D. Our aggressive energy need not explode directly against its source. We learn to inhibit direct retaliation, especially when others might disapprove of us or punish us; instead we displace our hostilities to safer targets. Displacement occurs in the old anecdote about a man who, because he is humiliated by his boss, berates his wife, who yells at their son, who kicks the dog, which bites the mail carrier.

(David G. Myers, *Social Psychology*, 9/e, 2008)

______ 8. The author in the last sentence of this paragraph uses which of the following?
   a. comparison
   b. classification
   c. cause and effect
   d. definition

E. What kinds of stimuli act as aggressive cues? They can range from the most obvious, such as the presence of weapons, to the subtlest, such as the mere mention of the name of an individual who has behaved violently in the past. For example, in one experiment, angered subjects were more aggressive when in the presence of a rifle and a revolver than in a similar situation in which no guns were present. It appears, then, that frustration does lead to aggression, at least when aggressive cues are present.

(Robert S. Feldman, *Understanding Psychology*, 11/3, 2013)

______ 9. Which of the following does the author *not* use in this paragraph?
   a. an example
   b. a contrast
   c. a definition
   d. a cause-and-effect statement

_____ 10. The main idea expressed in this passage is that
a. frustration can more easily lead to aggression when aggressive cues are present.
b. aggressive cues can be subtle or obvious.
c. people behave more aggressively when in the presence of weapons.
d. psychologists don't know what kind of stimuli act as aggressive cues.

Chapter Summary and Review

In this chapter, you learned about the patterns of organization that authors use. You also learned to recognize transition words and phrases. Based on the material in Chapter 6, answer the following.

Short Answer

Directions: List three or four transition words that signal the following patterns of paragraph organization.

1. Comparison ________________________________
2. Cause and effect ________________________________
3. Chronological order ________________________________
4. Classification ________________________________

Vocabulary in Context

Directions: Choose one of the following words to complete the sentences below. Use each word only once.

chronological conclusion contrast definitions examples

5. When you write a paper for class, you may want to give specific __________ that illustrate your point.
6. On a history test, you might be asked to place the major events leading up to World War II in __________ order.
7. A speaker at a graduation ceremony usually ends the speech with a(n) __________.
8. When minor league baseball players make it to the Major Leagues for the first time, they are sometimes surprised at the huge __________ between how the game is played in the major and minor leagues.
9. Sometimes authors of textbooks will give __________ for unusual words that they use.

CHAPTER

7 Patterns of Organization in Reading Selections

CHAPTER PREVIEW

In this chapter, you will

- Become familiar with the following patterns of organization in reading selections: comparison-contrast; examples and listing; categories and steps in a process; chronological order; and cause and effect.

Introduction to Patterns of Organization in Reading Selections

Once a writer has selected a mode of writing such as narrative, descriptive, expository, or persuasive, the writer needs to select one or more patterns of organization. The patterns of organization are (1) classification or division (categories), (2) listing, (3) comparison-contrast, (4) examples, (5) chronological order, (6) steps in a process, and (7) cause and effect. These categories should be familiar to you, because they previously appeared in this book as patterns of organization for paragraphs in Chapter 6.

For example, say that an author wishes to entertain the reader with a description of jobs that have not worked out well. So the author might give a chronological narrative of amusing events he or she witnessed while working. The author might then describe some "bad bosses" from the past. Or a writer who wishes to persuade the reader that it's time to pay college athletes for their work might narrate an account of the current system in college athletics. The writer could then provide examples of the hardships the athletes endure. The author might conclude by giving a chronological account of how college sports have evolved into such a big business.

Sometimes an author may organize an entire reading selection using only one pattern of organization. Often, however, multiple patterns are used. A writer selects the modes of writing and patterns of organization that will best achieve the goal of communicating with the audience. Being able to recognize the different modes of writing and patterns of organization will help you become both a better writer and reader.

In this chapter, you will have a chance to practice your skills with a variety of reading selections that illustrate the patterns of organization.

Comparison-Contrast

The reading selection that follows is a narrative written in 1994 by a nursing home resident. It illustrates a person and a situation with whom we are likely to empathize. Notice how the author compares and contrasts her life in the nursing home with her previous life outside it. Do you think nursing homes have changed for the better since this selection was published?

READING

"This is my world now. It's all I have left.
You see, I'm old."

TUNING IN TO READING Who cares for the elderly in your culture? Do relatives move them to nursing homes? Or do they care for them at home?

BIO-SKETCH Anna Mae Halgrim Seaver, who lived in Wauwatosa, Wisconsin, died in 1994.

NOTES ON VOCABULARY

Alzheimer's a progressive form of dementia involving impaired memory

Great Depression a long and severe worldwide economic depression that began when the New York Stock Market crashed in 1929 and continued through the 1930s

MY WORLD NOW BY ANNA MAE HALGRIM SEAVER

This is my world now. It's all I have left. You see, I'm old. And I'm not as healthy as I used to be. I'm not necessarily happy with it, but I accept it. Occasionally, a member of my family will stop in to see me. He or she will bring me some flowers or a little present, maybe a set of slippers—I've got 8 pair. We'll visit for a while and then they will return to the outside world and I'll be alone again.

2 Oh, there are other people here in the nursing home. Residents, we're called. The majority are about my age. I'm 84. Many are in wheelchairs. The lucky ones are passing through—a broken hip, a diseased heart, something has brought them here for rehabilitation. When they're well, they'll be going home.

3 Most of us are aware of our plight—some are not. Varying stages of Alzheimer's have robbed several of their mental capacities. We listen to endlessly repeated stories and questions. We meet them anew daily, hourly, or more often. We smile and nod gracefully each time we hear a retelling. They seldom listen to my stories, so I've stopped trying.

4 The help here is basically good, although there is a large turnover. Just when I get comfortable with someone, he or she moves on to another job. I understand that. This is not the best job to have.

5 I don't much like some of the physical things that happen to us. I don't care much for a diaper. I seem to have lost the control so diligently acquired as a child. The difference is that I am aware and embarrassed, but I can't do anything about it. I've had three children, and I know it isn't pleasant to clean another's diaper. My husband used to wear a mask when he changed the kids. I wish I had one now.

6 Why do you think the staff insists on talking baby talk when speaking to me? I understand English. I have a degree in music and am a certified teacher. Now I hear a lot of words that end in "y." Is this how my kids felt? My hearing aid works fine. There is little need for anyone to position their face directly in front of mine and raise their voice with those "y" words. Sometimes it takes longer for a meaning to sink in; sometimes my mind wanders when I am bored. But there is no need to shout.

I tried once or twice to make my feelings known. I even shouted once. 7 That gained me the reputation of being "crotchety." Imagine me, crotchety. My children never heard me raise my voice. I surprised myself. After I've asked for help more than a dozen times and received nothing more than a dozen condescending smiles and a "Yes, deary, I'm working on it," something begins to snap. That time I wanted to be taken to the bathroom.

I'd love to go out for a meal, to travel 8 again. I'd love to go to my own church, sing with my own choir. I'd love to visit my friends. Most of them are gone now, or else they are in different "homes" of their children's choosing. I'd love to play a good game of bridge, but no one here seems to concentrate very well.

My children put me here for my own 9 good. They said they would be able to visit me frequently. But they have their own lives to lead. That sounds normal. I don't want to be a burden. They know that. But I would like to see them more often. One of them is here in town. He visits as much as he can.

Something else I've learned to ac- 10 cept is my loss of privacy. Quite often I'll close my door when my roommate—imagine having a roommate at my age—is in the TV room. I do appreciate some time to myself and believe that I have earned at least that courtesy. As I sit thinking or writing, one of the aides invariably opens the door unannounced and walks in as if I'm not there. Sometimes she even opens my drawers and begins rummaging around. Am I invisible? Have I lost my right to respect and dignity? What would happen if the roles were reversed? I am still a human being. I would like to be treated like one.

11 The meals are not what I would choose for myself. We get variety, but we don't get a choice. I am one of the more fortunate ones who can still handle utensils. I remember eating with such cheap utensils in the Great Depression. I worked hard so I would not ever have to use them again. But here I am.

12 Did you ever sit in a wheelchair over an extended period of time? It's not comfortable. The seat squeezes you in the middle and applies constant pressure to your hips. The armrests are too narrow, and my arms slip off. I am luckier than some. Others are strapped into their chairs and abandoned in front of the TV. Captive prisoners of daytime soap opera, talk shows, and commercials.

13 One of the residents died today. He was a loner who, at one time, started a business and developed a multimillion-dollar company. His children moved him here when he could no longer control his bowels. He didn't talk to most of us. He often snapped at the aides as if they were his employees. But he just gave up; willed his own demise. The staff has made up his room and another man has moved in.

A typical day. Awakened by the woman in the next bed wheezing—a former chain smoker with asthma. Call an aide to wash me and place me in my wheelchair to wait for breakfast. Only 67 minutes until breakfast. I'll wait. Breakfast in the dining area. Most of the residents are in wheelchairs. Others use canes or walkers. Some sit and wonder what they are waiting for. First meal of the day. Only 3 hours and 28 minutes until lunch. Maybe I'll sit around and wait for it. What is today? One day blends into the next until day and date mean nothing. 14

Back to my semi-private room for a little semi-privacy or a nap. I do need my beauty rest; company may come today. What is today, again? The afternoon drags into early evening. This used to be my favorite time of the day. Things would wind down. I would kick off my shoes. Put my feet up on the coffee table. Pop open a bottle of Chablis and enjoy the fruits of my day's labor with my husband. He's gone. So is my health. *This* is my world. 15

(Newsweek, June 27, 1994)

COMPREHENSION CHECKUP

Short Answer

Directions: Answer the questions briefly, in a few words or sentences as appropriate, on the lines provided.

1. The notes that make up this reading were found in Mrs. Halgrim Seaver's room after her death by her son. Why do you think he published them?

____

____

2. How might this selection serve as an argument for providing better care for the elderly?

____

____

3. How would you describe the last paragraph of the selection? How would you describe the feeling expressed in the last three sentences of the selection?

____

True or False

Directions: Write **T** for each true statement and **F** for each false statement.

______ 1. Mrs. Seaver has three children who live close to her nursing home.

______ 2. Mrs. Seaver has a degree in music and used to sing in her church choir.

______ 3. Mrs. Seaver has received eight pairs of slippers from visitors.

______ 4. Mrs. Seaver is lucky to have a private room.

______ 5. Because Mrs. Seaver can no longer hear very well, she is grateful to the staff for speaking in a loud voice.

______ 6. Mrs. Seaver's husband wore a mask when he changed diapers.

______ 7. Mrs. Seaver has gained weight because of the high-fat diet at the nursing home.

______ 8. Mrs. Seaver was originally placed in the nursing home by her children.

______ 9. Mrs. Seaver's mind occasionally wanders when she gets bored.

______ 10. Sometimes, Mrs. Seaver would like to have a mask to wear.

Multiple Choice

Directions: Write the letter for the correct answer to each question.

______ 1. The author's purpose in this essay is to
a. inform others about what life in a nursing home is really like.
b. persuade relatives to reconsider putting their loved ones in nursing homes.
c. entertain the reader with amusing stories about life in a nursing home.
d. describe the abuses nursing home residents have to put up with.

______ 2. The author's main idea is that
a. nursing homes are a good place to be if you have nowhere else to go.
b. the nursing home experience isn't for everyone.
c. nursing homes need to focus on entertaining the residents.
d. life in a nursing home can be boring, lonely, and humiliating.

______ 3. The author's words indicate that she
a. feels lucky to still be alive.
b. is somewhat accepting of her living conditions.
c. is grateful to have outlived her friends and husband.
d. feels a great deal of bitterness toward her family.

______ 4. The author's feelings as expressed in paragraph 8 can best be described as
a. longing.
b. sarcastic.
c. arrogant.
d. angry.

______ 5. In paragraphs 15 and 16, Mrs Seaver describes a typical day by using
a. listing.
b. chronological order.
c. definition.
d. classification and division.

_____ 6. All of the following describe Mrs. Seaver **except**
a. she uses a wheelchair.
b. she has lost control of her bladder.
c. she wears a diaper.
d. she is 86 years old.

_____ 7. All of the following describe Mrs. Seaver **except**
a. she would like her family members to visit more frequently.
b. she would like to visit her friends.
c. she would like to play the piano again.
d. she would like to play bridge.

_____ 8. Mrs. Seaver experiences all of the following in the nursing home **except**
a. the lack of privacy.
b. the high turnover of staff.
c. the opportunity to share a bottle of wine.
d. the loss of close companions to talk to.

_____ 9. We can conclude that Mrs. Seaver
a. misses her husband.
b. is just passing through the nursing home.
c. is pleased to be so well taken care of.
d. has diminished mental capacities.

_____ 10. We can conclude that Mrs. Seaver
a. likes the caregivers to speak loudly so that she can hear them clearly.
b. dislikes being confined to a wheelchair.
c. is very fond of the food at the nursing home.
d. finds the days filled with varied activities that she enjoys.

Vocabulary in Context

Directions: Look through the paragraphs indicated in parentheses to find the word that matches each of the definitions below.

1. the greater part or larger number (2) __________
2. restoration to good health or useful life (2) __________
3. a bad or unfortunate situation (3) __________
4. powers to learn or retain knowledge (3) __________
5. a shift in personnel; a shake-up (4) __________
6. characterized by painstaking effort (5) __________
7. a cross, irritable, or unpleasant attitude (7) __________
8. displaying a superior attitude; patronizing (7) __________
9. always, without exception (10) __________
10. an article, tool, or container used in the kitchen (11) __________
11. confined (12) __________
12. one who avoids the company of other people (13) __________
13. death (13) __________
14. merges into one (14) __________

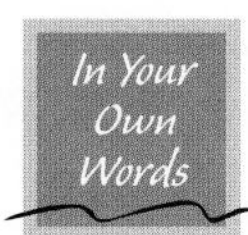

In Your Own Words

1. Do you think Mrs. Seaver was receiving "quality" care? Why or why not?
2. How are the elderly and infirm treated in your culture? Do you think they are treated worse or better than Mrs. Seaver in your culture?
3. Some nursing homes provide "pet" visits (short visits from dogs or cats). Do you think this might be a good idea to help alleviate the boredom of some nursing home residents?
4. Why does Mrs. Seaver put the word "homes" in quotes in paragraph 8? What does she mean to imply?

Written Assignment

What could have been done to improve the quality of Mrs. Seaver's life in the nursing home? For instance, do you think introducing nursing home residents to the computer could help them maintain contact with the outside world?

Internet Activity

1. Do some research on nursing homes in your area. What percentage of the elderly reside in nursing homes? Are nursing homes regulated? How expensive are they?
2. Do some research on hospice care for the elderly. What are the goals of hospice care? What is the difference between hospice care and a nursing home?

STUDY TECHNIQUE 11: COMPLETING A COMPARISON-CONTRAST CHART

One technique for organizing information pertaining to similarities and differences is to create a comparison-contrast chart. Some material, such as that in "My World Now," lends itself nicely to this type of graphic organizer.

Following is a comparison-contrast chart to complete. It will help you compare and contrast Anna Mae Halgrim Seaver's life in the nursing home to her life before in her own residence. The first columns (columns go up and down) list the categories to be compared and contrasted. The second column is for the information before the move to the nursing home, and the third column is for the information after the move. We have filled in the first three rows (rows go across) for you. Your assignment is to fill in the remaining two rows by scanning the reading selection.

Category	Before the Move	After the Move
Physical Limitations	Had control of her bladder. Walked unaided.	Must wear a diaper. Mind wanders. Confined to a wheelchair. Losing weight.
Personality	Never raised her voice.	Tries to make feelings known. Even shouted once. Considered crotchety.
Activities	Sang with her choir. Traveled. Played bridge and visited with friends.	Can't concentrate well enough to play bridge. No real friends.
Privacy		
Meals		

Examples and Listing

The reading selection that follows is written in an expository mode. The author gives examples of methods identity thieves use to obtain personal information, and then lists precautions individuals can take to avoid becoming a victim.

READING

"In the course of a week, you probably give away all sorts of information about yourself without even thinking about it."

TUNING IN TO READING Identity theft is a crime that is on the rise. This is probably because many people don't understand how widespread it is and as a result don't take proper precautions to protect themselves. Today it is relatively easy for a determined criminal to obtain personal data without going to the trouble of breaking into someone's home. Sometimes thieves simply eavesdrop on phone conversations when a person gives a credit card number to a hotel, rental car company, or others who request it. The following selection discusses tactics that identity thieves use to obtain personal information, and then lists steps you can take to protect yourself from identity theft.

BIO-SKETCH Glen J. Coulthard is a professor of business at Okanagan University in British Columbia, Canada. Since 1991 he has been a best-selling author for McGraw-Hill on the subjects of computers and information technology.

NOTES ON VOCABULARY

Trojan horse In classical mythology, the term referred to a large, hollow wooden horse used by the Greeks to win the Trojan War. The Greeks hid soldiers inside the horse and left it just outside the gates of Troy as a parting gift. The Trojans pulled it inside the city's gates. Late at night, Greek soldiers emerged from the horse and opened the gates for the invading army. Today, the term refers to a free program that looks like useful software but will do a lot of damage once it's installed on your computer.

Excerpt from

COMPUTING NOW

By Glen J. Coulthard

Identity Theft and How to Avoid It

If someone impersonates you by using your name, Social Security number, or other personal information to obtain documents or credit in your name, you are a victim of identity theft. With the right information, an identity thief can effectively "become" the victim, obtaining a driver's license, bank accounts, mortgages, and other items in the victim's name.

Identity theft cost the U.S. economy $54 billion in 2009. That year alone, more than 11 million Americans became victims of ID theft. Beyond monetary losses, however, victims of ID theft pay in other ways, spending many hours trying to repair the financial damages and regain their good reputation. 2

Below are some examples of methods identity thieves use to obtain the information they need. 3

Shoulder surfing. A trick known as **shoulder surfing** is as simple as watching someone enter personal identification information for a private transaction, such as an ATM. 4

Snagging. In the right setting, a thief can try **snagging** information by listening in on a telephone conversation while the victim gives credit card or other personal information to a legitimate agent. As more and more people carelessly hold loud, private conversations on their cell phones in public areas, snagging is easier than ever. 5

Dumpster diving. A popular low-tech approach is **dumpster diving.** Thieves can go through garbage cans, dumpsters, or trash bins to obtain canceled checks, credit cards, and utility statements, or bank account information that someone has carelessly thrown out. They win when they find items that have account numbers or personal information. Some ID thieves are brazen enough to swipe documents right out of your mailbox. 6

Social engineering. Thieves can use social engineering tactics both by pretending to represent your bank, utility company, or even the government; and by pretending to be you when contacting your bank or utility company. Their goal is to convince someone with private information about you that they have a legitimate purpose to receive that information. 7

High-tech methods. Sophisticated ID thieves can get information using a computer and Internet connection. For instance, Trojan horses can be planted on a system, or a person's identity may be snagged from unsecured Internet sites. Users providing private financial data via an unsecured "HTTP" Web page are especially vulnerable to the theft of data. 8

Victims of identity theft stand to lose large sums of money, suffer damage to their credit and reputation, and can possibly even lose possessions if the situation is not handled properly. It's important to remember that, even if you don't make transactions yourself, you may still be held responsible for them unless you take action quickly. 9

Because ID thieves mainly use nontechnical methods to get the information they need, most of the precautions you can take against ID thieves are low-tech. Further, they are all matters of common sense; you should do these things anyway, even if ID theft were not even possible. 10

From the moment they enter your mailbox until they reach the landfill, valuable documents such as account statements, financial records, bills and credit card applications are vulnerable. By handling them wisely, you can keep them out of the hands of an ID thief: 11

- **Guard your mail.** Pick up your mail as soon as possible after it arrives. Never allow mail to sit for a long time in your mailbox. If ID theft is a problem in your area, get a P.O. box and have sensitive documents delivered there. Also, put important outgoing mail in a public mailbox or take it to the post office, where no one can steal it.
- **Check your statements immediately.** Open and check your bank and credit card statements as soon as you get them. Look for suspicious charges, ATM transactions, or checks you did not write. If you find one, report it immediately. The sooner you report suspicious activity, the greater the chance

that the company will be able to help you. Some financial institutions place a time limit on reporting unauthorized transactions; after the time limit, your bank or credit card company may require you to pay for the charge.

- **Discard important documents wisely.** When you are ready to get rid of important documents, do it right. Shred any document that contains sensitive information such as your Social Security number, account numbers, or passwords.

In the course of a week, you probably give away all sorts of information about yourself without even thinking about it. It pays to be careful when sharing personal information to make sure it doesn't fall into the wrong hands. All of the following are good tips to remember: 12

- Never give anyone an account number over the phone unless you are sure he or she is a legitimate agent. Remember, a bank or legitimate business will never call you and ask for an account number. They should already have this information; if they need it, they will notify you by mail.
- Never give out account numbers, passwords, or other personal information via e-mail. E-mail is not a secure way to transmit data. It can be intercepted, or the recipient can forward it to someone else. Banks and legitimate businesses won't ask you to provide such information via e-mail.
- When buying something online, make sure the Web site is secure before entering any personal information into a form. Secure Web pages start their URL with "HTTPS", and the browser will display a lock icon, change the color of the title bar, or in some other way indicate that a secure connection has been made.

(Glen J. Coulthard, *Computing NOW*, 2013, p. 272–274)

COMPREHENSION CHECKUP

Short Answer

1. Of all the tips presented by Glen J. Coulthard, list the three that you find most helpful. Give reasons for your choice.

   a. ____________________

   b. ____________________

   c. ____________________

True or False

Directions: Indicate whether each statement is true or false by writing **T** or **F** in the space provided.

______ 1. To protect against identity theft, you should be careful in disposing of documents that contain personal information such as your Social Security number and bank account numbers.

______ 2. Most threats to your privacy are high-tech.

______ 3. An ID thief can sometimes find what he or she needs in your trash can.

______ 4. When you are using an ATM, you should be on the lookout for shoulder surfers.

______ 5. E-mail is generally a secure way to transmit information.

Multiple Choice

Directions: For each item, write the letter corresponding to the best answer.

______ 6. Which of the following best states the main idea of the selection?
a. It's easy to become an unwitting victim of identity theft.
b. Identity theft is a larger problem than experts suspected.
c. Identity theft is a large problem, but there are ways to combat it.
d. Identity theft is a federal crime.

______ 7. The author suggests all of the following ways to combat identity theft **except**
a. shred material containing personal information.
b. refrain from putting personal information in an e-mail.
c. don't carry personal information in your wallet or purse.
d. check your bank statements as soon as you get them.

______ 8. According to the author, a "dumpster diver" does all of the following **except**
a. goes through garbage cans, dumpsters, and trash bins.
b. searches for copies of checks, credit card, or bank statements.
c. steals information over the Internet.
d. uses a low-tech approach to steal personal information.

______ 9. The transition word *further* in paragraph 10 indicates
a. conclusion.
b. addition.
c. comparison.
d. cause and effect.

______ 10. The transition words *such as* in paragraph 11 are used to signal
a. an example.
b. a comparison.
c. a definition.
d. a list.

______ 11. The author mentions that an ID thief might do all of the following **except**
a. break into parked cars.
b. search through the trash.
c. solicit information over the telephone.
d. listen in on cell phone conversations.

______ 12. In paragraph 11 the transition word *also* indicates
a. addition.
b. spatial order.
c. reversal.
d. conclusion.

______ 13. The organizational pattern in paragraph 11 could be described as listing for all of the following reasons **except**
a. the use of a colon.
b. the use of the words *first, second,* and *third.*
c. the use of bullets.
d. the information is given without regard to order.

______ 14. A low-tech ID thief might resort to all of the following except
a. shoulder surfing.
b. dumpster diving.

c. snagging.
d. planting a Trojan horse on a computer system.

_____ 15. The author's main purpose in writing the selection is to
a. entertain.
b. persuade.
c. inform.
d. analyze.

Vocabulary in Context

Directions: Match the vocabulary words in Column A with the definitions in Column B. Place the correct letter on the line provided.

Column A	Column B
_____ 1. impersonates	a. steal
_____ 2. monetary	b. requiring specialized skill or knowledge
_____ 3. legitimate	c. rightful
_____ 4. brazen	d. pretends to be another person
_____ 5. swipe	e. relating to money
_____ 6. sophisticated	f. exposed to the possibility of being harmed
_____ 7. vulnerable	g. relating to private personal matters
_____ 8. sensitive	h. bold

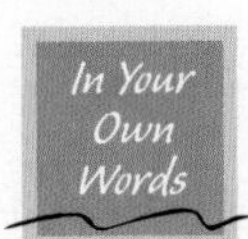

In Your Own Words

1. What are some things you should do if you become a victim of identity theft?
2. Identity theft is especially prevalent on college campuses. What reasons can you think of to account for this?

Written Assignment

1. Have you ever been a victim of identity theft? Do you know someone who was? Write a paragraph describing what happened.
2. Can identity theft be prevented? Come up with some new solutions to the problem.

Internet Activity

1. The Federal Trade Commission's identity theft site provides information to help you "deter, detect, and defend" against identity theft. You can access it at:

   www.ftc.gov/opa/reporter/idtheft

   Which of the site's suggestions will be most helpful to you?
2. Another government site is sponsored by the Department of Justice. You can access it at:

   www.usdoj.gov/criminal/fraud/websites/idtheft.html

   Which of the two government sites do you think provides the best information on the topic?
3. To check out scam alerts, consult the Identity Theft Resource Center at:

   www.idtheftcenter.org

   Their slogan is "Who's in your wallet?" Write a short paragraph describing a recent scam.

REVIEW TEST 6: Transition Words and Patterns of Organization

Seems like I've been having a lot of bad luck lately. First, I get this e-mail from my bank that says that there's been some suspicious activity in my account lately, and the bank wants me to confirm my account number and password. Always thoughtful, my bank provides a link in the e-mail that takes me directly to its Web site where I can do the confirmation.

Second, I get another e-mail message from my Internet service provider tell- 2
ing me that there's been a problem with my credit card, and if I don't update my account information immediately, it will terminate my service. Fortunately for me there's a link in the e-mail that takes me to its Web site. Finally, if that weren't enough, I get another e-mail from eBay saying I have to go through a mandatory registration, or it'll close my account. To make it easier for me, the e-mail has a link to the eBay site. What did I do to get so unlucky?

Actually, nothing. The above examples are just three illustrations of the Inter- 3
net scam known as "phishing." According to the Anti-Phishing Work Group, phishing is a form of online identity theft that uses fake e-mails designed to lure recipients to fraudulent Web sites, which attempt to trick them into divulging personal information, such as credit card numbers, passwords, Social Security numbers, and financial data.

Phishing isn't new. It first showed up decades ago when scammers used 4
bogus phone calls that tried to get people to give out personal information. The growing popularity of e-mail, however, has given this swindle a whole new life. In 2012, there were nearly 45,000 known phishing sites on the Web, and the number was increasing about 25 percent per month. It is estimated that about a quarter-million phishing messages are sent every month. One 2004 survey disclosed that about 3 percent of the people who get these phishing messages take the bait and provide personal information to the identity thieves. Banks and credit card companies estimate that phishing cost them about $1.2 billion in 2004, a cost that eventually got passed on to the consumer.

Phishing is bad enough, but a new scam called "pharming" is even scarier. 5
Pharming doesn't involve clicking on a link to a Web site. A person simply opens an e-mail and triggers a software program that actually rewrites the addresses of legitimate commercial Web sites. When a person, for example, types in the correct address of a credit card company, he or she is automatically and unknowingly sent to a bogus site that looks exactly like the legitimate site.

As they say, you can't be too careful. Make sure you keep up-to-date with 6
the latest security patches.

On a more general level, these schemes illustrate that the Internet has brought 7
us both positive and negative consequences. On the one hand, it entertains us, informs us, links us with friends and family, provides us with the world's greatest reference library, and stimulates commerce. On the other hand, it opens up whole new areas of concern: identity theft, fraud, deceptive advertising, pornography, and invasion of privacy.

For better or for worse, the Internet has become firmly embedded in the 8
nation's communication repertoire. It is hard to imagine how we ever got along without e-mail, e-commerce, e-dating, and eBay.

(Joseph R. Dominick, *The Dynamics of Mass Communication*, 9/e, McGraw-Hill, 2007, p. 261)

COMPREHENSION CHECKUP

Directions: Write the letter of the correct answer on the line provided.

_____ 1. In the first two paragraphs, the author gives _______ examples of e-mail messages he has received.
a. 2
b. 3
c. 4
d. 5

_____ 2. The first two paragraphs use the transition words *first, second,* and *finally.* These words are used to indicate
a. classification and division.
b. comparison.
c. contrast.
d. steps in a process and chronology.

_____ 3. In paragraph 3, the transition words *such as* are used to indicate
a. cause and effect.
b. examples.
c. definition.
d. contrast.

_____ 4. In paragraph 4, the transition word *however* signals a
a. contrast.
b. comparison.
c. definition.
d. cause and effect.

_____ 5. In paragraph 5, the transition word *but* signals a
a. definition.
b. comparison.
c. contrast.
d. classification and division.

_____ 6. In paragraph 5, the author provides an example of
a. "pharming."
b. "phishing."
c. someone being sent to an illegitimate site without their knowledge.
d. both a and c

_____ 7. In paragraph 7, the transition words *on the other hand* illustrate
a. comparison.
b. steps in a process.
c. contrast.
d. example.

_____ 8. Negative consequences of the Internet include all of the following **except:**
a. identity theft.
b. connects us to friends and family.
c. fraud.
d. invasion of privacy.

______ 9. In paragraph 8, the words *better* and *worse* are
a. synonyms.
b. homonyms.
c. antonyms.
d. none of the above

______ 10. The main idea of the selection is
a. the Internet is a valuable tool, but caution must be exercised in using it.
b. the author feels that he is a very unlucky person.
c. phishing and pharming are scams that cost the consumer a lot of money.
d. it is important to keep up with security measures.

Categories and Steps in a Process

In the following expository selection, the discussion of intimate relationships is divided into two categories—forming romantic relationships (getting in) and ending romantic relationships (getting out). The discussion then describes stages of communication that relationships pass through.

READING

"Many relationships stay stagnant for long periods of time."

TUNING IN TO READING The following excerpt on the stages of development in a romantic relationship comes from a popular communications textbook. Behavioral researcher Mark Knapp divided the rise and fall of romantic relationships into 10 stages, which are described below. According to Knapp, one stage predominates at any given time, though elements of other stages may be present. Not all romantic relationships will include all of the steps. Instead, some will stop at one place or another along the way.

BIO-SKETCH Kory Floyd is a professor of communication at Arizona State University. His research focuses on the communication of affection in personal relationships.

NOTES ON VOCABULARY

screen review for the purpose of including or excluding

Excerpt from

INTERPERSONAL COMMUNICATION

By Kory Floyd

Getting In: Forming Romantic Relationships

Romantic relationships don't develop overnight. Like many important relationships, they evolve, and researchers have found that people follow fairly consistent steps when they form romantic relationships. Communications scholar Mark Knapp, for instance, has suggested that relationship formation involves five stages: initiating, experimenting, intensifying, integrating, and bonding.

INITIATING. The **initiating stage** occurs when people meet and interact for the first time. For instance, you make eye contact with someone on the first day of class and decide to introduce yourself, or you might find yourself sitting next to someone on [an] airplane and strike up a conversation. "What's your name?" and "Where are you from?" are common questions people ask at this initial stage. 2

EXPERIMENTING. When you meet someone in whom you're initially interested, you might move to the **experimenting stage,** during which you have conversations to learn more about that person. Individuals at the experimenting stage might ask questions such as "What movies do you like?" and "What do you do for fun?" to gain basic information about a potential partner. This stage helps individuals decide if they have enough in common to move the relationship forward. 3

INTENSIFYING. During the **intensifying stage,** people move from being acquaintances to close friends. They spend more time together and might begin to meet each other's friends. They start to share intimate information with each other, such as their fears, future goals, and secrets about the past. They also increase their commitment to the relationship and may express that commitment verbally through statements such as "You're really important to me." 4

INTEGRATING. The **integrating stage** occurs when a deep commitment has formed, and the partners share a strong sense that the relationship has its own identity. At this stage, the partners' lives become integrated with each other, and they also begin to think of themselves as a pair—not just "you" and "I" but "we." Others start expecting to see the two individuals together and begin referring to the pair as a couple. 5

BONDING. The final stage in Knapp's model of relationship development is the **bonding stage,** in which the partners make a public announcement of their commitment to each other. That might involve moving in together, getting engaged, or having a commitment ceremony. Beyond serving as a public expression of a couple's commitment, bonding also allows individuals to gain the support and approval of people in their social networks. 6

Getting Out: Ending Romantic Relationships

Just as romantic relationships develop over time, they come apart over time. According to Mark Knapp, there are five stages that relationships go through when they end: differentiating, circumscribing, stagnating, avoiding, and terminating. 7

DIFFERENTIATING. Partners in any romantic relationship are similar to each other in some ways and different in other ways. In happy, stable relationships, partners see their differences as complementary. At the **differentiating stage,** however, they begin to see their differences as undesirable or annoying. 8

CIRCUMSCRIBING. When romantic partners enter the **circumscribing stage,** they begin to decrease the quality and the quantity of their communication with each other. Their purpose in doing so is to avoid dealing with conflicts. At the circumscribing stage, partners start spending more time apart. When they're together, they usually don't talk about problems, disagreements, or sensitive issues in their relationship and instead focus on safe topics and issues about which they agree. 9

STAGNATING. If circumscribing progresses to the point where the partners are barely speaking to each other, the relationship enters the **stagnating stage,** at which time the relationship stops growing and the partners feel as if they are just "going through the motions." Partners avoid communicating about anything 10 important because they fear it will only lead to conflict. Many relationships stay stagnant for long periods of time.

AVOIDING. When partners decide they are no longer willing to live in a stagnant relationship, they enter the **avoiding stage,** during which they create physical and emotional distance between themselves. Some partners take a direct route to creating distance, such as by moving out of the house or saying "I can't be around you right now." Others create distance indirectly, such as by making up excuses for being apart ("I have company in town all next week, so I won't be able to see you") and curtailing availability to the other person by screening phone calls or not responding to instant messages. 11

TERMINATING. The last stage in Knapp's model of relationship dissolution is the **terminating stage,** at which point the relationship is officially judged to be over. In non-marital relationships, that usually involves one or both partners' moving out if the couple shared a residence. It also involves dividing property, announcing to friends and family that the relationship has ended, and negotiating the rules of any future contact between the partners. For legally married partners, relational termination means getting a divorce. In the United States today, approximately 40 percent of all marriages end in divorce. 12

(Kory Floyd, *Interpersonal Communication,* 2/e, McGraw-Hill, 2012, pp. 323–324, 330–331)

"I'm leaving you, Gilbert. You can keep the bowl, but I'm taking the water and all the colored stones!"

COMPREHENSION CHECKUP

Completion

Directions: Complete the following steps-in-a-process diagram.

Step 5: Bonding	Differentiating: Step 1
Step 4: Integrating	Circumscribing: Step 2
Step 3: Intensifying	__________: Step 3
Step 2: Experimenting	__________: Step 4
Step 1: Initiating	__________: Step 5

Multiple Choice

Directions: For each item, write the letter corresponding to the best answer.

_____ 1. All of the following are examples of events that might happen in the initiating stage **except**
a. discussions about the weather.
b. handshakes.
c. soulful kisses.
d. discussions about where you are from.

_____ 2. All of the following are typical of the experimenting stage **except**
a. gaining more information about others.
b. discovering interests in common.
c. deciding whether it is worthwhile to get to know each other better.
d. spending large amounts of time with each other.

_____ 3. The transition words *for instance* in paragraph 2 indicate
a. addition.
b. summary.
c. example.
d. reversal.

_____ 4. Which stage is marked by spending increasing amounts of time together and making introductions to close friends and family members?
a. intensifying
b. initiating
c. experimenting
d. circumscribing

_____ 5. You could conclude all of the following from paragraph 8 **except**
a. the need to differentiate does not always indicate the relationship is weakening.
b. partners don't always enjoy the same activities.
c. having differences of opinion in a relationship is always undesirable.
d. people need to be individuals as well as part of a relationship.

_____ 6. The stagnation stage is marked by
a. increased interest and commitment.
b. interacting without any real emotional involvement.
c. confronting each other over problems and negotiating solutions.
d. continuing to grow in small but significant ways.

_____ 7. "Going through the motions" implies
a. being completely engaged.
b. a lack of real interest.
c. behaving in a mechanical fashion.
d. both b and c

_____ 8. If the author were reading this selection aloud, he would probably sound
a. optimistic.
b. objective.
c. sarcastic.
d. perplexed.

______ 9. The author's primary purpose in writing this selection was to
   a. inform readers of the difficulties in maintaining successful relationships.
   b. persuade readers to delay marriage until they have reached a mature age.
   c. tell a dramatic story about romantic relationships.
   d. explain the stages that a romantic relationship may pass through.

Vocabulary in Context

Directions: In the space provided, indicate whether each statement is true (**T**) or false (**F**).

______ 1. If you are wearing *complementary* colors, the colors of your clothes clash.

______ 2. A *scholar* is someone with little intellectual curiosity.

______ 3. If you are sharing *intimate* details of your life with someone, you are probably revealing information that you would ordinarily keep private.

______ 4. Bullies tend to be *sensitive* to the problems and feelings of others.

______ 5. Childcare experts say that being *consistent* is a key to effective discipline.

______ 6. When a person's thinking *evolves,* it remains about the same.

______ 7. When you *interact* with someone, you leave that person alone.

______ 8. A person in *stable* condition is likely to die shortly.

______ 9. An engagement ring usually symbolizes a personal *commitment.*

______ 10. A judge could *curtail* the visitation rights of a parent who is abusive.

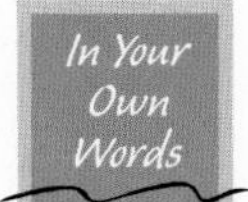

In Your Own Words

1. Considering the information provided in this selection, do you think it's possible to live "happily ever after"? Explain your answer.
2. Based on your own personal observations, do you think that "opposites attract"? Or is it more likely that "two birds of a feather flock together"? Explain your reasons.
3. Do you think living together is more likely or less likely to lead to marriage? Why?
4. Which proverb do you think is more accurate: "out of sight, out of mind" or "absence makes the heart grow fonder"? Give reasons for your answer.
5. What sorts of personality traits do you think lead to success in marriage? What factors do you think are associated with increased likelihood of divorce? Why do you think the divorce rate is higher today than in the past?

Written Assignment

1. Write a one- or two-sentence summary of each of the stages of a romantic relationship.
2. In the initiating stage, two people are probably attracted to each other on the basis of characteristics such as physical appearance, social standing, reputation, dress, race, age, personality, intelligence, education, religion. Which of these characteristics do you feel are most important to the typical male? To the typical female? Which are most important to you?

3. Breaking up is always hard to do, and doing it in person is almost always better than using a phone call, an instant message, or an e-mail. However, for those who just can't cope with the in-person ordeal, the authors of the popular *Dating and Sex Handbook* provide an example of a rejection letter. The trick, according to them, is to be kind, but firm.

   Dear ________________, [their name]

   I won't be able to make it this Saturday, or any Saturday, in fact. The truth is, I just can't be in a committed relationship right now. It's not you, it's me. I'm just not able to appreciate all you have to give.

   I feel like we've been spinning our wheels these last few years/months/weeks/days. I can't believe how wonderful you've been to me and how much you've put up with. You deserve better. I can't put you through this anymore and I can't give you what you need/want/deserve right now. I need more space, and I need time to figure out who the real [your name here] is.

   It may take some time, but I hope we can still be friends.

   Sincerely,

   ________________ [your name here]

   (Joshua Piven et al., The Worst-Case Scenario Survival Handbook: Dating and Sex. Chronicle Books, 2001, p. 154)

Just for fun, try writing your own rejection letter. Use concrete examples, but don't be too nasty!

Internet Activity

Professor Robert Sternberg developed the widely used triangular theory of love based on the components of intimacy, commitment, and passion. Enter a search for "Robert Sternberg" (now the president of the University of Wyoming) or "triangular theory of love." There is also a "Measure Your Love" questionnaire that you might find interesting.

You might also want to take an Internet relationships test. Enter a search for "relationships tests." Take a test that suits your needs (and make sure it's free!). Write a paragraph about what you found out about your relationships. Does the test correlate with the stages of romantic relationships you read about in the reading selection?

Chronological Order

The following short story by Langston Hughes is told in chronological order.

READING

"The woman said, 'Pick up my pocketbook, boy, and give it here.'"

TUNING IN TO READING What would you do if someone attempted to steal your purse or wallet? After reading the first paragraph of this short story, what do you think is going to happen next?

As you read this narrative, notice how the action of the story is told in sequence, with a clear beginning, middle, and end. Try to discover the larger message about relationships that the author is illustrating.

BIO-SKETCH Langston Hughes (1902–1967) is one of the best-known African American writers of the 20th century and the first to live solely from his writings and lectures. Shortly after his birth in Joplin, Missouri, his parents were divorced. As a result, Hughes spent much of his early childhood living in poverty with his maternal grandmother. In the following short story, the character of Mrs. Jones is most probably based on his grandmother. Hughes, a graduate of Lincoln University, was a prolific writer of poems, short stories, and plays. He also wrote two books. Throughout his literary career, he was sharply criticized by other African American writers who believed that he portrayed an unattractive view of African American life.

NOTES ON VOCABULARY

thank you, ma'm a small bump in the road sometimes put there to force drivers to go slowly. In earlier times, if a young couple went out riding, the male was entitled to a kiss every time he hit one of the bumps. He acknowledged that kiss with a polite *"Thank you, ma'm."*

pocketbook the original *pocketbook* was a man's purse that resembled an open book with a clasp at the top and that conveniently fit into the owner's pocket.

Thank You, Ma'm

LANGSTON HUGHES

She was a large woman with a large purse that had everything in it but a hammer and nails. It had a long strap, and she carried it slung across her shoulder. It was about eleven o'clock at night, dark, and she was walking alone, when a boy ran up behind her and tried to snatch her purse. The strap broke with the sudden single tug the boy gave it from behind. But the boy's weight and the weight of the purse combined caused him to lose his balance. Instead of taking off full blast as he had hoped, the boy fell on his back on the sidewalk and his legs flew up. The large woman simply turned around and kicked him right square in his blue-jeaned sitter. Then she reached down, picked the boy up by his shirt front, and shook him until his teeth rattled.

After that the woman said, "Pick up my pocketbook, boy, and give it here." 2

She still held him tightly. But she bent down enough to permit him to 3
stoop and pick up her purse. Then she said, "Now ain't you ashamed of yourself?"

Firmly gripped by his shirt front, the boy said, "Yes'm." 4

The woman said, "What did you want to do it for?" 5

The boy said, "I didn't aim to." 6

She said, "You a lie!" 7

By that time two or three people passed, stopped, turned to look, and 8
some stood watching.

"If I turn you loose, will you run?" asked the woman. 9

"Yes'm," said the boy. 10

"Then I won't turn you loose," said the woman. She did not release him. 11

"Lady, I'm sorry," whispered the boy. 12

"Um-hum! Your face is dirty. I got a great mind to wash your face for you. 13
Ain't you got nobody home to tell you to wash your face?"

"No'm," said the boy. 14

"Then it will get washed this evening," said the large woman, starting up 15
the street, dragging the frightened boy behind her.

He looked as if he were fourteen or fifteen, frail and willow-wild, in tennis 16
shoes and blue jeans.

The woman said, "You ought to be my son. I would teach you right 17
from wrong. Least I can do right now is to wash your face. Are you hungry?"

"No'm," said the being-dragged boy. "I just want you to turn me loose." 18

"Was I bothering *you* when I turned that corner?" asked the woman. 19

"No'm." 20

"But you put yourself in contact with *me*," said the woman. "If you think 21
that that contact is not going to last awhile, you got another thought coming.

When I get through with you, sir, you are going to remember Mrs. Luella Bates Washington Jones."

Sweat popped out on the boy's face and he began to struggle. Mrs. Jones stopped, jerked him around in front of her, put a half nelson about his neck, and continued to drag him up the street. When she got to her door, she dragged the boy inside, down a hall, and into a large kitchenette-furnished room at the rear of the house. She switched on the light and left the door open. The boy could hear other roomers laughing and talking in the large house. Some of their doors were open, too, so he knew he and the woman were not alone. The woman still had him by the neck in the middle of her room. 22

She said, "What is your name?" 23

"Roger," answered the boy. 24

"Then, Roger you go to that sink and wash your face," said the woman, whereupon she turned him loose—at last. Roger looked at the door—looked at the woman—looked at the door—*and went to the sink.* 25

"Let the water run until it gets warm," she said. "Here's a clean towel." 26

"You gonna take me to jail?" asked the boy, bending over the sink. 27

"Not with that face, I would not take you nowhere," said the woman. "Here I am trying to get home to cook me a bite to eat, and you snatch my pocketbook! Maybe you ain't been to your supper either, late as it be. Have you?" 28

"There's nobody home at my house," said the boy. 29

"Then we'll eat," said the woman. "I believe you're hungry—or been hungry—to try to snatch my pocketbook!" 30

"I want a pair of blue suede shoes," said the boy. 31

"Well, you didn't have to snatch *my* pocketbook to get some suede shoes," said Mrs. Luella Bates Washington Jones. "You could of asked me." 32

"Ma'm?" 33

The water dripping from his face, the boy looked at her. There was a long pause. A very long pause. After he had dried his face, and not knowing what else to do, dried it again, the boy turned around, wondering what next. The door was open. He could make a dash for it down the hall. He could run, run, run, *run!* 34

The woman was sitting on the daybed. After a while she said, "I were young once and I wanted things I could not get." 35

There was another long pause. The boy's mouth opened. Then he frowned, not knowing he frowned. 36

The woman said, "Um-hum! You thought I was going to say *but,* didn't you? You thought I was going to say, *but I didn't snatch people's pocketbooks.* Well, I wasn't going to say that." Pause. Silence. "I have done things, too, which I would not tell you, son—neither tell God, if He didn't already know. Everybody's got something in common. So you set down while I fix us something to eat. You might run that comb through your hair so you will look presentable." 37

An icebox was what people used before electricity. It literally held a block of ice to keep food cold.

In another corner of the room behind a screen was a gas plate and an icebox. Mrs. Jones got up and went behind the screen. The woman did not watch the boy to see if he was going to run now, nor did she watch her purse, which she left behind her on the daybed. But the boy took care to sit on the far side of the room, away from the purse, where he thought she could easily see him out of the corner of her eye if she wanted to. He did not trust the woman *not* to trust him. And he did not want to be mistrusted now. 38

"Do you need somebody to go to the store," asked the boy, "maybe to get some milk or something?" 39

"Don't believe I do," said the woman, "unless you just want sweet milk yourself. I was going to make cocoa out of this canned milk I got here." 40

"That will be fine," said the boy. 41

She heated some lima beans and ham she had in the icebox, made the cocoa, and set the table. The woman did not ask the boy anything about where he lived, or his folks, or anything else that would embarrass him. Instead, as they ate, she told him about her job in a hotel beauty shop that stayed open late, what the work was like, and how all kinds of women came in and out, blonds, red-heads, and Spanish. Then she cut him a half of her ten-cent cake. 42

"Eat some more, son," she said. 43

When they were finished eating, she got up and said, "Now here. Take this ten dollars and buy yourself some blue suede shoes. And next time, do not make the mistake of latching onto *my* pocketbook *nor nobody else's*—because shoes got by devilish ways will burn your feet. I got to get my rest now. But from here on in, son, I hope you will behave yourself." 44

She led him down the hall to the front door and opened it. "Good night! Behave yourself, boy!" she said, looking out into the street as he went down the steps. 45

The boy wanted to say something else other than, "Thank you, Ma'm," to Mrs. Luella Bates Washington Jones, but he couldn't do so as he turned at the barren stoop and looked back at the large woman in the door. He barely managed to say, "Thank you," before she shut the door. And he never saw her again. 46

(Langston Hughes, "Thank You, Ma'm," 1996)

COMPREHENSION CHECKUP

Short Answer

Directions: Answer the question briefly, in no more than a sentence or two.

What is the main idea the author is trying to convey?

____

Sequencing

A narrative usually relates a series of events in chronological order. This enables a reader to understand how one event leads directly to another.

Directions: Number the sentences to put the events in the correct chronological (or *time*) sequence.

______ Roger tells Mrs. Jones that he wants some blue suede shoes.

______ Roger thanks Mrs. Jones.

______ Roger combs his hair.

______ Roger offers to go to the store for Mrs. Jones.

______ Mrs. Jones kicks Roger and shakes him roughly.

______ Mrs. Jones serves Roger dinner and tells him about her job.

______ Mrs. Jones drags Roger behind her.

______ Roger washes his face.

______ Mrs. Jones gives Roger ten dollars to buy some blue suede shoes.

______ Roger tries to steal Mrs. Jones's purse.

In Your Own Words

1. When did Mrs. Jones decide to take Roger home to her house?
2. Why didn't Mrs. Jones call the police? Do you think Roger had tried to steal anything before?
3. Why didn't Roger run when he finally was given the opportunity?
4. When they were finally at her home, why did Mrs. Jones give Roger the chance to steal her purse?
5. Why does Mrs. Jones want Roger to make himself "presentable"? How are her suggestions interpreted by Roger?
6. At the end of their meal together, why did Mrs. Jones give Roger the money to buy his blue suede shoes?
7. What lesson do you think Mrs. Jones was trying to teach Roger?
8. Look at the "Notes on Vocabulary" for an unusual meaning of the phrase "thank you, ma'm." What do you think Hughes means to imply by the title of this story? Do you think he made use of this special meaning?
9. Do you think a similar incident could happen today? Or are people too frightened to get involved in another person's life?

Written Assignment

1. Natural-sounding dialogue can reveal something about the character of the people in the narrative. What does the dialogue in this story reveal about Mrs. Jones and Roger?
2. Trace the character development of Roger. How does his behavior change as the result of Mrs. Jones's actions?
3. Discuss how you helped someone or someone helped you. Give details about what happened and how you felt.

Internet Activity

Discover more about Langston Hughes by going to the following Web site:

www.poets.org/poets/

Type in his name, read a short biography about him, and then read one of his poems. Print the poem and write a short paragraph discussing the meaning of the poem for you.

Cause and Effect

The following excerpt from a psychology textbook explains the cause-and-effect relationship between violence in the media and aggressive behavior in children.

READING

"Does observing violent and antisocial acts in the media lead viewers to behave in similar ways?"

TUNING IN TO READING The following excerpt is from *Understanding Psychology* by Robert S. Feldman. The author discusses the effects of media violence on children. While reading the selection, think of ways to limit aggression among children who frequently watch TV or play video games. Would you support a ban on aggressive video games for children?

BIO-SKETCH Robert S. Feldman is a professor of psychology at the University of Massachusetts. Dr. Feldman has written numerous books and articles. He is also noted for his research on honesty and deception.

NOTES ON VOCABULARY

mobster a member of a criminal gang.

henchman originally meant "trusted attendant or follower." In the 19th century, Scottish novelist Sir Walter Scott got the word confused with "haunchman," which meant "an obedient or unscrupulous follower." Thus, *henchman* today refers to a ruthless subordinate, often a gang member.

dismember to divide into parts; to cut up.

copycat to imitate or mimic. The origins of this word are uncertain. *Copycat* may simply be derived from the actions of a kitten mimicking its mother.

VIOLENCE IN TELEVISION AND VIDEO GAMES: DOES THE MEDIA'S MESSAGE MATTER?

Robert S. Feldman

In an episode of "The Sopranos," a former television series, fictional mobster Tony Soprano murdered one of his associates. To make identification of the victim's body difficult, Soprano, along with one of his henchmen, dismembered the body and dumped the body parts.

A few months later, in real life, two real-life half brothers in Riverside, 2 California, strangled their mother and then cut her head and hands from her body. Victor Bautista, 20, and Matthew Montejo, 15, were caught by police after a security guard noticed that the bundle they were attempting to throw in a dumpster had a foot sticking out of it. They told police that the plan to dismember their mother was inspired by the "Sopranos" episode.

Like other "media copycat" killings, the brothers' cold-blooded brutality 3 raises a critical issue: Does observing violent, antisocial acts in the media lead viewers to behave in similar ways? Because research on modeling shows that people frequently learn and imitate the aggression that they observe, this question is among the most important being addressed by psychologists.

Certainly, the amount of violence in the mass media is enormous. By the 4
time of elementary school graduation, the average child in the United States will have viewed more than 8,000 murders and more than 800,000 violent acts on network television.

Most psychologists agree that watching high levels of media violence makes 5
viewers more susceptible to acting aggressively, and recent research supports this claim. For example, one survey of serious and violent young male offenders incarcerated in Florida showed that one-fourth of them had attempted to commit a media-inspired copycat crime. A significant proportion of those teenage offenders noted that they paid close attention to the media.

Violent video games have also been linked with actual aggression. In one 6
of a series of studies by psychologist Craig Anderson and his colleagues, for example, college students who frequently played violent video games were more likely to have been involved in delinquent behavior and aggression. Frequent players also had lower academic achievement.

Several aspects of media violence may contribute to real-life aggressive 7
behavior. For one thing, experiencing violent media content seems to lower inhibitions against carrying out aggression—watching television portrayals of violence or using violence to win a video game makes aggression seem a legitimate response to particular situations. Exposure to media violence also may distort our understanding of the meaning of others' behavior, predisposing us to view even non-aggressive acts by others as aggressive. Finally, a continuous diet of aggression may leave us desensitized to violence, and what previously would have repelled us now produces little emotional response. Our sense of the pain and suffering brought about by aggression may be diminished.

What about real-life exposure to *actual* violence? Does it also lead to 8
increases in aggression? The answer is yes. Exposure to actual firearm violence (being shot or being shot at) doubles the probability that an adolescent will commit serious violence over the next two years. Whether the violence is real or fictionalized, then, observing violent behavior leads to increases in aggressive behavior.

(Robert S. Feldman, *Understanding Psychology,* 11/e, 2013)

COMPREHENSION CHECKUP

Multiple Choice

Directions: For each item, write the letter corresponding to the best answer on the line provided.

______ 1. The author's main idea is that
- a. displays of violence in the media are quite common.
- b. *The Sopranos* is a violent television program.
- c. parents should watch violent television programs with their young children rather than let them view such programs by themselves.
- d. there is a significant association between observing violent acts and behaving in an aggressive manner.

_____ 2. The word *modeling* as used in paragraph 3 means
a. imitating.
b. observing.
c. extending.
d. preserving.

_____ 3. The transition word *finally* in paragraph 7 indicates a
a. comparison.
b. contrast.
c. addition.
d. conclusion.

_____ 4. An *insensitive* person is one who
a. shows consideration for others.
b. lacks creativity.
c. is not affected by the suffering of others.
d. feels a great deal of pain.

_____ 5. The author would agree with all of the following **except** for which?
a. Observing aggression in the media increases the likelihood that viewers will act aggressively.
b. Viewing programs such as *Sesame Street* is unlikely to lead to aggressive behavior in young children.
c. There is little actual violent material on television.
d. Exposure to media violence desensitizes viewers to acts of aggression.

_____ 6. After watching a violent program, a person might
a. mistake a nonthreatening act for a threatening one.
b. become overly sensitive to the suffering of others.
c. respond in a threatening way to a slight by another person.
d. both a and c.

_____ 7. The author's purpose in writing this selection is to
a. explain.
b. persuade.
c. entertain.
d. define.

_____ 8. According to recent research, all of the following are associated with playing violent video games **except**
a. lower academic achievement.
b. delinquent behavior.
c. personal generosity.
d. acts of aggression.

Vocabulary in Context

Directions: Choose one of the following words to complete the sentences on the following page. Use each word only once.

antisocial	desensitized	diminished	distorts	incarcerated
inhibitions	linked	proportion	repelled	susceptible

1. Margaret has missed a great deal of school because she is especially ______________ to colds and flu.

2. Because the coach frequently berated him, Nick had a(n) ______________ interest in continuing with the team.

3. To be able to participate in karaoke, people need to overcome their ______________ about performing in public.
4. After having been ______________ for over 20 years, Carlos was set free when DNA evidence conclusively proved he could not have committed the murder.
5. His ______________ behavior was responsible for his lack of close friends.
6. What ______________ of the population favors tax reform?
7. After years of hearing his crude jokes, Blanca had become ______________ to their impact.
8. Scientists at the University of California have ______________ infant exposure to pesticides to the development of autism.
9. Duc was so ______________ by the foul odor in the air that he had to leave the building immediately.
10. Presidential candidates frequently complain that the press ______________ what they say.

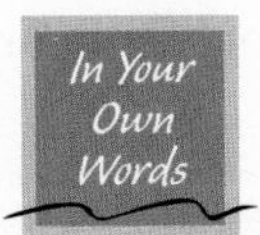

In Your Own Words

1. Assuming that there is a cause-and-effect relationship between watching violent programs in the media and engaging in violent behavior, can you think of ways to help solve this problem? Is there anything the media could do? What about parents?
2. Can you think of some desirable traits in children that are fostered by television? By playing video games?

Written Assignment

Recent studies indicate that most children spend well over three hours per day watching television. This is contrary to the American Academy of Pediatrics' (AAP) recommendation—that children spend no more than two hours per day with *all* screen media. According to the AAP, excessive viewing by children is associated with physical, academic, and behavioral problems. The AAP recommends that parents try to follow these guidelines:

- Pay attention to how much time children spend using all screen media (television, computer, and video game screens).
- Eliminate background television.
- Do not put a television set in a child's bedroom.
- Limit television on school days.
- Do not put a television in household eating areas, and do not connect television viewing with eating of any sort, including snacks and meals.

What do you think of these suggestions? Are they likely to work? Write a short essay discussing the AAP suggestions. Try to include a few suggestions of your own.

Internet Activity

LimiTV is a nonprofit North Carolina corporation formed in 1995 to educate parents, teachers, and children about the effects of excessive television viewing, including the relationship between TV violence and aggressive behavior. Go to its Web site at:

www.limitv.org

Find an article on the site of interest to you, and summarize the information.

Chapter Summary and Review

In Chapter 7, you became familiar with several patterns of organization in reading selections. Based on the information in Chapter 7, answer the following.

Vocabulary in Context

Directions: Choose one of the following terms to complete the sentences below. Use each term only once.

cause/effect	chronological-order	communicate	compare/contrast
multiple	one	selections	

1. Sometimes an author may organize an entire reading selection using only _______________ pattern of organization.
2. However, frequently an author uses _______________ patterns.
3. An author's goal is to _______________ with the audience.
4. Patterns of organization in paragraphs are the same as patterns in longer reading _______________.
5. An author who wants to tell a story in correct time order might use the _______________ pattern.
6. An author who wants to show similarities and differences between two things might use the _______________ and _______________ pattern.
7. An author who wants to discuss the effects of poor diet on disease might use the _______________ and _______________ pattern.

Interpreting What We Read

PART 3

CHAPTERS IN PART 3

Piano Deconstructed by Jim Reynolds

CHAPTER

8 Inference

CHAPTER PREVIEW

In this chapter, you will

- Practice drawing inferences from a variety of sources.

Introduction to Drawing Inferences

The details in the photograph below will help you answer the following questions. Answer each question the best you can and write down the clues from the photo that helped you find your answer. Write "can't tell" after any question that you can't answer on the basis of the clues provided.

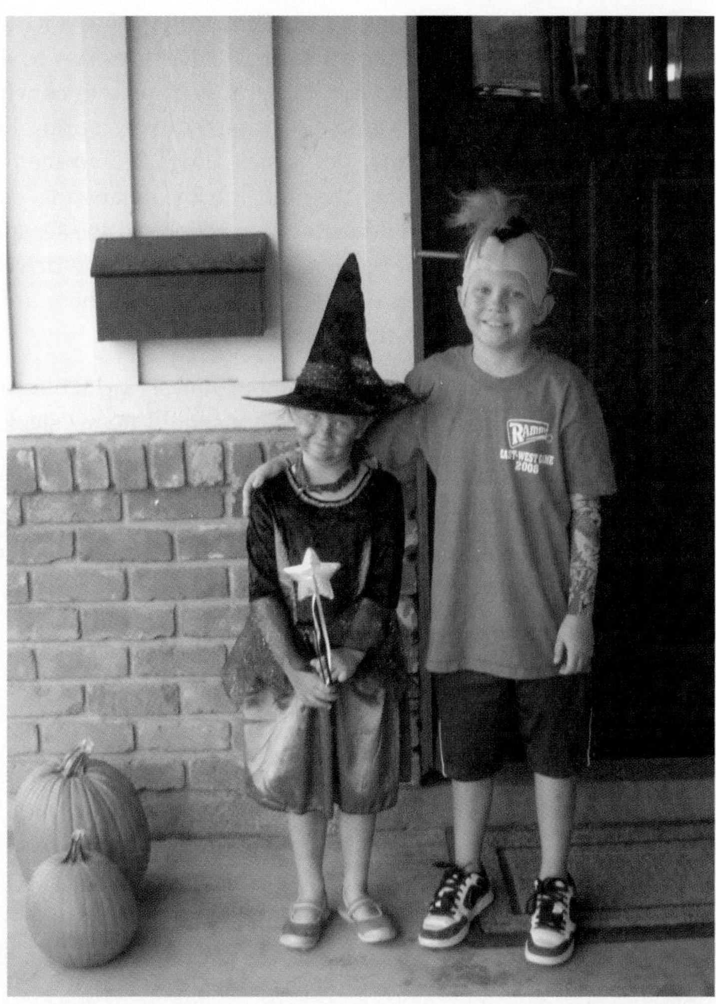

1. How old are the children? __________
2. What are the children's names? __________
3. Are the children in the same grade? __________
4. Where are the children going? __________
5. Are the children happy or sad? __________

When you answered these questions, you were making **inferences** from the picture. This means you made educated guesses and drew conclusions based on clues you found in the photograph. You had to draw inferences from the photo because it does not directly tell you the answers.

From this photo, you could answer only questions 4 and 5 with reasonable certainty. The children are probably going either trick-or-treating or to a Halloween party. We can draw this conclusion because they are wearing costumes and there are pumpkins to the side of the girl indicating the season of the year. You can reasonably infer that the boy is happy because he is smiling. The girl's half-smile is more difficult to decipher. She might just be dutifully smiling for the camera. The photo doesn't give us enough information to do anything but guess the answers to questions 1, 2, and 3.

Drawing Inferences in Everyday Life

We make inferences, or intelligent guesses, every day of our lives. If a teacher sees a student looking at a watch and tapping a foot impatiently, the teacher will likely conclude that the student is eager for class to end. If someone comes home from work and slams the door, most of us will conclude that the person is upset about something. If Maria's previously lively puppy lies on the floor all day, she'll likely conclude that her pet is sick and needs to see the vet.

We negotiate through life by means of "cues." We are constantly "reading" situations and adjusting our actions. If we see a car weaving down the road late at night, we will become concerned that the driver could be intoxicated, and so we try to stay out of the way. Inferences, then, are evidence-based. What might you logically infer from the following?

1. Your next-door neighbor has set up tables in her carport. On each table she places miscellaneous household items, stacks of baby clothes, and toys.

   Your inference: ______________________________

2. Ten people are seated at a table in a restaurant. At the end of the meal, a waitress brings a small cake with one candle and sets it directly in front of one of the people.

   Your inference: ______________________________

Inferences in Reading

The ability to make accurate inferences is an essential part of reading critically. Drawing inferences from written material requires the same kind of thinking as drawing inferences from real-life situations. You must study the available clues and come to a reasonable conclusion. By doing so, you find the idea that is present in what you are reading but not directly stated. When you "draw inferences," you make educated guesses using the clues provided by the writer, your own experience, and logic. In the words of S. I. Hayakawa, "an inference is a statement about the unknown made on the basis of the known." Reading for inferences is often called "reading between the lines."

To understand the short reading passage below, you must infer the meaning of the word *hora,* which can be accomplished by reading the last two sentences. After reading the passage, write the letter of the most logical answer on the line provided.

HORA

A corporate president recently made a visit to a nearby reservation as part of his firm's public relations program. "We realize that we have not hired any Native Americans in the five years our company has been located in this area," he told those assembled, "but we are looking into the matter very carefully." "Hora, hora," said some of the audience. "We would like to eventually hire 5 percent of our total workforce from this reservation," he said. "Hora, hora," shouted more of the audience. Encouraged by their enthusiasm, the president closed his short speech by telling them that he hoped his firm would be able to take some hiring action within the next couple of years. "Hora, hora, hora," cried the total group. With a feeling of satisfaction the president left the hall and was taken on a tour of the reservation. Stepping in a field to admire some of the horses grazing there, the president asked if he could walk up closer to the animals. "Certainly," said his driver, "but be careful not to step in the hora."

(John Langan, *Ten Steps to Improving Reading Skills,* 4/e, 2003)

______ 1. To get the main point of the passage, we must infer
a. the location of the reservation.
b. the kind of company the president headed.
c. the meaning of the word *hora.*

______ 2. From the president's speech, we can infer that
a. his firm had great interest in hiring Native Americans.
b. his firm had little interest in hiring Native Americans.

______ 3. From the passage, we can infer that
a. the audience believed the president's speech.
b. the audience did not believe the president's speech.

______ 4. From the passage, we can infer that the president
a. thought the Native Americans deserved to be hired.
b. thought his company should not hire the Native Americans.
c. misinterpreted the Native Americans' reaction to his speech.

______ 5. From the passage, we can infer that the main reason the president spoke to the Native Americans about jobs was that
a. they needed the jobs.
b. he thought promising jobs to Native Americans would make his company look good.
c. he thought hiring Native Americans would be good for his company.

If we understand the meaning of the word *hora,* we realize that the Native Americans recognized early on that the corporate president was engaging in "empty promises" and had no intention of hiring very many of them. We noted the fact that the firm had been in the area for five years and had not yet hired a single Native American. Moreover, the president was not promising to remedy the situation immediately, but was promising 5 percent employment within "the next couple of years," again indicating no real commitment on his firm's part.

You can see how experience can play a role in our ability to understand inferences. Those of us who know more about how businesses sometimes handle problems with community relations may more easily see the cues indicating the president's lack of sincerity. In this case, the joke was on the corporate president, whose feeling of satisfaction with his speech was completely unjustified.

As you proceed through the exercises that follow, keep the following guidelines in mind.

- Base your inferences on the facts that are presented.
- Apply what you already know about the subject to help you determine the correct inference.
- Consider all possible interpretations before coming to a final conclusion.

Exercise 1: Drawing Inferences from Jokes

Jokes often require you to read between the lines in order to get the point being made. They may be funny because of what is deliberately left unsaid. Study the two jokes below. What inference makes each joke humorous?

JOKE 1

A student was standing near the college mailroom with a package in her hands and a depressed look on her face. Her friend came by and said, "What's the matter? You look pretty sad for getting a package from home." The student replied, "My dad played a cruel trick on me. I wrote and asked for $200 for a dictionary, and he sent me a dictionary."

Inference: ____

____

JOKE 2

Mother: Why did you get such a low mark on that test?

Son: Because of absence.

Mother: You mean you were absent on the day of the test?

Son: No, but the kid who sits next to me was.

Inference: ____

Exercise 2: Drawing Inferences from Cartoons

Explain the inference that makes each of the following cartoons funny.

CARTOON 1

"Kenny hasn't spoken to me in six months, he won't return my calls and he goes out with all my friends. Do you think I should break up with him?"

Inference: ____

____

CARTOON 2

"I'd like some dry broiled fish, sliced cucumbers, and fresh mixed berries. If you don't have that, I'll take a triple bacon cheeseburger, jumbo fries and a cookie dough shake!"

Inference: ______________________________

Exercise 3: Drawing Inferences from a Mystery

Directions: In order to solve this short mystery, you must put together all the available clues.

"WIDE O-" BY ELSIN ANN PERRY

Maybe I'll put my head under the pillow—no, that's no good at all. I can imagine him, whoever he is, sneaking up on me. Okay, that does it! I'm going to get up and stay up, put the lights on in the living room, turn on the television. Oh, I hate going into the dark . . . there! Overhead light on, floor light on, TV on, nice and loud. Now I'll just sit down and relax and watch the—

1. The speaker seems mainly to be feeling ________.
   a. tired
   b. afraid
   c. sick

2. The sentence that gives the best clue as to why she feels this way is the one beginning ________.
   a. "Maybe I'll put my head. . . ."
   b. "I can imagine him. . . .
   c. "Now I'll just sit down. . . ."

3. In the last sentence, she is planning to watch the ________.
   a. front door
   b. clock
   c. television

Hey, what was that? Oh. Old houses creak, remember? If it creaked when Russell was here, it'll creak when he's away, and it's just—just something in the house. It's only your imagination, that's what it is. And the more sleepy you get, the more vivid your imagination will get.

4. The speaker says, "Hey, what was that?" because ________.
   a. she heard a noise
   b. she felt something touch her
   c. she saw something strange on TV

5. She is speaking to ________.
   a. her mother
   b. Russell
   c. herself

6. At this point, who do you think Russell is? ________________

All the doors are locked, right? And all the windows, too. Okay, then. So I feel like an idiot, trying to stay up all night. Well, sitting here in the living room is a lot better than doing what I did the last time Russ was away overnight! Locking myself in the bathroom and staying there all night, for heaven's sake—

7. She has locked all the doors and windows ________.
   a. to make herself feel safer
   b. because they were rattling
   c. because she felt a draft

8. She is trying to control her emotions by using her ________.
   a. common sense
   b. emotions
   c. imagination

Oh! Oh, the furnace clicked on, and that's all *that* was. Calm down, calm down! The trouble with you is, you read the newspapers. You should read the comics and stop there. No, I have to read *Mother of Three Attacked by Intruder* and *Woman Found Beaten to Death in Home*. But oooh, they were so close to us! That old lady lived—what was it, only three—four blocks away? But she lived alone and nobody knows I'm alone tonight. I hope.

9. She says, "Oh, the furnace clicked on, that's all *that* was," because ________
   a. she heard another noise
   b. she suddenly felt warm
   c. she turned it on herself

10. She has read *Mother of Three Attacked by Intruder* and *Woman Found Beaten to Death in Home* and now she thinks ________.
    a. they made good stories
    b. something like that might happen to her
    c. she has wasted her time

11. "That old lady" was ________.
    a. a character in a story
    b. a relative
    c. a murder victim

What is the matter with me, anyway? I'm acting like a child. Other women live alone—for years, even—and here I have to stay by myself for just one measly little night, and I go all to pieces. Oh, it sure seems cold in here. The furnace was on—still is on, in fact. Must be my nerves. I'll go into the kitchen and make myself a nice hot cup of tea. Good idea! Maybe that'll warm me up.

Now where is that light switch . . . there . . . well, no *wonder* I'm cold, with the back door standing wide o—

12. This is the end of the story, and yet the last word is left unfinished. What should it be? ________

13. Why doesn't the speaker finish the last word? In your own words, tell what you think must be happening at this moment.

____

____

("Wide O-" copyright 1968 by Elsin Ann Perry, *Ellery Queen's Mystery Magazine*, September 1968)

Exercise 4: Drawing Inferences from Fables

Nesreddin Hodja was born in Turkey in the early 13th century. He served as a religious leader (*imam*) and judge in his village. His fables are famous throughout the Middle East, Turkey, Hungary, Russia, and parts of Africa. All of his stories use humor to teach a fundamental lesson about human relationships.

The following Hodja stories are from Tales of the Hodja retold by Charles Downing (OUP, 1964), copyright © Charles Downing 1964, reprinted by permission of Oxford University Press)

Directions: Read the Nasreddin Hodja fables and answer the questions that follow.

A. Nesreddin was poor in those days, so he went looking for a job. A rich man needed a tiled path for his home, so Nesreddin offered to build him one for a gold coin. His offer was accepted. After he had built the path, he was given a silver coin. Nesreddin accepted the coin grudgingly. In two months, the rich man came back to him, saying, "Oh Nasreddin, your path is so beautiful I want another one. I will pay you another gold coin."

Nasreddin replied, "Fool me once, shame on you. Fool me twice, shame on me."

______ 1. We can infer that Nasreddin
   a. was about to make the same mistake.
   b. was eager to work for free.
   c. had learned an expensive lesson.

B. Nesreddin Hodja opened a booth with a sign above it that read:

TWO QUESTIONS ON ANY SUBJECT ANSWERED FOR ONLY 100 LIRAS

A man who had two very urgent questions handed over his money, saying, "A hundred liras is rather expensive for two questions, isn't it?"

"Yes," said Nesreddin, "and the next question, please?"

______ 2. We can infer that
   a. the man wasted his first question.
   b. Nesreddin was going to let the man ask two more questions.
   c. Nesreddin is not going to make much money on his booth.

C. One day a neighbor came to Nesreddin's house fresh from hunting, bringing a hare as a gift. Delighted, Nesreddin cooked the hare in a stew and shared it with his guest.

Soon, however, one countryman after another started to call, and each one was the relative of the man who had brought him the hare. No one brought any additional presents. Nevertheless, Nesreddin heated some more soup and shared it with all of his guests.

Many days later yet another stranger appeared saying, "I am the relative of the relative who brought you the hare."

He sat down at the table, like all the rest, expecting a nice meal. Nesreddin handed him a bowl of hot water mixed with a little salt and some spices.

"What kind of soup is this?" asked the stranger.

"You are the relative of the relative of my neighbor," Nesreddin said. "And that is the soup of the soup of the hare which was brought by him."

______ 3. We can infer that
- a. Nesreddin is a poor cook.
- b. Nesreddin felt that his hospitality had been abused.
- c. Nesreddin was happy to have more visitors.

D. One day Nesreddin went to town to buy new clothes. First he tried on a pair of pants. He didn't like the pants, so he gave them back to the shopkeeper. Then he tried on a robe, which had the same price as the pants. Nesreddin was pleased with the robe, and he left the shop. Before he climbed on his donkey to ride home, the shopkeeper and the shop-assistant ran out.

"You didn't pay for the robe!" said the shopkeeper.

"But I gave you the pants in exchange for the robe, didn't I?" replied Nesreddin.

"Yes, but you didn't pay for the pants either!" said the shopkeeper.

"But I didn't buy the pants," replied Nesreddin. "I am not so stupid as to pay for something that I never bought."

______ 4. We can infer that Nesreddin got to the shop
- a. on foot.
- b. by camel.
- c. by donkey.

______ 5. We can infer that the item Nesreddin liked best was
- a. the robe.
- b. the hat.
- c. the pants.

______ 6. We can infer that the shopkeeper was angry with Nesreddin because
- a. he didn't pay for the pants.
- b. he didn't pay for the robe.
- c. he left in a hurry.

______ 7. We can infer that Nesreddin paid for
- a. nothing.
- b. the robe.
- c. the pants.

E. One day Nesreddin borrowed a pot from his neighbor Ali. The next day he brought it back with another little pot inside. "That's not mine," said Ali. "Yes it is," said Nesreddin. "While your pot was staying with me, it had a baby."

Some time later Nesreddin asked Ali to lend him a pot again. Ali agreed, hoping that he would once again receive two pots in return. However, days passed and Nesreddin had still not returned the pot. Finally Ali lost patience and went to demand his property. "I am sorry," said Nesreddin. "I can't give you back your pot, since it has died." "Died!" screamed Ali. "How can a pot die?" "Well," said Nesreddin, "you believed me when I told you that your pot had had a baby."

______ 8. We can infer that the owner of the pot was
a. Nesreddin.
b. Ali.
c. the baby.

______ 9. How did Ali feel about lending the pot to Nesreddin the second time?
a. pleased
b. reluctant
c. angry

______ 10. Why did Ali lend Nesreddin the pot the second time?
a. He wanted an additional pot.
b. He was a good neighbor.
c. He had many pots to spare.

______ 11. Why was Ali annoyed with Nesreddin?
a. Nesreddin tried to play a trick on him.
b. Nesreddin tried to keep Ali's property.
c. both a and b

______ 12. What can we assume happened to the little pot?
a. Nesreddin kept it.
b. Ali gave it back to Nesreddin.
c. Ali kept it.

READING

"(My grandmother) said to me: 'You must learn to do some good work, the making of some item useful to man.'"

TUNING IN TO READING Have your grandparents ever given you advice about how to conduct your life? Was it advice that you agreed or disagreed with?

BIO-SKETCH William Saroyan (1908–1981) was an American writer of Armenian descent. Throughout his long and prolific career, he drew upon his heritage to provide him with inspiration for his short stories, novels, and plays. He is best known for the short story collection *The Daring Young Man on the Flying Trapeze;* the play *The Time of Your Life,* which won the Pulitzer Prize; and the novel *The Human Comedy.* In many of his stories, Saroyan invents a family life much different from his own. At the age of 3, he lost his father and was placed in an orphanage by his mother. At the age of 8, he began selling newspapers and working at a variety of odd jobs. He learned to read at the age of 9 and shortly afterward began to write. Eventually, at the age of 15, he left school altogether. Over the years, he has said, it was his writing that kept him sane.

NOTES ON VOCABULARY

humble to lower in condition, rank, or position. *Humble* is derived from the Latin word *humilis,* which in turn comes from *humus,* meaning "soil." The literal meaning of *humble* is "not far above the ground" or "low."

dungeon a dark underground cell, vault, or prison.

The Shepherd's Daughter

WILLIAM SAROYAN

IT IS THE OPINION OF MY GRANDMOTHER, God bless her, that all men should labour, and at the table, a moment ago, she said to me: You must learn to do some good work, the making of some item useful to man, something out of clay, or out of wood, or metal, or cloth. It is not proper for a young man to be ignorant of an honourable craft. Is there anything you can make? Can you make a simple table, a chair, a plain dish, a rug, a coffee pot? Is there anything you can do?

And my grandmother looked at me with anger. 2

I know, she said, you are supposed to be a writer, and I suppose you are. 3
You certainly smoke enough cigarettes to be anything, and the whole house is full of the smoke, but you must learn to make solid things, things that can be used, that can be seen and touched.

Ancient Persia was located in the Middle East where Iran is today.

There was a king of the Persians, said my grandmother, and he had a son, 4
and this son fell in love with a shepherd's daughter. He went to his father and he said, My Lord, I love a shepherd's daughter, and I would have her for my wife. And the king said, I am king and you are my son, and when I die you shall be king, how can it be that you would marry the daughter of a shepherd? And the son said, My Lord, I do not know but I know that I love this girl and would have her for my queen.

The king saw that his son's love for the girl was from God, and he said, 5
I will send a message to her. And he called a messenger to him and he said, Go to the shepherd's daughter and say that my son loves her and would have her for his wife. And the messenger went to the girl and he said, The king's son loves you and would have you for his wife. And the girl said, What labour does he do? And the messenger said, Why he is the son of the king; he does no labour. And the girl said, He must learn to do some labour. And the messenger returned to the king and spoke the words of the shepherd's daughter.

The king said to his son, The shepherd's daughter wishes you to learn some 6
craft. Would you still have her for your wife? And the son said, Yes, I will learn to weave straw rugs. And the boy was taught to weave rugs of straw, in patterns and in colours and with ornamental designs, and at the end of three days he was making very fine straw rugs, and the messenger returned to the shepherd's daughter, and he said, These rugs of straw are the work of the king's son.

And the girl went with the messenger to the king's palace, and she became 7
the wife of the king's son.

One day, said my grandmother, the king's son was walking through the 8
streets of Baghdad, and he came upon an eating place which was so clean and cool that he entered it and sat at the table.

This place, said my grandmother, was a place of thieves and murderers, 9
and they took the king's son and placed him in a large dungeon where many great men of the city were being held, and the thieves and murderers were killing the fattest of the men and feeding them to the leanest of them, and making sport of it. The king's son was of the leanest of the men, and it was not known that he was the son of the king of the Persians, so his life was spared, and he said to the thieves and murderers, I am a weaver of straw rugs and these rugs have great value. And they brought him straw and asked him to weave and in three days he weaved three rugs, and he said, Carry these to the palace of the king of the Persians, and for each rug he will give you a hundred gold pieces of money. And the rugs were carried to the palace of the king, and when the king saw the rugs he saw that they were the work of his son and he took the rugs to the shepherd's daughter and he said, These rugs were brought to the palace and they are the work of my son who is lost. And the shepherd's daughter took each rug and looked at it closely and in the design of each rug she saw in the written language of the Persians a message from her husband, and she related this message to the king.

And the king, said my grandmother, sent many soldiers to the place of the 10
thieves and murderers, and the soldiers rescued all the captives and killed all the thieves and murderers, and the king's son was returned safely to the palace of his father, and to the company of his wife, the little shepherd's daughter. And when the boy went into the palace and saw again his wife, he humbled himself before her and he embraced her feet, and he said, My love, it is because of you that I am alive, and the king was greatly pleased with the shepherd's daughter.

Now, said my grandmother, do you see why every man should learn an 11
honourable craft?

I see very clearly, I said, and as soon as I earn enough money to buy a saw 12
and a hammer and a piece of lumber I shall do my best to make a simple chair or a shelf for books.

(William Saroyan, *The Shepherd's Daughter*, 1934)

COMPREHENSION CHECKUP

Multiple Choice

Directions: For each item, write the letter corresponding to the best answer.

______ 1. We can infer that at first the king of the Persians
   a. was pleased by his son's selection of a bride.
   b. was puzzled by his son's selection of a bride.
   c. ignored his son's selection of a bride.
   d. was angered by his son's selection of a bride.

______ 2. We can infer that the messenger was of the opinion that
   a. a king's son must do the bidding of a shepherd's daughter.
   b. a king's son is above doing tasks of manual labor.
   c. the shepherd's daughter should not be made queen.
   d. the king's son should not marry someone of a lowly station.

______ 3. We can infer that the grandson is going to please his grandmother
a. by giving up his smoking habit.
b. by learning to weave straw rugs.
c. by abandoning his desire to be a writer.
d. by earning enough money by writing to enable him to build something.

______ 4. The king's son was initially spared by the thieves and murderers because
a. he was lean.
b. it was considered unwise to kill the son of a king.
c. he was overweight.
d. he was a well-known weaver.

______ 5. We can infer all of the following **except**
a. prior to hearing the story of the shepherd's daughter, the grandson had not found it necessary to learn any craft.
b. the king of the Persians loved his son very much.
c. the grandson has now decided to learn carpentry.
d. the grandson is narrating the story of the shepherd's daughter.

True or False

Directions: Indicate whether each statement is true or false by writing **T** or **F** in the space provided.

______ 6. The grandmother has the most respect for someone who can create something useful.

______ 7. The grandmother saved the life of the king's son.

______ 8. Before the shepherd's daughter agreed to marry the king's son, she required that he learn a craft.

______ 9. The grandmother approves of her grandson's chosen profession.

______ 10. The king's son was grateful to the shepherd's daughter for helping rescue him.

Vocabulary in Context

Directions: Look through the given paragraph and find a word that matches the definition.

1. view (paragraph 1) ______________________
2. work (paragraph 1) ______________________
3. lacking in knowledge or training (1) ______________________
4. worthy of respect (1) ______________________
5. expected to (paragraph 3) ______________________
6. a person who carries information (paragraph 5) ______________________
7. decorative (6) ______________________
8. a dark prison (paragraph 9) ______________________
9. without much flesh or fat (9) ______________________

10. not subjected to harm or death (9) ____________________
11. hugged (10) ____________________

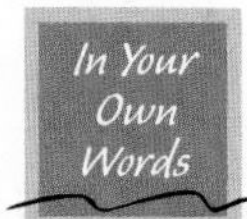

In Your Own Words

1. What is the main idea of the story?
2. According to the grandmother, what kind of work is admirable? Would the grandmother think that the practice of law is honorable? Include the supporting details from the story that helped you answer this question.
3. What character in the fable has the same attitude toward work as the grandmother?
4. What is the significance of the ending of the fable?
5. What is meant by the last sentence of the story? How will the grandson earn the money for the materials to build a chair or a bookshelf?
6. How much respect is given to the advice of elders in your family?

Written Assignment

Directions: Write a paragraph discussing one of the following.

1. Why is it necessary to learn a craft? What craft do you know? How do you think it is helpful to you?
2. Benjamin Franklin said, "He that hath a trade hath an estate." Compare Franklin's view with that of the grandmother and the shepherd's daughter.
3. Write a brief summary of "The Shepherd's Daughter."

Internet Activity

Directions: Complete the following:

The ancient Persian Empire was located in western Asia. At the height of its power, it encompassed much of what today is known as the Middle East, extending east to India and west to the Aegean Sea. Its great cities were Babylon and Persepolis, and its great leaders were Cyrus the Great, Darius the Great, and Xerxes. The Persian Empire lasted for more than 200 years. It was conquered about 330 B.C. by Alexander the Great. Until 1935, Persia was the official name of Iran.

Use the Internet to find additional information about the Persian Empire. Briefly summarize what you learn.

Exercise 5: Drawing Inferences from Literature

Directions: Read each of the following excerpts and use inferential reasoning to answer the questions that follow.

A. I suppose it was inevitable that my brother and I would get into one big fight which also would be the last one. When it came, given our theories about street fighting, it was like the Battle Hymn, terrible and swift. There are parts of it I did not see. I did not see our mother walk between us to try to stop us. She was short and wore glasses and, even with them on, did not have good vision. She had never seen a fight before or had any notion of how bad you can get hurt by becoming mixed up in one. Evidently, she just walked between her sons. The first I saw of her was the gray top of her head, the hair tied in a big knot with a big comb in it; but what was most noticeable was that her head was so close to Paul I couldn't get a good punch at him. Then I didn't see her anymore.

(Norman Maclean, *A River Runs Through It*, 1992)

1. What happened to the boys' mother? ______________________________

B. All he would have to do would be to slip the translation out of his desk, copy it, put it away, and he would pass the examination. All of his worries would be over. His father would be happy that he passed the examination. He wouldn't have to go to summer school. He and Charlie could go out to Colorado together to work on that dude ranch. He would be through with Latin forever. The Latin grade would never pull his average down again. Everything would be all right. Everything would be fine. All he would have to do would be to copy that one paragraph. Everyone cheated. Maybe not at V.P.S. But in other schools they bragged about it. . . . Everyone cheated in one way or another. Why should that one passage ruin everything? Who cared what problems the Romans had!

(C.D.B. Bryan, "So Much Unfairness of Things," 1962, 1964)

1. What subject is the student having difficulty with? ______________________

2. How is he rationalizing his decision? ______________________________

C. "C'mon, mama's boy," Bull whispered. "Bring little mama's boy up to Daddy Bull." Right hand, left hand, right hand, left hand, the ball drummed against the cement as Ben waited for his father to move out against him and Bull held back, fearing the drive to the basket. At the foul line, Ben left his feet for the jump shot, eyed the basket at the top of his leap, let it go softly, the wrist snapping, the fingers pointing at the rim and the ball spinning away from him as Bull lunged forward and drove his shoulder into Ben's stomach, knocking him to the ground. Though he did not see the ball go in, he heard the shouts of his mother and sisters; he saw Matthew leaping up and down on the porch. He felt his father rise off him slowly, coming up beaten by a son for the first time in his life. Screaming with joy, Ben jumped up and was immediately flooded by his family, who hugged, slapped, pummeled, and kissed him.

(Pat Conroy, *The Great Santini*, 1994.)

1. What kind of relationship does Ben have with his father? ________________

2. Is the family rooting for the father or the son? ______________________

3. What can we infer about Bull's character from this excerpt? ______________

____

____

D. A blur outside the car . . . Sherman grabbed the door pull and with a tremendous adrenal burst banged it shut. Out of the corner of his eye, the big one—almost to the door on Maria's side. Sherman hit the lock mechanism. *Rap!* He was yanking on the door handle—CELTICS inches from Maria's head with only the glass in between. Maria shoved the Mercedes into gear and squealed forward. The youth leaped to one side. The car was heading straight for the trash cans. Maria hit the brakes. Sherman was thrown against the dash. A vanity case landed on top of the gear shift. Sherman pulled it off. Now it was on his lap. Maria threw the car into reverse. It shot backward. He glanced to his right. The skinny one. . . . The skinny boy was standing there staring at him . . . pure fear on his delicate face. . . . Maria shoved it into first gear again. . . . She was breathing in huge gulps, as if she were drowning. . .

Sherman yelled, "Look out!"

The big one was coming toward the car. He had the tire up over his head. Maria squealed the car forward, right at him. He lurched out of the way . . . a blur . . . a terrific jolt. The tire hit the windshield and bounced off, without breaking the glass. . . .

Maria cut the wheel to the left, to keep from hitting the cans. . . . The skinny one standing right there. . . . The rear end fishtailed . . . *thok!* . . . The skinny boy was no longer standing. . . . Maria fought the steering wheel . . . a clear shot between the guard rail and the trash cans. . . . She floored it. . . . A furious squeal. . . . The Mercedes shot up the ramp.

(Tom Wolfe, *The Bonfire of the Vanities*, 1987)

1. Which person is wearing something that says "CELTICS"? ____________
2. How many people are inside the car? ____________
3. Who is driving the car? ____________
4. Describe the two people outside the car. Give an identifiable characteristic for each one. ____________
5. What happened to the skinny boy? ____________
6. What is the probable location of this incident? ____________
7. What is the likely emotion of those in the car? ____________

   How do you know? ____________
8. What can we infer about the motives of the two outside the car? ____________

   ____
9. Write a title that is descriptive of the contents of the passage. ____________

Directions: The following paragraphs are taken from the short story "Flight" by John Steinbeck; intervening paragraphs have been omitted. Answer the questions following each paragraph by using the clues provided by the author.

E. Without warning Pepe's horse screamed and fell on its side. He was almost down before the rifle crash echoed up from the valley. From a hole behind the struggling shoulder, a stream of bright crimson blood pumped and stopped and pumped and stopped. The hooves threshed on the ground. Pepe lay half stunned beside the horse. He looked slowly down the hill. A piece of sage clipped off beside his head and another crash echoed up from side to side of the canyon. Pepe flung himself frantically behind a bush.

   1. What is the probable fate of the horse? ____________

      ____
   2. Why is Pepe behaving in a frantic manner? ____________

F. The whole side of the slope grew still. No more movement. And then a white streak cut into the granite of the slit and a bullet whined away and a crash sounded up from below. Pepe felt a sharp pain in his right hand. A sliver of granite was sticking out from between his first and his second knuckles and the point protruded from his palm. Carefully he pulled out the sliver of stone. The wound bled evenly and gently. No vein nor artery was cut.

3. What is the likely setting of the story? ______________________________

4. How has Pepe been injured? ______________________________

5. Is the injury life-threatening? ______________________________

G. A moment later Pepe heard the sound, the faint far crash of horses' hooves on gravel. And he heard something else, a high whining yelp of a dog.

6. In what way has Pepe's situation become more desperate? ______________

____

H. He sat up and dragged his great arm into his lap and nursed it, rocking his body and moaning in his throat. He threw back his head and looked up into the pale sky. A big black bird circled nearly out of sight, and far to the left another was sailing near.

7. What can we infer about the status of his injury? ______________

____

8. What is the significance of the circling birds? ______________

____

I. Pepe bowed his head quickly. He tried to speak rapid words but only a thick hiss came from his lips. He drew a shaky cross on his breast with his left hand. It was a long struggle to get to his feet. He crawled slowly and mechanically to the top of a big rock on the ridge peak. Once there, he arose slowly, swaying to his feet, and stood erect. Far below he could see the dark brush where he had slept. He braced his feet and stood there, black against the morning sky.

9. What can we infer about how Pepe is feeling physically? ______________

____

10. Is Pepe religious? ______________________________

11. What is Pepe's solution to his dilemma? ______________________________

____

J. There came a ripping sound at his feet. A piece of stone flew up and a bullet droned off into the next gorge. The hollow crash echoed up from below. Pepe looked down for a moment and then pulled himself straight again.

12. Why did Pepe stand erect again? ______________________________

K. His body jarred back. His left hand fluttered helplessly toward his breast. The second crash sounded from below.

13. What was the end result of Pepe's flight? ______________________________

(John Steinbeck, "Flight," 1938)

Exercise 6: Drawing Inferences from Textbook Material

Directions: Read each of the following excerpts from textbooks, and use inferential reasoning to answer the questions that follow.

A. The beer people drink today is an alcoholic beverage made by fermenting grains and usually incorporating hops, but the process of making it was discovered nearly 8,000 years ago, around 6,000 B.C.E., in Sumeria. The Sumerians made beer out of half-baked crusty loaves of bread, which they crumbled into water, fermented, and then filtered through a basket. Surviving records indicate that as much as fifty percent of each grain harvest went into the production of beer.

Literally hundreds of surviving tablets contain recipes for beer, including for a black beer, a wheat beer, a white beer, and a red beer. One surviving tablet, which is similar to modern advertising slogans, reads "Drink Ebla—the beer with the heart of a lion."

(Janetta Benton, *Arts and Culture,* 2/e)

______ 1. We can infer that
   a. beer-making is a recent phenomenon.
   b. a key process involved in making beer is fermentation.
   c. beer-making consumed a small amount of the typical Sumerian grain harvest.
   d. none of the above

______ 2. We can infer that
   a. even in the past, good cooks sought to preserve their recipes by writing them down.
   b. the beer made by the Sumerians had a bitter taste.
   c. in Sumeria, only one type of beer was available.
   d. the Sumerians liked wine more than beer.

B. Coffee is made primarily from the seeds of *Coffea arabica,* a tree native to the mountains of Ethiopia. Consumption of coffee has a long history. One popular myth states that goats actually discovered the stimulating properties of the plant. Let out to graze, they came back one day friskier than normal. Investigating, the goatherd discovered animals had been eating the berries of a nearby tree. Trying some himself, he enjoyed the same stimulating effect and introduced the fruit to others. The fame of this berry soon spread. At first, coffee beans were eaten whole. The practice of roasting the seeds and producing what we would recognize as coffee began in the thirteenth century in Yemen. It was first used to keep worshippers awake through long vigils. By the late fifteenth century, coffee had spread to the Muslim cities of Medina and Mecca. Venetian traders introduced coffee to Europe in 1615, and by 1700 coffeehouses could be found throughout Europe. The first of the North American coffeehouses opened in Boston in 1669. Today coffeehouses are extremely popular in the United States, specializing in gourmet and exotic blends. Thousands of coffeehouses have opened in Japan in the last 30 years. Coffee may soon become the most popular stimulating beverage in the world.

(Estelle Levetin and Karen McMahon, *Plants and Society,* 6/e)

______ 1. We can infer that coffee
   a. was discovered by accident.
   b. is an extremely popular drink.

c. leads to an increase in energy.
d. all of the above

______ 2. We can infer that
a. coffee is a Western invention.
b. coffee beans can be eaten without causing death.
c. goats become ill when they eat coffee beans.
d. it took coffee a long time to become popular because of its bitter taste.

C. One-third of adults in the United States will suffer significant damage to their hearing by the time they are 65. Hearing damage can occur after eight hours of exposure to sounds louder than 80 decibels. Regular exposure for longer than one minute to more than 100 decibels can cause permanent hearing loss. Children may suffer damage to their hearing at lower noise levels than those at which adults suffer damage. Two common sources of excessive noise are the workplace and large gatherings of people at sporting events, rock concerts, and movie theaters. The Occupational Safety and Health Administration (OSHA) sets legal standards for noise in the workplace, but no laws exist regulating noise levels at concerts, which can be much louder than most workplaces. To avoid exposing yourself to excessive noise:

- Wear ear protectors when working around noisy machinery.
- When listening to music on a headset, keep the volume no louder than 6. Your headset is too loud if you are unable to hear people around you speaking in a normal voice.
- Don't sit or stand near speakers at a concert.
- Don't play music in your car so high that you can't hear the traffic.

(Paul M. Insel and Walton T. Roth, *Core Concepts in Health,* 13/e)

______ 1. We can infer that
a. a professional musician playing in a rock band might be at increased risk of suffering hearing loss in later years.
b. a person who operates a jackhammer or leaf blower without ear plugs might be at increased risk of suffering hearing loss in later years.
c. hearing loss only affects people who are 65 and older.
d. both a and b

D. On April 10, 1912, the ocean liner *Titanic* slipped away from the docks of Southampton, England, on its first voyage across the North Atlantic to New York. A proud symbol of the new industrial age, the towering ship carried 2,300 passengers, some enjoying more luxury than most travelers today could imagine. Poor people crowded the lower decks, journeying to what they hoped would be a better life in the United States.

Two days out, the crew received reports of icebergs in the area but paid little notice. Then, near midnight, as the ship steamed swiftly westward, a stunned lookout reported a massive shape rising out of the dark ocean directly ahead. Moments later, the *Titanic* collided with a huge iceberg, as tall as the ship itself, that split open its side as if the grand vessel were a giant tin can.

Seawater flooded into the ship's lower levels, pulling the ship down by the bow. Within twenty-five minutes of impact, people were rushing for the lifeboats. By 2:00 A.M., the bow was completely submerged, and the stern rose high above the water. Clinging to the deck, quietly observed by those in lifeboats, hundreds of helpless passengers and crew solemnly passed their final minutes before the ship disappeared into the frigid Atlantic.

The tragic loss of more than 1,600 lives made news around the world. However, some categories of passengers had much better odds of survival than others. Those on the upper decks, passengers traveling on first-class tickets, were more likely to be saved. Very few of the third-class passengers, on the lower decks, escaped drowning. And it was an advantage to be a woman or a child since they boarded the lifeboats first.

(John C. Macionis, *Society*, 11/e)

_____ 1. We can infer that
   a. passengers on the *Titanic* were more likely to survive if they were wealthy.
   b. passengers on the *Titanic* were more likely to survive if they were poor.
   c. the captain and crew members of the *Titanic* were more likely to survive.
   d. small children on the *Titanic* were more likely to perish because they didn't know how to swim.

_____ 2. We can infer that
   a. despite its massive size, the *Titanic* sank within a few hours.
   b. the *Titanic* sank within 25 minutes of hitting the iceberg.
   c. the crew bears no blame for the sinking of the *Titanic*.
   d. the *Titanic* split into two pieces as it sank in the freezing water.

E. The band strikes up—trumpets blaring, drums pounding, flutes trilling. Dancers whirl and gymnasts cavort. Then the players parade into the stadium, and the crowd goes wild, cheering their favorites. So many magnificent athletes trained to win, looking all the more formidable in their heavily padded gear. Which team will carry the day? A great deal is at stake for both players and spectators—honor, wealth, perhaps even life itself. The outcome hangs on the arc of a ball.

The Super Bowl? The World Series? Good guesses, because those present-day athletic spectacles bear striking resemblances to the scenes described above: the beginning of a ball game in pre-Columbian Mesoamerica. Those contests, with all their accompanying fanfare, consumed the attention of both elites and commoners for many centuries.

It was the Olmecs who got the ball rolling (and flying) around 1500 B.C.E. In the main plazas of their cities, they built ornate stone ball courts for teams to compete and celebrated star athletes with towering stone sculptures sometimes shown wearing helmets presumed to have been worn in their ancient ball games. Even as civilization rose and fell in Mesoamerica, the passion for playing ball, following the games, and gambling on their outcome not only endured but even spread to the Hohokam in the American Southwest. Archaeological digs have revealed that nearly every city built by the Maya, Toltecs, and Aztecs boasted its ball court: the most impressive were larger than present-day football fields, painted in vivid colors, and decorated with intricately carved birds, jaguars, and skeletal heads. Renowned players inspired artists to paint murals or to fashion clay figurines depicting ballplayers in full athletic regalia.

In most cultures the rules of the game dictated that players could only use their hips, buttocks, or knees to bounce the ball against the parallel walls of the court and the alley lying between. And after about A.D. 800 the game became even more challenging: teams earned the most points by shooting hoops—that is by sending the ball through a stone ring set in the center of the side walls. No mean feat, since players could not use their hands or feet, and the impact of a flying ball—about six pounds of solid rubber—could inflict serious and even fatal injuries.

(James West Davidson et al., *Experience History: Interpreting America's Past*, 7/e)

______ 1. We can infer that
   a. helmets are a 20th-century invention.
   b. ball games were very popular in pre-Columbian Mesoamerica.
   c. skilled athletes received little compensation or recognition.
   d. because of extensive padding, Mesoamerican ball players did not have to worry about serious injury.

______ 2. We can infer that
   a. it was easy to score in ancient ball games.
   b. Mesoamerican ball games sometimes involved gambling.
   c. hands could only be used when a contest was close.
   d. the Mayans did not participate in ball games.

READING

"Don't complain."

TUNING IN TO READING What do you do when life doesn't go your way? Do you get angry? Do you complain? Or do you try to make the best of the situation and even find something positive in it? The following reading describes a specific "life lesson" that was taught by a very special grandmother.

BIO-SKETCH Maya Angelou is best known as the author of *I Know Why the Caged Bird Sings,* an account of the early years of her life. She has published five collections of poetry, including the inspirational poem "On the Pulse of Morning," which she read at the inauguration of President Bill Clinton. Dr. Angelou passed away in her home on May 28, 2014, at the age of 86. At her eulogy, her son said, "She left this mortal plane with no loss of acuity and no loss in comprehension."

NOTES ON VOCABULARY

cut one's eyes at a rural expression meaning to glance at someone or something.

cooling board a board used to hold a dead body. In the winter months in rural areas, it might be impossible to bury the dead because the ground is frozen, so a body is wrapped and propped up in a barn until the ground is sufficiently thawed out.

winding sheet a sheet in which a corpse is wrapped for burial; similar to a shroud.

Complaining

WHEN MY GRANDMOTHER WAS RAISING me in Stamps, Arkansas, she had a particular routine when people who were known to be whiners entered her store. Whenever she saw a known complainer coming, she would call me from whatever I was doing and say conspiratorially, "Sister, come inside. Come." Of course I would obey.

My grandmother would ask the customer, "How are you doing today, Brother Thomas?" And the person would reply, "Not so good." There would be a distinct whine in the voice. "Not so good today, Sister Henderson. You see it's this summer. It's this summer heat. I just hate it. Oh, I hate it so much. It just frazzles me up and frazzles me down. I just hate the heat. It's almost killing me." Then my grandmother would stand stoically, her arms folded, and mumble, "Uh-huh, uh-huh." And she would cut her eyes at me to make certain that I had heard the lamentation. 2

At another time a whiner would mewl, "I hate plowing. That packed-down dirt ain't got no reasoning, and mules ain't got good sense. . . . Sure ain't. It's killing me. I can't ever seem to get done. My feet and my hands stay sore, and I get dirt in my eyes and up my nose. I just can't stand it." And my grandmother, again stoically with her arms folded, would say, "Uh-huh, uh-huh," and then look at me and nod. 3

As soon as the complainer was out of the store, my grandmother would call me to stand in front of her. And then she would say the same thing she had said at least a thousand times, it seemed to me. "Sister, did you hear what Brother So-and-So or Sister Much to Do complained about? You heard that?" And I would nod. Mama would continue, "Sister, there are people who went to sleep all over the world last night, poor and rich and white and black, but they will never wake again. Sister, those who expected to rise did not, their beds became their cooling boards, and their blankets became their winding sheets. And those dead folks would give anything, anything at all for just five minutes of this weather or ten minutes of that plowing that person was grumbling about. So you watch yourself about complaining, Sister. What you're supposed to do when you don't like a thing is change it. If you can't change it, change the way you think about it. Don't complain." 4

It is said that persons have few teachable moments in their lives. Mama seemed to have caught me at each one I had between the age of three and thirteen. Whining is not only graceless, but can be dangerous. It can alert a brute that a victim is in the neighborhood. 5

(Maya Angelou, *Wouldn't Take Nothing for My Journey Now,* 1993)

COMPREHENSION CHECKUP

Multiple Choice

Directions: For each item, write the letter corresponding to the best answer.

______ 1. Which one of the following character traits most accurately defines Angelou's grandmother in this excerpt?
a. pessimistic
b. wise
c. whiny
d. self-pitying

_____ 2. When Angelou says that her grandmother told her the same thing "at least a thousand times," she is
a. exaggerating.
b. expressing compassion.
c. expressing surprise.
d. being cheerful.

_____ 3. Angelou most likely feels __________ toward her grandmother.
a. amusement
b. resentment
c. disinterest
d. gratitude

_____ 4. We can infer that the words "cooling boards" and "winding sheets" have something to do with
a. graduation ceremonies.
b. death and dying.
c. farming practices.
d. running a small store.

_____ 5. A person who is behaving *stoically*
a. is excitable.
b. is impatient.
c. is calm and unaffected.
d. is distressed.

_____ 6. A *lamentation* is
a. an expression of joy and happiness.
b. a discussion.
c. an expression of grief.
d. a eulogy.

_____ 7. What is Angelou's main purpose in sharing this anecdote?
a. She wishes to make fun of those individuals inclined to complain about their lot in life.
b. She wants to share an important lesson she learned from her grandmother.
c. She wants to honor her grandmother.
d. She wants to demonstrate that the simple life has more value than a complicated one.

_____ 8. We can infer that the story takes place in
a. a large urban city.
b. a rural area.

_____ 9. We can infer from the story that
a. Angelou's grandmother did not respect complainers.
b. Angelou learned not to complain because of her grandmother's teachings.
c. Angelou had a great deal of respect for her grandmother.
d. All of the above.

_____ 10. Which of the following best states Angelou's grandmother's philosophy as expressed in this story?
a. Life is a never-ending series of problems that must be endured until we die.
b. Strive to always be cheerful.

c. Try to solve the problem, and if that fails, change your attitude toward it.
d. A complainer is not likely to have many friends.

True or False

Directions: Indicate whether each statement is true or false by writing **T** or **F** in the space provided.

______ 11. Angelou's grandmother took delight in embarrassing the complainers.

______ 12. Angelou sometimes referred to her grandmother as "mama."

______ 13. Angelou's grandmother referred to her customers as "brother" or "sister" because they were all close relatives.

______ 14. Angelou learned that in certain situations whining is a good idea.

______ 15. When Angelou's grandmother "cut her eyes" at her, she wanted to make sure she had Angelou's complete attention.

______ 16. Angelou's grandmother taught life lessons by words and example.

______ 17. A *brute* is likely to be a sensitive person.

______ 18. If you are *frazzled*, you are likely exhausted both physically and emotionally.

______ 19. According to Angelou, whining about a problem might lead to further harm.

______ 20. One of the complainers mentioned in the story disliked the heat and the other disliked plowing.

In Your Own Words

1. What specific lessons did Angelou's grandmother teach her? How did she convey those lessons?
2. How does Angelou's grandmother view life?

Written Assignment

Write a short paragraph discussing the meaning of the following quotation by Dr. Maya Angelou.

> "Complaining is dangerous for your prosperity and it's dangerous to your posterity."

Internet Activity

Have you ever heard of complaint-free bracelets? To find out more about them and to discover how Maya Angelou was the inspiration behind them, search the Internet for "Angelou and the 6 millionth bracelet."

READING

"Prepare for a crop, and make a crop, and you go to work for the best money wages . . . that you can get."

TUNING IN TO READING In the following letter, Abraham Lincoln, our 16th president, is trying to persuade his stepbrother, John D. Johnston, to change his attitude toward work.

READING (continued)

BIO-SKETCH Lincoln was president of the United States during the bloody Civil War. Although he was largely self-taught, Lincoln managed to read the classics such as the Bible and Shakespeare, which helped him develop his distinctive speaking and writing style. His two most famous speeches are the Gettysburg Address and the Second Inaugural Address, both noted for their brevity and the beauty and clarity of their language. Lincoln was assassinated by John Wilkes Booth while attending a play at Ford's Theater, plunging the nation into mourning. Today we remember him when we celebrate President's Day in February.

NOTES ON VOCABULARY

comply to do what is asked or demanded; yield; submit to

Abraham Lincoln Denies a Loan

BY ABRAHAM LINCOLN

December 24, 1848

Dear Johnston:

Your request for eighty dollars, I do not think it best to comply with now. At the various times when I have helped you a little, you have said to me, "We can get along very well now," but in a very short time I find you in the same difficulty again. Now this can only happen by some defect in your conduct. What that defect is, I think I know. You are not *lazy,* and still you are an *idler*. I doubt whether since I saw you, you have done a good whole day's work, in any one day. You do not very much dislike to work, and still you do not work much, merely because it does not seem to you that you could get much for it.

This habit of uselessly wasting time, is the whole difficulty; it is vastly important 2 to you, and still more so to your children, that you should break this habit. It is more important to them, because they have longer to live, and can keep out of an idle habit before they are in it, easier than they can get out after they are in.

You are now in need of some ready money; and what I propose is, that you 3 shall go to work, "tooth and nail," for somebody who will give you money for it.

Let father and your boys take charge of your things at home—prepare for 4 a crop, and make the crop, and you go to work for the best money wages, or in discharge of any debt you owe, that you can get. And to secure you a fair reward for your labor, I now promise you that for every dollar you will, between this and the first of May, get for your own labor either in money or your own indebtedness, I will then give you one other dollar.

By this, if you hire yourself at ten dollars a month, from me you will get 5 ten more, making twenty dollars a month for your own work. In this, I do not mean you shall go off to St. Louis, or the lead mines, or the gold mines in California, but I mean for you to go at it for the best wages you can get close to home—in Coles County.

Now if you will do this, you will soon be out of debt, and what is better, you will have a habit that will keep you from getting in debt again. But if I should now clear you out, next year you will be just as deep in as ever. You say you would almost give your place in Heaven for $70 or $80 dollars. Then you value your place in Heaven very cheaply, for I am sure you can with the offer I make you get the seventy or eighty dollars for four or five months' work. You say if I furnish you the money you will deed me the land, and if you don't pay the money back, you will deliver possession— 6

Nonsense! If you can't now live *with* the land, how will you then live without it? You have always been kind to me, and I do not now mean to be unkind to you. On the contrary, if you will but follow my advice, you will find it worth more than eight times eighty dollars to you. 7

Affectionately

Your brother
A. Lincoln

COMPREHENSION CHECKUP

1. What distinction does Lincoln make between being a lazy person and being an idler? ______________________________

____

2. What can you infer from this letter about Lincoln's attitude toward work?

____

3. What point is Lincoln making when he refers to Johnston's children?

____

____

4. What can you infer about why Lincoln wants Johnston to stay close to home?

____

____

5. Why does Lincoln tell Johnston that he must value his place in Heaven very cheaply? ______________________________

6. What can you infer about Lincoln's feelings for Johnston? ______________________________

____

7. What can you infer about Johnston's attitude to Lincoln?

____

Directions: Write the letter for the correct answer to each question on the lines provided.

_____ 8. The expression "tooth and nail" means
   a. elderly or old.
   b. with all one's strength or resources.
   c. a very small pointed stick for getting bits of food free from between the teeth.
   d. pleasing to the taste.

_____ 9. As used in the selection, the expression "clear you out" means
   a. settle your debts.
   b. prove you innocent.

c. move you out.
d. harvest your crop.

______ 10. A synonym for "fair" as in "a fair reward" is
a. heavenly.
b. just.
c. clear.
d. excessive.

Directions: Match the vocabulary words in Column A with their definitions in Column B. Place the correct letter in the space provided.

Column A	Column B
______ 1. defect	a. behavior
______ 2. vastly	b. supply
______ 3. conduct	c. flaw
______ 4. propose	d. agree to
______ 5. furnish	e. greatly
______ 6. comply with	f. suggest

In Your Own Words

1. Do you think Lincoln's offer made sense? Is it what Johnston expected? Why or why not?
2. Do you think Johnston will accept Lincoln's offer?
3. Give a short description of Johnston's character based on Lincoln's comments about him.

Written Assignment

1. Choose one of the following statements by Abraham Lincoln and explain its meaning in a paragraph. How does the statement relate to the selection?

   "Always bear in mind that your own resolution to succeed is more important than any other."

   "I'm a slow walker but I never walk back."

   "You cannot build character and courage by taking away a man's initiative and independence."

   "You cannot escape the responsibility of tomorrow by evading it today."

   "You cannot help men permanently by doing for them what they could and should do for themselves."

2. If you haven't already seen it, watch the highly acclaimed movie *Lincoln* (2012) by Steven Spielberg. Daniel Day-Lewis received the Academy Award for best actor for his portrayal of Lincoln's final four months in office. Explain your reaction to the movie. Include your opinion on the performances of the key actors.

Internet Activity

Search the Internet for information on one of the following topics:

"Lincoln's struggle with depression," "Lincoln's views on race," "the story of Mary Todd Lincoln," or "the origin of the Lincoln bedroom in the White House." After your search, write a short paragraph discussing something you didn't previously know about Lincoln.

READING

"In the Mexican worldview, death is another phase of life, and those who have passed into it remain accessible."

TUNING IN TO READING From pre-Columbian times, the Day of the Dead has been celebrated in Mexico and other Latin American countries. Every November first and second, the living gather to honor and remember their departed loved ones. In the United States, *el Dia de los Muertos* is often confused with Halloween, but unlike Halloween, the Mexican holiday is not considered scary or macabre. Actually, *el Dia de los Muertos* most closely resembles U.S. Memorial Day because both holidays show honor and respect for the dead.

BIO-SKETCH Both Paul M. Insel and Walton T. Roth are professors at Stanford University Medical School.

NOTES ON VOCABULARY

indigenous originating from a particular country or region

dogma a specific tenet or doctrine

EL DIA DE LOS MUERTOS: THE DAY OF THE DEAD

by Paul M. Insel and Walton T. Roth

In contrast to the solemn attitude toward death so prevalent in the United States, a familiar and even ironic attitude is more common among Mexicans and Mexican Americans. In the Mexican worldview, death is another phase of life, and those who have passed into it remain accessible. Ancestors are not forever lost, nor is the past dead. This sense of continuity has its roots in the culture of the Aztecs, for whom regeneration was a central theme. When the Spanish came to Mexico in the sixteenth century, their beliefs about death, along with such symbols as skulls and skeletons, were absorbed into the native culture.

Mexican artists and writers confront death with humor and even sarcasm, depicting it as the inevitable fate that all—even the wealthiest—must face. At no time is this attitude toward death livelier than at the beginning of each November on the holiday known as *el Dia de los Muertos,* "the Day of the Dead." This holiday coincides with All Souls' Day, the Catholic commemoration of the dead, and represents a unique blending of indigenous ritual and religious dogma. 2

Festive and merry, the celebration in honor of the dead typically spans two days—one day devoted to dead children, one to adults. It reflects the belief that the dead return to Earth in spirit once a year to rejoin their families and partake of holiday foods prepared especially for them. The fiesta usually begins at midday on October 31, with flowers and food—candies, cookies, honey, milk—set out on altars in each house for the family's dead. The next day, family groups stream to the graveyards, where they have cleaned and decorated the graves of their loved ones, to celebrate and commune with the dead. They bring games, music, and special food—chicken with mole sauce, enchiladas, tamales, and *pan de muertos,* the "bread of the dead," sweet rolls in the shape of bones. People sit on the graves, eat, sing, and talk with the departed ones. Tears may be shed as the dead are remembered, but mourning is tempered by the festive mood of the occasion. 3

During the season of the dead, graveyards and family altars are decorated with yellow candles and yellow marigolds—the "flower of death." In some Mexican villages, yellow flower petals are strewn along the ground, connecting the graveyard with all the houses visited by death during the year. 4

Does this more familiar attitude toward death help people accept death and come to terms with it? Keeping death in the forefront of consciousness may provide solace to the living, reminding them of their loved ones and assuring them that they themselves will not be forgotten when they die. Yearly celebrations and remembrances may help people keep in touch with their past, their ancestry, and their roots. The festive atmosphere may help dispel the fear of death, allowing people to look at it more directly. Although it is possible to deny the reality of death even when surrounded by images of it, such practices as *el Dia de los Muertos* may help people face death with more equanimity. 5

(Paul M. Insel and Walton T. Roth, *Core Concepts in Health,* brief 10/e update, McGraw-Hill, 2008, p. 359)

COMPREHENSION CHECKUP

Multiple Choice

Write the letter of the correct answer in the blank provided.

______ 1. Which sentence best expresses the main idea of the selection?
   a. The festival of the Day of the Dead typically begins on October 31.
   b. Mexicans tend to view death as a part of life and have a yearly celebration to remember and honor their loved ones who have died.
   c. Mexican artists treat death with humor and sarcasm.
   d. The souls of deceased children and deceased adults return on separate days.

______ 2. The author's primary purpose is to
- a. persuade Americans to interact more with family members.
- b. entertain the reader with personal stories celebrating a unique ritual.
- c. inform the reader of the ways in which death is dealt with around the world.
- d. explain the Day of the Dead celebration.

______ 3. The authors infer that
- a. accepting death as inevitable is a positive thing.
- b. the Day of the Dead celebration has little to recommend it.
- c. not much is gained from having a sense of one's roots.
- d. all of the above

______ 4. In paragraph 2, the author says that Mexican artists and writers depict death as something "that all—even the wealthiest—must face." This means that
- a. "for certain is death for the born." (Gita)
- b. "as men we are all equal in the presence of death." (Syrus)
- c. "death is certain to all; all shall die." (Syrus)
- d. all of the above

______ 5. We can infer from the selection that the authors probably feel that
- a. a graveyard is no place for a celebration.
- b. poking fun at death is in poor taste.
- c. yearly celebrations such as the Day of the Dead may help people cope with their own inevitable death.
- d. unlike the lighthearted attitude toward death reflected in U.S. culture, Mexicans exhibit an exceedingly solemn attitude.

______ 6. *Indigenous* ritual, as described in paragraph 2, is likely to be
- a. native.
- b. inborn.
- c. unnatural.
- d. creative.

______ 7. From this selection you could conclude that
- a. the Day of the Dead celebrations are no longer popular with Mexican immigrants to the United States.
- b. the Day of the Dead celebration is popular only with non-Christians.
- c. family and community members participate in the Day of the Dead celebrations.
- d. both a and c

______ 8. A synonym for the word *equanimity* as used in paragraph 5 is
- a. excitability.
- b. indifference.
- c. calmness.
- d. evasion.

______ 9. The word *tempered* as used in paragraph 3 means
- a. properly mixed.
- b. tuned.
- c. made less intense.
- d. having a pleasant disposition.

_____ 10. The Mexican celebration features all of the following **except**
a. bread of the dead.
b. a mournful attitude throughout.
c. aromatic flowers.
d. vigils to honor loved ones.

Topics and Supporting Details

Directions: Using the paragraph numbers in the text, match each paragraph with its topic.

1. Uses for the "flower of death" _____
2. Psychological and social benefits of the holiday _____
3. Introduction and origin of the holiday _____
4. Description of food and activities that make up the celebration _____
5. Lively depiction of death by artists and writers _____

Below are additional sentences about *el Dia de los Muertos.* Using your inference skills, determine the paragraph number in which the sentences are most likely to fit.

6. Mexican marigolds, called *zempascuchitl,* are particularly suited for the Day of the Dead festivities because of the strong pungent aroma. _____
7. Concepts of death and afterlife existed in the ancient Maya and Aztec cultures. _____
8. Mexican poets often write about death, comparing the fragility of life to a dream, a flower, a river, or a passing breeze. _____

Synonyms

Directions: Match each word in column A with its synonym in column B.

	Column A	Column B
_____	1. accessible	a. native
_____	2. unique	b. obtainable
_____	3. depicting	c. common
_____	4. equanimity	d. comfort
_____	5. indigenous	e. spread
_____	6. inevitable	f. unavoidable
_____	7. partake	g. participate
_____	8. prevalent	h. unusual; very special
_____	9. solace	i. portraying
_____	10. strewn	j. calmness

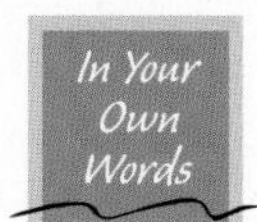

In Your Own Words

1. The goal of the ancient Greeks was to live a full life and then die with glory. What is your definition of a full life?
2. In the United States many people reach adulthood without having seen any close family member or friend die. This stands in direct contrast to other parts of the world where death is visible daily. Do you think an early experience with death changes one's attitude toward the dying process? In what way?

3. Many psychologists and other medical professionals say that the United States as a whole is a nation of "death deniers" and "death avoiders." They point out that many avoid even saying the word "died" and prefer to use expressions such as "passed on." They also note that many in our culture are in a constant search for the elusive "fountain of youth." These individuals are willing to use whatever cosmetic or surgical means are available to avoid looking their age. How do you feel about these issues of death and youth?

Written Assignment

Directions: Write a few paragraphs discussing one of the following questions.

1. Are some cultures better at providing emotional support to people who have lost a loved one?
2. What are the after-death practices of your specific culture? What are the funeral rites in your culture?

Internet Activity

To learn more about the Day of the Dead celebrations, consult the following Web sites:

www.public.iastate.edu/~rjsalvad/scmfaq/muertos.html

www.dayofthedead.com/html/traditions.htm#skullsandskeletons

REVIEW TEST 7: Main Ideas, Details, Purpose, Transitions, Patterns of Organization, and Inference

The following paragraphs are taken from college textbooks. The general purpose of each author is to present information about the topic or to explain a specific idea.

Directions: Read each paragraph. Then write the letter corresponding to the best answer for each question on the line provided.

A. Psychologist John Reisman divides enduring friendships into three types: "associative," "receptive," and "reciprocal." An *associative friendship* endures because of circumstances that bring the partners together. Associative friendships include relationships with colleagues at work, at church, at school and members of the same club, athletic team, fraternity, or sorority. The sense of commitment that each partner feels toward the other is due to the situation (belonging to the same club). A *receptive friendship* is based on a difference in status or control. One member is the giver and the other is the taker. Leaders and followers create receptive friendships, as do instructors and students, mentors and trainees, masters and apprentices, or any sets of people whose relationship is based on a relational difference of complementary roles in which one person is the giver and the other is the receiver. A very close relationship is most likely to be a *reciprocal friendship* rather than an associative or receptive one. Partners in a reciprocal friendship feel a commitment specifically to their interpersonal relationship. Moreover, reciprocal friends tend to consider themselves as equals in the relationship. They will switch back and forth between giving and receiving roles and will typically not maintain one role throughout the relationship.

(B. Aubrey Fisher and Katherine L. Adams, *Interpersonal Communication*, 2/e, 1994)

_____ 1. The organizational pattern used in this paragraph is
a. cause and effect.
b. classification and division.
c. comparison-contrast.
d. chronological order.

_____ 2. Your relationship with a supervisor at work would be an example of which type of friendship?
a. associative
b. receptive
c. reciprocal

_____ 3. You work as a teacher's aide at a local high school and have become friends with a fellow teacher's aide. The two of you often take lunch and recess breaks together. This is an example of a(n) __________ friendship.
a. associative
b. receptive
c. reciprocal

B. The Beatles—the singer-guitarists Paul McCartney, John Lennon, and George Harrison, and the drummer Ringo Starr—have been the most influential performing group in the history of rock. Their music, hairstyle, dress, and lifestyle were imitated all over the world, resulting in a phenomenon known as Beatlemania. All four Beatles were born during the early 1940s in Liverpool, England, and dropped out of school in their teens to devote themselves to rock. Lennon and McCartney, the main songwriters of the group, began working together in 1956 and were joined by Harrison about two years later. In 1962 Ringo Starr became their new drummer. The group gained experience by performing in Hamburg, Germany; and in Liverpool, a port to which sailors brought the latest American rock, rhythm-and-blues, and country-and-western records. In 1961, the Beatles made their first record, and by 1963 they were England's top rock group. In 1964, they triumphed in the United States, breaking attendance records everywhere and dominating the record market. Audiences often became hysterical, and the police had to protect the Beatles from their fans. Beatle dolls, wigs, sweatshirts, and jackets flooded the market. Along with a steady flow of successful records, the Beatles made several hit movies: *A Hard Day's Night, Help!*, and *Yellow Submarine.*

(Roger Kamien, *Music: An Appreciation*, 9/e, 2008)

_____ 1. For this paragraph, the author uses an organizational pattern that
a. gives examples to support a point.
b. describes a series of events in chronological order.
c. compares and contrasts key details.
d. defines key terms.

_____ 2. You can infer from this paragraph that the Beatles
a. took college classes in music theory.
b. had little effect on rock music.
c. were well-known musicians before joining the group.
d. changed the course of rock music.

______ 3. Ringo Starr
a. was the Beatles' first drummer.
b. was born in the late 1940s.
c. joined the group after the Beatles released their first record.
d. was one of the group's main songwriters.

C. Appearance counts when you are communicating on the Internet. You won't be judged by your physical appearance, your race, your hair color, or your age. But you will be judged by how you appear *in your writings.* You never know who might be lurking or how looking your best could benefit you. People have received job offers, internship and study opportunities, book contracts, and even marriage proposals, all based on their appearance on the Net.

Here is a list of some guidelines for looking your best when you send a personal e-mail message or post a message to a discussion group:

(1) Be professional about what you say and how you say it. Know what you are talking about and be sure that what you are saying is correct to the best of your knowledge.
(2) Make sure that your message is clear and logical. Focus on one subject per message. Don't be long-winded.
(3) Use informative subject headings and present the most important information in your first several sentences.
(4) Keep your paragraphs short and to the point. Include line breaks between your paragraphs.
(5) Add some color. Using *asterisks* around words and phrases to emphasize a point, or a smiley :-) to indicate an emotion, can make your post more interesting to read. But don't overdo it and PLEASE AVOID SHOUTING.
(6) Be careful when using sarcasm and humor. In the absence of face-to-face communication, your joke could cause offense. It can also be very difficult for people from other cultures to understand "native" humor.

(Nancy E. Willard, *The Cyber Ethics Reader*, 1997)

______ 1. The organizational pattern used in this paragraph could be described as
a. description.
b. comparison-contrast.
c. cause and effect.
d. listing.

______ 2. The main idea expressed in this paragraph is that
a. although you will not be judged by your physical appearance on the Internet, you will be judged by your written appearance.
b. humor is cultural and can easily be misunderstood.
c. brevity counts on the Internet.
d. presenting a good appearance on the Internet can lead to financial success.

______ 3. The author's primary purpose is to
a. warn readers about the dangers of e-mail.
b. inform readers of proper behavior for communicating on the Internet.

c. explain the meaning of communication.
d. entertain readers by comparing the Internet to face-to-face communication.

_____ 4. The author would agree with all of the following *except* for which?
a. Sloppiness in writing on the Internet does not make a good impression.
b. We should not use all capital letters.
c. It's not necessary to include a subject heading.
d. We should be careful when using jokes or wisecracks as they are easily misunderstood.

D. When you are a *speaker,* you are the source, or originator, of a message that is transmitted to a listener. Whether you are speaking to a dozen people or 500, you bear a great responsibility for the success of the communication. The key question that you must constantly ask yourself is not "Am I giving out good information?" or "Am I performing well?" but rather "Am I getting through to my listeners?" The *listener* is defined as the recipient of the message sent by the speaker. The true test of communication is not whether a message is delivered by the speaker, but whether it is accurately received by the listener. The message is whatever the speaker communicates to the listeners. The message is sent in the form of *symbols*—either *verbal* or *nonverbal.* The *channel* refers to the medium used to communicate the message. A speech can reach an audience by means of a variety of channels: radio, television, the Internet, a public address system, or direct voice communication. *Feedback* means the response that the listeners give the speaker. Sometimes it is *verbal,* as when a listener asks questions or makes comments during a lecture. Listeners also give *nonverbal* feedback. If they are smiling and nodding their heads, they are obviously in agreement with your remarks. If they are frowning and sitting with their arms folded, they more than likely disagree with what you are saying. *Interference* refers to anything that blocks or hinders the accurate communication of a message. When you are a speaker, watch for any signs of interference and if possible take steps to overcome the problem.

(Hamilton Gregory, *Public Speaking for College and Career,* 10/e, 2013)

_____ 1. The organizational pattern used in this paragraph is
a. sequence/process.
b. time order.
c. definition and example.
d. cause and effect.

_____ 2. The author implies that
a. successful communication requires a listener to accurately receive a message.
b. a speaker need be concerned only with presenting a message.
c. a message can be expressed either verbally or nonverbally.
d. both a and c

_____ 3. According to the author, feedback
a. can be negative as when a listener frowns at something the speaker says.
b. can be positive as when a listener nods to agree with a speaker.

c. can be verbal as when a listener asks questions.
d. all of the above.

E. One of the most striking contrasts between the United States and Brazil, the two most populous nations of the Western Hemisphere, is in the meaning and role of the family. Contemporary North American adults usually define their families as consisting of their husbands or wives and their children. However, when middle-class Brazilians talk about their families, they mean their parents, siblings, aunts, uncles, grandparents, and cousins. Later they add their children, but rarely the husband or wife, who has his or her own family. The children are shared by the two families. Because middle-class Americans lack an extended family support system, marriage assumes more importance. The husband–wife relationship is supposed to take precedence over either spouse's relationship with his or her own parents. This places a significant strain on North American marriages. Living in a less mobile society, Brazilians stay in closer contact with their relatives, including members of the extended family. Residents of Rio de Janeiro and São Paulo, two of South America's largest cities, are reluctant to leave those urban centers to live away from family and friends. Brazilians find it hard to imagine, and unpleasant to live in, social worlds without relatives. Contrast this with a characteristic American theme: learning to live with strangers.

(Conrad Phillip Kottak, *Anthropology: The Exploration of Human Diversity*, 14/e, 2011)

______ 1. The dominant pattern of organization in this paragraph is
a. cause and effect.
b. contrast.
c. classification.
d. listing.

______ 2. The writer of this paragraph probably believes that
a. spouses in the United States are not as involved with their own extended families as spouses in Brazil.
b. Brazilians find it more difficult to live away from their relatives than persons in the United States.
c. the father's side has more involvement with the children in a Brazilian family than the mother's side.
d. both a and b

______ 3. The author's main idea in this paragraph is that
a. the Brazilian system of marriage stands in contrast to the prevailing system in the United States.
b. Brazilians don't like to work too far away from their relatives.
c. an extended family is important to the Brazilians.
d. the U.S. system of families should become more like the Brazilian system.

F. Among the middle and upper classes of the industrialized nations, some people suffer from a condition called anorexia nervosa. Anorexic individuals suffer from a mistaken perception of their body size. Because they imagine themselves to be heavier than they really are, they desire to be thinner as a result. Anorexia is most common among Caucasian women between the ages of 15 and 30 with an average or above-average level of education. Anorexia is all but unknown among people living in poverty or in undernourished populations anywhere. It never seems to occur where food is scarce, or in times of famine. Anorexia was once extremely rare. Several experts say its marked increase in the United States since World War II is caused by a general standard of beauty that has increasingly glorified thinness, as measured by such criteria as waist and hip measurements of Miss America contestants, *Playboy* centerfolds, and models and ballet dancers generally. In fact, women in professions like modeling and ballet dancing are particularly likely to develop anorexia. Also, female athletes in sports like rowing where competition is organized by weight classes are at high risk for developing anorexia.

(Eli Minkoff and Pamela J. Baker, *Biology Today*, 1996)

_____ 1. The author suggests that
- a. anorexia is a frequent disease of the poor.
- b. anorexia primarily occurs among well-fed populations.
- c. anorexia rarely occurs in times of famine.
- d. both b and c

_____ 2. The writer of this paragraph probably believes that anorexia might be caused by
- a. an inability to accurately "see" one's size.
- b. an identification of thinness with beauty.
- c. the mass media's reliance on role models who are inappropriately thin.
- d. all of the above

_____ 3. According to the author, the person most likely to suffer from anorexia is
- a. a Black female age 15–30.
- b. a Caucasian male with an above-average education.
- c. a middle-class Caucasian female age 15–30.
- d. a person who participates in aerobics.

_____ 4. The dominant pattern of organization in this paragraph is
- a. cause and effect.
- b. time order.
- c. listing.
- d. classification.

G. Innocent victims trigger more compassion if personalized. In a week when a soon-forgotten earthquake in Iran kills 3,000 people, a lone boy dies, trapped in a well shaft in Italy, and the whole world grieves. The projected death statistics of a nuclear war are impersonal to the point of being incomprehensible. So international law professor Roger Fisher proposed a way to personalize the victims:

It so happens that a young man, usually a navy officer, accompanies the President wherever he goes. This young man has a black attaché case which contains the codes that are needed to fire nuclear weapons.

I can see the President at a staff meeting considering nuclear war as an abstract question. He might conclude, "On SIOP Plan One, the decision is affirmative. Communicate the Alpha line XYZ." Such jargon keeps what is involved at a distance.

My suggestion, then, is quite simple. Put that needed code number in a little capsule and implant that capsule right next to the heart of a volunteer. The volunteer will carry with him a big, heavy butcher knife as he accompanies the President. If ever the President wants to fire nuclear weapons, the only way he can do so is by first, with his own hands, killing one human being.

"George," the President would say, "I'm sorry, but tens of millions must die." The President then would have to look at someone and realize what death is—what an *innocent* death is. Blood on the White House carpet: it's reality brought home.

When I suggested this to friends in the Pentagon, they said, "My God, that's terrible. Having to kill someone would distort the President's judgment. He might never push the button."

(David G. Myers, *Social Psychology*, 9/e, 2008)

_____ 1. The organization pattern used by the author in this paragraph
a. gives an illustration to support a point.
b. demonstrates a cause-and-effect relationship.
c. lists ideas without regard to order.
d. defines key terms.

_____ 2. International law professor Roger Fisher probably believes that
a. in times of war, jargon is used to create distance from one's actions.
b. it may be easier to bomb an entire village from 40,000 feet than to shoot a single helpless villager face-to-face.
c. people responsible for killing other people are sometimes emotionally detached from the human reality of their decisions.
d. all of the above

_____ 3. The main idea expressed in this paragraph is that
a. personalizing the destruction that a nuclear war would cause may help prevent one.
b. people are sometimes unresponsive to great tragedies.
c. people are more likely to treat compassionately those they personally relate to.
d. people are least likely to be compassionate to persons they bomb from the air.

Chapter Summary and Review

In Chapter 8, you learned how to draw inferences from a variety of sources, such as textbook material, literature, and cartoons. Based on the material in Chapter 8, answer the following.

Short Answer

Directions: Answer the following briefly, in a few words or phrases.

1. Explain what an inference is. ________________________________

____

Vocabulary in Context

Directions: Choose one of the following words to complete the sentences. Use each word only once.

directly experiences inferences lines

2. In drawing inferences, we make use of our ___________ in life.
3. To figure out an idea that is not ___________ stated, we have to read between the ___________.
4. We draw ___________ every day of our lives.

CHAPTER

9

Figurative Language

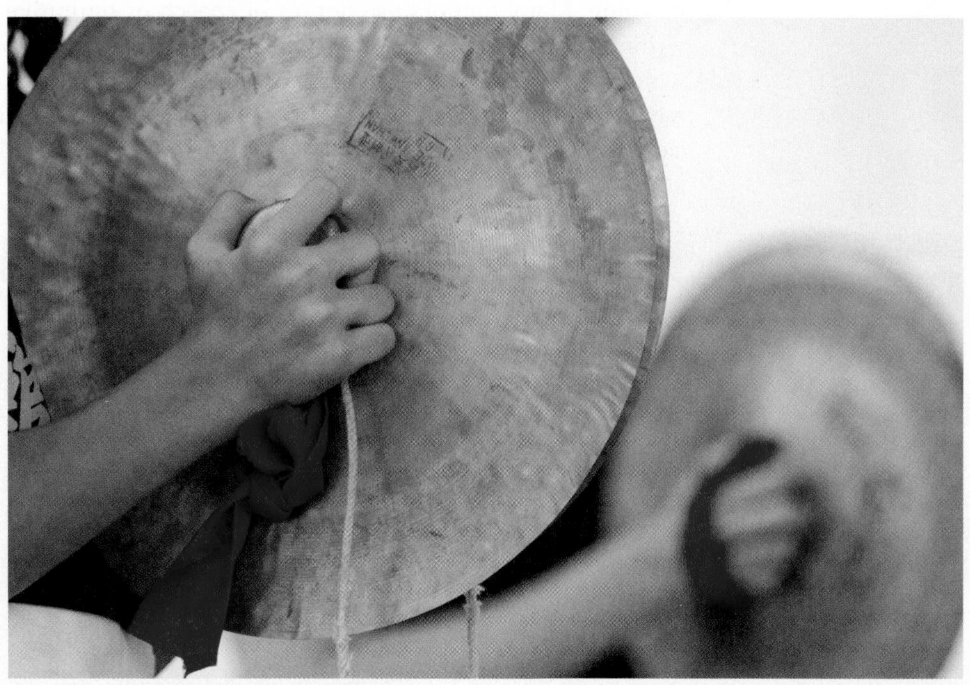

CHAPTER PREVIEW

In this chapter, you will

- Learn about similes, metaphors, and personification.
- Learn about extended metaphors.
- Become familiar with the use of symbolism in writing.
- Become familiar with literary allusions.
- Become familiar with imagery.

Figures of Speech—Similes, Metaphors, and Personification

In order to read well, you must become a *critical* reader. This means understanding not only the author's literal meaning but also the author's implied or inferential meaning. Many authors use figures of speech or figurative language to make their writing more colorful and interesting. These **figures of speech** are expressions in which words are used regardless of their true meanings in order to create a special meaning or effect. Often this specialized language enables the author to more clearly convey meaning by making a comparison to something that is more familiar or readily understood.

Literal Versus Figurative Comparisons

COMPARISONS

Literal

(Compares things from the same category)

1. Angie is as skinny as her sister.

Figurative

(Compares things from different categories)

1. Angie is as skinny as a telephone pole. (Simile: A is like B.) Uses *like, as,* or *as if* to make the comparison
2. Angie is a telephone pole. (Metaphor: A is B.) Uses a state of being verb to make the comparison—*am, is, are, was, were*
3. The telephone pole reaches its long arms to the sky. (Personification: Something that is not alive takes on human attributes or "person" characteristics.) Note: Personification is a special kind of metaphor.

Shoe—New business © 1996 MacNelly. Dist. by King Features Syndicate.

Shoe

When words are used conventionally and mean exactly what they say, they are being used *literally.* In figurative language, the words have been stretched to mean something beyond what they say. As an illustration of the difference between literal and figurative, study the *Shoe* cartoon above. In it, Loon takes something literally that is meant to be a figurative expression.

Now look at the sentences below. In each example, the first expression is a figurative one, and the second is literal.

Example 1

Our teacher is such a shrimp.

She is small.

Example 2

The test was a piece of cake.

The test was pretty easy.

Writers provide clues to the meaning of their figurative expressions, so the critical reader must study the entire context of the expression to infer its meaning. Three common kinds of figures of speech are similes, metaphors, and personification.

Similes

A **simile** is a figure of speech that compares two unlike things. Similes usually use the words *like, as,* or *as if* to show the comparison. "Sam is as energetic as Mary" is a comparison, not a simile. This is because it compares two things from the same category—people. "Sam is as energetic as the Energizer bunny" is a simile. Similes appear in both poems and prose. For example, a writer might describe a stormy sky by saying, "The sky darkened and storm clouds towered like skyscrapers against the horizon." In this case, the writer is comparing the clouds to tall buildings to convey the sense of how large and menacing the clouds appear.

Explain the meaning of each of these similes:

1. She is as confused as a rat in a maze. ______________________
2. His muscles are like iron bands. ______________________
3. The fullback charged as if he were a locomotive. ______________________

Metaphors

Metaphors state the comparison between two unlike things directly using a state-of-being verb. One thing is spoken of as though it were something else. The phrases *like, as,* or *as if* are not used. So, instead of saying "Life is *like* a roller coaster," which is a simile, a metaphor says "Life *is* a roller coaster." As another example, someone might say, "Life is a bed of thorns for Megan" in reference to a friend who is struggling to simultaneously work, get through school, and bring up a family. The person is comparing a "bed of thorns," a vision of pain and discomfort, to the hectic pace of Megan's life to highlight the difficulties she is having.

In "Dreams," the poet Langston Hughes uses metaphors to show the hopelessness of life without any dreams:

Hold fast to dreams
For if dreams die
Life is a broken-winged bird
That cannot fly.

Hold fast to dreams
For when dreams go
Life is a barren field
Frozen with snow.

An **extended metaphor** sustains the comparison for several lines or for the entire poem or story.

In the following excerpt from *How Good Do We Have to Be?*, Rabbi Harold S. Kushner uses an extended metaphor to express his feelings about life. What comparison is he making?

> Life is not a spelling bee, where no matter how many words you have gotten right, if you make one mistake you are disqualified. Life is more like a baseball season, where even the best team loses one-third of its games and even the worst team has its days of brilliance. Our goal is not to go all year without ever losing a game. Our goal is to win more than we lose, and if we can do that consistently enough, then when the end comes, we will have won it all.

(Rabbi Harold S. Kushner, *How Good Do We Have to Be?* 1996)

Now create your own metaphor for life. Include a short explanation of why you have chosen this metaphor.

Example: Life is a tidal wave; it doesn't stop for anybody or anything.

____

____

____

____

____

Personification

Personification is a kind of figurative language in which nonhuman or inanimate objects are given human traits or attributes. If you were to say, "The ocean stretched lazily, caressing the shore with gentle waves," you would be using personification. The ocean is not a person, but in the sentence it is being described as acting like one. When the poet Longfellow said, "Time has laid his hand upon my heart, gently," he was personifying the concept of time and his feelings about growing old. In the poem "The Eagle" by Alfred, Lord Tennyson, the first line of each stanza makes use of personification:

> **He clasps the crag with crooked hands;**
> Close to the sun in lonely lands,
> Ringed with the azure world he stands.
>
> **The wrinkled sea beneath him crawls;**
> He watches from his mountain walls,
> And like a thunderbolt he falls.

1. What figure of speech is the last line of the poem? ______________________
2. What does it mean to fall like a thunderbolt? ______________________

Now choose five inanimate objects, and write a sentence giving each object a human attribute.

Example: My computer sighed, wheezed, and then expired.

1. ____
2. ____

3. ______________________________

4. ______________________________

5. ______________________________

Finally, can you find the figures of speech in the cartoon below?

Shoe by Chris Cassatt and Gary Brookins

Shoe—New business © 2001 MacNelly. Dist. by King Features Syndicate.

Exercise 1: Literal or Figurative Comparisons

Directions: Indicate whether the comparison is literal or figurative by writing **L** or **F** in the space provided.

Reminder: Not all comparisons are figures of speech. A *figure of speech* makes a comparison between unlike things. A *literal comparison* compares things that are from the same category.

Example:
Lucille is as thin as a bookmark. (F) Different categories
Lucille is as thin as her grandmother. (L) Same category

______ 1. Evergreen trees bent *like people leaning out of the window.*

______ 2. The baby's breathing was choked and rough, like something pulled through tightly packed gravel.

______ 3. She was as strong-willed as her father.

______ 4. The animal was as white as cream cheese.

______ 5. He was eating as well and sleeping as well as the other students.

______ 6. I am a willow swaying gently in the wind.

______ 7. The waves beside them danced.

______ 8. He complained all day as if no one had anything better to do than listen to him.

______ 9. Like her brother before her, she chose to live at home while attending college.

______ 10. A gray mist rose on the sea's face.

List the numbers of the sentences containing a personification. ______

List the number of the sentence containing a metaphor. ______

Change the words in italics in sentence 1 to make an original simile.

Reminder: You need something that bends or is bent.

New simile: ______________________________

Exercise 2: Creating Original Comparisons

Comparisons are considered to be **clichés** when they are trite, overused, worn, or hackneyed. To better understand a cliché, read the following riddles. What do these riddles have in common?

1. Why did the judge wear a catcher's mitt?

   The ball was in his court.

2. How come a pickle doesn't sweat?

   It's cool as a cucumber.

3. When does a tea bag tremble?

   When it's in hot water.

Answer: They all have clichés as punch lines.

(Patricia T. O'Conner, *Woe Is I Jr.*, 2007)

Directions: Read the following clichés and try to create a fresh or original comparison.

1. thin as a rail ______________________________
2. red as a beet ______________________________
3. flat as a pancake ______________________________
4. nutty as a fruitcake ______________________________
5. light as a feather ______________________________

Now rewrite this paragraph by substituting original comparisons of your own for the italicized trite expressions.

It was late at night, and I was working alone at the office. *Quick as a flash,*

____

a robber dashed in and pulled a gun on me, demanding that I open the office safe. I managed to stay *cool as a cucumber* despite his gun at my temple

____

and his *grip like a vise* around my chest. Unfortunately, while escorting me

____

over to the wall safe, he knocked my glasses off my face and stepped on them with a resounding crunch. There I was *blind as a bat,* unable to see

____

the numbers well enough to open the lock. I began to *sweat like a pig,*

____

realizing I would soon be *dead as a doornail,* when without any warning

____

the police came to my rescue. To conclude my story, I am now as *happy as a lark.*

A special type of comparison is called an **analogy.** A writer uses an analogy to make something understandable or clear by comparing it to something that is different from it but that has something in common with it. Sometimes, however, an attempt to create a fresh and original comparison can go too far. These analogies recently posted on the Internet were labeled "the worst ever written in high school essays." Try conveying the same information in a meaningful comparison of your own.

1. Her hair glistened in the rain like nose hair after a sneeze.

2. He was as tall as a six-foot-three-inch tree.

3. The politician was gone but unnoticed, like the period after the Dr. on a Dr Pepper can.

4. His thoughts tumbled in his head, making and breaking alliances like underpants in a dryer without Cling Free.

5. The little boat gently drifted across the pond exactly the way a bowling ball wouldn't.

Exercise 3: Analyzing Figurative Comparisons

Directions: Each of the following sentences contains a figurative comparison. In the space provided, write down the real subject, what it is compared to, and the meaning of the sentence.

Example

Oliver Wendell Holmes once attended a meeting in which he was the shortest man present. "Doctor Holmes," quipped a friend, "I should think you'd feel rather small among us big fellows."

"I do," retorted Holmes, "I feel like a dime among a lot of pennies."

Subject: Dr. Holmes

Compared to: dime among pennies

Meaning: Dr. Holmes did not let his short stature bother him. Just as a dime, though smaller than a penny, is worth more, Holmes is "worth more" than his friends.

1. Whenever I try to speak to him, his mind wanders everywhere, like a cow following green grass.

   Subject: __________

   Compared to: __________

   Meaning: __________

2. Her face looked like it had just come out of a dryer and needed to be pressed.

   Subject: __________

Compared to: ____________________

Meaning: ____________________

3. He bobbed through life's turbulences like driftwood on the sea.

Subject: ____________________

Compared to: ____________________

Meaning: ____________________

4. His grandparents' home was like a giant security blanket.

Subject: ____________________

Compared to: ____________________

Meaning: ____________________

5. He struggled to extricate himself from the powerful undertow like a fly caught in a spider's web.

Subject: ____________________

Compared to: ____________________

Meaning: ____________________

6. The car ran the red light like a bull charging a matador.

Subject: ____________________

Compared to: ____________________

Meaning: ____________________

Exercise 4: Analyzing Figurative Comparisons in Song Lyrics

Directions: Each of the song lyrics below contains a figurative comparison. In the space provided, identify the real subject, indicate what it is being compared to, and explain the meaning of the lyric.

Example: You're my kryptonite (One Direction, "One Thing")
Subject: girlfriend
Compared to: kryptonite
Meaning: She is his weakness.

1. Do you ever feel like a plastic bag drifting through the wind, wanting to start again? (Katy Perry, "Firework")

Subject: ____________________

Compared to: ____________________

Meaning: ____________________

____

2. Do you ever feel, feel so paper thin like a house of cards, one blow from caving in? (Katy Perry, "Firework")

Subject: ____________________

Compared to: ____________________

Meaning: ____________________

____

3. Baby, you're a firework (Katy Perry, "Firework")

   Subject: ______________________________

   Compared to: ______________________________

   Meaning: ______________________________

4. He's like a curse, he's like a drug, you'll get addicted to his love (Carrie Underwood, "Cowboy Casanova")

   Subject: ______________________________

   Compared to: ______________________________

   Meaning: ______________________________

5. Loving him is like driving a new Maserati down a dead-end street (Taylor Swift, "Red")

   Subject: ______________________________

   Compared to: ______________________________

   Meaning: ______________________________

6. You, with your words like knives and swords and weapons that you use against me (Taylor Swift, "Mean")

   Subject: ______________________________

   Compared to: ______________________________

   Meaning: ______________________________

7. Life's a dance you learn as you go, sometimes you lead, sometimes you follow (John Michael Montgomery, "Life's a Dance")

   Subject: ______________________________

   Compared to: ______________________________

   Meaning: ______________________________

8. A day without you is like a year without rain (Selena Gomez, "A Year Without Rain")

   Subject: ______________________________

   Compared to: ______________________________

   Meaning: ______________________________

Exercise 5: Figurative Comparisons in Literature

Directions: The figures of speech (set in **boldface**) in the following excerpts were chosen by the authors because they create a fresh effect or demonstrate a new insight. Determine whether the expression is a metaphor, a simile, or a personification, and then decide what image or insight the author is trying to convey.

A. Until I was thirteen and left Arkansas for good, the Store was my favorite place to be. Alone and empty in the mornings, **it looked like an unopened present from a stranger. Opening the front doors was pulling the ribbon off the unexpected gift.** The light would come in softly (we faced north), easing itself over the shelves of mackerel, salmon, tobacco, thread. It fell flat on the big vat of lard and by noontime during the summer the grease had softened to a thick soup. **Whenever I walked into the Store in the afternoon, I sensed that it was tired. I alone could hear the slow pulse of its job half done.** But just before bedtime, after numerous people had walked in and out, had argued over their bills, or joked about their neighbors, or just dropped in "to give Sister Henderson a 'Hi y'all,'" the promise of magic mornings returned to the Store and spread itself over the family in washed life waves.

(Maya Angelou, *I Know Why the Caged Bird Sings*, 1970)

1. What does Angelou mean when she refers to the Store as "an unopened present"? Is this a simile or a metaphor? ______________________

____

2. To what does Angelou compare the opening of the front doors? Does this comparison involve a simile or a metaphor? ______________________

3. What figure of speech does the following phrase use: "I sensed that it [the Store] was tired"? ______________________

B. Once a week Grandma Mazur went to the beauty parlor and had her hair shampooed and set. Sometimes Dolly would use a rinse and Grandma would have hair the color of an anemic apricot, but mostly Grandma lived with her natural color of steel gray. Grandma kept her hair short and permed with orderly rows of curls marching across her shiny pink scalp. The curls stayed miraculously tidy until the end of the week, when they'd begin to flatten and blend together.

I'd always wondered how Grandma had managed this feat. And now I knew. Grandma rolled her pillow under her neck so barely any skull touched the bed. And Grandma slept like the dead. Arms crossed over her chest, body straight as a board, mouth open. Grandma never moved a muscle, and she snored like a drunken lumberjack.

(Janet Evanovich, *Four to Score*, 1998)

1. To what does Evanovich compare her grandmother's curls? Is this comparison a simile, metaphor, or personification? ______________________

____

2. What are three similes in this excerpt?

____

____

____

Exercise 6: Figurative Comparisons in Nonfiction

Not all figures of speech come from literature. Many writers of nonfiction also use figurative language in their writing. For example, to convey information to readers who are not well versed in scientific procedures, a science writer will often construct an appropriate metaphor. Keeping in mind that the word *metaphor* literally means "to transfer or bring across," Ted Anton and Rick McCourt, editors of *The New Science Journalists,* state that "almost every piece of really good science writing will connect its subject to an unexpected object or larger meaning."

Directions: Each of these figures of speech is taken from a scientific article. Determine what the figurative language suggests in each example, and then indicate whether the statements that follow are true or false by writing **T** or **F** in the space provided.

A. A DESCRIPTION OF A COMMON ROUNDWORM

Through a microscope, they look like tiny crystal serpents, curving and slithering across the dish with an almost drugged sluggishness, doubling back on themselves as though discovering their tails for the first time, or bumping up against a neighbor clumsily and then slowly recoiling.

(Natalie Angier, "The Very Pulse of the Machine," 1995)

_____ 1. The roundworm moves quickly in a purposeful fashion.

_____ 2. The roundworm appears well coordinated.

B. A DESCRIPTION OF PROTEINS

The concentration of proteins in the cell is as thick as honey, and young proteins must be sequestered from the surrounding ooze. During the early stages of folding, the polypeptide may form characteristic corkscrew shapes, or linked loops that resemble a Christmas bow, or slender fingerlike projections.

(Natalie Angier, "Chaperoning Proteins," 1995)

_____ 1. The ooze might jeopardize the development of the young proteins.

_____ 2. Proteins are highly concentrated in cells.

C. A DESCRIPTION OF A BAT CAVE

The air screams, rustling movements feather against the skin, squeaks and screeches bounce off the stone walls, and a sweet acrid stench rolls across the room. My mouth chews the darkness like a thick paste. . . . The rock walls feel like cloth to the touch. . . . The feces and urine continue to shower down, the mites tickle the surface of my body, the atmosphere tastes like a bad meal and always the air drifting like a thick fog promises the whisper of rabies.

(Charles Bowden, "Bats," 1995)

_____ 1. Bat caves are quiet, pleasant-smelling environments.

_____ 2. Visibility is good inside the cave.

_____ 3. Visitors emerging from a bat cave are likely to be covered in excrement.

D. A DESCRIPTION OF THE BRAIN

Brain is easy to define: It is the wet, oatmeal-colored organ, weighing about three pounds, that resides inside the skull. . . . Mind is not the all-knowing ruler of the brain, but a little circle of firelight in a dark, Australia-sized continent where the unconscious brain processes carry on.

(Timothy Ferris, "The Interpreter," 1995)

_____ 1. The conscious mind forms a much smaller part of the operations of the brain than the unconscious.

_____ 2. The mind is not really "running the show."

E. A DESCRIPTION OF CHROMOSOMES

Human chromosomes, shaped like cinch-waisted sausages and sequestered in nearly every cell of the body, are famed as the place where human genes reside.

(Natalie Angier, "A Clue to Longevity," 1995)

______ 1. The chromosomes contain human genetic material.

______ 2. Chromosomes reside in only a few dominant areas of the human body.

______ 3. The chromosome is smallest at the top and at the bottom.

F. A DESCRIPTION OF THE YELLOW JACKET

August is official yellow jacket month, as a number of entomologists have proclaimed on their Internet Web pages, and as anybody within range of a public trash can will attest. This is the season when the wretched little biblical plagues boil forth in force, bobbing and weaving like drunken marionettes, poking in fruit stands, crash-landing on soda cans, and haughtily, viciously, wickedly stinging any human who dares to protest. Actually, it turns out that yellow jackets are not the mean-spirited vermin their victims assume them to be, but instead are family values types that struggle selflessly to support and defend their kin. They just happen to crave the same junk food we do.

(Natalie Angier, "Selfless, Helpful, and Intelligent: The Wasp," 1999)

______ 1. August is the month when yellow jackets are out in force.

______ 2. Yellow jackets fly in direct routes.

Extended Metaphors

In an extended metaphor, the figurative comparison is developed throughout the entire article. This lengthy comparison helps readers visualize the event much more clearly. As you read the following article, note the extended metaphor and then answer the questions that follow.

READING

"It became a love/hate relationship."

TUNING IN TO READING What do you know about group support networks such as Weight Watchers and Alcoholics Anonymous? What techniques do these organizations use to help people change their destructive behaviors?

The following letter, by Robert L. Rodgers, made a powerful impression on the readers of the late syndicated advice columnist Ann Landers. It is included in *The Best of Ann Landers.*

BIO-SKETCH Until her death in 2002, Ann Landers (Eppie Lederer) was the most widely syndicated columnist in the world. During the course of her long career (1955–2002), she dispensed witty advice to help solve the personal problems of millions of people. Her column, which ran seven days a week, ended with her death. Reflecting on her long career, she said that "while it can be a headache, it's never a bore."

NOTES ON VOCABULARY

heart-breaking causing severe emotional pain or grief. This form of hyperbole (exaggeration) first appeared in the works of Chaucer and Shakespeare. In 1913, George Bernard Shaw wrote a play titled *Heartbreak House.* And of course there is the song recorded by the king himself, Elvis Presley, titled "Heartbreak Hotel."

guts pluck and perseverance in the face of opposition or adversity. The term dates from the mid-1900s.

been around been present or active; gained experience or sophistication. The term dates from the first half of the 1900s and over time has acquired a negative meaning.

common-law a marriage without a civil or religious ceremony based on a couple's living together continuously as husband and wife.

The Love of My Life

DEAR ANN LANDERS: I first met her in high school. She was older than I, and exciting. She'd been around. My parents warned me to have nothing to do with her. They claimed no good could come from our relationship.

But I kept meeting her on the sly. She was so sophisticated and worldly. It made me feel grown up just being with her. It was fun to take her to a party in those days. She was almost always the center of attention. 2

We began seeing more of each other after I started college. When I got a place of my own, she was a frequent guest. It wasn't long before she moved in with me. It may have been common-law, but it was heart-breaking for my parents. I kept reminding myself I wasn't a kid anymore. Besides, it was legal. 3

We lived together right through college and into my early days in business. I seldom went anywhere without her, but I wasn't blind. I knew she was unfaithful to me. What's worse, I didn't care. As long as she was there for me when I needed her (and she always was), it didn't matter. 4

The longer we lived together, the more attached I became. But it wasn't mutual. She began to delight in making me look foolish in front of my friends. But still I couldn't give her up. 5

It became a love/hate relationship. I figured out that her glamour was nothing more than a cheap mask to hide her spite and cynicism. I could no longer see her beauty after I came to know her true character. 6

But old habits are hard to break. We had invested many years in each other. Even though my relationship with her made me lose a little respect for myself, she had become the center of my life. We didn't go anywhere. We didn't do anything. We didn't have friends over. It was just the two of us. I became deeply depressed and knew that she was responsible for my misery. I finally told her I was leaving for good. It took a lot of guts, but I left. 7

I still see her around. She's as beautiful as when we met. I still miss her 8
now and then. I'm not boasting when I say she'd take me back in a minute. But by the grace of God, I'll never take up with her again.

Forty percent of eighth graders have consumed an alcoholic beverage.

If you see her, give her my regards. I don't hate her. I just loved her too 9
much.

Chances are you know her family. The name is Alcohol. 10

Robert L. Rodgers, Waco, Texas

Dear Robert L. Rodgers: I have never met her personally, but a great 11
many people who have been intimately involved with your old love have written to say she ruined their lives. She has no class and no character and is totally ruthless.

You didn't mention one of the main problems she creates. It's financial. 12
Almost everyone who becomes a victim of her charms ends up with money trouble. She's an expensive "hobby."

Nor did you mention what your companion of the past did to your health. 13
Many of her close friends develop heart trouble, stomach problems, and cirrhosis of the liver.

I'm glad you had the strength to end the relationship. You didn't say 14
whether you had help from Alcoholics Anonymous. Thousands of readers have told me it was the only way they could get out of her clutches.

Incidentally, I heard from a good source that she hated to lose you but 15
she's not lonesome. She's on millions of guest lists around the country. In fact, they wouldn't dream of having a party without her! Funny that someone so evil and destructive continues to be so popular.

(*The Best of Ann Landers,* 1996)

COMPREHENSION CHECKUP

Multiple Choice

Directions: For each item, write the letter corresponding to the best answer.

_____ 1. Rodgers is comparing "Alcohol" to
- a. his parents.
- b. a girlfriend.
- c. a trusted friend.
- d. none of the above

_____ 2. Rodgers began drinking in
- a. elementary school.
- b. high school.
- c. college.
- d. his twenties.

_____ 3. Rodgers rationalized his drinking by saying that
- a. as an adult he was legally able to drink.
- b. alcohol made him feel mature.
- c. alcohol made things exciting.
- d. all of the above

_____ 4. Which of the following does Ann Landers wonder about?
a. Did Rodgers consult a self-help group for assistance in overcoming his addiction?
b. Did Rodgers's alcoholism cause him health problems?
c. Did Rodgers get into trouble with the law?
d. Both a and b

_____ 5. Which of the following is not mentioned specifically by either Rodgers or Landers as a possible consequence of misuse of alcohol?
a. financial difficulties
b. health complications
c. looking foolish in front of others
d. causing accidents

_____ 6. The idiomatic expression "on the sly" means that
a. Rodgers was using alcohol secretly.
b. Rodgers was using alcohol furtively.
c. Rodgers was using alcohol frequently.
d. both a and b

_____ 7. The phrase that most closely means the opposite of "sophisticated and worldly" is
a. inexperienced and naive.
b. smart and powerful.
c. lazy and ignorant.
d. cheerful and knowledgeable.

_____ 8. When Rodgers says that "he wasn't blind," he means that
a. he was in a no-win situation.
b. he was ignorant of what was going on.
c. he was aware of what was going on.
d. he was feeling his way in the relationship.

_____ 9. Ann Landers implies that
a. she has never used alcohol.
b. she uses alcohol on an infrequent basis.
c. she is a frequent user of alcohol.
d. she fails to understand how someone could become addicted to alcohol.

_____ 10. Why does Ann Landers put the word *hobby* in quotation marks in paragraph 12?
a. She is quoting from someone.
b. She likes the way the word looks.
c. She means that alcohol is not really a hobby because it is destructive.
d. She doesn't approve of hobbies.

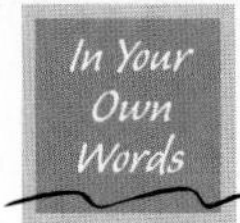

In Your Own Words

1. "It is estimated that between 9 and 10 million Americans are either alcoholics or problem drinkers" (*Targeting Wellness*, p. 246). What are some factors mentioned by Rodgers that influence the use of alcohol? How did alcohol help Rodgers relate to people?
2. Although it is often desirable to change patterns of behavior, it is seldom easy. In what ways does the letter from Rodgers illustrate the hidden pressures *not* to change?

3. Neither Rodgers nor Ann Landers mentioned two other destructive effects of alcohol: accidents and violence. Are you aware of any recent situations in which alcohol led to a serious accident? Are you aware of any recent situations in which alcohol was associated with violent or antisocial conduct? What should be the punishment for driving while intoxicated?
4. "A number of psychological traits have been closely associated with alcoholism, including deep-seated feelings of inadequacy, anxiety, and depression." How does Rodgers's letter illustrate these traits?
5. Do you think that Ann Landers's answer is what Rodgers expected? Why or why not?
6. What do you think the expression "love/hate relationship" means?
7. A surprisingly large number of young people are first exposed to either alcohol or drugs by relatives. What is your reaction to such incidents? If the child becomes addicted, should the relatives be held responsible?

Written Assignment

Directions: Complete one of the following:

1. Break into groups of four. Two students will write a paraphrase of Rodgers's letter, and two will write a paraphrase of Ann Landers's response. When you are finished, read your completed paraphrases to the class.
2. Give a short description of the consequences of being addicted to "Alcohol" that Rodgers mentions in his letter. What additional consequences are mentioned by Ann Landers?
3. The Oscar-nominated actor Robert Downey, Jr., was first introduced to marijuana at the age of 6 by his father Robert Downey, Sr. Since then he has waged a very public battle with drug addiction that has included numerous stays in drug rehabilitation facilities and jail. What do you think should be done with individuals such as Robert Downey, Jr., and Lindsay Lohan, who are nonviolent drug offenders? Write a few paragraphs giving your opinion.
4. Write a short letter to someone giving him or her your advice on how to deal with drug or alcohol addiction.
5. Do you personally know anyone who has had a problem with either alcohol or drugs? How did that person first get involved? Did the person seek help? Was he or she able to conquer that addiction? If so, how did he or she succeed?

Internet Activity

1. A major problem on college campuses is binge drinking. Using a search engine, type in "college binge drinking." Locate a Web site that discusses the problems associated with this type of drinking, and then write a paragraph summarizing the information. What is the relevance of this article for you, your friends, or your college?
2. In the past few years, many resource and support groups have become available to help problem drinkers. However, Alcoholics Anonymous still sets the standard for self-help groups. The Web site for this organization is:

   www.alcoholics-anonymous.org

   Go to this Web site to take an alcohol assessment test. For other self-assessment tests related to alcohol, go to a search engine and type in "tests for alcoholism."

The Use of Symbols

A **symbol** is a person, an object, or an event that stands for more than its literal meaning. It is representative of something else. A good symbol captures in a simple form a more complicated reality. For example, a white dove symbolizes peace, a flag symbolizes a country's values and aspirations, a budding flower may symbolize birth and new beginnings, and a logo on a shirt may signify wealth and status. Writers use symbols to create a particular mood or to reinforce a specific theme.

In his poem "The Road Not Taken," Robert Frost uses an extended metaphor to compare life to a journey along a road.

THE ROAD NOT TAKEN

Two roads diverged in a yellow wood,
And sorry I could not travel both
And be one traveler, long I stood
And looked down one as far as I could
To where it bent in the undergrowth;

Then took the other, as just as fair,
And having perhaps the better claim,
Because it was grassy and wanted wear;
Though as for that the passing there
Had worn them really about the same,

And both that morning equally lay
In leaves no step had trodden black.
Oh, I kept the first for another day!
Yet knowing how way leads on to way,
I doubted if I should ever come back.

I shall be telling this with a sigh
Somewhere ages and ages hence:
Two roads diverged in a wood, and I—
I took the road less traveled by,
And that has made all the difference.

The fork in the road is a more specific symbol that represents a major decision in life—a decision that must be made and that likely cannot be taken back. To preserve its symbolic value, the poem does not discuss the particulars of a decision or choice. In this way, the choice made in the poem can stand for any important choice made in life.

The ancient Greeks started the tradition of wearing wedding rings around the third finger of the left hand. They believed that finger contained a vein of love that runs directly to the heart. In actuality, blood flows to the heart through veins in all fingers on both hands.

Exercise 6: Identifying Symbols

Directions: Identify what each of these common symbols represents.

1. wedding ring ____________________
2. white wedding dress ____________________
3. rabbit's foot ____________________
4. American flag ____________________
5. Lexus or Infiniti ____________________
6. Springtime ____________________
7. skull and crossbones ____________________
8. gavel ____________________

READING

"The Germans bombed the town of Guernica. . . . Guernica was devastated and its civilian population massacred."

TUNING IN TO READING To learn more about one of the greatest achievements of 20th-century art, read the following selection from an art history textbook.

BIO-SKETCH Although Pablo Picasso (1881–1973) was born in Spain, he spent most of his adult life in France. His early works revealed his strong compassion for those who were poor and suffering. He once said, "Painting is stronger than me, it makes me do what it wants." One of Picasso's finest paintings, *Guernica,* is a passionate expression of social protest, which Picasso painted during the Spanish Civil War (1937). It is hard to view *Guernica* (pictured below) without vicariously experiencing the agony and destruction of war. Picasso was a dominant figure in Western art in the 20th century and is credited with helping to bring back storytelling to art.

"The more horrifying the world becomes, the more art becomes abstract."
—Pablo Picasso

NOTES ON VOCABULARY

fury from Latin *furia* meaning "violent passion, rage, or madness." In classical mythology, the three Furies were winged female monsters with snakes for hair. Their goal was to pursue and punish those who had committed evil deeds.

procrastinate to put off doing something unpleasant or burdensome until a future time. The word *procrastinate* can be broken down into parts, *pro* meaning "toward" and *cras* meaning "tomorrow." So when you *procrastinate,* you are pushing something toward tomorrow.

GUERNICA

Mark Getlein

[*Guernica*] was created by an artist whose sympathies lay with those not in power, an artist who took up his brush with a sense of fury at the "ins" who caused devastation. From his fury came one of the great masterpieces of 20th-century art. The artist was Picasso, and the painting is called *Guernica.*

It is necessary to know the story behind *Guernica* to understand its power. 2
In 1937 Europe was moving toward war, and a trial run, so to speak, occurred

in Spain, where the forces of General Francisco Franco waged civil war against the established government. Franco willingly accepted aid from Hitler, and in exchange he allowed the Nazis to test their developing air power. On April 28, 1937, the Germans bombed the town of Guernica, the old Basque capital in northern Spain. There was no real military reason for the raid; it was simply an experiment to see whether aerial bombing could wipe out a whole city. Being totally defenseless, Guernica was devastated and its civilian population massacred.

At the time Picasso, himself a Spaniard, was working in Paris and had been commissioned by his government to paint a mural for the Spanish Pavilion of the Paris World's Fair of 1937. For some time he had procrastinated about fulfilling the commission; then, within days after news of the bombing reached Paris, he started *Guernica* and completed it in little over a month. Despite the speedy execution, however, this was no unreasoning outburst of anger. Picasso controlled his rage, perhaps knowing that it could have better effect in a carefully planned canvas, and he made many preliminary drawings. The finished mural had a shocking effect on those who saw it; it remains today a chillingly dramatic protest against the brutality of war. 3

At first encounter with *Guernica* the viewer is overwhelmed by its presence. The painting is huge—more than 25 feet long and 12 feet high—and its stark, powerful imagery seems to reach out and engulf the observer. Picasso used no colors; the whole painting is done in white and black and shades of gray, possibly to create a "newsprint" quality in reporting the event. Although the artist's symbolism is very personal (and he declined to explain it in detail), we cannot misunderstand the scenes of extreme pain and anguish throughout the canvas. At far left a shrieking mother holds her dead child, and at far right another woman, in a burning house, screams in agony. The gaping mouths and clenched hands speak of disbelief at such mindless cruelty. 4

Another victim is the dying horse to the left of center, speared from above and just as stunned by the carnage as any of the human sufferers. Various writers have interpreted the bull at upper left in different ways. Picasso drew much of his imagery from the bullfight, an ingrained part of his Spanish heritage. Perhaps the bull symbolizes the brutal victory of the Nazis; perhaps it, like the horse, is also a victim of carnage. There is even more confusion about the symbols of the lamp and the light bulb at top center. These may be indications that light is being cast on the horrors of war, or they may be signals of hope. Picasso did not tell us, so we are free to make our own associations. 5

Guernica is like no other painting in the world. Enormous in size, stark in its black-and-white tones, shocking in its images of brutality, vehement in its political protest—Picasso's great work stands alone in the history of art. Although Picasso was prolific as an artist, he never made another picture like *Guernica.* This uniqueness, then, presents a problem: How can the painting be kept from harm? How does one protect a one-of-a-kind masterpiece? 6

Picasso always intended *Guernica* as a gift to the people of Spain, his homeland, but at the time of its creation in 1937, he did not trust the Spanish government. So, he shipped the picture off to the Museum of Modern Art in New York, where it was to be held "on extended loan" until such time as a "democratic" government was established in Spain. 7

In New York, *Guernica* was simply hung on a wall—a large wall to be sure. 8
Its impact was staggering when the viewer came around a corner and, suddenly, there it was. If the museum guards decided you were all right, and if you held your breath carefully, you could get quite close to the canvas. Or you could stand far back to take in the whole work at a gulp. So the situation remained for forty years. Only one unpleasant event marred the open relationship between artwork and viewers. In 1974 an Iranian artist splashed the *Guernica* with red paint as a political protest, but no permanent damage was done.

By 1981, eight years after Picasso's death, there was general agreement 9
that Spain's government had become sufficiently "democratic" to satisfy the artist's conditions. Under tight security *Guernica* was sent to Madrid, where it was installed in an annex of the Prado museum. The Prado was taking no chances with its newly acquired masterpiece. *Guernica* was quickly sealed up in what some observers called a "cage"—an immense riot-resistant enclosure under an armor-plated ceiling, with bulletproof glass set some 14 feet in front of the canvas's surface. Obviously, one could no longer move in close to study details. Museum visitors complained that glare on the glass prevented any overall view of the painting. Some grumbled that the protective box dominated the picture, making even a 25-foot-wide painting seem puny. *Guernica* was safe, all right, but at what cost to its expression?

The controversy escalated in 1992, when *Guernica* was moved yet again, 10
this time to the Reina Sofia museum a mile or so from the Prado. This new journey had all the drama of a spy movie. A special steel box, climate-controlled and weighing 3,500 pounds, was built to carry the painting. The transport company practiced its run down the road for weeks in advance, using stand-in paintings. Finally, on the fateful day, an armored truck carried *Guernica* through heavily guarded streets to its new home. The trip took half an hour and cost $200,000. Arriving intact at the Reina Sofia, *Guernica* was once again secured behind bulletproof glass.

One cannot help wondering what Picasso would have thought about all 11
this hullabaloo. His eldest daughter has accused the Spanish art ministry of "murdering" *Guernica.* Perhaps "jailing" it would be a better term. The issue is one of balance. If *Guernica* should be damaged or destroyed, there is no way ever to replace it. But what is the point of keeping this masterpiece so very safe that no one can properly see it?

(Mark Getlein, *Living with Art*, 10/e, 2013)

COMPREHENSION CHECKUP

True or False

Directions: Indicate whether each statement is true or false by writing **T** or **F** in the space provided.

______ 1. Franco's collaboration with Hitler resulted in the bombing of Guernica.

______ 2. Picasso's painting required many months to complete.

______ 3. The colorful painting is generally thought to be very large.

_____ 4. Picasso was a Spaniard by birth.

_____ 5. The light bulb at the top of the painting may be seen as a sign of hope.

_____ 6. Picasso intended *Guernica* to be a gift from him to the people of Spain.

_____ 7. Originally *Guernica* was loaned to the Louvre in France.

_____ 8. *Guernica* survived an incident in which red paint was splashed on it.

_____ 9. Today *Guernica* is secured behind glass.

_____ 10. Picasso's oldest daughter feels that the painting has been "murdered."

Vocabulary in Context

Directions: Indicate whether the italicized word is used correctly or incorrectly by writing **C** or **I** in the space provided.

_____ 1. The cruel loss of his five children was *devastating.*

_____ 2. Because the price of gas in the United States keeps *escalating,* people are no longer going on long car trips.

_____ 3. When someone has an *outburst,* they are especially calm.

_____ 4. If you cannot swim and are *engulfed* by a wave, you might need a lifeguard immediately.

_____ 5. It is considered to be especially polite to *gape* at someone.

_____ 6. At car speeds of over 100 miles an hour, an *impact* with a wall can cause serious injury.

_____ 7. Stephen King is a *prolific* writer who has written over 30 bestsellers.

_____ 8. AIDS, a worldwide epidemic, has killed a *staggering* number of human beings.

_____ 9. His *clenched* fist and scowling face indicated his happiness with his math grade.

_____ 10. Millions of bats were *massacred* because the townspeople feared rabies.

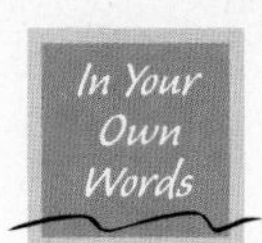

In Your Own Words

1. How does the author feel about the way the Spanish government chose to exhibit Picasso's *Guernica* prior to 1995? What clues enable you to make this inference?
2. How do you think Picasso might feel about the safe-keeping of his masterpiece?
3. The author suggests that Picasso might have painted *Guernica* in black, white, and shades of gray to create a "newsprint" effect. What other reasons might Picasso have had for using this color scheme?
4. Picasso was fascinated by the ancient sport of bullfighting. The author mentions several things that the bull in the painting might symbolically represent. What do you think the bull in *Guernica* represents?
5. Why is the light bulb such a prominent feature?
6. The bombing of Guernica happened during the day. Why did Picasso portray it as happening at night?
7. What is the subject matter of the painting? Death? Suffering? War?

Internet Activity

View some of Picasso's paintings by visiting

www.abcgallery.com/P/picasso/picasso.html (Olga's Gallery)

or

www.pablopicasso.org

To learn more about Pablo Picasso, visit his official Web site at:

www.picasso.fr

Then choose a favorite painting and write a brief description of it.

READING

"If you can't do the time, don't do the crime"

TUNING IN TO READING Today, many people use yellow ribbons to welcome home soldiers or to serve as a reminder for those who are missing. What does a yellow ribbon symbolize to returning soldiers? Why do families with soldiers who are POWs or MIAs wear or display yellow ribbons?

BIO-SKETCH Pete Hamill (1935–) was born in Brooklyn and attended Catholic schools as a child. He left school at the age of 16 to become a sheet-metal worker and later joined the United States Navy. The G.I. Bill of Rights helped him pay for his education at Mexico City College. In 1960, he began his career in journalism at the *New York Post* and later served as its editor in chief. He also became editor in chief for the *New York Daily News*. As a journalist, he covered wars in Vietnam, Nicaragua, Lebanon, and Northern Ireland. He has written several fiction and nonfiction books, including *The Drinking Life* and *Downtown: My Manhattan*. "The Yellow Ribbon," originally written for the *Post*, became the inspiration for a TV movie and a song by Tony Orlando titled "Tie a Yellow Ribbon 'Round the Old Oak Tree."

NOTES ON VOCABULARY

solitude the state of being solitary or alone. It comes from the Latin word *solus*, meaning "sole" or "alone." It is often used to describe the state of being cut off from human contact. The loneliness of such a situation is sometimes stressed.

THE YELLOW RIBBON BY PETE HAMILL

They were going to Ft. Lauderdale, the girl remembered later. There were six of them, three boys and three girls, and they picked up the bus at the old terminal on 34th Street, carrying sandwiches and wine in paper bags, dreaming of golden beaches and the tides of the sea as the gray cold spring of New York vanished behind them. Vingo was on board from the beginning.

2 As the bus passed through Jersey and into Philly, they began to notice that Vingo never moved. He sat in front of the young people, his dusty face masking his age, dressed in a plain brown ill-fitting suit. His fingers were stained from cigarettes and he chewed the inside of his lip a lot, frozen into some personal cocoon of silence.

3 Somewhere outside of Washington deep into the night, the bus pulled into a Howard Johnson's, and everybody got off except Vingo. He sat rooted in his seat, and the young people began to wonder about him, trying to imagine his

life: Perhaps he was a sea captain, maybe he had run away from his wife, he could be an old soldier going home. When they went back to the bus, the girl sat beside him and introduced herself.

4 "We're going to Florida," the girl said brightly. "You going that far?"

5 "I don't know." Vingo said.

6 "I've never been there," she said. "I hear it's beautiful."

7 "It is," he said quietly, as if remembering something he had tried to forget.

8 "You live there?"

9 "I did some time there in the Navy. Jacksonville."

10 "Want some wine?" she said. He smiled and took the bottle of Chianti and took a swig. He thanked her and retreated again into his silence. After a while, she went back to the others, as Vingo nodded in sleep.

11 In the morning they awoke outside another Howard Johnson's, and this time Vingo went in. The girl insisted that he join them. He seemed very shy and ordered black coffee and smoked nervously, as the young people chattered about sleeping on the beaches. When they went back on the bus, the girl sat with Vingo again, and after a while, slowly and painfully and with great hesitation, he began to tell his story. He had been in jail in New York for the last four years, and now he was going home.

12 "Four years!" the girl said. "What did you do?"

13 "It doesn't matter," he said with quiet bluntness. "I did it and I went to jail. If you can't do the time, don't do the crime. That's what they say and they're right."

14 "Are you married?"

15 "I don't know."

16 "You don't know?" she said.

17 "Well, when I was in the can I wrote to my wife," he said. "I told her, I said, Martha, I understand if you can't stay married to me. I told her that. I said I was gonna be away a long time, and that if she couldn't stand it, if the kids kept askin' questions, if it hurt her too much, well, she could just forget me. Get a new guy—she's a wonderful woman, really something—and forget about me. I told her she didn't have to write me or nothing. And she didn't. Not for three-and-a-half years."

"And you're going home now, not 18
knowing?"

"Yeah," he said shyly. "Well, last 19
week, when I was sure the parole was coming through I wrote her. I told her that if she had a new guy, I understood. But if she didn't, if she would take me back she should let me know. We used to live in this town, Brunswick, just before Jacksonville, and there's a great big oak tree just as you come into town, a very famous tree, huge. I told her if she would take me back, she should put a yellow handkerchief on the tree, and I would get off and come home. If she didn't want me, forget it, no handkerchief, and I'd keep going on through."

"Wow," the girl said. "Wow." 20

She told the others, and soon all of 21
them were in it, caught up in the approach of Brunswick, looking at the pictures Vingo showed them of his wife and three children, the woman handsome in a plain way, the children still unformed in a cracked, much-handled snapshot. Now they were 20 miles from Brunswick and the young people took over window seats on the right side, waiting for the approach of the great oak tree. Vingo stopped looking, tightening his face into the ex-con's mask, as if fortifying himself against still another disappointment. Then it was 10 miles, and then 5 and the bus acquired a dark hushed mood, full of silence, of absence, of lost years, of the woman's plain face, of the sudden letter on the breakfast table, of the wonder of children, of the iron bars of solitude.

Then suddenly all of the young 22
people were up out of their seats, screaming and shouting and crying, doing small dances, shaking clenched fists in triumph and exaltation. All except Vingo.

23 Vingo sat there stunned, looking at the oak tree. It was covered with yellow handkerchiefs, 20 of them, 30 of them, maybe hundreds, a tree that stood like a banner of welcome blowing and billowing in the wind, turned into a gorgeous yellow blur by the passing bus. As the young people shouted, the old con slowly rose from his seat, holding himself tightly, and made his way to the front of the bus to go home.

(Pete Hamill, "The Yellow Ribbon," 1972)

COMPREHENSION CHECKUP

Multiple Choice

Directions: For each item, write the letter corresponding to the best answer.

_____ 1. The main idea expressed in this article is that
a. a prison sentence can easily ruin a marriage.
b. young people on vacation can meet interesting people.
c. love is better the second time around.
d. after serving his time in prison, Vingo returned to Brunswick and discovered that his wife wanted him back after all.

_____ 2. The author's primary purpose in writing this article is to
a. inform readers about unjust prison sentences.
b. explain to readers how prison disrupts family life.
c. entertain readers with a heartwarming story.
d. persuade readers to show compassion for those returning from prison.

_____ 3. The pattern of organization used in this article is
a. classification and division.
b. comparison-contrast.
c. chronological order.
d. cause and effect.

_____ 4. You can conclude that Pete Hamill obtained the information needed to write this article by
a. interviewing Vingo.
b. interviewing a girl who was on the bus with Vingo.
c. interviewing Vingo's family and friends.
d. interviewing the boys who were riding on the bus.

_____ 5. We can infer that the young people aboard the bus are going to Florida
a. to visit relatives.
b. to get married.
c. to interview for jobs.
d. to take a vacation.

_____ 6. We can infer that Vingo's wife was
a. willing to forgive Vingo.
b. angry for having to raise their children alone.
c. a compassionate and caring woman.
d. both a and c

_____ 7. We can infer that the young people began their trip in
a. Washington, DC.
b. New York.
c. Florida.
d. Pennsylvania.

_____ 8. In paragraph 3, the word *rooted* in "He sat rooted in his seat" means
a. to become established or anchored.
b. to search about.
c. to work hard.
d. to dig.

_____ 9. In paragraph 21, the word *fortifying* in "as if fortifying himself against still another disappointment" means
a. strengthening.
b. weakening.
c. praising.
d. condemning.

True or False

Directions: Indicate whether each statement is true or false by writing **T** or **F** in the space provided.

_____ 10. Vingo was in prison for four years before being paroled.

_____ 11. There were eight young people and two chaperones making the trip.

_____ 12. Vingo had never been to Jacksonville before.

_____ 13. Vingo looked at the pictures of his wife and children a lot.

_____ 14. Vingo felt that you shouldn't commit crimes if you aren't willing to do the time.

The Yellow Ribbon: Summary

Following is an incomplete summary of "The Yellow Ribbon." Write the letters of the missing sentences on the lines provided.

(1) Vingo has just been released from a New York prison and is taking a bus home to his wife in Brunswick, Florida. (2) Some young people are on the bus heading to the beaches of Fort Lauderdale. (3) Just outside Washington, everybody gets off the bus except Vingo. (4) _____ (5) The next morning, the girl again converses with Vingo, and this time he tells his story. (6) _____ (7) He hasn't heard from his wife in three-and-a-half years. Vingo recently wrote to Martha again when he was certain he would be released from prison. (8) _____ 9. If there was no handkerchief, he wouldn't get off the bus. (10) The young people become caught up in the excitement and look at the pictures of Vingo's family that he shows them. (11) As they approach Brunswick, the atmosphere inside the bus becomes very tense. (12) Then all of a sudden the young people are celebrating while Vingo stays in his seat stunned. (13) _____

a. He told Martha to put a yellow handkerchief on a well-known tree on the outskirts of town if she would take him back.
b. Vingo doesn't know whether or not he is married, because he told his wife, Martha, that he would understand if she found another man while he was away.
c. The oak tree is covered with yellow handerchiefs and stands as a banner of welcome as Vingo makes his way home.
d. The young people become curious about Vingo, and when they get back on the bus one of the girls introduces herself and engages him in conversation.

In Your Own Words

1. In the last paragraph, Hamill says that the tree covered with yellow handkerchiefs "stood like a banner of welcome." In Vingo's case, what does the tree symbolically represent?
2. Make a profile sketch of Vingo by listing his key character traits. Some traits are directly stated in the text, and others must be inferred from the evidence presented. Be able to justify each of your traits by citing specific passages.
3. What does it mean to be "frozen into some personal cocoon of silence"?
4. What does Vingo's face look like when he tightens it "into the ex-con's mask"?
5. What inference can you make about why Vingo's wife did not keep in regular contact with him while he was in prison? What kind of woman do you think she is?

Written Assignment

All of us make assumptions about other people just by looking at them. We also judge people by their friends. You can often tell a lot about a person from the people he or she associates with. What do your friends "say" about you? That is, what can someone tell *about you* from knowing or observing your friends? Write a paragraph about yourself from this perspective.

Internet Activity

Many people wear ribbons or bracelets to support various causes. Can you think of some examples? What colors are used? Many people across the United States display yellow ribbons as an expression of solidarity with our troops. Others display these ribbons as a reminder of loved ones in danger and a desire for their safe return home. To learn more about the tradition of wearing yellow ribbons, go to

www.loc.gov/folklife/ribbons

or type "origins of yellow ribbons" into a search engine. Write a paragraph summarizing the information you find.

Literary Allusions

A **literary allusion** is a reference to something that is supposed to be common cultural knowledge. Allusions are a technique writers use to quickly express a complex thought or evoke a certain image or reaction. In this sense, they are much like symbols. To fully understand a literary work, you need to be able to recognize and understand the allusions used by the author. Often, research must be done to discover the meaning of an allusion.

Study the following example from the opening stanza of "Travel" by Robert Louis Stevenson:

I should like to rise and go
Where the golden apples grow;—
Where below another sky
Parrot islands anchored lie,
And, watched by cockatoos and goats,
Lonely Crusoes building boats;—

The word *Crusoe* refers to the main character of Daniel Defoe's 18th-century novel *Robinson Crusoe.* In the novel, Crusoe is shipwrecked and washed ashore on an uninhabited island. Crusoe has come to symbolize a person who can overcome hardships and survive in isolation. The second literary allusion, Parrot islands, refers to the Canary Islands, located in the Atlantic Ocean directly off the northwest coast of Africa. The Canaries, because of their beauty and relative isolation, symbolize serenity. Thus, in the beginning of this poem, the poet is expressing a longing to journey to a remote area.

Cultural Literacy Assignment

Directions: Form groups of four. Each group will then be assigned either Quiz A or Quiz B. You are allowed to help each other.

CULTURAL LITERACY QUIZ A

Mythology and Folklore

1. A weak or sore point in a person's character. A ______ h______
2. A magician who acted as King Arthur's primary advisor. M______

Proverbs

3. Physical beauty is superficial. B______ is ______ ______ d______.
4. If we want to achieve our goal, we must get an early start. The ______ b______ catches the w______.

Idioms

5. A disgrace to the family. B______ sh______
6. If something can go wrong, it will. M______ L______

Literature

7. Author of *Diary of a Young Girl.* A______ F______
8. "I'll huff and I'll puff, and I'll blow your house down." T______ ______ P______
9. A novel by J. D. Salinger recounting the adventures of the young Holden Caulfield. *The Catcher in the R______*

Art

10. The creator of the paintings on the ceiling of the Sistine Chapel. M______
11. The statue features the words "Give me your tired, your poor, your huddled masses." S______ of L______

History

12. A king of England who beheaded two wives. H______ the ______
13. The ancient Roman leader who was murdered on March 15. Julius C______
14. The inventor of the lightning rod, bifocal glasses, and a stove. B______ F______
15. A seamstress who made flags in Philadelphia during the Revolutionary War. B______ R______
16. A battle between Custer and Native Americans. L______ B______
17. The championship game of the NFL held in January. S______ B______

Bible

18. The principle of justice that requires punishment equal in kind to the offense. An ______ for an ______

19. "Do unto others as you would have them do unto you." The G______ R______

Science

20. Large, white, puffy clouds—some carry rain. C______

21. A shuttle that exploded in space. C______ / ______

CULTURAL LITERACY QUIZ B

Mythology and Folklore

1. The king of the Greek gods. Z______
2. Small men who resemble elves capable of revealing the whereabouts of a pot of gold at the end of the rainbow. L______

Proverbs

3. Apples keep us healthy. An ______ a day k______ the d______ a______.
4. Don't assume that you'll get the things you want until you have them. D______ c______ y______ ch______ b______ they h______.

Idioms

5. Smooth, flattering talk (Irish derivation). B______
6. To blow an event out of proportion. Don't m______ a m______ out of a m______ h______.

Literature

7. Ali Baba and the ______ Thieves.
8. "All animals are equal, but some animals are more equal than others." A______ F______
9. "Elementary, my dear Watson." Sh______ H______

Art

10. A painting by Leonardo da Vinci of a woman with a mysterious smile. M______ L______
11. The Spanish painter of *Guernica.* P______

History

12. The queen of Egypt famed for her beauty; lover of Marc Antony. C______
13. A female French military leader who claimed God spoke to her in voices. J______ of A______
14. An English nurse of the 19th century, and a symbol for all nursing. F______ N______
15. The commander of the Confederate troops. R______ E. L______
16. His most famous speech is "I Have a Dream." M______ L______ K______, Jr.
17. The oldest and most famous of the college "bowl games." R______ B______

Bible

18. The reason people of the earth speak different languages. The T______ of B______
19. The first children of Adam and Eve. C______ and A______

Science

20. Lacy or wispy clouds that form at high altitudes. C______
21. A very "unlucky" space mission. A______

Imagery

In addition to the figures of speech mentioned earlier, writers use **imagery** to create word pictures. This means that they describe a person, an object, or a setting by relying on sensory images. The words or phrases that they use may emphasize any one, or all, of our five senses—sight, sound, taste, touch, and smell. Readers must be able not only to recognize these images but also to understand the author's intent in presenting a particular image. For example, in "The Runner," the poet Walt Whitman uses imagery to convey the sensation of running. The descriptive words in the poem primarily appeal to our visual sense.

> On a flat road runs the well-train'd runner;
> He is lean and sinewy, with muscular legs;
> He is thinly clothed—he leans forward as he runs,
> With lightly closed fists, and arms partially rais'd.

The excerpt below creates a visual picture of sea travel in the 18th century.

> A mountain of water swelled from the Atlantic, towered over the *Jamaica Packet,* then toppled over the small wooden passenger ship. The impact hurled Janet Schaw and her maid about their cabin like rag dolls. As seawater surged in, the ship pitched wildly, "one moment mounted to the clouds and whirled on the pointed wave," the next plunging into the heaving ocean. For more than two days, the *Jamaica Packet* hurtled in the gale's grip. Then its foremast splintered, and the ship flipped onto its side. Schaw found herself "swimming amongst joint-stools, chests and tables" in her cabin and listening to the sound of "our sails fluttering into rags." It would have been the end of the *Jamaica Packet* if, at that moment, its masts had not washed overboard. With the weight of the masts gone, the ship righted itself.
>
> Schaw, "a lady of quality" was traveling by the finest accommodations from Great Britain to America in the age of sail. For passengers who could not pay for a private cabin, the storm was worse. Like thousands of others who came to America in the eighteenth century, they were consigned to steerage, the between-decks area or "upper hold."
>
> Perhaps four to five feet high, that space was crowded with narrow wooden bunks arranged in tiers about two feet apart. It was impossible for most people to stand in steerage or to sit up in a bunk, where as many as four people huddled together at night. Sanitary facilities consisted of a few wooden buckets filled with seawater; candles and fish-oil lanterns supplied the only light. The sole source of air was the hatch opening onto the deck.

When the storm struck, the hatch was fastened tightly to keep the holds from filling with water. But as waves dashed over the decks, water streamed into steerage, forcing its occupants to stand, clutching their children to keep them from being crushed, drowned or suffocated. For days they stood in water, without a fire or any food except raw potatoes and moldy biscuits. And they were without light or fresh air.

Although there are no reliable statistics for shipboard mortality during the eighteenth century, estimates range from 3 percent to as high as 10 to 15 percent of all passengers. For all who traveled abroad, transatlantic travel was tedious and dirty at best, hazardous and horrific at worst. With good reason, those who risked the crossing routinely made out wills and sought the prayers of loved ones. On the high seas, disease and misfortune took a heavy toll.

(James West Davidson et al., *Experience History*, McGraw-Hill, 2011, p. 116)

READING

"My clothes have failed me."

TUNING IN TO READING Growing up poor in South Fresno, California, Gary Soto often felt as if he didn't fit in. He explores that feeling of self-consciousness in the following selection. Have you ever felt as though your clothes (or something else) set you apart from others? How did you deal with the situation? How did that experience make you feel about yourself?

BIO-SKETCH Gary Soto, a Mexican American writer, has won numerous awards with his autobiographical writings and poetry. He has written over 35 books, which have sold nearly four million copies. His life as a writer is featured in the Gary Soto Literary Museum at Fresno City College, where he began his writing life in 1972 as a student.

NOTES ON VOCABULARY

Braille a system of writing for the blind consisting of raised dots interpreted by touch.

camouflage fabric dyed with patches of green, brown, black, or tan (earth tones) intended to make the wearer hard to distinguish from a natural, outdoor background.

The Jacket

GARY SOTO

My clothes have failed me. I remember the green coat that I wore in sixth grade when you either danced like a champ or pressed yourself against a greasy wall, bitter as a penny toward the happy couples.

When I needed a new jacket and my mother asked what kind I wanted, I described something like bikers wear: black leather and silver studs, with enough belts to hold down a small town. We were in the kitchen, steam on the windows from her cooking. She listened for so long while stirring dinner that I thought she understood for sure the kind I wanted. The next day when 2

I got home from school, I discovered draped on my bedpost a jacket the color of day-old guacamole. I threw my books on the bed and approached the jacket slowly, as if it were a stranger whose hand I had to shake. I touched the vinyl sleeve, the collar, and peeked at the mustard-color lining.

From the kitchen mother yelled that my jacket was in the closet. I closed the door to her voice and pulled at the rack of clothes in the closet, hoping the jacket on the bedpost wasn't for me but my mean brother. No luck. I gave up. From my bed, I stared at the jacket. I wanted to cry because it was so ugly and so big that I knew I'd have to wear it a long time. I was a small kid, thin as a young tree, and it would be years before I'd have a new one. I stared at the jacket, like an enemy, thinking bad things before I took off my old jacket, whose sleeves climbed halfway to my elbow. 3

I put the big jacket on. I zipped it up and down several times and rolled the cuffs up so they didn't cover my hands. I put my hands in the pockets and flapped the jacket like a bird's wings. I stood in front of the mirror, full face, then profile, and then looked over my shoulder as if someone had called me. I sat on the bed, stood against the bed, and combed my hair to see what I would look like doing something natural. I looked ugly. I threw it on my brother's bed and looked at it for a long time before I slipped it on and went out to the backyard, smiling a "thank you" to my mom as I passed her in the kitchen. With my hands in my pockets, I kicked a ball against the fence, and then climbed it to sit looking into the alley. I hurled orange peels at the mouth of an open garbage can, and when the peels were gone I watched the white puffs of my breath thin to nothing. 4

I jumped down, hands in my pockets, and in the backyard, on my knees, I teased my dog, Brownie, by swooping my arms while making bird calls. He jumped at me and missed. He jumped again and again, until a tooth sunk deep, ripping an L-shaped tear on my left sleeve. I pushed Brownie away to study the tear as I would a cut on my arm. There was no blood, only a few loose pieces of fuzz. Damn dog, I thought, and pushed him away hard when he tried to bite again. I got up from my knees and went to my bedroom to sit with my jacket on my lap, with the lights out. 5

That was the first afternoon with my new jacket. The next day I wore it to sixth grade and got a D on a math quiz. During the morning recess, Frankie T., the playground terrorist, pushed me to the ground and told me to stay there until recess was over. My best friend, Steve Negrete, ate an apple while looking at me, and the girls turned away to whisper on the monkey bars. The teachers were no help: they looked my way and talked about how foolish I looked in my new jacket. I saw their heads bob with laughter, their hands half covering their mouths. 6

Even though it was cold, I took off the jacket during lunch and played kickball in a thin shirt, my arms feeling like Braille from goose bumps. But when I returned to class I slipped the jacket on and shivered until I was warm. I sat on my hands, heating them up, while my teeth chattered like a cup of crooked dice. Finally warm, I slid out of my jacket but put it back on a few minutes later when the fire 7 bell rang. We paraded out into the yard where we, the sixth graders, walked past all the other grades to stand against the back fence. Everybody saw me. Although they didn't say out loud, "Man, that's ugly," I heard the buzz-buzz of gossip and even laughter that I knew was meant for me.

And so I went, in my guacamole-colored jacket. So embarrassed, so hurt, I couldn't even do my homework. I received C's on quizzes and forgot the state capitals and the rivers of South America, our friendly neighbor. Even the girls who had been friendly blew away like loose flowers to follow the boys in neat jackets. 8

I wore that thing for three years until the sleeves grew short and my forearms stuck out like the necks of turtles. All during that time no love came to me—no little girl in a Sunday dress she wore on Monday. At lunchtime I stayed with the ugly boys who leaned against the chainlike fence and looked around with propellers of grass spinning in our mouths. We saw girls walk by alone, saw couples, hand in hand, their heads like bookends pressing air together. We saw them and spun our propellers so fast our faces were blurs. 9

I blame that jacket for those bad years. I blame my mother for her bad taste and her cheap ways. It was a sad time for the heart. With a friend I spent my sixth-grade year in a tree in the alley, waiting for something good to happen to me in that jacket, which had become the ugly brother who tagged along wherever I went. And it was about that time that I began to grow. My chest puffed up with muscle and, strangely, a few more ribs. Even my hands, those fleshy hammers, showed bravely through the cuffs, the fingers already hardening for the coming fights. But that L-shaped rip on the left sleeve got bigger, bits of stuffing coughed out from its wound after a hard day of play. I finally Scotch-taped it closed, but in rain or cold weather the tape peeled off like a scab and more stuffing fell out until the sleeve shriveled into a palsied arm. That winter the elbows began to crack and whole chunks of green began to fall off. I showed the cracks to my mother, who always seemed to be at the stove with steamed-up glasses, and she said that there were children in Mexico who would love that jacket. I told her that this was America and yelled that Debbie, my sister, didn't have a jacket like mine. I ran outside, ready to cry, and climbed the tree by the alley to think bad thoughts and watch my breath puff white and disappear. 10

But whole pieces still casually flew off my jacket when I played hard, read quietly, or took vicious spelling tests at school. When it became so spotted that my brother began to call me "camouflage," I flung it over the fence into the alley. Later, however, I swiped the jacket off the ground and went inside to drape it across my lap and mope. 11

I was called to dinner: steam silvered my mother's glasses as she said grace; my brother and sister with their heads bowed made ugly faces at their glasses of powdered milk. I gagged too, but eagerly ate big rips of buttered tortilla that held scooped-up beans. Finished, I went outside with my jacket across my arm. It was a cold sky. The faces of clouds were piled up, hurting. I climbed the fence, jumping down with a grunt. I started up the alley and soon slipped into my jacket, that green ugly brother who breathed over my shoulder that day and ever since. 12

(Gary Soto, *Effects of Knut Hamson on a Fresno Boy*)

COMPREHENSION CHECKUP

Multiple Choice

Directions: For each item, write the letter corresponding to the best answer.

_____ 1. When the narrator states that his chest "puffed up with muscle and, strangely, a few more ribs," he is providing an image that primarily appeals to our sense of
a. smell.
b. sight.
c. taste.
d. hearing.

_____ 2. Which one of the following sentences lends a tone of sadness to the selection?
a. "That winter the elbows began to crack and whole chunks of green began to fall off."
b. "And so I went, in my guacamole-colored jacket."
c. "There was no blood, only a few loose pieces of fuzz."
d. "It was a cold sky. The faces of clouds were piled up hurting."

_____ 3. "Bits of stuffing coughed out from its wound" is an example of
a. simile.
b. metaphor.
c. personification.
d. symbol.

_____ 4. All the following are similes **except**
a. "bitter as a penny."
b. "white puffs of my breath thin to nothing."
c. "flapped the jacket like a bird's wings."
d. "my forearms stuck out like the necks of turtles."

_____ 5. "Tape peeled off like a scab" is an example of
a. personification.
b. simile.
c. synonym.
d. antonym.

_____ 6. When the narrator said that he wanted a jacket "with enough belts to hold down a small town," he was using
a. exaggeration.
b. understatement.
c. hyperbole.
d. both a and c

True or False

Directions: Indicate whether each statement is true or false by writing **T** or **F** in the space provided.

_____ 7. The narrator wore the jacket for five years.

_____ 8. The narrator suggests that fighting is in his future.

_____ 9. The narrator's brother calls him "camouflage" because of the jacket's appearance.

_____ 10. The narrator has numerous girlfriends during the period he describes.

_____ 11. The narrator's mother reminds her son that there are others who would feel fortunate to have his jacket.

_____ 12. In sixth grade, the narrator is small and thin.

Short Answer

Directions: Answer the following questions briefly, in a few words, phrases, or sentences, as appropriate.

1. What is the main idea? ____________________
____
2. What is the author's purpose? ____________________
____
3. What words demonstrate that the jacket had a profound effect on the narrator's life even after he no longer had to wear it? ____________________
____
4. The narrator blames his jacket for many of his misfortunes. What are four things that go wrong in the narrator's life after receiving the jacket? ________
____
____
____
5. What details in the story indicate that the narrator comes from a background where money is not plentiful? ____________________
____
____
____
____
6. What is the narrator's relationship with his mother during the period described in the story? ____________________
____
7. In what ways does the narrator demonstrate his insecurity while wearing the jacket? ____________________
____
8. What does the narrator mean when he describes the jacket as an ugly brother breathing over his shoulder? ____________________

Vocabulary in Context

Directions: Choose the correct definition of each word according to how it is used in the sentence.

_____ 1. An artist drawing your *profile* will show a view from the
   a. front.
   b. back.
   c. side.

_____ 2. If something is *bobbing*, it is
a. dangling.
b. stationary.
c. moving up and down.

_____ 3. If something *shrivels*, it
a. shrinks.
b. expands.
c. festers.

_____ 4. A *forearm* is located
a. between the elbow and the shoulder.
b. between the wrist and the elbow.
c. between the wrist and the knuckles of the hand.

_____ 5. If your friend is *moping*, she is
a. dejected.
b. in low spirits.
c. both a and b

_____ 6. A *vicious* spelling test is one that is
a. easy.
b. brutal.
c. dangerous.

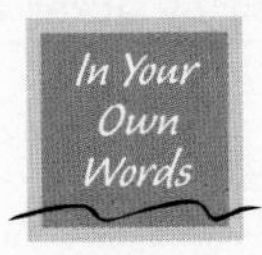

In Your Own Words

1. The narrator feels that his clothes have failed him. Do you think clothes that are not of your own choosing, but instead are forced upon you, can have an adverse effect on self-confidence? On happiness?
2. What is your opinion about the saying "Clothes make the man"?
3. In your opinion, how important are possessions to overall happiness?

Written Assignment

Directions: Choose one of the following quotations and write a few short paragraphs giving your opinion.

> "If most of us are ashamed of shabby clothes and shoddy furniture, let us be more ashamed of shabby ideas and shoddy philosophies. . . . It would be a sad situation if the wrapper were better than the meat wrapped inside it.
> —Albert Einstein
>
> "People seldom notice old clothes if you wear a big smile." —Lee Mildon
>
> "What a strange power there is in clothing. —Isaac Bashevis Singer
>
> "There is much to support the view that it is clothes that wear us and not we them." —Virginia Woolf

Internet Activity

Check out Gary Soto's Web site at www.garysoto.com.

What new information about Soto did you learn? Write a short paragraph summarizing Soto's personal and literary accomplishments.

STUDY TECHNIQUE 12: PRACTICE WITH TIME LINES

A time line is a specialized way of organizing information. Time lines are useful when material needs to be organized chronologically. When you are working with historical articles, or other kinds of articles that describe a sequence of events, it sometimes helps to prepare a time line.

All that a time line does is place events in chronological order along a line and then assign information to the dates. You can make a time line vertically (up and down) or horizontally (across). How specific you want to make a time line in terms of the number of dates and the amount of information you assign to each date depends on the reading material and your needs.

The following time line shows important events in Gary Soto's life.

1952	date of birth
1956	father is killed in an accident
1972	took his first poetry-writing class
1974	graduated from college with a bachelor's degree in English
1975	married Carolyn Oda
1977	began teaching at the University of California at Berkeley
1978	collection of poetry is nominated for a Pulitzer Prize
1985	publishes first book of prose
1995	is a finalist for the National Book Award
2010	Gary Soto Literary Museum established at Fresno City College

COMPLETION

Directions: Reorder the following events so that they follow the same sequence as in the story. Write the events in the correct order in the following box. We have done the first event for you.

a. The boy Scotch-tapes the L-shaped rip closed.
b. Brownie rips a hole in the jacket.
c. The boy discovers the jacket draped on his bedpost.
d. The boy's brother calls him "camouflage" because the jacket is so spotted.
e. The boy gets a D on a math test and gets pushed to the ground at recess.
f. The boy's mother asks what kind of jacket he wants.

1. The boy's mother asks what kind of jacket he wants.
2. ______
3. ______
4. ______
5. ______
6. ______

Chapter Summary and Review

In Chapter 9, you learned about the use of figurative language, including similes, metaphors, and personification. You also became familiar with extended metaphors, literary allusions, and imagery.

Short Answer

Directions: Give an example for each of the following.

1. Simile: ______
2. Metaphor: ______
3. Personification: ______

Vocabulary in Context

Directions: Choose one of the following words to complete the sentences below. Use each word only once.

inanimate language literally personification unlike visual

4. ______________ occurs when human characteristics are assigned to ______________ objects.
5. Both fiction and nonfiction writers use figurative ______________ in their writing.
6. Descriptive poems often appeal to readers' ______________ sense.
7. Figures of speech should not be taken ______________.
8. Similes and metaphors find a similarity in two ______________ things.

CHAPTER

10 Tone

CHAPTER PREVIEW

In this chapter, you will

- Learn to recognize an author's tone.
- Learn to recognize irony.
- Become familiar with satirical devices.

Inferring Tone

It is not so much what you say as the manner in which you say it;
It is not so much the language you use as the tone in which you convey it.
"Come here," I sharply said, and the child cowered and wept.
"Come here," I sweetly said, and to my lap he crept.
Words may be mild and fair but the tone may pierce like a dart;
Words may be soft as the summer air but the tone may break my heart;
For words come from the mind, grow by study and art—
But tone leaps from the inner self, revealing the state of the heart.
Whether you know it or not, whether you mean it or care,
Gentleness, kindness, love and hate, envy and anger are there.

—Anonymous

The poem above describes the importance of tone. The word **tone** refers to the emotional quality of a piece of written material. Just as a speaker's voice can convey a wide range of feelings, so can a writer's **voice.** Authors vary tone to express their attitude toward a topic. In this way, authors can express an opinion without directly stating it. Understanding tone is crucial to interpreting what the author has written.

To appreciate the differences in tone that writers employ, read the following versions of a murder confession. Notice how the choice of words and details lead to contrasting tones.

"I just shot my husband five times in the chest with this .357 Magnum." (Tone: matter-of-fact, objective)

"How could I ever have killed him? I can't believe I did that!" (Tone: surprised)

"Oh, my God. I've murdered my husband. How can I ever be forgiven for this dreadful deed?" (Tone: regretful)

"That dirty rat. He's had it coming for years. I'm glad I finally had the nerve to do it." (*Tone:* revengeful)

(John Langan, *Improving Reading Comprehension Skills,* Townsend Press, 1992, p. 308)

Words Used to Describe Tone

Tone is expressed by the words and details an author selects and can often be described by a single adjective. Following is a list of words that are sometimes used to describe tone. Brief definitions are provided.

1. admiring (thinking of with delight or approval; respecting)
2. admonishing (criticizing in a mild way)
3. alarmed (suddenly afraid or anxious; frightened)
4. amazed (feeling great wonder; astonished)
5. ambivalent (uncertain about a choice; showing mixed feelings)
6. amused (entertained; playful; humorous)
7. angry (feeling strong resentment)
8. appreciative (thankful; grateful)
9. arrogant (feeling superior or self-important)
10. awed (respect mixed with wonder)
11. befuddled (confused)
12. bitter (extremely resentful)
13. charming (very pleasing; attractive; delightful)
14. cheerful (full of cheer; glad; joyful)
15. compassionate (full of sympathy)
16. concerned (made anxious or uneasy; troubled)

continued

Words Used to Describe Tone—*continued*

17. congratulatory (happy for someone's success or good luck)
18. contemptuous (disdainful; scornful; showing little respect)
19. critical (finding fault with; disapproving)
20. cruel (causing great pain; brutal)
21. cynical (doubting that people are ever sincere, honest, or good)
22. depressed (sad; gloomy; discouraged)
23. dictatorial (inclined to be domineering; overbearing; tyrannical)
24. disapproving (feeling against someone or something)
25. disgusted (feeling strong distaste; nausea; loathing)
26. excited (stirred up)
27. exaggerating (making something seem larger, greater, or better than it is)
28. formal (not relaxed or familiar; stiff)
29. humorous (funny or amusing; comical)
30. impressed (affected by or influenced deeply)
31. impassioned (filled with or showing great emotion)
32. informal (casual; familiar)
33. instructive (educative; useful, informative)
34. ironic (meaning the opposite of what is expected or said)
35. irreverent (not showing respect)
36. loving (warmly affectionate)
37. motivating (encouraging)
38. nostalgic (longing for something that happened long ago or is now far away)
39. objective (without bias; neutral)
40. optimistic (looking on the bright side)
41. outraged (great anger aroused by something seen as an injury, insult, or injustice)
42. peevish (cross or irritable)
43. perplexed (filled with doubt; puzzled)
44. pessimistic (expecting the worst)
45. playful (lively; said in fun)
46. pleading (asking in a serious way; begging)
47. questioning (contesting; challenging)
48. remorseful (feeling great guilt or sorrow)
49. sarcastic (mocking, sneering, or cutting speech)
50. scolding (using sharp, angry words to find fault with someone; rebuking)
51. self-pitying (a self-indulgent attitude concerning one's own difficulties)
52. sentimental (having tender, gentle feelings)
53. serious (showing deep thought; not joking or fooling around)
54. solemn (very serious or grave)
55. sorrowful (filled with sadness or grief)
56. surprised (struck by a sudden feeling of wonder by something unexpected; shocked)
57. tragic (mournful; dreadful)
58. vindictive (said in revenge; wanting to get even)
59. warning (cautioning)
60. whiny (complaining or begging in a way that lacks dignity)
61. witty (clever in an amusing way)

Exercise 1: Tone—At the Restaurant

Directions: The following conversations took place at a local restaurant at lunchtime. Choose one of the following words to identify the tone in each numbered passage. Use key words and punctuation as clues, and be able to justify your choices.

amazed	appreciative	cheerful	dictatorial	disgusted
nostalgic	outraged	perplexed	scolding	sorrowful

__________ 1. "Don't you dare talk to me like that! I'm your mother and you owe me a little respect. Sit up straight, stop slouching, and please chew with your mouth closed. Don't you have any manners?"

__________ 2. "Wow! This is really a nice restaurant. From the outside it certainly doesn't look like much."

__________ 3. Mike looks up at the servers singing Happy Birthday and says, "What is this? What's going on? It's not my birthday."

__________ 4. "Mommy, I hate this macaroni," Susie said with a sob. "I don't want to be here anymore," she cried. "Please take me home."

_______ 5. "I'd like to speak to your manager. You've completely ignored me while you've flirted with the young men at the next table. I want you to know I've never been treated like this before. You're going to be sorry your behavior was so rude when you're out of a job."

_______ 6. "Gene, clean up the spill at table 6 and then take four glasses of water to table 7."

_______ 7. "We hope you had a pleasant time and will come back soon. Please tell all your friends about us. We've only been open for two weeks and are grateful for all new customers."

_______ 8. "Hello, everybody! How are you all today? I'm Susan, your server! The tuna looks terrific today! Can I get you an appetizer to start off?"

_______ 9. "This food is awful! My lettuce is soggy and it's turning brown. There's a hair in my tomato soup and my sandwich is burned!"

_______ 10. "Oh, honey. Look at that picture on the wall. Remember when we were in Italy? We were so young then and we had such a wonderful time. I wish we could go back to those carefree days."

Exercise 2: Tone—At the Movie Theater

Directions: Choose one of the following words to identify the tone in each numbered passage. Use key words and punctuation as clues, and be able to justify your choices.

admiring	alarmed	angry	appreciative	compassionate
dictatorial	disgusted	ironic	self-pitying	whining

_______ 1. "I know this has been an especially difficult time for you. This movie will be good for you. You won't have to concentrate on a complex plot. It's just pure light-hearted entertainment. Relax and enjoy yourself and let me take care of everything."

_______ 2. "Is this seat taken? Whoops, I didn't mean to step on your foot. I'm as graceful as a dancing elephant!"

_______ 3. "What a wonderful actress. No matter what role she plays, she always does a beautiful job. It's such a pleasure to attend one of her movies. I don't think she's ever been in a bad one. And she's so lovely, too. Her smile lights up the screen."

_______ 4. "Oh my goodness. I don't think I remembered to lock the door. I had the key right there in my hand, but I don't think I used it. What am I going to do?"

_______ 5. "What is the matter with me? I can't seem to do even the simplest thing right. Things certainly haven't been easy for me lately. Car problems, school problems, health problems, and now this."

_______ 6. "Sit there and hold our seats. Don't move. I'll go get the popcorn and drinks."

_______ 7. "What's this? I like plain popcorn, not buttered. And I don't like Junior Mints at all. I like to eat Raisinettes at the movies. And this drink. You know I don't like diet drinks."

_______ 8. "Ooh yuck. Somebody must have spilled their drink. There's something sticky all over the floor. And now it's on my shoes. This place is a pit. Doesn't anybody clean up in here? Look, even the seats are a mess."

_______ 9. "Are you the manager? Listen here, young man, I want my money back. I demand a refund. This whole evening has been a disaster."

_______ 10. "Thank you so much for going with me to the movie. This is just what I needed. You are such a good friend to think of me. I don't know what I'd do without you."

Exercise 3: Tone—Do Any of These Sound Familiar?

Directions: For each question, write the letter for the word that best describes the tone of the passage quoted.

_____ 1. "Hey, it's not my problem. It's your problem. I'm going to do what I'm going to do. You don't like it, that's just tough."
a. excited
b. self-pitying
c. contemptuous

_____ 2. "I can't decide if I should stay in school or drop out and get a job."
a. peevish
b. ambivalent
c. playful

_____ 3. "Oh, thank you for the necklace. It's lovely. It's just what I've always wanted."
a. informal
b. appreciative
c. objective

_____ 4. "Don't feel bad about forgetting my birthday, sweetie. I know you've been busy. It's really not that important."
a. forgiving
b. amused
c. bitter

_____ 5. "You're late to pick me up again. This is the fifth time this week! Don't give me your excuses. I don't want to hear it."
a. tragic
b. surprised
c. outraged

_____ 6. "Well, of course you're right and I'm wrong. I keep forgetting that someone as brilliant as you say you are is never wrong."
a. informal
b. sarcastic
c. humorous

_____ 7. "Of all the nerve. Can you believe some people? Hey, lady! I'm next in line. Wait your turn."
a. angry
b. befuddled
c. sorrowful

_____ 8. "Mike, you're making far too many errors in your papers. I suggest you proofread them more carefully."
a. surprised
b. witty
c. critical

_____ 9. "He's had all kinds of problems and yet he just keeps on trying. I have nothing but respect for the guy."
a. admiring
b. solemn
c. cheerful

_____ 10. "Tina was so sweet. She used to make little flowers and smiley faces for me when she was three. She was such a loving child."
a. charming
b. nostalgic
c. amused

_____ 11. "Mommy, why does Ann always get to sit next to the window? I want to sit next to the window. You never let me sit there. It's not fair! And I'm hungry, too."
a. optimistic
b. formal
c. whining

_____ 12. "I hate to loan you my car. Something bad always happens to it. I know it's not going to be any different this time either. Why should it be?"
a. ironic
b. nostalgic
c. cynical

Exercise 4: Tone in Textbook Passages

Directions: Read the following short passages taken from college textbooks. Then find a word (or words) in the list of tone words at the beginning of the chapter that best describes the tone of each speaker. Write the word on the blank provided. Use key words and punctuation as clues, and be able to explain your choices.

1. Nathan was only five years old when the fever struck him. At first no one knew what was wrong. No one knew that parasites inside his body had infected his red blood cells. No one knew those cells were clumping together, choking the flow of blood through his body and damaging his vital organs. No one knew his kidneys would soon fail and seizures would begin. No one knew he would wind up in a coma. The parasites in Nathan's body came from a mosquito bite, a bite that gave him malaria. And Nathan is not alone. The World Health Organization tells us the horrible truth: In Africa, a child dies from malaria every 30 seconds. Isn't it time we tried to do something to help children like Nathan?

   (Stephen Lucas, *The Art of Public Speaking,* 10/e, McGraw-Hill, 2009, p. 372)

   Tone: ______________________

2. Financial wellness doesn't refer to being rich but rather to managing your financial resources appropriately. Money doesn't guarantee good health and

happiness, but financial difficulties can strain physical, emotional, and social dimensions of wellness and thus reduce your overall well-being. Financial security provides peace of mind and reduces stress. What's the big message here? You must live within your financial means and, when possible, save for the future.

(Gary Liguori, *Questions and Answers*, 2/e, McGraw-Hill, 2014, p. 10)

Tone: ____________________

3. We see the beautiful, slim bodies of attractive people having an exciting and fun time in a lovely environment many times every day through the magic of television or the turn of a page in a popular magazine. Everyone and everything appears to be just right. Whether it's wrinkle cream, beer, exercise equipment, or the latest weight control product, advertisers are persuading people to buy products and services. Too often consumers must follow the concept of *caveat emptor*, a phrase that means "Let the buyer beware." In other words, it is the consumer's problem to determine if the advertisement is misleading, and she must make the decision to purchase at her own discretion or risk. This is just Not Fair! Consumers should be able to trust that the information presented by advertisements is accurate and truthful.

   (Cheryl A. Kolander, *Contemporary Women's Health*, 5/e, McGraw-Hill, 2014, p. 47)

   Tone: ____________________

4. It is a warm, sunny day out on the baseball field. You, playing shortstop, decide to taunt the upcoming batter with such comments as, "Easy out," "This one can't hit," "He runs like a girl," and so on. All of a sudden, there is a commotion in the stands. The game is called to a halt as a fistfight in the stands ends with your father in critical condition. Seems the father of the "easy out" started calling you names, and it all spun out of control. Something like this would never happen, though, would it? Unfortunately, this is becoming an all-too-common scenario in the area of Little League and high school sports.

   (Paul Nelson, et al. *iSpeak: Public Speaking for Contemporary Life*, McGraw-Hill, 2013, p. 219)

   Tone: ____________________

5. Have you read your "Mountain Dew" bottle? Your "Diet Pepsi" bottle? Your "Classic Coke" can? If you take the time to read your bottle or can, you will find an interesting message, sometimes in distinctive red print. That message says: "Phenylketonurics: Contains Phenylalanine." Is this a message to aliens who dwell among us? Have you ever personally met a "phenylketonuric"? Do you know what this label means and why you should read the warning?

   (Paul Nelson, et al. *iSpeak: Public Speaking for Contemporary Life* McGraw-Hill, 2013, p. 219)

   Tone: ____________________

6. Tall (6 feet, 4 inches) and gangly, Lincoln had an awkward manner as he spoke, yet his logic and sincerity carried the audience with him. Born in the slave state of Kentucky, Lincoln had grown up mostly in southern Indiana and central Illinois. Yet his intense ambition lifted him above the backwoods from which he came. He compensated for a lack of schooling through disciplined self-education, and he became a shrewd courtroom lawyer of respectable social standing. When Lincoln took the oath of office, his national experience consisted of one term in the House of Representatives. But Lincoln was a shrewd judge of character and a superb politician. To achieve a common goal he willingly overlooked withering criticism and personal slights. He was not easily humbugged, overawed, or flattered and never

allowed personal feelings to blind him to his larger objectives. Few presidents have been better able to communicate with the average citizen.

(James West Davidson, *U.S.: A Narrative History,* 2/e, McGraw-Hill, 2012, p. 300, 312)

Tone: ____

7. In *The Faith Healers,* James Randi tells what happened to a youngster with twisted legs who attended televangelist Peter Popoff's "Miracle Crusade" with strong expectations that he would be made well:

   Following the spectacle, I saw that little boy outside the Civic Center again, perched on his crutches and staring down at the pavement. At the service the highly touted "healer" had not even come near the kid. The boy looked up as I approached him. His smile was gone, and I saw tears running down his face. His eyes were red from weeping. I began to speak, but I choked up and had to turn away. I will never forget that terrible moment, as the child realized that he had witnessed a cruel, callous hoax. Hundreds of people at that meeting had believed they would see miracles performed. Some few had been touched by the preacher, but none had been healed. Most had given cash or checks, some in envelopes sent to them by mail before they attended. One way or another, they were all swindled.

   (Stephen Barrett, *Consumer Health,* 9/e, McGraw-Hill, 2013, p. 38)

   Tone: ____

8. The book you are about to read is a superior piece of work! It demonstrates the sheerest true excellence in its treatment of one of the outstanding important topics of our time! You will find every moment informative and entertaining to a degree you have never before encountered in the world of fine literature! This much applauded volume has earned for its author a rightful place as one of the top writers on the contemporary scene!

   (Stephen Barrett, *Consumer Health,* 9/e, McGraw-Hill, 2013, p. 48)

   Tone: ____

9. Today, Americans spend billions of dollars per year for herbal capsules and tablets, bulk herbs, and herbal teas used for supposed medicinal qualities. Most are purchased over-the-counter. Many herbs contain hundreds or even thousands of chemicals that have not been completely cataloged. While some may ultimately prove useful as therapeutic agents, others could well prove toxic. Most herbal products sold in the United States are not standardized, which means that determining the exact amounts of their ingredients can be difficult or impossible. Moreover, many herbal practitioners are not qualified to make appropriate diagnoses or to determine how herbs compare to proven drugs. Many herbal products are marketed as "dietary supplements," even though they have little or no nutritional value. No legal standards exist for their processing, harvesting, or packaging. In many cases, contents and potency are not accurately disclosed on the label. Many products marketed as herbs contain no useful ingredients, and some even lack the principal ingredient for which people buy them.

   (Stephen Barrett, *Consumer Health,* 9/e, McGraw-Hill, 2013, p. 215)

   Tone: ____

10. There is much to be worried about in our global environment. Evidence is growing relentlessly that we are degrading our environment and consuming resources at unsustainable rates. Biodiversity is disappearing at a pace unequaled since the end of the age of dinosaurs 65 million years ago. Irreplaceable topsoil erodes from farm fields, threatening global food supplies.

Ancient forests are being destroyed to make newsprint and toilet paper. Rivers and lakes are polluted with untreated sewage, while soot and smoke obscure our skies. Even our global climate seems to be changing to a new regime that could have catastrophic consequences.

(William P. Cunningham and Mary Ann Cunningham, *Environmental Science,* 12/e, McGraw-Hill, 2012, p. 2)

Tone: ______________________________

11. Today, worldwide public awareness of—and support for—environmental protection is at an all-time high. Over the past 50 years, human ingenuity and enterprise have brought about a breathtaking pace of technological innovations and scientific breakthroughs. We have learned to produce more goods and services with less material. The breathtaking spread of communication technology makes it possible to share information worldwide nearly instantaneously. Since World War II, the average real income of developing countries has doubled; malnutrition has declined by almost one-third; child death rates have been halved; average life expectancy has increased by 30 percent; and the percentage of rural families with access to safe drinking water has risen from less than 10 percent to almost 75 percent.

(William P. Cunningham and Mary Ann Cunningham, *Environmental Science,* 12/e, McGraw-Hill, 2012, p. 2)

Tone: ______________________________

READING

"The old man sighed and said nothing."

TUNING IN TO READING This well-known Russian folktale has been retold many times, most notably by the Brothers Grimm. The version below is by well-known Russian author Leo Tolstoy. Although it is a very short narrative, it conveys a lot of emotion in just a few words.

BIO-SKETCH Count Lev Nikolayevich Tolstoy (1828–1910), also known as Leo Tolstoy, is considered to be one of history's greatest writers. He is best known for his classic novels *Anna Karenina and War and Peace.*

The Old Grandfather and His Little Grandson

BY LEO TOLSTOY

The grandfather had become very old. His legs would not carry him, his eyes could not see, his ears could not hear, and he was toothless. When he ate, bits of food sometimes dropped out of his mouth. His son and his son's wife no longer allowed him to eat with them at the table. He had to eat his meals in the corner near the stove.

2 One day they gave him his food in a bowl. He tried to move the bowl closer; it fell to the floor and broke. His daughter-in-law scolded him. She told him that he spoiled everything in the house and broke their dishes, and she said that from now on he would get his food in a wooden dish. The old man sighed and said nothing.

3 A few days later, the old man's son and his wife were sitting in their hut, resting and watching their little boy playing on the floor. They saw him putting together something out of small pieces of wood. His father asked him, "What are you making, Misha?"

4 The little grandson said, "I'm making a wooden bucket. When you and Mamma get old, I'll feed you out of this wooden dish."

5 The young peasant and his wife looked at each other and tears filled their eyes. They were ashamed because they had treated the old grandfather so meanly, and from that day on they again let the old man eat with them at the table and took better care of him.

(Leo Tolstoy, Twenty-Two Russian Tales for Young Children, trans. Miriam Morton. Simon and Schuster, 1969)

COMPREHENSION CHECKUP

Short Answer

1. What is the author's tone? ______________________________

2. Give two reasons to support your choice.

   a. ______________________________

   b. ______________________________

In Your Own Words

1. How do the man and his wife treat the grandfather at the beginning of the story? ______________________________
2. What activity on the part of the grandson makes the couple change their attitude toward the grandfather? ______________________________
3. What did the couple realize about their behavior toward the grandfather? ______________________________
4. What does Tolstoy suggest about how the elderly should be treated when they can no longer care for themselves? ______________________________

5. What is the author's main idea? ______________________________

____

6. How easy or difficult is it to treat elderly parents well? ______________

7. Is it easy to grow old in today's society? Why or why not? ______________

Written Assignment

1. Describe each of the characters in the story with a single word. Provide a short explanation for each of your choices.
2. In this story, a child's actions lead to changes in his parents' behavior toward another person. Do you think parents can learn things about themselves by observing how their children behave? Can you think of some specific example from your own life?
3. Use your imagination and the clues provided by the author to answer the following questions about the old grandfather. Provide quotes from the story to support your answers.
   a. What does the grandfather look like?
   b. How does the grandfather behave?
   c. How do you think the grandfather feels?
   d. What do you think the grandfather fears?

Internet Activity

1. Find the life expectancy for people your own age. What is the predicted life expectancy for someone born in 2014?
2. Read a review of the 2009 movie *The Last Station,* which describes the last year of Tolstoy's life. Write a summary of the review.

READING

A 50-ton humpback was tangled in ropes and drowning. These brave volunteers risked their lives trying to free her.

TUNING IN TO READING Have you ever been involved in a rescue attempt of an animal that was threatened or in need? If so, how did the experience make you feel? The selection below describes the rescue of a humpback whale, a mammal that was hunted almost to the point of extinction. Today, even though it is still listed as an endangered species, it has made a dramatic comeback with a population now nearing 20,000.

BIO-SKETCH Anita Bartholomew is a freelance writer and editor whose specialties include health, science, social issues, politics, and personal profiles.

NOTES ON VOCABULARY

humpback whale A whale having a large round back and long flippers. Humpback whales communicate using complex, distinctive songs that identify individuals and play an important role in mating.

pectoral fin either of the pair of fins located behind the head. They help to control the direction of movement.

WHALE OF A RESCUE ANITA BARTHOLOMEW

A Risky Rescue Mission

The two divers in snorkel gear dropped backward off the inflatable boat into the Pacific Ocean. Cautiously they swam toward the humpback lying weak and exhausted in the waves. The water was 53 degrees, dark and frothy like the foam on a beer. They could barely tell the animal's head from its tail.

2 A huge flipper, eight or nine feet long—the whale's left pectoral fin—rose up a yard away. One slap could kill a man.

3 Thick nylon crab ropes, called blue steel because of their strength, wound around the fin, through the whale's mouth and over its head. In some spots the lines sliced so deeply they disappeared into the animal's flesh.

4 Left like this, the whale would die.

5 Professional dive master James Moskito spent about as much time in the water as he did on land. Still boyish-looking at 40, he now worked for a company that took people on shark adventures, up close and personal. From mid-September to mid-November, he led divers enclosed in steel cages down into the hunting grounds of great white sharks off the Farallon Islands, some 30 miles outside San Francisco Bay.

6 This Sunday in mid-December 2005, he and his girlfriend, Holly Drouillard, were planning something a little more mellow: a trip to his parents' home.

7 Before hitting the freeway, Moskito checked his voice mail and found a message from Mick Menigoz, the skipper of a charter fishing boat. A whale was trapped in crab lines and floundering at sea. Menigoz was putting together a group of divers to assist volunteers from the Marine Mammal Center in Sausalito. Would Moskito come with them?

8 "I'm in," Moskito said.

9 During his 26 years in the Air Force, Tim Young had parachuted out of helicopters and huge, four-engine C-130 airplanes—with full scuba gear and a load of medical supplies—to rescue people in precarious situations.

10 The summons from Menigoz that interrupted his family's Sunday breakfast, however, was unusual even for Young. Without hesitation, he tossed his diving equipment into the car and headed for the Emeryville harbor where Menigoz's boat, *Superfish,* was docked.

Cutting Through the Cat's Cradle

11 After picking up Frances Gulland, the Marine Center's veterinarian, and two volunteers across the bay in Sausalito, Menigoz motored out through the Golden Gate. He had the center's small inflatable craft with an outboard in tow.

12 By about 1:30 p.m., he was close to the GPS coordinates for the whale's location and told everyone to scan the horizon.

13 One volunteer, Jason Russey, pointed to a plume of water rising like cold steam from the sea—the spout of a humpback whale. "There it is," he yelled.

14 As they approached, they saw the domed top of a massive gray head—about the size of a large dining-room

table—just above the water. The humpback almost seemed to be anchored in place, not swimming, not even drifting with the current. And to Menigoz's trained eye, the animal was also listing to one side. The *Superfish* cautiously inched forward to within 100 feet.

15 Four buoys the size of gallon bleach bottles floated in the water around the whale. Each buoy was connected by a rope to a 100-pound metal and mesh crab trap on the ocean floor. Four traps shouldn't weigh down a whale that size, Moskito thought. Why wasn't it moving?

16 He and Young climbed into the inflatable and went to check. The rubberized craft bucked in the rolling sea. As they edged closer, a sea lion swimming nearby leaped out of the water over the floundering whale as if to mark the spot.

17 Moskito took it as a good sign—sea lions wouldn't swim where sharks were feeding.

18 Suited up, he and Young tested their snorkels, readied themselves, and then rolled backward into the sea.

19 Like so much scattered popcorn, small chunks of white blubber, gouged from the whale's body by the ropes, floated all around them, clouding the water. Young and Moskito made their first inspection, and then returned to the outboard to don scuba gear. They'd need air to work around—and maybe under—the humpback.

20 As Young swam back to the whale, one of the crab-trap ropes caught the sheath on his leg and snatched away the larger of his two dive knives. A glint of steel disappeared into the gloom.

21 Swimming downward, the two men saw the animal was a female, some 50 feet in length. Her tail was wrapped with about 20 ropes connected to a dozen or so 100-pound crab traps. That's what was anchoring her in place. The weights dragged her tail down at a 90-degree angle to her body. From the tail, the ropes wound upward around her flipper. She was hogtied—and using every ounce of strength just to keep her blowhole above water.

Moskito's heart sank as he looked at the tangled mess. There's no way we're going to save this whale, he thought, but realizing, too, that they had to try. 22

Back together on the surface, the two men mapped out a game plan. They'd start with the two ropes that were more loosely wound around the pectoral fin. 23

Taking their dive knives back underwater, they came body to body with the whale. Young began sawing at the half-inch blue rope. Moskito used a double-bladed knife that worked like scissors. 24

Instead of thrashing at them with her fin, the whale stopped moving completely, resting in the swells. Even after they cut her flipper free, she remained still and calm. 25

Both men surfaced and swam back to the inflatable to talk with the center's crew. "I think she knows we're trying to help her," Moskito said. The team turned the outboard around and motored to the *Superfish* for more supplies. 26

Moskito dove down to tackle the spaghetti tangle around the whale's tail. And Young traced the ropes, slippery with the humpback's blubber, to her mouth. The feel of the whale's skin, as soft as a wet chamois, surprised him. Patches of barnacles and other crustaceans had attached themselves to her body; he could see scars from earlier injuries. 27

The blue lines ran over her head and through her mouth from side to side like a gag. She had struggled so fiercely against the ropes that they'd sliced into her flesh. 28

Young severed the ropes, and then tugged with all his strength to remove the pieces. It was like pulling on giant dental floss. This had to be frightening her, hurting her, he thought. But amazingly, she remained calm. Young worked methodically, acutely aware of the danger of getting an arm, leg or a 29 piece of his gear tangled in the cat's cradle of lines that surrounded her. If the humpback should dive, she would take him down with her.

30 His swim fins resting lightly against her flipper for leverage, Young floated eye-to-eye with the wounded animal. In utter stillness, with that eye as large as a human fist, the whale watched him as he tackled the lines.

31 At the tail, Moskito sliced through the nylon bonds as quickly as he could. Each time he cut one, the humpback eased her tail into position again.

A Fantastic Moment

32 While Moskito and Young worked, the Marine Mammal Center's crew picked up Jason Russey and Ted Vivian, two more volunteer divers from the *Superfish,* and returned to the whale. They dropped into the water in snorkel gear and began the job of removing pieces of rope from the whale's mouth.

33 Instead of teeth, humpbacks have thick, hair-like bristles called baleen that hang from the gum and serve as a food-filtration system. Ropes had gouged their way into the whale's mouth and were tangled in the baleen.

34 Floating just inches from her giant maw, Russey gripped the whale's lower lip and reached inside her mouth to tug out pieces that could keep her from feeding. The huge mammal opened and closed her mouth as he tugged, but remained motionless in the water.

35 It had been well over an hour since the rescuers arrived on the scene when Moskito got down to the last few ropes. They were deeply embedded in the blubber of the tail, and he couldn't pry them loose. Not knowing what the animal would do, he shoved his knife in and began to cut away. "I'm almost there," he mumbled through his breathing apparatus. "Just two more. I'll be done and you'll be free."

36 He made the last cut and watched a buoy dangling below spiral down into the darkness. Then he surfaced and shouted out a celebratory "Whoo-hoo. She's free!" The other three men joined in the hooting and hollering.

37 Finally liberated, the whale did a shallow dive. Moskito turned around: "Where'd it go? Where'd it go?" he called.

38 The next thing he knew, she was coming up from below and straight at him. Hey, I just saved you, he thought, relief turning to fear as she rushed him.

39 The humpback stopped a foot from his chest. She nudged him, then turned away and swam in a circle around the divers. One by one she grazed by each of the four men.

40 Trying to explain the whale's behavior scientifically, Frances Gulland, the vet at the Marine Mammal Center, thinks that she probably swam in circles because her body had been kinked for so long. The divers just happened to be there while she was exercising.

41 But the men disagree. She swam with them for a good ten minutes. They all say, as Moskito does, that it was one of the "most fantastic moments" of their lives.

42 And Tim Young, who's had more than his share of adrenaline adventures, says this: "I spent 26 years in the military doing high-risk rescues. Nothing's been more gratifying than this one. Nothing."

(From *Reader's Digest,* May 2006)

COMPREHENSION CHECKUP

Short Answer

1. What tone words would you use to describe the whale's plight?

2. What tone words would you use to describe how the volunteers felt during the rescue attempt?

____

3. What tone words would you use to describe how the volunteers felt after successfully freeing the whale?

____

Multiple Choice

Directions: Write the letter of the correct answer on the blank provided.

_____ 1. The reader can infer all of the following about the whale rescue **except**
a. rescuing a floundering whale is dangerous work.
b. the rescuers were motivated primarily by monetary gain.
c. the rescuers were moved by the whale's plight.
d. there are people who are ready and willing to help save the life of a whale.

_____ 2. In paragraph 1, the phrase "frothy like the foam on a beer" is an example of
a. synonym.
b. simile.
c. metaphor.
d. personification.

_____ 3. The selection mentions all of the following about the whale **except**
a. the whale is a female.
b. she is approximately 50 feet in length.
c. her coloration is black and white.
d. she has scars and barnacles on her skin.

_____ 4. When the author refers to the whale's skin as being "as soft as a wet chamois" she is using a(n)
a. antonym.
b. metaphor.
c. personification.
d. simile.

_____ 5. All of the following demonstrate the whale's cooperation with the divers **except**
a. she did not thrash at them with her fin.
b. she dived only a few times while waiting to be freed.
c. she remained calm even though she was probably being hurt by the removal of the ropes.
d. she allowed divers to pull ropes out of her mouth.

_____ 6. All of the following statements indicate the dangerous aspects of the rescue attempt **except**
a. the whale charged the divers repeatedly.
b. the men had to work in close proximity to a large, frightened whale.
c. the whale's fin was so large that one slap could kill a man.
d. if she had decided to dive, she would have taken a man tangled in the ropes down with her.

_____ 7. The reader can infer that the size of the whale
a. was not in the least intimidating to the divers.
b. caused her to be trapped in the first place.
c. made it much harder to rescue her.
d. made her a likely tourist attraction.

_____ 8. The selection is primarily about
a. the rescue of a trapped whale by concerned persons.
b. the hardships experienced by the divers during the attempted rescue.
c. the dangers involved in attempting the rescue of any trapped animal.
d. the attachment that developed between the divers and the whale.

_____ 9. The selection uses the following images to describe the whale's plight as she is trapped by ropes: "the spaghetti tangle under the whale's tail," and "the cat's cradle of lines that surrounded her." These are images that appeal to our sense of
a. smell.
b. sight.
c. touch.
d. hearing.

_____ 10. Paragraph 41 serves as a(n) ____________ paragraph 40.
a. comparison to
b. example of
c. definition of
d. contrast to

Sequencing

Directions: Number the following sentences in correct time-order sequence.

_____ Young was eye-to-eye with the whale.

_____ Young and Moskito spotted a sea lion swimming close to the whale.

_____ The two divers freed the whale's pectoral fin.

_____ Jason Russey spotted the spout of the whale.

_____ The whale swam in circles around the divers.

_____ Moskito gave a celebratory shout when he freed the whale.

_____ Moskito checked his voice mail and discovered a message from Menigoz.

_____ Menigoz motored out through the Golden Gate.

True or False

Directions: Indicate whether the statement is true or false by writing **T** or **F** on the blank provided.

_____ 1. To *scan the horizon* means to look it over quickly or broadly.

_____ 2. We can infer that the individuals mentioned in the story felt a sense of accomplishment after rescuing the whale.

_____ 3. If an animal is *hogtied,* it is likely immobile and helpless.

_____ 4. According to the selection, sea lions aren't likely to swim in an area where sharks are lurking.

_____ 5. Humpback whales have very large teeth.

_____ 6. Four divers worked in the water to free the whale.

_____ 7. The whale has an eye about as big as a human fist and a head the size of a large dining-room table.

_____ 8. Tim Young and James Moskito were responsible for cutting the ropes that bound the whale.

_____ 9. Frances Gulland's primary job was to take tourists on shark adventures.

_____ 10. After being freed from the ropes, the whale swam with the divers for more than 30 minutes.

Vocabulary in Context

Directions: In the space provided, write the letter of the definition that best fits the way the italicized word or phrase is used in each of the following sentences.

_____ 1. *Frothy* water is likely to be
- a. frivolous.
- b. unsubstantial.
- c. bubbling and foamy.
- d. worthless.

_____ 2. A *mellow* day could be described as all of the following **except**
- a. unhurried and relaxed.
- b. pleasant and agreeable.
- c. juicy and sweet.
- d. laid back.

_____ 3. If a whale is *floundering* at sea, it is
- a. traveling swiftly.
- b. leaping into the air.
- c. having trouble staying afloat.
- d. feeding on fish.

_____ 4. A *precarious* situation is one that is
- a. dangerous and uncertain.
- b. blissfully happy.
- c. steady and reliable.
- d. comfortable and secure.

_____ 5. The *summons* from Menigoz that interrupted his family's Sunday breakfast was a
- a. warning.
- b. call for help.
- c. order.
- d. traffic ticket.

_____ 6. We can infer that a whale's *blowhole* is similar to __________ in a human being.
- a. an arm
- b. an eye
- c. an ear
- d. a nostril

______ 7. A synonym for *listing* as in "the animal was also *listing* to one side" is
a. leaning.
b. tilting.
c. inclining.
d. all of the above

______ 8. If you've *mapped out a game plan,* you
a. have a strategy for achieving your objective.
b. are going to improvise.
c. are going to pull things together hurriedly.
d. have drawn a picture.

______ 9. Saying that Young worked *methodically* means he worked
a. in a hurried, chaotic way.
b. in an orderly and systematic fashion.
c. thoughtlessly.
d. according to what a book recommended.

______ 10. To say that the whale was *liberated* means that she was
a. restrained.
b. made free.
c. uncontrolled.
d. discharged.

In Your Own Words

Considering the danger of the rescue attempt and the fact that the rescuers were not going to be paid for their time and effort, why do you think they dropped everything that Sunday and came to the aid of a trapped whale?

Written Assignment

1. There is a great deal of interest in whales and other large mammals like dolphins. Why do you think they are so fascinating to so many people? Have you had any close-up experience with them? Do you think they can communicate with one another? With humans? Write a few paragraphs giving your opinion.
2. One of the most famous humpback whales is Humphrey, who was rescued twice by concerned groups. In 1985, Humphrey swam into San Francisco Bay and then up the Sacramento River. In 1990, Humphrey again swam into San Francisco Bay and became stuck on a mudflat. In both instances, Humphrey was successfully guided back to the Pacific Ocean. However, both rescue efforts were very costly and time-consuming. How do you feel about spending large amounts of money and rescue workers' time on rescue missions such as these? Write a few paragraphs giving your opinion. Consider how your position on this topic will affect the tone of your writing.

Internet Activity

Do an Internet search for information on the two humpback whales named Delta and Dawn. What was the ultimate outcome of the rescue attempt?

Identifying Irony

When there is a contrast between what people say and what they actually mean, they are using **verbal irony.** Since the meaning is usually expressed indirectly, you must use inference to understand this *reversed* meaning, or you will misinterpret the author.

Another form of irony is **situational.** In this form, there is a contrast between what is expected to occur and what actually does happen. Many stories or poems that end with an unexpected twist are based on this type of irony.

Directions: Examine the cartoon below and then answer the following questions.

RUBES. © 1995 by Leigh Rubin. By permission of Leigh Rubin and Creators Syndicate, Inc.

1. Locate the word in the cartoon that best expresses irony. ____________

2. What can you infer has happened in the cartoon?

   ____

3. What key point is being made in the cartoon? What situation is being criticized?

   ____

4. Describe the tone or attitude you think is really being expressed in the cartoon.

   ____

The "Forest" cartoon concerns the environment. The sign proclaims the new headquarters of a forest conservation group. This cartoon is ironic because, instead of preserving timberland, the foundation has cleared ground to erect another building. The foundation has destroyed what it was supposed to be protecting. This action has defeated the group's fundamental goal. This is the exact *opposite* of what we would reasonably expect. In the cartoon, the meaning is expressed indirectly, so you must use inference to decipher the reversed meaning.

Look at the sign in the following below. What inferences can be drawn from the words and the picture? In what way is the sign ironic?

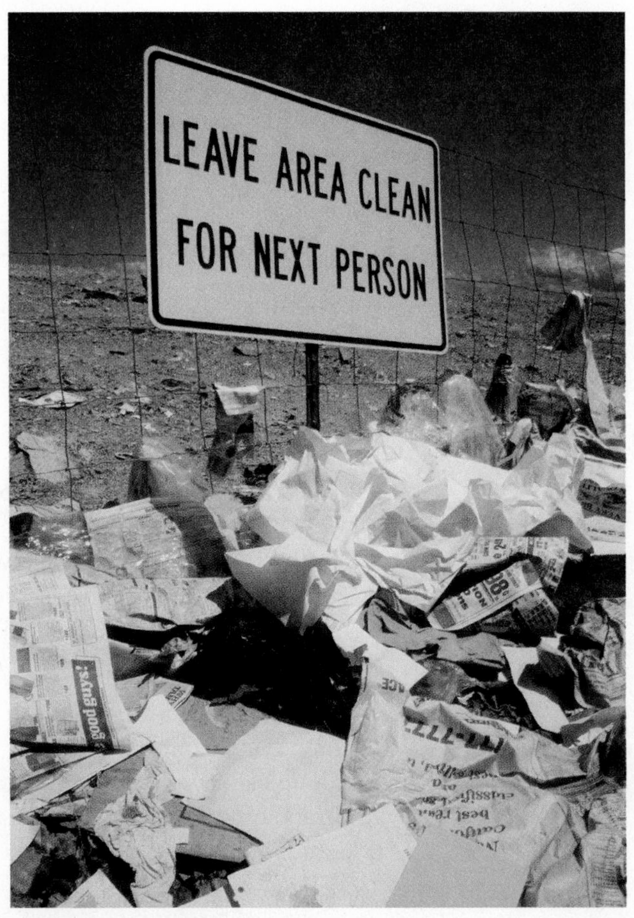

Exercise 5: Detecting Irony

Directions: Read the fable and then answer the questions that follow.

"The only two things in life that are guaranteed are death and taxes."
—Benjamin Franklin

Once, a long time ago, Death came riding into the city of Baghdad looking for Ali Haj, a proud and wealthy merchant. Death was in no hurry to meet Ali Haj, for he had many other old friends whom he wished to honor by a visit. On hearing that Death was in the town and had already called on some of his friends, Ali Haj, who had not gained his riches by stupidity, spoke to his old, blind servant:

"There is a great prince come to town, whom I am eager to see, for I wish to give him a rare jewel to win his friendship. Unfortunately, I cannot hope he would visit the poor home of a humble merchant like myself. Therefore I shall go to seek him. But if he should by chance come here while I am away, welcome him with the choicest of food and drink, and beg him only to wait for me a little while. But see you keep him here."

Then Ali Haj gathered his favorite treasures, his wives and children, and fled on his swiftest horses to Damascus.

When Death knocked at his door the next day, the blind servant appeared. "I seek your master, Ali Haj," Death said.

"He has gone out to seek a great prince to give him a precious jewel," answered the servant. "But if you, my lord, are that prince, then my master begs you to consider this house your own and to stay only a little while till he returns."

"There are many who call me Prince," said Death, "but few so joyful to greet me as Ali Haj. But that is what I expected of him." Then he stared at the ancient man, who was indeed rich in white hairs and wrinkles. "Since you are sure to see him soon, kindly remind him that he need not have gone out today to seek me, for I wished only to ask him to meet me tomorrow in Damascus."

Multiple Choice

Directions: For each item, write the letter corresponding to the best answer.

_____ 1. Ali Haj succeeds in fooling all of the following **except**
a. himself.
b. the old, blind servant.
c. death.
d. his wives and children.

_____ 2. All of the following are true statements according to the fable **except** for which?
a. Death had many old friends whom he wished to visit.
b. The old servant is going to die soon.
c. Ali Haj is trying to avoid Death.
d. Ali Haj is going to be able to outsmart Death.

_____ 3. The main organizational pattern used in this fable is
a. comparison-contrast.
b. example.
c. chronological order.
d. definition.

_____ 4. The author's purpose in writing this fable is to
a. inform.
b. persuade.
c. entertain.
d. convince.

_____ 5. All of the following are descriptive of Ali Haj **except**
a. he is clever.
b. he is rich.
c. he is proud.
d. he is brave.

_____ 6. In context the word *rich* (paragraph 6) means
a. owning much money and property.
b. deep and brilliant.
c. having a lot.
d. full and mellow.

Written Assignment

Directions: Write a brief response to each question.

1. What is the fable saying about Death?
2. What is ironic about Ali Haj's departure? Why does he ask the servant to keep Death well entertained in Baghdad? What does Death mean when he says he expected this type of welcome from Ali Haj?
3. Is Ali Haj going to succeed in avoiding Death? Explain your answer.
4. What does Death mean when he tells the old servant that he is sure to see his master, Ali Haj, soon?

READING

"God: of the money that I asked for, only seventy pesos reached me. Send me the rest, since I need it very much."

TUNING IN TO READING Irony is a form of commentary by an author. In this story, pay close attention to the situation described by the author.

BIO-SKETCH Gregorio Lopez y Fuentes (1897–1966) was a highly acclaimed author who received Mexico's National Prize for Literature in 1935. As the son of a small farmer, he understood the difficulties farmers faced in trying to make a living off the land. This story was translated from Spanish by Donald A. Yates.

NOTES ON VOCABULARY

mortify the word *mortify* comes from the Latin words *mortis,* meaning "death," and *facere* meaning "to make." Today, *mortify* means "to humiliate or shame."

locusts migratory grasshoppers that strip vegetation from large areas.

prodigy something that excites wonder or amazement.

A Letter to God

GREGORIO LOPEZ Y FUENTES

THE HOUSE—THE ONLY ONE IN THE ENTIRE VALLEY—sat on the crest of a low hill. From this height one could see the river and, next to the corral, the field of ripe corn dotted with the kidney-bean flowers that always promised a good harvest.

The only thing the earth needed was a rainfall, or at least a shower. 2
Throughout the morning Lencho—who knew his fields intimately—had done nothing else but scan the sky toward the northeast.

"Now we're really going to get some water, woman." 3

The woman, who was preparing supper, replied: 4

"Yes, God willing." 5

The oldest boys were working in the field, while the smaller ones were 6
playing near the house, until the woman called to them all:

"Come for dinner . . ." 7

It was during the meal that, just as Lencho had predicted, big drops of 8
rain began to fall. In the northeast, huge mountains of clouds could be seen approaching. The air was fresh and sweet.

The man went out to look for something in the corral for no other reason 9
than to allow himself the pleasure of feeling the rain on his body, and when he returned he exclaimed:

"Those aren't raindrops falling from the sky, they're new coins. The big 10
drops are ten-centavo pieces and the little ones are fives. . . ."

With a satisfied expression he regarded the field of ripe corn with its kidney- 11
bean flowers, draped in a curtain of rain. But suddenly a strong wind began to blow and together with the rain very large hailstones began to fall. These truly did resemble new silver coins. The boys, exposing themselves to the rain, ran out to collect the frozen pearls.

"It's really getting bad now," exclaimed the man, mortified. "I hope it 12
passes quickly."

It did not pass quickly. For an hour the hail rained on the house, the gar- 13
den, the hillside, the cornfield, on the whole valley. The field was white, as if covered with salt. Not a leaf remained on the trees. The corn was totally destroyed. The flowers were gone from the kidney-bean plants. Lencho's soul was filled with sadness. When the storm had passed, he stood in the middle of the field and said to his sons:

"A plague of locusts would have left more than this. . . . The hail has left 14
nothing: this year we will have no corn or beans. . . ."

That night was a sorrowful one: 15

"All our work, for nothing!" 16

"There's no one who can help us!" 17

"We'll all go hungry this year. . . ." 18

But in the hearts of all who lived in that solitary house in the middle of 19
the valley, there was a single hope: help from God.

"Don't be so upset, even though this seems like a total loss. Remember, 20
no one dies of hunger!"

"That's what they say: no one dies of hunger. . . ." 21

All through the night, Lencho thought only of his one hope: the help of 22
God, whose eyes, as he had been instructed, see everything, even what is deep in one's conscience.

Lencho was an ox of a man, working like an animal in the fields, but still 23
he knew how to write. The following Sunday, at daybreak, after having convinced himself that there is a protecting spirit, he began to write a letter which he himself would carry to town and place in the mail.

It was nothing less than a letter to God. 24

"God," he wrote, "if you don't help me, my family and I will go hungry 25
this year. I need a hundred pesos in order to resow the field and to live until the crop comes, because the hailstorm . . ."

He wrote "To God" on the envelope, put the letter inside and, still troubled, 26
went to town. At the post office he placed a stamp on the letter and dropped it into the mailbox.

One of the employees, who was a postman and also helped at the post 27
office, went to his boss laughing heartily and showed him the letter to God. Never in his career as a postman had he known that address. The postmaster—a fat amiable fellow—also broke out laughing, but almost immediately he turned serious and, tapping the letter on his desk, commented:

"What faith! I wish I had the faith of the man who wrote this letter. To 28
believe the way he believes. To hope with the confidence that he knows how to hope with. Starting up a correspondence with God!"

So in order not to disillusion that prodigy of faith, revealed by a letter that 29
could not be delivered, the postmaster came up with an idea: answer the letter. But when he opened it, it was evident that to answer it he needed something more than good will, ink and paper. But he stuck to his resolution: he asked for money from his employee, he himself gave part of his salary, and several friends of his were obliged to give something "for an act of charity."

It was impossible for him to gather together the hundred pesos, so he was 30
able to send the farmer only a little more than half. He put the bills in an envelope addressed to Lencho and with them a letter containing only a single word as a signature: GOD.

The following Sunday Lencho came a bit earlier than usual to ask if there 31
was a letter for him. It was the postman himself who handed the letter to him, while the postmaster, experiencing the contentment of a man who has performed a good deed, looked on from the doorway of his office.

Lencho showed not the slightest surprise on seeing the bills—such was his 32
confidence—but he became angry when he counted the money. . . . God could not have made a mistake, nor could he have denied Lencho what he had requested!

Immediately, Lencho went up to the window to ask for paper and ink. On 33
the public writing table, he started in to write, with much wrinkling of his brow, caused by the effort he had to make to express his ideas. When he finished, he went to the window to buy a stamp which he licked and then affixed to the envelope with a blow of his fist.

The moment that the letter fell into the mailbox the postmaster went to 34
open it. It said:

"Better to accept whatever happens."
—Horace

"God: of the money that I asked for, only seventy pesos reached me. 35
Send me the rest, since I need it very much. But don't send it to me through the mail, because the post-office employees are a bunch of crooks. Lencho."

(Gregorio López y Fuentes, "A Letter to God")

COMPREHENSION CHECKUP

Recognizing Irony

Directions: Answer the questions briefly, in a few words, phrases, or sentences, as appropriate.

1. Record your first impressions about Lencho, his wife, the postman, and the postmaster. Give a brief description of each.

____

____

2. Study the following list of key details and explain what could reasonably be inferred from each.

   a. Lencho knows his fields "intimately."

   ____

   b. Lencho's only hope is "the help of God."

   ____

c. The postman goes to his boss "laughing heartily."

d. Never had the postman "known that address."

e. The postmaster answers the letter "in order not to disillusion that prodigy of faith."

f. The postmaster experiences "the contentment of a man who has performed a good deed."

g. Lencho affixes the stamp "with a blow of his fist."

3. Why does Lencho react the way he does? Would you react as Lencho does? Explain why or why not.

4. Identify and explain a simile and a metaphor in the story.

5. In what way is the story ironic? Explain your answer.

Written Assignment

Have you ever tried to help someone, and it turned out that the person resented your efforts? If so, how did you feel about that person? Describe your experience in a short paragraph.

Recognizing Satire

Satire is a kind of writing that uses ridicule to create awareness of flaws and to bring about change. Almost anything can be satirized, including people, institutions, and ideas. Because it relies on exaggeration and distortion, satire often has a humorous effect.

Caricature

Caricature is a form of satire in which certain characteristics, such as physical features, are exaggerated. In the 15th century, when Leonardo da Vinci sketched the faces of clerics and nobles, the "charged portrait" was an important means of political and social criticism. Biting portraits provided a way to tear down a public figure. But the social impact of the political cartoon is not as potent as it used to be. As the 20th century wore on, politicians and other targets of political cartoons began to embrace and benefit from their own caricatures. Most U.S. presidents have become ardent collectors of political cartoons about themselves. President Lyndon

Johnson reportedly liked seeing himself in cartoons so much that he didn't care whether they were flattering or not.[1] Look at the following caricature of President George Washington. Which of the features are distorted? How do these distortions satirize Washington?

© Don Tywoniw, www.dontywoniw.com

Hyperbole (Overstatement)

Hyperbole is language that exaggerates. It comes from the Greek word *hyperbole,* meaning "excess or extravagance." We are using hyperbole when we say, "He is as strong as a bull." In Mark Twain's classic novel *The Adventures of Huckleberry Finn,* the author uses hyperbole when he gives readers the following warning at the start of the book:

> *NOTICE: Persons attempting to find a motive in this narrative will be prosecuted; persons attempting to find a moral in it will be banished; persons attempting to find a plot in it will be shot.—By Order Of The Author*

Another word for hyperbole is **overstatement.** In overstatement the subject is magnified beyond reality by using adjectives (*big, longer, best*) and sweeping generalizations (*every, always, never*). Look at this example:

> He stood there, tall and proud—taller than Mount Everest and prouder than New England on the day the Patriots won their first Super Bowl.

"A satirist is a man who discovers unpleasant things about himself and then applies it to other people."
—Peter McArthur

Much of our humor is comic overstatement. Look at the following example:

> Virginia's young son had been living in the back of his pickup truck for so long she decided to give it an address.

Understatement

The satirist may also use **understatement,** which is saying less about something than is expected. As an example of understatement, consider Mark Twain's comment in the following story. In 1897, Samuel Clemens (Mark Twain) was staying

[1]Information from Week in Review, *New York Times,* June 17, 2001, section 4, p. 16.

in London at the same time as his cousin, Dr. James Ross Clemens. Dr. Clemens became ill and died, but the press mistakenly reported that it was Mark Twain who had died. To untangle the mix-up, Twain sent a cable from London to the Associated Press that read, "The reports of my death are greatly exaggerated."

Jonathan Swift, well-known satirist of the 18th century and author of *Gulliver's Travels* and *A Modest Proposal,* gave this example:

> Last week I saw a woman flayed alive, and you will hardly believe how it altered her appearance for the worse.

The long-running TV show *The Simpsons* received the prestigious George Foster Peabody Award for excellence in television. *The Simpsons* was cited for satire and social commentary. If you have not seen the show, try watching an episode or two. What kinds of things does Matt Groening, creator of *The Simpsons,* satirize? For example, using the "Grandpa" character, what is Groening saying about how elderly people are treated in this country?

When reading satire, pay close attention to the goals of the satirist, the devices used to accomplish his or her goals, and the tone. While a satire can have any tone, the most common are ironic and humorous.

READING

"'There are a lot of people in this country who only use a handgun once or twice a year. . . . So we'll rent them a gun for a day or two.'"

TUNING IN TO READING This article, written in a satirical style, argues for stronger gun-control legislation.

BIO-SKETCH Art Buchwald was one of the foremost humorists in the United States. His job, as he saw it, was to expose us to our failings as human beings and as members of society. Buchwald wrote numerous books and was a regular contributor to a syndicated newspaper column. He was also a recipient of the Pulitzer Prize.

What is the play on words in Hurts Rent-A-Gun?

NOTES ON VOCABULARY

chicken out lose one's nerve; back out of something because of fear. *Chicken* is a slang term for "cowardly."

Russian roulette loading a bullet into one chamber of a revolver, spinning the cylinder, and then pulling the trigger while pointing the gun at one's own head.

gutted destroyed; removed the vital or essential parts from something.

dream come true wild fancy or hope that is realized.

Directions: Answer the questions in the margins as you are reading the article.

Hurts Rent-A-Gun

By ART BUCHWALD

Is Buchwald optimistic or pessimistic about the possibility of gun control? (paragraph 1)

THE SENATE RECENTLY passed a new gun-control bill, which some observers consider worse than no bill at all. Any serious attempt at handgun registration was gutted, and Senate gun lovers even managed to repeal a 1968 gun law controlling the purchase of .22 rim-fire ammunition.

2 After the Senate got finished with its work on the gun-control bill, I

Why does Buchwald make the last name of his friend "Hurts"? (paragraph 2)

____

____

Is Buchwald serious about proposing rent-a-gun counters at gas stations? (paragraph 8)

____

____

What is Buchwald saying in paragraphs 12 and 13?

____

____

____

____

What is Buchwald's concern here? (paragraphs 20–21)

____

____

____

received a telephone call from my friend Bromley Hurts, who told me he had a business proposition to discuss with me. I met him for lunch at a pistol range in Maryland.

3 "I think I've got a fantastic idea," he said, "I want to start a new business called Hurts Rent-A-Gun."

4 "What on earth for?" I asked.

5 "There are a lot of people in this country who only use a handgun once or twice a year, and they don't want to go to all the expense of buying one. So we'll rent them a gun for a day or two. By leasing a firearm from us, they won't have to tie up all their money."

6 "That makes sense," I admitted.

7 "Say a guy is away from home on a trip, and he doesn't want to carry his own gun with him. He can rent a gun from us and then return it when he's finished with his business."

8 "You could set up rent-a-gun counters at gas stations," I said excitedly.

9 "And we could have stores in town where someone could rent a gun to settle a bet," Hurts said.

10 "A lot of people would want to rent a gun for a domestic quarrel," I said.

11 "Right. Say a jealous husband suspects there is someone at home with his wife. He rents a pistol from us and tries to catch them in the act. If he discovers his wife is alone, he isn't out the eighty dollars it would cost him to buy a gun."

12 "Don't forget the kids who want to play Russian roulette. They could pool their allowances and rent a gun for a couple of hours," I said.

"Our market surveys indicate," Hurts said, "that there are also a lot of kids who claim their parents don't listen to them. If they could rent a gun, they feel they could arrive at an understanding with their folks in no time." 13

"There's no end to the business," I said. "How would you charge for Hurts Rent-A-Gun?" 14

"There would be hourly rates, day rates, and weekly rates, plus ten cents for each bullet fired. Our guns would be the latest models, and we would guarantee clean barrels and the latest safety devices. If a gun malfunctions through no fault of the user we will give him another gun absolutely free." 15

"For many Americans it's a dream come true," I said. 16

"We've also made it possible for people to return the gun in another town. For example, if you rent the gun in Chicago and want to use it in Salt Lake City, you can drop it off there at no extra charge." 17

"Why didn't you start this before?" 18

"We wanted to see what happened with the gun-control legislation. We were pretty sure the Senate and the White House would not do anything about strong gun control, especially during an election year. But we didn't want to invest a lot of money until we were certain they would all chicken out." 19

"I'd like the franchise for Washington's National Airport," I said. 20

"You've got it. It's a great location," Hurts said. "You'll make a fortune in hijackings alone." 21

(Art Buchwald, *I Never Danced at the White House*, 1972, 1973)

COMPREHENSION CHECKUP

Multiple Choice

Directions: For each item, write the letter corresponding to the best answer.

______ 1. The topic of the article is

a. car rental agencies.
b. gun control.
c. domestic violence.
d. free enterprise.

______ 2. Buchwald chose the name Bromley Hurts because
   a. his wife's cousin has the same name.
   b. it is a "play" on Hertz Rent-A-Car.
   c. it indicates that guns can cause "hurt."
   d. both b and c

______ 3. The author's primary purpose in writing this satire is to
   a. persuade readers to stop buying guns.
   b. condemn the new gun-control bill.
   c. persuade readers to buy handguns.
   d. describe a lucrative business opportunity.

______ 4. The tone of this article could best be described as
   a. sentimental and sad.
   b. humorous and ironic.
   c. angry and vindictive.
   d. cautious and logical.

______ 5. According to the article, which of the following people would benefit from the fictitious Hurts Rent-A-Gun?
   a. a jealous spouse
   b. a man away from home on a trip
   c. a person wanting to settle a bet
   d. all of the above

______ 6. You can infer from the article that Buchwald believes that
   a. people can be trusted to use guns responsibly.
   b. people cannot be trusted to use guns responsibly.
   c. people who use guns should practice at pistol ranges.
   d. disposable guns are the wave of the future.

______ 7. The statement "for many Americans it's a dream come true" is an example of
   a. literary allusion.
   b. caricature.
   c. ironic exaggeration.
   d. understatement.

True or False

Directions: Indicate whether each statement is true or false by writing **T** or **F** in the space provided.

______ 8. Buchwald likely favors strong gun-control legislation.

______ 9. Buchwald is really happy with the new gun-control bill.

______ 10. Leasing a gun is the same as owning one.

Short Answer

1. What details indicate Buchwald's desire for a stronger gun-control bill?

____

____

2. Who is Buchwald most critical of in this article? ______________________

____

3. Describe the tone of Buchwald's satire. ______________________
4. Buchwald implies an analogy between renting a gun and renting a car. List the details that show how Hertz Rent-A-Car, or any other car rental agency, is similar to Hurts Rent-A-Gun. ______________________

____

____

____

5. What are the specific uses for rental guns mentioned in the article? Why are these uses included in the article? ______________________

____

____

6. Does Buchwald believe that the country will be a less or a more dangerous place if handguns are more closely regulated? Give supporting reasons.

____

____

____

Vocabulary in Context

Directions: Underline the word or phrase in the second sentence that helps explain the meaning of the italicized word in the first sentence.

1. I can't imagine that Stephanie would fall for Joshua's *proposition.* After all, she already suffered from his last proposed scheme.
2. Do you think it is likely that they are going to *repeal* that law? They should revoke it because it makes no sense.
3. Doing *domestic* chores is one of my least favorite activities. However, if you don't take care of your home, it will fall apart.
4. Greg's computer *malfunctioned* again causing the loss of valuable data. If it fails to work one more time, I think he should get a new computer.
5. Sutin has the *franchise* for three Baskin-Robbins ice cream stores. As the owner of the right to operate the stores, he is expecting to make a lot of money.
6. Let's *pool* our money and buy some lottery tickets. We'll increase our chances of winning by putting our money together.

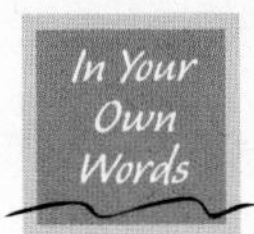

In Your Own Words

Do you think the easy availability of guns contributes to the higher rates of violent crime in the United States? Are you in favor of more gun control? Why or why not?

Internet Activity

You can find newspaper columns and articles written by Art Buchwald at www.washingtonpost.com. Type in "Buchwald." Select one of his pieces, print it, and explain what he is satirizing.

Exercise 6: Detecting Satire

Directions: The following cartoon offers an opposing viewpoint to the one expressed by Art Buchwald in the previous article. On the line provided, give the main idea of the cartoon.

Jerry L. Barnett, *The Indianapolis Star.* Reprinted with permission of the cartoonist.

The main idea of this cartoon is: ______________________________

____

Internet Activity

1. To obtain additional information about the issue of gun control, visit both of the following Web sites. One site presents the pro position on gun control, and the other site presents the con position. Write a summary paragraph contrasting these two viewpoints on this issue. Which viewpoint do you find more appealing?

   www.bradycampaign.org (The Brady Campaign to Prevent Gun Violence)
   www.nra.org (National Rifle Association)

2. You must be able to draw inferences to understand any cartoon, but political or editorial cartoons require a level of sophistication about current events. Find an editorial cartoon on one of the two Web sites given below, print it, and identify the cartoonist's main idea. What background knowledge on your part was required to interpret the cartoon? What inferences were you able to draw about the cartoonist's viewpoint?

   www.comicspage.com
   www.creators.com

Chapter Summary and Review

In Chapter 10, you learned how to recognize the tone of an article. You also became familiar with irony, satire, hyperbole, caricature, and understatement. Based on the material in Chapter 10, answer the following.

Short Answer

Directions: Give synonyms for each of the following tone words.

1. arrogant ____________________
2. whining ____________________
3. optimistic ____________________
4. pessimistic ____________________
5. vindictive ____________________
6. dictatorial ____________________

Directions: Define the following word.

7. Satire ____________________

   ____

Vocabulary in Context

Directions: Choose one of the following words to complete the sentences below. Use each word only once.

caricatures emotional hyperbole satire

8. The phrase "strong as an ox" is usually an example of __________.
9. Tone refers to the __________ quality of an article.
10. Political cartoonists often like to draw __________ of our presidents.
11. __________ relies on exaggeration and distortion and often has a humorous effect.

PART 4

Reading Critically

CHAPTERS IN PART 4

CHAPTER

11 Fact and Opinion

CHAPTER PREVIEW

In this chapter, you will

- Develop strategies to help you tell the difference between fact and opinion.

Introduction to Fact and Opinion

Fact

A **fact** is a statement that can be proved to be true or false in some objective way. You can prove it yourself, or you can turn to some objective authority such as records, tests, or historical or scientific documents. Statements of fact often rely on concrete data or measurements. Here are some examples of facts and how they can be proved.

Statements of Fact	Sources of Proof
1. Abraham Lincoln was the 16th president of the United States.	History book
2. Sara is taller than Kate.	Measurement
3. My favorite candidate won the election.	Counting votes
4. The movie is playing at 6:15.	Looking at movie listings

It is important to realize that statements of fact can sometimes be false. At one time in the past, it was considered to be a "fact" that the earth was at the center of the universe. Of course, we now know this is not true. Until recently, the following statement was considered to be a fact.

Star Wars is the top domestic money-earner of all time.

This is no longer a true "fact" because in 1997, the movie *Titanic* surpassed *Star Wars* in box office receipts. Now *Avata*r has surpassed *Titanic*.

Some ""statements of fact" are false because they are based on erroneous information. Comedians like to joke that if you ask most women over 40 their age, you're going to get a false answer. Other "facts" that are based on numbers and statistics may be false because data of this sort can be easily manipulated. In evaluating such information, it is best to keep in mind what Mark Twain famously said: "There are lies, damn lies, and statistics."

Opinion

"So many men, so many opinions."
—Terence

Opinions are statements of belief or judgment that cannot be proved by any objective means. Any statement that deals with probabilities or future events is an opinion because it cannot be proved. For example, if I said that the United States will do better in the next World Cup tournament, I would be expressing an opinion. Opinions often rely on words that express a value judgment. Below are some examples of opinions. While some people may agree with these statements, others will disagree. The words that express value judgments are in italics.

Statements of Opinion

1. Abraham Lincoln was a *great* president. (value judgment)
2. It's *better* to be tall than to be short. (value judgment)
3. My candidate was the *most interesting*. (value judgment)
4. The movie is a *good* one. (value judgment)
5. He is going to get the most votes in the next election. (future event)
6. She is the nicest person in the world. (exaggeration)

The following are some examples of words that signal an opinion.

Words and Phrases That Signal an Opinion

I believe	Perhaps	This suggests
Apparently	In my view	Presumably
It seems likely	Many experts agree	In my opinion
One interpretation is	One possibility is	

Following are some examples of words that can signal value judgments.

Words That Signal Value Judgment

necessary	interesting	effective
beautiful, attractive, *etc.*	highest *or* lowest	most *or* least
best *or* worst	bad	nice
greatest	successful	wonderful

Some opinions have more validity than others. Opinions that are backed up by facts belong to this category. To make a case for Abraham Lincoln being a great president, I could talk about his many achievements. My statement would still be an opinion, only now it would be well supported. Opinions given by experts are more reliable than opinions given by someone lacking specialized knowledge. For instance, Michael Jordan's opinion on basketball would carry more weight than that of someone who has never played the game.

Much of what we read and hear is a combination of fact and opinion. To evaluate such information, we need to be able to distinguish between the two.

Exercise 1: Thinking about Facts and Opinions

Directions: Using complete sentences, write six facts about yourself. Then think about some opinions you have, and write down six of them.

Facts about You

1. ______________________________

2. ______________________________

3. ______________________________

4. ______________________________

5. ______________________________

6. ______________________________

Your Opinions

1. ______________________________

2. ______________________________

3. ______________________________

4. ______________________________

5. ______________________________

6. ______________________________

Exercise 2: Recognizing Facts and Opinions

Directions: Place an **F** in the blank for those statements that are mostly factual and an **O** in the blank for those statements that are mostly opinion. Circle the abstract or value judgment words in the statements of opinion.

______ 1. The community college is a better place to attend school for the first two years than a university or a four-year school.

______ 2. *U.S. News & World Report* found that 100 percent of the students at Harvard University were in the top quarter of their high school graduating class.

______ 3. David McCullough's *John Adams* is a convincing portrait of one of the dominant men of the Revolutionary War.

______ 4. According to Sharon Thompson's 2013 research study, teenagers' rates of drug use, eating disorders, depression, and suicide are rising.

______ 5. The book I'm reading now is number one after its second week on the *New York Times* fiction best-seller list.

______ 6. At $13.95 a copy, the book is a real bargain.

______ 7. In a 2013 study, the American Medical Association reported that drinking is heaviest among singles and the newly divorced.

______ 8. A 2013 study by A. C. Nielsen Company showed that home use of the Internet has cut TV viewing, with wired homes watching an average of 13 percent less television.

______ 9. According to data reported in *Retirement Places Rated,* Las Vegas, with a grade of 84.5, is America's number-one retirement destination.

______ 10. Researchers from the University of Arizona recently tested 500 used kitchen dishcloths and found that two-thirds contain bacteria that can make people sick.

______ 11. Toothpaste containing peroxide and baking soda is far better at producing clean and attractive teeth.

______ 12. Researchers at Ohio State University found that women experience anxiety and depression about 30 percent more often than men.

______ 13. Women have greater burdens and limitations placed on them in both the workplace and the family.

Exercise 3: More Recognizing Facts and Opinions

Directions: Read the following sentences and put an **O** in the blank if the statement is an opinion or an **F** if the statement is a fact. Circle the opinion words that indicate probabilities or future events.

______ 1. The Victoria's Secret catalog offers 45 items in satin.

______ 2. You will learn more from reading books than you will from watching television.

______ 3. By the year 2020, we will be unable to function as a society without computers.

_____ 4. A recent Ohio State study showed that playing the violin or the cello burns 40 percent more calories than watching TV.

_____ 5. In 1923, F. Scott Fitzgerald called a collection of his short stories *Tales of the Jazz Age.*

_____ 6. The National Highway Department, in its 2013 study, concluded that elderly drivers (those over the age of 70) are responsible for the majority of driving fatalities in the United States.

_____ 7. The United States is certain to do better in the next Olympic competition.

_____ 8. The United Nations Human Development Program reports that the divorce rate in the United States is now the highest of any major industrialized nation.

_____ 9. An Education Department survey showed that 70 percent of 5,500 secondary school principals approve of requiring school uniforms.

_____ 10. Schools that maintain a dress code will tend to have fewer instances of assault, robbery, and vandalism, and at the same time will tend to report improved academic performance.

Exercise 4: Rewriting Opinion Statements

Directions: Working in a group, determine whether the given statement is a fact (**F**) or an opinion (**O**), and write your answer on the line provided. Then on a separate piece of paper rewrite all statements of opinion as statements of fact. Be sure to eliminate all abstract and value judgment words. Your fact sentence should use concrete words and be verifiable.

Example:

Opinion: My current house is **too small** for my family.

Fact: I have a one-bedroom house and 10 people in my family.

or

Fact: I have a 900-square foot home and 10 people in my family.

_____ 1. My husband and I took a three-mile hike on Sunday.

_____ 2. My spring break was much too short.

_____ 3. My Honda Accord gets excellent gas mileage.

_____ 4. The yearly salary for the principal of John F. Kennedy School is $75,000.

_____ 5. He is a reckless and irresponsible driver.

_____ 6. The iMac computer was very reasonably priced.

_____ 7. The temperature in the oven is 375 degrees.

_____ 8. My English teacher graded my last essay unfairly.

_____ 9. Of all my college classes, my computer class has been the most helpful.

_____ 10. Tiger Woods is the best golfer in Professional Golf Association (PGA) history.

Exercise 5: Distinguishing Fact from Opinion

Many writers try to convince readers of the wisdom of their arguments by combining facts and opinions, often within the same sentence. The following sentences contain both fact and opinion. The facts have been italicized.

1. *With half of all American marriages failing,* it appears that "till death do us part" simply means until the going gets rough.
2. *A* USA Today *poll showed that 65 percent of Americans were unable to identify* the Bill of Rights, thus demonstrating the widespread ignorance of the population at large.

Directions: After reading each sentence, underline only the facts.

1. With the National Institute on Drug Abuse estimating that at least 500,000 high school students use or have used steroids, it is obvious that something needs to be done about the growing drug threat among teens.
2. Immediately after divorce, the income of households with kids declines by 21 percent, thereby creating an unfortunate new class of people in poverty—divorced women with children.
3. Male adults who enjoy light or moderate drinking should keep right on enjoying imbibing, since research by Serge Renaud of the National Institutes of Health on 36,000 middle-age men demonstrated that those who drank two to four glasses of wine a day had a 30–40 percent reduction in mortality from all causes.
4. In the state of Illinois, the delicate balance between a boss's right to know what's going on in the office and an employee's right to privacy has been upset by a 1995 state law that permits bosses to eavesdrop on employees' work telephones.
5. California, the state where 1.8 million civil lawsuits were filed in 2010, perhaps should have a new motto emblazoned on all license plates—Home of Litigators.
6. In 1981, the product NutraSweet was introduced to the public as a boon to the overweight, yet the Centers for Disease Control and Prevention recently reported that U.S. obesity rates have actually increased since that time.
7. Despite the fact that many physicians, scientists, and consumer advocates regard homeopathic medicines as ineffective at best and dangerous at worst, the National Center for Homeopathy reports that Americans are spending more than $165 million annually on homeopathic preparations.

READING

"Robinson received death threats, his family was harassed, and some hotels barred him from staying with the team."

TUNING IN TO READING

Ethnic prejudice has no place in sports, and baseball must recognize that truth if it is to maintain stature as a national game."

—Branch Rickey

READING (continued)

Branch Rickey, general manager of the Brooklyn Dodgers, took the most significant action of his career when he hired Jackie Robinson to be the first African American to play in the major leagues. Until that point, whites and blacks played in separate leagues.

Shortly before Rickey's death in 1965 at age 83, he sent a telegram to Jackie Robinson, who by that time was retired from baseball and involved in the civil rights movement with Martin Luther King Jr.

Wheelchair bound, Rickey apologized to Robinson for not joining him at the march on Selma, Alabama. Robinson responded with a letter that read: "Mr. Rickey, things have been very rewarding for me. But had it not been for you, nothing would be possible. Even though I don't write to you much, you are always on my mind. We feel so very close to you, and I am sure you know our love and admiration is sincere and dedicated. Please take care of yourself. We know where your heart is. We will take care of the Selma Alabamas and do the job."

BIO-SKETCH James West Davidson, a well-known historian, is the author of numerous books. He is also the co-editor of the *Oxford New Narratives in American History*.

NOTES ON VOCABULAR

Jim Crow laws laws that required segregation between the races in such places as churches, hotels, restaurants, and bathrooms

cold war nonviolent conflict between the United States and the Soviet Union that began after World War II

Okinawa and Guadalcanal islands in the Pacific Ocean that were captured from the Japanese after bloody battles during World War II

court-martial a court for people in the military accused of breaking military law

BEFORE YOU READ Did you happen to see the movie *42* starring Chadwick Boseman as Jackie Robinson and Harrison Ford as Branch Rickey? In a recent interview, Rachel Robinson, Jackie's widow, described how difficult it was for her husband to cope with the pressure of racism. As vividly depicted in the movie, Jackie relied a great deal on his wife for emotional support. When you are reading this selection, think about how well you would have handled abuse of the sort that Robinson endured.

JACKIE ROBINSON INTEGRATES BASEBALL

James West Davidson

After World War II, Branch Rickey of the Brooklyn Dodgers was determined to break the color line in baseball. For years he had wanted to give black players the opportunity to play in the majors. Equally to the point, he was convinced that this action would improve his team. "The greatest untapped reservoir of raw material in the history of the game is the black race," he explained, adding, "The Negroes will make us winners for years to come."

In the early years of professional baseball African Americans had played on 2
several major league teams. In 1887, however, as Jim Crow laws spread across the South, the threat of a boycott by some white players caused team owners to adopt an unwritten rule banning black players. That ban stood for 60 years.

World War II created a new climate. The hypocrisy of fighting racism abroad while promoting it at home was becoming harder for team owners to ignore. "If a black boy can make it on Okinawa and Guadalcanal," Commissioner Albert "Happy" Chandler told reporters in April 1945, "hell, he can make it in baseball." Economic factors played a role as well. The African American migration to northern cities during World War II created a new, untapped audience for major league baseball. Growing cold war tensions added another factor. Even a Mississippi newspaper saw blacks in the major leagues as "a good answer to our communist adversaries who say the Negro has no chance in America." 3

Rickey recognized the enormous hostility that the first black player would face. He found the ideal prospect in Jackie Robinson, a World War II veteran and a remarkable athlete who had lettered in four sports at UCLA. Rickey told Robinson in 1945, "I need a man that will take abuse, insults." Robinson would be carrying "the flag for [his] race." 4

Robinson was willing. He had risked court-martial during the war to fight segregation. "Nobody's going to separate bullets and label them 'for white troops' and 'for colored troops,'" Robinson told a superior officer. But he assured Rickey, "If you want to take this gamble I will promise you there will be no incident." Rickey assigned him to Montreal, where he led the Dodgers' farm team to a championship. 5

When the Dodgers invited Robinson to spring training, several southern-born players circulated a petition stating their opposition to playing with a black man. But manager Leo Durocher bluntly warned them they would be traded if they refused to cooperate. Robinson would make them all rich, Durocher insisted. 6

On April 15, 1947, Robinson made his debut with the Dodgers at Ebbets Field. A black newspaper, *The Boston Chronicle,* proclaimed, TRIUMPH OF WHOLE RACE SEEN IN JACKIE'S DEBUT IN MAJOR LEAGUE BALL. 7

But the abuse heaped on Robinson was worse than Rickey had anticipated. Robinson received death threats, his family was harassed, and some hotels barred him from staying with the team. He secretly wore a protective lining inside his hat in case he was beaned (he was hit a record nine times during the season, 65 times in seven years). Through it all, Robinson kept his temper, though not without difficulty. Once when a Cubs player kicked him, Robinson started to swing, then stopped. "I knew I was kind of an experiment," he recalled; ". . . the whole thing was bigger than me." 8

In Robinson's first year, the Dodgers won the pennant and he was named Rookie of the Year. Two years later, he was named the Most Valuable Player in the National League. After he retired in 1957, the skill and dignity he brought to the game earned him a place in baseball's Hall of Fame. 9

In the wake of his success, other teams added African Americans. Professional basketball and football followed baseball's lead. Still, the pace of integration was slow, and it was not until 1959 that all major league teams had at least one black member. Thanks to the vision of Branch Rickey and the courage of Jackie Robinson, baseball had become truly a national game. 10

(James West Davidson et al., *Experience History: Interpreting America's Past,* McGraw-Hill, 2011, p. 765)

Fact and Opinion

Directions: Identify statements of fact with an **F** and statements of opinion with an **O**.

_____ 1. That ban stood for 60 years.

_____ 2. World War II created a new climate.

_____ 3. Rickey assigned him to Montreal, where he led the Dodgers' farm team to a championship.

_____ 4. When the Dodgers invited Robinson to spring training, several southern-born players circulated a petition stating their opposition to playing with a black man.

_____ 5. On April 15, 1947, Robinson made his debut with the Dodgers at Ebbets Field.

_____ 6. A black newspaper, *The Boston Chronicle,* proclaimed, TRIUMPH OF WHOLE RACE SEEN IN JACKIE'S DEBUT IN MAJOR LEAGUE BALL.

_____ 7. Through it all, Robinson kept his temper, though not without difficulty.

_____ 8. Once when a Cubs player kicked him, Robinson started to swing, then stopped.

Directions: In the following sentences, underline the words that indicate an opinion.

9. He found the ideal prospect in Jackie Robinson, a World War II veteran and a remarkable athlete who had lettered in four sports at UCLA.

10. The African American migration to northern cities during World War II created a new, untapped audience for major league baseball.

11. After he retired in 1957, the skill and dignity he brought to the game earned him a place in baseball's Hall of Fame.

12. Thanks to the vision of Branch Rickey and the courage of Jackie Robinson, baseball had become truly a national game.

Short Answer

1. What is the main idea of the selection? _______________

____

2. What is the primary pattern of organization of the selection? _______________

What clues helped you determine the organizational pattern? Write several on the lines provided. _______________

3. Branch Rickey had several motives for wanting a black player on the Dodgers. What were these motives? Use specific details from the selection to support your answer. _______________

____

____

4. Rickey told Robinson in 1945, "I need a man that will take abuse, insults." Why do you think Branch Rickey wanted Jackie Robinson to retreat from all confrontations? What were his reasons for demanding a nonviolent approach?

____

5. How might things have gone differently if Jackie Robinson had reacted with physical or verbal anger to the taunts and abuse he was subjected to?

____

6. Rickey said that Robinson would be carrying "the flag for [his] race." What did he mean by that statement?

____

7. What were the special set of circumstances that led to 1947 being the year that baseball was integrated?

____

Vocabulary in Context

Directions: Choose the best definition for the italicized word according to its context in the selection.

_____ 1. *reservoir* (paragraph 1)
   a. a place where something, especially water, is collected and stored for use
   b. a container for a liquid
   c. a large supply

_____ 2. *ban* (paragraph 2)
   a. to say that something is wrong
   b. an official order forbidding something

_____ 3. *climate* (paragraph 3)
   a. the average weather conditions of a place
   b. how hot or cold it is on a particular day
   c. a general feeling, spirit, or atmosphere

_____ 4. prospect (paragraph 4)
   a. the act of looking forward to something
   b. the likely chance of succeeding at getting something
   c. a person who has a chance of succeeding
   d. a wide view

_____ 5. gamble (paragraph 5)
   a. a game in which the players make bets
   b. to bet or wager
   c. the risk of losing something in order to gain something
   d. taking an action that may or may not succeed

_____ 6. *debut* (paragraph 7)
   a. first appearance before the public
   b. the formal entering of a young woman into high society

_____ 7. *pace* (paragraph 10)
   a. a step in walking or running
   b. the length of a step or stride
   c. the rate of speed at which something moves or develops
   d. a certain way of walking or running

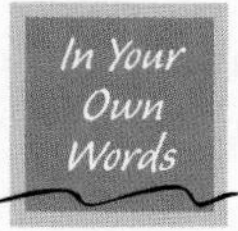

In Your Own Words

1. Even though the players on teams in professional sports are ethnically diverse today, management and ownership in professional sports lag behind in diver-

sity. Do you think that ethnic prejudice is still being felt in professional sports? What can be done to improve ethnic balance at all levels of professional sports?

2. Only Jackie Robinson has had the honor of having his jersey, No. 42, retired from all baseball teams. Recently several Latino groups have lobbied to have Roberto Clemente's No. 21 jersey similarly retired. What do you think? Should this honor be reserved for the man who originally broke the color barrier?

Written Assignment

What sorts of personal characteristics lead someone to want to break cultural or social barriers? Choose an occupation and write a short essay describing how you would handle being a role model.

Internet Activity

Jackie Robinson is well known for being the first African American to play professional baseball in the National League. For a bit of trivia, type "Larry Doby" in any search engine and find out what he did.

Fact and Opinion Quiz 1

Directions: Indicate whether the statement is a fact or an opinion by writing **F** or **O** in the blank provided.

_____ 1. According to a study of kids age 12–17 conducted by the Pew Internet & American Life Project, 73 percent of kids in the United States are online.

_____ 2. Using fire department and medical examiner reports, the *New England Journal of Medicine* found that risk of harm from house fires was 2.8 times higher for elderly people.

_____ 3. The simplest way to have psychologically healthy children is to avoid divorce.

_____ 4. Rudeness is the worst problem in the U.S. workplace because it damages the mental health and productivity of employees.

_____ 5. The National Fatherhood Initiative reports that about 4 out of 10 first marriages end in divorce.

_____ 6. Workers who bring their lunches from home and eat them at their desks make a big mistake because they end up working longer hours without a break.

_____ 7. Over half of criminal behavior nationally is committed by individuals under the influence of drugs, according to studies by the National Institute of Justice.

_____ 8. Astrology is a good method for predicting future events and identifying individual characteristics.

_____ 9. In a government survey of 5,001 youngsters, one in five adolescents who regularly socialize on the Internet encountered a stranger who wanted "cybersex."

_____ 10. Women who date strangers should hire a private detective to run a background check on potential suitors.

_____ 11. Capital punishment is immoral.

_____ 12. The Internet is not likely to become as essential as the telephone and the television are today.

_____ 13. The research of California State University psychologist Diane Halpern demonstrates that men are likely to be better than women at finding their destinations in unfamiliar settings.

_____ 14. Oprah Winfrey is a positive role model for television watchers.

_____ 15. According to the Bureau of Justice Statistics, the number of local, state, and federal prisoners has risen by 676,000 since 1990.

Fact and Opinion Quiz 2

Directions: Indicate whether the statement is a fact or an opinion by writing **F** or **O** in the blank provided.

_____ 1. Sixteen-year-olds shouldn't be allowed to drive because they are involved in too many accidents.

_____ 2. The Insurance Institute for Highway Safety reported that the death rate for 16-year-old drivers has nearly doubled.

_____ 3. According to a recent study by Dr. Bruce Pomeranz, bad reactions to prescription and over-the-counter medicines kill more than 100,000 Americans and seriously injure 2.5 million more each year.

_____ 4. Middle-class families with children have a lot less money to spend.

_____ 5. If young children know the difference between right and wrong, they won't be bothered by violence on TV.

_____ 6. The U.S. Justice Department survey showed that 78 percent of all jail inmates reported using marijuana at some point in their lives.

_____ 7. The most difficult job for the working parent is balancing the demands of work with those of family.

_____ 8. Many people make the mistake of not becoming vegetarians until they have experienced a major health crisis.

_____ 9. In 1997 Diana, Princess of Wales, was killed in a car crash.

_____ 10. Today's workers have to work harder and faster, and they never seem to have enough time to get everything done.

_____ 11. Compact cars are a lot more practical than full-size cars.

_____ 12. Recent proposals by elementary school districts across the country to eliminate recess are part of an alarming trend in education.

_____ 13. According to the Census Bureau, nearly a third of young children under the age of 5 are cared for in day care centers.

_____ 14. Parents should search a teenager's bedroom only if they suspect the teen has been abusing drugs.

_____ 15. Researchers in Scotland cloned an adult mammal, a lamb named Dolly, who is a genetic copy of her mother.

READING

"With that said, there are many people who would say that when it comes to happiness, there are many things more important than money."

TUNING IN TO READING There is an ancient fable about happiness that is common to many cultures.

A long time ago there was an old king who was greatly worried about his son. This young prince was terribly unhappy, and although the king tried everything in his power, he could not convince his son to enjoy life. In despair, the king called his advisors to him. They counseled him by saying that the only cure for unhappiness was to obtain the shirt of a happy man and present it to the young prince. The king, thinking this to be a simple task, was greatly relieved. He eagerly sent his messengers out to search. For two years, they roved far and wide throughout the kingdom, visiting every town and village. At last, they rejoiced in locating one supremely happy man. Unfortunately, for the king and the young prince, the poor farmer, though gloriously happy, possessed no shirt.

The moral of this fable is that happiness does not depend upon material possessions, can't be given to another, and above all, is elusive. The writer Nathaniel Hawthorne once said: "Happiness is a butterfly, which when pursued, is always just beyond your grasp, but which, if you will sit down quietly, may alight upon you."

While the Declaration of Independence says that everyone has the right to "life, liberty, and the pursuit of happiness," only recently have psychologists begun to explore what makes people happy. A study conducted at the University of Illinois by Edward Diener and Martin Seligman found that students reporting the highest levels of happiness had strong ties to friends and family. The researchers concluded that close relationships with others are important for happiness. They also discovered that some people are more likely to be happy than others. In general, those who have an optimistic personality are more likely to label themselves as happy. Read the following selection to find out what else correlates with happiness.

BIO-SKETCH David Olson is professor emeritus of family social science at the University of Minnesota. He has written or edited more than 20 books.

NOTES ON VOCABULARY

cohabiting defined by the federal government as two unrelated adults of the opposite sex sharing the same living quarters. A broader definition includes both heterosexual and same-sex unmarried couples who have an emotional and sexual relationship.

FACTORS AFFECTING HAPPINESS

David H. Olson

Money and Happiness

Do money and happiness go together? It seems likely that when rich and very poor people are compared, the rich are happier. However, apparently once people are out of poverty, the differences in happiness are relatively weak.

Some recent reports indicate that there is a strong relationship between money and happiness. In an international study asking people how satisfied they are with their life on a scale of 1 to 10, in general people in wealthier 2 nations (the United States, Europe, Japan, Saudi Arabia) reported being more happy than those from poor countries (primarily African countries). These findings were also true when it came to looking at those who were wealthy and those who were poor within countries—the wealthy people were happier. Another study conducted by the Pew Research Center indicates that globally, countries that have had rising economic growth have also had rising happiness levels. This report also showed that once people reach a certain level of income, happiness levels off. Some studies say that after families reach a household income of $50,000, the relationship between money and happiness is no longer strong.

Another study, which was done in the United States, also showed that money and happiness go together. In this study, one-third of participants said they were very happy, with another 50 percent indicating they were pretty happy. According to this study, these numbers have been stable over the past 35 years. The Pew Research Center also found that annual family income correlated with people's happiness responses. For example, only 24 percent of those with annual family incomes of less than $30,000 said they were very happy, whereas 49 percent of families making $100,000 or more said they were very happy. However, just because money and happiness go together does not mean one causes the other. Maybe money leads to happiness, or happiness leads to money. This study also showed that those who were healthiest were more likely to be very happy and those who had poor health were least happy. It may be that those with poor health make less money, and it was health that made the difference, not money. One might ask: Is it the money that makes the difference or is it things that go along with having money that make the difference, such as home ownership, less stress, or having more choices? All we know from these studies is that wealth and happiness seem to go together. With that said, there are many people who would say that when it comes to happiness, there are many things more important than money. In fact, two of the wealthiest men in the United States, Warren Buffett and Bill Gates, have weighed in on this issue. Buffett has said, "The true measure of success is the number of people who genuinely care about and respect you when you near the end of your life." Bill Gates said, "My goal for success outside of work is definitely raising a family. So far I haven't caused any damage; they seem to be doing OK." 3

Children and Happiness

In regard to having a family, there is conflicting information about the effects of children on individual and couple happiness. A recent study by Bradford Wilcox, using large data sets, looked at these issues, and the findings provide new information. 4

Most people want to have children, and yet, children can often create personal stress. Wilcox found that married men and women were equally happy regardless of their parental status. Parents who are cohabiting are next in terms of happiness, and single parents are least happy. Wilcox concluded that those with a partner, whether that person is a spouse or a person in a cohabiting relationship, have a higher degree of personal happiness raising children than do single parents. 5

When it came to being depressed, Wilcox found that married parents and cohabiting parents had an equal likelihood of being depressed, and single parents had a higher likelihood of being depressed. On the basis of these results, one might speculate that sharing the work, responsibility, financial costs, and stress of raising children is made easier when one has someone with which to share it. 6

According to Wilcox, although marital happiness does decline over time for all couples, it decreases more suddenly for parents versus nonparents. Childless couples have a more gradual decline in marital happiness, whereas for couples with children there is a significant decline that coincides with the birth of their first child. 7

Are there benefits to having children? Both married men and women, according to Wilcox, are more likely to indicate that their life has an important purpose than married couples who do not have children. It appears that although marital happiness may decline with the addition of children, a sense of purpose may replace the marital satisfaction. 8

Wilcox also explored differences in the number of children and marital happiness. He found that couples who had no children and couples who had four or more children were happiest. 9

(David H. Olson et al., *Marriages and Families*, 8/e, McGraw-Hill, 2014, pp. 221–223, 330–331)

COMPREHENSION CHECKUP

Fact and Opinion

Identify each of these statements from the excerpt as either a fact or an opinion. Write your answer in the space provided.

1. "Wilcox also explored differences in the number of children and marital happiness." ____________

2. "He found that couples who had no children and couples who had four or more children were happiest." ____________

3. "Both married men and women, according to Wilcox, are more likely to indicate that their life has an important purpose than married couples who do not have children." ____________

4. "According to Wilcox, although marital happiness does decline over time for all couples, it decreases more suddenly for parents versus nonparents."

____

______ 5. Which of the following statements is an opinion?

a. In this study, one-third of participants said they were very happy, with another 50 percent indicating they were pretty happy.
b. There are many things more important than money.
c. Wilcox found that couples who had no children and couples who had four or more children were happiest.
d. For example, only 24 percent of those with annual family incomes of less than $30,000 said they were very happy, whereas 49 percent of families making $100,000 or more said they were very happy.

______ 6. Which of the following statements is a fact?
   a. Most people want to have children, and yet, children can often create personal stress.
   b. Wilcox found that married men and women were equally happy regardless of their parental status.
   c. It appears that although marital happiness may decline with the addition of children, a sense of purpose may replace the marital satisfaction.
   d. On the basis of these results, one might speculate that sharing the work, responsibility, financial costs, and stress of raising children is made easier when one has someone with which to share it.

______ 7. What word(s) in the following statement help you to determine that it is an opinion?
   "It seems likely that when rich and very poor people are compared, the rich are happier."
   a. rich
   b. very poor
   c. seems likely
   d. happier

______ 8. What word in the following statement helps you to determine that it is an opinion?
   "However, apparently once people are out of poverty, the differences in happiness are relatively weak."
   a. apparently
   b. poverty
   c. differences
   d. weak

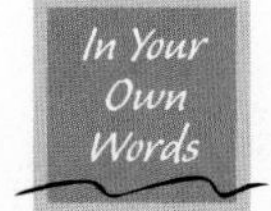

In Your Own Words

1. What kinds of stresses do parents face today? List the problems that couples are likely to confront in adjusting to parenthood. Do you think raising children today is harder or easier than it was a generation ago?
2. Do you think the transition to parenthood is more difficult for older or younger couples? Do you think the transition to parenthood is easier for couples who have been married longer?
3. Do you think that couples today have an unrealistic or romanticized view of parenthood? For instance, most new parents appear to underestimate the amount of sacrifice that a new baby requires, including less opportunity for sleeping or doing other things. How often do you think parents discuss these potential problems before the birth of a child?
4. Are you surprised that people above a certain income level are happier than people below it? How do you account for these findings?
5. Do you think that acting happy or putting on a happy face helps you to feel happy or become happy?
6. Rank the following traits for their importance to happiness—wealth, parenthood, health, social activity, religious commitment, marriage, and work. Explain your ranking. Try to come to some sort of conclusion about what happiness means to you.

Written Assignment

Directions: Write a short essay discussing one of the following.

1. According to sociological research, happiness rates vary from country to country. The five nations that score the highest on the happiness index are Costa Rica, Denmark, Iceland, Switzerland, and Norway. The five countries that score the lowest are Togo, Tanzania, Burundi, Benin, and Zimbabwe. The United States ranks 21st out of 149 nations. Are you surprised that the United States is not ranked higher? Can you give reasons to explain why some countries might rank high and others low?
2. Studies suggest that more money, a larger home, exotic vacations, and better jobs don't really make us happier in the long run. Do you agree based on your own experiences and the experiences of those around you?

Internet Activity

Ed Diener, a psychology professor at the University of Illinois, has developed "The Satisfaction with Life Scale." To take the quiz for yourself, consult his Web site at

http://www.psych.uiuc.edu/~ediener

Explain what you learned about yourself. Did the quiz confirm what you already knew about yourself? Did it give you new insight into your personality?

Graphic Organizers

Directions: Answer the following questions based on the pie graph and bar graph below.

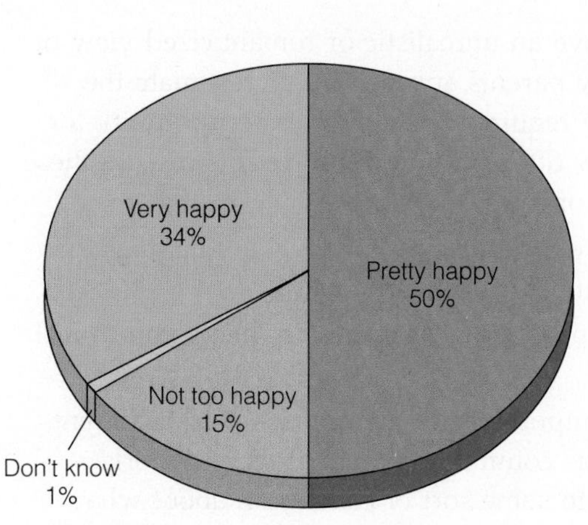

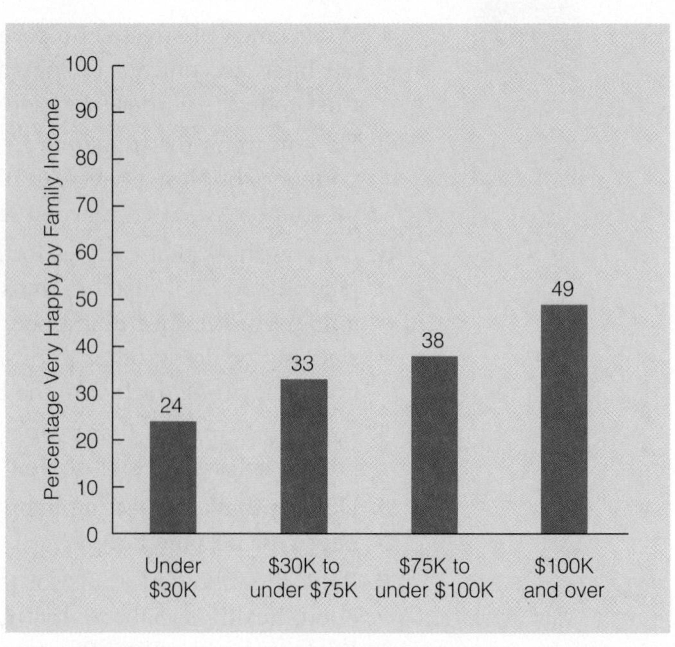

Source: David H. Olson et al., *Marriages and Families*, 8/e, McGraw-Hill, 2014, p. 222.

1. What percentage of Americans are pretty happy? ______
2. What percentage of Americans are not too happy? ______
3. What percentage of those with annual family incomes of less than $75,000 said they were very happy? ______
4. What percentage of those with annual family incomes of less than $100,000 said they were very happy? ______

Exercise 6: Identifying Fact and Opinion in a Movie Review

THE BLIND SIDE MOVIE REVIEW

An Overview

Named one of the top 10 sports movies of all time by film critics, *The Blind Side* is perfect family fare for all but the very youngest. The movie depicts the inspirational story of Michael Oher, currently an offensive lineman for the Baltimore Ravens. Oher, born to a mother addicted to crack, is one of 13 children. He spent his early years being placed in, and running away from, various foster homes. As a result of the trauma of his early upbringing, Oher struggled with reading and writing and with an inability to trust others to help him. "Big Mike's" story began to change when he encountered the Tuohy family (Sean, Leigh Anne, Collins, and S.J.). The Tuohys, a well-to-do evangelical Christian family, put their faith to the test when they set out to help the 16-year-old Michael succeed in academics and life.

The Acting in *The Blind Side*

The heart of the movie is the very talented Sandra Bullock. She has starred in a number of romantic comedies, such as *Miss Congeniality* and *While You Were Sleeping*, and also the dramas *Crash*, *Speed*, and *A Time to Kill*. Bullock won the 2010 Best Actress Academy Award for her portrayal of the strong-willed Leigh Anne Tuohy. Bullock was initially hesitant to accept the role, claiming she didn't think she could accurately portray Leigh Anne. Thankfully, she put her misgivings aside because her performance is powerful. Her Leigh Anne Tuohy is a person of great compassion, relentless drive, and fierce loyalty. Bullock's forthright portrayal is both refreshing and quite funny. She was well-deserving of an Oscar.

A pleasant surprise is well-known country singer Tim McGraw in the role of Sean Tuohy. He makes Sean come across as well-meaning, likable, and supportive. Academy Award-winning actress Kathy Bates has a small but pivotal role as Miss Sue, Michael's tutor. With Miss Sue's patient guidance and unconventional teaching methods, Michael is able to raise his GPA to 2.52, making him eligible to play college football.

Children are sure to enjoy the performance of Jae Head as S.J. (Sean Tuohy Jr.). The scenes where S.J. helps get Michael into top physical condition, asks for numerous "small favors" from the college coaches recruiting Michael, and survives a horrific car accident thanks to Michael's protective instincts and quick reflexes are some of the most memorable in the movie.

The movie also stars Quinton Aaron as the troubled African American homeless teen Michael Oher, who eventually becomes a college All-American and first-round NFL draft pick. Although Aaron has relatively few lines, he manages to convey a lot of emotional depth, particularly in the scenes when he begins to doubt his adopted parents' selfless love for him. The Tuohys and Miss Sue are all graduates of the University of Mississippi (Ole Miss). As an impressively gifted athlete, Michael Oher is heavily recruited by college coaches across the country, including by Notre Dame's Lou Holtz playing himself. When Oher makes a decision to attend his adoptive parents' alma mater, an NCAA investigation is launched to determine the motives of the Tuohy family. Was their decision to adopt him really as selfless as it had originally appeared? Or were the Tuohys motivated by a desire to help their beloved university produce a championship season? Here is where Quinton Aaron shines as an actor. He manages to convey all of the scarred, reclusive teen's emotional agony over the possible betrayal of a family he has come to love and trust.

Although *The Blind Side* was nominated for a best picture Academy Award, it did not win. Still, it has become a classic feel-good movie. When it was originally screened, moviegoers routinely clapped at the end. To date more than 3 million DVD copies have been sold. Sales of the book by Michael Lewis, upon which the movie is based, have also been impressive.

The Present

Leigh Anne Tuohy, Sean Tuohy, and Michael Oher have published books about the experiences depicted in the movie. In 2010, the Tuohys published *In a Heartbeat: Sharing the Power of Cheerful Giving*. Michael Oher's memoir, published in 2011, is titled *I Beat the Odds: From Homelessness to The Blind Side and Beyond*. Both books aim to inspire others to charitable giving.

Oher continues to thrive as a left tackle for the Baltimore Ravens, protecting the blind side of quarterback Joe Flacco. The Tuohys continue to see as many of his games as possible. Now they'll all have a renewed interest in being in Maryland. Sean Tuohy Jr. has decided to play college basketball at Loyola University in Maryland. While breaking with tradition was wrenching (his father was a guard at Ole Miss), both S.J. and Michael see a positive in his decision to attend Loyola. He and Michael will be living only fifteen minutes away from each other. Now S.J. can easily attend Michael's games, and Miichael can easily attend S.J.'s. The two siblings are looking forward to seeing more of each other!

The Blind Side

Color/128 minutes, rated PG-13

One scene involves brief violence, drugs, and sexual references.

Fact and Opinion

Directions: The following sentences contain both fact and opinion. After reading each sentence, underline only the facts.

1. Named one of the top 10 sports movies of all time by film critics, *The Blind Side* is perfect family fare for all but the very youngest.
2. The movie depicts the inspirational story of Michael Oher, currently an offensive lineman for the Baltimore Ravens.
3. A pleasant surprise is well-known country singer Tim McGraw in the role of Sean Tuohy.
4. With Miss Sue's patient guidance and unconventional teaching methods, Michael is able to raise his GPA to 2.52, making him eligible to play college football.

Directions: Indicate whether each statement is a fact or an opinion by writing **F** or **O** in the blank provided.

______ 5. Oher, born to a mother addicted to crack, is one of 13 children.

______ 6. He spent his early years being placed in, and running away from, various foster homes.

______ 7. The Tuohys and Miss Sue are all graduates of the University of Mississippi (Ole Miss).

______ 8. He makes Sean come across as well-meaning, likable, and supportive.

______ 9. Children are sure to enjoy the performance of Jae Head as S.J. (Sean Tuohy Jr.).

______ 10. When Oher makes a decision to attend his adoptive parents' alma mater, an NCAA investigation is launched to determine the motives of the Tuohy family.

______ 11. Here is where Quinton Aaron shines as an actor.

______ 12. He manages to convey all of the scarred, reclusive teen's emotional agony over the possible betrayal of a family he has come to love and trust.

______ 13. Although *The Blind Side* was nominated for a best picture Academy Award, it did not win.

______ 14. To date more than 3 million DVD copies have been sold.

______ 15. Leigh Anne Tuohy, Sean Tuohy, and Michael Oher have published books about the experiences depicted in the movie.

Directions: Label each numbered sentence in the following paragraph as (F) for fact, (O) for opinion, or (B) for both.

(1) The heart of the movie is the very talented Sandra Bullock. (2) She has starred in a number of romantic comedies, such as *Miss Congeniality* and *While You Were Sleeping*, and also the dramas *Crash*, *Speed*, and *A Time to Kill*. (3) Bullock won the 2010 Best Actress Academy Award for her portrayal of the strong-willed Leigh Anne Tuohy. (4) Bullock was initially hesitant to accept the role, claiming she didn't think she could accurately portray Leigh Anne. (5) Thankfully, she put her misgivings aside because her performance is powerful. (6) Her Leigh Anne Tuohy is a person of great compassion, relentless drive, and fierce loyalty. (7) Bullock's forthright portrayal is both refreshing and quite funny. (8) She was well-deserving of an Oscar.

Sentence 1 ______________

Sentence 2 ______________

Sentence 3 ______________

Sentence 4 ______________

Sentence 5 ______________

Sentence 6 ______________

Sentence 7 ______________

Sentence 8 ______________

READING

"Toothpaste manufacture is a very lucrative occupation."

TUNING IN TO READING Most of us attempt to maintain healthy teeth and good oral hygiene by brushing at least once a day. But have you ever stopped to consider what's actually in the toothpaste we're using? Are those ingredients that we can't pronounce good for us, or at least not causing us harm?

READING (continued)

In June 2007, the U.S. Food and Drug Administration (FDA) advised consumers to avoid certain brands of toothpaste manufactured in China after batches of Chinese-made toothpaste were found to contain the poisonous chemicals diethylene glycol (also called diglycol or DEG). The chemical is used in antifreeze as a solvent, and ingesting it is potentially fatal. As stated on most tubes, toothpaste is not intended to be swallowed. In fact, it can be harmful especially to children.

When you examine the ingredients on the label of your own tube of toothpaste, you may see the following: hydrated silica (sand), which is the abrasive found in most gel toothpastes; common detergents such as sodium lauryl sulfates and lauryl sarcosinate; sodium carbonate peroxide or titanium dioxide for whitening; and triclosan, a controversial chemical, which is found in some brands.

BIO-SKETCH David Bodanis earned a degree in mathematics from the University of Chicago. Bodanis has a talent for explaining complex topics in simple, easy-to-understand language. Some of the books he has written are *E* = *MC*[2], *The Secret Family, The Secret Garden, The Body Book,* and *The Secret House,* from which this excerpt is taken.

NOTES ON VOCABULARY

hunker down to settle in a location for an extended period; hide out; hold firm. The phrase is from the Old Norse word ***hokra,*** meaning "to crouch."

errant straying; wayward. From Old French ***errer,*** meaning "to travel about."

dollop a small portion or amount. From the Norwegian word ***dolp,*** meaning "lump."

gustatory of or relating to the sense of taste. From the Latin ***gustare,*** meaning "to taste."

What's in Your Toothpaste?

DAVID BODANIS

INTO THE BATHROOM GOES OUR MALE RESIDENT, and after the most pressing need is satisfied, it's time to brush the teeth. The tube of toothpaste is squeezed, its pinched metal seams are splayed, pressure waves are generated inside, and the paste begins to flow. But what's in this toothpaste, so carefully being extruded . . .?

Water mostly, 30 to 45 percent in most brands: ordinary, everyday simple tap water. It's there because people like to have a big glob of toothpaste to spread on the brush, and water is the cheapest stuff there is when it comes to making big globs. Dripping a bit from the tap onto your brush would cost virtually nothing. Whipped in with the rest of the toothpaste, the manufacturers can sell it at a neat and accountant-pleasing $4 per pound equivalent. Toothpaste manufacture is a very lucrative occupation. 2

Second to water in quantity is chalk: exactly the same material children use to draw on sidewalks. It is collected from the crushed remains of long-dead 3 ocean creatures. In the Cretaceous seas, chalk particles served as part of the wickedly sharp outer skeletons that these creatures had to wrap around themselves to keep from getting chomped by all the slightly larger ocean creatures they met. Their massed graves are our present chalk deposits.

The individual chalk particles—the size of the smallest mud particles in your garden—have kept their toughness over the eons, and now on the toothbrush they'll need it. The enamel outer coating of the tooth they'll have to face is the hardest substance in the body—tougher than skull, or bone, or nail. Only the chalk particles in toothpaste can successfully grind into the teeth during brushing, ripping off the surface layers like an abrading wheel grinding down a boulder in a quarry. 4

The craters, slashes, and channels that the chalk tears into the teeth will also remove a certain amount of built-up yellow in carnage, and it is for that polishing function that it's there. A certain amount of unduly enlarged extra-abrasive chalk fragments tear such cavernous pits into the teeth that future decay bacteria will be able to hunker down there and thrive; the quality control people find it almost impossible to screen out these errant super-chalk pieces, and government regulations allow them to stay in. 5

In case even the gouging doesn't get all the yellow off, another substance is worked into the toothpaste cream. This is titanium dioxide. It comes in tiny spheres, and it's the stuff bobbing around in white wall paint to make it come out white. Splashed around onto your teeth during the brushing, it coats much of the yellow that remains. Being water soluble, it leaks off in the next few hours and is swallowed, but at least for the quick glance up in the mirror after finishing, it will make the user think his teeth are truly white. Some manufacturers add optical whitening dyes—the stuff more commonly found in washing machine bleach—to make extra sure that the glance in the mirror shows reassuring white. 6

These ingredients alone would not make a very attractive concoction. They would stick in the tube like a sloppy white plastic lump, hard to squeeze out as well as revolting to the touch. Few consumers would savor rubbing in a mixture of water, ground-up blackboard chalk, and the whitener from latex paint first thing in the morning. To get around that finicky distaste the manufacturers have mixed in a host of other goodies. 7

To keep the glop from drying out, a mixture including glycerine glycol—related to the most common anti-freeze ingredient—is whipped in with the chalk and water, and to give *that* concoction a bit of substance (all we really have so far is wet colored chalk), a large helping is added of gummy molecules from the seaweed *Chondrus crispus.* This seaweed ooze spreads in among the chalk, paint, and anti-freeze, then stretches itself in all directions to hold the whole mass together. A bit of paraffin oil (like fuel that flickers in camping lamps) is pumped in with it to help the moss ooze keep the whole substance smooth. 8

With the glycol, ooze, and paraffin we're almost there. Only two major chemicals are left to make the refreshing, cleansing substance we know as 9 toothpaste. The ingredients so far are fine for cleaning, but they wouldn't make much of the satisfying foam we have come to expect in the morning brushing.

To remedy that, every toothpaste on the market has a big dollop of deter- 10
gent added too. You've seen the suds detergent will make in the washing machine. The same substance added here will duplicate that inside the mouth. It's not particularly necessary, but it sells.

The only problem is that by itself this ingredient tastes, well, too like deter- 11
gent. It's horribly bitter and harsh. The chalk put in toothpaste is pretty foul-tasting too for that matter. It's to get around that gustatory discomfort that the manufacturers put in the ingredient they tout perhaps the most of all. This is the flavoring, and it has to be strong. Double rectified peppermint oil is used—a flavor so powerful that chemists know better than to sniff it in the raw state in the laboratory. Menthol crystals and saccharine or other sugar simulators are added to complete the camouflage operation.

Is that it? Chalk, water, paint, seaweed, anti-freeze, paraffin oil, detergent, 12
and peppermint? Not quite. A mix like that would be irresistible to the hundreds of thousands of individual bacteria lying on the surface of even an immaculately cleaned bathroom sink. They would get in, float in the water bubbles, ingest the ooze and paraffin, maybe even spray out enzymes to break down the chalk. The result would be an uninviting mess. The way manufacturers avoid that final obstacle is by putting something in it to kill the bacteria. Something good and strong is needed, something that will zap any accidentally intrudant bacteria into oblivion. And that something is formaldehyde—the disinfectant used in anatomy labs.

So it's chalk, water, paint, seaweed, anti-freeze, paraffin oil, detergent, pep- 13
permint, formaldehyde, and fluoride (which can go some ways toward preserving children's teeth)—that's the usual mixture raised to the mouth on the toothbrush for a fresh morning's clean. If it sounds too unfortunate, take heart. Studies show that thorough brushing with just plain water will often do as good a job.

(David Bodanis, *The Secret House*, 2003)

COMPREHENSION CHECKUP

Short Answer

Directions: Answer the questions briefly.

1. What is the topic of the selection? ______________________________
2. What is the selection's main idea? ______________________________
____
3. List three details supporting the author's main idea. ______________________________
____
____

Fact and Opinion

Directions: Determine whether the paragraph indicated is primarily one of fact (**F**) or opinion (**O**).

______ 4. Paragraph 3

______ 5. Paragraph 7

Directions: Identify each numbered sentence in the following paragraphs as either a fact (**F**) or an opinion (**O**).

(1) "With the glycol, ooze, and paraffin we're almost there." (2) "Only two major chemicals are left to make the refreshing, cleansing substance we know as toothpaste." (3) "The ingredients so far are fine for cleaning, but they wouldn't make much of the satisfying foam we have come to expect in the morning brushing."

______ 6. Sentence 1

______ 7. Sentence 2

______ 8. Sentence 3

(1) "So it's chalk, water, paint, seaweed, anti-freeze, paraffin oil, detergent, peppermint, formaldehyde, and fluoride (which can go some ways towards preserving children's teeth)—that's the usual mixture raised to the mouth on the toothbrush for a fresh morning's clean." (2) "If it sounds too unfortunate, take heart. (3) Studies show that thorough brushing with just plain water will often do as good a job."

______ 9. Sentence 1

______ 10. Sentence 2

______ 11. Sentence 3

Directions: In each of the following sentences, underline the words that indicate an opinion.

12. "Only two major chemicals are left to make the refreshing, cleansing substance we know as toothpaste."
13. "Whipped in with the rest of the toothpaste, the manufacturers can sell it at a neat and accountant-pleasing $4 per pound equivalent."
14. "Toothpaste manufacture is a very lucrative occupation."

Multiple Choice

Directions: For each item, write the letter corresponding to the best answer.

______ 1. The main ingredient in toothpaste is
a. water.
b. chalk.
c. formaldehyde.
d. none of the above.

______ 2. Which of the following is true, according to the selection?
a. The chalk in toothpaste comes from long-dead ocean creatures.
b. Toothpaste gels are healthier than regular paste.
c. It's a good idea to brush after each meal.
d. Children should be encouraged to chew gum to clean their teeth.

_____ 3. From the selection, you could conclude that
a. toothpaste contains only harmful ingredients.
b. toothpaste contains only healthful ingredients.
c. toothpaste contains many unappetizing ingredients.
d. toothpaste contains lead and other metals.

_____ 4. According to the selection, the enamel in teeth
a. is very prone to yellowish stains.
b. is water soluble.
c. is the hardest substance in the body.
d. should be scraped clean on a regular basis.

_____ 5. According to information presented in the selection
a. seaweed is added to toothpaste to create a refreshing taste.
b. the chalk in toothpaste is unlike the kind children play with.
c. titanium dioxide is found in Windex.
d. detergent is added to toothpaste to create foam.

True or False

Directions: Indicate whether each statement is true or false by writing **T** or **F** in the space provided.

_____ 6. Formaldehyde is added to toothpaste to kill bacteria.

_____ 7. Peppermint oil is added to toothpaste to counter the taste of detergent and chalk.

_____ 8. Chalk particles may be responsible for creating holes in teeth.

_____ 9. Whitening agents added to toothpaste make teeth permanently white.

_____ 10. Toothpaste manufacturers add some ingredients to camouflage the taste of other ingredients.

Vocabulary in Context 1

Directions: Use the context clues from the paragraph indicated to determine the meaning of the italicized words. (Remember, no looking in the dictionary.)

1. Paragraph 1: *pressing*
   Definition: ____________________
2. Paragraph 2: *extruded*
   Definition: ____________________
3. Paragraph 2: *lucrative*
   Definition: ____________________
4. Paragraph 5: *unduly*
   Definition: ____________________
5. Paragraph 5: *cavernous*
   Definition: ____________________
6. Paragraph 6: *bobbing*
   Definition: ____________________

7. Paragraph 6: *soluble*

   Definition: ____________________

8. Paragraph 6: *reassuring*

   Definition: ____________________

9. Paragraph 7: *revolting*

   Definition: ____________________

10. Paragraph 10: *remedy*

    Definition: ____________________

11. Paragraph 10: *duplicate*

    Definition: ____________________

12. Paragraph 12: *immaculately*

    Definition: ____________________

Vocabulary in Context 2

Directions: Choose one of the following words to complete each of the sentences below. Use each word only once. Be sure to pay close attention to the context clues provided.

camouflage	carnage	concoction	eons
finicky	gouging	ingests	oblivion
savor	screen out	thrive	tout

1. No longer heard on the radio, many songs from the 1930s and 1940s have passed into __________.
2. If a child __________ poison, it may be necessary to induce vomiting.
3. Dinosaurs roamed the earth __________ ago.
4. Most house plants will __________ if they receive enough water and proper light.
5. The goal of the company was to __________ half of the applicants after the initial interview.
6 Using only the ingredients she had on hand, Stella created a savory __________ for dinner.
7. After winning the primary, the politician took time to __________ his success.
8. She was so __________ about her food that she ended up eating very little.
9. Many studies __________ the benefits of adding fluoride to toothpaste.
10. The army wanted to __________ the tanks with green and brown paint to help them blend into their surroundings.
11. The battle at Gettysburg resulted in dreadful __________ with thousands of soldiers killed or wounded.
12. The little children were __________ out enough sand on the beach to make a castle.

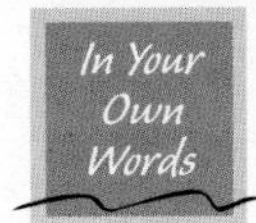

In Your Own Words

1. If you couldn't brush your teeth with toothpaste, how else would you do it?
2. Do you think the FDA should be more zealous in evaluating toothpaste and other products manufactured in foreign countries?
3. Would you be willing to brush your teeth with a foul-tasting substance if it had all-natural ingredients and would not harm your health?
4. What do you think the author's attitude toward toothpaste is? Do you think he uses toothpaste himself?

Written Assignment

Do you think it's a good idea to know more about the ingredients of everyday products? Write a paragraph giving your opinion.

Internet Activity

1. Try to find out who invented toothpaste or who first marketed it successfully. Use your favorite search engine to discover the facts, and write a brief paragraph summarizing your findings.
2. Toothpaste has a history that stretches back thousands of years. Do some research to determine what the ancient Egyptians and Chinese used to clean their teeth. Write a paragraph presenting a brief history.
3. Bodanis suggests in the final paragraph that toothpaste is an unnecessary product. Many of the products we buy and use routinely are, strictly speaking, unnecessary. What are some other examples of unnecessary products? Why do we use them?
4. Personal care products such as toothpaste are not the only products containing chemical additives. Most food products do as well. Read the labels on several kinds of packaged food. List the most frequently occurring additives, and then look those additives up to learn what purpose they serve. Visit the Web site of the U.S. Food and Drug Administration (www.fda.gov/).

   Triclosan is considered by many to be a worrisome chemical in toothpaste. Do some research to identify toothpastes that contain this chemical and to see whether scientists consider it safe for daily use.

Chapter Summary and Review

In Chapter 11, you learned how to tell the difference between fact and opinion. Based on the material in Chapter 11, answer the following.

Short Answer

Directions: Answer the following briefly.

1. Write three factual statements.

   a. ______________________________

   b. ______________________________

   c. ______________________________

2. Write three opinion statements.

   a. ______________________________

   b. ______________________________

   c. ______________________________

Vocabulary in Context

Directions: Choose one of the following words to complete the sentences below. Use each word only once.

fact opinion signal value

3. *Perhaps, presumably,* and *apparently* are words that ___________ a(n) ___________.

4. It is a(n) ___________ that the title of this book is *Reading and All That Jazz.*

5. If you said that *Titanic* was the best movie of all time, you would be making a(n) ___________ judgment.

CHAPTER

12 Bias

CHAPTER PREVIEW

In this chapter, you will

- Develop familiarity with writing that has a biased viewpoint.
- Learn to distinguish between denotative and connotative meanings.
- Learn to identify positive and negative connotations.
- Learn to recognize euphemisms.
- Learn to recognize bias in magazines, newspapers, and textbooks.

Introduction to Bias

In the previous chapter, we learned how important it is to be able to distinguish between fact and opinion. To be critical readers, we also need to be aware of our biases and the biases of others. A **bias** is defined as a strong leaning in either a positive or a negative direction.

Authors have biases, and it is the critical reader's job to discover what they are. A careful reader will study the author's line of reasoning, notice whether opinions have been supported by facts and reasons, and then decide if the author's bias has prevented the making of a good argument.

In the drawing of "The Investigation" shown below, the suspect in the investigation is in the center. Each of the individuals (and the Martian life-form?) briefly describes the suspect's appearance and gives his or her point of view. **Point of view** is defined as an opinion, an attitude, or a judgment on the part of an individual.

Notice how the descriptions they give the interviewer reflect their personal biases. Can you list some of these biases? Now read the essay "The Defendant's Characteristics" while noting the effect bias can have on legal judgments.

john jonik. Reprinted with permission.

READING

"There is a physical attractiveness stereotype: Beautiful people seem like good people."

TUNING IN TO READING Have you ever served on a jury? Did you enjoy the experience? Can you think of any instances when a jury verdict was not popular with the public? Was the defendant found guilty or not guilty? Can you explain the difference between popular perception and the verdict?

BIO-SKETCH David G. Myers is an active writer with many articles and books to his credit, including the textbook *Social Psychology,* from which this excerpt is taken. He is the John Dirk Werkman Professor of Psychology at Hope University in Michigan.

NOTES ON VOCABULARY

Clarence Darrow a lawyer known for his legal writings and for his defense of unpopular causes in the late 19th and early 20th centuries. Darrow was the defense attorney in the famous *Scopes* trial of 1925. John Scopes, a high school biology teacher, was arrested for teaching the theory of evolution to his students. Although Scopes was eventually found guilty and had to pay a $100 fine, Darrow was considered to be the winner in the trial.

Cicero a famous orator and statesman who lived in Rome from 106 B.C. to 43 B.C. He is known as one of ancient Rome's finest writers of prose. Many of his essays on philosophy are based on the works of Aristotle and Plato.

THE DEFENDANT'S CHARACTERISTICS

David G. Myers

According to the famed trial attorney Clarence Darrow, jurors seldom convict a person they like or acquit one they dislike. He argued that the main job of the trial attorney is to make the jury like the defendant. Was he right? And is it true, as Darrow also said, that "facts regarding the crime are relatively unimportant"?

Darrow overstated the case. One study of more than 3,500 criminal cases and some 4,000 civil cases found that 4 times in 5 the judge agreed with the jury's decision. Although both may have been wrong, the evidence usually is clear enough that jurors can set aside their biases, focus on the facts, and agree on a verdict. Darrow was too cynical; facts do matter. 2

Nevertheless, when jurors are asked to make social judgments—would *this* defendant commit *this* offense? intentionally?—facts are not all that matter. Communicators are more persuasive if they seem credible and attractive. Jurors cannot help forming impressions of the defendant. Can they put these impressions aside and decide the case based on the facts alone? To judge from the more lenient treatment often received by high-status defendants it seems that some cultural bias lingers. But actual cases vary in so many ways—in the type of crime, in the status, age, gender, and 3 race of the defendant—that it's hard to isolate the factors that influence jurors. So experimenters have controlled such factors by giving mock jurors the same basic facts of a case while varying, say, the defendant's attractiveness or similarity to the jurors.

There is a physical attractiveness stereotype: Beautiful people seem like good people. Michael Efran wondered whether this stereotype would bias students' judgments of someone accused of cheating. He asked some of his University of Toronto students whether attractiveness should affect presumption of guilt. They answered: "No, it shouldn't." But did it? Yes. When Efran gave other students a description of the case with a photograph of either an attractive or an unattractive defendant, they judged the most attractive as least guilty and recommended that person for the least punishment. 4

To see if these findings extend to the real world, Chris Downs and Phillip Lyons asked police escorts to rate the physical attractiveness of 1,742 defendants appearing before 40 Texas judges in misdemeanor cases. Whether the misdemeanor was serious (such as forgery), moderate (such as harassment), or minor (such as public intoxication), the judges set higher bails and fines for less-attractive defendants. What explains this dramatic effect? Are unattractive people also lower in status? Are they indeed more likely to flee or to commit crime, as the judges perhaps suppose? Or do judges simply ignore the Roman statesman Cicero's advice: "The final good and the supreme duty of the wise man is to resist appearance." 5

If Clarence Darrow was even partly right in his declaration that liking or disliking a defendant colors judgments, then other factors that influence liking should also matter. Among such influences is the principle that likeness (similarity) leads to liking. When people pretend they are jurors, they are indeed more sympathetic to a defendant who shares their attitudes, religion, race, or (in cases of sexual assault) gender. For example, when Cookie Stephan and Walter Stephan had English-speaking people judge someone accused of assault, they were more likely to think the person not guilty if the defendant's testimony was in English, rather than translated from Spanish or Thai. 6

So it seems we are more sympathetic toward a defendant with whom we can identify. If we think *we* wouldn't have committed that criminal act, we may assume that someone like us is also unlikely to have done it. 7

Ideally, jurors would leave their biases outside the courtroom and begin a trial with open minds. So implies the Sixth Amendment to the U.S. Constitution: "The accused shall enjoy the right to a speedy and public trial by impartial jury." In its concern for objectivity, the judicial system is similar to science: Both scientists and jurors are supposed to sift and weigh the evidence. Both the courts and science have rules about what evidence is relevant. Both keep careful records and assume that others given the same evidence would decide similarly. 8

When the evidence is clear and jurors focus on it, their biases are indeed minimal. The quality of the evidence matters more than the prejudices of the individual jurors. 9

(David G. Myers, *Social Psychology*, 9/e, 2008)

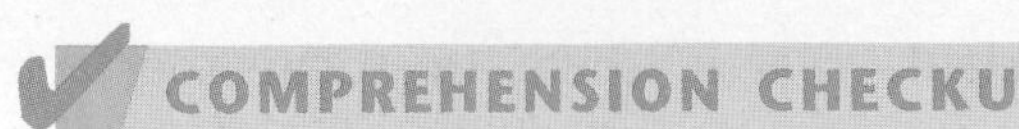

Multiple Choice

Directions: For each item, write the letter corresponding to the best answer.

_____ 1. The main idea expressed in this selection is that
a. jurors can be influenced by the physical appearance and actions of a defendant.
b. jurors are unlikely to pay attention to the physical characteristics of a defendant.
c. in Texas, judges were affected by the attractiveness of the defendants.
d. jurors are unlikely to be sympathetic to those who are like them.

_____ 2. Paragraph 2 contains the following statement: "Darrow overstated the case." This is a statement of
a. fact.
b. opinion.

_____ 3. As used in paragraph 3, the word *credible* means
a. easily deceived.
b. believable.
c. childish.
d. doubtful.

_____ 4. In paragraph 4, the example of Efran's University of Toronto students was used to illustrate that
a. attractive people receive more lenient sentences in court.
b. the way we treat attractive and unattractive people shapes the way they think about themselves.
c. attractive people are thought to be less likely to have committed a crime.

_____ 5. In paragraph 5, the author helps readers understand the different types of misdemeanors by providing
a. definitions.
b. examples.
c. cause-and-effect relationships.
d. chronological order.

_____ 6. Based on Cicero's statement, readers can conclude that he would advise jurors to
a. carefully consider the appearance of the defendant during jury deliberations.
b. disregard the appearance of the defendant during jury deliberations.

_____ 7. Paragraph 8 contains the following statement: "Ideally, jurors would leave their biases outside the courtroom and begin a trial with open minds." This is a statement of
a. fact.
b. opinion.

_____ 8. The mode of writing used in this selection is
a. narrative.
b. descriptive.
c. expository.
d. persuasive.

Short Answer

Directions: Answer the following questions briefly.

1. According to the selection, what are some biases that can affect a jury's ability to reach a fair decision? ______________________________

   ______________________________.

2. According to the context clues in paragraph 2, what does the word *cynical* mean?
   "Darrow was too *cynical;* facts do matter."
   Cynical means ______________________________.
3. In paragraph 3, what does the transition word *nevertheless* signal?
   Nevertheless signals ______________________________.
4. According to the context clues in paragraph 6, what does the word *colors* mean?
   "If Clarence Darrow was even partly right in his declaration that liking or disliking a defendant *colors* judgments . . ."
   Colors means ______________________________.
5. What two things are being compared in paragraph 8?
   ____________________ and ____________________.
6. According to the context clues in paragraph 8, what does the word *objectivity* mean?
   "In its concern for *objectivity* . . ."
   Objectivity means ______________________________.

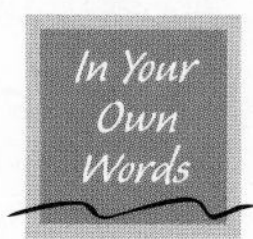

In Your Own Words

1. Do you think jurors are capable of setting aside their biases and deciding cases on the facts and law alone? What leads you to your conclusion?
2. Do you think jurors are less likely to convict someone who seems similar to them?

Written Assignment

The reading selection mentions a physical attractiveness stereotype. Do you think an attractive appearance gives someone a big advantage in life? Or do you think people are unlikely to be influenced by superficial qualities because they believe that "beauty is only skin deep" and "you can't judge a book by its cover"? Write a short essay giving your opinion.

Internet Activity

Consult the Web site titled "Teaching Tolerance" developed by the Southern Poverty Law Center. It explores the topic of stereotypes and prejudices and provides a test you can take to discover if you have any unconscious or hidden biases.

www.tolerance.org/hiddenbias

Denotation and Connotation

When you look up a word in your dictionary, you are determining its **denotation,** or dictionary meaning. However, words also have **connotations,** or meanings beyond simple dictionary definitions. These words carry an extra emotional "charge." We can think of these words as being positive, negative, or neutral.

For example, even though the words *thin, slender,* and *skinny* all have similar dictionary definitions, they have different connotative meanings. Most of us think *slender* has a positive connotation and *skinny* a negative one. *Thin* has a more neutral meaning. In using words that have connotative meanings, we reveal our personal biases.

Authors can do exactly the same thing as speakers by choosing one particular word over another. If an author begins a novel by referring to the title character as someone who is *thrifty,* what picture of that person comes to your mind? How about if the author refers to the title character as *cheap* or *stingy*?

In the following cartoon, the word *problems* and the word *challenges* have very similar denotative meanings. However, as the son points out to his dad, they have very different connotative meanings.

One Big Happy

Exercise 1: Spotting Biased Words

Directions: Read the following comments from a parent–teacher conference and, for each word pair, circle the word with the more positive connotation.

> I am very proud of Tommy and his *diligent/plodding* effort to improve his arithmetic grade. He does seem to have a(n) *self-confident/arrogant* approach toward the work at this grade level. However, he is not placing enough emphasis on producing quality homework. It is done in a(n) *sloppy/untidy* way. In general, he is a very *able/gifted* child. He does, however, need to improve his social and emotional conduct. His contributions to the class are made in a(n) *enthusiastic/hyperactive* way, and he is sometimes *rude/insensitive* in his comments to others. He does seem *eager/willing* to participate in most activities in the classroom, but he needs to learn to do so in a less *assertive/aggressive* manner. On the playground and in his relations with his peers, he is often *shy/reserved,* but he is beginning to be asked to enter into new activities. I enjoy having Tommy in my room and I hope we can make the rest of the year a pleasant one.

Exercise 2: Positive and Negative Connotation

Directions: Below are two versions of the same speech. One uses positive words to favor Senator X and the other uses words slanted against him. Read both speeches and circle all of the biased words or phrases. Then rewrite the speech as a neutral observer reporting only facts rather than giving opinions or making value judgments. As a guideline answer *who, what, where, when, why,* and *how* questions. Be careful not to substitute your own biased words for the ones you eliminate.

In Favor of Senator X

In a well-reasoned statement to an admiring audience, the dignified and courtly Senator X today forcefully argued for his proposal to limit violence in the media. The auditorium filled with laughter as the esteemed senator showed his trademark dry wit. By disarming the opposition, it looks like the senator will emerge triumphant and his insightful proposal will carry the day.

Against Senator X

In his usual dour style, the aging Senator X today sought to persuade the crowd in the auditorium to accept his proposal to limit violence in the media. The audience, clearly repulsed by his crude, cynical attempts at humor, appeared to be laughing more at the senator than with him. Frightened by his threats, the opposition will probably be goaded into backing his program.

Neutral Version

____

____

____

____

____

Euphemisms

When we substitute inoffensive words or phrases for ones that are likely to offend someone, we are using **euphemisms.** Generally, we use euphemisms to be polite or to avoid controversy. For example, a euphemism such as "passed away" might be substituted for the word "died."

The use of euphemisms to purposely mislead others and obscure the truth is called **doublespeak.** In the working world, layoffs have become commonplace, but because the word "layoff" has a negative connotation, many new euphemisms have been created both to appease the person being fired and to mislead the general public. Thus, when a company fires a large group of workers and announces a "force reduction program," they are guilty of doublespeak. Read the following information on doublespeak and inflated language from Hamilton Gregory's *Public Speaking for College and Career.*

BEWARE OF DOUBLESPEAK

When some federal and state legislators raise taxes, they don't refer to their action as "raising taxes." To do so might anger taxpayers. No, timidly and sneakily, they say they voted for "revenue enhancement."

"Revenue enhancement" is an example of **doublespeak.** Here are some additional examples:

- After one of its planes crashed, National Airlines described the event—in its annual report to stockholders—as an "involuntary conversion of a 727," a legal term designed to conceal the truth.
- When politicians in Washington, DC, slashed funding for national parks in 2004, they asked park superintendents to call the budget cuts "service level adjustments."

Euphemisms become harmful when they mask a problem that should be dealt with. When homeless people are called "urban nomads," does this romantic euphemism cause the public to turn its eyes from a problem that needs attention?

The best advice is this: Use euphemisms if tact and kindness require them, and avoid them if they serve to deceive or confuse.

In his book *The New Doublespeak,* William Lutz discusses another type of doublespeak called **inflated language.** Lutz says, "inflated language is designed to make the ordinary seem extraordinary; to make everyday things seem impressive; to give an air of importance to people, situations, or things that would not normally be considered important." For example:

- A used car is advertised as a *preowned car* or *pre-enjoyed automobile.*
- A seafood restaurant calls its servers *seafood specialists.*
- A magazine refers to elderly people as the *chronologically gifted.*
- A national pizza delivery chain announces that its drivers will henceforth be known as *delivery ambassadors.*

Some inflated language seems harmless. If garbage collectors prefer to be called *sanitation engineers,* most people will not criticize too strenuously. If they believe that the term dignifies their valuable but unglamorous work, most won't object to the use of the term. But the problem is that inflated language is spreading rapidly into all areas of life, causing misunderstanding and confusion. If you saw an advertisement for a *grief therapist,* wouldn't you envision a counselor for a mourning individual whose loved one has just died? If so, you'd be wrong, because *grief therapist* is an inflated term for an undertaker. How are we to know that an *excavation technician* is a ditch digger? That a *communications monitor* is a switchboard operator? That a *customer engineer* is a salesperson? That a *corrosion control specialist* is the person who sends your car through a car wash?

An inflated term may begin in kindness, but it often ends in confusion. Avoid its use unless you know that it is clearly understood.

(Hamilton Gregory, *Public Speaking for College and Career,* 10/e, 2013)

Note: William Lutz suggests that people fight doublespeak by becoming "first-rate crap detectors." One way to accomplish this is to start collecting and trading examples of doublespeak. Try to bring in examples to your class on a topic such as the economy, unemployment, or foreign aid.

Exercise 3: Euphemisms

Directions: Give euphemisms for each of the following words or phrases.

1. older person ____________________
2. toilet ____________________

3. drunk ______________________
4. pregnant ______________________
5. lazy ______________________
6. pornography ______________________

Directions: Turn these euphemistic words or phrases into regular words.

1. to be temporarily without funds ______________________
2. lingerie ______________________
3. cemetery ______________________
4. mixed-breed dog ______________________
5. preowned vehicle ______________________
6. chemically dependent ______________________
7. to misappropriate the company's funds ______________________
8. nightclub ______________________
9. telemarketing ______________________
10. to score below average on a test ______________________
11. vertically challenged ______________________
12. to stretch the truth somewhat ______________________
13. learning resources center ______________________
14. to depart from this life ______________________

Bias in Magazines, Newspapers, and Textbooks

Many people think of magazines and newspapers—and especially textbooks—as being free of bias and of being an objective presentation of the facts. But this is far from true, as the excerpts below illustrate.

Exercise 4: Detecting Bias in Magazines, Newspapers, and Textbooks

Directions: For each passage, write the letter corresponding to words that suggest the writer's bias on the line provided.

______ 1. Citizenship today is in a precarious state. For much of the past half century, the involvement of citizens in their communities has dwindled, voter turnout has remained well below that of other advanced democracies, and the level of trust between citizens and elected national leaders has reached historic lows. We believe that citizenship today is at a crossroads: we can build on recent gains in voter interest and reconstruct the reciprocal bonds of trust between citizen and government, or we can watch these bonds continue to fray. We can either begin finding solutions to the pressing problems that endanger our future or watch these problems continue to worsen. There are some signs that young people are ready to open a dialogue about how to construct a more vibrant democracy that works for all citizens. That is our hope.

(Joseph Losco, *AM GOV*, McGraw-Hill, 2013–2014, p. 5)

a. citizens, turnout, trust, bonds
b. reciprocal, involvement, democracy, dialogue
c. precarious, dwindled, fray, endanger

______ 2. Who ever would have thought that good old PB&J could be a health hazard? Sad but true: the peanut-butter-and-jelly sandwich is under assault, along with its cousin the fluffer nutter, the peanut-butter cracker, the Reese's Piece, the peanut M&M and all the other delectable forms the humble peanut comes in. At the Breck School in Minneapolis, PB&J sandwiches must now be eaten at separate tables. The Bradstreet Early Childhood Center in North Andover, Massachusetts, is one of many kindergartens to have created peanut-free classrooms this fall, and the Trinity School in New York City has expelled all forms of the peanut from the premises. Why the frenzy over goobers? Because 1 percent of American children are now estimated to have a peanut allergy.

(John Sedgwick, "Goodbye to the Goober," 1996)

a. hazard, sad, expelled, frenzy, assault
b. goobers, separate, peanut-free, premises
c. cracker, estimated, allergy, health

______ 3. Any work is potentially censorable by someone, someplace, sometime, for some reason. Nothing is permanently safe from censorship, not even most books most teachers and librarians would regard as far removed from censorial eyes—not *Hamlet*, *Julius Caesar*, *Treasure Island*, or anything else. If one book is removed from a classroom or library, no book is safe any longer. If a censor succeeds in getting one book out, every other person in the community who objects to another book should, in courtesy, be granted the same privilege. When everyone has walked out of the library carrying all those objectionable books, nothing of any consequence will be left no matter how many books remain. Some books are certain to offend some people and be ardently defended by others. Indeed, every library has books offensive to someone, maybe everyone. After all, ideas do offend many people.

(Alleen Pace Nilsen and Kenneth L. Donelson. *Literature for Today's Young Adults*, 8/e, 2009)

a. offend, offensive, objectionable, censorship
b. courtesy, granted, someplace, potentially
c. classroom, library, removed, reason

______ 4. In a society almost as dependent on email as on the U.S. Postal Service, junk email—better known as "spam"—has become more than a mere annoyance. For Internet-connected individuals, it's a persistent, time-consuming, and offensive aggravation. In the business world it's a crisis, draining resources and bandwidth and laying networks vulnerable to numerous security hazards. Today, unsolicited email accounts for nearly a staggering 80 percent of worldwide email traffic. The vast majority of the spam messages being sent are advertisements for products of dubious origin or attempts to steal personal information.

(Glen J. Coulthard, *Computing Now*, McGraw-Hill, 2013, p. 185)

a. annoyance, offensive, aggravation, staggering
b. society, resources, vast, attempts
c. dependent, vulnerable, origin, steal

_____ 5. Querulous, funny, serious, playful, fearless, caring, and curious—the roadrunner sports a jaunty outlook wrapped in a bundle of tan, white, black, and metallic bronze. The roadrunner earned its name when settlers traveling westward first discovered that this odd, vivacious bird liked to race their wagons. But Mexicans were calling the bird *corre camino* ("it runs the road") long before Europeans settled the lands in the southwestern United States. It measures just 22 to 24 inches in length—half of which is tail—but has earned quite a reputation and many names from many cultures. In Texas, it goes by the name "chaparral cock," in New Mexico it's known as "snake eater," and in Mexico it's dubbed *paisano* ("compatriot" or "countryman"). Confident and crowned with a feather crest, the roadrunner earns king-of-the-road bragging rights. So swift of foot that it rarely takes flight, this clever member of the cuckoo family snatches airborne insects and smaller birds with leaps up to 6 feet in the air.

(Carrie M. Miner, "Roadrunner Facts & Fantasy," 2001)

a. jaunty, vivacious, confident, clever
b. wrapped, reputation, names, dubbed
c. outlook, metallic, crest, rights

_____ 6. White-coated experts at the Faster Living Institute, alarmed by a nationwide study that showed the average American constantly running behind schedule, have just announced the results of their drive to isolate the cause and find a solution. Where does all the time go? It's stolen, is the institute's shocking answer, by our own medicine chests and the obsolete nineteenth-century medication-taking process. "Don't let that innocent-looking little bathroom cabinet fool you," says one college-trained researcher. "It's a diabolical time trap. You can finally stop torturing yourself about always running late when you realize that two minutes per day, fourteen minutes per week, fifty-six minutes per month, or twelve hours per year, are wasted in finding, selecting, uncapping, and ingesting medication."

(Bruce McCall, "Hurry-Up Experts Say Medicine Chest Doomed," 2001)

a. white-coated, constantly, isolate
b. stolen, shocking, diabolical
c. nationwide, average, ingesting

_____ 7. Teachers undergo many perplexing stresses every day. The demands on their time are diverse and contradictory. Conflicts arise from serving as an instructor, a disciplinarian, and an employee of a school district at the same time. In too many schools, discipline means dealing with violence. Burnout is one of these stresses: between a quarter and a third of new teachers quit within their first three years, and as many as half leave poor urban schools in their first five years. Teachers' salaries vary considerably from state to state. Nevertheless, the economic reward for teaching is miniscule compared to some career options. In fact, salaries are significantly lower than those of many professionals and skilled workers. As a result, many teachers have become disappointed and frustrated and have left the educational world for careers in other professions.

(Richard T. Schaeffer, *Sociology*, 12/e, McGraw-Hill, 2010, p. 369)

a. conflicts, discipline, urban, reward
b. perplexing, burnout, demands, violence
c. contradictory, employee, miniscule, career

______ 8. The scientific evidence for global climate change is clear, consistent, and compelling, yet public opinion polls show that people remain skeptical. Despite the potential catastrophic risks, 48 percent of Americans believe that the seriousness of global warming is generally exaggerated. Ironically, many of those who are now calling for a reduction in the human activity that contributes to global climate change are located in core nations, which have contributed disproportionately to the problem. (The United States produces 19 percent of the world's carbon dioxide.) We want our hamburgers, but we decry the destruction of the rain forests to create grazing land for cattle. We want inexpensive clothes and toys, but we condemn developing countries for depending on coal-fired power plants, the number of which is expected to increase 46 percent by 2030.

(Jon Witt, *SOC*, McGraw-Hill, 2012, p. 371)

a. evidence, climate change, seriousness, ironically
b. reduction, disproportionately, clear, developing
c. decry, compelling, destruction, catastrophic risks

Exercise 5: Detecting Bias: "Who Gets In?"

The college can admit only 5 more students. As a member of the board, it is your responsibility to rank the 10 students listed on the following page according to who most deserves to be accepted. Descriptions of their precollege situation and performance are given.

In your group, keep in mind the following factors as you select the **5** you consider the most deserving:

1. The person's potential, abilities, or capabilities
2. The person's motivation to perform
3. The probability of successful completion of a college education

Your group must be in complete agreement about your choices. After selecting your 5, write a brief sentence or two explaining the rationale for your choices. When everyone has completed the assignment, the group leader should write the selections on the board. Be prepared to defend your selections to the rest of the class.

L'Tisha

Very intelligent; senior class valedictorian; has won awards in the National Science Fair for exhibits; has definite plans to major in chemistry; high school counselor says she has difficulty relating to others; she was involved in several disputes with high school classmates over chemistry experiments.

Julio

An all-state center in high school; plans to play college basketball and would help the team; scored poorly on the college admittance test although his high school grades were average; plans to become a physical therapist.

Jill

Ranked in the middle of her graduating class; did well in high school math; has good study habits; high school counselor says she has interfering, confrontational parents.

Carolyn

A divorced mother with two children; 24 years old, trying to return to college to continue her education after dropping out six years ago; works and raises her family; no financial support from her former husband; will need financial aid; wishes to become an elementary school teacher.

Dominique

An applicant from Venezuela; has already earned a degree in her own country; did very well academically; she wants to enroll to experience our lifestyle and perfect her English; not interested in any specific subject; plans to return home.

Juan Carlos

High school counselor says he is outgoing and well-liked among his peers; poor grades; studied little in high school and has poor study skills; test results reveal a very high IQ.

Howard

Ranked in the top 5 percent of his graduating class; high school counselor says he is a loner who lacks social skills; had no extracurricular activities in high school; has a great deal of academic potential; wants to be a doctor like his father.

Jiao

Had attendance problems in high school; grades were mediocre; worked in excess of 40 hours a week; IQ in gifted range; will need financial aid.

Evelyn

She is 58 years old; worked in a day care center for the past 15 years; prior to that she was a housewife and mother; wants to earn a degree in child psychology; high test scores.

Dakin

Average grades; works 28 hours a week to pay for his education; is aiming for a degree in engineering; high potential in math; a very hard worker.

(David B. Ellis, *Becoming a Master Student*, 7/e, 1994)

Exercise 6: Detecting Bias—Sex-Based Words

A. Each word or phrase below is usually associated with only one sex. Using your knowledge of cultural history, determine why these phrases are associated with one sex but not with the other.

Feminine Based	Masculine Based
1. mother nature ______________	1. old man winter ______________
2. black widow spider __________	2. daddy longlegs spider __________
3. *The Clarissa* (clipper ship) ______	3. LA-Z-BOY lounging chair ________
4. the statue of justice __________	4. man-of-war (battleship) ________
5. a ladybug ______________	5. a father of modern science ______

THE FAMILY CIRCUS. By Bil Keane

"How come we don't hear anything about FATHER Nature?"

Write a general statement about your findings.

____

____

B. The (animal) words listed below are nearly always associated with one sex or the other. Mark **M** for the terms you would most likely use with males and **F** for terms you would most likely use with females. See if you can come to any conclusions as to how the two lists differ and what they show about cultural expectations for males and females.

______	1. a beast	______	1. to be mousy
______	2. a bird	______	2. a rat
______	3. to be bullheaded	______	3. a loan shark
______	4. a social butterfly	______	4. a fox
______	5. to be catty	______	5. a tiger
______	6. a chick	______	6. a tigress
______	7. a donkey	______	7. a vixen
______	8. to be kittenish	______	8. a vulture
______	9. a hog	______	9. a wolf
______	10. a lamb	______	10. doe eyes

Conclusions: ____

____

____

C. Change the following "man words" to "gender-inclusive" alternatives.

Example: congressman—congressional representative

1. workman ____
2. anchorman ____

Herman

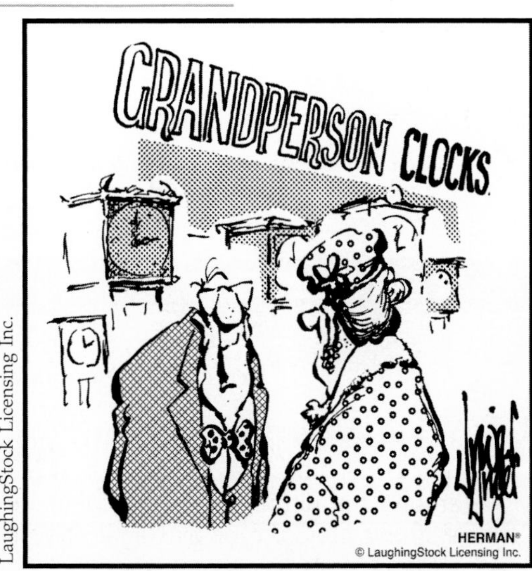

"We're living in very strange times, Martha."

3. the best man for the job ______
4. weatherman ______
5. foreman ______
6. businessman ______
7. salesman ______
8. mailman ______
9. insurance man ______
10. fireman ______
11. cameraman ______
12. freshman ______
13. spokesman ______
14. man-sized job ______
15. sportsmanship ______

D. Change the following "female words" to "gender-inclusive" alternatives.

1. cleaning lady ______
2. housewife ______
3. ladylike ______

E. Change the following titles, used to distinguish female workers from males, to neutral terms for both men and women.

1. lady doctor ______
2. stewardess ______
3. policewoman ______
4. waitress ______

F. What is the problem with using language that is sexist or biased?

____

____

____

(Alleen Pace Nilsen, *Changing Words in a Changing World,* 1980)

READING

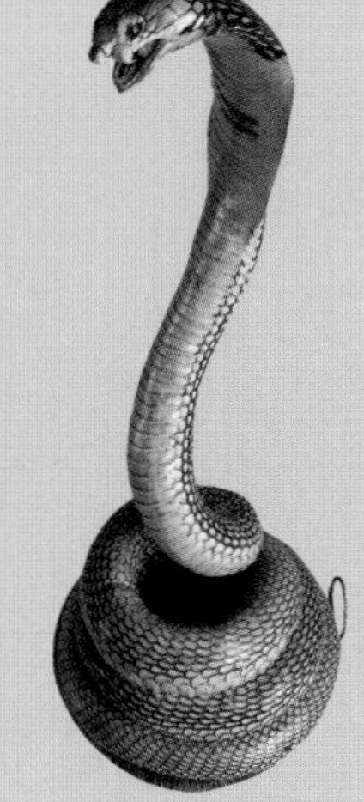

"He realizes there must be a cobra in the room."

TUNING IN TO READING This short story by Mona Gardner takes place during the time when India was a British colony. As the characters are gathered around the dinner table, the colonel makes a provocative statement that exhibits a strong prejudice or bias against women. The story is concluded in a very ironic way.

NOTES ON VOCABULARY

attachés people on the diplomatic staff of an ambassador to another country

cobra a poisonous snake native to Asia and Africa capable of expanding the skin of the neck to form a hood

sobers calms, makes more serious

rupees basic monetary unit of India

THE DINNER PARTY BY MONA GARDNER

The country is India. A colonial official and his wife are giving a large dinner party. They are seated with their guests—army officers, government attachés with their wives, and a visiting American naturalist—in their spacious dining room. It has a bare marble floor, open rafters, and wide glass doors opening onto a veranda.

2 A spirited discussion springs up between a young girl who insists that women have outgrown the jumping-on-a-chair-at-the-sight-of-a-mouse era and a colonel who says that they haven't.

3 "A woman's unfailing reaction in any crisis," the colonel says, "is to scream. And while a man may feel like it, he has that ounce more of nerve control than a woman has. And that last ounce more is what counts."

4 The American does not join in the argument but watches the other guests. As he looks, he sees a strange expression come over the face of the hostess. She is staring straight ahead, her muscles contracting slightly. With a slight gesture, she summons the native boy standing behind her chair and whispers to him. The boy's eyes widen, and he quickly leaves the room.

5 Of the guests, none except the American notices this or sees the boy place a bowl of milk on the veranda just outside the open doors.

6 The American comes to with a start. In India, milk in a bowl means only one thing—bait for a snake. He realizes there must be a cobra in the room. He looks up at the rafters—the likeliest place—but they are bare. Three corners of the room are empty,

and in the fourth the servants are waiting to serve the next course. There is only one place left—under the table.

7 His first impulse is to jump back and warn the others, but he knows the commotion would frighten the cobra into striking. He speaks quickly, the tone of his voice so arresting that it sobers everyone.

8 "I want to know just what control everyone at this table has. I will count to three hundred—that's five minutes—and not one of you is to move a muscle. Those who move will forfeit fifty rupees. Ready!"

9 The twenty people sit like stone images while he counts. He is saying "two hundred and eighty" when, out of the corner of his eye, he sees the cobra emerge and make for the bowl of milk. Screams ring out as he jumps to slam the veranda doors safely shut.

"You were right, Colonel!" the host exclaims. "A man has just shown us an example of perfect control." 10

"Just a minute," the American says, turning to his hostess. "Mrs. Wynnes, how did you know the cobra was in the room?" 11

A faint smile lights up the woman's face as she replies. "Because it was crawling across my foot." 12

(*The Saturday Review,* January 31, 1942)

COMPREHENSION CHECKUP

Multiple Choice

Directions: Write the letter of the correct answer in the blank provided.

_____ 1. Which of the following is the author's main idea?
   a. Tragedy often awaits those who least suspect it.
   b. The difference between a good outcome and a bad one is often only a matter of inches.
   c. Courage is not a trait that belongs to only one sex.
   d. People working together can accomplish great things.

_____ 2. What does the hostess reveal at the end of the story?
   a. She felt the colonel should be soundly criticized for his old-fashioned philosophy about women's abilities.
   b. She had displayed remarkable courage by remaining calm and level-headed when a cobra crawled across her foot.
   c. She was angry with her husband's prejudiced viewpoint.
   d. She disliked the American's display of bad manners.

_____ 3. Sensing danger, what action does the American take to help prevent it?
   a. He summons help to remove the cobra.
   b. He challenges the colonel to prove his point.
   c. He supplies the cobra with food and drink.
   d. He creates a diversion to keep everyone still and calm until the cobra has left the area.

_____ 4. In the "battle between the sexes," whose viewpoint does the host support?
   a. the American's viewpoint
   b. his wife's viewpoint
   c. the colonel's viewpoint
   d. the young girl's viewpoint

_____ 5. Which of the following is a statement of opinion?
a. A woman's unfailing reaction in any crisis is to scream.
b. The American does not join in the argument but watches the other guests.
c. The country is India.
d. The hosts are seated with their guests.

_____ 6. When the author describes the 20 people sitting like stone images, she
a. is using a simile.
b. is using personification.
c. is describing the stillness of their posture.
d. both a and c

_____ 7. We can infer all of the following from the behavior of both the American naturalist and Mrs. Wynnes **except**
a. cobras are likely to strike when there is sudden movement.
b. cobras are fond of milk.
c. cobras are wary of loud sounds.
d. cobras aren't fond of heights.

_____ 8. A *naturalist* is someone who
a. inspects homes to determine if there is a bug or rat infestation.
b. specializes in natural history, especially in the study of plants and animals in their natural surroundings.
c. likes to argue points of philosophy.
d. visits foreign countries to learn more about the language and culture.

_____ 9. As described in the story, a *veranda* is
a. an outside porch.
b. a place where children like to play.
c. similar to a living room.
d. where people gather to shop.

_____ 10. To *forfeit* something means to
a. throw it overboard.
b. demand it.
c. surrender or lose it.
d. gain or win it.

Vocabulary in Context

Directions: Look through the paragraphs indicated in parentheses to find the word that matches each of the definitions below.

1. ample; roomy (1) ____________________
2. lively (2) ____________________
3. food used as a lure (6) ____________________
4. inclination; urge (7) ____________________
5. disturbance (7) ____________________
6. impressive; commanding (7) ____________________
7. come into view (9) ____________________

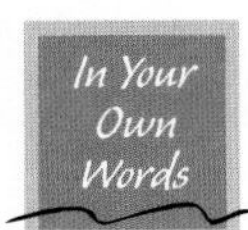

In Your Own Words

1. Why does the American suggest that everyone remain still? Why doesn't he tell the dinner guests the real reason he wishes them to be silent?
2. What traits does the American display that indicate that he is well suited to his profession of naturalist, someone who studies nature?
3. Why does the hostess have a faint smile on her face at the end of the story?
4. What is ironic about the situation described in the story?
5. In what ways does the author illustrate the negative effects of stereotypes?

Written Assignment

Do you think men are better in a crisis than women? Give your opinion in a few paragraphs.

Internet Activity

Consult the following Web site to discover some fascinating information about the cobra. Write a short paragraph describing what you learned.

www.nationalgeographic.com/features/97/kingcobra/index-n.html

Exercise 7: Bias in Publications

Directions: Study the list of publications and the given topic. Would you expect the publication to be biased or objective (neutral) on this particular topic? Write an **O** for objective or a **B** for biased in the space provided.

Publication	Topic	
1. *Los Angeles Times* editorial	marijuana	_____
2. *The New England Journal of Medicine*	marijuana	_____
3. *The Catholic Star Church Newsletter*	marijuana	_____
4. *American Medical Association Complete Medical Encyclopedia*	marijuana	_____
5. *The Partnership for a Drug-Free America Newsletter*	marijuana	_____
6. *The Scourge of Drugs* by Wendell Collins	marijuana	_____
7. *Sociology* by James N. Henslin	marijuana	_____
8. *Understanding Psychology* by Charles G. Morris	marijuana	_____

READING

"Next time you make a bag of Orville Redenbacher's, you'll be repeating an experiment that heralded the dawning of the age of microwave cooking."

TUNING IN TO READING Do you own a microwave? If you have one in your home, do you use it for more than reheating coffee or leftovers? By 1997, 90 percent of all American households had a microwave. If you were forced to eliminate one of your appliances, which one could you most easily do without, and why?

Practice your SQ3R techniques with this reading selection. Survey the material by reading the first two paragraphs, the last two paragraphs, and the bio-sketch.

READING *(continued)*

BIO-SKETCH Ira Flatow, National Public Radio's science correspondent, is the host of *Talk of the Nation's* "Science Friday." In his book *They All Laughed,* "he demonstrates that truth is stranger than fiction." Each of the stories, including this one about the invention of the microwave, is really a story about inquisitive people who won't take no for an answer. While doing research about inventors, Flatow discovered that most of them are hearty souls, unafraid of appearing ridiculous by asking silly questions. He calls this the "quack like a duck" discovery method. If something looks like a duck, walks like a duck, but doesn't quack like a duck, these bold inventors want to know why. In this excerpt, Perry Spencer, noticing the melted candy bar in a lab coat he'd been wearing all day long, should have assumed his own body temperature had been the culprit. Because that answer didn't make "quack noises," Spencer went on to invent the microwave oven.

Early Microwave oven

NOTES ON VOCABULARY

nuke slang for cooking food in a microwave oven.

cynical disbelieving; sarcastic, sneering. In ancient Greece, a *Cynic* was a member of a school of philosophers who believed that being virtuous was the highest good. Because *cynics* had contempt for worldly needs and pleasures, they were extremely critical of the rest of society. Today the word refers to anyone who questions the motives or actions of other people.

maven an expert, a really knowledgeable person. The word *maven* comes from Yiddish.

FROM A MELTED CANDY BAR TO MICROWAVES

Ira Flatow

Next time you nuke a bag of Orville Redenbacher's, you'll be repeating an experiment that heralded the dawning of the age of microwave cooking.

Almost 50 years ago, 1946 to be exact, one of the great minds in the history of electronics accidentally invented microwave popcorn. 2

"Little minds are interested in the extraordinary; great minds in the commonplace."
—Elliot Hubbard

Shortly after World War II, Percy L. Spencer, electronic genius and war hero, was touring one of his laboratories at the Raytheon Company. Spencer stopped in front of a magnetron, the power tube that drives a radar set. Suddenly he noticed that a candy bar in his pocket had begun to melt. 3

Most of us would have written off the gooey mess to body heat. But not Spencer. Spencer never took anything for granted. During his 39 years with Raytheon, he patented 120 inventions. When England was battered by German bombs in the 1940 Battle of Britain, Spencer turned his 4 creative mind toward developing a better version of the British invention radar. His improved magnetron allowed radar tube production to be increased from 17 per week to 2,600 per day. His achievements earned him the Distinguished Service Medal, the U.S. Navy's highest honor for civilians.

So when this inquisitive, self-educated, and highly decorated engineer who 5
never finished grammar school came face to face with a good mystery, he didn't merely wipe the melted chocolate off his hands and shrug off the incident. He took the logical next step. He sent out for popcorn. Holding the bag of unpopped kernels next to the magnetron, Spencer watched as the kernels exploded.

The next morning Spencer brought in a tea kettle. He wanted to see what 6
microwaves would do to raw eggs. After cutting a hole in the side of the kettle, Spencer placed an uncooked egg into the pot. Next he placed a magnetron beside the kettle and turned on the machine.

An unfortunate (cynical?) engineer poked his nose into the pot and was 7
greeted by an explosion of yolk and white. The egg had been blown up by the steam pressure from within. Spencer had created the first documented microwave mess—an experiment to be inadvertently repeated by countless thousands of microwave cooks. He had also shown that microwaves had the ability to cook foods quickly.

Legend has it that this demonstration was reproduced before unsuspect- 8
ing members of Raytheon's board of directors who had trouble visualizing exactly what microwaves could do to food. The ensuing egg shower convinced the board of directors to invest in the "high frequency dielectric heating apparatus" patented in 1953.

That demo and the fact that the military no longer needed 10,000 mag- 9
netron tubes per week for radar sets helped shape the future of microwaves. What better way to recover lost sales than to put in every American home a radar set disguised as a microwave oven?

But first the device needed a better name. Raytheon's marketing mavens 10
felt few people would demand a high-frequency dielectric heating apparatus for their kitchens even if they could pronounce it. A contest followed to rename the apparatus. Seeing as how the oven owed its roots to radar, the winning entry suggested "Radar Range." The words were later merged to Radarange. But no words could hide the woeful inadequacies of this first-generation oven.

Weighing 750 pounds and standing five and a half feet [tall], the Radarange 11
required water—and plumbing—to keep its hefty innards cool. Hardly the compact unit that fits under today's kitchen cabinets. The early 1953 design—with its three-thousand-dollar price tag—was strictly for restaurants, railroads (the Japanese railroad system bought 2,500), and ocean liners. These customers would be Raytheon's prime market for two decades.

The microwave oven was no pleasure to cook with, either. Culinary 12
experts noticed that meat refused to brown. French fries stayed white and limp. Who could eat this ugly-looking food? Chefs were driven to distraction. As chronicled in *The Wall Street Journal,* "the Irish cook of Charles Adams, Raytheon's chairman, who turned his kitchen into a proving ground, called the oven 'black magic' and quit."

It would take decades before the consumer oven was perfected. The Tappan 13
Company took an interest in the project and helped Raytheon engineers shrink the size of the magnetron. A smaller power unit meant the hideous plumbing could be done away with and air cooling fans could take over.

Then someone had the brilliant idea that perhaps the magnetron should 14
not be pointed directly at the food but rather out of sight. That's it. Put the food in a box, put the microwave source at the back, and lead the microwaves into the box via a pipe. Now we could truly call it an oven.

And that's what happened. In 1955 Tappan introduced the first consumer 15
microwave oven. Did you have one? Hardly anyone did. It was still too big and costly. Then came 1964 and a breakthrough. From Japan, the country that had a reputation for making "transistorized" (read: small) products out of everything, came an improved electron tube. Smaller than the old magnetron, it put Raytheon on track to placing a microwave oven under everyone's kitchen cabinet.

Needing a consumer-oriented vehicle to sell its new ovens, Raytheon 16
bought up Amana Refrigeration, Inc., in 1965 and put out its first affordable ($495), compact, and practical microwave oven in 1967.

The specter of little microwaves leaking out of the oven scared a lot of 17
people. Their worst fears were realized in 1968 when a test of microwave ovens at Walter Reed Hospital found microwaves did indeed leak out. Federal standards set in 1971 solved that problem.

Today more homes have microwave ovens than dishwashers. And we owe 18
it all to an inquisitive man with a melted candy bar in his pocket and egg on his face.

(Ira Flatow, *They All Laughed . . .*, 1992)

COMPREHENSION CHECKUP

Multiple Choice

Directions: For each item, write the letter corresponding to the best answer.

______ 1. What is the main idea of the selection?
- a. Spencer, a highly inquisitive man with little formal education, is credited with inventing the microwave oven.
- b. Spencer never took anything for granted, including a gooey chocolate bar.
- c. In 1946, Spencer invented microwave popcorn.
- d. Spencer patented 120 inventions.

______ 2. The author's primary purpose is to
- a. inform us of hazards involved in the use of microwaves.
- b. persuade people to buy microwaves.
- c. explain how a microwave oven works.
- d. explain the events leading to the creation of the modern microwave.

______ 3. The original Radarange achieved little acceptance in which of the following situations?
- a. restaurants
- b. ocean liners
- c. railroads
- d. small kitchens

_____ 4. The original Radarange had all of the following qualities **except** for which?
a. cooked food to perfection
b. had large size and weight
c. required water for cooling
d. was very expensive

_____ 5. All of the following led to our modern microwave oven **except** for which?
a. Japan reduced the size of the electron tube.
b. Air cooling fans were introduced.
c. The microwave source was placed at the back.
d. Microwave-safe dishes were invented.

_____ 6. The main idea of paragraph 12 is stated in the first sentence. All the following details support the main idea **except** for which?
a. The meat refused to brown.
b. French fries stayed white and limp.
c. Chefs were driven to distraction.
d. Charles Adams, Raytheon's chairman, turned his kitchen into a proving ground.

_____ 7. In paragraphs 2 and 3, the writer's point of view toward Percy Spencer is
a. favorable.
b. unfavorable.

_____ 8. As used in paragraph 5, the words *inquisitive, self-educated,* and *highly decorated* have a
a. negative connotation.
b. positive connotation.

_____ 9. As used in paragraph 10, the words *woeful* inadequacies have a
a. negative connotation.
b. positive connotation.

_____ 10. The organizational pattern in paragraphs 16 and 17 could be described as
a. listing pattern.
b. spatial order.
c. chronological order.
d. compare and contrast.

True or False

Directions: Indicate whether each statement is true or false by writing **T** or **F** in the space provided.

_____ 11. The magnetron caused the candy bar in Spencer's pocket to melt.

_____ 12. Spencer performed additional experiments with the magnetron using unpopped kernels and raw eggs.

_____ 13. The microwave oven was perfected quickly.

_____ 14. Spencer was chosen to select an appropriate name for his new invention.

_____ 15. Chefs were eager to work with the new oven.

_____ 16. Initially, microwaves leaked out of the ovens.

_____ 17. Homes are more likely to have a dishwasher than a microwave oven.

Vocabulary in Context

Directions: Look through the given paragraph and find a word that matches the definition.

1. announced (1) ____________
2. pessimistic (7) ____________
3. unintentionally (7) ____________
4. resulting (8) ____________
5. experts (10) ____________
6. pitiful (10) ____________
7. kitchen (12) ____________
8. object of fear (17) ____________

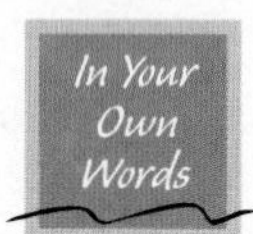

In Your Own Words

1. What does the author admire about Spencer?
2. How was the timing of Spencer's discovery beneficial to the military?
3. What does context tell us about the meaning of the word *inquisitive* in the last sentence of the reading? In paragraph 5?

Written Assignment

Although Spencer lacked formal education, he was a highly successful engineer. In the world today, how likely is it that a person without formal education could achieve success in a technical field? Write a few paragraphs giving your opinion.

Internet Activity

To read a biography of Ira Flatow, check out the following Web site:

www.iraflatow.com/IraFlatow/Home.html

READING

"The public image of policing is heavily influenced by stereotypes about police officers: about who they are, what they believe, and how they act."

TUNING IN TO READING Almost all of us have a point of view about the police that is dependent on our own personal experiences or the experiences of people we know. What image of the police springs to your mind? Is it of the officer pulling someone over to write a ticket for speeding? Is it of the cop breaking up a party of underage drinkers? Is it of a police officer hitting someone with a nightstick? Is it of a detective tracking down a killer or robber or rapist? Are your feelings about the police in the United States largely negative, positive, or neutral?

BIO-SKETCH Dr. Samuel Walker is Isaacson Professor of Criminal Justice at the University of Nebraska at Omaha. He is the author of numerous books and journal articles on policing, criminal justice, and civil liberties. He is currently engaged in research on police accountability systems. Dr. Charles Katz is an associate professor in the Department of Criminal Justice and Criminology at Arizona State University West. He is currently engaged in research on the police response to gangs and police organizational theory.

NOTES ON VOCABULARY

Rorschach The Rorschach inkblot test was developed by the Swiss psychiatrist Hermann Rorschach. A series of inkblots are presented to the individual being tested. He or she then suggests what the inkblots represent. The therapist analyzes the results and makes an assessment about the patient's personality traits.

BEYOND STEREOTYPES OF COPS

Samuel Walker and Charles Katz

How many times have you heard someone make a statement such as "All cops are ___________"? How many jokes have you heard about police officers spending all their time at donut shops? How often have you heard someone say that people became cops because they like to use force? Statements and jokes of this sort reflect negative stereotypes about police officers.

At the same time, how many times have you heard someone say that police officers do no wrong or, more likely, that they have such dangerous and stressful jobs that we should never criticize them for maybe using a little too much force in some situation? This point of view reflects a positive stereotype about police officers. 2

The public image of policing is heavily influenced by stereotypes about police officers: about who they are, what they believe, and how they act. These stereotypes fall into two categories. On the one side, a negative stereotype views officers as uneducated, untrained, prejudiced, brutal, and corrupt. On the other side, a positive stereotype views them as heroic saints, risking their lives in the 3

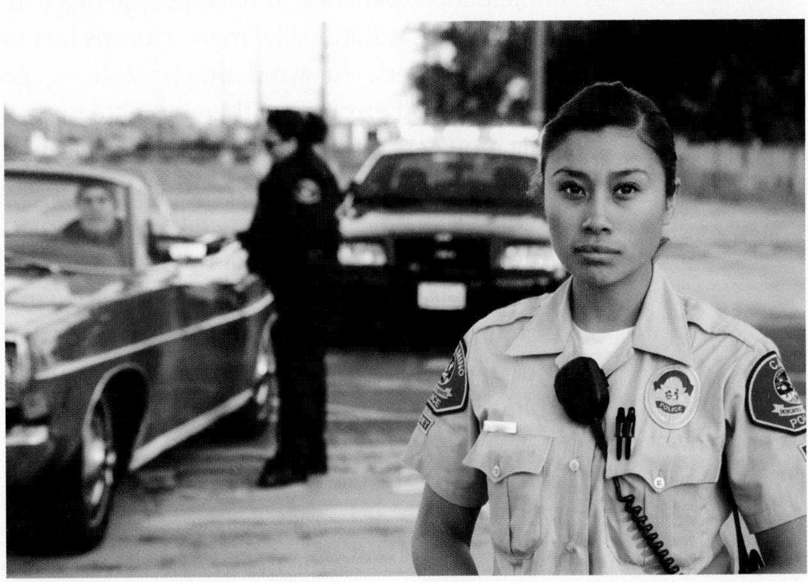

face of hostility from the public, the media, and the courts. Arthur Niederhoffer characterizes the police officer as a "Rorschach in uniform." "To people in trouble the police officer is a 'savior,' but to others he is a 'fierce ogre.'"

Neither stereotype is accurate. As Bayley and Mendelsohn conclude in their 4 study of police–community relations in Denver, the average police officer is rather average. Police officers do not differ significantly from the general population in terms of their values and political beliefs. The special nature of police work does, however, encourage certain attitudes and behavior, and there is a distinct police subculture among officers.

Inaccurate stereotypes about policing affect the recruitment of new officers. 5 The National Center on Women and Policing argues that stereotypes emphasizing officer use of force and the need for physical size and strength discourage women from considering careers in policing. In reality, most police work is uneventful, and police-citizen encounters primarily require communication skills.

Reality Shock: Beginning Police Work

Police officer attitudes toward the public change significantly during the first 6 weeks and months on the job. McNamara found that the percentage of officers agreeing with the statement "Patrolmen almost never receive the cooperation from the public that is needed to handle police work properly" rose from 35 percent at the beginning of academy training to 50 percent after two years on the job. A similar change in attitudes occurred among new Detroit police officers. After four months on the job, officers gave substantially lower ranking to the importance of "listening attentively when the victim expresses feelings or emotions."

Changes in officers' attitudes are the result of several different aspects of 7 police work. Officers encounter some hostility from citizens. This is a shock because officers tend to choose law enforcement as a career because they want to work with people and help the community. Officers also experience being stereotyped, with citizens reacting to the uniform, the badge, and the gun, rather than to them as individuals. As in the case with racial stereotyping, it is an unpleasant experience to have people react to you as a category rather than as an individual. Additionally, many citizens feel uncomfortable around a person with arrest powers. To avoid these reactions, police officers tend to socialize primarily with other officers, thereby increasing their isolation from the public.

Police officers' attitudes also change because they perform society's "dirty 8 work," handling unpleasant tasks that no one else wants to perform or is able to handle. The police see humanity at its worst. They are the first people to find the murder victim, for example. Officers encounter the victims of serious domestic abuse, child abuse, and rape firsthand. In one study, for example, officers ranked dealing with an abused child as the most stressful kind of situation they encounter. These experiences accumulate over time, and eventually give officers a very negative view of humanity.

Police–Community Relations

Conflict between the police and racial and ethnic minority communities is one 9 of the most serious problems in American policing. The focus of the problem in recent years has been the controversy over "driving while black" or "driving while brown" (DWB)—the allegation that the police single out African-American or Hispanic drivers for traffic stops on the basis of their race or ethnicity rather than suspected criminal conduct.

In a survey of Cincinnati residents, 46.6 percent of African-Americans indicated they had been personally hassled by the police, compared with only 9.6 percent of whites. Hassled was defined as being "stopped or watched closely by a police officer, even when you had done nothing wrong." Additionally, 66 percent of African-Americans reported that someone they knew had been hassled, compared with only 12.5 percent of whites. Among many African-American families there is much fear of the police. A *New York Times* article in 1997 described how some African-American and Hispanic parents made a special effort to teach their children to be very respectful of police officers, primarily because they were afraid their children might be arrested, beaten, or even shot if they displayed any disrespect to an officer. 10

The use of deadly force has been the source of major conflict between minorities and the police. James Fyfe concluded that "blacks and Hispanics are everywhere overrepresented among those on the other side of police guns." One of the most controversial incidents in recent years was the fatal shooting of Amadou Diallo by New York City police officers in 1999 (and the subsequent acquittal of officers on criminal charges). Diallo, a Haitian immigrant, was unarmed, and apparently shot while standing in the doorway of his apartment. This shooting, together with other incidents of police misconduct, created a strong feeling among many minorities in the city that they are the target of systematic police abuse. 11

Allegations of police brutality, defined as the use of excessive physical force, represent the most common complaint voiced by minorities about the police. The issue of excessive physical force is particularly complex. Police officers are authorized by department policies to use force in certain situations: to protect themselves, to effect an arrest, to overcome resistance, and to bring a dangerous situation under control. The relevant question is, "when is the use of force excessive?" Officers are supposed to "use only the force necessary to accomplish lawful objectives." 12

Whether or not a certain level of force is necessary in a particular situation is frequently a matter of opinion. It often involves conflicting perceptions of whether a person was resisting arrest, or whether he or she posed a threat to the safety of the officer. The Bureau of Justice Statistics found that police officers used some kind of force in less than 1 percent of all encounters with citizens. About two-thirds of all uses of force are justified, given the circumstances, and about one-third are unjustified, or excessive. Thus, police use excessive force in an estimated one-third of 1 percent (0.3 percent) of all encounters with citizens. 13

Many people believe the 1 percent estimate is too low. The 1 percent estimate, however, acquires a different meaning when examined more closely. The Bureau of Justice Statistics estimate of 421,000 force incidents per year translates into 1,100 per day. Thus, there are about 360 excessive force incidents every day of the year. The result is that a sizable number of racial and ethnic minorities experience police misconduct at one time or another. 14

Summary

Conflict between the police and racial and ethnic communities remains a seri- 15
ous problem in American policing. This problem persists despite general improvements in policing. Many of these problems are the responsibility of the police themselves. At the same time, conflict between police and minorities is a product of the larger structure of racial discrimination in American society.

(Samuel Walker and Charles M. Katz, *The Police in America*, 8/e, 2013)

COMPREHENSION CHECKUP

Multiple Choice

Directions: For each item, write the letter corresponding to the best answer.

_____ 1. In paragraph 3, the authors
- a. discuss positive and negative stereotypes of police officers.
- b. mention that the public's view of the police is influenced by stereotypes.
- c. use antonyms to describe officers as either savior or ogre.
- d. all of the above.

_____ 2. The authors present information that supports all of the following **except** for which?
- a. Police officers do not differ significantly from the populace as a whole.
- b. The majority of police work is high-risk and exciting.
- c. A distinct police subculture does exist.
- d. Women are discouraged from applying for positions as police officers because of the emphasis on brute strength.

_____ 3. Police attitudes toward the public at large
- a. change little over the course of their careers.
- b. change significantly during the first weeks and months on the job.
- c. become more positive.
- d. none of the above

_____ 4. All of the following are true about police officers **except** for which?
- a. Officers frequently encounter hostility from the citizenry they are hired to protect.
- b. Officers tend to choose police work for altruistic reasons.
- c. Officers are treated as individuals.
- d. Officers frequently socialize with other officers.

_____ 5. The police are called upon
- a. to do society's unpleasant tasks.
- b. to deal with victims of domestic abuse.
- c. to deal with murder victims.
- d. all of the above

_____ 6. Minorities frequently say that they are
- a. stopped or watched closely by a police officer even when they have committed no crime.
- b. the victims of excessive force on the part of the police.
- c. treated fairly by the police.
- d. both a and b

______ 7. Officers are authorized by law to use force
a. to protect themselves from danger.
b. to bring control to a possibly dangerous situation.
c. to overcome resistance on the part of a suspect.
d. all of the above

______ 8. The authors mention Amadou Diallo to illustrate
a. videotaped beatings.
b. excessive deadly force.
c. problems with New York City police officers.
d. problems with the Los Angeles Police Department.

True or False

Directions: Indicate whether each statement is true or false by writing **T** or **F** in the space provided.

______ 9. The job of policing tends to isolate the police from the public at large.

______ 10. Among officers there is a distinct police subculture.

______ 11. African Americans are more likely to be hassled by the police than Whites.

______ 12. An officer may properly use as much force as the officer wants regardless of the circumstances.

Fact and Opinion

Directions: Indicate whether each sentence is a statement of fact or expresses an opinion by writing **F** or **O** in the blank provided.

______ 1. Neither stereotype [about police officers] is accurate.

______ 2. As Bayley and Mendelsohn conclude in their study of police–community relations in Denver, the average police officer is rather average.

______ 3. Police officers do not differ significantly from the general population in terms of their values and political beliefs.

______ 4. Officers encounter the victims of serious domestic abuse, child abuse, and rape firsthand.

______ 5. As is the case with racial stereotyping, it is an unpleasant experience to have people react to you as a category rather than as an individual.

______ 6. In one study, for example, officers ranked dealing with an abused child as the most stressful kind of situation they encounter.

______ 7. In a survey of Cincinnati residents, 46.6 percent of African Americans indicated they had been personally hassled by the police, compared with only 9.6 percent of whites.

______ 8. The issue of excessive physical force is particularly complex.

______ 9. The Bureau of Justice Statistics found that police officers used some kind of force in less than 1 percent of all encounters with citizens.

______ 10. At the same time, conflict between police and minorities is a product of the larger structure of racial discrimination in American society.

Vocabulary in Context

Directions: Match each word to its definition. Use each word only once.

acquittal	controversy	corrupt	excessive	hassled
heroic	incidents	isolation	ogre	relevant

1. in fairy tales, a flesh-eating monster or giant ______________
2. found not guilty in a court of law ______________
3. too much or too great ______________
4. by itself; separated ______________
5. pertinent; to the point ______________
6. dispute or disagreement ______________
7. larger than life; brave ______________
8. dishonest; debased ______________
9. annoyed, harassed, disturbed ______________
10. occurrences ______________

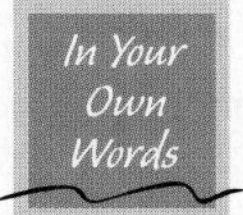

In Your Own Words

1. Many people express anger at the way they feel the police have treated them. In general, do you think the police treat people respectfully or rudely?
2. Although the United States already has the highest percentage of its population in prison of any country in the world, many people say we need to get tougher on crime. What is your opinion?
3. In Youngstown, Ohio, seven principles were established to guide police forces in both established and emerging democracies around the world. Principle 7 is: "The police are expected to discharge their duties in a nondiscriminatory manner." Do you think American police forces are successful in respecting this principle? Why or why not?
4. What is your opinion of reality-based police television shows? Do these shows help the public understand the nature of police work? Or do they offer a one-sided view of police work?
5. How important do you think it is to have a police department that mirrors America? Should police departments strive to actively recruit more women and minorities? How important is it to have bilingual officers?

Written Assignment

Do you think the police are more likely to discriminate against minorities, males, the poor, and the young? Or do you think these groups are more likely to be the ones involved in situations that attract the attention of the police? Write a short essay giving your opinion.

Internet Activity

Consult the following Web site that serves police officers:

www.officer.com

Pull up material of interest to you and write a few paragraphs about it. Does the Web site reflect a general bias? Can you find a more specific bias in each of the topics discussed?

Exercise 8: Scanning an Essay

Directions: The following exercise makes use of a reading selection titled "The American Environment: 'Silent Spring'" found below. Scan the essay to locate the date that corresponds to each of the following statements. Write the date on the line.

TIME LINE FOR "THE AMERICAN ENVIRONMENT: 'SILENT SPRING'"

_________ Gypsy moths are accidentally introduced to the Boston area.

_________ Paul Muller discovers DDT's toxicity to insects.

_________ American scientists become aware of Muller's discovery.

_________ DDT is used on a typhus outbreak in Italy.

_________ DDT enters the marketplace.

_________ Muller is awarded the Nobel Prize in Medicine; DDT-resistant housefly appears.

_________ A DDT-resistant mosquito appears.

_________ Rachel Carson publishes *The Sea Around Us.*

_________ The nature sanctuary behind Olga Huckins's house is sprayed with DDT; a letter is sent to the newspaper and Rachel Carson.

_________ Rachel Carson publishes *Silent Spring.*

_________ Rachel Carson dies of cancer.

_________ The United States bans the sale of DDT.

Now carefully read the essay and answer the questions that follow.

READING

"Silent Spring became one of the most controversial books of the 1960s."

TUNING IN TO READING Rachel Carson in her landmark book, *Silent Spring,* presented a simple message: Artificial pesticides, particularly DDT, are harmful to the health of people, wildlife, and ecosystems. At the time of her book's publication, pesticides were being indiscriminately sprayed over residential neighborhoods, parks, and beaches in the belief that they would cause no harm. Her book is credited with awakening the public to the possible negative effects of both pesticides and industrial chemicals.

BIO-SKETCH Alan Brinkley is the Alan Nevins Professor of History at Columbia University and the author of many books on American history, including *Voices of Protest* (1982), *The End of Reform* (1995), and *Eyes of a Nation* (1998).

NOTES ON VOCABULARY

sanctuary a refuge for wildlife

voracious having a huge appetite; ravenous

wreaking havoc causing great devastation or destruction

THE AMERICAN ENVIRONMENT: "SILENT SPRING"

Alan Brinkley

One summer day in 1957, a small plane flew over the nature sanctuary behind Olga Huckins's house in Duxbury, Massachusetts. It sprayed the land below with an oily mist and then vanished. The next day, Huckins found seven dead songbirds, their beaks gaping in apparent agony. She was so furious that she wrote an angry letter to a local newspaper; as an afterthought, she sent a copy to her friend Rachel Carson. It was one of those small events that alters the course of history.

Carson was a biologist and a gifted writer. Educated at Johns Hopkins University at a time when few women became scientists, she had gone to work for the government as an aquatic biologist, where—despite her painful shyness—she distinguished herself as a writer able to explain scientific issues to a wider public. In the meantime, she began to write popular essays about her special love, the ocean. In 1951 she published *The Sea Around Us.* It became an international best seller, bringing Carson a fame she never imagined and enough income to retire from government. By 1957, when she received Huckins's letter, she was one of the most popular nature writers of her generation. 2

The mist that the plane had sprayed behind Huckins's house was a mixture of ordinary fuel oil and a chemical called dicholoro-diphenyl-trichloroethane: DDT. In 1939, a Swiss chemist named Paul Muller had discovered that although DDT seemed harmless to human beings and other mammals, it was extremely toxic to insects. American scientists learned of Muller's discovery in 1942, just as the army was grappling with the insect-borne tropical diseases—especially malaria and typhus—that threatened American soldiers. 3

Under these circumstances DDT seemed like a godsend. It was first used on a large scale in Italy in 1942–1944 during a typhus outbreak, which it quickly helped end. Soon it was being sprayed in mosquito-infested areas of Pacific islands where American troops were fighting the Japanese. No soldiers suffered any apparent ill effects from the spraying, and the incidence of malaria dropped precipitously. DDT quickly gained a reputation as a miraculous tool for controlling insects, and it undoubtedly saved thousands of lives. For its discovery, Paul Muller was awarded the Nobel Prize in medicine in 1948. With so many benefits and no obvious drawbacks, the new chemical was first released for public use in 1945. DDT entered the marketplace billed as an extraordinarily safe and effective poison, the ultimate weapon against destructive insects. 4

For the next decade, the new chemical continued to live up to its early billing. It helped farmers eliminate chronic pests and was widely used to control mosquitoes. One of its most impressive successes was in virtually eliminating the gypsy moth, a voracious insect that had been stripping the leaves from northeastern forests ever since being accidentally introduced to the Boston area in 1868. 5

By the time Rachel Carson received Olga Huckins's letter, however, signs of trouble were beginning to appear in areas that had been sprayed with the 6 chemical. For one, its effectiveness against certain insects declined as they developed resistance to its effects, so that higher doses were needed to produce the same lethal effect. A resistant housefly had appeared as early as 1948, and a resistant mosquito in 1949.

More worrisome were the chemical's effects on larger animals. Some were killed outright, like the birds in Olga Huckins's back yard. But DDT also seemed to inhibit some animals' ability to reproduce. It would later be learned that the eggshells of certain birds were so thinned by the chemical that young birds were crushed in their nests even before they hatched. The extraordinary persistence of DDT in the environment, and its tendency to accumulate in fatty tissues, meant that animals could concentrate surprising quantities in their flesh. This was especially true of those at the top of food chains—eagles, trout, and, not least, people. Many bird lovers were noting a general reduction in bird populations, and people who fished were catching fewer fish. As the woods became emptier and more silent, DDT seemed the most likely culprit. Rachel Carson had worried about pesticides for years, but it was not until reading Olga Huckins's letter that she decided to do something about them. Meticulously gathering the best available data, she wrote a book that was published in 1962, *Silent Spring.* In it, she warned that the indiscriminate use of pesticides was wreaking havoc with the web of life, destroying wildlife populations, and threatening human health. She wrote of a landscape in which sickness and death threatened animals and people alike, in which "a strange stillness" had replaced the familiar songs of birds. Her eloquence was made all the more urgent by her private knowledge as she finished the book that she herself was dying of cancer. 7

Silent Spring became one of the most controversial books of the 1960s. It sold nearly half a million copies within six months of its publication and was discussed everywhere. The chemical industry was outraged. After first trying to suppress the book's publication altogether and threatening lawsuits against its author and publisher, pesticide manufacturers began a long campaign to discredit Carson and repair the damage her book had done. In the end, though, Carson won at least a partial victory: the U.S. finally banned the sale of DDT in 1972. More important, her book raised public awareness about the threats human activities pose to the natural environment. Although she died in 1964, no single person would be more important in shaping environmental policies over the next thirty years. 8

(Alan Brinkley, *American History*, 11/e, 2003)

COMPREHENSION CHECKUP

True or False

Directions: Indicate whether the statement is true or false by writing **T** or **F** in the space provided.

______ 1. Rachel Carson had a special fondness for the ocean.

______ 2. DDT was responsible for saving thousands of lives.

______ 3. DDT was initially thought to be both safe and effective.

______ 4. Rachel Carson wrote *Silent Spring* to make the public aware of the helpful effects of pesticide use.

______ 5. DDT is toxic to both beneficial and harmful species.

______ 6. As a result of her exposure to pesticides, Rachel Carson contracted cancer.

______ 7. DDT was first used to eradicate typhus in Germany.

______ 8. Some mosquitoes became resistant to DDT.

______ 9. Rachel Carson was praised by the chemical industry.

______ 10. Rachel Carson was a nature writer.

Short Answer

1. What is the author's main idea? ______________________________
____
2. What is the author's position on *Silent Spring?* ______________________
3. Write the words or phrases that suggest the author's position. ____________
____
4. What is the author's position on Rachel Carson? ____________________
5. Write the words that indicate the author's attitude toward Carson ________
____
____
6. Does the author have a bias? If so, what is it? _____________________
____

In Your Own Words

1. Many developing nations continue to apply DDT to control crop pests and to kill mosquitoes because they transmit malaria. Do you think the United Nations should try to end the use of DDT throughout the world?
2. Although the United States banned the use of DDT, U.S. companies still manufacture and export the compound to developing nations. Thus, pesticide-laden food may find its way back to the United States. Environmentalists refer to this as the "circle of poison." How do you feel about this?

Written Assignment

Many scientists credit Rachel Carson and others for making people more environmentally aware. We in the industrialized world consume an enormous quantity of natural resources. What do you think we can do to consume less and reduce our impact on the environment? Write a few paragraphs giving specific suggestions that the average person could implement.

Internet Activity

To read a critical account of Rachel Carson, use a search engine to locate "Rachel Carson's Deadly Fantasies." Write a few paragraphs giving your opinion. What are the author's specific biases? How credible does this information seem to you?

REVIEW TEST 8: Identifying Author Bias

Directions: Use what you learned about connotation and denotation, euphemism, point of view, and fact versus opinion to identify the author's bias. Then state this bias briefly in your own words.

1. Tropical forests (home for 66% of the plant species, 90% of nonhuman primates, 40% of birds of prey, and 90% of insects), used to cover 6–7% of the total land surface of the Earth—an area roughly equivalent to our contiguous 48 states. Every year, humans destroy an area of forest equivalent to the size of Oklahoma.

   At this rate, these forests and the species they contain will disappear completely in just a few more decades. The destruction of tropical rain forests gives only short-term benefits but is expected to cause long-term problems. If tropical rain forests are preserved, the rich diversity of plants and animals will continue to exist for scientific and pharmacological study. One fourth of the medicines we currently use come from tropical rain forests. It is hoped that many of the still unknown plants will provide medicines for other human ills. Worldwide, without tropical rain forests, there could be changes in climate that would affect the entire human race. Preserving these forests is a wise investment. Such action promotes the survival of most of the world's species—indeed, the human species, too.

   (Sylvia S. Mader, *Human Biology,* 8/e, 2004)

   Bias: ____

   ____

2. I can think of some pretty good reasons why vouchers for private schools are a bad idea. First of all, and probably most important, these schemes deprive public schools of the support they deserve. Parents who choose to send their kids to private school still have a responsibility to support public education, not the other way around. Pat Robertson, one of the biggest endorsers of voucher schemes, has said: "They say vouchers would spell the end of public schools in America. To which we say, so what?" What in the world is he thinking? Look, 42 million of our kids go to public school each day. Their future is America's future. No matter what we choose for our own kids, we all have a stake in the success of public education.

   There's something else I want you to understand. Just because vouchers are public money doesn't mean that the participating private schools will be accountable to the public. Wondering about the curriculum at the David Koresh Academy? How about the expulsion policy at the Louis Farrakhan School? Well, stop wondering. It ain't any of your business now, and it will never get to be your business, even if they used your tax dollars to send somebody to these schools.

   (James Carville, *We're Right, They're Wrong,* 1996)

   Bias: ____

   ____

3. Girls today are much more oppressed. They are coming of age in a more dangerous, sexualized and media-saturated culture. They face incredible

pressures to be beautiful and sophisticated, which in junior high means using chemicals and being sexual. As they navigate a more dangerous world, girls are less protected.

As I looked at the culture that girls enter as they come of age, I was struck by what a girl-poisoning culture it was. The more I looked around, the more I listened to today's music, watched television and movies and looked at sexist advertising, the more convinced I became that we are on the wrong path with our daughters. America today limits girls' development, truncates their wholeness, and leaves many of them traumatized.

(Mary Pipher, *Reviving Ophelia,* 1994)

Bias: ______________________________

4. The information age has brought us many wonders, but it has also made possible an unprecedented level of record keeping and high-tech snooping into the lives of others. While we dazzle ourselves in virtual worlds and strange new digital communities that stretch around the globe, it's easy to forget that the same technology that connects us can keep track of us as never before.

   Employers have more freedom to infringe on the privacy of employees than do the police, who still need court approval to tap most telephone or data lines, notes Andre Bacard, author of the *Computer Privacy Handbook.* Supervisors, he says, "can tap an employee's phones, monitor her e-mail, watch her on closed-circuit TV, and search her computer files, without giving her notice."

   (Reed Karaim, "The Invasion of Privacy," 1996)

   Bias: ______________________________

5. As college students you are exposed to loud music and other noise all the time. You go to parties, clubs, and concerts where the volume is so loud you have to shout so the person next to you can hear what you are saying. You turn your personal CD players so high they can be heard halfway across the room. And you seldom give it a second thought. But you should, because excessive noise can have a serious impact on your health and well-being. Noise-induced hearing loss can begin as early as 10 years of age. There are now 21-year-olds walking around with hearing-loss patterns of people 40 years their senior. The problem with hearing loss is that it creeps up on you. Today's hard-rock fans won't notice the effect of their hearing loss for another 15 years. And then it will be too late. Unlike some physical conditions, hearing loss is irreversible. Loud noise damages the microscopic hairs in the inner ear that transmit sound to the auditory nerve. Once damaged, those hairs can never recover and can never be repaired. Now are you convinced? At least think about the possible consequences the next time you are set to pump up the volume on your personal CD player.

   (Stephen E. Lucas, *The Art of Public Speaking,* 8/e, 2004)

   Bias: ______________________________

   ____

6. Super Bowl beer ads, and beer ads in general, have for many years seemed to be directed toward juveniles. Whether or not advertisers do this intentionally, children pick up on them. This kind of advertising impact is especially troublesome because young people see nearly 2,000 commercials for beer and wine each year. For every public service announcement with a message like "Just say no" or "know when to say when," teens will view 25 to 50 beer and wine commercials that say essentially "Drinking is cool." Meanwhile, underage drinking remains a widespread problem. Many young people are beginning to consume alcohol around age 13, and a large majority will do their heaviest drinking before their 21st birthday. Beer advertisements in particular often glamorize drinking and provide no information about the potential negative effects alcohol has on the body, including nausea, blackouts, and liver disease.

   (George Rodman, *Mass Media in a Changing World,* 4/e, 2012)

   Bias: ____

   ____

7. For more than 200 years, America has been known as the "Land of Opportunity" where anyone who works hard can enjoy both material success and the freedom of living in a democracy. Indeed, millions of immigrants from all around the globe have poured into the United States eager to work, learn, and build a better future for themselves and their families. However, for many immigrants and refugees who come to America, the hard work they hope will be the path to the good life often puts them at risk for workplace-related illness and injury. Immigrants who have little education and lack work and language skills often are forced to take jobs that are low-paying, hazardous, or both. They sew for long hours in garment sweatshops, work with hazardous materials like asbestos or toxic chemicals without adequate protection, or labor in settings where they are targets of violent crime. Clearly, all workplaces should be safe and healthy environments for their workers. Just as clearly, immigrants with low levels of skill and education must be protected from a host of workplace hazards that can cause illness, injury, and even death.

   (Wayne A. Payne and Dale B. Hahn, *Understanding Your Health,* 6/e, 2000)

   Bias: ____

8. Thanks to the Internet, many of us have gotten back in touch with old friends; shared photos, histories, and enthusiasms; and become better acquainted with people whom we might never have gotten to know offline. But there are dangers too. If we're not careful our online interactions can hurt our real-life relationships. For example, many of us are too busy to pick up the phone or even write a decent email, yet we spend hours on social-networking sites, uploading photos of us and our friends, forwarding inane quizzes, posting quirky, sometimes nonsensical jokes, or tweeting unimportant information about our latest whereabouts.

   (Brian K. Williams and Stacey C. Sawyer, *Using Information Technology,* 10/e, McGraw-Hill, 2013)

   Bias: ____

   ____

   ____

Chapter Summary and Review

In Chapter 12, you learned to identify writing that has a biased viewpoint and to recognize an author's personal bias. You also learned about the difference between denotative and connotative meanings and between positive and negative connotations. Based on the material in Chapter 12, answer the following.

Short Answer

Directions: List three organizations you think may have a biased point of view, and indicate their bias.

Name of Organization	Bias of Organization
1. ____________________	____________________
2. ____________________	____________________
3. ____________________	____________________

Vocabulary in Context

Directions: Choose one of the following words to complete the sentences below. Use each word only once.

bias euphemism positive

4. Some cities do not admit that they have potholes. Instead, they use a __________ and call their potholes "pavement deficiencies."
5. Three driver-training teachers became part of a jury pool in a drunk-driving case. The judge dismissed them from serving as jurors because of their presumed __________ against drunk drivers.
6. The term *administrator* has a more __________ connotation than the term *bureaucrat.*

CHAPTER 13

Propaganda Techniques, Logical Fallacies, and Argument

CHAPTER PREVIEW

In this chapter, you will

- Learn about persuasive writing techniques.
- Become familiar with common propaganda techniques and logical fallacies.
- Become familiar with the structure of an argument.
- Recognize valid and invalid arguments.
- Become familiar with inductive and deductive reasoning.
- Evaluate persuasive writing selections.

Introduction to Persuasive Writing Techniques

Instead of using neutral, objective language, authors who are trying to persuade sometimes use language designed to arouse readers emotionally. This is often a sign of bias on the author's part and serves as a signal to you that the author is trying to influence you. Authors may use any or all of the following persuasive techniques.

1. **Emotionally loaded language** (connotative language) designed to appeal directly to your feelings rather than your reasoning abilities

In the example below, the boldfaced words have strong emotional power:

> **The promise** of America **sparkles** in the eyes of every child. Their dreams are the **glittering dreams** of America. When those dreams are **dashed,** when **innocent hopes** are **betrayed,** so are the **dreams and hopes** of the entire nation.
>
> (Stephen E. Lucas, *The Art of Public Speaking,* 10/e)

2. **Tear-jerking stories** or references to people and causes that you empathize with

In the example below, the author describes a very sad situation.

> Nathan was only five years old when the fever struck him. At first, no one knew what was wrong. No one knew that parasites inside his body had infected his red blood cells. No one knew those cells were clumping together, choking the flow of blood through his body and damaging his vital organs. No one knew his kidneys would soon fail and seizures would begin. No one knew he would end up in a coma.
>
> The parasites in Nathan's body came from a mosquito bite, a bite that gave him malaria. And Nathan is not alone. The World Health Organization tells us the horrible truth. In Africa, a child dies from malaria every 30 seconds.
>
> (Stephen E. Lucas, *The Art of Public Speaking,* 10/e)

3. **Manipulation of tone**

The author uses irony in the following description of an execution:

> It didn't quite go as planned in Florida recently. The humming of the electricity was joined by a more ominous crackling sound like cellophane crinkling. Then great waves of gray smoke poured out and flames leaped from the prisoner's head. The smell of cooked human flesh and burning hair became pronounced. Despite the evidence to the contrary, proponents of capital punishment hasten to insist that the execution was not "cruel and unusual."

4. **Psychological appeals**

This technique is used frequently by the media to create ads that appeal directly to our desire for safety, power, prestige, sex, or popularity.

> For example, People for the Ethical Treatment of Animals (PETA) used "sex appeal" when it had a series of well-known models and actresses, such as Pamela Anderson, Eva Mendes, Audrina Partridge, and Khloe Kardashian, pose naked to protest the buying of fur coats.

5. Moral appeals

Authors may seek to appeal to your sense of morality or fair play.

C. S. Lewis was a professor of English literature at Oxford and Cambridge Universities. He is known for his writings on Christianity and morality. His tales for children include the popular *The Lion, the Witch, and the Wardrobe* in the Chronicles of Narnia series. Here is Lewis, arguing against experimental surgery on animals:

> If we cut up beasts simply because they cannot prevent us and because we are backing our own side in the struggle for existence, it is only logical to cut up imbeciles, criminals, enemies, or capitalists for the same reason.
>
> (C. S. Lewis, "Vivisection," 1947, 1991)

6. Appeal to authority

Authors may call attention to their own integrity, intelligence, or knowledge—or that of others—to convince you to trust their judgment and believe them.

Judge Alex Kozinski wrote an article for *The New Yorker* magazine supporting the death penalty. Near the beginning of the article, he established his authority on this topic by saying:

> As a judge on the United States Court of Appeals for the Ninth Circuit, I hear cases from nine states and two territories spread over the western United States and Oceania.

When evaluating an appeal to authority, be sure to note the author's affiliations. Look for information that reveals the author's connections with particular people or organizations, as with Kozinski and the U.S. Court of Appeals.

In addition to the persuasive techniques discussed above, authors also may use propaganda or logical fallacies to manipulate the reader.

What Are Propaganda Techniques and Logical Fallacies and How Are They Used?

We have learned the difference between fact and opinion, and we have also discussed bias. Now we are going to look at the related topic of propaganda.

The word *propaganda* was first used by Pope Urban VIII (1623–1644), who created a "congregation for propagating the faith." Thus, **propaganda** originally meant spreading the Christian faith with missionary activity throughout the world. Today *propaganda* refers to the spreading of ideas to further a cause. Political parties often use *propaganda* to persuade people to vote for their candidates or support their programs. Advertising is a form of propaganda designed to persuade consumers that certain products or brands are superior.

Because modern propaganda often makes use of distortion and deception, the word *propaganda* now has a negative sound to it. But propaganda is sometimes destructive and sometimes beneficial. Tobacco companies use propaganda to persuade people to smoke, and more specifically to persuade people to smoke particular brands of cigarettes. Many people would characterize this use of propaganda as destructive because smoking is damaging to health. But in recent years, propaganda has been used in antismoking campaigns to inform people of the dangers of smoking and to try to persuade them to stop smoking. These antismoking campaigns use propaganda for a positive, beneficial purpose.

Propaganda works by using certain techniques to manipulate reason and emotion. Because propaganda is manipulative, it is important for you to be familiar with these techniques so that you will know when propaganda is being directed at you. Once you are aware that propaganda techniques are being used, your knowledge of these techniques will also help you evaluate the accuracy and fairness of the message. Does the message really make sense? Is the cause being promoted by the propaganda something that you want to support? Our special focus is on the use of propaganda techniques in written material. You want to know when a writer is using propaganda techniques so that you can more accurately and fairly evaluate what is being said.

The Institute for Propaganda Analysis was formed in 1937 to study propaganda and educate the American public about it. The institute identified seven propaganda techniques. Other techniques have since been added to the list, including logical fallacies (errors in reasoning). We will discuss the main propaganda techniques and logical fallacies in this chapter and give you some practice in identifying them.

Original Seven Propaganda Techniques

1. **Name-calling (personal attack, ad hominem).** This technique consists of attaching a negative label to a person or thing. Politicians routinely attack one another for changing a position on an issue by calling the offender a "flip-flop." When politicians engage in name-calling, they are usually trying to avoid supporting their own position with facts. Rather than explain what they believe in, they try to tear their opponent down. Many of us engage in the same type of technique when someone disagrees with us. We might call someone we disagree with "radical," "reactionary," "foolish," or "stupid."
2. **Glittering generalities**. This technique involves important-sounding "glad words" that have little or no real meaning. When glad words are used, it is hard to prove or disprove a statement. The words "good," "honest," "fair," and "best" are examples of glad words. When an automobile manufacturer says in an advertisement that its cars are the "best," what does the manufacturer really mean? Does one particular model have the "best" safety record? Have the "best" warranty? Get the "best" mileage?
3. **Transfer**. In this technique, an attempt is made to transfer the prestige of a positive symbol to a person or an idea. At both the Republican and the Democrat national conventions, the backdrop is always the American flag. Politicians want us to think that they are patriotic and will do what is right for the country. Advertising also makes use of transfer. Both the U.S. Postal Service Express Mail and a nationwide legal firm specializing in injury and wrongful death use an eagle in their advertisements.
4. **Testimonial**. This technique is easy to understand. Often big-name models and athletes, as well as movie and TV stars, are paid huge amounts of money to endorse a product. Whenever you see someone famous endorsing a product, ask yourself how much that person knows about the product, and what he or she stands to gain by promoting it. In the area of politics, national political leaders often give ringing endorsements of members of their party who are running for office at the state or local level. They hope to use their prestige to influence the voting.
5. **Plain folks**. This technique uses a folksy approach to persuade us to support someone or something. At election time, politicians appear at local diners,

coffee shops, or malls to prove they are just like us. A man or a woman running for president will be photographed making breakfast, taking out the garbage, or grocery shopping. To sell products such as headache remedies, cereal, or toilet bowl cleaners, advertisers will depict ordinary-looking people doing ordinary activities.

6. **Card stacking**. This term comes from the act of stacking a deck of cards in your favor. Propagandists effectively use card stacking to slant the message. Key words or unfavorable statistics may be omitted in an ad or commercial, leading to a series of half-truths. An advertisement stating that "four out of five dentists surveyed recommend Zest toothpaste" may be true, but it may also fail to disclose that only five dentists were actually contacted, and of those five, four accepted money to provide an endorsement. Keep in mind that an advertiser is under no obligation "to tell the truth, the whole truth, and nothing but the truth." If you go into a car dealership to purchase a new car, the salesperson is not likely to inform you that the model you are interested in has a problem with paint discoloration. The telemarketer trying to solicit funds to feed hungry children in Asia is unlikely to reveal how much of your donation goes to pay his salary and other administrative costs.
7. **Bandwagon (ad populum)**. The bandwagon approach encourages you to think that because everyone else is doing something, you should do it, too, or you'll be left out. When soft drink or beer ads show many attractive people having fun on a beach, they are using bandwagon propaganda. Ads urging you to live it up because it's "Miller time" are using a bandwagon appeal. The technique embodies a "keeping up with the Joneses" philosophy. If a commercial says, "No wonder six million people bought our product last year," they're using the bandwagon technique to exploit the fear of missing out on something.

Exercise 1: Identifying Propaganda Techniques

Directions: The following statements make use of the propaganda techniques we've just studied. For each statement, identify the propaganda technique used. Some techniques will be used more than once.

1. Vote for Jack Hazelhurst. Governor Brown is voting for him. ______________
2. E-Z LIVING recliners are the best that money can buy. ______________
3. Before giving his speech, Senator Jones had the band play "The Star-Spangled Banner." ______________
4. Basketball star Michael James says, "You should buy QuickLift tennis shoes. They'll help you lift off for a great day." ______________
5. Congressional candidate Fred Goodwin says that people should vote for him because he is fair, honest, and kind. ______________
6. In a recent interview, Governor Herman said that those who oppose his reform measures are "misguided, arrogant fools." ______________
7. Hurry down to our car dealership before we sell our last sale car. ______________
8. Governor Swellguy put on a hard hat and took a tour of the new mining operations at National Mining Company. ______________
9. All the guys down at Barney's Bar drink Blitz beer. ______________

10. Brightwhite toothpaste makes your smile bright again. It gets rid of ugly discoloration caused by coffee and tea. It makes that special person in your life eager to get close. ______________

11. Mayor Walker is for the little guy. You don't see him driving an expensive car or sending his daughter to a private school. ______________

12. My opponent has been stingy in helping the nation's unemployed. And he ignorantly voted against all the bills to build a rapid transit system. ______________

More Propaganda Techniques and Logical Fallacies

The following were not part of the original seven techniques identified by the Institute for Propaganda Analysis in 1937. They were added at a later date and are known as both propaganda techniques and *logical fallacies or errors in reasoning.*

8. **False analogy (false comparison).** In this fallacy, two things that may or may not really be similar are portrayed as being similar. The store brand can of peas may look like the name brand, but is it exactly the same? We have to ask ourselves several questions to determine the answer. For instance, are the peas of the same quality? Are they the same size? Are there as many peas in the can? In most false analogies, there is simply not enough evidence available to support the comparison.
9. **Either/or fallacy.** This fallacy is also called "black-and-white thinking" because only two choices are given. You are either for something or against it; there is no middle ground or shades of gray. People who exhibit this type of thinking have a "bumper sticker" mentality. They say things like "America—love it or leave it" and "Put up or shut up." According to this line of reasoning, you are either in favor of gun control or against it, or in favor of abortion or opposed to it. When we attempt to polarize an issue, we negate all attempts to find a common ground.
10. **Circular reasoning (begging the question).** In this fallacy, the conclusion simply restates the information presented as evidence. Here's an example: "She lost the election because she didn't get enough votes." Here's another example: "The team is in first place because they've won more games than the other teams."
11. **Red herring.** This fallacy involves directing attention away from a debatable point to one that is irrelevant (the red herring). By changing the topic, the discussion goes in a new, unhelpful direction. Here's an example: "I know I forgot to buy groceries, but nothing I do ever pleases you." This is similar to what students do when they try to distract the teacher with lots of questions in order to postpone a scheduled test.
12. **Hasty generalization (stereotyping).** In this fallacy, assumptions are made about a whole group based on an inadequate sample. Stereotypes fall into this category. Here are some examples of hasty generalizations. Mark hears that both Tracy and Melanie were in accidents, so he says that "women drivers are worse than men." Or Roberta sees that all her female friends are struggling with math but her male friends are doing well, so she says that "men are better than women in math." In both of these examples, the sample population is just too small to support the broad conclusion.
13. **Faulty cause and effect.** This fallacy suggests that because B follows A, A must *cause* B. When we hear people say, "I know it's going to rain today

because I just washed my car," they are guilty of faulty cause and effect. Remember, just because two events or two sets of data are related does not necessarily mean that one caused the other to happen. It is important to evaluate the data carefully and not jump to the wrong conclusion. Is the man in the cartoon guilty of faulty cause and effect?

ZAHN
"WILL YOU SHUT THAT THING OFF? THE MAN IS PUTTING!"

Bob Zahn. www.cartoonfile.net. Reprinted with permission.

Exercise 2: Identifying Propaganda Techniques and Logical Fallacies

Directions: The following statements make use of propaganda techniques and logical fallacies 8–13. For each statement, identify the technique used. Some techniques will be used more than once.

1. You are either part of the solution or part of the problem. ______________
2. Jeremy saw Mike hanging out with Tim, who has just gotten out of jail. "Now Mike will end up in jail, too," he said. ______________
3. Having a pit bull or a Rottweiler in the home around small children is dangerous because it's unsafe. ______________
4. Yang Chow Chinese dinners are just as good and appetizing as what is served in expensive Hong Kong restaurants. ______________
5. All college students have a lot of credit card debt. ______________
6. I feel lucky today, so my favorite basketball team is going to win. ______________
7. We can communicate effectively with people all the way around the world, so it should be easy for parents to communicate with their own kids in their own house. ______________
8. People shouldn't get upset when drivers who are texting cause traffic accidents. After all, drivers cause accidents when they eat in the car, too. ______________
9. College students today are lazy and irresponsible. ______________
10. Either he is a genius or he is a fraud. ______________

Exercise 3: Analyzing a Propaganda Technique

What propaganda technique does the "got milk?" ad illustrate? To whom do you think the ad is likely to appeal? Write your answers on the lines below the ad.

The taste of fame.
Center stage, silver screen, joyful new mom. How do I keep this show on the road? Milk. Its wholesome goodness helps make my family strong at every stage. Talk about a powerful performance.
got milk?
whymilk.com/jenniferhudson

REVIEW TEST 9: Propaganda Techniques and Logical Fallacies

Directions: For each passage, identify the propaganda technique being used.

______________ 1. "Get behind the wheel of the most popular car on the road today!"

______________ 2. "You need a toothpaste that does it All. All toothpaste fights cavities, plaque, bad breath, and gingivitis. Plus it brightens your smile. Face your day the All-prepared way!"

______________ 3. "Either this community votes to fund mass transit or all of us will be personally affected by gridlock on our streets."

______________ 4. Sports star: "I've tried every brand of pain relief medication on the market, and, believe me, nothing out there works better than Pain-away."

______________ 5. Politician running for election: "When I was very young, my father died, leaving my mother with debt and no way to support our family. Unlike my opponent, I know what it's like to struggle to put food on the table and pay the bills. Give me your vote on election day."

______________ 6. Broncos fan watching the Super Bowl on TV: "I better go away. Every time I come in to watch the game, the Packers score a touchdown."

______________ 7. "My opponent for the school board has the morals of an alley cat. Maybe his wife can tolerate his 'affairs' but the rest of us should not allow him to become a role model to our children."

______________ 8. "A lot of us want only the best—the best house, in the best neighborhood, with the best car in our garage. Don't you think it's about time to be thinking about the best phone service? Call 1-800-BEST for a free consultation."

______________ 9. "Your sister has always gotten good grades and worked part-time to pay for her expenses. Don't you think you should be doing the same?"

______________ 10. "This is Chuck Jones standing in front of 'Old Faithful' in Yellowstone National Park. Remember to use Old Faithful laxative if you have problems with irregularity."

______________ 11. "How dare my opponent accuse me of fraud when I'm working hard for the American people!"

______________ 12. Mark's girlfriend left him for somebody else, so he said to his friend Mike, "You just can't trust women."

______________ 13. Marijuana should not be legalized because it's against the law to legalize drugs.

READING

"To be a careful and informed health consumer, you need to consider the effects that alcohol advertisements have on you."

TUNING IN TO READING Alcohol is considered by many health experts to be the most widely used and destructive drug in the United States. It is currently the third leading cause of early death. Alcohol is considered to be destructive because of the devastating effects of drinking and driving and the consequences of increased crime, physical and sexual abuse, and destroyed family relationships associated with overindulgence in alcohol. It is estimated that over 17 million people in the United States have a significant problem with alcohol. To learn more about the effects of alcohol advertising, read the following excerpt and then answer the questions that follow.

BIO-SKETCH Both Paul M. Insel and Walton T. Roth are professors at Stanford University Medical School.

NOTES ON VOCABULARY

nonconformist a person who refuses to conform to established customs, attitudes, or ideas

logo a graphic representation or symbol of a company name or trademark

ALCOHOL AND ADVERTISING

by Paul M. Insel and Walton T. Roth

Our society teaches us attitudes toward drinking that contribute to alcohol-related problems. Many of us have difficulty expressing disapproval about someone who has drunk too much, and we are amused by the antics of the "funny" drunk. We accept the alcohol industry's linkage of drinking with virility or sexuality. And many people treat nondrinkers as nonconformists in social settings. To be a careful and informed health consumer, you need to consider the effects that alcohol advertisements have on you. Are alcohol ads harmless fun? Or can they have more serious effects? How do such ads affect you?

Alcohol manufacturers spend $2 billion every year on advertising and promotions. They claim that the purpose of their advertising is to persuade adults who already drink to choose a certain brand. But in reality, ads cleverly engage young people and children—never overtly suggesting that young people should drink, but clearly linking alcohol and good times. Alcohol ads are common during televised sporting events and other shows popular with teenagers. Studies show that the more TV adolescents watch, the more likely they are to take up drinking in their teens. New alcoholic drinks geared to the taste of young people are heavily promoted. "Hard lemonade" and other fruity or sweetened drinks ("alcopops" or "low-alcohol refreshers") have been described by teens as a way to get drunk without suffering the bitter taste of most alcoholic beverages. Though only recently introduced, these drinks have been tried by almost half of 14–18-year-olds. 2

Alcohol manufacturers also reach out to young people at youth-oriented activities like concerts and sporting events. Product logos are heavily marketed through sales of T-shirts, hats, and other items. Many colleges allow alcohol manufacturers to advertise at campus events in exchange for sponsorship. 3

What is the message of all these advertisements? Think about the alcohol ads you've seen. Many give the impression that drinking alcohol is a normal part of everyday life and good times. This message seems to work well on the young, many of whom believe that heavy-duty drinking at parties is normal and fun. The use of famous athletes or actors in commercials increases the appeal of alcohol by associating it with fame, wealth, sex, and popularity. Many beer advertisements, for example, portray beer drinking as a critical part of one's success in finding an attractive mate. 4

What ads don't show is the darker side of drinking. You never see hangovers, car crashes, slipping grades, or violence. Although some ads include a brief message such as "know when to say when," the impact of such cautions is small compared to that of the image of happy, attractive young people having fun while drinking. 5

The next time you see an advertisement for alcohol, take a critical look. What is the message of the ad? What audience is being targeted, and what is the ad implying about alcohol use? Be aware of its effect on you. 6

(Paul M. Insel and Walton T. Roth, *Core Concepts in Health,* 12/e, McGraw-Hill, 2011, pp. 291–292)

COMPREHENSION CHECKUP

______ 1. Which of the following best expresses the main idea of the excerpt?
   a. "Alcohol manufacturers also reach out to young people at youth-oriented activities like concerts and sporting events."
   b. "We accept the alcohol industry's linkage of drinking with virility or sexuality."
   c. "To be a careful and informed health consumer, you need to consider the effects that alcohol advertisements have on you."
   d. "You never see hangovers, car crashes, slipping grades, or violence."

______ 2. Which of the following can be inferred from the excerpt?
   a. The author is not likely to approve of alcohol-related ads featuring rock stars and beach party scenes.
   b. The author would be more comfortable with alcohol ads if they didn't feature rock stars.
   c. The author thinks that many young people are not aware of the effect of alcohol advertising on them.
   d. both a and c

______ 3. Which of the following statements best states the author's bias?
   a. "Alcohol ads are common during televised sporting events and other shows popular with teenagers."
   b. "Our society teaches us attitudes toward drinking that contribute to alcohol-related problems."
   c. "Product logos are heavily marketed through sales of T-shirts, hats, and other items."
   d. "New alcoholic drinks geared to the taste of young people are heavily promoted."

_____ 4. Which of the following sentences is a statement of fact?
   a. "But in reality, ads cleverly engage young people and children—never overtly suggesting that young people should drink, but clearly linking alcohol and good times."
   b. "Alcohol advertisers spend $2 billion every year on advertising."
   c. "What ads don't show is the darker side of drinking."
   d. "We accept the alcohol industry's linkage of drinking with virility or sexuality."

_____ 5. In this excerpt, the author shows bias against
   a. alcohol manufacturers.
   b. the American teen.
   c. college fraternities and sororities.
   d. televised sporting events.

_____ 6. The author of this excerpt has created a tone that could be described as
   a. humorous.
   b. serious.
   c. ambivalent.
   d. ironic.

_____ 7. Which of the following can we infer from the reading?
   a. The author thinks that television advertising is not likely to have much effect on the behavior of young people.
   b. The author thinks that parental figures are likely to have the most influence on a young person's attitude toward drinking alcohol.
   c. The author thinks that long-term exposure to advertising promoting alcohol affects the behavior of young people.
   d. none of the above

_____ 8. The statement "Studies show that the more TV adolescents watch, the more likely they are to take up drinking in their teens" implies a
   a. cause-and-effect relationship.
   b. compare and contrast relationship.
   c. classification and division relationship.
   d. definition and example relationship.

_____ 9. A famous actor is promoting alcohol in an advertisement that features an extravagant party on a yacht. This ad makes use of __________ propaganda techniques.
   a. bandwagon and testimonial
   b. glittering generality and plain folks
   c. name-calling and false analogy
   d. none of the above

_____ 10. The television shows *Cougar Town*, *Jersey Shore*, and *The Real Housewives* feature a great deal of drinking. Critics of the show contend that the drinking is portrayed as a harmless and sociable activity. Which idea from the excerpt do these TV shows illustrate?
   a. "the darker side of drinking"
   b. "alcohol and good times"
   c. "know when to say when"
   d. "low-alcohol refreshers"

Vocabulary in Context

Directions: Use the context clues in the sentences below to determine the meaning of the italicized word.

1. Many of us have difficulty expressing *disapproval* about someone who has drunk too much. (paragraph 1)

   disapproval: ______________________

2. we are amused by the *antics* of the "funny" drunk (paragraph 1)

   antics: ______________________

3. We accept the alcohol industry's *linkage* of drinking with virility or sexuality. (paragraph 1)

   linkage: ______________________

4. ads cleverly engage young people and children—never *overtly* suggesting that young people should drink, but clearly linking alcohol and good times. (paragraph 2)

   overtly: ______________________

5. New alcoholic drinks *geared* to the taste of young people are heavily *promoted.* (paragraph 2)

   geared: ______________________

   promoted: ______________________

6. Many beer advertisements, for example, *portray* beer drinking as a critical part of one's success in finding an attractive mate. (paragraph 4)

   portray: ______________________

7. the *impact* of such cautions is small (paragraph 5)

   impact: ______________________

8. What audience is being *targeted,* and what is the ad *implying* about alcohol use? (paragraph 6)

   targeted: ______________________

   implying: ______________________

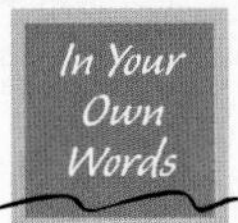

In Your Own Words

1. What do you think about lowering the legal drinking age from 21 to 18? Will allowing 18-year-olds to possess alcohol make it easier for those younger than 18 to have easy access to alcohol?
2. What do you think is the effect of a parent's permissiveness about teenage drinking on teenage drinking behavior? Do you think parental attitudes toward drinking influence drinking behavior in college?

Written Assignment

What do you think about ignition-interlock devices for prevention of DUI (driving under the influence [of alcohol]) offenses? These devices use an infrared sensor to detect blood alcohol (BAC) levels. When the driver of a vehicle pushes the start button, the infrared sensor will detect the BAC level. If the driver has a BAC greater than 0.08, the car will not start. Do you think installation of this technology in all cars would be a justified safety measure, or do you think it would be a violation of civil liberties?

Internet Activity

Consult one of the following Web sites. Write a list of the best tips you receive from the site.

www.collegedrinkingprevention.gov
http://camy.org/
www.health.org

READING

"The rush to smoke was also fueled by the fight for suffrage; women wanted equality."

TUNING IN TO READING More than 226,000 Americans were diagnosed as having lung cancer in 2012. Lung cancer kills more people than the combined death toll from alcohol, cocaine, heroin, homicide, suicide, automobile accidents, and AIDS. Although smoking in the United States has declined markedly, millions of Americans—particularly the young—still smoke. Smoking is also more common among people who are highly stressed, divorced or separated, unemployed, or in the military.

BIO-SKETCH Dr. Stanley J. Baran has had a long and distinguished academic career. He currently teaches at Bryant College in Rhode Island, where he is chair of the Communications Department. In addition to earning numerous awards for both research and teaching excellence, Dr. Baran has published over 10 books.

NOTES ON VOCABULARY

suffrage the right to vote in political elections. The U.S. Constitution states, "No state shall be deprived of its equal *suffrage* in the Senate."

crusade a vigorous movement or enterprise on behalf of a cause. Originally, the word referred to the Crusades, which were European military expeditions in the 11th–13th centuries to "recover" the Holy Lands from the Muslims.

coup a highly successful act. *Coup* came from the French word meaning "blow" or "stroke," as in *coup d'état.* Among the Plains Indian tribes, *coup* referred to a daring deed performed by a warrior in battle against an enemy.

taboo something prohibited or forbidden. In Fijian, a Polynesian language, the word originally meant "marked as holy." The first *taboos* were prohibitions against the use or mention of certain things. Violating a *taboo* was believed to make the gods angry.

BOOSTING SMOKING AMONG WOMEN AND CHILDREN

Stanley J. Baran

Into the early 1900s, smoking was seen as an unsavory habit, permissible for men, never for women. But with the turn of the century, women too wanted to light up. Advertising campaigners first began targeting female smokers in

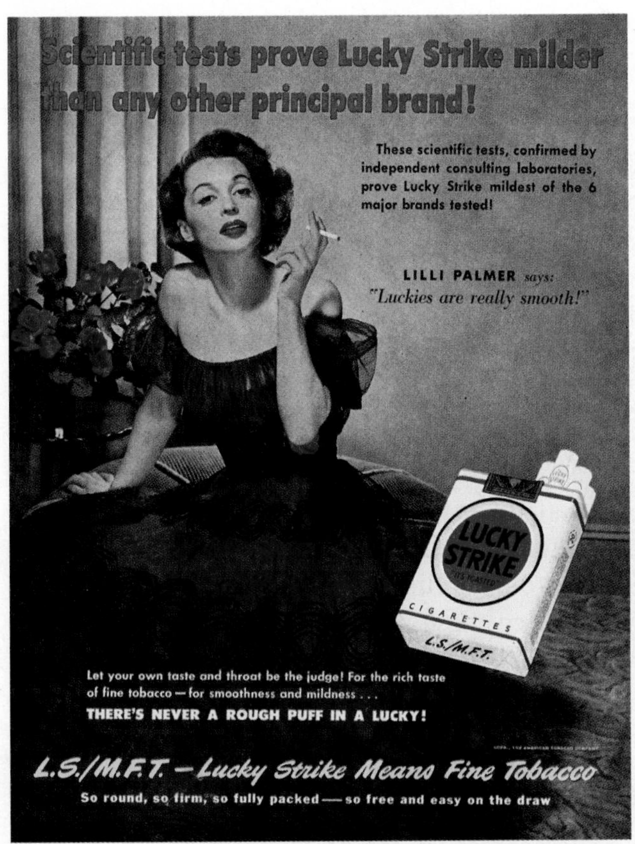

Lucky Strike used advertising and an effective public relations campaign to break the taboo on women smokers.

1919. The American Tobacco Company slogan "Reach for a Lucky instead of a sweet," along with ads designed to help women understand that they could use cigarettes to keep their figures, was aimed at this new market. The rush to smoke was also fueled by the fight for suffrage; women wanted equality. The right to vote was an important goal, but if men could smoke without a fight, why couldn't women?

As more women began to smoke, anti-smoking crusades attempted to deter them. The protection of women's morality, not their health, inspired the crusaders. Many cities forbade the use of tobacco by women in public places. Yet the number of women who started smoking continued to grow. George Washington Hill, head of American Tobacco, wanted this lucrative market to continue to expand, and he wanted to own as large a part of it as possible. He turned to public relations and Edward Bernays. 2

A nephew of Sigmund Freud, Bernays was employed to conduct psychological research aimed at understanding the relationship between women and cigarettes. He learned that women saw cigarettes as symbols of freedom, as the representation of their unfair treatment in a man's world, and as a sign of their determination to be accepted as an equal. 3

Bernays had several objectives: (1) to let the public know that it was quite all right for women to smoke; (2) to undercut the bans on public smoking by women that existed in many places; and (3) to position Lucky Strike cigarettes as a progressive brand. 4

In meeting these goals, Bernays perpetrated a publicity stunt that is still heralded as a triumphant coup among public relations practitioners. New York City had a ban on public smoking by females. Because of, rather than despite this, Bernays arranged for 10 socially prominent young women to enter the 1929 annual Easter Parade down Fifth Avenue as "The Torches of Liberty Contingent." As they marched, the debutantes lit their Lucky "torches of freedom" and smilingly proceeded to puff and walk. For reporters on the scene, this made for much better news and photos than the usual little kids in their spring finery. The blow for female emancipation was front-page news, not only in New York, but nationally. The taboo was dead. 5

Later in his life, Bernays would argue that had he known of the link between cigarette smoking and cancer and other diseases, he would never have taken on American Tobacco as a client. 6

In the 1980s as U.S. levels of smoking continued to decline, R. J. Reynolds introduced a new campaign for its Camel brand cigarettes. The campaign 7

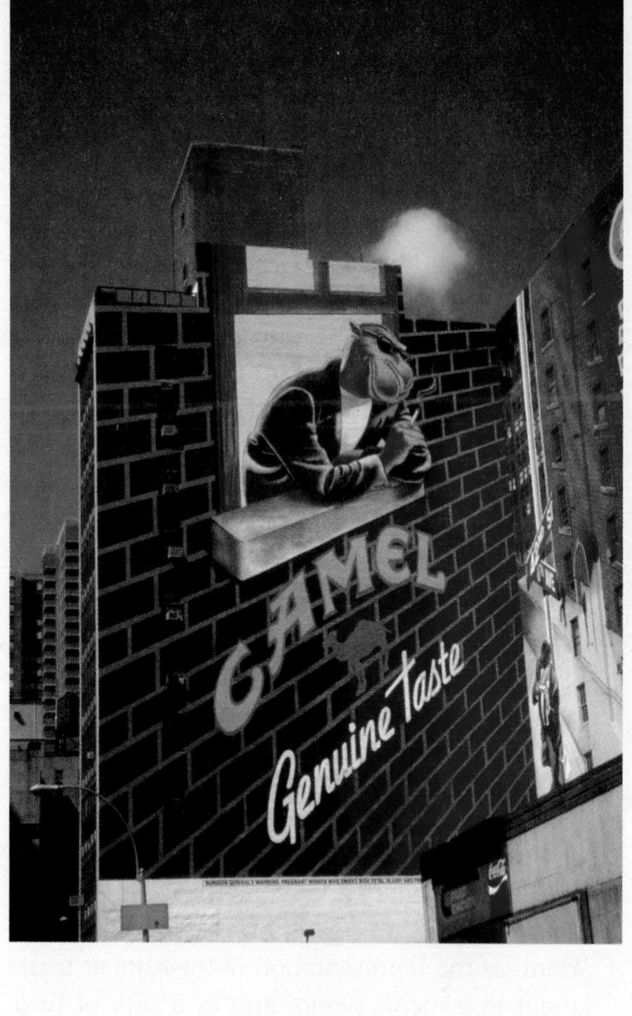

featured a sun-bleached, cool, and casual camel who possessed human qualities. Joe Camel, as he was called, was debonair, in control, and the center of attention, whether in a pool hall, on a dance floor, leaning against his convertible, or lounging on the beach. He wore the hippest clothes. He sported the best sunglasses. R. J. Reynolds said it was trying a new campaign to boost brand awareness and corner a larger portion of a dwindling market. But antismoking groups saw in Joe Camel the echo of Edward Bernays' strategy to open smoking to an untapped market. They accused the company of attempting to attract young smokers—often adding that these were the lifelong customers the tobacco company needed to replace those it was killing.

The battle heated up in 1991, and an entire 8
issue of the *Journal of the American Medical Association* was devoted to the impact of smoking on the culture. One of the articles reported on a study of Joe Camel's appeal to youngsters. Researcher Dr. Joseph DiFranza had discovered that Joe Camel was the single most recognizable logo in the country. Children as young as 3 years old could recognize Joe, and more kids could identify him than could identify Mickey Mouse.

R. J. Reynolds attempted to discredit the study and its author and claimed 9
that it had a First Amendment right to advertise its legal product any way it wanted. Nonetheless, soon after the publication of the *JAMA* issue, antismoking activist Janet Mangini filed a lawsuit in San Francisco against the tobacco company. Several California counties and cities joined the suit, alleging that the Joe Camel campaign violated state consumer protection laws designed to protect minors from false or misleading tobacco advertising.

Just before it was to go to trial in 1997, the country's second largest 10
tobacco company, while admitting no wrongdoing, agreed to settle out of court with a payment of $10 million. It also agreed to a court order to suspend the Joe Camel campaign, the first time in history that a tobacco company had been forced to abandon an advertising campaign. What may have encouraged the cigarette company to cooperate were internal memos in the hands of the court that would later be made public. An R. J. Reynolds Tobacco memo from 1975 said: "To ensure increased and long-term growth for Camel Filter, the brand must increase its share penetration among the 14–24 age group." Other memos identified target smokers as young as 12 years old!

(Stanley J. Baran, *Introduction to Mass Communication*, McGraw-Hill, 7/e, 2013)

COMPREHENSION CHECKUP

Multiple Choice

Directions: For each item, write the letter corresponding to the best answer on the line provided.

_____ 1. All of the following are true according to the selection **except** for which?
a. Women wanted men to quit smoking.
b. Women wanted to enjoy the same privileges as men.
c. Women viewed smoking as a liberating activity.
d. Women worried about their weight.

_____ 2. We can conclude that Edward Bernays
a. always took pride in his association with American Tobacco.
b. helped change public attitudes about women and smoking.
c. masterminded a public relations success.
d. both b and c

_____ 3. By using "10 socially prominent young women" to smoke their "torches of freedom" in the Easter Parade, Bernays employed all of the following propaganda techniques **except**
a. testimonial.
b. name-calling.
c. bandwagon.
d. transfer.

_____ 4. For women in the early 1900s, Lucky Strike cigarettes were associated with all of the following **except**
a. emancipation.
b. slimness.
c. glamour.
d. disease.

_____ 5. In paragraph 5, "the taboo was dead" suggests that
a. women were now permitted to vote.
b. women were now free to smoke in public places.
c. women no longer received less pay for the same work.
d. women were free to work outside the home.

_____ 6. In paragraph 7, the word *debonair* means
a. suave.
b. careless.
c. crotchety.
d. none of the above

_____ 7. In paragraph 7, the word *But* signals
a. classification and division.
b. definition.
c. example.
d. contrast.

_____ 8. As used in paragraph 7, "corner a larger portion" means to
a. relinquish a part of.
b. engender awareness of.
c. push to the side.
d. gain control of.

_____ 9. R. J. Reynolds Tobacco
a. felt that it should be allowed to advertise cigarettes any way that it desired.
b. tried to discredit DiFranza's study.
c. agreed to discontinue using Joe Camel in its advertisements.
d. all of the above

True or False

Directions: Indicate whether each statement is true or false by writing **T** or **F** in the space provided.

_____ 10. Smoking was once seen as a man's activity.

_____ 11. "Cool" Joe Camel was designed to appeal to the young.

_____ 12. DiFranza discovered that Mickey Mouse was the most recognized logo in the United States.

_____ 13. Just one California city sued R. J. Reynolds.

_____ 14. R. J. Reynolds admitted to targeting children with its Joe Camel campaign.

Vocabulary in Context

Directions: Use context clues to determine the meaning of the italicized word, and then write a definition for that word in the space provided.

1. smoking was seen as an *unsavory* habit (paragraph 1)
Definition: ____________________

2. the rush to smoke was also *fueled* by the fight (paragraph 1)
Definition: ____________________

3. antismoking crusades attempted to *deter* them (paragraph 2)
Definition: ____________________

4. wanted this *lucrative* market to continue to expand (paragraph 2)
Definition: ____________________

5. a publicity stunt that is still *heralded* as a triumphant coup (paragraph 5)
Definition: ____________________

6. the *echo* of Edward Bernays's strategy (paragraph 7)
Definition: ____________________

7. corner a larger portion of a *dwindling* market (paragraph 7)
Definition: ____________________

8. most recognizable *logo* in the country (paragraph 8)
Definition: ____________________

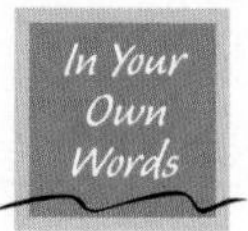

In Your Own Words

1. Whose responsibility is it to educate young people about the dangers of smoking? Parents? The public school system? The federal government? Cigarette manufacturers?

2. The ad on page 455 features the movie star Lilli Palmer. What propaganda techniques are being used here to promote the Lucky Strike brand?
3. In 2010, more than 30% of PG-13 films featured tobacco imagery, a disturbing trend given that the National Cancer Institute concluded that adolescents imitate the smoking they see in the movies. What propaganda technique is being used by the tobacco industry? Do you think that movies rated for young people should be smoke-free?
4. Although smoking has declined in the United States, it has actually increased in the rest of the world, partly because of aggressive marketing campaigns by U.S. tobacco companies. Because many of the poorest countries do not warn their citizens about the dangers of smoking, children as young as 7 and 8 smoke in these countries. Should tobacco companies be required to inform the citizens of all countries about the health risks of smoking?

Written Assignment

The Virginia Slims brand of cigarettes was introduced by Philip Morris in 1968. Throughout the 1970s and 1980s, Philip Morris promoted this product with the slogan "You've come a long way, baby." One panel of the ad would depict women stacking wood for stoves or washing the laundry by hand and then hanging it out on clotheslines to dry. The other panel would depict a stylish, sexy woman doing modern activities. Do some research on the original ad campaign. Why do you think the word "slim" was included in the brand name of the cigarette? Can you identify other brands that are designed to appeal to specific segments of society? Should tobacco companies be allowed to target particular groups?

Internet Activity

The character of Joe Chemo, a camel who wished he'd never smoked, was developed by Scott Pious, a psychology professor at Wesleyan University. Check out the Joe Chemo Web site at:

www.joechemo.org

Then test your tobacco IQ in the 10-item test to get your "smoke-o-scope." Do you think the tips on quitting are likely to help long-term smokers?

The Structure of an Argument

An argument takes one side of an issue that people disagree about. For instance, the question "Do many athletes use performance-enhancing drugs?" is not a debatable issue. We can answer it with research and statistical evidence. However, if we change the question to "Should performance-enhancing drugs be allowed in sports?" we have a debatable issue. That is because drug use in sports is a controversial topic. Some people will support allowing performance-enhancing drugs in sports and others will oppose it.

The Parts of an Argument

An argument has four parts or characteristics: the issue, the claim, the evidence, and the assumptions.

Issue: a controversial or debatable subject. It must be something about which people have differing opinions, such as illegal immigration or the death penalty.

Claim: the key point. This is what the author is trying to prove. All the following are claims: Convicted felons should be allowed to vote. The space shuttle program should be continued. Illegal immigrants should be allowed a path to citizenship.

Evidence: support given by the author for the claim. It can be almost anything that could be persuasive, such as facts, statistics, expert opinion, research, personal experience, or experiences of others.

Assumptions: things that the author believes to be true but may or may not be true. If someone is always checking books out of the library, we assume they like to read. If someone exercises three times a week, we assume that this person values fitness. Authors sometimes do not state their assumptions.

Exercise 4: Writing Opposing Claims

Directions: For each of the following claims, write an opposing claim.

EXAMPLE

Claim: Schools should have programs that help students stay physically fit.

Opposing Claim: Schools should keep their focus exclusively on academic goals.

1. **Claim:** Texting while driving should be made illegal.

   Opposing Claim: ______________________________

2. **Claim:** The death penalty should be abolished in the United States.

   Opposing Claim: ______________________________

3. **Claim:** The use of marijuana for medical purposes should be prohibited.

   Opposing Claim: ______________________________

4. **Claim:** The selling of beef from cattle that were given growth hormones should be banned.

   Opposing Claim: ______________________________

5. **Claim:** State lotteries should be abolished.

   Opposing Claim: ______________________________

Exercise 5: Identifying the Evidence That Supports the Claim

Directions: Each group of sentences below begins with a claim. Some of the sentences directly support the claim and some don't. Put an **S** (for support) on the line next to a sentence that directly supports the claim. Leave the other sentences blank.

EXAMPLE

Claim: High schools should use iPads instead of textbooks as learning tools.

______ The iPad is just a cool new toy that students will play with for a while before becoming bored by it.

______ In contrast to textbooks, iPads allow students to correspond with their teachers, file papers and homework assignments, and keep a digital record of their work.

______ The educational value of iPads has yet to be demonstrated.

______ iPads extend the learning experience beyond what can be found between the covers of a textbook.

______ The money spent on iPads would be better spent trying to recruit, train, and retain teachers, says Larry Cuban, professor of education at Stanford University.

______ iPads are lightweight and offer students relief from hauling around heavy textbooks that weigh down their backpacks.

1. **Claim:** Colleges should make more of an effort to reduce excessive drinking by students.

______ When school administrations try to further regulate drinking, they simply make students more secretive about it.

______ The National Institute on Alcohol Abuse and Alcoholism estimates that 1,700 college students between ages 18 and 24 die of alcohol-related causes each year, while about 600,000 suffer from alcohol-related injuries.

______ Nearly 25 percent of all college students report academic consequences of excessive drinking, including missing class, falling behind, doing poorly on exams or papers, and receiving lower grades overall.

______ Most college drinking takes place off campus.

______ There are practical steps that colleges can take to reduce excessive drinking by students, such as requiring incoming freshmen to attend an orientation session on alcohol abuse.

2. **Claim:** College students should be taught to be cautious in their use of online social network sites such as Facebook.

______ Students can easily be drawn into spending too much time on such sites, causing their studies to suffer.

______ These sites give students an easy, convenient way to keep in touch with friends and relatives.

______ Students are well aware of the advantages of these sites, but they have little understanding of their dangers.

______ Activities on these sites that students view as harmless fun may be held against them years later by a potential employer doing a background check.

______ These sites can provide students with a way to relieve the stress of college life.

3. **Claim:** States should legalize all forms of gambling.

______ Legalizing gambling would boost a state's economy by creating jobs and generating tax revenue.

______ Gambling is an evil that has a corrupting influence on society.

______ People should be free to do what they want with their money so long as it does not directly harm others.

______ Too many people whose money would best be spent on basic necessities waste it on gambling.

______ Gambling is simply another form of entertainment.

______ Gambling can be as destructive and addictive as alcohol.

4. **Claim:** Animal testing of drugs should be prohibited.

______ Animal testing aids researchers in developing drugs and treatments that improve health and save lives.

______ According to the Humane Society of the United States, 92 percent of drugs that pass animal testing fail human safety trials.

______ Treatments for cancer, HIV drugs, antibiotics, and vaccines have been made possible by animal testing.

______ The reaction of a drug in an animal's body is often quite different from what happens in a human body.

______ Humans can consent to testing; animals cannot.

______ Animal testing of drugs is important in ensuring the safety of drugs on the market.

______ Animal testing of drugs too often subjects animals to horrible cruelty and even death.

______ The benefits of animal testing of drugs outweighs its drawbacks.

5. **Claim:** It should be more difficult for people to obtain credit cards.

______ Credit cards are handy for dealing with life's emergencies.

______ It can take five years to pay off $1,000 of credit card debt if you make only the minimum payment.

______ Using a credit card wisely helps people build a good credit rating so that they can later obtain loans for such important purchases as a home or a car.

______ The easy convenience of credit cards too often causes some people to sink deeply into debt.

______ Credit cards make it too easy for people to make impulse purchases of things they don't really need.

______ People need credit cards to be able to make purchases online.

______ Credit cards are much more convenient than carrying cash or writing checks.

______ Banks take advantage of credit card holders by charging excessive fees and high interest rates.

Exercise 6: Identifying the Assumptions

Now let's look at an additional argument. Notice that in this example the assumption the author is making is included.

Claim: The driving age should be raised to age 18.

Evidence: Statistics show 16-year-olds are more likely to cause accidents than those 18 or older.

Assumption: There would be fewer accidents if the driving age were raised to age 18.

Directions: Identify the assumptions for the following claims from Exercise 5. Write your answers below.

1. **Claim**: Colleges should make more of an effort to reduce excessive drinking by students.

   Assumption: ______________________________

   ____

2. **Claim**: College students should be taught to be cautious in their use of online social network sites such as Facebook.

   Assumption: ______________________________

   ____

3. **Claim**: Animal testing of drugs should be prohibited.

   Assumption: ______________________________

   ____

4. **Claim:** It should be more difficult for people to obtain credit cards.

   Assumption: ______________________________

   ____

Valid or Invalid Arguments

Many authors support their arguments with a combination of facts and opinions. The trick is to determine which reasons cited by the author are strong and support the argument and which are weak or irrelevant and fail to support the argument. Propaganda techniques and errors in reasoning are commonly used in arguments that are intended to convince the reader by any means necessary. An argument that relies too much on such devices is a poor or invalid argument.

Exercise 7: Recognizing Valid or Invalid Arguments

Directions: Read the passages and answer the questions that follow.

A. (1) Drowsy drivers should be held criminally liable for the crashes they cause. (2) An estimated 60 million Americans are operating vehicles each day without adequate sleep. (3) The National Highway Traffic Safety Administration estimates that 100,000 police-reported crashes are the direct result of driver-fatigue each year, resulting in 1,550 deaths and 71,000 injuries. (4) AAA reports that driving while sleep-deprived can have some of the same hazardous effects on the driver as being drunk. (5) Its studies concluded that coordination, reaction-time, and judgment are all impaired by lack of sufficient sleep. (6) The next time you're tempted to get in a car and drive when you're sleepy, just remember you're putting yourself and others at risk.

_____ 1. The author's claim is given in which sentence?
a. Sentence 1
b. Sentence 4
c. Sentence 5
d. Sentence 6

_____ 2. What type of support is offered for the author's claim?
a. primarily facts
b. primarily opinions

_____ 3. What is the author not taking into account with this argument?
a. Drowsy driving is difficult to detect by police officers.
b. Too many people wouldn't be honest about how little sleep they've had.
c. How would the prosecution be able to prove that a person was too sleepy to drive?
d. All of the above

_____ 4. AAA's conclusion stated in sentence 4 is an example of
a. a fact.
b. an opinion.
c. a propaganda device.
d. an assumption.

B. (1) More than 5,000 teens die each year in car crashes. (2) The rate of crashes per mile driven for 16-year-old drivers is almost 10 times the rate for drivers ages 30 to 59, according to the National Highway Traffic Safety Administration. (3) Statistics show 16-year-olds are more likely to cause accidents than those 18 or older. (4) Many countries in Europe and elsewhere have a driving age of 17 or 18. (5) Americans increasingly favor raising the driving age, according to Gallup polls. (6) If we prohibit 16-year-olds from purchasing a handgun, we also need to prohibit them from being in control of a car, which has the potential to become a deadly weapon. (7) This issue is not really debatable any longer. (8) We should raise the driving age to 18.

_____ 1. The author's claim is given in which sentence?
a. Sentence 1
b. Sentence 4
c. Sentence 5
d. Sentence 8

_____ 2. Sentence 3 is an example of
a. a fact.
b. an opinion.

_____ 3. Sentence 6 is an example of
a. a fact.
b. an opinion.

_____ 4. Sentence 7 is an example of
a. a fact.
b. an opinion.

_____ 5. Sentence 5 is an example of which propaganda technique?
a. name-calling
b. bandwagon
c. transfer
d. card stacking

_____ 6. Which of the following are important issues that the author fails to fully take into account?
a. All teenagers do not mature at the same time.
b. Perhaps the problem is the lack of driver's training and practice for teenagers.
c. If teenagers aren't able to drive at 16, how will they get to jobs and school and social activities.
d. All of the above

_____ 7. The author notes that 5,000 teens die each year in car crashes. How well does this statement support the author's argument?
a. Not much, because the author doesn't tell us in how many of these accidents teens were the drivers.
b. A lot, because the reader should assume that a teen was the driver in all these accidents.

C. (1) The start time for high school should not be changed to accommodate the needs of high school students who have trouble getting up early in the morning. (2) Changing the school start time so that self-indulgent, lazy high school students can sleep later does nothing but reinforce the notion among spoiled teenagers that the world revolves around them. (3) A more vigorous approach to parental discipline would yield a much better result in the long run than changing school hours. (4) Children are responsible for their actions, such as staying up too late. (5) They can learn the hard way that there are negative consequences for the poor choices they make. (6) Changing the start of the school day to allow kids to stay up late isn't teaching children the right life lesson.

_____ 1. The author's claim is given in which sentence?
a. Sentence 1
b. Sentence 3
c. Sentence 4
d. Sentence 6

_____ 2. Sentence 2 is an example of
a. a fact.
b. an opinion.

_____ 3. Sentence 2 is an example of which propaganda device?
a. bandwagon
b. transfer
c. name-calling
d. testimonial

_____ 4. The author's claim is
a. adequately supported with factual evidence.
b. inadequately supported because it depends primarily on personal opinion.

D. (1) Almost half of all U.S. marriages end in divorce. (2) McGeorge and Carlson (2006) compared 1,000 couples exposed to an 8-week course of marriage preparation with those who did not take such a course and found a greater readiness for marriage among the first group. (3) Kirby (2006) upon testing over 1,000 married couples found that those who had taken a course in marriage preparation scored higher in marital satisfaction. (4) Everybody knows that couples who attend premarital courses communicate with each other better than those who do not. (5) To reduce the divorce rate, high school students should attend classes where they are taught about the responsibilities of marriage. (6) Sure, teachers complain about being overworked, but this would be time and money well spent.

______ 1. The author's claim is given in which sentence?
a. Sentence 1
b. Sentence 2
c. Sentence 4
d. Sentence 5

______ 2. Sentence 2 is an example of
a. a fact.
b. an opinion.

______ 3. Sentence 4 is an example of
a. a fact.
b. an opinion.

______ 4. Which of the following is the author of this argument not likely to agree with?
a. This is an area of education best left to churches.
b. This is an area of education best left to community groups.
c. Schools should be responsible for teaching students only reading, writing, and mathematics.
d. All of the above

______ 5. The author fails to take into account all the following *except* for which?
a. Many high schools lack a teacher qualified to teach marriage preparation courses.
b. Giving couples planning to get married a marriage course increases marital satisfaction.
c. It could be years before the high school students who take the course get married, if they get married at all.
d. The research was conducted on couples and not on individual high school students who may or may not be in a relationship.

______ 6. Is the author leaping to a conclusion in arguing that courses in marriage preparation given in high school will reduce divorce rates?
a. yes
b. no

______ 7. If someone says, "Why bother to teach students about relationships when a lot of them don't even know who Abraham Lincoln is?" that person is
a. giving an opinion.
b. expressing a fact.

Drawing Conclusions: Inductive and Deductive Reasoning

In the final step of analyzing a selection, readers must evaluate the soundness of the author's reasoning.

All of us draw conclusions based on what we think is reasonable and acceptable. Often these conclusions are based on inductive or deductive reasoning.

Inductive Reasoning

The word parts for "inductive" are *in* meaning "into" and *duc* meaning "to lead." In **inductive reasoning,** specific examples, evidence, or propositions lead to a more general conclusion. We reason inductively all the time.

An example of inductive reasoning is the following:

> It's time for me to plan my vacation. The last time Steve flew on Snoozy Airlines, they lost his luggage. My friend Greg says Skyloft is never on time. Tony says RightAir is always too crowded. Ryan and Bonnie have flown many miles on SureFlight and have never had any problems. Therefore, I think I'll fly on SureFlight too.

As this example implies, a conclusion reached by inductive reasoning is only as valid as the specific information on which it is based. Maybe if I had talked to more people, I would have heard some critical comments about SureFlight or some flattering comments about Snoozy or SkyLoft.

So you can see that inductive reasoning leads to a conclusion that is only probably correct. A conclusion becomes more likely to be correct when the specific information on which it is based improves.

Deductive Reasoning

Deductive reasoning goes in the opposite direction from inductive reasoning. *De* means "away from," and **deductive reasoning** moves away from the general to the specific. A conclusion reached through deductive reasoning is seen as following logically from more general propositions or statements. Just as we often reason inductively, we also often reason deductively.

A **syllogism** is a common kind of deductive reasoning. The following is an example of a syllogism:

> All men are mortal.
>
> Brad Pitt is a man.
>
> Brad Pitt is mortal.

Here is another example of a syllogism:

> "All of the comedies starring Ben Stiller are really enjoyable. He's starring in the movie *Night at the Museum 3*. This movie is going to be really enjoyable."

You can see that whether the conclusion drawn by deductive reasoning is valid depends on whether the general statements on which it is based are correct. If not all Ben Stiller comedies really are enjoyable—maybe some were boring—then it does not follow that his movie *Night at the Museum 3* has to be enjoyable. Or maybe all Ben Stiller comedies are enjoyable, but he is not really starring in *Night at the*

Museum 3 and instead is just playing a supporting role, Again, the conclusion would not follow.

Does the *Zits* cartoon shown here make use of a syllogism? Is the conclusion a valid one?

Zits

READING

According to the A. C. Nielsen Company, the average American watches 3 hours and 46 minutes of television each day (more than 52 days of nonstop television watching per year). By age 65, the average American will have spent nearly 9 years glued to the tube.

"On television things that are not visually interesting, such as thinking, reading and talking, are ignored."

TUNING IN TO READING How has TV affected you positively? Negatively? How much TV do you watch in a typical day? In the following excerpt, written in a persuasive mode, the author compares and contrasts the community of the past with the new MTV community. She offers personal and other evidence in an effort to change how we think about the media.

BIO-SKETCH Dr. Mary Pipher is a clinical psychologist, part-time instructor at the University of Nebraska, nationwide lecturer, and best-selling author. Her book *Reviving Ophelia,* published in 1994, explored the stresses placed on teenage girls by modern society. In 1999, Pipher published *Another Country,* a book about elderly people in America. She observes that "to grow old in the U.S. is to inhabit a foreign country, isolated, disconnected, and misunderstood." In her 1996 book *The Shelter of Each Other,* from which this excerpt is taken, Pipher turns her attention to the stresses placed on the family as a whole. In Pipher's view, the family is so burdened with problems that it can no longer protect family members from the "enemy within," which she defines as inappropriate stimulation from a variety of sources, with TV being at the top of her list.

NOTES ON VOCABULARY

Romeo and Juliet a tragedy by William Shakespeare about two ill-fated lovers whose romance ends in death because of the feud between their two families.

persona a character in a fictional work; the public role or personality a person assumes. In Latin, the word for "mask" was *persona.* In ancient Rome, actors wore masks that covered the entire face. Each Roman god was represented by a particular mask so that the audience always knew what god an actor was portraying.

nuance a slight difference or distinction. The term was borrowed from French and originally referred to a slightly different shade of color.

decry to denounce or disparage openly.

rule of thumb a practical method or principle that is based on the wisdom of experience. The expression dates from the 1600s and originally referred to making rough estimates of measurements by using one's thumb.

Tonga Islands a group of islands in the southwest Pacific Ocean slightly east of Fiji. They are also known as the Friendly Islands.

TV

MARY PIPHER

IN A COLLEGE CLASS I ASKED, "What would it be like to grow up in a world without media?" A student from the Tonga Islands answered, "I never saw television or heard rock and roll until I came to the United States in high school." She paused and looked around the room. "I had a happy childhood. I felt safe all the time. I didn't know I was poor. Or that parents hurt their children or that children hated their parents. I thought I was pretty."

Television has probably been the most powerful medium in shaping the new community. The electronic community gives us our mutual friends, our significant events and our daily chats. The "produced" relationships of television families become our models for intimacy. We know media stars better than we know our neighbors. Most of us can discuss their lives better than we can discuss those of our relatives. We confuse personas and persons. That is, we think a man who plays a doctor on TV actually knows something about medicine. We think a chatty talk show host is truly good-natured. This confusion is especially common with young children, who are developmentally incapable of distinguishing between reality and fantasy. But even adults get mixed up about this. 2

Most real life is rather quiet and routine. Most pleasures are small pleasures—a hot shower, a sunset, a bowl of good soup or a good book. Television suggests that life is high drama, love and sex. TV families are radically different from real families. Things happen much faster to them. On television things that are not visually interesting, such as thinking, reading and talking, are ignored. Activities such as housework, fund raising and teaching children to read are vastly underreported. Instead of ennobling our ordinary experiences, television suggests that they are not of sufficient interest to document. 3

"Television has proved that people will look at anything rather than each other."
—Ann Landers

These generalizations even fit the way TV portrays the animal kingdom. Specials on animals feature sex, births and killing. Dangerous and cuddly-looking animals are favored. But in reality, most animals are neither dangerous nor cute. Sharks and panda bears are not the main species on the planet. Most animals, like most people, spend most of their time in rather simple ways. They forage and sleep. 4

5 TV isolates people in their leisure time. People spend more time watching music videos but less time making music with each other. People in small towns now watch international cable networks instead of driving to their neighbor's house for cards. Women watch soaps instead of attending church circles or book clubs. When company comes, the kids are sent to the TV room with videos. Television is on during meals and kids study to television or radio.

Forty percent of 2-year-olds watch three or more hours of TV every day.

6 Parents are not the main influences in the lives of their children. Some of the first voices children hear are from the television; the first street they know is Sesame Street. A child playing Nintendo is learning different lessons than a child playing along a creek or playing dominoes with a grandfather. Many children have been conditioned via the media into having highly dysfunctional attention spans.

7 Adults too have diminished concentration. Neil Postman in *Amusing Ourselves to Death* writes of the 1858 Lincoln/Douglas debates. The average citizen sat for up to seven hours in the heat and listened to these two men discuss issues. People grasped the legal and constitutional issues, moral nuances and political implications. In addition, they could listen to and appreciate intricate and complex sentences. In the 1990s President Clinton's speeches were decried by the press and the public when they lasted more than an hour. To an audience socialized to information via sound bite, an hour seems like a long time.

8 The time devoted to violence on TV in no way reflects its importance in real life. In real life, most of us exercise, work, visit our friends, read, cook and eat and shop. Few of us spend any significant amount of our time solving murders or fleeing psychotic killers. On television there are many more detectives and murderers than exist in the real world. A rule of thumb about violence is "If it bleeds, it leads." Violence captures viewer attention. Our movies have become increasingly violent, and as James Wolcott wrote in *The New Yorker,* "Violence is the real sex now."

9 Some might argue that there is nothing new under the sun. Of course, in a narrow sense, they are correct. There have always been murderers and rapists, and stories about violence have been themes of literature and song. But things are different now. Children, including toddlers, are exposed to hundreds of examples of violence every day. The frequency and intensity of these images is unprecedented in the history of humanity. We have ample documentation that this exposure desensitizes children, makes it more likely they will be violent and increases their fear levels about potential violence.

10 Another difference is in the attitudes about violence. *Romeo and Juliet,* for example, was a tragedy. The deaths in the play were presented as a cause of enormous suffering to friends and families and as a terrible waste. When Juliet and Romeo died, something momentous happened in the universe. The very gods were upset. Often today, death is a minor event, of no more consequence than, say the kicking of a flat tire. It's even presented as a joke.

11 It is one thing to read Shakespeare, which at least requires that the person can read. It's another to, day after day, see blood splattered across a screen by "action heroes." It is one thing to show, as Shakespeare did, that violence can be the tragic consequence of misunderstandings, and another to show violence

as a thrill, as a solution to human problems or merely as something that happens when people are slightly frustrated or men need to prove they are men.

12 Of course, one could argue that parents can keep televisions out of their homes. This is extremely hard for the average parent to do. Even if they succeed, their children go from these "protected environments" to play with children who have watched lots of TV and who behave accordingly.

13 I don't often go to violent movies, but I do have a stake in them. I don't like living in a world where thousands of teenage boys, some of whom own guns, have been reared on them. Walking city streets, I may be accosted by a youth who has spent most of his life watching violent media. Unfortunately, needy children are the ones most affected. Children with the least available parents watch the most TV. Violent television is like secondhand smoke; it affects all of us.

14 Heavy viewers develop the "mean world syndrome." This leads to a vicious-cycle phenomenon. Because children are afraid and the streets are not safe, they come home right after school and stay indoors. They watch more TV, which makes them more afraid and thus more likely to stay indoors. With everyone indoors the streets are less safe. Families watch more TV and are more fearful and so on.

15 Television and electronic media have created a new community with entirely different rules and structures than the kinds of communities that have existed for millions of years. Families gather around the glow of the TV as the Lakota once gathered around the glow of a fire on the Great Plains or as the Vikings once huddled around fires in the caves of Scandinavia. They gather as New England families gathered in the 1800s around a fireplace that kept them warm and safe. But our TVs do not keep us warm, safe and together. Rapidly our technology is creating a new kind of human being, one who is plugged into machines instead of relationships, one who lives in a virtual reality rather than a family.

(Mary Pipher, *The Shelter of Each Other,* 1996)

COMPREHENSION CHECKUP

Short Answer

Directions: Answer the following questions briefly, in no more than a sentence or two.

1. Write the main idea in paragraph 1.

____

2. Write the main idea that is directly stated in paragraph 2. Explain what Pipher means when she says we have trouble distinguishing between "personas and persons." Are children the only ones who have trouble with this?

____

____

____

3. Summarize the key points that Pipher makes in paragraph 3. How does what you see on the evening local or national news reinforce Pipher's argument?

4. In paragraph 4, Pipher says that TV distorts our impression of animals. How does TV do this?

5. What does Pipher say in paragraph 5 about what is happening to our sense of belonging to a community? Is the Internet likely to create strong community ties or weaken them?

6. Do you agree with Pipher's assertion that parents are not the primary influences in their children's lives? Why or why not? How do the media contribute to children's short attention spans?

7. Paragraphs 8–13 are devoted to a discussion of violence on TV. Why does television portray so much violence? What are some of the effects of violent TV programs on the young?

8. Pipher compares and contrasts the modern media's attitude to violence and death with that portrayed in *Romeo and Juliet*. What is the difference she perceives?

9. Many people would suggest that parents are responsible for their own children and so should restrict the amount of time their kids spend watching TV. What is Pipher's response to these critics?

10. Explain the cause-and-effect relationships in paragraph 14.

    Cause:

    Effect:

    Cause:

    Effect:

11. This article is written in the persuasive mode. What are the key points that Pipher is trying to persuade readers to accept?

12. Paragraph 15 compares and contrasts two communities. List the similarities and differences between the two. Then fill in the Venn diagram *on the next page* with your details.

____

____

STUDY TECHNIQUE 13: VENN DIAGRAM

Making a Venn diagram is a good way to compare and contrast two things. Create a Venn diagram to compare and contrast pre-TV and post-TV communities. First, list everything about the pre-TV community in area A. Next, do the same with the post-TV community in area C. Then, list everything that A and C have in common in area B. When you are finished, the outer areas will show how the two communities are different, and the overlapping area in the middle will show the similarities between the two communities. Use the information in your Venn diagram to write a paragraph comparing and contrasting the two communities.

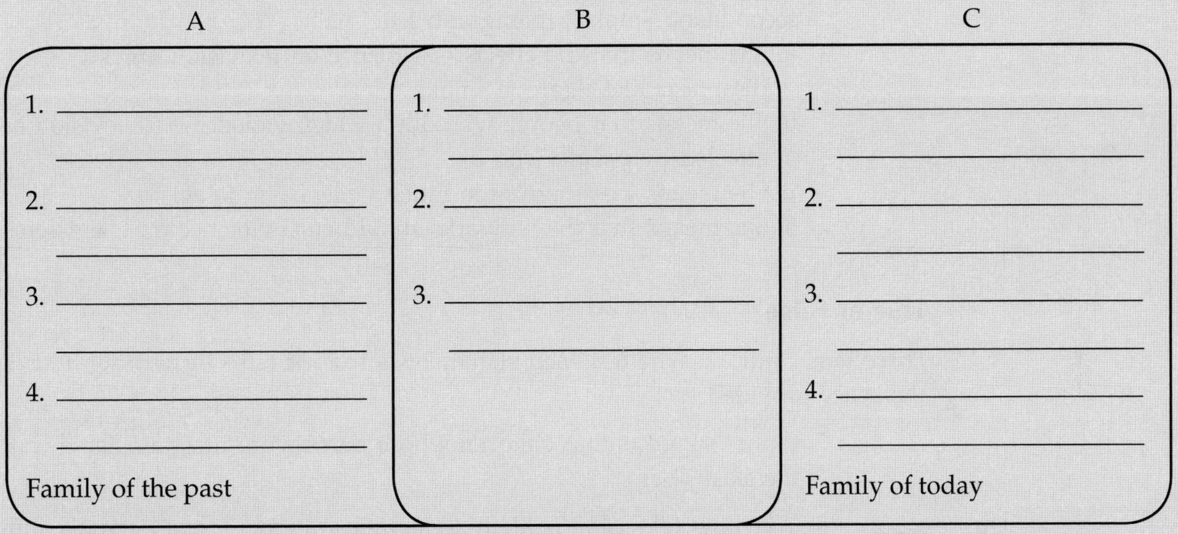

A	B	C
1. ______________	1. ______________	1. ______________
2. ______________	2. ______________	2. ______________
3. ______________	3. ______________	3. ______________
4. ______________		4. ______________
Family of the past		Family of today

Multiple Choice

Directions: For each item, write the letter corresponding to the best answer.

______ 1. The organizational pattern used in paragraph 2 is
a. main idea, details.
b. details, main idea, details.
c. details, main idea.
d. no directly stated main idea.

______ 2. What does Pipher mean by the term "protected environments" in paragraph 12?
a. She is referring to homes that are middle class.
b. She is referring to homes in gated communities.
c. She is referring to homes that have only one television.
d. She is referring to homes that do not have a television.

______ 3. From this selection you could conclude that
a. no one should watch TV.
b. people should limit the amount of television they and their families watch.
c. people should spend more time on the Internet.
d. the government should regulate the content of TV programs.

______ 4. A likely title for this selection would be
a. "TV—The Cause of Violence."
b. "TV versus Shakespeare."
c. "TV in the Tonga Islands."
d. "TV and Its Effects on Relationships."

______ 5. If the author was reading this selection orally, her tone of voice would probably be
a. admiring.
b. optimistic.
c. critical.
d. amused.

______ 6. What does Pipher mean when she says that "Violent television is like secondhand smoke" (paragraph 13)?
a. She means that the effects of violence on television quickly disappear like cigarette smoke.
b. She means that people who don't watch violence on television are affected by people who do.
c. She means that there's too much violence on television.
d. She means that the networks should curb violence on television.

True or False

Directions: Indicate whether each statement is true or false by writing **T** or **F** in the space provided.

______ 7. Pipher suggests that children whose parents are most available watch the least TV.

______ 8. Watching television is likely to significantly increase a person's ability to concentrate.

______ 9. According to Pipher, things happen much more quickly in real life.

______ 10. Pipher believes that violence on television causes children to view the world as mean and unsafe.

Vocabulary in Context

Directions: Use the context clues to determine the meaning of the italicized word, and then write a definition for the word in the space provided.

1. Roxana is living a *fantasy* life, buying clothes, cars, and jewelry she cannot afford.

____

2. Gladys is such a *chatty* person that Yoko feels a deep need for solitude after spending only a short while with her.

____

3. Wild animals sometimes enter towns to *forage* for food.

____

4. Children like to sleep with their cute and *cuddly* teddy bears.

____

5. The *implication* of running a red light could be a car accident or a ticket.

____

6. She was trying to pretend that she was not angry, but *nuances* in her behavior told you that she was.

____

7. Something *momentous* happened to Tamotsu yesterday—he won the lottery!

____

8. Sandy decided to give up jogging late at night after she was *accosted* by a stranger for the second time in a week.

____

Drawing Inferences

Directions: Study the following cartoon carefully, then consider the statements below. If the statement appears to be a valid inference based on the details found in the cartoon, mark it **Y** for yes. If it seems to be an unlikely conclusion, mark it **N** for no.

_____ 1. The people standing in line are purchasing tickets to a violent movie.

_____ 2. They are expecting the film to foster decent values.

_____ 3. The cartoonist feels the general public is responsible for the decline in high moral standards in the entertainment industry.

Non Sequitur

Written Assignment

1. Summarize the information presented in a local news show. Identify the subject of each story (murder, robbery, fire, accident, etc.) and the approximate amount of time given to coverage of the story.

2. Watch a TV drama, detective show, soap opera, or movie, and keep track of how many specific acts of violence the show portrays.
3. Is Mary Pipher making a deductive or inductive argument? Write a short essay stating your reasons.
4. How does the cartoon support Mary Pipher's argument?

Evaluating the Evidence: Editorials

In contrast to news stories, which try to be objective, an **editorial** is a statement of personal opinion. As such, editorials are much more subjective than textbook selections or newspaper and magazine articles. The purpose of an editorial is to persuade readers to believe one thing rather than another. Editorials are found in magazines, in newspapers, and also on radio, television, and the Internet. Editorials tend to be short and direct, and so they are particularly appealing to those who dislike lengthy articles and complex analyses.

Tips for Evaluating Editorials

While most editorials provide a quick update of a topic, it is generally advisable to have some knowledge of the topic being discussed in advance so that you are in a better position to evaluate the material. When you are reading or listening to an editorial, it is sometimes helpful to engage in a mental dialogue with the author. When you are having a discussion (or an argument) with a friend, you might ask such questions as "Is that so?" "Where did you get that information?" and "But, what about this?" You might try to ask similar questions when you are evaluating an editorial. Here are some additional tips for reading editorials.

1. Think about the author. How authoritative is he or she? Is this topic within the author's area of expertise? Editorials, being personal in nature, reveal a lot about the author. Is he or she someone you respect?
2. Read the title of the editorial first. The title may reveal the author's position at the outset.
3. While a good editorial is passionate, it is your job as reader to identify the author's biases and determine whether or not you agree with the positions presented. Try to determine the author's predispositions or biases as you read.
4. Consider how the author of the editorial handles opposing positions. Does he or she acknowledge other positions? Does he or she attempt to rebut the opposing arguments?
5. Consider whether the editorial writer differentiates between important and trivial arguments. Make a list to see whether you can determine which arguments are important to making the case and which are not.
6. Consider whether the author recommends a solution to the problem. If so, is the solution reasonable or practical? Can it be implemented? If the problem cannot be solved, does the author provide constructive suggestions for improving the situation?

Marijuana Isn't Harmless—Especially for Kids

My Turn

BY SHEILA POLK

SEPT. 13, 2013

2 Odds are you know someone with an addiction: 2.3 million people over the age of 12 sought substance/alcohol treatment in 2011, according to the U.S. Substance Abuse and Mental Health Services Administration. Add those not seeking or unable to afford treatment and the numbers escalate.

3 Marijuana dependence/abuse is twice as prevalent as other drugs—4.2 million Americans (2011), nearly two-thirds of Arizona's population. Nation-

ally, treatment admissions skyrocketed 21 percent (2000–2010), with an average age of 25 and nearly three quarters male. In Arizona, marijuana treatment has surpassed methamphetamine.

4 Marijuana withdrawal has the same symptoms as other drugs—cravings, irritability, low self-confidence, despondency, depression and suicidal thoughts.

5 I see public opinion swaying toward marijuana legalization and scratch my head. Recovery is possible, but why mainstream a substance of addiction? One in 11 new users will become addicted—one in six who start as teens and up to one in two who smoke it daily.

6 As we strive for global competitiveness and lament poor school performance in comparison to our international peers, we must face the truth about pot. It is more crucial than ever to challenge the impression many teens have that marijuana is a benign, unfairly demonized substance.

7 Regular marijuana use jeopardizes a young person's chance of success—in school and in life. The National Institute of Drug Abuse warns that habitual teen marijuana use is linked to a significant decrease in IQ of seven to eight points, not to mention school dropout or failure, future drug use, and mental health problems. An eight IQ point drop is titanic, sinking a person of average intelligence into the lowest third of the range.

8 Nationally, one in 15 high-school seniors are regular pot users. The 2012 Arizona Youth Survey found that one in five of Arizona's high-school seniors used pot in the past 30 days and a 14.4 percent cumulative increase in past 30-day use since 2008 for grades 8, 10, and 12.

Parents tell me of their pot-using teens falling behind in school while insisting that marijuana is "medicine." Unlike methamphetamine, heroin, and the horrific synthetics (bath salts/spice), marijuana's harms are not readily apparent: no life-threatening overdose or deterioration into a gaunt and ravaged figure. 9

The effects are rather subtle: downward life trajectory, erosion of IQ, impaired cognitive development, mental health issues, low education attainment, and the escalation of delinquency. Disintegration over months or years is not easily identified nor does it garner headlines. 10

I see the harms—child abuse inflicted by the neglectful pot-smoking parent; traffic fatalities by the marijuana-impaired driver. 11

I see the subtle signs of destruction in the growing number of addicted young adults. 12

Our job as adults is to create an environment to fuel our kids' success. To that end, we must educate them and the voting public about the value of the brain and the damage of marijuana. 13

Already an uphill battle, the legalization movement feeds teens' perception that marijuana is safe. We can't sit passively by and watch this slow decline. 14

Marijuana is harmless? Think again. 15

Sheila Polk is the Yavapai County Attorney and co-chairwoman of MAT-Force, the Yavapai County Substance Abuse Coalition. 16

(*Arizona Republic,* September 13, 2013)

Exercise 8: Evaluating the Use of Persuasive Techniques in an Editorial

Directions: Answer the following questions about the editorial.

1. **Author's purpose.** Is it the author's primary purpose to inform or to persuade? Why do you think so?

___

___

___

___

2. **Emotional appeals.** Where does the author use language that is meant to appeal to your emotions? Give an example of material that is included in the editorial for its emotional appeal.

3. **Ethical appeals.** Does the editorial cite any experts? What do the experts have to say about the topic of the editorial? How much trust should you put in what the experts say? Might other experts have different opinions?

4. **Logical appeals.** What logical or reasonable arguments are included in the editorial? Does the editorial make use of inductive or deductive reasoning?

5. **Psychological appeals.** Does the editorial say anything that is intended to manipulate you psychologically by appealing to your need for acceptance, power, prestige, and so forth?

6. **Tone.** What is the author's tone? Is the tone meant to influence or manipulate you? Give specific examples of how the author uses tone to affect you.

7. **Bias.** What is the author's specific bias? Where does this bias appear in the editorial—at the beginning, the middle, or the end?

Evaluating the Evidence: Political Cartoons

A political (or editorial) cartoon is a drawing that has a political or social message. Most political cartoons employ satire or humor to communicate a specific point of view about a current event or issue. Many political cartoons feature caricatures of prominent public figures. They also often make use of common symbols. For instance, the Democratic Party is represented by a donkey, and the Republican Party by an elephant. A drawing of Uncle Sam stands for the United States as a whole.

Political cartoons can be difficult to decipher. Understanding them often requires a knowledge of current events. It also helps to be familiar with social and political issues.

Exercise 9: Evaluating a Political Cartoon

Directions: Study the cartoon below to determine what the cartoonist, Scott Stantis, has to say about the war on drugs. What is his point of view on the topic? Is he for the current policy or against it?

Chapter Summary and Review

In Chapter 13, you became familiar with propaganda techniques and logical fallacies. You also learned about persuasive writing techniques, evaluated persuasive writing selections, and became familiar with deductive and inductive reasoning. Based on the material in this chapter, answer the following.

Short Answer

Directions: From advertising or your own experience, give an example of the following propaganda techniques. Explain how your example illustrates the technique.

Propaganda Technique	Example	Explanation
1. Name-calling	______________	______________
2. Transfer	______________	______________
3. Glittering generalities	______________	______________
4. False analogy	______________	______________
5. Either/or fallacy	______________	______________

Directions: Answer the following questions briefly, using no more than a few words or sentences as appropriate.

1. Give an example of deductive reasoning. ______________________________

   ____

2. Give an example of inductive reasoning. ______________________________

   ____

Vocabulary in Context

Directions: Choose one of the following words or phrases to complete the sentences below. Use each word only once.

authority	deductive	plain folks
bandwagon	inductive	testimonial

1. When a person who is giving an opinion on cloning says that she is a professor of bioethics, she is making an appeal to ______________.
2. Trying to draw conclusions from a hypothesis or a general principle is ______________ reasoning.
3. ______________ reasoning begins with gathering evidence and then draws a conclusion from the evidence.
4. A famous model promoting a particular line of cosmetics is an example of a(n) ______________.
5. When a politician puts on a hard hat and goes into a coal mine, he is demonstrating the ______________ technique.
6. An example of the ______________ technique is a commercial featuring a bar filled with people who are drinking one particular brand of beer.

PART 5

Vocabulary Units

VOCABULARY Unit 1 Homonyms and Other Confusing Words

U.S. Capitol

Homonyms are words that sound the same but may have different spellings or meanings. There are other words that could be added to our list of homonyms below, but these are the ones students most commonly have trouble with. Mastering these words will help you make a good impression in written assignments. *Affect* and *effect* are discussed in a separate box because they are especially difficult.

accept a verb meaning "to receive, take, or hold." Did you *accept* the money given to you by your rich uncle?

except a preposition meaning "without." Everyone *except* you was invited to the party.

expect a verb meaning "to look forward to an event." *Expect* is not technically a homonym, but students sometimes confuse it with *except.* I *expect* to get an A in English, but if I don't do well on the final I might end up with a B.

capitol a noun meaning "the physical building where laws are made." From now on, you should use this word for the actual building. The *capitol* building in Washington, DC, has two branches, the Senate and the House of Representatives.

capital a noun or an adjective meaning "most important or most serious," including the *capital* city, money, *capital* letters, *capital* punishment, and the top of a column of a building. What is the *capital* city of your state?

Think about This Sentence: Your state *capitol* building is located in the *capital* city of your state.

know a verb meaning "to understand." Did you *know* all the important information for the test?

no an adverb, sometimes an adjective, used to express something negative. Did you stay up all night studying for the test? *No,* you went to bed.

knew a verb, past tense of the verb *know.* I *knew* the material for the test.

new an adjective meaning "present, modern"; an antonym of *old.* Did you spend your money on a *new* car?

past a noun meaning "former time." In the *past* you did not study as much as you should have.

an adjective meaning "former." One of our *past* presidents was Thomas Jefferson.

an adverb meaning "beyond something." Did you walk *past* the library on the way to the student union?

passed the past tense of the verb *pass.* The quarterback *passed* the ball to the tight end, who ran for a touchdown. The student *passed* the test with an A. My father *passed* away. Each of these sentences uses the word *passed* as a verb expressing action.

Think about This Sentence: Most of our *past* presidents have *passed* away.

principal a noun meaning "head of a school, or other person who is the main person."

a noun meaning "sum of money." When you buy a house, you will pay on *principal* and interest.

an adjective meaning "main" or "chief." Was the *principal* cause of the Civil War the desire to abolish slavery or the need to keep our country unified?

principle a noun meaning "fundamental moral beliefs." Cheating people out of their money should go against the *principles* your parents taught you.

a noun meaning "fundamental theory," as in physics. A fundamental *principle* in physics is that the atoms or molecules in gases are more widely spaced than in solids or liquids.

Think about This Sentence: Your *principal* beliefs are the *principles* you live by.

quiet an adjective meaning "silent." Are you a *quiet* person?

quite an adverb meaning "very" or "extremely." The line of cars trying to get into the parking lot of the football stadium was *quite* long.

quit a verb meaning "to discontinue" or "give up." This word is not really a homonym, but is often confused with *quiet* and *quite.* The student *quit* her job at McDonald's so that she could devote more time to her studies.

their an adjective indicating possession; the possessive form of "they." *Their* car was stolen from the parking lot.

there an adverb indicating direction, meaning "in that position." Notice how the word *here* appears in the word *there.* The computer lab is located over *there.*

a pronoun used to begin a sentence or phrase. *There* are a few students absent from class today.

they're a contraction for "they are." *They're* going to the party after the game.

to a preposition indicating direction, and meaning "toward." Are you going *to* your house after you finish class?

part of a verb indicating an infinitive statement. Unless you are independently wealthy, you will need *to* work for a living. You may want *to* study in the library.

Think about This Sentence: You are going *to* work because you need *to* work for a living. The first *to* is a preposition indicating direction; the second *to* is part of the verb "to work."

too an adverb meaning "also" or "excessively." He, *too,* was allowed to leave class early. She drank *too* much at the party.

two the number 2. The baseball team scored *two* runs in the fifth inning.

threw the past tense of the verb *throw.* The shortstop *threw* out the runner at first base.

through a preposition indicating direction. The drunk driver drove *through* the red light.

a preposition meaning "finished." When the student was *through* with the test, he took it to the instructor at the front of the class.

Finish the sentence: The boy *threw* the ball *through* the ______.

Affect versus *Effect*

Now for the difference between *affect* and *effect.* The key to working with these words is knowing the difference between a noun and a verb. Remember that a verb indicates *action* or *state of being.* A noun is a person, place, or thing; remember that things can be intangible (for example, feelings, causes, and hopes).

action The team *won* the game last night.

affect a verb meaning "influence." This word will *almost always* be used as a verb. If one thing *affects* something else, it influences it. If you are using one of these words as a verb, you will use *affect* 95 percent of the time. Weather *affects* our personalities and how we feel. (The weather is influencing your personality.)

In psychology, *affect* can be used as a noun meaning "emotional response." After her mother died, Maria became depressed and had a flat *affect.*

state of being The team *is* excellent because its players *are* quick and play good defense.

effect Ninety-nine percent of the time this word will be a noun. *Effect* as a noun usually means "the result of an action." What will be the *effect* on you if Congress cuts back the financial aid program?

Using *effect* as a verb is very tricky, but on the positive side you will probably need to use it this way very rarely. As a verb, *effect* means "to cause or bring about." Congress may *effect* a change in the income tax laws.

weather a noun meaning "temperature, climate." The *weather* was so hot that you just had to stay inside with the air conditioner running.

whether a conjunction similar to "if." Some people believe it really doesn't make much difference *whether* we have a Republican or a Democratic president.

were a past tense of the verb *be.* We *were* in the mountains when the fire broke out.

we're a contraction for *we are. We're* going to go to the store.

wear a verb meaning "to have on the body" or "to diminish." What are you going to *wear* to the party on Saturday? You are going to *wear* out the carpet walking back and forth so much.

where an adverb, a conjunction, or a noun indicating location. *Where* did I leave my books?

Now write your own sentences using *affect* and *effect.* (You may find it helpful to refer to the sample sentences above.)

____

____

____

Homonym Exercise 1

Directions: For each exercise, complete the following sentences using the correct homonym.

1. Did she _______________ the marriage proposal?
   accept/except

2. In the United States, the issue of _______________ punishment is controversial.
   capitol/capital

3. I don't _______________ what to do to help you study for that quiz.
   know/no

4. That room definitely needs _______________ paint.
   knew/new

5. In the ________________, I was not available to work on Tuesdays.
   past/passed

6. My ________________ include not speaking harshly of anyone.
   principals/principles

7. I want you to ________________ making that very annoying noise.
   quit/quite

8. While I am the talkative one in the family, my husband is the ____________ one.
   quiet/quite

9. The noise was ________________ loud and as a result gave me a headache.
   quite/quit

10. Write a sentence of your own using *capital* correctly.

    ____

Homonym Exercise 2

1. People don't realize they are ________________ by advertising.
   affected/effected

2. What possible ________________ does drinking alcohol have on teenagers?
   affects/effects

3. Special ______________ in the movie *Star Wars* look tame by today's standards.
   affects/effects

4. The teacher told me my absences ________________ my grade in her class.
   affected/effected

5. The ________________ forecast today shows a chance of showers in the north.
   weather/whether

6. It doesn't matter ________________ I exercise or not; I still can't lose weight.
   weather/whether

7. It's not possible to ________________ all of the material for the quiz.
   know/no

8. I don't know ________________ to turn in my finished essay.
   were/where

9. They ________________ not able to attend the luncheon held in their honor.
   were/where

10. The babysitter wants to give the children ________________ lunch at noon.
    their/there

11. ______________ are too many people enrolled in the nine o'clock English class.
    their/there

12. Jan said that she wanted to come to the party ________________.
    to/too/two

13. I am not able ________________ visit him in the hospital today.
    to/too/two

14. Her resignation from the position was ________________ by her supervisor.
    accepted/excepted

15. The hostess ________________ my apologies when I declined the invitation.
    accepted/excepted

Vocabulary Unit 1 Crossword Puzzle

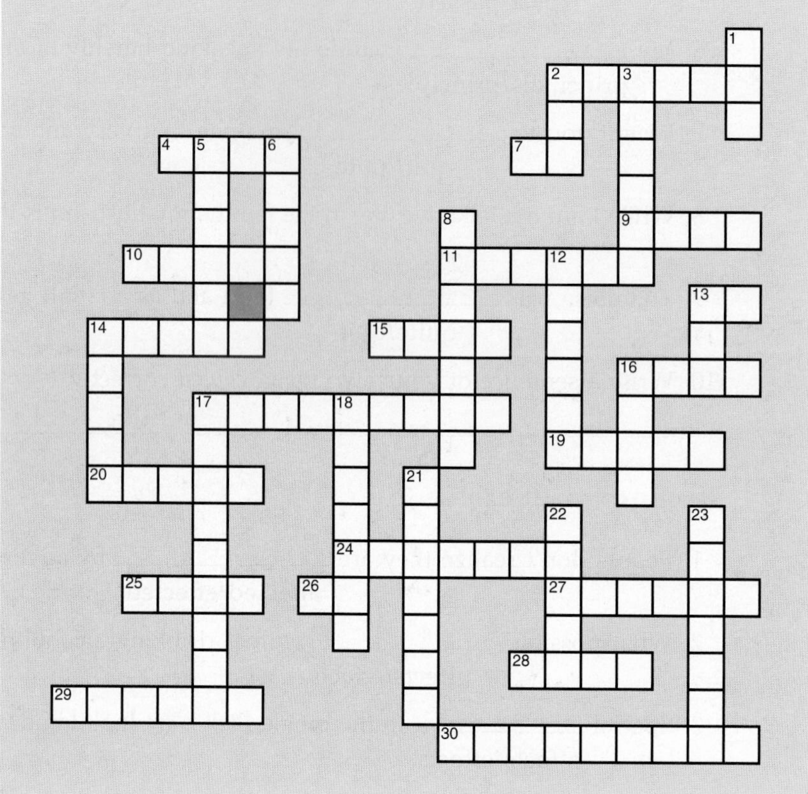

ACROSS CLUES

2. _____ on their way to class.
4. We have all done things in the _____ that we later regretted.
7. All students need _____ study several times each week for each class.
9. Did you drive your car _____ the exit on the freeway?
10. _____ is a good program on TV tonight.
11. Will you _____ your friend's invitation to the party?
13. Will you go _____ your graduation ceremony?
14. The student was _____ upset when he was withdrawn from class.
15. Many students _____ college before they graduate.
16. Do you _____ who won the game last night?
17. One of the _____ ingredients in soda is sugar.
19. Why were you over _____ when you should have been over here?
20. _____ house was broken into several times last summer.
24. You must walk _____ the hallway to get to the classroom.
25. Did you _____ your job?
26. _____, I do not want any more ice cream.
27. Everyone _____ you received an A on the test.
28. _____ you at home last night studying?
29. The elderly person _____ away.
30. One _____ of life is to do unto others as you would want them to do unto you.

DOWN CLUES

1. We went to Wal-Mart to buy _____ clothes.
2. There are _____ wheels on a typical bike.
3. All of the student's grades were A's _____ for the B on the final.
5. Studying hard should positively _____ your grade.
6. The basketball player _____ the ball out-of-bounds, by accident.
8. What is the _____ city of your state?
12. Using drugs will have a negative _____ on a person.
13. _____ little sleep will probably make you drowsy and cranky.
14. Was the room _____ while students were taking the test, or was it too noisy?
16. The student _____ all the important information for the test.
17. Religious books lay down basic _____s of life.
18. Where is the _____ building located?
21. When will you be _____ with your work and able to go home?
22. _____ is the closest McDonald's?
23. The first letter of a sentence should be a(n) _____ letter.

Vocabulary Unit 1: Additional Practice with Homonyms and Other Confusing Words

Directions: Write the correct word on the lines provided.

1. ____________ home is no longer ____________ because it was demolished by the hurricane. (**their, there**)
2. ____________ do you like to ____________ a suit and tie? **(wear, where)**
3. I'll go ____________ the restaurant early ____________ get a table for ____________, unless you think Eric and Megan want to come ____________. **(to, too, two)**
4. At a meeting of school ____________, one of them said that she hoped they all stuck to their ____________. **(principals, principles)**
5. I will ____________ any job ____________ one that involves heavy lifting. **(accept, except)**
6. I was wondering ____________ you thought you ____________ going? **(were, where)**
7. What is the ____________ of not turning in my homework on time? Can it ____________ my grade adversely? **(affect, effect)**
8. He ____________ better than to buy a brand ____________ car, but the salesperson talked him into it anyway. **(knew, new)**
9. Hugo Chavez, the ____________ president of Venezuela, ____________ away in 2013. **(passed, past)**
10. I'll need to ____________ my job if the baby doesn't ____________ down and go to sleep. **(quiet, quit)**

VOCABULARY Unit 2 Word Parts Dealing with Numbers

The Greeks and Romans came up with a system for creating words by putting together smaller word parts. They used three types of word parts: prefixes, suffixes, and roots. *Pre* means "before," and so it makes sense that a prefix comes before the main part of a word. *Suf* means "after," and so a suffix comes at the end of a word. A root word is the main part of a word and usually comes in the middle. Many English words are composed of at least one root, and many have one or more prefixes and suffixes.

Part of the Greek and Roman system was a set of prefixes that represented numbers. There are many words in English derived from specific numbers. One way to help you remember many of these number prefixes is to think of the months of the year. For example, October has the prefix *oct*, meaning "eight." That might help you remember what *oct* means, except for one big problem—October is not the 8th month, but the 10th. How can this be? The answer is that our calendar evolved from the original Roman calendar, which began in March instead of January and had only 10 months. The months of Januarius and Februarius were added later, around 700 B.C. You can see that making March the first month makes October the eighth month.

Vocabulary Units 2 and 3 will draw on your knowledge of the numbering system. Make sure that you remember that the calendar began in March.

Now we are going to learn some number prefixes.

uni—one	tetra—four	oct—eight
mono—one	quint—five	nov—nine
bi—two	pent—five	dec—ten
duo—two	sex—six	lat—side
di—two	hex—six	ped—foot
tri—three	sept—seven	pod—foot
quad—four	hept—seven	

biped *Ped* means "foot" as in *pedal* and *pedestrian*, so a *biped* is an animal with two feet, such as a bird.

tripod Sometimes there are slight variations in the spellings of word parts. *Pod* also means "foot," so a *tripod* has three feet. An example would be a stand for a camera.

quadruped An animal with four feet, such as a dog or a cat.

hexapod An organism with six feet, such as an insect. Why aren't spiders *hexapods?* Because they have eight feet.

hexapod—There are over five million species of insects in the world. The total insect population of the world is at least 1 quintillion (1 followed by 18 zeros).

unicorn That mythical animal with one horn.

unison An instance of sounding the same note at the same time.

monopoly A company that has no competition is called a *monopoly.* The electric and gas companies in your area are probably *monopolies* because they are the only companies allowed to give you service.

monolog(ue) *Log* means "to speak," so a *monolog* is one person speaking without anyone responding. Jay Leno and David Letterman give *monologs* at the beginning of their shows. Why is the "ue" in parentheses? Words such as *monologue, dialogue,* and *catalogue* are in the process of losing their last two letters. As time passes, there is a tendency to drop unneeded letters from words. A dictionary 50 years from now will probably not list any of these words with the "ue" at the end.

lateral Toward the side, sideways. The quarterback threw a *lateral* pass.

unilateral One-sided. The mother made a *unilateral* decision and told her child to go to bed. This was not a decision that was made by discussing it with the child.

bilateral Two-sided. We signed a *bilateral* agreement with Russia.

bicuspids Your teeth with two points.

dual Two of a kind, such as *dual* mufflers.

duel—In 1804, Alexander Hamilton, whose picture you will find on a $10 bill, fought a famous duel with Aaron Burr.

duel A formal combat with weapons fought between two people in the presence of witnesses.

duet A musical composition written for two musicians to perform simultaneously.

duo Two musical performers; a pair.

trio Three people in a group.

quartet Four people in a group. A jazz *quartet* has four musicians.

quintuplets Five children of the same mother born at one time.

biplane—The first plane flight by Orville Wright lasted 12 seconds, went to a height of 8 to 12 feet, and traveled 120 feet. The name of this plane, flown at Kitty Hawk, North Carolina, was Bird of Prey.

sextuplets Six children of the same mother born at one time.

octuplets Eight children of the same mother born at one time. In 2009 in California, Nadya Suleman gave birth to octuplets.

monoxide One oxygen atom, as in carbon *monoxide* (CO).

dioxide Two oxygen atoms, as in carbon *dioxide* (CO_2).

biplane A plane with two sets of wings, one over the other, such as the one the Wright brothers flew.

triplane A plane with three sets of wings, one over the other. The Germans, and specifically the "Red Baron," flew *triplanes* for a short period during World War I, but they were not practical for combat.

tetrahedron A four-sided, three-dimensional object.

Tetrahedron

pentagon A five-sided figure. The Defense Department has its headquarters in this five-sided building located in Virginia just across the Potomac River from Washington, DC.

Pentateuch The first five books of the Old Testament (Genesis, Exodus, Leviticus, Numbers, and Deuteronomy) are called the *Pentateuch.* The Jews consider these books central to their faith and call them the Torah (law).

hexagon—All snow crystals are hexagonal.

hexagon A six-sided figure.

octagon An eight-sided figure.

octave Eight notes of the musical scale.

octane You know it has to do with gas, but *octane* acquired its name because it has eight carbon atoms in its chemical formula (C_8H_{18}).

A Typical Triplane

decade	A 10-year period.
decimal	Our numbering system is called a *decimal* system because it is based on units of 10.
September	Originally the seventh month.
October	Originally the eighth month.

Pentagon—The Pentagon has 17.5 miles of corridors, 7,754 windows, and 23,000 people working there.

The Pentagon

November Originally the ninth month.

December Originally the tenth month.

biathlon Two events, usually sporting.

triathlon An endurance race combining three consecutive events, usually swimming, bicycling, and running. The Hawaii *Triathlon* requires participants to swim 2 miles, ride a bike 100 miles, and, last but not least, run 26 miles—all of which is done in one day.

heptathlon An athletic contest for women that requires participants to take part in seven events: 100-meter hurdles, shot put, high jump, 200-meter dash, long jump, javelin throw, and 800-meter run. Jackie Joyner-Kersee won the gold medal in the *heptathlon* at the Olympics in 1988 and 1992.

decathlon An athletic contest in which each contestant takes part in 10 events: 100-meter dash, 400-meter dash, long jump, 16-pound shot put, high jump, 110-meter hurdles, discus throw, pole vault, javelin throw, and 1500-meter run. The decathlon winner is usually proclaimed "the world's greatest athlete."

sexagenarian A person in his or her sixties.

septuagenarian A person in his or her seventies.

octogenarian A person in his or her eighties.

nonagenarian A person in his or her nineties.

Exercise 1

Directions: Write the definition of each prefix.

1. di ______
2. quad ______
3. oct ______
4. ped ______
5. tetra ______
6. duo ______
7. dec ______
8. lat ______
9. nov ______
10. pod ______
11. bi ______

Directions: Read the definition and then write the correct prefix(es).

12. seven—(2) ______ ______
13. five—(2) ______ ______
14. one—(2) ______ ______
15. three—(1) ______ ______
16. six—(2) ______ ______

Exercise 2: A "Prefixed" Fairy Tale

Directions: Replace the prefix with its definition, and write it in the blank provided.

Once upon a time there was a young (pent, ______) -year-old girl named Little Red Riding Hood. She had a grandmother who was (nov × nov, ______) years old. Grandmother lived in a house (dec, ______) blocks from Little Red's home. (Mono, ______) day Little Red set off for Grandma's house. She took a route that was only (di, ______) miles long instead of (tri, ______) miles. Before she left, she packed a basket filled with (sept, ______) or (oct, ______) goodies. She had gone almost (bi, ______) miles, and had been walking about (hept × hept), ______) minutes when she came upon a large wolf. He put out his paw and leaned against her (lat, ______). After a brief struggle of (quad, ______) or (quint, ______) minutes, she noticed Grandma and the woodman. The (duo, ______) of them quickly came to her rescue. The woodman knocked out the wolf, and soon the wolf slept peacefully for (hex, ______) hours under a tree. Finally, Little Red was happy after all, but she wouldn't go for a walk on (pod, ______) again for at least (tetra, ______) to (sex, ______) weeks.

Exercise 3: Vocabulary in Context

Directions: In the blanks below, write the word that best completes the sentence. Use each word only once.

bicuspid	biped	decade	dual	monolog
monopoly	nonagenarian	octagon	pentagon	quartet

1. A stop sign is called an ____________ because it has eight sides.
2. Bill Gates, the chair of Microsoft, was accused of creating a(n) ____________ in the software industry.
3. The opening act of the play featured a(n) ____________ spoken by one of the actors.
4. The ____________ teeth arrive when a child is about 10–12 years old.
5. The ____________ houses the offices of the five U.S. military services: the Air Force, Army, Navy, Marines, and Coast Guard.
6. A kangaroo is considered to be a(n) ____________ because it has two feet.
7. Together, John, Paul, George, and Ringo formed the Beatles, the famous musical ____________ of the 60s.
8. Carlos has ____________ citizenship; he has legal rights in both Spain and the United States.
9. A(n) ____________ is more likely than someone younger to suffer from Alzheimer's disease.
10. The Roaring Twenties was a(n) ____________ of jalopies, flappers, speakeasies, and jazz.

Exercise 4: Vocabulary in Context

Directions: In the blanks below, write the word that best completes the sentence. Use each word only once.

bilateral	decathlon	duo	hexagonal
lateral	monoxide	octane	octave
quadrupeds	triathlon	triplane	unison

1. Many quartz crystals have a(n) ____________ shape.
2. At the football game, the crowd yelled in ____________, "Defense, defense, defense!"
3. After failing to be promoted to assistant principal, the teacher made a(n) ____________ move to a teaching position at another school.
4. The ____________ was a popular flying machine from about 1905 to 1910.
5. Dogs, cats, and horses are all examples of ____________.
6. Batman and Robin are a dynamic, crime-fighting ____________.
7. The Beatles' song "Can't Buy Me Love" (1964) sounds entirely different when sung a(n) ____________ lower.
8. The winner of the grueling ____________ is often featured on the cover of Wheaties, Breakfast of Champions.
9. The old Plymouth needed high- ____________ gas to run well.
10. Because of a gas leak and poor ventilation, the family died of carbon ____________ poisoning.
11. In 1987, a historic ____________ disarmament agreement was reached between Ronald Reagan of the United States and Mikhail Gorbachev of the Soviet Union.
12. In the ____________, Frank placed high in swimming and bicycling but made a poor showing in distance running.

Now that you have studied Vocabulary Unit 2, practice your new knowledge by trying the crossword puzzle.

Expanding Your Word Power

The words listed below are not found in this Vocabulary Unit, but they are derived from the vocabulary word parts that you have studied. All of them would be good words for you to learn. See if you can guess the meaning of each word from its word parts.

1. unitard
2. unitarian
3. universal
4. monolingual
5. monosyllabic
6. monotheism
7. monotonous
8. binoculars
9. bipolar
10. deuce
11. triage
12. triceratops
13. tricolor
14. trigonometry
15. trimester
16. quadriplegic
17. impede
18. pedicure
19. podiatrist
20. arthropod

Vocabulary Unit 2 Crossword Puzzle

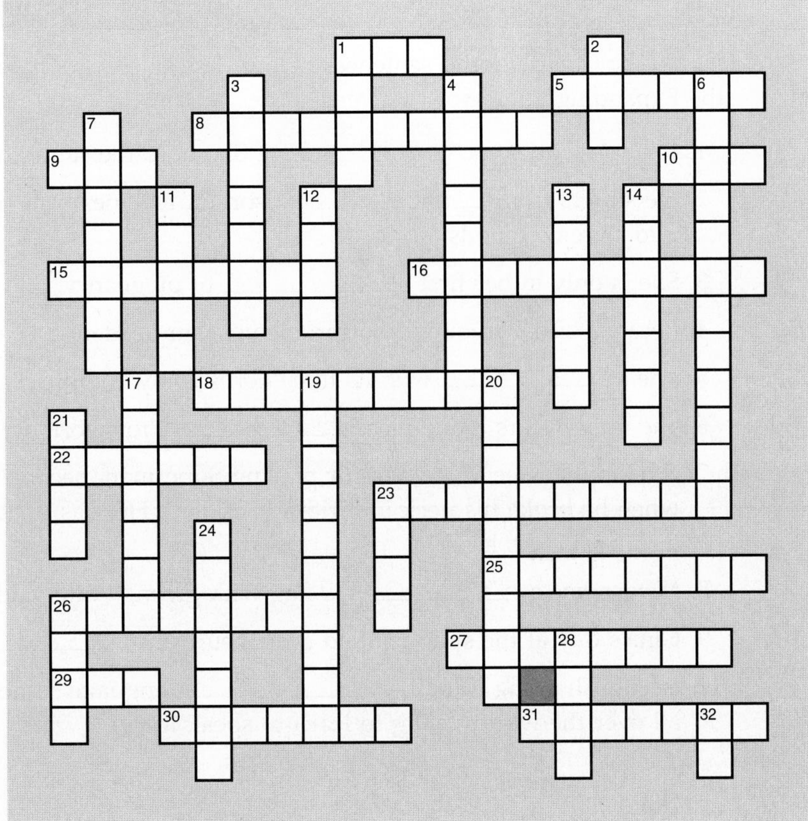

ACROSS CLUES

1. The abbreviation for what was once the 10th month.
5. A chemical found in gas.
8. The Torah, or first five books of the Old Testament.
9. A word part meaning "side."
10. A word part meaning "one."
15. What the Red Baron flew in World War I.
16. One of five children born at one time.
18. Teeth with two points.
22. All the voices or instruments together.
23. A contest involving seven track events.
25. A business that has no competition.
26. Carbon _____ is one thing that comes out of a car exhaust pipe.
27. The building in Washington, DC, where the military has its headquarters.
29. The abbreviation for what was once the 9th month.
30. What David Letterman delivers at the start of the show.
31. We exhale carbon _____.

DOWN CLUES

1. Two of a kind.
2. The abbreviation for what was once the 8th month.
3. A numbering system that is based on units of 10.
4. An animal with four legs.
6. A person in his or her nineties is a(n) _____.
7. Passing the ball to the side is a(n) _____.
11. An animal with two legs.
12. What Aaron Burr and Alexander Hamilton fought.
13. The eight notes of the musical scale.
14. What the Wright Brothers flew.
17. The mythical animal with one horn.
19. A decision made without consulting the other party is _____.
20. What was originally the 7th month.
21. A musical piece written for two musicians to perform at the same time.
23. A word part meaning "seven."
24. A scientific name for insects.
26. A word part meaning "one."
28. Three in a group.
32. A word part meaning "two."

Vocabulary Unit 2: Additional Practice with Expanding Your Word Power

Directions: Complete the sentences below with one of the vocabulary words from the Expanding Your Word Power list.

1. Jolana's work is so ______________. She does the same thing day after day.
2. He suffers from ______________ disorder. He goes back and forth between two extreme moods.
3. She is only in her first ______________ of pregnancy. She has two more to go.
4. Because of her frequent foot problems, Kim needed to see a ______________.
5. The ______________ with its three horns is my favorite plant-eating dinosaur.
6. She often wears a one-piece ______________ for working out.
7. Christopher Reeve, known for playing Superman, became a ______________ when he broke his neck in a riding accident. He was unable to move either his arms or his legs.
8. Mexico has a ______________ flag with green, white, and red.
9. Gina's day at the spa included a manicure and a ______________.
10. Is English going to be the ______________ language some day? Are people all over the world trying to learn to speak it?

VOCABULARY Unit 3 Word Parts Dealing with Number and Amount

What does the word quadricentennial *mean?*

When will your state celebrate its quadricentennial?

In this unit, we will continue working with word parts involving number and amount.

centi—100 milli—1,000

century 100 years. In the year 2001, we entered the 21st *century.*

centennial A 100-year anniversary. *Ann* and *enn* mean "year." Since *centi* means "100" and *enn* means "year," we are simply putting word parts together to make a word meaning 100 years. In 1876, we celebrated the first *centennial* of our independence from England.

bicentennial A 200-year anniversary.

tricentennial A 300-year anniversary.

cent A penny is called a *cent* because it is 1/100 of a dollar.

Giant Centipede

centipede—The largest centipede in the world, Himantarum gabrielis, has 171 to 177 pairs of legs and is found in southern Europe.

centipede *Centi* means "100" and *ped* means "foot," so a *centipede* would be an animal with 100 feet. *Actually,* centipedes don't have 100 feet; they just look like they do.

centigrade Divided into 100 parts. On the centigrade, or Celsius, scale, water freezes at 0 degrees and boils at 100 degrees. While most other nations use the *centigrade* scale, the United States uses the Fahrenheit scale. On this scale, water freezes at 32 degrees and boils at 212 degrees.

centimeter A unit of length in the metric system; 1/100 of a meter, or approximately two-fifths of an inch.

centenarian A 100-year-old person. There are more women who are *centenarians* than there are men.

millennium A period of 1,000 years.

millipede An animal that looks like it has 1,000 feet. The technical difference between a *centipede* and a *millipede* is that a *millipede* has two pairs of legs on each segment, while a *centipede* has only one pair of legs on each segment.

millimeter 1/1000 of a meter. Metric wrenches used for working on bikes and cars made in Europe and Asia are measured in *millimeters.*

million The word *million* was probably derived by multiplying 1,000 × 1,000. Maybe this will help you remember that *milli* means "1,000."

multi—many graph—write
poly—many gam—marriage

multiply A system of repeating addition many times (3 × 3 = 3 + 3 + 3).

multimedia A combination of many media. A *multimedia* computer presentation might appeal to more than one of our senses simultaneously, with film, music, and special lighting all in one performance.

multilateral Many-sided. Remember that *lat* means "side." A treaty signed by more than two nations would be a *multilateral* treaty.

polygon A many-sided figure. A decagon is a *polygon* that has 10 sides and 10 angles. The simplest *polygon* is the triangle.

polygraph You probably know that *polygraph* machines are used on someone suspected of lying. *Graph* means "write." The machine works by recording (writing) the many bodily changes (blood pressure, respiration, pulse rate, perspiration) thought to occur when a person lies in answering questions.

polygamy Being married to more than one person at the same time.

polyglot Speaking or writing several languages.

semi—half demi—half hemi—half

semester Half an academic year.

semicircle Half a circle.

semiprofessional Not fully professional. The baseball player was not good enough to play professionally, so he played in a *semiprofessional* league, or what is commonly called the semipros.

semicentennial Half of 100 years, or 50 years; a 50th anniversary. Here you are just putting together *semi* meaning "half," *cent* meaning "100," and *enn* meaning "year."

semilunar Shaped like a half-moon; crescent-shaped.

hemisphere Half of a sphere or a globe. We live in the Western *Hemisphere.* The word *hemisphere* is also used when referring to the left half or right half of our brain.

demitasse A small (half) cup. This cup is used for drinking very strong black coffee similar to espresso. A *demitasse* is usually served following dinner.

equi—equal

Don't get *equi* confused with *equus,* which means "horse." *Equestrian* competition involves horse-riding.

equal Evenly proportioned.

equator—The earth is not a perfect sphere because it is slightly flattened at the poles. The greatest circumference of the earth is at the equator and is 24,902 miles.

equator The imaginary line around the middle of the earth that splits it into two equal parts.

equidistant Equally distant.

equinox *Equi* meaning "equal" and *nox* meaning "night." The *equinox* happens twice a year, once in March and then again in September, when day and night are of exactly *equal* length.

equilibrium The state of being evenly balanced. Your *equilibrium,* or balance, is controlled by your inner ear.

equilateral A figure having *equal* sides. A square is an *equilateral.*

omni—all

omnivorous Eating all sorts of food, especially both animal and vegetable food. Human beings are *omnivorous.*

omnipotent All-powerful. Many religions consider God to be *omnipotent.*

omniscient All-knowing. The professor thought he was *omniscient* in his subject area.

omnipresent Present in all places at the same time. Cartoons are *omnipresent* on TV on Saturday mornings.

ambi, amphi—both; around

These two word parts have the same meaning, one coming from Latin and the other from Greek.

ambidextrous Able to use both hands equally well.

ambiguous Vague; having two or more meanings. Because the teacher's directions were *ambiguous,* many students failed to complete the assignment correctly.

ambivalent *Ambi* means "both" and *valens* means "worth," so *ambivalent* means "an inability to decide between two conflicting feelings or thoughts." My parents are *ambivalent* about my getting a job. On the one hand, they would like me to earn money; on the other, they think my grades will suffer.

amphibian An organism that is able to live or operate on land and in the water. A salamander is an *amphibian.*

An Outdoor Amphitheater in Greece

amphitheater A type of theater or stadium that has seats going all around the stage or arena. The Greeks and Romans built outdoor *amphitheaters,* many of which are still in use today. You may have an *amphitheater* in your hometown for summer concerts.

Exercise 1

Directions: In the blanks below, write the word from the list that best completes the sentence. Use each word only once.

ambidextrous	amphitheater	centenarian	century	equal
equilibrium	million	multilateral	polygraph	semester

1. Sarah Delany, the co-author of *Having Our Say—The Delany Sisters' First 100 Years,* is a good example of a ________________.
2. While many religions consider the wife to be ________________ to the husband in the spousal relationship, some religions say a wife "should submit herself graciously" to her husband's leadership.
3. Because of her work for the poor of India, *Time* magazine named Mother Teresa one of the most inspirational people of the 20th ________________.
4. The special prosecutor wants those individuals requesting immunity from prosecution to submit to a complete ________________ examination.
5. If a basketball player can dribble and pass the ball equally well with either hand, we would probably call the player ________________.
6. Marcus was relieved to have the spring ________________ of college over so that he could relax over a long summer break.
7. A retired couple just won over a(n) ________________ dollars in the New Jersey Lottery.
8. The old movie classic *Ben-Hur* has a famous chariot race that takes place in a Roman ________________.
9. A(n) ________________ environmental treaty was signed by six nations.
10. In order to perform well on the balance beam, a gymnast must have a superb sense of ________________.

Exercise 2

Directions: In the blanks below, write the word from the list that best completes the sentence. Use each word only once.

ambiguous	centigrade	centimeters	centipede	equator
hemisphere	omnipresent	omniscient	omnivorous	polygamy
polyglot	semiprofessional			

1. We turned down the wrong street because the directions that the attendant at the gas station gave us were ________________.
2. Young children believe their parents to be ________________ because they expect them to know the answers to any question that they ask.
3. The ________________ thermometer, devised by Swedish astronomer Anders Celsius, is now used throughout most of the world.

4. The United States and Canada are located in the Western _______________.
5. If _______________ were allowed in the United States, do you think many men would have more than one wife?
6. Ants seem to be _______________ at most picnics.
7. The _______________ is a segmented, nocturnal animal known for its poisonous bite.
8. The _______________ is equidistant from the North Pole and the South Pole.
9. My dog Cookie is _______________; she'll eat anything.
10. A college teacher who speaks five languages fluently qualifies as a(n) _______________.
11. The movie *Bull Durham,* starring Kevin Costner, is about a(n) _______________ baseball team.
12. A typical pencil is 19 _______________ long.

Expanding Your Word Power

The words listed below are not found in this Vocabulary Unit, but they are derived from the vocabulary word parts that you have studied. All of them would be good words for you to learn. See if you can guess the meaning of each word from its word parts.

1. bicoastal
2. semiannual
3. semiautomatic
4. semifinal
5. semisweet
6. equivalent
7. ambient

Vocabulary Unit 3 Crossword Puzzle

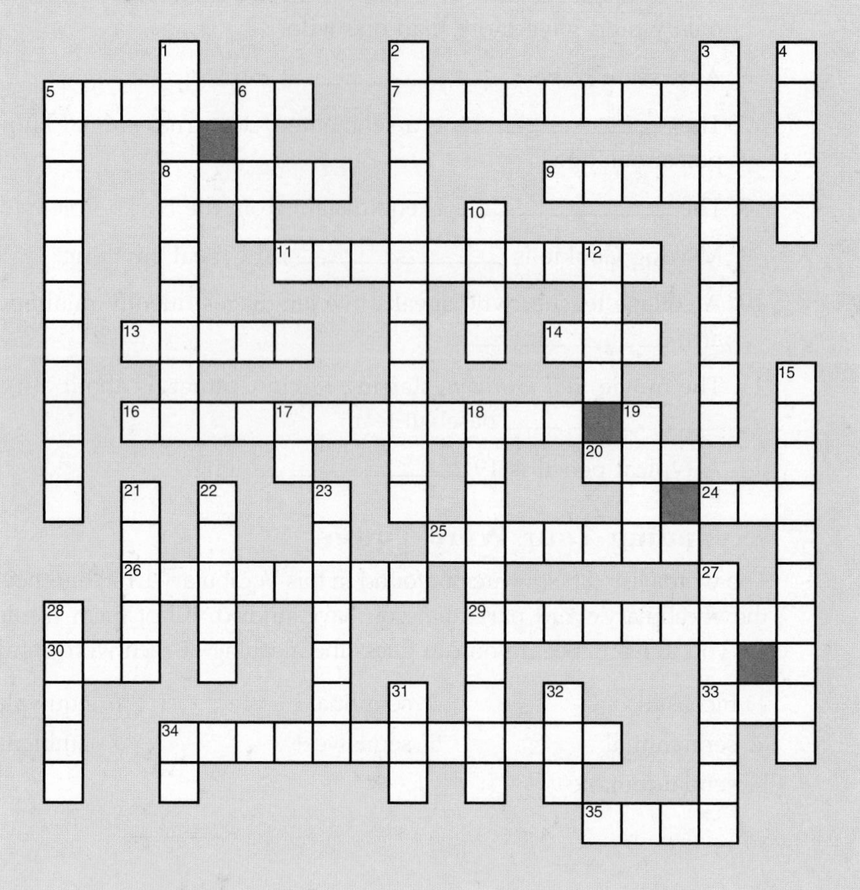

ACROSS CLUES

5. This event happens in September and March.
7. This "critter" has two pairs of legs on each of its segments.
8. A root word meaning "moon."
9. The imaginary line dividing the Northern and Southern Hemispheres.
11. 1/100 of a meter.
13. A word part meaning "1,000."
14. A word part meaning "two."
16. Being able to use both hands equally well.
20. The abbreviation for what was once the ninth month.
24. The abbreviation for what was once the eighth month.
25. 1,000 × 1,000.
26. A person who can speak many languages.
29. A "critter" that appears to have 100 legs.
30. A word part meaning "one."
33. A word part meaning "three."
34. 200-year anniversary.
35. A word part meaning "many."

DOWN CLUES

1. 1,000 years.
2. In ancient Greece, you might have gone to a(n) ______ to watch a play.
3. Water freezes at 0 degrees on this scale.
4. A word part meaning "four."
5. A square is a(n) _____ figure.
6. Word part meaning "all."
10. A word part meaning "both."
12. A word part meaning "equal."
15. Movies are ______ experiences because they combine images and sound.
17. A word part meaning "two."
18. All-knowing.
19. A word part meaning "one."
21. A word part meaning "both."
22. A word part for "many."
23. A figure with many sides.
27. In the year 2001, we entered the 21st _____.
28. A word part meaning "five."
31. An abbreviation for what was once the 10th month.
32. A word part meaning "marriage."
34. A word part meaning "two."

Vocabulary Unit 3: Additional Practice with Expanding Your Word Power

Directions: Match the vocabulary word in Column A with its definition in Column B. Place the correct letter in the space provided. Column A words are from the Expanding Your Word Power list.

	Column A	Column B
______	1. ambient	a. occurring or existing on two coasts
______	2. bicoastal	b. a person who hates marriage
______	3. bigamy	c. multicolored
______	4. equivalent	d. occurring twice a year
______	5. misogamist	e. an algebraic expression having two or more terms
______	6. monogamy	f. the next to last round in an elimination tournament
______	7. polychromatic	g. slightly sweetened
______	8. polynomial	h. entering into a marriage with one person while still legally married to another
______	9. semiannual	i. not fully automatic
______	10. semiautomatic	j. equal in value, amount, or function
______	11. semifinal	k. an encompassing environment; the immediate surroundings of something
______	12. semisweet	l. the state of having a single mate

VOCABULARY Unit 4 Word Parts Dealing with the Senses, Size, and Writing

In Vocabulary Unit 3, you learned that *enn* and *ann* mean "year." In this unit, you will study some more words using these word parts. We will also introduce word parts related to the five senses, size, and writing.

Sunflower

ann—year enn—year

anniversary The yearly return of a date or event, as in a wedding *anniversary*.

annual *Annual* usually means "yearly," but it is also a term used to describe a plant living only one year or season. A sunflower is an example of an *annual* because it completes its life cycle, produces seeds, and dies after growing only one season. *Annual* flowers will not bloom again.

biannual Happening twice a year. The equinox is a *biannual* event.

biennial Happening every two years; also a plant that lasts for two years. Congressional elections take place *biennially*.

perennial Continuing for a long time; year after year; also a plant that has roots that remain alive during the winter and that blooms year after year, such as the iris. The New York Yankees are *perennially* a good baseball team.

anno Domini (A.D.) *Anno* means "year," and *Domini* means "Lord," so *A.D.* does not mean "after death," but "Year of Our Lord." The Civil War began in *A.D.* 1860.

audio—hear ology—the study of; the science of spec(t) —to see

audience A group of people gathered to hear (and see) a speaker, play, or concert; also a formal interview with someone in a high position. The local parish priest was granted an *audience* with the pope.

audiology The science of hearing.

auditorium A room where an audience usually gathers to listen.

audition A hearing to judge the skills of a musician or actor for a job. When you *audition* for a part in a play, the director will be interested in hearing how you read your lines. There were no microphones in ancient Greece, so actors who were in plays had to be able to say their lines loud enough so that the people in the back row of the amphitheaters could hear them.

auditory Having to do with the sense of hearing; also your listening skills. In the first part of this textbook, you discovered whether you were an *auditory* learner.

spectator A person who sees or watches something without being an active participant. You might be a *spectator* at a football game.

spectrum—One beautiful spectrum, the rainbow, occurs when light hits moisture in the air at a certain angle.

speculate To mentally see something in a serious way. Are you *speculating* about what you are going to do tonight?

spectrum A *spectrum* is a range of color, as in a rainbow or in light shining through a prism. The word also sometimes refers to a range of ideas. In the college classroom, there was a wide *spectrum* of opinion on the subject of abortion.

vis—see in—not; into, within

visible Capable of being seen. The mountains were *visible* from a great distance.

"Vision is the art of seeing things invisible."
—Jonathan Swift

invisible Not capable of being seen. Here *in* means "not." The Latin prefix *in* appears in many English words. Sometimes it means "not," and other times it means "into." When you come to a word using *in*, you may need to use context clues or your dictionary to determine the correct meaning.

vista A view or outlook seen from some distance.

visionary Looking into the future. He had a *visionary* scheme to create human colonies on Mars. *Visionary* also means a prophet or seer. In the Old Testament, prophets were *visionaries* because they looked into the future.

audio-visual Involving both hearing and seeing. DVD recorders are examples of *audio-visual* equipment.

phono—sound

phonograph A device for reproducing sound recorded in a turning record. The word literally means "sound written down." We used to listen to records on a *phonograph*. What's the modern-day equivalent of the *phonograph*?

phonics The study of speech sounds and their written symbols (letters). Your teacher might have taught you *phonics* when you were learning to read.

Thaves

Frank and Ernest used with the permission of Thaves and The Cartoonist Group. All rights reserved.

macro—large micro—small, or one-millionth part; enlarging, amplifying bio—life scope—an instrument for seeing

microwave A small electromagnetic wave; also an oven that cooks with *microwaves*. The literal meaning is "small wave."

micrometer One-millionth of a meter.

microphone An instrument for amplifying sound. In this word, *micro* means "amplifying what is small or weak."

microscope An instrument for making very small objects look larger. In this word, *micro* means "enlarging what is small."

microeconomics An economic analysis of small-scale parts of the economy, such as the growth of a single industry or demand for a single product.

macroeconomics The part of economic theory that deals with the larger picture, such as national income, total employment, and total consumption.

microbiology The branch of biology that deals with small life organisms.

magna—large mega—large; one million tele—distance

magnify To make larger.

megaphone A device for magnifying the voice; literally means "large sound." Police may use *megaphones* to be heard over the noise of the crowd.

megabyte One million pieces of information; loosely one million bytes.

telescope An optical device for seeing distant objects; use of a *telescope* makes these distant objects appear to be closer.

telephone A device for transmitting speech or computerized information over distances; "sound from a distance."

telephone—The first telephone book was published in 1878 in New Haven, Connecticut. It listed only 50 names.

telephoto A camera lens that magnifies a distant object so that it appears to be close. A photographer working for a tabloid magazine was able to get a picture of Prince William by using a camera equipped with a *telephoto* lens.

telepathy Mind reading; knowledge communicated from one person to another without using any of the five senses; "feeling from a distance."

teleconference A conference of persons in different locations by means of the telephone or TV.

television—"All television is educational television. The question is: what is it teaching?"

—Nicholas Johnson

television "Seeing from a distance."

scribe, script—write biblio—book pre—before post—after

scribble To write carelessly, quickly.

inscription Something engraved; a short, signed message. (Here *in* means "into.") Because Thomas Jefferson wanted to be remembered for the things he had left to the people, and not for the high offices he had held, the *inscription* on his tomb reads: "Here was buried Thomas Jefferson, author of the Declaration of American Independence, of the Statute of Virginia for religious freedom, and father of the University of Virginia."

prescription Something advised or ordered; a written direction for the preparation and use of medicine; "written before." Following her attack of the flu, her doctor's *prescription* was lots of fluids and complete bed rest.

postscript A note written after the signature in a letter (P.S.).

scribe A writer, author, or secretary. Before the invention of printing, the *scribes* were professional penmen who copied manuscripts and documents.

Scripture Any sacred writing or book; a Bible passage.

Bible—The Bible is the best-selling book in the world. The entire Bible has been translated into at least 337 languages.

Bible The sacred book of Christianity; the Old Testament and New Testament.

bibliography Since *graph* means "write," a *bibliography* literally means "books written down." A *bibliography* is a list of sources of information on a particular subject. When you write a research paper for one of your classes, you will include a *bibliography* at the end of your paper listing the books and articles you used for your research.

Exercise 1: Word Parts

Directions: Write sentences using the following words. Add whatever endings are necessary.

1. audiologist ______________________________
____
2. perennial ______________________________
____
3. speculate ______________________________
____
4. scribe ______________________________
____
5. biennial ______________________________
____
6. visionary ______________________________
____
7. telepathy ______________________________
____
8. scribble ______________________________
____

Exercise 2: Word Parts

Directions: In the blanks below, write the word from the list that best completes the sentence. Use each word only once.

audition	biannual	bibliography	inscription	invisible
magnify	microwave	perennial	phonics	scribbles

1. Marco decided to fill his garden with ______________ plants that don't have to be replaced year after year.

2. The former employees of the department store hold a(n) ______________ luncheon in January and July of every year.

3. Educators have not decided whether it is better to teach young children to read by the whole-language approach or to use ______________ to teach them the sounds the letters make.

4. The mother saved all of her child's drawings, although most were little more than colorful ______________.

5. Marla's research paper was excellent, but she received a D because she forgot to include a complete list of her sources in a(n) ______________.

6. The ______________ on the wedding ring read, "To my beloved Luz, the light of my life."

7. Millions of baby boomers need glasses to ______________ the small print in books.

8. The young actor's ______________ for the play apparently did not go well because he did not get the role.

9. A chameleon can make itself almost ______________ by changing colors to match its surroundings.

10. The ______________ is a more popular appliance than the dishwasher.

Exercise 3: Word Parts

Directions: In the blanks below, write the word from the list that best completes the sentence. Use each word only once.

biennial	megaphone	microphones	postscript	spectators
spectrum	teleconference	telepathy	visionary	vista

1. I would think that if anyone could communicate by means of ______________ it would be identical twins.

2. The police officer, who was using a ______________ to be heard over the crowd, urged the soccer fans to disperse quickly and quietly.

3. Rather than waste time, energy, and money flying to New York to go over the details of the will, all of the parties agreed to hold a ______________ instead.

4. Marta's daughter wrote her a wonderful letter for Mother's Day, and as a ______________ she wrote, "I love you."

5. Although the number of ______________ actually attending the World Series has not declined, the number of viewers watching on TV certainly has.

6. During the televised debate, both candidates' ______________ went dead for over 10 minutes.

7. The pansy is a ______________ plant that produces a flower in the second year.

8. After the arduous climb to the top of Mount Everest, we were rewarded with a sweeping ______________ of Southeast Asia.

9. The polls certainly revealed a wide ______________ of opinion about future tax cuts.

10. In his book *The Road Ahead,* Bill Gates clearly demonstrates why he is the leading communications ________________ of the 21st century.

Expanding Your Word Power

The words listed below are not found in this Vocabulary Unit, but they are derived from the vocabulary word parts that you have studied. All of them would be good words for you to learn. See if you can guess the meaning of each word from its word parts.

1. auditor
2. inaudible
3. auspicious
4. conspicuous
5. spectacular
6. introspection
7. perspicacious
8. envision
9. visage
10. vis-à-vis
11. visitation
12. cacophony
13. symphony
14. telegenic
15. manuscript
16. describe
17. conscription
18. precede
19. precook
20. prehistoric
21. presume
22. prejudge
23. precocious
24. predispose
25. prerequisite
26. postdate
27. postpartum
28. posterior
29. posthumous
30. postmortem

Vocabulary Unit 4 Crossword Puzzle

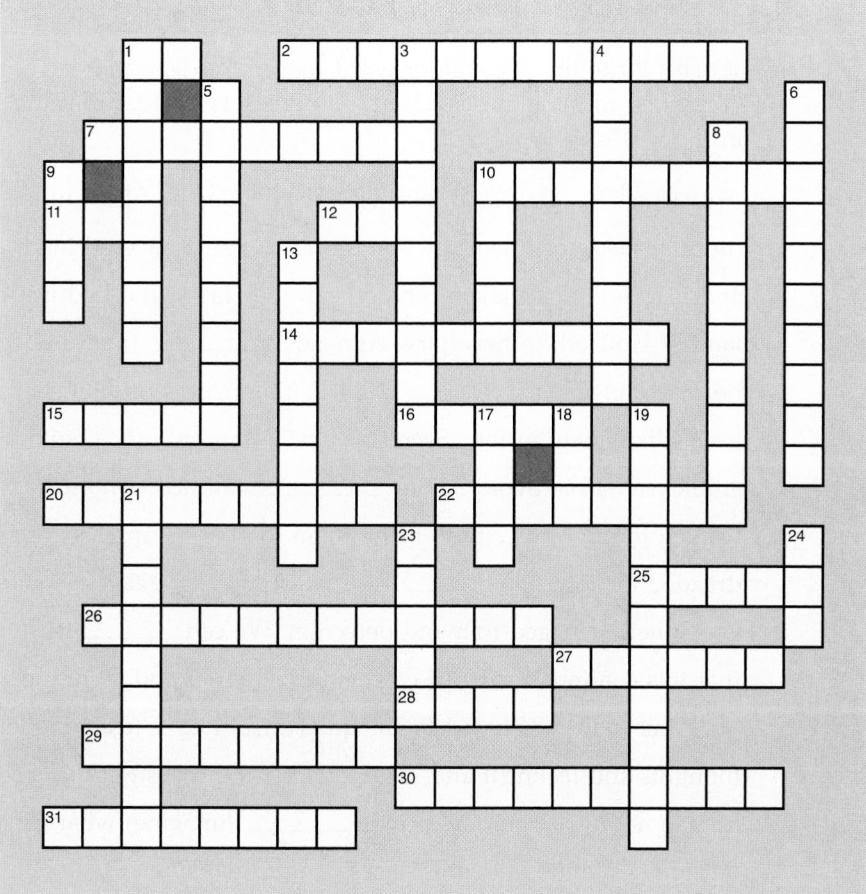

ACROSS CLUES

1. A word part meaning "two."
2. Written before.
7. Instrument to see from a distance.
10. Roses are ______ flowers. They bloom year after year.
11. A word part meaning "year."
12. A word part meaning "side."
14. "Year of Our Lord" (no space between words).
15. The sacred book of Christianity.
16. A word part meaning "to see."
20. A person who looks into the future.
22. The ______ for the Opening Ceremony of the Winter Olympics was one of the largest in history.
25. View seen from a distance.
26. A list of books or references at the end of a paper.
27. A writer.
28. A word part meaning "half."
29. Your listening skills.
30. P.S.
31. A range of light or ideas.

DOWN CLUES

1. Every other year.
3. A group that watches an event.
4. Sound from a distance.
5. Police might use one of these.
6. Seeing from a distance.
8. An instrument for amplifying sound.
9. A word part meaning "1,000,000."
10. A word part meaning "sound."
13. The equinox is a(n) ______ event.
17. A word part meaning "the same amount or size."
18. A word part meaning "three."
19. Happening once a year, such as a wedding ______.
21. Sacred writing.
23. A word part meaning "write."
24. A word part meaning "marriage."

Vocabulary Unit 4: Additional Practice with Expanding Your Word Power

Directions: Write the vocabulary word that makes sense in each blank. Definitions are provided in parentheses. Use the vocabulary words from the Expanding Your Word Power list.

In 1944, a __________ (published after the death of the author) __________ (unpublished document) by Anne Frank was discovered in an attic where she and her family had taken refuge from the Nazis who had invaded her homeland of Holland. In her diary, Anne, a __________ (mature beyond that of a normal age) 13-year-old, __________ (the process of telling—past tense) what it was like living in the "Secret Annex" of an old office building. Their loyal employee had to avoid being __________ (attracting notice or attention) as she walked through the city to bring them food and supplies. The thing they dreaded most was a __________ (visit) by the Nazis to the attic. For two years they managed to avoid detection. We can __________ (take for granted) that this continual fear caused them much grief and suffering.

Anne's diary is noted for its quiet __________ (examination of one's thoughts and feelings) and __________ (astute; insightful) observations of human nature. Anne dared to __________ (imagine) what life would be like outside her limited circumstances. Unfortunately, her __________ (impressive; striking) promise as an author was cut short when she and her family were discovered and sent to the Bergen-Belsen concentration camp. Anne Frank died at age 15 of typhus two months before the camp's liberation. Over the years, her diary became a classic tribute to human endurance and her __________ (face) has become one of the most widely recognized in the world.

VOCABULARY Unit 5 Word Parts Dealing with Direction and Position

All the word parts in this unit are related to either direction or position.

super—above or over
sub—under, below, beneath

supersonic—Chuck Yeager made the first supersonic flight October 14, 1947, over Edwards Air Force Base in California.

supersonic *Super* means "above," and *sonus* means "sound," so *supersonic* means moving at a speed greater than that of sound.

supervisor A person who oversees or directs work or workers. The original meaning of the word was "to see from above."

superscript A figure, letter, or symbol written above the line. In math, 10 squared would be written 10^2, with the 2 being a *superscript*.

subscript A figure, letter, or symbol written below the line. The chemical formula for water, H_2O, has a *subscript*.

subscribe To agree to pay for a service or periodical. Originally, when you *subscribed* to a magazine, you signed your name at the bottom of the contract on the dotted line.

subliminal *Limen* means "threshold." If something is *subliminal*, it is below the threshold of consciousness. The sale of audiocassette tapes with *subliminal* self-help messages is a big business in the United States. While you are sleeping, you could listen to a weight-loss tape with a *subliminal* message saying "eat less."

retro—backward, back, behind

retroactive Having an effect on things that are past; going back in time. If you received *retroactive* pay, you would be paid for work that was done in the past.

retrorocket A small rocket that produces a backward thrust in order to reduce speed.

retrogress To move backward toward an earlier or worse condition; to decline. After learning new study techniques, the student *retrogressed* to her old methods of studying and just read the chapter the night before the quiz.

retrospect To see back in time; hindsight. In *retrospect*, the cook should have added more garlic to her soup.

ante(i)—before, in front of, prior to
ad—toward

Sometimes spellings of word parts change over the years. In the word part *ante*, sometimes the "e" changes to "i." This causes confusion with the word part *anti* meaning "opposite of." What do you think was the original meaning of the word *antifreeze*? Sometimes you have to use the context of a sentence to determine the meaning of a word part. When in doubt, consult a dictionary.

anticipate To look forward to something before it happens. She was *anticipating* a pleasant two-week vacation in Hawaii.

ante In poker, each player must *ante* up (place a bet) before receiving cards.

anteroom A small room before a larger or more important room. *Anterooms* can be lobbies, vestibules, or waiting rooms.

antecedent Coming before in time, order, or logic. In English grammar, the *antecedent* of a pronoun is the noun to which the pronoun refers. In the sentence "The team will win the game if it plays well," the *antecedent* of the pronoun "it" is the word "team."

antebellum *Bellum* means "war," so *antebellum* means "before the war." The word is often used in relation to the American Civil War. The *antebellum* days of the South were approximately 1820–1860.

advance *"Ance"* originally came from *ante,* and so the word *advance* literally translates as "toward before." The hurricane rapidly *advanced* on the helpless town.

adolescent A person moving toward adulthood or maturity.

advent *Ven* means "come," so *advent* means "to come toward." To Christians, the season of *Advent* includes the four Sundays before Christmas.

advertise *Vert* means "to turn," so *advertise* means "to turn toward." *Advertising* praises a service or product so that people will want to turn toward it, or buy it.

circ—ring; around cycle—circle; wheel

circulate—In one year, the human heart circulates 770,000 to 1.6 million gallons of blood. This is enough to fill 200 tank cars, each with a capacity of 8,000 gallons.

circumference—The circumference of a quarter has 119 grooves; a dime has one fewer.

circle A *circle* is a plane figure, but the word also means "to surround" or "move around."

circulate To move in a circle and return to the same point; to move around freely. Blood *circulates* through the body.

circumference The measure of the distance around a circle.

circumnavigate To sail or fly around, as in *circumnavigating* the earth. The first American to *circumnavigate* the earth in a space vehicle was John Glenn.

circumscribe To draw a line around. The student *circumscribed* the correct answer on the quiz by drawing a circle around it.

circumspect To look all around or to consider all circumstances before deciding.

circadian Relating to a person's daily biological cycle.

circa *Circa* means "around" or "approximately," in reference to a period of time or the date of an event, especially when the exact dates are not known. Jazz began in the United States *circa* 1920.

bicycle To ride or travel on a two-wheeled vehicle.

cyclorama No, not a track for bicycles. A *cyclorama* is a series of large pictures put on the wall of a circular room so that a spectator standing in the middle can see all around (360 degrees). If you have been to Disneyland, you might have seen a movie in a *cyclorama.*

cyclical Moving or occurring in a circular pattern. Fashions in clothing tend to be *cyclical.* Men's ties gradually become wider, and then gradually become narrower, and then start the cycle over.

pan—all; every; around   peri—around; about

Panavision® See all around. The movie was in *Panavision.* Movies in *Panavision* are not really all around you, but are simply on a large screen.

Panasonic® Sound all around. Do you think you really get sound all around you from a *Panasonic* transistor radio?

panorama A wide view. A synonym for *panorama* is *vista.* From the top of the mountain, the sunset produced a beautiful *panorama.*

panacea A cure-all; or the act of going around the problem. Owners of sports teams often resort to firing the coach as a *panacea* for the team's failure to win enough games. Some people view building more prisons as a *panacea* to the crime problem.

Pan-American—The Pan-Am Highway is the longest driveable road in the world. It is 15,000 miles long. It goes from northwest Alaska, down through Santiago, Chile, east through Argentina, and ends in Brasilia, Brazil.

Pan-American Common to North, South, and Central America together. The diplomats negotiated a *Pan-American* treaty to deal with poaching of endangered species.

perimeter The outer boundary or measurement around a figure or area. The soldiers guarding the camp walked along its *perimeter.*

peripheral Lying at the outside. Because he has so much money already, it is of only *peripheral* importance to him whether he gets a job. You might have your driver's license revoked if you have poor *peripheral* vision.

periscope An optical instrument used on submarines that goes up to the surface and allows a person to "look around."

Exercise 1

Directions: In the blanks below, write the word from the list that best completes the sentence. Use each word only once.

adolescent	anteroom	anticipating	circulate	circumspect
panacea	perimeter	retrospect	subscribe	supervisor

1. Ginny can't seem to get along with her ______________ at work, so she's going to have to start looking for another job.
2. Oscar was ______________ his 21st birthday because his friends were taking him to Las Vegas to celebrate.
3. There is no easy ______________ for the problem of poverty in the United States because every possible solution creates a host of unforeseen complications.
4. In trying to win a sweepstakes award, many people ______________ to a large number of magazines they don't really want.
5. In ______________, Herminia should have known that the free, all-expenses-paid vacation to the Bahamas was too good to be true.

6. The legislator waited in the _______________ for about 30 minutes talking to the president's secretary before being admitted to the president's private study.
7. At a wedding reception, it's considered good manners for the bride and groom to _______________ among all of their guests.
8. Many parents find it difficult to understand and cope with a(n) _______________ and are glad when the teenage years finally end.
9. Since his last brush with the law, Mark has behaved in a very _______________ manner, going out of his way to stay out of trouble.
10. Bandit patrols the _______________ of his yard to make sure no other dog has dared trespass.

Exercise 2

Directions: Write the word from the list that best completes the sentence. Use each word only once.

advent	antebellum	antecedent	circa	circumference
circumscribe	cyclical	panorama	peripheral	retroactive

1. The most famous and probably most photographed _______________ mansion in Louisiana is Oak Alley, where parts of *Interview with a Vampire* and *Primary Colors* were filmed.
2. Does the _______________ of a person's head have anything to do with how smart the person is? Some studies suggest there may be a correlation.
3. Only one item has been in the White House since the very beginning—the Gilbert Stuart painting of George Washington _______________ 1800.
4. The cab crashed because of a number of _______________ events, including the cab company's failure to replace faulty brakes and its hiring of a careless driver.
5. With the _______________ of winter, Victor knew he would soon have to put snow tires on his car.
6. After a six-month training period at Bank of America, Diarra received a salary of $9 an hour. She also got some back pay, because her new salary was _______________ to when she first started her training.
7. Watching her young daughter go out the door in a tank top and bell bottoms reminded Charlene of clothes she had worn as an adolescent. She realized just how _______________ fashion is.
8. Edwin stood on the edge of the Grand Canyon and looked at the _______________ spread before him. The breathtaking view filled him with awe.
9. My father, who is in his eighties, is no longer allowed to drive because of an impairment of his _______________ vision.
10. The teacher told the student to look on the map of California and _______________ Santa Clara County in red ink.

Expanding Your Word Power

The words listed below are not found in this Vocabulary Unit, but they are derived from the vocabulary word parts that you have studied. All of them would be good words for you to learn. See if you can guess the meaning of each word from its word parts.

1. superimpose
2. superstar
3. supernatural
4. substandard
5. subconscious
6. subway
7. subjugate
8. subversion
9. retrofit
10. antechamber
11. anterior
12. antacid
13. antipathy
14. antithesis
15. antisocial
16. circuitous
17. circumvent
18. pandemic
19. pandemonium
20. panopoly
21. peistalsis
22. periodontal
23. peripatetic

Vocabulary Unit 5 Crossword Puzzle

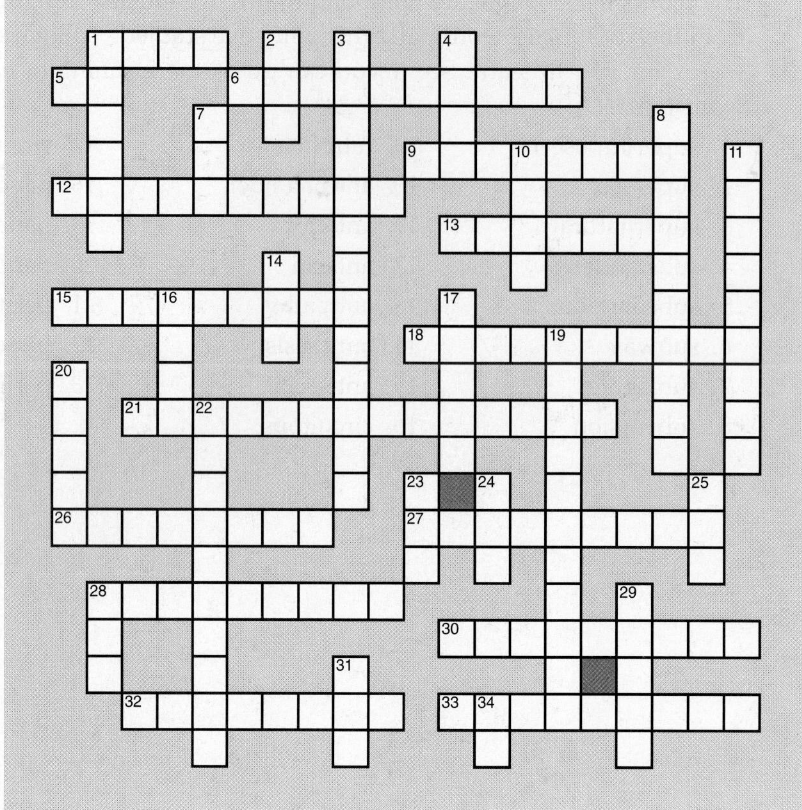

ACROSS CLUES

1. What you might do at the beginning of a poker game before receiving your cards.
5. A word part meaning "toward."
6. ______ vision is to the side.
9. You might see a beautiful ______ (synonym for *vista*) from the top of a mountain.
12. The ______ days of the South were those preceding the Civil War.
13. A cure-all.
15. To sign your name at the bottom of a contract.
18. A person who oversees.
21. John Glenn was able to ______ the earth.
26. A lobby or vestibule.
27. Your daily biological rhythm is your ______ cycle.
28. The formula for carbon dioxide has a(n) ______ in it.
30. An outer boundary is called a(n) ______.
32. Occurring in cycles.
33. The literal meaning is "to turn toward."

DOWN CLUES

1. The period of time before Christmas.
2. The abbreviation for what was once the 10th month.
3. The distance around a circle.
4. A word part meaning "large."
7. A word part meaning "under."
8. The movie was in ______.
10. A word part meaning "all."
11. Large pictures all around you in a circular room.
14. A word part meaning "see."
16. A word part meaning "half."
17. A word part meaning "hear."
19. Back pay is ______.
20. The antique was ______ 1900.
22. In hindsight or ______.
23. The abbreviation for what was once the 8th month.
24. A word part meaning "three."
25. A word part meaning " one."
28. A word part meaning "six."
29. A word part meaning "100."
31. A word part meaning "around."
34. A word part meaning "two."

Vocabulary Unit 5: Additional Practice with Expanding Your Word Power

Directions: Give an answer for each of the following. The vocabulary words are from the Expanding Your Word Power list.

1. Name two people who are *superstars.* ________________.
2. Who would you turn to for help if you had *periodontal* disease? ________________
3. Who is more likely to tear his *anterior* cruciate ligament, someone who is sedentary or someone who is active? ________________
4. If you are *peripatetic,* are you likely to stay in one place for a long time? ________________
5. If your home was built with *substandard* materials, are you going to be pleased or angry when you find out? ________________
6. Do people who live in a society in which they are *subjugated* tend to be contented or discontented? ________________
7. If you wanted to *circumvent* the backup on the freeway, would you get off it or stay on it? ________________
8. Does a *pandemic* involve a few people or many? ________________
9. If you feel *antipathy* toward a political candidate, are you likely to vote for or against her? ________________
10. Does an *antisocial* person enjoy social gatherings or try to avoid them? ________________

VOCABULARY Unit 6 Word Parts Dealing with Opposing Meanings

This unit begins with the word part *auto,* found in many English words. It then looks at word parts having opposing meanings, such as "over" and "under," and "same" and "different." The last section covers some words that are commonly confused.

auto—self or same

automobile *Auto* means "self," so an *automobile* is a self-moving vehicle.

autograph *Graph* means "write," and *auto* means "self," so an *autograph* is a person's own signature. The literal meaning is self-written.

automaton Acting unthinkingly or automatically, like a robot. After the police officer had informed the Millers of their daughter's murder, the couple acted like *automatons* in making arrangements for her funeral.

autonomous *Auto* means "self" and *nomos* means "law," so the literal meaning of *autonomous* is "self law." The word refers to self-government or being independent. The United States is an *autonomous* country. Individual states in the United States are not totally *autonomous* because they are part of the United States. Are individual citizens in the United States *autonomous?*

co, com, con—with, together
contra—against; opposite

cooperate To act or work together with another or others.

committee A group of people chosen to work together on a particular matter.

consensus Comes from *con* meaning "with" and *sentire* meaning "to think or feel." It refers to a thinking together or a general agreement.

compare *Par* means "make equal," so if you *compare* two things, you are technically showing their similarities. But people, including college instructors, often use this word when they really mean to show similarities and differences. If one of your instructors asks you to do a *comparison,* find out whether the instructor wants you to show similarities only, or really wants you to show similarities and differences.

contrast *Contra* means "against," so *contrast* means "to point out differences," or how one thing goes against another.

contradict Comes from *contra* meaning "against" and *dict* meaning "say," as in *diction* and *predict.* The literal meaning of *contradict* is "say against." To *contradict* means "to deny the statement" of another person.

contraband *Ban* originally meant "to officially forbid," so *contraband* means "to forbid against." Today it refers to something that is illegal to import or export. Cocaine would be considered *contraband.*

extra—over; more than; beyond
ultra—over; more; beyond
infra—under, below, beneath

extramarital Relating to a sexual relationship with someone other than one's spouse.

extraterrestrial *Terra* means "earth," so an *extraterrestrial* is a being from outside the earth's limits. The title character from the movie *E.T.* was an *extraterrestrial.* Scientists are actively searching for signs of *extraterrestrial* intelligence.

extrasensory Some people believe that they have a power of perception beyond the normal senses. They credit this *extrasensory* perception, or ESP, for their ability to predict the future, read someone else's thoughts, or visualize an unknown event. For example, have you ever felt that something tragic has happened to a close friend, and it turned out you were right? That might be ESP. Scientists, though, are very skeptical about the validity of ESP.

ultraviolet *Ultraviolet* light is above violet on the color spectrum. It is invisible because its wavelengths are too short. The ozone layer blocks most, but not all, of the harmful *ultraviolet* radiation, which is what causes sunburns.

ultramicroscope An instrument that allows a person to see things too small to be seen by an ordinary microscope.

infrared *Infrared* light is below red on the color spectrum. It is invisible because its wavelengths are too long for the human eye. The army uses *infrared* light to see at night. TV remote controls use *infrared* light.

infrastructure The basic structure or underlying foundation of something. The *infrastructure* of a house is its foundation and framing. The *infrastructure* of a community is its roads, schools, power plants, and transportation and communication systems.

trans—across

transportation *Port,* as in portable, port-a-potties, and import, means "to carry." So, *transportation* refers to the act of carrying something from one place to another.

transmission *Mis,* as in missile and missionary, means "to send," so *transmission* means "the act of sending across." The *transmission* of a car sends energy from the engine across the drive shaft to the wheels. You can also *transmit* a message to another person by writing a letter, using e-mail, voice mail, or text messaging.

transsexual A person who undergoes surgery and hormone treatments to change his or her sex. So, it could be said that a *transsexual* goes across sexual boundaries.

transvestite A *transvestite* dresses in the clothing of the opposite sex. So, a *transvestite* dresses across sexual boundaries. If you can't remember the difference between this word and the one above, keep in mind that a vest is a piece of clothing. It comes from *vestire,* which means "to dress."

homo—same; equal; like
hetero—different

homosexual Having sexual desire for the same sex.

heterosexual Having sexual desire for the opposite sex.

homogeneous The same in structure or quality; having similar parts. Your class is fairly *homogeneous* in terms of age if you are all of a comparable age.

heterogeneous Dissimilar; composed of unlike parts. Your class may be *heterogeneous* because you come from different backgrounds, cultures, and countries.

homogenization The *homogenization* process of milk mixes the fat particles of the cream evenly throughout so that the cream doesn't separate. In milk taken straight from the cow, the lighter cream rises to the top. This is different from the process of pasteurization, named after inventor Louis Pasteur, which uses heat to kill bacteria.

Here are some words that are often confused with one another. Though some may appear to use the word parts mentioned in this unit, they really do not.

compliment Something said in praise; to make a nice remark about someone.

complement That which completes or makes whole or perfect; to balance. The team plays well because the players *complement* each other; they fit together well. Steve needs to get his date a corsage that will *complement* the color of her dress.

supplement Comes from *sub* meaning "under" and *plere* meaning "to fill," and refers to something added to make up for a lack. Physicians often prescribe vitamin *supplements* to pregnant women.

council A group of people called together to make decisions, such as a city council.

counsel A mutual exchange of ideas; to give or take advice.

consul A government official appointed to live in a foreign country and look after his or her country's citizens who are in the foreign country. If you were in a foreign country and having passport problems, you might go to the U.S. *consulate* for help. If you are from another country, you may wish to visit your country's *consulate.*

continuous Going on without any interruption; unbroken. Think of "ous" to help you remember the meaning of this word, as in "one uninterrupted sequence." The cars backed up in a *continuous* line on the freeway.

continual Repeated often; over and over again but with interruptions. The weather forecaster predicted *continual* showers over the Labor Day weekend.

Exercise 1: Writing Sentences

Make up your own sentences using each of the following words:

complement ______________________________

____

homogeneous ______________________________

____

autonomous ______________________________

____

infrastructure ______________________________

____

continuous ______________________________

____

extrasensory ______________________________

____

automaton ______________________________

____

Exercise 2 Word Parts: Opposing Meanings

Directions: In the blanks below, write the word from the list that best completes the sentence. Use each word only once.

autograph	automaton	committee	compare	complement
consul	contraband	extramarital	heterogeneous	homogeneous

1. After Duy's daughter was killed in a drive-by shooting, he performed his job like a(n) ______________, just going through the motions.
2. To address morale problems in the school district, a(n) ______________ was formed composed of teachers, parents, administrators, and students.
3. Many educators believe that a national test in reading and math is needed so that people can ______________ student performance in their state with what is happening in other states.
4. Many major league baseball stars will only sign a(n) ______________ for a child.
5. Drug traffickers often use "mules" to transport ______________ into the United States.
6. People who form successful partnerships often have individual traits that ______________ each other.
7. Stranded in Brazil with no money and no passport, Kathleen sought help from the U.S. ______________.
8. In the workplace today, diversity is widespread, creating a(n) ______________ mix of people and ideas.
9. In the past few years, the media has often exposed the ______________ affairs of leading political candidates.
10. A high school composed solely of Catholic boys age 14–18 would have a(n) ______________ student body.

Exercise 3 Word Parts: More Opposing Meanings

Directions: In the blanks below, write the word from the list that best completes the sentence. Use each word only once.

autonomous	complimented	consensus	continual	continuously
contradict	council	counsel	extraterrestrials	supplement

1. We all ______________ my daughter-in-law, Bonnie, and her friend, Kathleen, on the outstanding meal they had prepared.

2. The teacher was not going to be able to attend class on Monday. She told her students that if they could achieve a(n) ______________ about doing an extra assignment, she would agree to cancel class. Otherwise, she would have to get a substitute.

3. Betsy, a battered wife, sought ______________ on how to get a restraining order against her husband.

4. The city ______________ passed an ordinance requiring those under the age of 18 to be home by 10:00 P.M. on weekdays and by midnight on weekends.

5. While working at the preschool with the two- and three-year olds, Elvira had a(n) ______________ headache.

6. The Colorado River flows ______________.

7. If Bart wanted to be completely ______________ and his own man, why did he call his parents every Sunday asking for money?

8. A president needs to have advisors willing to ______________ him. It is not a good idea for him to be surrounded by a bunch of "yes men."

9. Many police officers ______________ their incomes by working in department stores as security guards on their days off.

10. He won an award for his science fiction story about ______________ on Mars.

Expanding Your Word Power

The words listed below are not found in this Vocabulary Unit, but they are derived from the vocabulary word parts that you have studied. All of them would be good words for you to learn. See if you can guess the meaning of each word from its word parts.

1. autoimmune
2. autism
3. extraneous
4. extrapolate
5. extraordinary
6. extravagant
7. transcendent
8. transient
9. translation
10. transfuse
11. transfiguration
12. coauthor
13. cohabitate
14. contraceptive

Vocabulary Unit 6 Crossword Puzzle

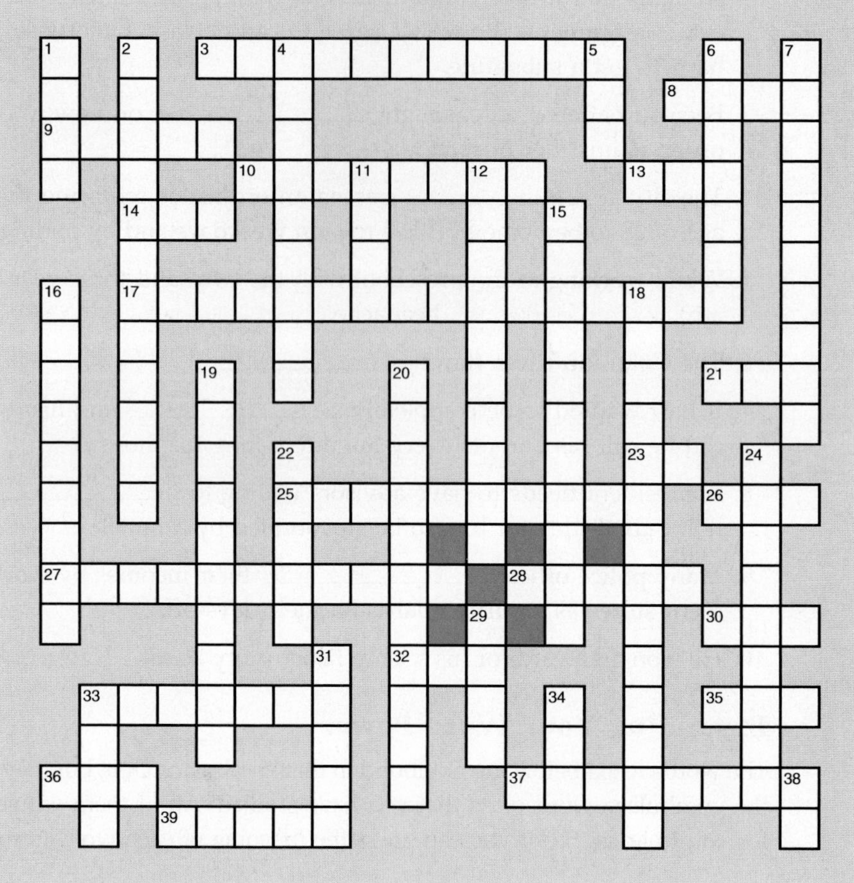

ACROSS CLUES

3. A person who has had a sex change operation.
8. A word part meaning "same."
9. A word part meaning "across."
10. To point out differences.
13. A word part meaning "around."
14. A word part meaning "below."
17. E.T.
21. An abbreviation for what was once the 10th month.
23. A word part meaning "toward."
25. Your state is not ______ because it is part of the United States.
26. A word part meaning "two."
27. ______ milk has been heated to kill bacteria.
28. A word part meaning "back."
30. An abbreviation for what was once the 8th month.
32. A word part meaning "year."
33. A group called together for discussion.
35. A word part meaning "see."
36. A word part meaning "three."
37. ______ light has wavelengths longer than ordinary light.
39. A word part meaning "over, more, beyond."

DOWN CLUES

1. A word part meaning "self."
2. A person who wears the clothing of the opposite sex.
4. Self-written.
5. A word part meaning "side."
6. To give advice.
7. To deny the statement of someone.
11. A word part meaning "distance."
12. A person who directs work or workers.
15. Light that causes sunburn.
16. The chemical formula for water has a(n) ______ in it.
18. The foundation and frame of a building.
19. That which completes; to balance.
20. In a(n) ______ group, the members are alike.
22. A word part meaning "large."
24. To sign your name at the bottom of a document.
29. A word part meaning "before."
31. A word part meaning "more or over."
33. A word part meaning "around."
34. A word part meaning "with."
38. A word part meaning "two."

Vocabulary Unit 6: Additional Practice with Expanding Your Word Power

Directions: Match the vocabulary word in Column A with its antonym in Column B. Place the correct letter in the space provided. Column A words are from the Expanding Your Word Power list.

	Column A	Column B
______	1. extraordinary	a. a. permanent
______	2. extravagant	b. commonplace
______	3. transient	c. essential
______	4. extraneous	d. economical

Directions: Match the vocabulary words in Column A with their synonym in Column B. Place the correct letter in the space provided.

	Column A	Column B
______	1. translation	a. preventive
______	2. extrapolate	b. sublime
______	3. transcendent	c. adaptation
______	4. contraceptive	d. deduce

VOCABULARY Unit 7 Word Parts Dealing with More Opposing Meanings

This vocabulary unit will continue with word parts having opposite or nearly opposite meanings. Some of these, such as *hyper* and *hypo,* and *inter* and *intra,* are commonly confused. The middle section discusses word parts having to do with phobias. The last section discusses a word part meaning "false."

syn—same; together pro—for
anti—opposite, against nym—name

synonym—There are 2,660 synonyms for being intoxicated, more than for any other condition or object.

symphony—Beethoven was totally deaf when he wrote his Ninth Symphony.

synonym Same name. *Synonyms* are words that have the same or similar meanings. For example, *vista* and *panorama* are synonyms.

antonym Different name. *Antonyms* are words having opposite meanings. *Homogeneous* and *heterogeneous* are words with opposite meanings.

symphony *Sym* means "together" and *phono* means "sound," so a *symphony* orchestra produces music by blending sounds together.

antiphony Opposition of sounds. An *antiphony* is a musical piece that has half of a choral group singing in front of the audience and half in back. Such singing was popular in the Middle Ages.

analyze To separate into its parts. *Ana* means "up" and *lyze* means "to loosen," so the literal meaning of the word is "to loosen something up." When you *analyze* why you did not do very well on your psychology test, you try to take apart what happened to see what went wrong.

synthesize *Syn* means "together," and so *synthesize* means to form a whole by bringing together the separate parts. What does a *synthesizer* do in music? It combines different sounds to produce a new sound.

antithesis *Anti* means "opposite," so an *antithesis* is something that is in opposition. The *antithesis* of segregation is integration.

pro-choice *Pro* means "in favor of," so a person who is *pro-choice* is supportive of a woman's right to *choose* legal abortion.

anti-abortion If you are *anti-abortion,* you are opposed to legal *abortion.*

antidote *Dote* comes from the root word meaning "to give," so an *antidote* is something given to counteract something else. If your child drinks a toxic liquid that is acidic, the container may give instructions recommending bicarbonate of soda as an *antidote.* (Remember that you should still call a doctor.)

syndicated *Syn* means "same" and *dic* means "to say," so *syndicated* means "saying the same thing." If something is *syndicated,* it appears in many newspapers, magazines, or radio or TV stations. *Garfield* is a *syndicated* cartoon that appears in newspapers around the country.

hypo—under, below hyper—above, over, excessive

hyperactive A *hyperactive* child is excessively active. If you were *hyperactive* as a child, there's a good chance you still are.

hypoactive Meaning "underactive." Depressed people are often *hypoactive.*

Calvin and Hobbes

hypothermia—A person may die of hypothermia when the body temperature is 95 degrees or less.

hyperthermia The state of being overheated or too hot; very high temperature. Long-distance runners in hot weather need to be careful to drink enough water to avoid *hyperthermia.*

hypothermia The state of being too cold or of having a below-normal body temperature. A person lost in a snowstorm might die of *hypothermia.*

hypodermic Many of you know that *derm* means "skin," so a *hypodermic* needle is one that goes under the skin.

hyperbole A *hyperbole* is an exaggeration, such as "strong as an ox." In the cartoon *on the following page,* Calvin says that his bad day makes him feel as though he has been run over by a train. This is an example of *hyperbole. Hyperbole* is discussed in the section on satire.

mania—craving
phobia—irrational fear of something

phobias—Twenty-five percent of women and 12 percent of men have at least one type of phobia. Some of the most common phobias are related to injections, the dentist, and heights.

claustrophobia Irrational fear of small, tightly enclosed places.

acrophobia Fear of high places. Acrobats obviously do not have this *phobia.*

monophobia Fear of being alone.

homophobia Fear of homosexuals (gay men and lesbians) or homosexuality.

pyromania A compulsion to start fires.

monomania An excessive interest in one thing. A *monomaniac* has a mental disorder characterized by preoccupation with one subject.

intra—within or inside inter—between or among

intercollegiate Between or among colleges or universities. Your college's *intercollegiate* baseball team plays other colleges.

intramurals Literally, this word means "within the walls," so an *intramural* sports program would be one that takes place within the walls of your college. In *intramural* athletics, student teams play against each other.

interstate Between or among states. The *interstate* highway system connects 48 states.

intrastate Within a state. Your telephone bill may have a list of your *intrastate* calls.

international Between or among nations.

intravenous Within or directly into a vein, such as an *intravenous* injection or IV bottle.

para—alongside, beside, side; partial; similar

parallel *Parallel* lines run side by side. *Parallel* ideas are similar thoughts.

paraphrase Literally, a similar phrase. When you *paraphrase* something, you put it into your own words.

paraprofessional Alongside a professional. This word refers to a person who is not a member of a given profession but who assists those who are. *Paramedics* and *paralegals* are *paraprofessionals.*

paramedic A person with limited medical duties such as a nurse's aide; a person trained to rescue others.

paralegal Persons trained to aid lawyers but not licensed to practice law.

paranoid *Para* means "beside" and *noid* refers to the mind. *Paranoia* is characterized by extreme suspiciousness or delusions of persecution.

paraplegic A *paraplegic* has a paralysis of the lower half of the body, or is partially paralyzed.

quadriplegic Total paralysis of the body from the neck down; having all four limbs paralyzed.

pseudo—false

pseudoscience A false science; a system of theories that presumes without warrant to have a scientific basis. Astrology, which studies the placement of the moon, sun, and stars to predict the future, is considered by many to be a *pseudoscience.* Astronomy is the real scientific study of the universe.

pseudonym A false name; a fictitious name, such as a pen name used by a writer to preserve anonymity. The book *Primary Colors,* describing an insider's look at the American political system, was written by Joe Klein using the *pseudonym* of Anonymous. Who is the most famous American author to write under a *pseudonym?* Hint: His two most well-known books are *The Adventures of Tom Sawyer* and *The Adventures of Huckleberry Finn.*

alias Also a false name, but usually used by criminals to disguise their identity.

misnomer To attach the wrong name to a person or a thing. What do you call that cuddly, tree-dwelling little animal from Australia? If you called this animal a koala bear, you have just used a *misnomer,* because koalas aren't bears at all. They are marsupials and carry their young in pouches like a kangaroo.

Exercise 1: Using Word Parts to Understand Meaning

Directions: Choose one of the following words to complete the sentences below. Use each word only once.

anti-abortion	claustrophobia	pseudoscience	hyperactive	hyperthermia
hypodermic	hypothermia	paraplegics	synonym	ultraviolet

1. A(n) ________________ for *irritate* is *annoy*.
2. Too much exposure to ________________ radiation can cause skin cancer.
3. The goal of the ________________ group Operation Rescue was to shut down abortion clinics.
4. ________________ and other persons with disabilities who are in wheelchairs sometimes encounter physical barriers such as the lack of ramps.
5. Most of the victims of ________________ are elderly people who have poorly heated homes.
6. A(n) ________________ child is impulsive, is full of energy, and sleeps less than other children.
7. Many people consider palm reading and fortune telling to be a form of ________________.
8. When he was 3 years old, Jeremy was locked in a closet. Now he suffers from ________________ and has trouble riding in an elevator.
9. After spending three days in the Arizona-Sonora desert without water, Brandon was suffering from ________________ and was transported to the Tucson Medical Center.
10. AIDS can be spread when drug users inject themselves with unsterile ________________ needles.

Exercise 2: Using Word Parts to Understand Meaning

Directions: Choose one of the following words to complete the sentences below. Use each word only once.

acrophobia	antidote	antonym	hyperbole	hypoactive
misnomer	parallel	paraphrase	pseudonyms	syndicated

1. *Peanuts* is a nationally ________________ cartoon that appears in hundreds of newspapers across the country.
2. The men who clean the windows on the Empire State Building most likely do not suffer from ________________.
3. The chair of the Federal Reserve Board cut interest rates as a(n) ________________ for a slowing economy.
4. Because a whale is a mammal, to call it a fish would be a(n) ________________.
5. "Be true to yourself" is a(n) ________________ of "To thine own self be true."
6. The young child diagnosed as ________________ appeared to lack energy and rarely ran around and played with other children.
7. It is a(n) ________________ to say that Dave is as tall as a tree.

8. *Introvert* is a(n) ______________ of *extrovert*.
9. Many famous authors, such as O Henry, whose real name is William Sydney Porter, used ______________ to keep their identities secret.
10. You can choose to travel on the coastal route or the interstate; the two run ______________ to each other.

Exercise 3: Using Word Parts to Make Words

Directions: Make a word using each of the following word parts. Then in your own words, define or explain the meaning of your word. Do not create any nonsense words.

Word Part	Your Word	Meaning
1. syn	______________	______________
2. sym	______________	______________
3. anti	______________	______________
4. phobia	______________	______________
5. mania	______________	______________
6. inter	______________	______________
7. intra	______________	______________
8. pro	______________	______________

Expanding Your Word Power

The words listed below are not found in this Vocabulary Unit, but they are derived from the vocabulary word parts that you have studied. All of them would be good words for you to learn. See if you can guess the meaning of each word from its word parts.

1. hypocrisy
2. hypochondriac
3. hypothetical
4. hypercritical
5. hypersensitive
6. hyperextend
7. hypertension
8. paranormal
9. paramilitary
10. paradigm
11. paradox
12. paragon
13. parameter

Vocabulary Unit 7 Crossword Puzzle

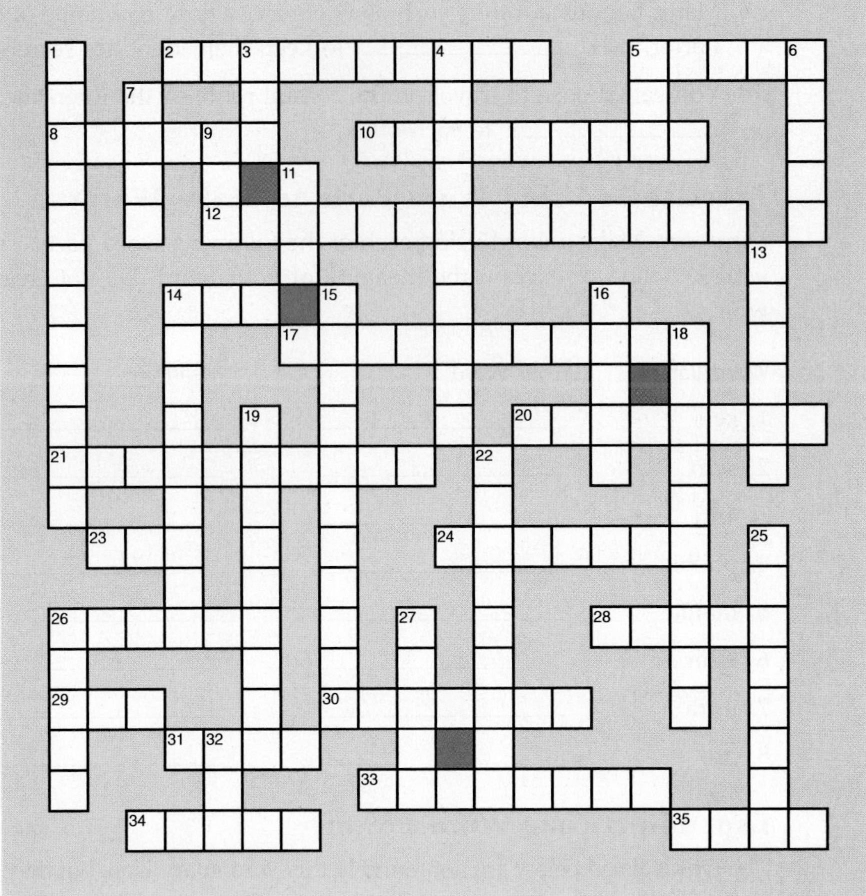

ACROSS CLUES

2. Underactive.
5. A word part meaning "above."
8. A word part meaning "false."
10. An opposition of sounds.
12. The fear of enclosed spaces.
14. A word part meaning "six."
17. Team sports on campus.
20. A person with delusions of persecution.
21. Within a state.
23. A word part meaning "two."
24. To separate into parts.
26. A word part meaning "different."
28. Used by a criminal to disguise identity.
29. A word part meaning "all around."
30. A(n) ______ for *vista* might be a *panorama*.
31. A word part meaning "same."
33. Lines running side by side.
34. A word part meaning "within" or "inside."
35. A word part meaning "alongside."

DOWN CLUES

1. Overheated.
3. A word part meaning "in favor of."
4. Between or among states.
5. A word part meaning "same."
6. A word part meaning "back."
7. A word part meaning "around" or "about."
9. An abbreviation for what was once the 10th month.
11. A word part meaning "marriage."
13. A word meaning "irrational fear."
14. An exaggeration.
15. IV.
16. A word part meaning "large."
18. To bring elements together.
19. Mark Twain is the ______ of Samuel Clemens.
22. An excessive interest in one thing.
25. The wrong name for an object.
26. A word part meaning "above" or "over."
27. A word part meaning "craving."
32. An abbreviation for what was once the 8th month.

Vocabulary Unit 7: Additional Practice with Expanding Your Word Power

Directions: Use the context to determine the meaning of the italicized word. The vocabulary words are from the Expanding Your Word Power list.

1. The gravestone of the *hypochondriac* said: "See, I told you I was sick."

   Definition of hypochondriac: ______________________________

2. She suffers from *hypertension* and must take blood pressure medication to control it.

   Definition of hypertension:

   ____

3. Was Mother Teresa a *paragon* of virtue? She certainly embodied the traits of generosity and selflessness.

   Definition of paragon: ______________________________

4. It's a *paradox* that sometimes you have to be cruel to be kind.

   Definition of paradox: ______________________________

   ____

5. While skin is not usually irritated by daily activities, people with *hypersensitive* skin may need to see a dermatologist.

   Definition of hypersensitive: ______________________________

6. In a blatant example of *hypocrisy,* the politician who was a strong advocate of family values was carrying on an affair with a woman who was not his wife.

   Definition of hypocrisy: ______________________________

   ____

7. Do you believe in telepathy, extrasensory perception, fortune-telling, and other *paranormal* phenomena?

   Definition of paranormal: ______________________________

8. The Commission on Presidential Debates lays out the *parameters* for each debate. Then it is up to the moderator to enforce them.

   Definition of parameters: ______________________________

VOCABULARY Unit 8 Word Parts and Review

Vocabulary Word Parts

Following is a list of the word parts we have studied.

Word Parts	Meaning	Examples
ad	toward	advance
ambi	both	ambiguous, ambidextrous
amphi	both	amphibian
ann, enn	year	annual, biennial
ante(i)	before	anteroom, anticipate
anti	against	antiperspirant
audio	hear	audience, auditory
auto	self	automobile, autograph
bi	two	bicycle, biathlon
biblio	book	Bible, bibliography
centi	hundred, 1/100	century, centimeter
circ	around, ring	circle, circumference
co, com, con	with	coordinate, compare, connect
contra	against	contradict, contrast
cycle	circle, wheel	bicycle
dec	ten	December, decade
demi	half	demitasse
di	two	dioxide
duo	two	duet, duel
equi	half	equator, equinox
extra	over, above	extraordinary, extraterrestrials
gam	marriage	polygamy
graph	write	polygraph
hemi	half	hemisphere
hetero	different	heterosexual, heterogeneous
homo	same	homogenized
hyper	over, above	hyperactive, hyperventilate
hypo	under, below	hypoactive, hypothermia
in	in, not	inside, invisible
infra	under	infrared, infrastructure
inter	between, among	intercollegiate, interstate
intra	within	intravenous, intrastate

Word Parts	Meaning	Examples
lat	side	lateral
macro	large	macroeconomics
magna	large	magnify, magnificent
mania	craving	pyromania
mega	large, 1,000,000	megabucks, megabyte
micro	small, 1/1,000,000	microwave, micrometer
milli	thousand, 1/1000	millennium, millimeter
mono	one	monologue, monoxide
multi	many	multicultural
nov, non	nine	November, nonagenarian
oct	eight	October, octopus
ology	study of	sociology, psychology
omni	all	omnipotent, omnivorous
pan	around	panorama, Panasonic
para	beside, partial, similar	parallel, paralegal, paraphrase
ped, pod	foot	pedal, pedestrian
pent	five	Pentagon, pentathlon
peri	around	periscope, perimeter
phobia	fear	claustrophobia, acrophobia
phono	sound	phonograph, phonics
poly	many	polygon
post	after	postscript, postnatal
pre	before	pre-test, prenatal
pro	for	pro-democracy
pseudo	false	pseudoscience, pseudonym
quad, quar	four	quartet, quadrangle
quint	five	quintuplets, quintet
retro	backward	retroactive
scope	instrument for seeing	microscope, telescope
scrib, script	write	inscribe, scripture
semi	half	semicircle
sept, hept	seven	September, septuplet, heptathlon
sex, hex	six	sextuplet
spect	see	spectator, spectrum
sub	under, below	subtract, subscript
super	above, over	supersonic, superscript

Word Parts	Meaning	Examples
syn	same	synonym, symphony
tele	distance	television
tetra	four	tetrahedron
trans	across	transportation
tri	three	tricycle, triangle
ultra	over, more, beyond	ultraconservative, ultrasonic
uni	one	unicycle, unison
vis	see	vision, visionary

Vocabulary Review Exercise

Directions: Complete the following sentences with words from the vocabulary list on the preceding pages.

1. Your telephone bill may list ________________ calls that you have made to other cities within your state.
2. If you eat a salad with your hamburger, you are eating both meat and plants, and so you are ________________.
3. A jazz ________________ would have five members.
4. The ________________ occurs twice a year, once in March and once in September.
5. You now know that if you went to a nursery and bought some ________________ flowers, they would not bloom again next year.
6. Most whole milk that you purchase at the store is called ________________ because the milk and the cream are mixed together.
7. In Chapter 1, you learned about ________________, visual, and kinesthetic learning styles.
8. *Panorama* is a(n) ________________ for *vista.*
9. The chemical formula for water has a(n) ________________ in it.
10. People who believe in unidentified flying objects are likely also to believe that ________________ have visited us.
11. Many of us are ________________ to some extent because we use both our hands.
12. The ________________ in Washington, DC, houses the Defense Department.
13. Present-day jazz music is recorded on compact discs. Jazz used to be recorded on 78 rpm ________________ records that could hold only three minutes on a side.

Vocabulary Review Puzzle

Directions: Complete the puzzle on the following page with words from Vocabulary Units 1–7.

Vocabulary Unit 8 Crossword Puzzle

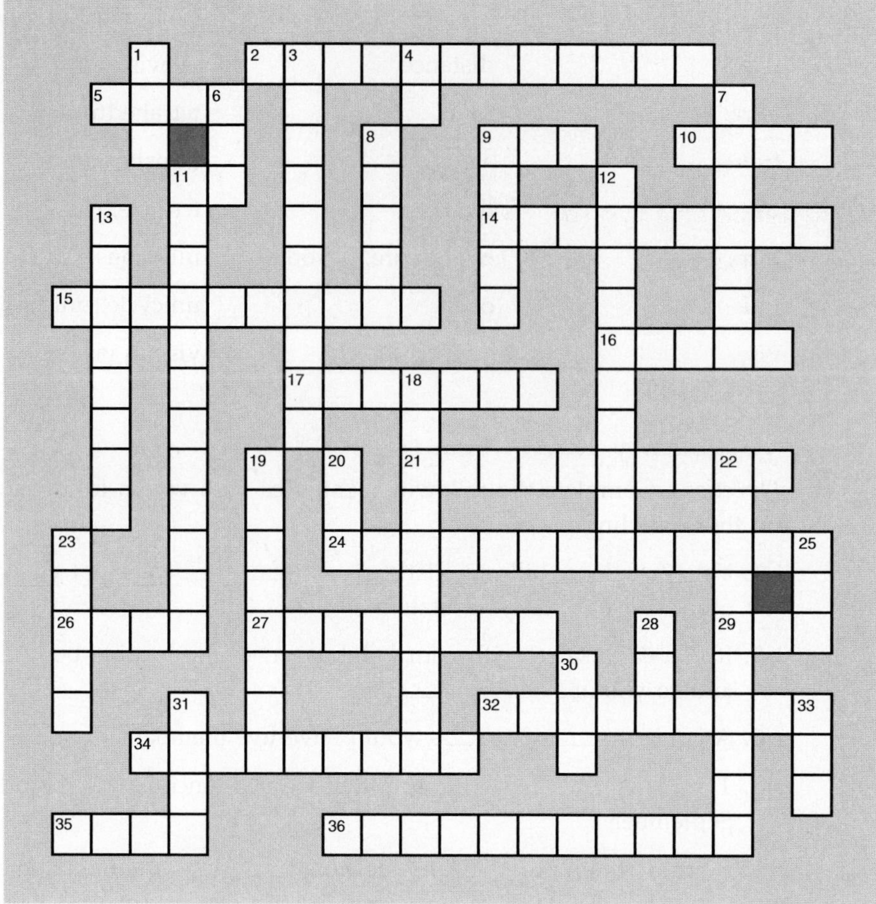

ACROSS CLUES

2. The ability to use both hands equally well.
5. A note written after the signature in a letter is a(n) ______script.
9. A word part meaning "six."
10. A(n) ______legal is a person trained to aid lawyers but not licensed to practice law.
11. A word part meaning "two."
14. A machine used on someone suspected of lying.
15. A one-sided decision.
16. A false name used by criminals to disguise their identity.
17. The time when day and night are of approximately equal length all over the earth.
21. "Seeing from a distance."
24. The measure of the distance around a circle.
26. A word part meaning "many."
27. Your listening skills; having to do with the sense of hearing.
29. A word part meaning "same; together."
32. A plant lasting more than two years.
34. An animal with four feet.
35. A word part meaning "same; equal; like."
36. A figure, letter, or symbol written above the line.

DOWN CLUES

1. Word part meaning "foot."
3. 1/1000 of a meter.
4. A word part meaning "two."
6. A word part meaning "three."
7. A cure-all; the act of going around the problem.
8. Pyro______ is a compulsion to start fires.
9. The state of being overheated or too hot is ______thermia.
11. Literally means "books written down."
12. A child with an energy level below normal could be called ______.
13. A five-sided building containing the U.S. military establishment.
18. Between or among states.
19. Light that is below red on the color spectrum.
20. Abbreviation for what was originally the 10th month.
22. "All-knowing."
23. A word part meaning "above or over."
25. A word part meaning "year."
28. A word part meaning "all; every; around."
30. A word part meaning "before."
31. A(n) ______maton acts unthinkingly or automatically, like a robot.
33. A word part meaning "side."

Appendices

We have chosen to include "Timed Reading Information," and "Test-Taking Techniques" in the Appendices. For these sections, we include an explanation of the topic, as well as practice exercises. At the end of the Appendices, you will find a summary of a reading selection and sample copies of some of the forms that appear in the text.

Timed Reading Rate Information, Readings, Questions, and Answers

Timed Reading Rate Information

The average adult reading rate on material of moderate difficulty is about 250 words per minute with 70 percent comprehension. All of the following readings are from college textbooks, and all are of about the same level of difficulty. The first five readings have approximately the same number of words.

Louis Armstrong (258 words)

Johnny Cash (248 words)

Elvis Presley (245 words)

Carlos Santana (246 words)

American Idol (252 words)

Jay-Z (571 words)

To practice increasing your reading speed, you may wish to time yourself on each of the readings. Or you could do this in groups or as a whole class. Stop reading after one minute has elapsed. Questions for each reading appear below. Try to get three to four questions correct for each reading.

For the first reading, read at your normal reading pace and then answer the questions without looking back at the material.

For the other readings, experiment with the following techniques to see if any of them help you.

- Read the material as rapidly as you can.
- Try not to reread any material.
- Keep your mind focused on the subject matter. Don't give in to distractions.
- Try to read silently without moving your lips.
- Don't read word by word, but instead try to read in phrases or thought units.
- Use your pen or pencil as a pacer by sweeping it underneath the words.

Readings

Louis Armstrong

Louis Armstrong (1901–1971) was born in New Orleans and from infancy heard the many forms of black music in that city. When he was 12, he was sent to the Colored Waifs' Home for Boys for shooting a pistol during New Year's festivities. It was at the home that Louis took up the bugle—later the cornet—and upon leaving at the age of 16, he began playing professionally. Joe Oliver, Kid Ory, and the other elders of the jazz scene gave young Armstrong guidance and employment. After Oliver's travels brought him to Chicago to form his Creole Jazz Band, he sent for Armstrong to play second cornet. Armstrong married the group's pianist, Lillian Hardin, who prepared him to leave Oliver and go out on his own as a freelance artist. From 1924 on, Armstrong appeared with many bands. During this period, Armstrong became the Johnny Appleseed of jazz, profoundly influencing his fellow musicians wherever he went. Armstrong had a rare technical and creative talent, which emerged in his trumpet playing performances. He was also a formidable force in American popular singing and influenced many popular singers. In 1964, at the height of Beatlemania in the United States, Armstrong's recording of "Hello Dolly" was the only American popular recording to compete with the Beatles for the top spot on the *Billboard* charts. His 1968 recording of "What a Wonderful World" is still popular today. Armstrong is truly a timeless musician and entertainer, honored even today by both the world of jazz artists and the popular audience. **(David Lee Joyner, *American Popular Music*, 3/e, 2009)**

Johnny Cash

Johnny Cash was one of the most remarkable artists in American popular music. While always true to himself musically, he managed to stay both commercially and artistically popular for four generations. His music could be uplifting and inspiring or even hilarious—as in the case of "A Boy Named Sue."

As portrayed in the 2005 biographical film *Walk the Line*, Johnny Cash had a humble beginning, born in rural Arkansas on February 26, 1932. He established his musical image as the dark loner in 1957 with "Folsom Prison Blues" and "I Walk the Line," his first No. 1 country hit. He appeared at the Grand Ole Opry dressed all in black, and the image blended so well with his dark ballads that he was dubbed "the man in black."

Going into the 1960s, Cash's hectic lifestyle led him to a dependence on prescription drugs. It cost him his first marriage, his freedom, and nearly ended his career and, indeed, his life. In the meantime, he had become attracted to June Carter who co-wrote Cash's "Ring of Fire." In 1980, he became the youngest inductee into the Country Music Hall of Fame, and in 1994 was inducted into the Rock and Roll Hall of Fame. Throughout his career, Cash influenced younger artists including U2 and Bruce Springsteen. When Johnny Cash passed away in 2003, just four months after the death of his beloved wife June, he was as successful and relevant as he had ever been. **(David Lee Joyner, *American Popular Music*, 3/e, 2009)**

Elvis Presley

Legendary Sam Phillips had a recording studio in Memphis, Tennessee, where he primarily recorded black urban blues singers. It was during this time that Phillips became aware of the new interest young whites had in rhythm and blues. He thought that if he could find a young white man with the black sound, he could make a million dollars.

Phillips found his dream in Elvis Presley. Through one of those fateful occurrences, young Presley, a truck driver, came by the studio in 1953 and recorded a couple of songs for his mother's birthday. Phillips called Presley back to the studio, and on the night of July 5, 1954, they recorded "That's Alright Mama," and Rockabilly came of age.

Presley was young and good looking, with a sexy and defiant look. He wore outrageous clothes, had equally outrageous body movements on stage, and could convincingly sing country, gospel, and blues songs. He quickly became a regional hit.

To get enough money to promote his other artists, Phillips sold Presley's recording contract to RCA Records in Nashville and his managerial contract to Colonel Tom Parker. Presley's first Nashville releases were "Heartbreak Hotel" and "Hound Dog" in 1956. Presley continued with a string of hits throughout the fifties. Then he entered military service, after which he vanished into Hollywood for an extended motion picture contract. Though he remained popular all his life, he never recaptured the spontaneity and natural exuberance of his original recordings. (David Lee Joyner, *American Popular Music,* 3/e, 2009)

Carlos Santana

The guitarist and songwriter Carlos Santana fuses rock with Latin and African rhythms as well as elements of jazz and the blues. A major figure in Spanish-language rock, and leader of the band Santana, he was inducted into the Rock and Roll Hall of Fame in 1998.

Santana, a fourth-generation musician, was born in 1947 in the town of Autlan de Navarra in Mexico. When he was 5 his father—a violinist and bandleader—began teaching him the violin, and at 8 he switched to the guitar. In 1955, Santana moved with his family to Tijuana, Mexico, where he sang and played guitar on the streets for tourists. At age 14, he moved to San Francisco, and five years later he formed the Santana Blues Band. A turning point in Santana's career came in 1969, when his band caused a sensation at the Woodstock rock festival. Its first album, *Santana,* was hailed by *Rolling Stone* magazine as "an explosive fusion of Hispanic-edged rock, Afro-Cuban rhythms, and interstellar improvisation." During the 1970s, Santana's band became one of the most famous in the world.

Besides recording with his band, Santana often records with star performers in other fields like Bob Dylan (folk rock) and Herbie Hancock and Wayne Shorter (jazz). Remarkable for a rock performer, at age 52, Santana created his biggest hit so far, the album *Supernatural* (1999), which was voted Best Rock Album of the Year and has sold over 21 million copies worldwide. (Roger Kamien, *Music,* 2008)

American Idol

In the imagination of the public, nothing is more compelling than the "star is born" scenario, where a hopeful unknown gets a big break, and becomes a celebrity. For decades this drama has been played out in television shows featuring amateur competition. Some contestants become sensations while mediocre performers are, at best, rejected and, at worst, subjected to ridicule and insults.

Premiering in the summer of 2002 on the FOX network, *American Idol* tapped into the current craze for "reality" television. It granted viewers a window into the lives of real people—in this case, someone trying to become a star, from start to finish. In the case of *American Idol,* the finish could come sooner rather than later. One of the show's more effective features was a harsh judge, successful British entertainment producer Simon Cowell, who not only accepted or rejected the hopeful, but mercilessly belittled the poor contestant who didn't meet his approval. The very first winner of *American Idol,* female vocalist Kelly Clarkson, went on to record two multi-platinum albums and was nominated for a Grammy Award. Winning second place wasn't bad either. In the second season, runner-up Clay Aiken became the sentimental favorite and his career eclipsed that of the winner, Ruben Studdard.

Carrie Underwood was the first major country star to have been a product of *American Idol*. She won the top spot on the show in 2005 and soon recorded her first album, *Some Hearts*, which featured the hit single "Jesus, Take the Wheel." (David Lee Joyner, *American Popular Music*, 3/e 2009)

Jay-Z

Shawn Carter, aka Jay-Z, should be no stranger to hip-hop fans. The 10-time Grammy winning artist has sold more than 45 million albums worldwide. He's bested only by the Beatles in terms of No. 1 albums on the billboard charts. Although Jay-Z still releases an album from time to time, today he's more concerned with his business ventures than with rap. For good reason, too: his businesses have earned him a net worth of 450 million.

But Jay-Z didn't turn from rapper to media mogul overnight. Many musicians attempt to translate their artistic success into a business empire only to fail from either a lack of knowledge or an unwillingness to adapt to the system. Jay-Z, on the other hand, used his entrepreneurial cunning along with his complete control over the Jay-Z brand to become one of the world's richest musicians. In fact, in a few years Jay-Z's fortune may exceed $1 billion, making him one of the richest people in the world.

Part of the reasons Jay-Z has been so successful is that he's been involved in the business side of music almost as long as he's been rapping. In 1996 no labels wanted to sign a 26-year-old low-profile personality known mostly through New York's local hip-hop scene. Out of necessity, he and two others founded Rock-A-Fella Records. The risk of starting his own business paid off big both for his career and his brand. Since he owned the company he rapped for, that made him more attractive to cost-cutting labels wanting to avoid traditional contracts. He eventually entered a joint venture with Def Jam Recordings, and together the two companies made millions from albums like *Reasonable Doubt* and *The Blueprint*.

As his stardom rose, Jay-Z did endorsements like any other pop star would. But unlike his industry peers, Jay-Z carefully considered which products he promoted, all while obtaining creative control over each ad. In a spot for HP computers, for instance, Jay-Z played the role of a professional commanding his empire in a sharp suit with his trusty computer. Each ad that played up his business side slowly wore down his Brooklyn bad boy image from his rap days and replaced it with that of a slick corporate player. By the time Jay-Z took up the mantle of CEO of Def Jam, few questioned the abilities of this rapper to take over the reins of a major company.

Jay-Z's branding expertise has served him as well in his clothing line. in the late 1990s he noticed that sales of Iceberg apparel rose after he mentioned the company in his raps. Jay-Z once again took the entrepreneurial route and started his own clothing brand called Rocawear. The line took off, and in 2006 Jay-Z sold it to a brand licensing company for $204 million. Jay-Z continues to own a stake in the Rocawear name.

Today Jay-Z's business holdings are almost too numerous to count. The international 40/40 nightclub chain, a partial ownership in the New Jersey Nets basketball team, and a footwear line with Reebok account for just a portion of his wide portfolio. His most ambitious entrepreneurial venture at the moment is his role as the CEO of Roc Nation, a joint project with concert giant Live Nation.

Although his popularity as a rapper helped launch his valuable brand, Jay-Z wouldn't be the success he is today without the entrepreneurial risks he took throughout his career. (William G. Nickels, *Understanding Business*, 10/e, McGraw-Hill, 2013, p. 147)

Questions for Louis Armstrong Reading

Directions: Without looking back at the selection, indicate whether each statement is true or false by writing **T** or **F** on the line provided.

_____ 1. Louis Armstrong learned to play the bugle and the cornet at the Colored Waifs' Home.

_____ 2. Armstrong is famous for his recordings of "Hello Dolly" and "What a Wonderful World."

_____ 3. Armstrong was born in San Francisco and grew up in California.

_____ 4. Armstrong gained a reputation as the "Johnny Appleseed" of jazz.

_____ 5. Armstrong's pistol-shooting incident occurred during a Mardi Gras celebration.

Questions for Johnny Cash Reading

Directions: Without looking back at the selection, indicate whether each statement is true or false by writing **T** or **F** on the line provided.

_____ 1. Johnny Cash once recorded a humorous song titled "A Boy Named John."

_____ 2. At one time, Cash became addicted to prescription drugs.

_____ 3. Cash was known as "the man in blue" because of the striking color of his eyes.

_____ 4. Cash was inducted into both the Country Music Hall of Fame and the Rock and Roll Hall of Fame.

_____ 5. Cash had a reputation as a dark loner who came from humble beginnings.

Questions for Elvis Presley Reading

Directions: Without looking back at the selection, indicate whether each statement is true or false by writing **T** or **F** on the line provided.

_____ 1. Elvis Presley was discovered by Sam Phillips.

_____ 2. Presley was discovered when he went to a sound studio to record a few songs for his wife's birthday.

_____ 3. Presley's distinctive sound was called "country-western."

_____ 4. After serving in the military, Presley went to Hollywood.

_____ 5. Presley had a number of hits throughout 1950s.

Questions for Carlos Santana Reading

Directions: Without looking back at the selection, indicate whether each statement is true or false by writing **T** or **F** on the line provided.

_____ 1. As a young boy, Carlos Santana played and sang on the streets in Tijuana, Mexico.

______ 2. The album *Supernatural* was recorded when Santana was in his 50s.

______ 3. Santana was extremely skilled on the drums.

______ 4. Santana's band performed at the Woodstock rock festival.

______ 5. Santana never performs with artists from other fields.

Questions for American Idol Reading

Directions: Without looking back at the selection, indicate whether each statement is true or false by writing **T** or **F** on the line provided.

______ 1. *American Idol* can rightly be called reality television.

______ 2. The British judge Simon Cowell was considered to be harsh on some contestants.

______ 3. Clay Aiken and Aretha Franklin are two successful past winners of *American Idol.*

______ 4. Kelly Clarkson was the very first *American Idol* winner.

______ 5. Carrie Underwood, a past *American Idol* winner, has gone on to success in country music.

Questions for Jay-Z Reading

Directions: Without looking back at the selection, indicate whether each statement is true or false by writing **T** or **F** on the line provided.

______ 1. Jay-Z's real name is Shawn Carter.

______ 2. Jay-Z involved himself in the business side of music.

______ 3. Jay-Z had little interest in doing endorsements.

______ 4. Jay-Z is associated with the Rocawear clothing line.

______ 5. Jay-Z took few business risks throughout his career.

Answers to the Questions for the Readings

Louis Armstrong	Johnny Cash	Elvis Presley
1. T	1. F	1. T
2. T	2. T	2. F
3. F	3. F	3. F
4. T	4. T	4. T
5. F	5. T	5. T
Carlos Santana	**American Idol**	**Jay-Z**
1. T	1. T	1. T
2. T	2. T	2. T
3. F	3. F	3. F
4. T	4. T	4. T
5. F	5. T	5. F

Test-Taking Techniques

How to Improve Your Performance

The Multiple-Choice Test

As a college student, you are going to have to take many multiple-choice and true/false tests and quizzes. While nothing substitutes for thoroughly knowing the material and preparing well, the following are some basic test-taking tips that you should be familiar with:

1. Read directions carefully.
2. Pay attention to oral instructions.
3. Look through the entire test, and plan your time accordingly.
4. Do not dwell on any question too long. If you can't answer the question, move on and come back to the question if you have time at the end.
5. If in doubt between two answers, go with your first gut-level reaction. Don't change an answer unless you are positive you are making the correct choice. You may be changing a right answer to a wrong answer. Your time can probably be better spent elsewhere on the test.
6. Even if you think you have more knowledge about the material than the author of the material or you think the author is wrong, go with what the author says, not what you think.
7. Read through all the answers before picking one.
8. If one of your choices is a combination of two or more answers (such as "A and B"), remember that all parts of the answer must be correct. (A must be a correct answer and B must also be a correct answer.)
9. When in doubt, and one answer includes language from the question, go with that answer. Also look for clues in the question that may help give away the answer.
10. Look at long answers first, especially if one answer is much longer than the others. A longer answer is more likely to be correct than a shorter answer. Why? It usually takes more words to write a correct answer because it needs to be phrased carefully. Also, right answers may need qualifying phrases to make them correct. Wrong answers are wrong anyway, so it doesn't matter how they are written.
11. When the question asks you to pick a missing word, use grammar clues such as *a* and *an.* An *a* goes with words beginning with consonants, and an *an* goes with words beginning with vowels.
12. Eliminate answers with all-inclusive words such as *all, everyone, none, always,* and *nobody.* Answers that include such words are quite likely wrong. Usually, the only time answers with such words are correct is when that is exactly what the author said. If there is one exception, the answer will be wrong.

13. When a question asks for the main idea of the selection or the best possible title, make sure your answer is broad enough to cover all parts of the selection.
14. Sometimes the last answer will be "All of the above." If you are fairly sure that two of the three answers are correct but are unsure about the third answer, go with "All of the above."
15. Two questions on the test may be similar. Use the correct answer for one question to help you find the correct answer for the other.
16. Allow at least a minute or two to check over your answer sheet. Is your name on it? Do you need to date it? Have you skipped any questions?
17. If you are putting your answers on a Scantron, make sure that you have completely erased any earlier answers. Scantrons will pick up incomplete erasures.

The True-or-False Test

Of course, you have a 50 percent chance of getting a true-or-false statement correct. However, you can increase your odds of getting the right answer if you realize that if any part of the statement is false, the entire statement must be false. Double-check the numbers, facts, and dates in true-or-false statements. Sometimes this information may be altered slightly, making the statement false.

Be careful when statements contain absolutes such as *all*, *always*, *everyone*, *never*, and *no one*. Statements are more likely to be false if they contain such words. For example, consider the following statement: "It is always a bad idea to change your answer to a question." The statement is false.

On the other hand, statements that include qualifiers such as *sometimes*, *perhaps*, and *maybe* are more likely to be true. For example, consider this statement: "It is sometimes a bad idea to change your answer to a question." This time the statement is true.

Unfortunately, none of these rules leads you to the correct answer all of the time.

The Matching Test

Read through all the choices before you actually begin matching. Then do the matches that you are absolutely sure of first. Put a check mark by the items that you have used rather than crossing them out completely. If new information occurs to you, you might have to go back and reassess your original answers. A completely crossed-out answer might be difficult to read.

The Short-Answer Test

The emphasis here is on expressing yourself briefly and concisely. Try jotting down a brief outline so that you can organize your answer before you begin writing. Remember to cover the main points.

The Essay Test

Before the Test

There is no substitute for simply knowing all of the course material well. But that can be a big task, and realistically, some parts of the material are probably more important, and more likely to appear on an essay test, than other parts.

One way to give your preparation some focus is to try to think of questions that might appear on the test. Because your teacher will likely be the one who writes the test, ask yourself what questions you think your teacher might ask. Review your class notes and any handouts to determine what the teacher emphasized in the course. What topics did the teacher spend the most time on? What topics did the teacher seem to care the most about?

Keep in mind that an essay question may ask for information on a specific topic or it may be directed at a general understanding of the course material. You need to prepare yourself for both kinds of questions.

General or "big picture" essay questions often deal with relationships among topics or concepts. A good way to prepare for these questions is to make an outline or map of the course material. Look at your class notes, any handouts, and your textbook, and organize this material into an outline. If your teacher has closely followed a textbook, the book's table of contents should give you a good start on making your outline.

Once you have come up with a list of possible questions, use some of your study time preparing answers to these questions. You may even want to practice writing out answers.

During the Test

Carefully read the question; you can't expect to write a good answer to a question you don't understand. In fact, you might write a wonderful essay, but if it doesn't answer the question, it will not do you much good. What is the question asking you to do? Does the question use any of the keywords discussed on pages A12–A13? If so, think about what that keyword means.

Once you understand the question, begin thinking about how best to answer it. It's probably not a good idea to start writing immediately. Give yourself some time to think first. What material from the course will the answer involve? What do you remember about this material? At this point, you might want to start jotting some notes. If you prepared well for the test, the more you think about this material, the more of it you will remember.

Organizing Your Answer

Once you have recalled the material you need in order to answer the questions, you need to begin thinking about how to organize your answer. Knowing the information goes a long way toward writing a good essay, but how you organize the information also counts. This is especially true for a "big picture" essay question. Your organization will show the teacher how well you understand what is important and what the relationships are among ideas and concepts.

A traditional essay has an introduction, a conclusion, and three paragraphs of development. This does not mean that a good essay cannot have more or less than three paragraphs of development, but ordinarily an essay that is three paragraphs long will say what needs to be said without saying too much. Usually the three paragraphs of the traditional essay are developed in the same order in which their main ideas are mentioned in the introductory statement.

Here is an example of an introductory statement:

> An increase in state financial aid for public education will raise student scores on standardized tests because (1) teacher salaries can be increased, which will attract more-talented people into teaching; (2) more teachers can be hired, which will reduce class size; and (3) school districts will have more money available for learning resources and activities.

So, the first paragraph of this essay would discuss the need for more-talented teachers and why the hiring of more-talented teachers should lead to an increase in the test scores. The second paragraph would discuss the need for smaller classes and how smaller classes should lead to increased scores. The third paragraph would discuss the need for more learning resources and activities and how improved resources and activities should boost test scores.

Often the secret to writing a good essay is constructing a good introductory statement, because once you have a good introductory statement, the rest of the essay follows from it. This is one reason it makes sense to do some thinking and organizing before you start to write.

To write a good introductory statement, it sometimes helps to take the question and rearrange it into an introductory statement. For example, assume that the question says the following:

> Discuss whether an increase in state financial aid for public education will raise student scores on standardized tests.

Then you might use the following introductory statement:

> An increase in state financial aid for public education will/will not raise student scores on standardized tests because . . .

Some Practical Pointers

1. Research shows that neatness counts, so write carefully and legibly. Try to avoid messy erasures, crossed-out words, and words written between lines and in the margins. You might want to consider using pens with erasable ink.
2. When a question has more than one part, make sure you answer all parts.
3. Remember that each paragraph should develop only one main idea.
4. Give specific examples to illustrate your points.
5. Answer in complete sentences.
6. Check to see if what you have written answers the questions *who, what, where, when, why,* and *how.*
7. Save some time to proofread your essay for spelling and other errors that are likely to produce a bad impression.
8. If you find you have no time to answer questions at the end of the test, write some notes in summary form. These will often earn you at least partial credit.
9. Make use of your returned test papers. You can learn a lot by reading the instructor's comments and correcting the answers.

Keywords That Often Appear in Essay Questions

Following is a list of keywords that often appear in essay questions. If you are going to write a good answer to an essay question that uses one of these terms, you need to know what the term means.

analyze to break down the subject into parts and discuss each part. You will want to discuss how the parts relate to each other.

comment on to discuss or explain.

compare to show differences and similarities, but with the emphasis on similarities.

contrast to show differences and similarities, but with the emphasis on differences.

criticize The narrow meaning of *criticize* is to examine something for its weaknesses, limitations, or failings. Does the theory, article, or opinion make sense? If not, why not? In a more general sense, *criticize* means to find both strengths and weaknesses. In this sense, the meaning of *criticize* is similar to that of *evaluate.*

define to state the meaning of a term, theory, or concept. You will want to place the subject in a category and explain what makes it different from other subjects in the category.

describe to explain what something is or how it appears. What you need to do is draw a picture with words.

diagram to make a chart, drawing, or graph. You also will want to label the categories or elements, and maybe give a brief explanation.

discuss to fully go over something. You will want to cover the main points, give different perspectives, and relate strengths and weaknesses.

enumerate to make a list of main ideas by numbering them.

evaluate to examine for strengths and weaknesses. You will need to give specific evidence and may wish to cite authorities to support your position.

explain to make clear; to give reasons. An explanation often involves showing cause-and-effect relationships or steps.

illustrate to use a diagram, chart, figure, or specific examples to further explain something.

interpret to indicate what something means. A question that asks for an *interpretation* usually wants you to state what something means to you. What are your beliefs or feelings about the meaning of the material? Be sure to back up your position with specific examples and details.

justify to give reasons in support of a conclusion, theory, or opinion.

list to put down your points one by one. You may want to number each of the points in your list.

outline to organize information into an outline, using headings and subheadings. Your outline should reflect the main ideas and supporting details.

prove to demonstrate that something is true by means of factual evidence or logical reasoning.

relate to discuss how two or more conclusions, theories, or opinions affect each other. Explain how one causes, limits, or develops the other.

review usually, to summarize. A narrower meaning is to analyze critically.

summarize to put down the main points; to state briefly the key principles, facts, or ideas while avoiding details and personal comments.

trace to follow the course of development of something in a chronological or logical sequence. You will want to discuss each stage of development from the beginning to the end.

Exercise: Essay Exam Skills

Read the explanations below. In the blank, write a term that the instructor might use when posing the question to the students in the class.

1. In class, the instructor has discussed the contributions of Auguste Comte, Herbert Spencer, and Max Weber to the field of sociology. On the essay exam, he wants the students to briefly go over the contribution of each of these persons while avoiding their own personal comments. What term will he use for this question?

   ____

2. In a child development class, the instructor has discussed the development of language from birth to 36 months. She now wants the students to present the process of language acquisition in chronological sequence. What term should she use?

   ____

3. In an art history class, the instructor wants the students to show the difference between engraving, drypoint, and etching. Which term will she use in the question?

   ____

4. In an American history class, the professor has discussed the Manhattan Project, which developed the atomic bomb during World War II. He now wants the students to examine the project for its weaknesses. What term will he use in the question?

   ____

5. In a biology class, the professor has explained the term "cloning." On a quiz, she wants to make sure her students understand the meaning of the concept. What term will she use in her question?

   ____

6. In an economics class, the professor wants the students to graph the 2000–2001 recession, showing the rise and fall of the unemployment rate and consumer spending. What term should she use on her exam?

   ____

7. In a geography class, the teacher wants the students to make clear how pollution caused harm to the Costa Rican rain forest. What term will he use?

   ____

8. In a psychology class, the instructor wants the students to describe the ways in which long-term memory and short-term memory are alike and the ways in which they are different. What term will she use?

   ____

9. In a reading class, the teacher wants the students to write down the steps of SQ3R one by one, numbering each. What term will she use in her question?

   ____

Sample Summary

Student Sample: Summary of "Students Who Push Burgers"

Who: high school and college students

What: are spending too little time studying and too much time working

Where: in the United States

When: the author compares attitudes in the '50s to attitudes in the late '80s

Why: students work to buy luxury items parents won't pay for

How: because of increased acceptance on the part of parents and teachers

Overall Main Idea

Student employment is a major cause of the decline in American education.

Other Main Ideas

1. Today student employment is widely accepted as normal for teens, but in the past going to school was a student's "job." (implied)
2. Working students have little time for homework. (directly stated)
3. Students work to buy luxury items and then feel they need to go out and have fun. (implied)
4. Thus, by the time they get to college, most students look upon studies as a spare-time activity. (directly stated)
5. The problem doesn't just affect the individual student, but the quality of education as a whole. (implied)

Student Summary

Walter S. Minot in his article "Students Who Push Burgers" feels that U.S. education has declined because students hold part-time jobs. Minot compares the educational system of the 1950s to that of the 1980s. In the past, kids only worked to help out their families financially. Today's students work to buy luxury items, fooling their parents into thinking that they are learning the value of a dollar. Because these students work so hard at their jobs, they feel they deserve to have a good time after work, and they don't have enough time or energy to do their homework. As a result, schools are finding it difficult to get quality work from their students, and have had to reduce their standards. Minot feels this problem doesn't just affect individual students or schools, but the quality of education as a whole.

Sample Sheets for Assignments and Schedules

ASSIGNMENTS
MONDAY
TUESDAY
WEDNESDAY
THURSDAY
FRIDAY
OTHER ASSIGNMENTS, TESTS, ETC.

MONTH ____________________

SUNDAY	MONDAY	TUESDAY	WEDNESDAY	THURSDAY	FRIDAY	SATURDAY

ASSIGNMENT SHEET

SUBJECT(S) ______________________________

DATE	ASSIGNMENTS	DUE	FINISHED

STUDY SCHEDULES

	MONDAY	TUESDAY	WEDNESDAY	THURSDAY	FRIDAY	SATURDAY	SUNDAY
6:00–7:00A.M.							
7:00–8:00A.M.							
8:00–9:00A.M.							
9:00–10:00A.M.							
10:00–11:00A.M.							
11:00–12:00P.M.							
12:00–1:00P.M.							
1:00–2:00P.M.							
2:00–3:00P.M.							
3:00–4:00P.M.							
4:00–5:00P.M.							
5:00–6:00P.M.							
6:00–7:00P.M.							
7:00–8:00P.M.							
8:00–9:00P.M.							
9:00–10:00P.M.							
10:00–11:00P.M.							
11:00–12:00A.M.							
12:00–1:00A.M.							

Credits

Text and Line Art Credits

Introduction Page 6: Robert S. Feldman, *P.O.W.E.R. Learning and Your Life: Essentials of Student Success*, 2nd ed., p. 73. Copyright © 2014 by McGraw-Hill Education. Reprinted with permission; **p. 8:** Robert S. Feldman, *P.O.W.E.R. Learning and Your Life: Essentials of Student Success*, 2nd ed., pp. 10–12. Copyright © 2014 by McGraw-Hill Education. Reprinted with permission; **p. 11:** Byron Pitts, *Step Out on Nothing*, pp. 37–47. © 2009 by Byron Pitts, used by permission of St. Martin's Press and the author.

Chapter 1 Page 27: Freda Adler, Gerhard O. W. Mueller, and William S. Laufer, *Criminal Justice*, 5th ed., p. 64. Copyright © 2009 by McGraw-Hill Education. Reprinted with permission; **p. 28:** Freda Adler, Gerhard O. W. Mueller, and William S. Laufer, *Criminal Justice*, 5th ed., pp. 389, 405, 60. Copyright © 2009 by McGraw-Hill Education. Reprinted with permission; **p. 29:** Freda Adler, Gerhard O. W. Mueller, and William S. Laufer, *Criminal Justice*, 5th ed., pp. 295, 64. Copyright © 2009 by McGraw-Hill Education. Reprinted with permission; **pp. 32, 33, 34–35:** From *The Random House Webster's College Dictionary* by Random House, Inc., copyright © 1995, 1992, 1991 by Random House, Inc. Used by permission of Random House Reference and Information Publishing, a division of Random House, Inc. Any third party use of this material, outside of this publication, is prohibited. Interested parties must apply directly to Random House LLC for permission.

Chapter 2 Page 41: Kory Floyd, *Interpersonal Communication*, 2nd ed., pp. 152–153. Copyright © 2012 by McGraw-Hill Education. Reprinted with permission; **p. 49:** Lowell Ponte, "The Two Most Dangerous Hours of Your Day." Reprinted with permission from *Reader's Digest*. Copyright © 1992 by The Reader's Digest Association, Inc.; **p. 60:** From *First Things First: The Rules of Being a Warner* by Kurt and Brenda Warner, pp. 65–69. Copyright © 2009 by Kurt and Brenda Warner. Used by permission of Tyndale House Publishers, Inc. All rights reserved; **p. 64:** From *First Things First: The Rules of Being a Warner* by Kurt and Brenda Warner, pp. 48–49. Copyright © 2009 by Kurt and Brenda Warner. Used by permission of Tyndale House Publishers, Inc. All rights reserved; **p. 70:** William G. Nickels, James M. McHugh, and Susan M. McHugh, *Understanding Business*, 10th ed., pp. 3, 5–7. Copyright © 2013 by McGraw-Hill Education. Reprinted with permission.

Chapter 3 Page 82: Diane E. Papalia and Ruth Duskin Feldman, *Experience Human Development*, 12th ed., p. 492. Copyright © 2012 by McGraw-Hill Education. Reprinted with permission; **p. 83:** Estelle Levetin and Karen McMahon, *Plants and Society*, 6th ed., p. 6. Copyright © 2012 by McGraw-Hill Education. Reprinted with permission; **p. 83:** Stephen E. Lucas, *The Art of Public Speaking*, 10th ed., p. 24. Copyright © 2009 by McGraw-Hill Education. Reprinted with permission; **p. 83:** Stephen E. Lucas, *The Art of Public Speaking*, 10th ed., p. 24. Copyright © 2009 by McGraw-Hill Education. Reprinted with permission; **p. 84:** Kitty O. Locker and Donna S. Kienzler, *Business and Administrative Communication*, 8th ed., p. 443. Copyright © 2008 by McGraw-Hill Education. Reprinted with permission; **p. 84:** Bethami A. Dobkin and Roger C. Pace, *Communication in a Changing World*, 2006 Edition, p. 169, 171, 164. Copyright © 2006 by McGraw-Hill Education. Reprinted with permission; **p. 85:** Terry Kwal Gamble and Michael Gamble, Communication Works, 9th ed., pp. 137, 150, 163. Copyright © 2006 by McGraw-Hill Education. Reprinted with permission; **p. 86:** Bethami A. Dobkin and Roger C. Pace, *Communication in a Changing World*, 2006 Edition, pp. 166, 167. Copyright © 2006 by McGraw-Hill Education. Reprinted with permission; **p. 87:** Kitty O. Locker and Donna S. Kienzler, *Business and Administrative Communication*, 8th ed., p. 441. Copyright © 2008 by McGraw-Hill Education. Reprinted with permission; **p. 87:** Stephen E. Lucas, *The Art of Public Speaking*, 10th ed., p. 23. Copyright © 2009 by McGraw-Hill Education. Reprinted with permission; **p. 92:** Jerrold S. Greenberg, *Comprehensive Stress Management*, 13th ed., p. 185. Copyright © 2013 by McGraw-Hill Education. Reprinted with permission; **p. 94:** David G. Myers, *Social Psychology*, 9th ed., pp. 158–159. Copyright © 2008 by McGraw-Hill Education. Reprinted with permission; **p. 96:** Kitty O. Locker and Donna S. Kienzler, *Business and Administrative Communication*, 8th ed., pp. 440–443. Copyright © 2008 by McGraw-Hill Education. Reprinted with permission; **p. 98:** Estelle Levetin and Karen McMahon, *Plants and Society*, 6th ed., p. 123. Copyright © 2012 by McGraw-Hill Education. Reprinted with permission; **p. 100:** Diane E. Papalia and Ruth Duskin Feldman, *Experience Human Development*, 12th ed., p. 163. Copyright © 2012 by McGraw-Hill Education. Reprinted with permission; **p. 100:** Estelle Levetin and Karen McMahon, *Plants and Society*, 6th ed., p. 89. Copyright © 2012 by McGraw-Hill Education. Reprinted with permission; **p. 101:** David G. Myers, *Social Psychology*, 9th ed., p. 157. Copyright © 2008 by McGraw-Hill Education. Reprinted with permission; **p. 101:** Kitty O. Locker and Donna S. Kienzler, *Business and Administrative Communication*, 8th ed., pp. 437–438. Copyright © 2008 by McGraw-Hill Education. Reprinted with permission; **p. 102:** Sylvia S. Mader, *Concepts of Biology*, 1st ed., p. 735. Copyright © 2009 by McGraw-Hill Education. Reprinted with permission; **p. 104:** Wendy Wilder Larsen and Tran Thi Nga, "Grandmother's Fable" from *Shallow Graves: Two Women and Vietnam*. New York: Random House, 1986. © 1986 by Wendy Wilder Larsen and Tran Thi Nga. Reprinted by permission of Leona P. Schecter Literary Agency on behalf of the authors; **p. 106:** Sylvia S. Mader, *Concepts of Biology*, 1st ed., pp. 2–3. Copyright © 2009 by McGraw-Hill Education. Reprinted with permission; **p. 110:** Diane E. Papalia and Ruth Duskin Feldman, *Experience Human Development*, 12th ed., p. 104. Copyright © 2012 by McGraw-Hill Education. Reprinted with permission; **p. 112:** David H. Olson and John DeFrain, *Marriage and Families*, 8th ed., pp. 233–234, 233, 240, 147, 148, 116, 364, 449, 450. Copyright © 2014 by McGraw-Hill Education. Reprinted with permission; **p. 117:** Robert S. Feldman, *Essentials of Understanding Psychology*, 10th ed., pp. 348–349. Copyright © 2013 by McGraw-Hill Education. Reprinted with permission; **p. 117:** Kory Floyd, *Interpersonal Communication*, 2nd ed., pp. 39, 84. Copyright © 2012 by McGraw-Hill Education. Reprinted with permission; **p. 123:** "Global Food Rules," from *Parenting Without Borders* by Christine Gross-Loh, copyright © 2013 by Christine Gross-Loh. Used by permission of Avery Publishing, an imprint of Penguin Group (USA) LLC, and Gillian MacKenzie Agency; **p. 126:** "Ban Cellphones – Unless You're Attacked by a Giant Squid" from *Boogers Are My Beat: More Lies, But Some Actual Journalism* by Dave Barry, copyright © 2003 by Dave Barry. Used by permission of Crown Books, an imprint of the Crown Publishing Group, a division of Random House LLC., and the author. All rights reserved. Any third party use of this material, outside of this publication, is prohibited. Interested parties must apply directly to Random House LLC for permission; **p. 129:** From Thorin Klosowski, "The Most Annoying Things You Do with Your Phone That You Should Quit (or At Least Be Aware Of)," Lifehacker.com. Reprinted by permission of Gawker Media.

Chapter 4 Page 132: Robert S. Feldman, *Essentials of Understanding Psychology*, 10th ed., pp. 206–209. Copyright © 2013 by McGraw-Hill Education. Reprinted with permission; **p. 137:** Robert S. Feldman, *P.O.W.E.R. Learning: Strategies for Success in College and Life*, 6th ed., pp. 207–216. Copyright © 2014 by McGraw-Hill Education. Reprinted with permission; **p. 148:** Robert S. Feldman, *P.O.W.E.R. Learning: Strategies for Success in College and Life*, 6th ed., Figure 8.1 (p. 215). Copyright © 2014 by McGraw-Hill Education. Reprinted with permission; **p. 149 top:** Robert S. Feldman, *Essentials of Understanding Psychology*, 10th ed., Figure 2 (p. 206). Copyright © 2013 by McGraw-Hill Education. Reprinted with permission. (Based on information in Atkinson & Shifrin, 1968); p. 149 bottom: Robert S. Feldman, *Essentials of Understanding Psychology*, 10th ed., Figure 6 (p. 225). Copyright © 2013 by McGraw-Hill Education. Reprinted with permission. (Based on data from Bahrick, et al., 1996); **p. 150:** Robert S. Feldman, *Psychology and Your Life*, 2nd ed., Figure 3 (p. 217). Copyright © 2013 by McGraw-Hill Education. Reprinted with permission. (Based on data from Rubin, 1985); **p. 151:** Slameka, N. J., & McElree, B. (1983). Normal forgetting of verbal lists as a function of their degree of learning. *Journal of Experimental Psychology: Learning Memory and Cognition*, 9, 384–397. Reprinted by permission of the American Psychological Association.

Chapter 5 Page 160: Jerrold S. Greenberg, *Comprehensive Stress Management*, 13th ed., pp. 385–386. Copyright © 2013 by McGraw-Hill Education. Reprinted with permission; **p. 161:** Estelle Levetin and Karen McMahon, *Plants and Society*, 6th ed., p. 81. Copyright © 2012 by McGraw-Hill Education. Reprinted with permission; **p. 162:** Hamilton Gregory, *Public Speaking for College and Career*, 7th ed., p. 427. Copyright © 2005 by McGraw-Hill Education. Reprinted with permission; **p. 164:** Rose Castillo Guilbault, "The Conveyor Belt Ladies" from *Farmworker's Daughter: Growing Up Mexican in America*. © 2005 by Rose Castillo Guilbault. Reprinted by permission of Heyday Books; **p. 169:** Jack R. Kapoor, Les R. Dlabay, and Robert J. Hughes, *Personal Finance*, 10th ed., pp. 172–174. Copyright © 2012 by McGraw-Hill Education. Reprinted with permission; **p. 173:** Jack R. Kapoor, Les R. Dlabay, and Robert J. Hughes, *Personal Finance*, 10th ed., Exhibit 6–3 (p. 177) . Copyright © 2012 by McGraw-Hill Education. Reprinted with permission; **p. 175:** Walter S. Minot, "Students Who Push Burgers" © 1988 by Walter S. Minot. Reprinted by permission of the author. From *Christian Science Monitor*, November 22, 1988; **p. 182:** From Gordon Grice, "The Black Widow." First published in *High Plains Literary Review*. Copyright © 1995 by Gordon Grice. Reprinted by permission of the author; **p. 187:** Freda Adler, Gerhard O. W. Mueller, and William S. Laufer, *Criminal Justice*, 5th ed., p. 192. Copyright © 2009 by McGraw-Hill Education. Reprinted with permission.

Chapter 6 Page 201: Robert S. Feldman, *Essentials of Understanding Psychology*, 10th ed., p. 134. Copyright © 2013 by McGraw-Hill Education. Reprinted with permission; **p. 202:** Richard Armour, "Money" from *Yours for the Asking, a Book of Light Verse*. Boston: B. Humphries, 1942. Reprinted by permission of Geoffrey Armour; **p. 202:** Robert S. Feldman, *Understanding Psychology*, 11th ed., p. 625. Copyright © 2013 by McGraw-Hill Education. Reprinted with permission; **p. 203:** David G. Myers, *Social Psychology*, 9th ed., pp. 355–356. Copyright © 2008 by McGraw-Hill Education. Reprinted with permission; **p. 204:** Diane E. Papalia and Ruth Duskin Feldman, *Experience Human Development*, 12th ed., p. 528. Copyright © 2012 by McGraw-Hill Education. Reprinted with permission; **p. 206:** Mark Getlein, *Living with Art*, 10th ed., p. 11. Copyright © 2013 by McGraw-Hill Education. Reprinted with permission; **p. 206:** Robert H. Bohm and Keith N. Haley, *Introduction to Criminal Justice*, 6th ed., pp. 29–30. Copyright © 2010 by McGraw-Hill Education. Reprinted with permission; **p. 208:** William Cole, "Lies, All Lies" from *A Boy Named Mary Jane, and Other Silly Verse*. New York: Watts, 1977. © 1977 William Cole. Reprinted by permission of the Estate of William Rossa Cole; **p. 213:** Jerrold S. Greenberg, *Comprehensive Stress Management*, 13th ed., p. 416. Copyright © 2013 by McGraw-Hill Education. Reprinted with permission; **p. 214:** Wayne A. Payne and Dale B. Hahn, *Understanding Your Health*, 6th ed., pp. 36, 230–231. Copyright © 2000 by McGraw-Hill

Education. Reprinted with permission; **p. 215:** Wayne A. Payne and Dale B. Hahn, *Understanding Your Health*, 6th ed., p. 139. Copyright © 2000 by McGraw-Hill Education. Reprinted with permission; **p. 216:** Diane E. Papalia and Ruth Duskin Feldman, *Experience Human Development*, 12th ed., pp. 128–129. Copyright © 2012 by McGraw-Hill Education. Reprinted with permission; **p. 216:** Hamilton Gregory, *Public Speaking for College and Career*, 7th ed., pp. 75–76. Copyright © 2005 by McGraw-Hill Education. Reprinted with permission; **p. 217:** Hamilton Gregory, *Public Speaking for College and Career*, 7th ed., p. 32. Copyright © 2005 by McGraw-Hill Education. Reprinted with permission; **p. 217:** David G. Myers, *Social Psychology*, 9th ed., p. 324. Copyright © 2008 by McGraw-Hill Education. Reprinted with permission; **p. 221:** Kory Floyd, *Interpersonal Communication*, 2nd ed. Copyright © 2012 by McGraw-Hill Education. Reprinted with permission; **p. 223:** Freda Adler, Gerhard O. W. Mueller, and William S. Laufer, *Criminal Justice*, 6th ed. Copyright © 2011 by McGraw-Hill Education. Reprinted with permission; **p. 230:** David G. Myers, *Social Psychology*, 9th ed., p. 349. Copyright © 2008 by McGraw-Hill Education. Reprinted with permission; David G. Myers, Social Psychology, 9th ed., both excerpts from p. 349. Copyright © 2008 by McGraw-Hill Education. Reprinted with permission; **p. 231:** Robert S. Feldman, *Understanding Psychology*, 11th ed., p. 626. Copyright © 2013 by McGraw-Hill Education. Reprinted with permission.

Chapter 7 Page 235: Anna Mae Halgrim Seaver, "My World Now: Life in a Nursing Home, from the Inside," *Newsweek*, June 27, 1994. Reprinted by permission of Richard H. Seaver, Sr.; **p. 240:** Glen J. Coulthard, *Computing NOW*, 1st ed., pp. 272–274. Copyright © 2013 by McGraw-Hill Education. Reprinted with permission; **p. 245:** Joseph R. Dominick, *The Dynamics of Mass Communication*, 9th ed., p. 261. Copyright © 2007 by McGraw-Hill Education. Reprinted with permission; **p. 247:** Kory Floyd, *Interpersonal Communication*, 2nd ed., pp. 323–324, 330–331. Copyright © 2012 by McGraw-Hill Education. Reprinted with permission; **p. 254:** "Thank you, M'am" from *Short Stories* by Langston Hughes. Copyright © 1996 by Ramona Bass and Arnold Rampersad. Reprinted by permission of Hill and Wang, a division of Farrar, Straus and Giroux, LLC, and Harold Ober Associates Incorporated; **p. 258:** Robert S. Feldman, *Understanding Psychology*, 11th ed., pp. 203–204. Copyright © 2013 by McGraw-Hill Education. Reprinted with permission.

Chapter 8 Page 269: Elsin Ann Perry, "Wide O-" © 1968 by Elsin Ann Perry. From *Ellery Queen's Mystery Magazine*, September 1968, pp. 116–117. Reprinted by permission of the author; **p. 274:** William Saroyan, "The Shepherd's Daughter," from *The Daring Young Man on the Flying Trapeze*. © 1934 by William Saroyan. Reprinted by permission of the Trustees of Leland Stanford Junior University c/o Stanford University Libraries; **p. 279:** from "Flight" from *The Long Valley* by John Steinbeck, copyright 1938, renewed © 1966 by John Steinbeck. Used by permission of Viking Penguin, a division of Penguin Group (USA) LLC; **p. 281:** Estelle Levetin and Karen McMahon, *Plants and Society*, 6th ed., pp. 263–264. Copyright © 2012 by McGraw-Hill Education. Reprinted with permission; **p. 283:** James West Davidson et al., *Experience History: Interpreting America's Past*, 7th ed., p. 6. Copyright © 2011 by McGraw-Hill Education. Reprinted with permission; **p. 284:** "Complaining" from *Wouldn't Take Nothing for My Journey Now* by Maya Angelou, copyright © 1993 by Maya Angelou. Used by permission of Random House, Inc., and Virago, an imprint of Little, Brown Book Group. Any third party use of this material, outside of this publication, is prohibited. Interested parties must apply directly to Random House LLC for permission; **p. 291:** Paul M. Insel and Walton T. Roth, *Core Concepts in Health*, Brief 10th ed. update, p. 359. Copyright © 2008 by McGraw-Hill Education. Reprinted with permission. **P. 298:** Hamilton Gregory, *Public Speaking for College and Career*, 10th ed. Copyright © 2013 by McGraw-Hill Education. Reprinted with permission; **p. 300:** David G. Myers, Social Psychology, 9th ed., p. 398. Copyright © 2008 by McGraw-Hill Education. Reprinted with permission.

Chapter 9 Page 305: Langston Hughes, "Dreams" from *The Collected Poems of Langston Hughes* by Langston Hughes, edited by Arnold Rampersad with David Roessel, Associate Editor, copyright © 1994 by the Estate of Langston Hughes. Used by permission of Alfred A. Knopf, an imprint of the Knopf Doubleday Publishing Group, a division of Random House LLC, and Harold Ober Associates Incorporated. All rights reserved. Any third party use of this material, outside of this publication, is prohibited. Interested parties must apply directly to Random House LLC for permission; **p. 320:** Mark Getlein, *Living with Art*, 10th ed., p. 58. Copyright © 2013 by McGraw-Hill Education. Reprinted with permission; **p. 324:** Pete Hamill, "The Yellow Ribbon." Reprinted by permission © 1971 by Pete Hamill. Used by permission. All rights reserved; **p. 331:** James West Davidson et al., *Experience History: Interpreting America's Past*, 7th ed., p. 116. Copyright © 2011 by McGraw-Hill Education. Reprinted with permission; **p. 332:** Gary Soto, "The Jacket" from *The Effects of Knut Hamson on a Fresno Boy*. Copyright © 1983, 1988, 2000 by Gary Soto. Reprinted with the permission of The Permissions Company, Inc. on behalf of Persea Books, Inc., New York, and BookStop Literary Agency, LLC, www.perseabooks.com.

Chapter 10 Page 345: Stephen E. Lucas, *The Art of Public Speaking*, 10th ed., p. 372. Copyright © 2009 by McGraw-Hill Education. Reprinted with permission; **p. 347:** Stephen Barrett, *Consumer Health: A Guide to Intelligent Decisions*, 9th ed., pp. 38, 48, 215. Copyright © 2013 by McGraw-Hill Education. Reprinted with permission; **p. 351:** Anita Bartholomew, "Whale of a Rescue." Reprinted with permission from *Reader's Digest*. Copyright © 2006 by The Reader's Digest Association, Inc.; **p. 361:** "A Letter to God," by Gregorio López y Fuentes, translated by Donald A. Yates. Reprinted by permission of Donald A. Yates; **p. 366:** © 1972 Tribune Media Services, Inc. All Rights Reserved. Reprinted with permission. From Art Buchwald, *I Never Danced at the White House*. New York: Putman, 1973. Appeared originally in *The Washington Post*, August 17, 1972.

Chapter 11 Page 380: James West Davidson et. al., *Experience History: Interpreting America's Past*, 7th ed., p. 765. Copyright © 2011 by McGraw-Hill Education. Reprinted with permission; **p. 386:** David H. Olson, John DeFrain, and Linda Skogrand, *Marriages and Families*, 8th ed., pp. 221–223, 330–331. Copyright © 2014 by McGraw-Hill Education. Reprinted with permission; **p. 390:** Figures from David H. Olson, John DeFrain, and Linda Skogrand, *Marriages and Families*, 8th ed., p. 222. Copyright © 2014 by McGraw-Hill Education. Reprinted with permission; **p. 394:** From David Bodanis, *The Secret House*, pp. 10–15. Copyright © 2003 by David Bodanis. Reprinted with permission of the Carol Mann Agency.

Chapter 12 Page 404: David G. Myers, *Social Psychology*, 9th ed., pp. 555–558. Copyright © 2008 by McGraw-Hill Education. Reprinted with permission; **p. 410:** Hamilton Gregory, *Public Speaking for College and Career*, 10th ed., pp. 243–244. Copyright © 2013 by McGraw-Hill Education. Reprinted with permission; **p. 412:** Glen J. Coulthard, *Computing Now*, 1st ed., p. 185. Copyright © 2013 by McGraw-Hill Education. Reprinted with permission; **p. 422:** "From a Melted Candy Bar to Microwaves" [pp. 57–60] from *They All Laughed…* by Ira Flatow. Copyright © 1992 by Ira Flatow. Reprinted by permission of HarperCollins Publishers; **p. 427:** Samuel Walker and Charles M. Katz, *The Police in America: An Introduction*, 8th ed., pp. 122–123, 219, 385, 394, 404–406, 157–158. Copyright © 2013 by McGraw-Hill Education. Reprinted with permission; **p. 434:** Alan Brinkley, *American History: A Survey*, 11th ed., pp. 876–877. Copyright © 2003 by McGraw-Hill Education. Reprinted with permission; **p. 439:** Wayne A. Payne and Dale B. Hahn, *Understanding Your Health*, 6th ed., p. 545. Copyright © 2000 by McGraw-Hill Education. Reprinted with permission.

Chapter 13 Page 442: Stephen E. Lucas, *The Art of Public Speaking*, 10th ed., pp. 371, 372. Copyright © 2009 by McGraw-Hill Education. Reprinted with permission; **p. 450:** Paul M. Insel and Walton T. Roth, *Core Concepts in Health*, 12th ed., pp. 291–292. Copyright © 2011 by McGraw-Hill Education. Reprinted with permission; **p. 454:** Stanley J. Baran, *Introduction to Mass Communication*, updated 7th ed., pp. 317, 335. Copyright © 2013 by McGraw-Hill Education. Reprinted with permission; **p. 469:** "TV" from *The Shelter of Each Other* by Mary Pipher, Ph.D., copyright © 1996 by Mary Pipher, Ph.D. Used by permission of G.P. Putnam's Sons, a division of Penguin Group (USA) LLC; **p. 476:** Sheila Polk, "Marijuana Isn't Harmless – Especially for Kids," *Arizona Republic*, September 13, 2013. © 2013 by Sheila Polk. Reprinted by permission of the author.

Appendices Page A2: Adapted from David Lee Joyner, *American Popular Music*, 3rd ed., pp. 80–81, 82. Copyright © 2009 by McGraw-Hill Education. Reprinted with permission; **p. A3:** David Lee Joyner, *American Popular Music*, 3rd ed., pp. 168–169. Copyright © 2009 by McGraw-Hill Education. Reprinted with permission; **p. A3:** David Lee Joyner, *American Popular Music*, 3rd ed., p. 188. Copyright © 2009 by McGraw-Hill Education. Reprinted with permission; **p. A4:** Adapted from David Lee Joyner, *American Popular Music*, 3rd ed., pp. 319–320. Copyright © 2009 by McGraw-Hill Education. Reprinted with permission; **p. A5:** William G. Nickels, James M. McHugh, and Susan M. McHugh, *Understanding Business*, 10th ed., p. 147. Copyright © 2013 by McGraw-Hill Education. Reprinted with permission.

Photo Credits

Part Openers 1: © Ingram Publishing/SuperStock RF; 2: © Education Images/UIG/Getty Images; 3: © Jim Reynolds www.jxreynolds.com jreynolds@jxreynolds.com; 4: © Darren Hopes/Getty Images RF; 5: © Illustration Works/Getty Images

Intro Opener: © Image Source/Getty Images RF; p. 6: © AFP/Getty Images; **p. 11:** © Walter Weissman/Corbis

Chapter 1 Opener: © Paul Bradbury/age fotostock RF

Chapter 2 Opener: © Ariel Skelley/Blend Images LLC; **p. 60:** © Michael Kovac/Getty Images for GQ

Chapter 3 Opener: © Mark Downey/Getty Images RF; p. 77 (top left): © Dimitrios Kambouris/WireImages/Getty Image; p. 77 (top right): © Jason LaVeris/FilmMagic/Getty Images; p. 77 (bottom left): © John Dominis/The LIFE Picture Collection/Getty Images; p. 77 (bottom right): © Jon Kopaloff/FilmMagic/Getty Images; **p. 106:** © Scott Harris/iStock/360/Getty Images RF; **p. 123:** © Dan Loh; p. 125: © AP Photo/Lynne Sladky

Chapter 4 Opener: © Markus Amon/Stone/Getty Images; p. 150 (top): © MO:SE/Alamy RF; p. 150 (middle 1): © iStock/360/Getty Images RF; p. 150 (middle 2): © photosindia/Getty Images RF; p. 150 (bottom): © Dream Pictures/Blend Images LLC RF; **p. 154:** © Steve Hix/Somos Images/Corbis

Chapter 5 Opener: © Digital Vision/Getty Images RF; **p. 165:** © Steve Jennings/WireImages/Hulton Archives/Getty Images; **p. 177:** © Photodisc/Getty Images RF

Chapter 6 Opener: © Comstock Images/Getty Images RF; **p. 207:** © The Gallery Collection/Corbis; **p. 223:** © Fancy/SuperStock RF

Chapter 7 Opener: © Radiums Images/360/Getty Images RF; p. 252: © McGraw-Hill Education./Mark A. Dierker, photographer; **p. 253:** © Robert W. Kelley/Time Life Pictures/Getty Images

Chapter 8 Opener: © Steve Ryan/The Image Bank/Getty Images; **p. 265:** © Bonnie McCarthy; **p. 273:** © Bettmann/Corbis; **p. 284:** © Alex Koester/Corbis; **p. 288:** © Ingram Publishing RF; **p. 291:** © iStock/360/Getty Images RF

Chapter 9 Opener: © McGraw-Hill Education; **p. 314:** © Time & Life Pictures/Getty Images; p. 320 (top): © Bettmann/Corbis; p. 320 (bottom): © The Gallery Collection/Corbis; **p. 324:** © AP Photo/Jim Cooper; **p. 332:** © MCT via Getty Images

Chapter 10 Opener: © anne de Haas/ E+/Getty Images RF; **p. 348:** © Sovfoto/Universal Images Group/Getty Images; **p. 359:** © Corbis RF; **p. 366:** © Frank Capri/ Hulton Archive/Getty Images

Chapter 11 Opener: © Hola Images/Getty Images RF; **p. 379:** © Time & Life Pictures/Getty Images

Chapter 12 Opener: © Juice Images/Corbis RF; **p. 418:** © Comstock Images/Alamy RF; p. 422: © Roy Stevens/Time & Life Pictures/Getty Images; **p. 427:** © Hill Street Studios/Beld Images LLC RF

Chapter 13 Opener: © C Flannigan/FilmMagic/Getty Images; **p. 448:** © Bridgette Sullivan/PhotoEdit; **p. 455:** © Hulton Archives/Getty Images; **p. 456:** © The Photo Works/Science Source; **p. 468:** © Keith Philpott/ Time Life Pictures/Getty Images

Vocabulary P. 482: Photographs in the Carol M. Highsmith Archive, Library of Congress, Prints and Photographs Division; **p. 491:** © George Hall/Corbis; **p. 491:** © Hisham Ibrahim/Photodisc/Getty Images RF; **p. 497:** © Dave Moyer RF; **p. 499:** Library of Congress Prints and Photographs Division [LC-USZ62-108921]; **p. 505:** © PictureQuest RF

Index